OUTREMER

OUTREMER

Studies in the history of the Crusading Kingdom of Jerusalem

Presented to JOSHUA PRAWER

Edited by B.Z. KEDAR, H.E. MAYER, R.C. SMAIL

YAD IZHAK BEN-ZVI INSTITUTE

JERUSALEM 1982

ACKNOWLEDGMENTS

The editors are deeply indebted to a number of friends and benefactors, without whose expertise and generosity this volume could not have appeared. They would like to express their particular thanks to Mr Yehuda Ben Porat, the director of Yad Izhak Ben-Zvi, Jerusalem, for his unwavering support and understanding; to Mr Alexander Peli of Massada Press, Jerusalem, for the initial backing and editorial support; to the Hebrew University of Jerusalem, the Jerusalem Institute for Israel Studies, Mr Teddy Kollek, Mayor of Jerusalem, and the University of Haifa, for generous grants which made publication possible; to Mr David Louvish, prince of copy-editors; to Mr Hananel Goldberg, of Yad Izhak Ben-Zvi, for his devoted care in preparing the book; to Mr Claudio Feimblatt, for permission to use his photograph of Joshua Prawer; to Dr Sylvia Schein, for dealing with all kinds of problems concerning the preparation and production of the book, which arose in Israel at times when no editor was in the country.

B.Z.K., H.E.M., R.C.S.

ISBN 965-217-010-0

MANUFACTURED IN ISRAEL

TABLE OF CONTENTS

JOSHUA PRAWER —
AN APPRECIATION

The work and personality of Joshua Prawer have earned him the the admiration not only of crusading historians, but of a still wider circle of scholars throughout the world. He came to Palestine in 1936 and made it his *patria*. As a medieval historian with a western outlook, he has devoted his principal work and interests to that part of the medieval past of his country and the neighbouring regions in which Europeans were most deeply involved: to the crusades and the crusader states.

When he began his career as a scholar, this field of study had not been neglected. The surface history of political and military events in Outremer had been written by Röhricht and, embedded in accounts of the major crusades, by René Grousset, who was to be followed by Sir Steven Runciman. These works were justly renowned, but what was still needed was detailed investigation of what lay below the surface, especially of the foundations of the leading crusader state, the kingdom of Jerusalem. In the nineteenth century pioneering work of this kind had been undertaken by scholars like Beugnot, Rey, Prutz and Dodu. The study made by the last-named of the monarchy of the Latin kingdom was superseded by the valuable monograph of John La Monte: but this is now fifty years old, its subject-matter is limited to the structure and working of the royal government, and its author may be thought to have relied to an excessive degree on the partisan evidence provided by the baronial jurists who wrote in the kingdoms of Jerusalem and Cyprus in the thirteenth century and after. Fresh work was needed, resting on a wider range of source materials than that used by earlier writers, and.dealing with aspects of crusader society in the Latin kingdom which lay even nearer than government to the bedrock.

Prawer holds an outstanding place among the small group of scholars, which includes Claude Cahen and Jean Richard, who have helped to meet these needs. The continued existence of any society depends ultimately on the effective operation of a scheme of law, and it is on the laws of the kingdom and on the courts in which those laws were interpreted and applied that some of Prawer's most distinguished research has been done. The number of papers on legal subjects in *Crusader Institutions* (1980), where they spill over into the section on social history, is sufficient evidence of the extent to which he has built on the earlier work of Grandclaude. In this part of his work Prawer has particularly concentrated on those European inhabitants of the kingdom who were known as burgesses, on the terms on which they held their property, on the laws under which they lived and on the courts in which their affairs were regulated. Of almost equal basic importance is human settlement on the land and in the towns and, as was to be expected from a pupil of Richard Koebner, Prawer is the author of major papers in this field. He also broke new ground by his revolutionary study of the agrarian and social history of the crusader lordship of Tyre, based as it is on a lengthy report made in 1243 to the Venetian government by its principal agent in Syria, supplemented by official statistics compiled by the Turkish administration early in the twentieth century and by a knowledge of the farming methods, until recently apparently changeless, of the *fellahin*.

To the subject of government he has contributed a fine trilogy of original papers. He has demonstrated the existence of a masterful and authoritarian royal government in the Latin kingdom during the earlier part of the twelfth century, and a changing balance of power between the monarch and the great vassals during the middle and later years of that century, with the balance increasingly tilting. in favour of the baronial magnates. He has further perceived that, in the changed conditions of the thirteenth century, government in the kingdom was no longer based to the same extent as formerly on the king and the great vassals. Other groups in society had grown to political importance. These included the Military Orders, the privileged organizations of Italian and Provençal merchants, and the Frankish burgesses, who often formed confraternities and acted through their agency. The nobility, the Military Orders, the European merchants and the Frankish burgesses were all groups in society with privileges and immunities secured to them by formal legal grant or by the laws of the kingdom or the Church, and there were political occasions of major importance in which all of them were present or represented. Prawer has been the first to show that the Latin kingdom's government in the thirteenth century came to depend less on feudal relationships and more on the participation of privileged groups, and he has studied with particular care those episodes in which political crisis impelled those groups to form a "community," a single association cemented by a common oath. The Latin kingdom thus provided, in Prawer's view, an early example of the process of transition *vom Lehnstaat zum Ständestaat*. This boldly original interpretation has won very wide, if not universal, acceptance; but even where it has not, it has given rise to creative controversy, and to have provoked such discussion is not the least of Prawer's many services to crusading studies.

The fundamental research embodied in his papers enabled him to write books which, because of his new insights into crusader society, set new standards in presenting the history of the crusades and of the Latin kingdom. The two volumes of his *Histoire du royaume latin de Jérusalem* (1969-70) contain not only the best account now available of certain major crusades, notably the Third, but a rewriting of much of the military history of the Latin kingdom. In this he has been helped by his first-hand knowledge of the geography of the country and by his penetrating view of geopolitical conditions in the Levant, sharpened by his close knowledge of those, which are in some respects remarkably similar, of the present time. In his book on *The Latin Kingdom of Jerusalem* (1972) he deepened his description of all aspects of crusader society, from the Crown to the ethnic and religious minorities.

Prawer's interests are not confined to the interpretation and evaluation of the written sources; he is keenly interested in crusader monuments. He initiated the excavation of St. Louis's wall and mural towers at Caesarea and the Hospitaller castle of Belvoir. The excursions he conducted to crusader sites from the 1950s onwards made thousands of Israelis aware of the remains of the Latin kingdom and the importance of their preservation.

As a teacher of medieval history at the Hebrew University Prawer had to grapple with the problem of introducing Israeli students to a civilization alien to them in language and religion. The freshmen's drill he evolved in response became a distinguishing feature of undergraduate historical studies in Jerusalem and has meanwhile been carried by his pupils into all Israeli universities. In his early years as a University teacher, he had to be a Jack-of-all-medieval-trades, but as the years passed he was able to concentrate increasingly on his teaching of crusading history. The impact of his classes on this subject is perhaps best reflected in contemporary Hebrew literature, in which history students are frequently depicted as working on some aspect of the crusades.

As deputy dean (1953-55) and dean (1961-65) of the Hebrew University's Faculty of Humanities, Prawer played a decisive role in devising the liberal arts curricula now normative in Israeli universities. During the same period he helped to establish the Hebrew University pre-academic unit, originally conceived to enable applicants of oriental origin to meet the requirements for admission, and later expanded to suit the needs of new immigrants and students from overseas. Prawer was also one of the founders of Haifa University, serving in the years 1966-68 as the first Academic Head of that institution. Later he assisted in the establishment of the country's youngest university at Beer Sheba. Between 1975 and 1978 he was prominent in the affairs of his own alma mater as pro-rector of the Hebrew University.

Prawer has been for many years an acute observer of the Israeli educational system. (In one of his articles he described it as being run by groups of educators each of which looks back in anger at its immediate predecessor.) In the years 1956-58 he served as chairman of the pedagogic secretariat of the Ministry of Education, working for the advancement of pupils of oriental origin and devising a system of graded tuition fees. Between 1964 and 1966 he headed the government-appointed Prawer Committee, which proposed to establish an interim stage between primary and secondary education; the reform plan was adopted by the Knesseth and is gradually being put into effect.

Though never engaging in party politics, Prawer has often taken a stand on current issues. Shortly after his arrival in Palestine in 1936 he joined the Haganah, the Jewish defence force; during the War of Independence he served as liaison officer between the Haganah and the Christian institutions in Jerusalem and was wounded while carrying out his duties. In later years he vigorously defended the freedom of archaeological research in connection with excavations in the City of David. Most recently he was one of the very first to call for a full judicial inquiry into the circumstances surrounding the Beirut massacre.

It is too early as yet to assess Prawer's overall role in Israel's intellectual life. Editor-in-chief of the *Encyclopaedia Hebraica* for many years, who recently brought the 32 volumes of that enterprise to a successful conclusion, chairman of the Humanities Section of the Israel Academy of Sciences and Humanities, academic chairman of the Jerusalem Institute for Israel Studies, member of the boards of the Israel Archaeological Society, the Yad Ben Zvi Institute, the Open University, participant in the negotiations which led to the conclusion of Israel's cultural agreements with several European countries — Prawer belongs to the small group of Israelis who, soon after the attainment of their country's independence in 1948, established frameworks of intellectual activity and managed them for decades. The international community of medieval historians is fortunate that one who has played a prominent part in the public and cultural life of his country has yet been able to make so significant and original a contribution, and at so high a level, to his chosen field of study.

B.Z. Kedar, H.E. Mayer, R.C. Smail

LIST OF ABBREVIATIONS

AOL	*Archives de l'Orient latin*
CC cont. med.	Corpus Christianorum. Continuatio mediaevalis
CSHB	Corpus Scriptorum Historiae Byzantinae
Delaville, *Cartulaire*	J. Delaville Le Roulx, ed., *Cartulaire général de l'Ordre des Hospitaliers de Saint-Jean de Jérusalem, 1100-1310.* 4 vols. Paris, 1894-1906.
Eracles	*Le Estoire de Eracles Empereur*, RHC HOcc. 2.
Ernoul	*Chronique d'Ernoul et de Bernard le Trésorier*, ed. L. de Mas-Latrie. Paris, 1871.
Mayer, *Bistümer*	H.E. Mayer, *Bistümer, Klöster und Stifte im Königreich Jerusalem*, Schriften der MGH 26. Stuttgart, 1977.
MGH SS	Monumenta Germaniae Historica. Scriptores
Müller, *Documenti*	G. Müller, ed., *Documenti sulle relazioni delle città toscane coll'Oriente cristiano*. Florence, 1879.
PL	Patrologia Latina
PPTS	Palestine Pilgrims' Text Society
Prawer, *Crusader Institutions*	J. Prawer, *Crusader Institutions*. Oxford, 1980.
Prawer, *Histoire*	J. Prawer, *Histoire du royaume latin de Jérusalem*. 2 vols. Paris, 1969-70.
Prawer, *Latin Kingdom*	J. Prawer, *The Latin Kingdom of Jerusalem. European Colonialism in the Middle Ages*. London, 1972.
RHC	Recueil des Historiens des Croisades
HOcc.	Historiens occidentaux
HOr.	Historiens orientaux
DArm.	Documents arméniens
RHDFE	*Revue historique de droit français et étranger*

RHGF	Recueil des historiens des Gaules et de la France
Richard, *Royaume*	J. Richard, *Le royaume latin de Jérusalem*. Paris, 1953.
RIS	Rerum Italicarum Scriptores
Ritterorden	*Die geistlichen Ritterorden Europas*, ed. J. Fleckenstein and M. Hellmann, Vorträge und Forschungen 26. Sigmaringen, 1980.
ROL	*Revue de l'Orient latin*
RRH	R. Röhricht, *Regesta regni hierosolymitani* and *Additamentum*. Innsbruck, 1893-1904.
RS	Rolls Series
Runciman, *Crusades*	S. Runciman, *A History of the Crusades*. 3 vols. Cambridge, 1951-54.
Sanudo, *Secreta*	Marino Sanudo Torsello, *Liber secretorum fidelium crucis*, in J. Bongars, *Gesta Dei per Francos*, vol. 2. Hanau, 1611. Reprinted, with a foreword by J. Prawer, Jerusalem, 1972.
WT	William of Tyre, *Historia rerum in partibus transmarinis gestarum*, RHC Hocc. 1.
ZDPV	*Zeitschrift des Deutschen Palästina-Vereins*

PUBLICATIONS OF JOSHUA PRAWER*

1941

1. "The role of Jews in Medieval Trade," *The Commerce of Gentiles and Jews* (Tel Aviv, 1941), pp. 74-92 (Hebrew).

1946

2. "The Jews in the Latin Kingdom of Jerusalem," *Zion* 11 (1946), 38-82 (Hebrew).

1947

3. *The Crusader Kingdom of Jerusalem (1099-1291)* (Jerusalem, 1947). 156 pp. (Hebrew).

4. "The Vicissitudes of the Jewish Quarter in Jerusalem in the Arabic Period," *Zion* 12 (1947), 136-148 (Hebrew).

5. "The Jewish Population in Palestine: Arab Rule; the Crusaders; the Mameluk Period (640-1516)," *Three Historical Memoranda submitted by the General Council of the Jewish Community of Palestine (Vaad Leumi)* (Jerusalem, 1947), pp. 27-51.

1948

6. "Toward the Critique of Letters from Jerusalem from the 15th and 16th Centuries," *Jerusalem. Quarterly for the Study of Jerusalem and its History* 2 (1948), 139-159 (Hebrew).

7. "The Friars of Mount Zion and the Jews of Jerusalem in the Fifteenth Century," *Bulletin of the Jewish Palestine Exploration Society* 14 (1948/49), 15-24 (Hebrew).

---

* The list does not contain articles in encyclopaedias or essays on public affairs. Neither does it contain publications in whose preparation Professor Prawer is currently engaged as author or editor. The list has been compiled by Sylvia Schein.

1951

8. "L'établissement des coutumes du marché à Saint-Jean d'Acre et la date de composition du *Livre des Assises des Bourgeois*," *RHDFE* 29 (1951), 329-351.

9. "Colonisation Activities in the Latin Kingdom of Jerusalem," *Revue belge de philologie et d'histoire* 29 (1951), 1063-1118 (revised version in no. 78).

10. "On Agriculture under the Crusaders," *Eretz-Israel* 1 (1951), 145-152 (Hebrew) (revised French and English versions in nos. 14, 78).

1952

11. "The *Assise de Teneure* and the *Assise de Vente*: A Study of Landed Property in the Latin Kingdom," *Economic History Review* 41 (1951/52), 77-87 (revised version in no. 78).

12. "Le muid royal de Saint-Jean d'Acre et les mesures arabes contemporaines," *Byzantion* 22 (1952), 58-61.

13. "The Settlement of the Latins in Jerusalem," *Speculum* 27 (1952), 490-503 (revised version in no. 78).

1953

14. "Étude de quelques problèmes agraires et sociaux d'une seigneurie croisée au XIIIe siècle," *Byzantion* 22 (1952), 1-61; 23 (1953), 143-170 (revised English version in no. 78).

15. "Historical Maps of Acre," *Eretz-Israel* 2 (1953), 175-184 (Hebrew).

16. Review article of: S. Runciman, *A History of the Crusades, 2. The Kingdom of Jerusalem and the Frankish East, 1100-1187* (Cambridge, 1952). In: *Byzantion* 23 (1953), 569-572.

1954

17. "Les premiers temps de la féodalité dans le royaume latin de Jérusalem," *Revue d'histoire du droit* 22 (1954), 401-424 (revised English version in no. 78).

18. "Étude préliminaire sur les sources et la composition du *Livre des Assises des Bourgeois*," *RHDFE* 32 (1954), 198-227, 358-382 (revised English version in no. 78).

19. Review article of: S. Runciman, *A History of the Crusades, 3. The Kingdom of Acre and the later Crusades* (Cambridge, 1954). In: *Byzantion* 24 (1954), 327-330.

20. Review article of: G. Kraemer, *Der Sturz des Königreichs Jerusalem (583/1187) in der Darstellung des 'Imād ad-Dīn al-Kātib al-Iṣfahānī* (Wiesbaden, 1952). In: *Erasmus* 7 (1954), 419-420.

21. Review article of: P.W. Topping, *Feudal Institutions as Revealed in the Assises of Romania, the Law Code of Frankish Greece* (Philadelphia, 1949). In: *RHDFE* 32 (1954), 129-133.

1955

22. (with Ch. Perrat:) "Une *tenure en bourgeoisie* de Morée au XIIIe siècle," *RHDFE* 33 (1955), 99-102.

1956

23. "Ascalon and the Ascalon Strip in Crusader Politics," *Eretz-Israel* 4 (1956), 231-251 (Hebrew).

1957

24. "Jerusalem, Capital of the Crusader Kingdom," in *Judah and Jerusalem. The Twelfth Archaeological Convention* (Jerusalem, 1957), pp. 90-104 (Hebrew).

1958

25. "The City and County of Ascalon in the Crusader Period," *Eretz-Israel* 5 (1958), 224-237 (Hebrew).

26. Review article of: R.C. Smail, *Crusading Warfare (1097-1193)* (Cambridge, 1956). In: *Revue belge de philologie et d'histoire* 36 (1958), 303-304.

1959

27. "La noblesse et le régime féodal du royaume latin de Jérusalem," *Moyen Age* 65 (1959), 41-74 (revised English versions in nos. 48, 78).

28. Review article of: K.M. Setton and M.W. Baldwin, eds., *The First Hundred Years* (Philadelphia, 1955) [=*A History of the Crusades*, 1]. In: *Revue belge de philologie et d'histoire* 37 (1959), 167-170.

1960

29. *Palestine during the Crusader Period.* Tel Aviv, 1960. 75 pp. (Hebrew).

30. (with M. Benvenisti:) "Crusader Palestine: Map and Index," in *Atlas of Israel* (Jerusalem, 1960; second ed., Jerusalem, 1972). Sheet 9.10.

31. Review article of: Gunther von Pairis, *Historia Constantinopolitana*, ed. and trans. E. Assman (Weimar, 1956). In: *Revue belge de philologie et d'histoire* 38 (1960), 658-659.

1961/62

32. "Étude sur le droit des *Assises de Jérusalem*: droit de confiscation et droit d'exhérédation," *RHDFE* 39 (1961), 520-551; 40 (1962), 29-42 (revised English version in no. 78).

33. Review article of: *Le traité d'Emmanuel Piloti sur le passage en Terre Sainte*, ed. E. Nauwelaerts and B. Nauwelaerts (Louvain—Paris, 1958). In: *Revue belge de philologie et d'histoire* 40 (1962), 1095-1097.

1963

34. *A History of the Latin Kingdom of Jerusalem,* 2 vols. Jerusalem, 1963; 2nd ed. Jerusalem, 1971. 602 + 547 pp. (Hebrew) (French trans. in no. 51).

35. "Sinai and the Red Sea in Crusader Policy," in *Elath. The Eighteenth Archaeological Convention* (Jerusalem, 1963), pp. 168-181 (Hebrew) (English version in no. 78).

36. "High Education, General Education and High Schools," in *Theory and Practice in*

Education. Studies in Memory of Abraham Arnon (Tel-Aviv, 1963), pp. 463-470 (Hebrew).

1964

37. "The Battle of Hattin," *Eretz-Israel* 7 (1964), 117-124 (Hebrew) (for French and English versions see nos. 39, 78).

38. Review article of: R.L. Wolff and H.W. Hazard, eds., *The Later Crusades, 1189-1131* (Philadelphia, 1962) [=*The History of the Crusades*, ed. K.M.A. Setton, 2]. In: *Revue belge de philologie et d'histoire* 42 (1964), 633-634.

39. "La bataille de Hattîn," *Israel Exploration Journal* 14 (1964), 160-179 (for Hebrew and English versions see nos. 37, 78).

1965

40. "The 'Lovers of Zion' in the Middle Ages: Immigrations to Palestine in the Crusader Period," in *Western Galilee and the Coast of Galilee. The Nineteenth Archaeological Convention* (Jerusalem, 1965), pp. 129-136 (Hebrew).

1966

41. "Estates, Communities and the Constitution of the Latin Kingdom," *Proceedings of the Israel Academy of Sciences and Humanities* 2 (1966), pp. 1-42 (repr. Jerusalem, 1969, 42 pp.) (for an enlarged version see no. 78; an abridged version appeared in F.L. Cheyette, ed., *Lordship and Community in Medieval Europe* [New York, 1968], pp. 156-179).

1967

42. "The History of the Castle of Belvoir," *Bulletin of the Jewish Palestine Exploration Society* 31 (1967), 236-249 (Hebrew).

43. "The Monastery of the Cross," *Ariel* 18 (1967), 59-62.

44. "Jewish Resettlement in Crusader Jerusalem," *Ariel* 19 (1967), 60-66.

45. "Crusader Jerusalem," *Qadmoniot* 1 (1967), 39-46 (Hebrew).

46. "The Lintels of the Holy Sepulchre," *Qadmoniot* 1 (1967), 47-51 (Hebrew).

1968

47. *Jerusalem. Living City.* Jerusalem, 1968 (English, French, German and Spanish editions).

48. "The Nobility and the Feudal Regime in the Latin Kingdom of Jerusalem," in Cheyette, ed., *Lordship* (no. 41 above), pp. 156-179 (English translation of no. 27; see also no. 78).

49. "Christianity Between Heavenly and Earthly Jerusalem," in *Jerusalem Through the Ages. The Twenty-Fifth Archaeological Convention* (Jerusalem, 1968), pp. 179-192 (Hebrew).

50. (with S.N. Eisenstadt:) "Feudalism," in *International Encyclopedia of the Social Sciences* 5 (New York, 1968), pp. 393-403.

1969

51. *Histoire du royaume latin de Jérusalem.* 2 vols. Paris, 1969-71; 2nd ed., Paris, 1975 (French trans. of no. 34).

52. "The Next Ten Years," in *The University and Social Welfare*, ed. I. Katz (Jerusalem, 1969), pp. 175-178.

1972

53. *The Latin Kingdom of Jerusalem. European Colonialism in the Middle Ages.* London, 1972. 587 pp. (for Hebrew version see no. 63).

54. *The World of the Crusades.* Jerusalem, 1972. 160 pp. (for German trans. see no. 59).

55. "Foreword: Life and Works of Marino Sanudo," in the photographic reproduction of Sanudo's *Liber Secretorum Fidelium Crucis* (Jerusalem, 1972), pp. V-XVII.

1973

56. "R. Ashtori Ha-Parhi. The First Jewish Geographer of Eretz-Israel," in *Eretz-Shomron. The Thirtieth Archaeological Convention* (Jerusalem, 1973), pp. 106-113 (Hebrew).

57. "Preface: Biographical Sketch of Ct M. de Vogüé," in the photographic reproduction of M. de Vogüé, *Les Eglises de la Terre Sainte* (Jerusalem, 1973), pp. III-VI.

58. "I Veneziani e le colonie veneziane nel Regno Latino di Gerusalemme," in *Venezia e il Levante fino al sec. XV*, ed. A. Pertusi (Florence, 1973), pp. 625-656 (enlarged English version in no. 78).

1974

59. *Die Welt der Kreuzfahrer.* Wiesbaden, 1974; 2nd ed. 1979. (German trans. of no. 54).

60. "A Crusader Tomb of 1290 from Acre and the Last Archbishops of Nazareth," *Israel Exploration Journal* 24 (1974), 241-251.

61. Review article of: R.C. Smail, *The Crusaders in Syria and the Holy Land* (London, 1973). In: *Antiquity* 48 (1974), 323-324.

1975

62. *Heiliges Land. Geschichte des Heiliges Landes in Text und Bild.* Bern—Stuttgart, 1975; second ed. 1977.

63. *The Crusaders: The Profile of a Colonial Society.* Jerusalem, 1975. 661 pp. (Hebrew version of no. 53).

1976

64. "The Armenians in Jerusalem under the Crusaders," in *Armenian and Biblical Studies*, ed. M.E. Stone (Jerusalem, 1976), pp. 222-236.

65. "Notes on the History of the Jews in the Latin Kingdom of Jerusalem," *Shalem* 2 (1976), 103-112 (Hebrew) (English trans. in no. 74).

66. "The Autobiography of Obadyah the Norman Convert," *Tarbiz* 45 (1976), 272-295 (Hebrew) (for English version see no. 73).

67. Review article of: T. Tobler, *Descriptiones Terrae Sanctae* (Leipzig, 1874, repr. Hildesheim, 1974). In: *Bulletin of the Institute of Jewish Studies (1976)*.

1977

68. "Jewish Quarters in Jerusalem," *The Israel Museum News* 12 (1977), 80-91.

69. "History, Faith and Beauty," *Jerusalem, Most Fair of Cities* (Jerusalem, 1977), pp. 4-16.

70. "The Earliest Commune of Tripoli and the Tower of the Mint," in *Studies in Memory of Gaston Wiet*, ed. M. Rosen-Ayalon (Jerusalem, 1977), pp. 171-177.

71. "Crusader Cities," in *The Medieval City*, ed. H.A. Miskimin et al. (New Haven and London, 1977), pp. 179-199.

1978

72. "The Jewish Community as a Force for Jewish Continuity: An Historical Perspective," *Journal of Jewish Communal Services* 55 (1978), 23-43 (French and Hebrew translations).

1979

73. "The Autobiography of Obadiah the Norman, a Convert to Judaism at the Time of the First Crusade," in *Studies in Medieval Jewish History and Literature*, ed. I. Twersky (Cambridge, Mass., 1979), pp. 110-134 (English version of no. 66).

74. "Notes on the History of the Jews in the Latin Kingdom of Jerusalem," *Immanuel* 9 (1979), 81-87 (English version of no. 65).

75. "Jérusalem terrestre, Jérusalem céleste. Jérusalem dans la perspective chrétienne et juive au haut Moyen Age et à la veille de la première croisade," *Jérusalem: l'Unique et l'Universel. Colloques d'intellectuels juifs de langue française* (Vandôme, 1979), pp. 17-27.

76. "Christian Distraught in the Realization of Claims for Inheritance of the Holy City," *Cathedra* 11 (1979), 135-136 (Hebrew).

77. "The Defense Doctrine of the Crusaders," *Elazar Papers* 2 (1979), 16-23 (Hebrew).

1980

78. *Crusader Institutions.* Oxford, 1980. 536 pp.

79. "Jerusalem in Jewish and Christian Thought of the Early Middle Ages," *Cathedra* 17 (1980), 40-72 (Hebrew) (for English version see no. 81).

80. "Military Orders and Crusader Politics in the Second Half of the XIIIth Century," *Die geistlichen Ritterorden Europas*, ed. J. Fleckenstein and M. Hellmann (Sigmaringen, 1980), pp. 217-229.

81. "Jerusalem in the Christian and Jewish Perspectives of the Early Middle Ages," in *Settimane di Studi sull' Alto Medio Evo* (Spoleto, 1980), pp. 1-57 (for Hebrew version see no. 79).

1981

82. "The Archaeological Research of the Crusader Period," in *Thirty Years of Archaeology in Israel. 1948-1978* (Jerusalem, 1981), pp. 117-128 (Hebrew).

83. "On Ya'akov," in *In Memoriam J.L. Talmon* (Jerusalem, 1981), pp. 40-47 (Hebrew).

84. (Editor) *The History of Eretz-Israel under Moslem and Crusader Rule (634-1291).* Jerusalem, 1981 (Hebrew).

FULFILLMENT AND DIVERSION IN THE EIGHT CRUSADES

ROBERT S. LOPEZ
Yale University

Only two of the many medieval crusades hit the bull's eye, Jerusalem and the Holy Sepulchre: the First (though an inordinate number of participants went astray) and the Sixth (carried out through diplomacy and no fighting by excommunicated Frederick II). One may perhaps suspend sentence on the Second Crusade, which did not have to conquer Jerusalem since the Latins still had it but did nothing to strengthen their hold. Qualified recognition must be granted to the Third Crusade, which left Jerusalem to the Muslims but helped the Latins to enlarge and consolidate their holdings along the coast. None of the other four expeditions included in the list of what might be called the regular crusades touched the soil of the Holy Land: the Fourth went to Constantinople, the Fifth and the Seventh to Egypt, the Eighth to Tunis. If one adds the crusades that never aimed at Jerusalem — religious massacres like the Albigensian and Bogomil wars, political affairs like the Guelph coalitions against Ghibelline rulers and the weird personal vendetta of Boniface VIII against the Colonna noblemen in Palestrina, combinations of both like the German conquest of the Baltic region — it becomes still clearer that, strictly speaking, diversion was not a freak but almost a habit.

Must we be shocked? I do not believe so. Never in history has performance lived up to principles; nor are we bound to the crusaders' practice of making war for the love of God. Above all, the burden of historians is not to pass moral judgments, but to understand both the motivations and the opportunities of every crusade, see whether or not the game was played according to the rules as far as the hand consented, and appraise the ability of the players in maneuvering their trump cards — all this, of course, while allowing for a reasonable amount of self-serving, expediency, error and cross-purpose, since perfection is not of this world. Unfortunately, these obvious canons of interpretation seem to lose their compelling power before the mystic spell, the epic stature and the conflicting emotions of the crusades. Most textbook authors and many prominent specialists yield to the temptation of espousing old prejudices or exposing their own. Granted that total impartiality is neither possible nor desirable, for there is no full understanding without some involvement, the comments that follow will strive to reconsider fulfillment and diversion, consistency and aberration solely according to the prevalent convictions of the contemporaries. One would like to say "to majority opinion," but the numerical majority cannot be found out, and, at any rate, was never consulted: equality on earth was not a crusader ideal. It would be both more feasible and less anachronistic to look for what a Bernard of Clairvaux and a Marsilius of Padua would have called "the opinion of the weightier part," *pars valentior*; but that conception of valid consensus does not serve the purpose of a dispassionate assessment, for the weight of each person and the wisdom of his opinion were differently reckoned depending on the scales, whether lay or ecclesiastic, noble or burgher, German or French, aggressive or moderate.

There is, however, one standard by which the achievements and failures of each crusade may be impartially evaluated: consistency or inconsistency with the officially proclaimed aims of the First Crusade. The original program was clearly spelled out in 1095 at Clermont, promptly approved by the widest and weightiest consensus ever brought together in medieval times, and never directly challenged later. Unquestionably, in spite of its tenuous and distant link with Peace of God movements and notwithstanding the euphemistic labels *iter* or *passagium* (voyage or pilgrimage) that usually designated it, a crusade was conceived as an act of war. Of limited war, however: extermination, expulsion or forced baptism of the Muslims, even if they had been feasible, were no more anticipated than the immediate conversion of the Jews; such final solutions had to wait for an explicit decree of God. The pogroms that accompanied some crusades, the massacres of Muslim prisoners that pleased so many crusaders were clearly inconsistent with the program of Clermont. So were the crusades against heretics and political enemies; whether or not their promoters felt justified in stretching the program, they were a different game with different rules and need not be considered on the same plane as the eight regular crusades.

The Clermont plan singled out two goals only, both aiming at recovery rather than expansion; the irredentist appeal of the second goal, returning to Christian rule Christ's own city with whatever territory might be needed to insure free access to its shrines, must not obscure the fact that it was adopted chronologically after the first. Long before any thought was given to the liberation of Jerusalem, Gregory VII had launched another appeal: it was urgent to help the Greeks to roll the Muslim invaders back to the old Anatolian frontier, and, as an implicit if tactfully unstated part of the bargain, to mend the recent, still mendable schism of 1054. The second part of the plan fitted snugly into the first: more than four centuries earlier, Heraclius had moved from Constantinople to recover Jerusalem, and one century earlier, John Tzimiskes had almost done it again. Anatolia was the gateway to Syria, the restored harmony of Rome and Constantinople could blast open a Christian-held *iter* all the way from the shrine of Compostela to the Holy Sepulchre. Organized in 1095 by Urban II, accepted both by Alexius Comnenus and Godfrey of Bouillon, lubricated by delicate religious and political compromises, the First Crusade took off from Constantinople, suspiciously but auspiciously. No doubt the hope that military cooperation would bring out the fraternal bonds was soon dimmed by the realization that actually it exasperated their sibling rivalry. Nevertheless the first goal was never ideally forgotten for the second. It seems proper to evaluate fulfillment and diversion with both goals in mind.

With reason, all historians of the crusades stress the innumerable internal conflicts that frustrated the efforts and often betrayed the spirit of Clermont; but this is what could be expected when so many combatants of so many nations and from all social classes are thrown together for such a long span of time. The Muslims also were disunited, and so have been the defenders of freedom in our own time. If only in order not to be drowned in detail, it will be necessary to recall only the most conspicuous and constant differences among crusaders; the Greeks, who were in turn co-belligerents and victims but not partners in the planning and hence not held to the objectives of Clermont, are irrelevant in that context. Probably the sharpest contrast, though not as sharp as the mutual dislike of Greeks and Latins, was that of feudal barons and maritime burghers. It was not complicated by religious and linguistic misunderstandings, but in some other ways it resembled the cleavage between Rome and Constantinople. In both cases the pride and prejudice of an older culture confronted the arrogance and unconventionality of successful upstarts. Bolstered by ecclesiastic and aristocratic bias against trade, the barons' assumption that the bourgeois thirst for money was more sordid than feudal greed for land stood in the way of their recognizing the townsmen's allergy to custom duties and unpaid bills, to say nothing of their unwillingness to cut their own throats by giving up commerce with all infidels at once. In turn the burghers' older and keener knowledge of foreign lands and customs, as well as their perception of being snubbed, kept them from collaborating wholeheartedly with the barons; they fought bravely, but had no taste for hopeless fights.

There was progress, however, in the course of time. Each party held one of the two trump cards that enabled mere handfuls of warriors to conquer and retain far-away territory surrounded by enemies and torn by internal dissension: a charge of ironclad knights pierced through any deployment of adversary troops in the open field, an onslaught of missile-throwing galleys overwhelmed any hostile fleet on the open sea. In the First Crusade, surprise and bravery, plus the gingerly help of the Greeks, made it possible for land fighters alone to make the first and decisive breakthrough as far as the northern Syrian frontier; but they might have perished there if the seamen, belatedly rushing to the rescue of the winners, had not joined them for the last lap with supplies and siege machines. With assistance all the way, but no longer surprise, the Second Crusade was a flop. By the third try, all but proud Barbarossa had learned the lesson: they traveled by sea, though most of the fight was on land, and so did the majority of the later crusaders. Thereafter, the survival of the tired and outnumbered knights depended more and more on the dwindling good will of the seamen, but even then each group held on to its priorities. It may be idle to speculate whether the tattered kingdom "of Jerusalem" in Acre could have been rescued if the seamen had been given the run of the show, but we know that the Genoese kept Chios until the sixteenth century and the Venetians kept Crete until the seventeenth.

Still another conflict of attitudes was prominent in the crusades, the antagonism between extremists and moderates. It was understandably difficult for the first crusaders not to identify furor with fulfillment and compromise with diversion; no matter how temperate the original program, the hot climate of Palestine has always produced more zealots than cool heads. Still, war for its own sake was not a Clermont goal. After the first stampede, with Jerusalem in Christian hands, it was possible and advisable to learn how to keep it without unnecessary bloodshed. Without neglecting the defense of the Holy Sepulchre, the kings after Godfrey had a chance to bring order and prosperity through toleration, befriend their subjects, cultivate good relations with Greek, Armenian and Syrian Christians, and find points of agreement with the Muslims (to say nothing of the Jews). If a Fulcher of Chartres was overoptimistic in 1125 when he wrote that "confidence reconciles the most strange races" and envisaged an affluent new nation growing through intermarriage between Westerners and Oriental Christians or even converted Muslims—the conquerors were too few and too haughty, the country too small and too ragged for such miracles—fifty years later, William of Tyre, archbishop and chronicler, pointed out with reason that commerce with the Egyptians "always yielded to us advantages and honor." In 1184 Ibn Jubayr, a Muslim pilgrim, summed up as follows his impression of the kingdom: "The soldiers attend to their wars, the population trade in peace, and the world belongs to whomever grabs it."

That, too, was an overstatement. Two years later, by grabbing too much, the irresponsible Rainald of Châtillon set in motion Saladin's *jihād* that nearly annihilated the kingdom of Jerusalem. Before and after the unnecessary disaster of Hattin, however, there always were many who strove for peaceful coexistence. But intransigence had its inflexible champions within the kingdom, and still more among one-shot visiting crusaders who gave a disapproving, uninformed once-over to the situation, quickly washed their sins in the blood of the closest infidels, and hastened back home to sin again, leaving to the residents the task of mending the broken pots. All things considered, a modern student of the crusades is tempted to call such people, who flaunted rashness as a blackmail against common sense, the most dangerous diversionists. They undermined the internal stability and external reputation of the kingdom.

Contemporary critics, however, tended to be lenient towards misguided aggressivity. The basic test of diversion, as was pointed out at the beginning, was an alliance with the wrong party or an unprovoked attack on the wrong front; but the dividing line between right and wrong was not consistently or unanimously drawn. So long as Muslim Syria was divided among quarreling petty states, it was obviously justifiable to gang up with a weaker bad neighbor against a more dangerous one. For many years the kings of Jerusalem cultivated the friendship of Damascus as a counterpoise to Aleppo, and occasionally even the Seljuq sultans of Anatolia came in handy to frighten an aggressive adversary: these and other quirks of local politics aroused no serious indignation back home. The outcry about diversion grew sharp only where a heavy moral and material commitment was involved, that is, concerning alliances with or side attacks against the major infidel or schismatic powers overshadowing the tough but tiny states of the crusaders: the Byzantine Empire, the Egyptian Caliphate or Sultanate, and, for a shorter period, the Mongol Khanate of Iran.

Inasmuch as helping the Greeks and thereby mending the schism was one of the original goals, Byzantium ought to have been the best prospect for the closest alliance; but religious rapprochement hardly made any progress after the First Crusade, while reciprocal misunderstanding, mistrust and scorn flouted all efforts at effective military entente thereafter. Even Amalric I, the only king of Jerusalem who consistently promoted collaboration with Byzantium, botched a promising combined land-and-sea expedition against Egypt in 1169 by quarreling ceaselessly with Manuel Comnenus' admiral, Contostephanus. Most crusaders came to hate the Greeks more than the Muslims while coveting their flaunted riches; Bohemond I of Antioch and Henry VI of Germany planned crusades against Byzantium, and the Fourth Crusade was probably the only one where seamen and knights shelved their social antipathy and forgot their recent quarrels in order to bring down the Greeks. Yet the spirit of Clermont had not waned: one should not make too much of Innocent III's protests against that crusade since he cashed its dividends, but Innocent IV tried to patch up differences with John Vatatzes, the conquering emperor of Nicaea, and Gregory X came closer than any of his predecessors to fulfilling the first goal of Clermont. In 1274 the Council of Lyons sanctioned the full reconciliation of the Greek and Latin churches, not as a by-product but as the prelude of a joint crusade with Michael Palaeologus, restorer of the Byzantine Empire. But Gregory died two years later, the West was not ready, the Greeks were not persuaded, and the next popes chose to excommunicate the emperor and bless Charles of Anjou's projected crusade to revive the Latin Empire for his own benefit.

Egypt was unquestionably an enemy, indeed the strongest and hardest to tackle; this largely explains the crusaders' wavering conduct and ultimate failure. Frontier clashes would barely scratch its periphery, commercial blockades would hurt it no more than the crusaders' own states and the maritime cities of the West, and a decisive blow at its heart in the Nile valley would require a greater effort than the crusaders were prepared or eager to make so far from their immediate front. In 1118 King Baldwin I led a raid along the coast as far as the easternmost branch of the Nile, but a conquest of Egypt by land was unthinkable without some help from within. This opportunity was offered in 1163-69 by the disorders that accompanied the disintegration of the Fatimid Caliphate. For a short time Amalric I, invited by one of the contenders, kept a garrison in Cairo and became almost the overlord of the country; but his misuse of the Byzantine fleet delivered Egypt to Saladin, who in the following twenty years annexed Syria and overran most of the kingdom. Paradoxically, his triumphs and the brisk reaction of the Third Crusade tended to increase the mutual respect of Latins and Muslims; it is sometimes easier to build bridges between strenuous enemies than between uncongenial allies. As early as 1191 Richard Coeur-de-Lion proposed his sister or his niece to Saladin's brother as a wife and peace token; that was premature, but by 1229 Saladin's nephew was ready to yield Jerusalem peacefully to Frederick II. That agreement, it is true, was sandwiched between two crusades that hurled two seaborne armies straight into Egypt, both times to victory followed by disaster; but it is significant that both times the surprised and frightened successors of Saladin began by offering Jerusalem in return for the evacuation of Egypt. By turning them down, the crusaders lost two more chances of fulfilling the second goal of Clermont, temporarily at least; by losing both wars, they made obvious to themselves and the Muslims that they could not knock Egypt down.

Elated by their triumph over Louis IX's grand expedition in 1250, encouraged by their surprise victory over the Mongols of Hulagu Khan in 1260, helped indirectly by the inglorious collapse of the Latin Empire which opened possibilities for a deal with the Greeks, the new Mamluk rulers of Egypt patently engaged in the systematic reduction of the remaining strongholds of the crusaders' kingdom. But the Mongols, though now divided into four rival khanates, were still a match for them. Hulagu's son and grandson, Abagha (1265-82) and Arghun (1284-91), were eager to revenge the defeat of 1260, and kept sending embassies to the West to propose a joint, synchronized offensive that might well turn the tide against the Muslims. They had some Christian schismatic blood and strong Christian sympathies that might lead them to full conversion if the alliance came through. Of course one could wish better associates than these polygamous, unstable descendants of dreaded Jenghiz Khan, but none other was available to the discordant and depressed crusaders; and the Mamluks were worse. Whether by lack of imagination or by fear, the popes and the Western monarchs wasted time in inconclusive negotiations; by 1283, the formerly intransigent Templars bought a truce from the Mamluks by promising to warn them against impending crusades or Mongol attacks. The kingdom of Jerusalem did not really die for the faith: it committed suicide.

This long yet sketchy summation of well known relevant facts has no other ambition than to justify what will be a short, tentative reevaluation of the eight crusades. Obviously, the First Crusade comes closest to a perfect score. There were diversions and defections on the part of splinter groups; there were deplorable acts of cruelty, no matter how exaggerated in the accounts of sadistic Latin and terrified Muslim writers (mass murder was technologically ill organized at that time). Yet, considering the inflammatory character of much crusading propaganda, the impossibility of imposing a uniform discipline on disparate assemblages of volunteers, and in general the novelty of the enterprise as well as the unfamiliarity of most crusaders with the theatre of operations, the waste was relatively small. That both goals of Clermont were kept in mind all the time and altogether attained should be ascribed in the first place to the intelligence, energy and moderation of the leaders, Godfrey of Bouillon and Alexius Comnenus—although most writers did then and still do tend to play down the truly remarkable patience of the latter.

The Second Crusade was almost the antithesis of the first. Suggested in the first instance by the fall of Edessa, a peripheral crusader principality, it needed not worry about the Clermont goals, that had already been achieved. Preached by the most admired persuader of the time, Bernard of Clairvaux, who stressed the need for discipline and warned against molesting the Jews; led by the most powerful monarchs in the West, Louis VII of France and Conrad III of Germany, both eager to prove their zeal; seconded by a Byzantine emperor according to already tested methods and rules, the crusade did not move to an unknown and hostile operational base, but to a well established kingdom of Jerusalem, whose rulers had succeeded even in gaining a reliable Muslim ally (Unur of Damascus). Nevertheless, it snatched failure out of promise. The best part of the Germans were beaten in two divergent columns before getting close to the kingdom; the French barely restrained those among them who would rather fight against the Greeks; Damascus was scared away from the alliance, and the lost principality was not recovered. Technically, however, there was no diversion—or rather, two diversions bore fruits not contemplated at Clermont: a group of English, Flemish and Frisian crusaders took Lisbon from the Muslims, and a group of Germans darted away to attack the pagan Wends beyond the Elbe.

The Third Crusade is hard to evaluate: fulfillment or diversion? Not everything had been lost at Hattin: ten days after the defeat, the arrival of Conrad of Montferrat had galvanized the knights and burghers of Tyre, other fortified seaports were untaken, and some help had come from Sicily. When the Third Crusade got going, Barbarossa's German army almost "vanished," as Joshua Prawer says, after the accidental death of the emperor at the threshold of Syria; but without the massive intervention of the French and English armies of Philip Augustus and Richard Coeur-de-Lion, strongly supported by Italian marines, no counteroffensive would have been possible. The crusade gave the kingdom another century of life, and room enough to live in relative security and comfort. By stopping short of Jerusalem, however, it enticed the resident crusaders to forsake the second goal of Clermont and settle for the name without the substance of a "kingdom of Jerusalem." Moreover, there was a fruitful diversion: King Richard, who had snatched Cyprus not from the Muslims but from a Byzantine pretender, through two successive resales delivered the island to the exiled Jerusalem king, who transformed it into a crusader haven beyond Muslim reach.

The Fourth Crusade, initially branded as a betrayal by Innocent III, who soon after the rape of Constantinople nonetheless celebrated it as "the Lord's doing, admirable in our eyes," has been so persistently called a diversion—the diversion par excellence—that one is tempted to let the misnomer stay. It certainly went astray; but none of its diversionary drifts was unprecedented and most of them were unexpected. Officially, the target was said to be Egypt, the crusader's arch-enemy and recent conqueror of Jerusalem: this was unimpeachable, for ever since Amalric I's time it was understood that the key to Jerusalem lay in the Nile Valley. Secretly, Boniface of Montferrat and the other barons who planned the expedition intended to stop on their way to restore on the Byzantine throne the legitimate emperor. In return, his son, Alexius IV, promised more than he could keep: eventually, to pay most expenses, supply food and soldiers for the conquest of Egypt, maintain a small standing force in the kingdom of Jerusalem, *and* bring to pass the reunion of the Greek with the Latin Church. Never before had such an attractive offer been tendered: the first Clermont goal plus cooperation towards the second. The Venetians agreed with the barons to participate with their Doge and the largest fleet they had ever assembled, and to supply at a prearranged price all ships needed by the other crusaders; there is no proof that they knew in advance of the planned detour, but they welcomed it when it was disclosed. The rest of the garbled story is too well known to require a detailed account, but it need be cleansed of the sinister interpretations heaped on it by centuries of aristocratic and ecclesiastic bias. Everything was fouled up, but there is no reason to assume that Boniface of Montferrat, whose family had an untarnished record in the previous crusades and in the service of the Byzantine imperial family, accepted Alexius' offers with the intention of betraying him; there is no ground to criticize the Venetians for exacting payment for unused ships they had built on order at tremendous expense; there is no fairness in damning the crusaders who ran amok when they captured for the second time the Byzantine capital where no emperor they could trust had remained. Had he lived longer, Henry VI would have treated Constantinople much worse under slighter provocation; the only flat diversion in the Fourth Crusade, the siege of Zara that had revolted against Venice, was just one of the minor transgressions committed by nearly every party in every crusade.

The Sixth, bloodless Crusade, too, deserves a less unfavorable treatment than it usually receives: it did attain the second goal of Clermont. Whether the compromise on Jerusalem between Frederick II and Sultan al-Kāmil reflected cynicism or toleration (very probably something of both), it was dictated by common sense, and had a chance to work. Since neither the Christians nor the Muslims were willing to give up a city sacred to both, they ought to share it as equally as possible. The Christians recovered full sovereignty over Jerusalem and a narrow strip connecting it with the rest of the kingdom — enough for secure access, not enough for aggressive build-ups. The Muslims preserved what may be called extraterritorial rights over their shrines just across their border, and free access everywhere else. Like most equitable compromises after a long struggle, this one was greeted as a disgrace by extremists on both sides; but the idea of negotiated agreement had long been in the air, and history teaches that no feud is eternal if an honorable truce is steadily renewed for a sufficient number of years. As in the Third Crusade, the kings did not stay long enough to consolidate their results: Frederick was especially sabotaged by most of the clergy, and the pope, who had excommunicated him, had invaded his home state; al-Kāmil, too, had to fight his infuriated imāms and his unreliable relatives who held vassal portions of Saladin's heritage. Nevertheless the arrangement was not disturbed until 1239, the end of the ten-year truce; then, after al-Kāmil had died, one of his quarreling relatives grabbed Jerusalem but another returned it with some territorial additions. In 1243 the normally intransigent Templars reopened negotiations to ask for something more, but in 1244 a band of Khwarezmian Turks in the pay of the new sultan of Egypt grabbed Jerusalem, sacked the city and evacuated it promptly. The Muslim rulers of Damascus, Homs and Kerak still honored the truce; flanked by them, the best army the resident crusaders could muster precipitously counterattacked Egyptians and Khwarezmians near Gaza. It was another Hattin, and Jerusalem was lost for the following seven centuries.

Obviously Jerusalem could not be held without Egypt's spontaneous or extorted consent. The Fifth and Seventh Crusades were aimed at cowing Egypt into submission. Amalric's attempt at marching in along the coast had failed; the new expeditions relied on naval superiority and surprise landing. They struck directly by sea at the same place where Amalric and the Byzantine fleet had ended their unsuccessful attempt: Damietta, at the central mouth of the Nile due north of Cairo, a most valuable seaport that could serve as a pawn for exchange with Jerusalem, or a beachhead for an advance toward the Egyptian capital, or a permanent military and commercial Christian enclave linked to the West by sea. Amalric had besieged it in vain; the Fifth Crusade captured it in 1219 after a long siege; the Seventh recaptured it in two days in 1249. The first conquest was carried out by a fairly large but motley expeditionary force, commanded by an inflexible papal legate and a more receptive king of Jerusalem (John of Brienne); one of its followers was St. Francis of Assisi, who preached to the Egyptians without success but may have mollified Sultan al-Kāmil enough to prepare him for the later agreement of the Sixth Crusade. The second conquest was carefully organized, powerfully manned and prestigiously led by St. Louis IX. Both in 1219 and in 1249, as was mentioned before, the fall of Damietta prompted an Egyptian offer to ransom it by yielding Jerusalem in its stead; both times the crusaders refused the swap, both because they doubted the sultan's intention or ability to deliver and because they hoped to keep their gains and dictate harsher terms in his capital; both times they were beaten, approximately at the same place not far up the Nile, and forced to trade Damietta merely for a chance to go home again.

The second defeat was far worse than the first because the investment and casualties had been larger, and in the end the king of France with a large part of his army had to pay ransom, while many prisoners were massacred. This notwithstanding, a time-honored tradition asserts that St. Louis' noble behavior earned him undying prestige among the Muslims; possibly so, but unimpeachable contemporary evidence indicates that Frederick II's prestige was greater. On the other hand Louis IX's devotion, endurance and practical talent shone in the four years he spent in the kingdom of Jerusalem, working for the liberation of captives still held in Egypt, improving fortifications and fostering harmony among the resident crusaders. Not unlike Frederick II, he now was not unwilling to attain by agreement with Muslims the goal he had missed by war: in 1252 he was ready to join in an attack against an-Nāṣir of Aleppo and Damascus with the new Mamluk ruler of Egypt, who offered once more Jerusalem as a reward; but the Caliph of Baghdad succeeded in reconciling the Muslim rivals — the last service he rendered to his faith before Hulagu Khan, in 1258, conquered the religious capital of Islam and put him to death. Two years later, Hulagu's Christian lieutenant Kitbugha made his triumphal entrance in Damascus, flanked by the Christian rulers of Armenia and Antioch, and sent detachments as far as Gaza. The second goal of Clermont, hopelessly out of reach for the crusaders, was now close at hand to the Mongols, who in Baghdad had made a point to spare the Christians while massacring the Muslims. Defeated by the Mamluks near Bethsan while the main army was engaged on another front, the Mongols evacuated most of Syria, but kept harassing the Muslims with probing incursions and solicited the Western rulers to participate in a major coordinated attack. As they gradually relented their impetus, they improved their diplomatic manners: at first they had replied to the feelers of Western envoys (including those of Louis IX) with orders to submit, now they treated on equal and amiable terms. Between 1267 and 1276 the solicitations of Abagha Khan were especially frequent; in 1270, having beaten the attacks of his Mongol rivals (the khans of the Golden Horde and of Turkestan) he wrote the King of France urging him to bring over a crusade and promising all help he could give. But St. Louis had sailed to Tunis that very year, and the encounter never took place.

Down to our days, St. Louis' well earned halo has dazzled rigorous historians, who have desperately tried to explain away what they could not deny. To keep the saint untarnished, they have wronged the family man, the lucid thinker and the great organizer that Louis IX was. Of course he desperately wanted the armed assistance of Charles of Anjou, his brother; he thought, not without reason, that restoration of the tribute paid by Tunis to Charles' predecessors was the only bait that could tempt his brother temporarily away from his grand plans of conquest in Italy and the Greek Empire; a detour on Tunis seemed to him justified by the needs of the crusade and the virtue of family ties, whose sanctity had led him (as he stated) to grant the king of England, a less close relative, an overgenerous peace treaty. The initiative must have been his, not Charles'; the latter's lack of enthusiasm and tragic delay in joining the crusaders in Tunisia indicates it, and St. Louis was the last man who would yield his convictions to anybody's pressure. To make the detour possible, however, he did not hesitate to deceive his allies of both crusades, the Genoese seamen and marines, who would not have helped him had they known in advance that they were to attack their good ally and customer, the Emir of Tunis. Joinville, Louis' devoted cousin, seneschal and fellow-crusader in Egypt, was one of many Frenchmen who refused to accompany their king. Further, there is no proof whatever that Louis believed the absurd rumor, spread to rationalize the detour, that the Emir intended to convert to Christianity nor is it believable that in his age of good nautical maps and intensive travel he did not realize the distance between Tunis and Egypt, let alone Jerusalem.

Truth, not flattery is owed to the memory of a saint. The Eighth Crusade was not a justifiable detour but an unmitigated diversion. Its only success was the temporary conquest by the Genoese of a small place that had once been Carthage. Louis died before he could see his brother arrive at long last, grab the tribute and hasten back home in time to confiscate the shipwrecked goods of his fellow crusaders who had lingered and been caught in a storm. But he was too intelligent and conscientious not to feel that his second crusade had been a mistake resembling a sin. It is said that St. Louis' last words were "Jerusalem, Jerusalem" and expressed regret. It may be more exact to say that they expressed remorse.[1]

---

1 This article had already gone to the press when I read the important contributions of P. Meyvaert, "An Unknown Letter of Hulagu, Il-Khan of Persia, to King Louis IX of France," *Viator* 11 (1980) and J. Richard, "Une ambassade mongole à Paris en 1262," *Journal des Savants* (1979, but actually 1980). By showing that Hulagu, eight years before St. Louis undertook his diversionist Tunis crusade, had made constructive proposal for a joint effort in Syria, these contributions implicitly place a heavier burden of neglect on the shoulders of the French monarch.

POPE GREGORY VII'S "CRUSADING" PLANS OF 1074

H.E.J. COWDREY
St. Edmund Hall, Oxford

Professor Prawer has observed that Pope Gregory VII's plans of 1074 to bring military help to the Byzantine Empire are not without a bearing upon the development of the crusading idea.[1] The plans are familiar and have often been discussed; it is, indeed, doubtful whether anything new can be said about them unless further information comes to light. It may nevertheless be useful to bring together more completely than has hitherto been done the relevant evidence from papal, Italian, and Byzantine sources, and to review its significance in the current state of scholarly opinion.

Gregory's plans had a twofold background—in his burgeoning hope for the reunion of the Eastern and Western Churches, and in his troubled dealings with Robert Guiscard, the Norman duke of Apulia and Calabria. The reunion of the Churches was an especial concern of Gregory's earliest years as pope,[2] and his concern was intensified by his impression of the plight of Eastern Christians following the Seljuq victory at Manzikert in 1071. He alluded to reunion in a letter of 9 July 1073 to the Eastern Emperor Michael VII Dukas (1071-8), in which he cordially acknowledged the emperor's written and verbal

---

1 Prawer, *Histoire,* 1:159-161; cf. Carl Erdmann, *Die Entstehung des Kreuzzugsgedankens* (1935; repr., Stuttgart, 1955), pp. 145-153, trans. Marshall W. Baldwin and Walter Goffart, *The Origin of the Idea of Crusade* (Princeton, 1977), pp. 160-169 [hereafter cited, from the trans., as Erdmann, *Origin*].

2 See esp. Richard Koebner, "Der Dictatus Papae," in *Kritische Beiträge zur Geschichte des Mittelalters. Festschrift für Robert Holtzmann zum sechzigsten Geburtstag* (Berlin, 1933), pp. 64-92; Julia Gauss, *Ost und West in der Kirchen- und Papstgeschichte des 11. Jahrhunderts* (Zürich, 1967), pp. 41-68.

messages brought by two eastern monks, Thomas and Nicholas. He affirmed his wish to renew the ancient concord of the Roman church and its daughter of Constantinople, and he expressed his intention of sending Patriarch Dominicus of Grado to discuss more fully the matters that he had raised. In the meantime his own messenger would convey and bring back messages.[3] However, nothing is known of consequent negotiations; although Dominicus was in Venice during September 1074, having presumably by then completed any journey that he made.[4]

Gregory's policy towards Byzantium was thus based upon good will; but his attitude to Robert Guiscard was one of gathering disenchantment. As Archdeacon Hildebrand he had helped to negotiate the treaty of Melfi (1059) and the alliance by which the Norman leaders Robert Guiscard and Prince Richard of Capua were together to become protectors of the apostolic see.[5] But by the late 1060s Norman expansion towards the papal lands in Central Italy was causing Pope Alexander II (1061-73) such anxiety that the papacy sought to control the Normans by playing upon their divisions.[6] When Gregory became pope in April 1073 he at first sought to negotiate with Robert Guiscard.[7] But by autumn he, too, was concerned to counter Robert Guiscard's expansiveness by seeking to divide him from Richard of Capua. On 14 September Richard took an oath of fealty to Gregory, who was at Capua from 1 September to 15 November. Writing on 27 September to Erlembald, the Patarene leader at Milan, Gregory rejoiced that the Normans, who had conspired together to the peril of the Roman church, would now make peace with each other only when he so willed.[8] Gregory clearly intended that his separate understanding with

3   Gregory VII, *Registrum* 1.18, ed. Erich Caspar, MGH Epp. sel. 1-2 [hereafter cited as *Reg.*], pp. 29-30. For Gregory's eastern policy, see esp. Walther Holtzmann, "Studien zur Orientpolitik des Papsttums und zur Entstehung des ersten Kreuzzuges," *Historische Vierteljahrschrift* 22 (1924), 167-199, repr. in *Beiträge zur Reichs- und Papstgeschichte des hohen Mittelalters. Ausgewählte Aufsätze von Walther Holtzmann,* Bonner historische Forschungen 8 (Bonn, 1957) [hereafter cited, from the reprint, as Holtzmann], pp. 51-78; and Georg Hofmann, "Papst Gregor VII. und der christliche Osten," *Studi Gregoriani* 1 (1947), 169-181.

4   See the charter in L.A. Muratori, ed., *Antiquitates italicae medii aevi,* 1 (1738), 243-246; also *Reg.* 2.39, 31 December 1074, pp. 175-176.

5   For papal relations with the Normans, see esp. Ferdinand Chalandon, *Histoire de la domination normande en Italie et Sicile,* 1 (1907; repr. New York, 1960); Josef Déer, *Papsttum und Normannen. Untersuchungen zu ihren lehnsrechtlichen und kirchenpolitischen Beziehungen,* Studien und Quellen zur Welt Kaiser Friedrichs II. 1 (Cologne, 1972); and David Whitton, "Papal Policy in Rome, 1012-1124" (Univ. of Oxford D. Phil. thesis, 1979).

6   Chalandon, *Domination normande,* 1:222.

7   Vincenzo de Bartholomaeis, ed., *Storia de' Normanni di Amato di Montecassino,* 7. 7-9, Fonti per la storia d'Italia 76 (Rome, 1935) [hereafter cited as Amatus], pp. 297-299. Amatus' work survives only in an early fourteenth-century French version.

8   Amatus, 7.10, 12, pp. 300, 303; *Reg.* 1. 21*a*, 25, pp. 35-36, 41-42.

Richard of Capua would set a curb upon Robert Guiscard. But at the end of 1073 Robert Guiscard's capture of Amalfi was a reminder of his power, and also a blow to Gregory's ally Prince Gisulf of Salerno.[9] In February 1074 Robert Guiscard attacked Benevento and Pandulf, the son and heir of Prince Landulf VI whom Gregory favoured, was killed.[10] The duke of Apulia was clearly an increasing danger to the papacy and its South Italian friends, which it was in Gregory's interest yet more strongly to counter.

Gregory's freedom of action with regard both to Byzantium and to South Italy appeared to be the greater because King Henry IV of Germany was preoccupied by the Saxon rising which had begun in 1073 and which he did not master until his victory at the Unstrut in June 1075. His situation had prompted Henry in the autumn of 1073 to send Gregory a submissive letter which convinced the pope of his good will and obedience.[11] Thus, by early 1074 Gregory saw the way open to embark upon wide-ranging plans which would advance his ends both in the Byzantine Empire and in South Italy.[12]

The earliest testimony to what he had in mind is a letter of 2 February 1074, which he sent to Count William of Upper Burgundy.[13] He recalled a solemn promise which the count had made at Rome in the days of Alexander II that, if he were summoned, he would return there to fight for the *res sancti Petri.* He urged William now to prepare a force of knights to uphold the liberty of the Roman church by coming with his army to Rome in St. Peter's service should that prove necessary. He was also to transmit the summons to Count Raymond of Saint-Gilles, the future leader of the First Crusade whom Gregory here described as Prince Richard of Capua's father-in-law, Count Amadeus II of Savoy who was the son of Marchioness Adelaide of Turin, and other *fideles sancti Petri* who had likewise made promises at St. Peter's tomb. If his own reply were positive, William was further to charge the messenger by whom he sent it to enlist the support of Countess Beatrice of Tuscany together with her

---

9   *Chronici Amalphitani fragmenta,* 22, in Muratori, *Antiq. ital.* 1:211; cf. Chalandon, *Domination normande,* 1:233-234. For Gregory's favour towards Gisulf, see *Reg.* 1.2, 23 April 1073, p. 4.

10 *Chronica sancti Benedicti,* MGH SS 3:203; *Annales Beneventani a.*1073, MGH SS 3:181; cf. Gerold Meyer von Knonau, *Jahrbücher des Deutschen Reiches unter Heinrich IV. und Heinrich V.,* 2 (1894; repr., Berlin, 1964), 340. For Gregory's treaty of 12 August 1073 with Landulf, see *Reg.* 1.18*a*, pp. 30-31.

11 *Reg.* 1.29*a*, pp. 47-49, cf. 1.25.

12 The most detailed modern analysis of the evidence is in Meyer von Knonau, *Jahrbücher,* 2:341-344, 441-442; see also Augustin Fliche, *La Réforme grégorienne,* 2 (Paris, 1926), 169-172.

13 *Reg.* 1.46, pp. 69-71; cf. Amatus, 7.12, p. 303.

daughter Matilda and Matilda's husband Duke Godfrey of Lorraine.[14] Gregory declared that, in seeking to recruit so considerable a force, he had a twofold purpose. First, it would serve to pacify the Normans, who would thereby be intimidated, without any shedding of Christian blood, into obedience to righteousness (*iustitia*). Secondly, Gregory planned to cross to Constantinople and help Christians who, being greatly vexed by the Saracens, eagerly besought his aid. His use of the first person plural confirms that he purposed himself to travel to the East. He underlined the centrality of Constantinople in his plan by adding—rather artificially after summoning the *fideles sancti Petri* for the defence of St. Peter's property in Italy—that the knights who were already with him would suffice to deal with the rebellious Normans. On 1 March 1074, Gregory followed up this letter with a general summons to all Christians who were prepared to defend their faith.[15] He described its bearer as a Western Christian recently returned from the East with an eye-witness account, similar to others that he had received, of Seljuq campaigns almost to the very walls of Constantinople and of the slaughter of Christians in their thousands. He urged his hearers to the defence of the Eastern Empire and its Christian subjects; they were to report back to him what divine mercy prompted them to do. In this summons Gregory made no reference to the Normans, nor did he say anything about the leadership or organization of his expedition.

Historians have often regarded Gregory's initiative in thus summoning an expedition to the East as a direct and deliberate response to the Emperor Michael VII's approach of 1073.[16] But Walther Holtzmann was undoubtedly correct to see in this approach nothing more than a background factor. At no time did Gregory refer to it, while in his summons of 1 March he declared that his information was from reports of western travellers. In 1073-4 the situation of the Byzantine Empire seems, in fact, to have given rise to no pressing and immediate need for western military help. There is no evidence that Michael VII asked for it in any way analogous to Alexius Comnenus' appeal read to the council of Piacenza (1095), and there is no reason to presume an appeal.[17] Gregory at this stage made no express reference to the reunion of the Churches

14 On 3 January 1074 Gregory had already invited Matilda to accompany her mother on a visit to Rome and referred to other correspondence: *Reg.* 1.40, pp. 62-63.

15 *Reg.* 1.49, pp. 75-76. This letter, like *Reg.* 1.46, bears the marks of Gregory's own dictation.

16 Paul Riant, "Inventaire critique des lettres historiques des croisades," *AOL* 1 (1881), 62-64; Meyer von Knonau, *Jahrbücher,* 2:340-341 (but cf. 2:274-275); *Reg.* 1.18, p. 29, n. 2; Peter Charanis, "Byzantium, the West and the Origins of the First Crusade," *Byzantion* 19 (1947), 17-36, at pp. 20-21.

17 Holtzmann, pp. 56-57. For the situation in the Byzantine Empire, see Riant, "Inventaire," pp. 61-65.

which might suggest that he was actively negotiating about it. Everything points to the plan being Gregory's own, devised at his own time and in his own way, and taking its cue from travellers' reports rather than diplomacy with the Byzantine authorities.

It was against the dissident Normans that Gregory in the first instance directed it. Erdmann went so far as to argue that he deliberately took as his model Pope Leo IX's ill-fated expedition against the Normans in 1053. Admittedly there are similarities: not only did Gregory seek Lotharingian help as Leo had sought German,[18] but his assertion to Count William of Burgundy that he intended to restrain the Normans by intimidation rather than by shedding Christian blood echoes Leo's own design.[19] Yet it is hardly likely that Gregory would take as his model a campaign that led to the *débâcle* at Civitate, while the similarity of tactics can be explained by the prevailing war ethic of the reform papacy. Gregory acted as seemed best in face of the depredations of Robert Guiscard's Normans. At his Lent council in March 1074 he prepared the ground by excommunicating the duke and his accomplices, as a means to bringing about their repentance for infringing papal interests.[20]

At some time after 9 May Gregory felt ready to begin his expedition.[21] He could hope to gather together a fairly impressive host. Amongst lay figures, Countess Matilda of Tuscany, Marquis Azzo II of Este, and Robert Guiscard's brother-in-law and implacable enemy Prince Gisulf of Salerno had attended his Lent council; Matilda and Gisulf, at least, appear to have stayed on at Rome. Archbishop Guibert of Ravenna, too, had stayed, having promised Gregory that after Easter (20 April) he would give great military help against the Normans and also against the counts of Bagnorea, which lay to the east of Lake Bolsena, and would personally join his expedition. Gregory counted upon the aid of Prince Richard of Capua, whom the Montecassino chronicler Amatus described as being at this time his friend and ally. But Amatus makes it clear that it was upon Countess Matilda of Tuscany that Gregory mainly relied for forces.[22] Robert Guiscard was Amatus' hero and Gisulf of Salerno his *bête noire*. He poured scorn upon Gregory's plan to intimidate the duke by weight of numbers, saying that, since Gregory could not find men to aid him, he

---

18 Although as early as 7 April Gregory chided Duke Godfrey of Lorraine for his failure to fulfil his promise to aid St. Peter and send knights for his warfare: *Reg.* 1.72, pp. 103-104.
19 Erdmann, *Origin,* pp. 123, 160-161, 169; see Leo IX, Ep. 103, PL 143:777-781, at col. 779AB.
20 *Reg.* 1.85a, p. 123.
21 9 May is the date of Gregory's last letter before he left Rome: *Reg.* 1.83, pp. 118-119.
22 Bonizo of Sutri, *Liber ad amicum,* 7, ed. Ernst Dümmler, MGH LdeL 1:602-604; Amatus, 7.12, pp. 303-304. Gregory also referred to his debt to Countesses Beatrice and Matilda in his letter to Empress Agnes of 15 June: *Reg.* 1.85, pp. 121-123.

sought the help of women. When Beatrice and Matilda of Tuscany promised to bring 30,000 knights who, to make victory quite sure, would include a stiffening of 500 Germans, Gregory replied that, with Prince Richard's help, 20,000 would suffice to vanquish the paltry Norman rabble. But the countesses insisted upon overwhelming forces, and Gregory deferred to their judgement and determination.[23]

Thus far Amatus; the facts of the campaign were more prosaic. Gregory at first travelled northwards from Rome to meet the Tuscan forces. (It is not clear that Archbishop Guibert of Ravenna had any part in determining the direction of the march, or even that he was still present.) In the week after Pentecost two of his letters, with the remarkable dating *Data in expeditione,* show him to have been, on 12 June, at Monte Cimino between Sutri and Viterbo and, on 15 June, at San Flaviano which is to the south-east of Lake Bolsena and on the road northwards from Viterbo.[24] Amatus named Monte Cimino as the assembly point of the army, but Bonizo of Sutri San Flaviano.[25] The expedition speedily ended in fiasco. Three reasons were given. First, according to Amatus, Prince Gisulf of Salerno failed in his role of paymaster; willing though he was to compass the destruction of Robert Guiscard he distributed only contemptible rewards — "Indian girdles and bands and cheap cloths, fit only for girding women and equipping servants or for adorning walls." Secondly, again according to Amatus, the Pisan contingent of the Tuscan army recalled old grievances against Gisulf; for his safety Gregory had to send him away secretly to a refuge in Rome. Thirdly, according to Bonizo of Sutri, a sudden insurrection stirred up by Gregory's Lombard enemies called Countesses Beatrice and Matilda back to Tuscany. With his objectives wholly unfulfilled Gregory had perforce to return to Rome, where he fell seriously ill.[26] He sought abortively to deal with Robert Guiscard by way of negotiation: the duke obeyed his summons to a meeting at Benevento bringing a strong retinue, but Gregory was unable to attend.[27] During the summer Robert Guiscard allied himself with Duke Sergius of Naples against the principality of Capua. This prompted the mediation of Abbot Desiderius of Montecassino and led to a reconciliation, albeit short-

23   Amatus, 7.12, pp. 303-304.
24   *Reg.* 1.84-85, pp. 119-123. De Bartholomaeis' identification of Gregory's *ad Sanctum Flabianum* (Amatus 7.13, p. 305, n. 1), seems preferable to the more usual Fiano, to the east of Viterbo near the River Tiber, e.g. *Reg.* 1.85, p. 123, n. 1.
25   Amatus, 7.13, pp. 305-306; Bonizo of Sutri, 7, p. 604.
26   Amatus, 7.13-14, pp. 305-307 and (for Pisan grievances against Gisulf) 8.4, pp. 346-347; Bonizo of Sutri, 7, p. 604.
27   Amatus, 7.14, pp. 306-307.

lived, between Robert Guiscard and Richard of Capua.[28] Gregory's expedition had come to nothing, and the political situation in South Italy which followed was evidently beyond his control.

An inevitable consequence was that his wider plan to help the Byzantine Empire could not as yet be pursued. It was further hindered in the autumn of 1074 because Gregory was engaged in a conflict with King Philip I of France, against whom he sought to enlist the French bishops and lay magnates.[29] Yet the Byzantine plan was not without an echo, for on 10 September Gregory wrote to Duke William of Aquitaine a letter praising his readiness for St. Peter's service, but stating that it was not convenient then to write further about his expedition to the East, "since rumour has it that the Christians across the sea have repelled the fierceness of their pagan adversaries, and [Gregory] was still awaiting the counsel of Providence as to his future course of action." [30]

Gregory again relied upon hearsay; there is no hint that he had received an official communication from Byzantium, nor is there evidence that a major victory had been won there. In fact, whether directly or indirectly, Gregory's uncertainty is likely to have been the result of Byzantine diplomacy, of which it is impossible to discern how far if at all he was ever aware.[31] For the Emperor Michael VII's assessment of his need for standing, rather than merely occasional, western help against the Turks had led him to look for a possible ally in Gregory's adversary Robert Guiscard.[32] Michael was prepared to pay the price of abandoning Byzantine claims to sovereignty over the South Italian themes of Longobardia and Calabria. It was, therefore, with Robert Guiscard rather than with Gregory that he maintained communication.[33] He continued the attempts of his predecessor Romanus IV Diogenes (1067-71) to conclude a marriage alliance. He at first sought the hand of one of Robert Guiscard's daughters for his brother Constantine.[34] He was undeterred by the duke's

28 Amatus, 7.15-17, pp. 307-309. For Gregory's hesitant attitude to Robert Guiscard, see his letter to Countesses Beatrice and Matilda, *Reg.* 2.9, 16 Oct. 1074, pp. 138-140, which also reflects his dismay that his earlier plan had come to nothing.
29 *Reg.* 2.5, to the French archbishops and bishops, 10 September, pp. 129-133; *Reg.* 2.18, to Duke William of Aquitaine, 13 November, pp. 150-151. See Erdmann, *Origin,* pp. 162-166.
30 *Reg.* 2.3, pp. 126-128; cf. the language of *Reg.* 2.9.
31 For Byzantine diplomacy at this time, see Chalandon, *Domination normande,* 1:235-236, 258-264; Charanis (as n. 16).
32 John Scylitzes, Continuation of George Cedrenus, *Synopsis historiarum,* ed. Immanuel Bekker, CSHB, 2 (Bonn, 1839), 724.
33 There is no evidence that Gregory induced Robert Guiscard to make peace with Byzantium in 1074: Steven Runciman, *The Eastern Schism* (Oxford, 1955), p. 59.
34 For his letters see Konstantinos N. Sathas, *Bibliotheca graeca medii aevi,* 5 (Paris, 1876), 385-392, nos. 143-144; they are listed by Franz Dölger, *Regesten der Kaiserurkunden des oströmischen Reiches von 565-1453,* 2 (Munich, 1925), 18, nos. 989-990.

reluctance, and after the birth in 1074 of his own son Constantine he proposed that this child should be betrothed. Robert Guiscard now agreed, in due course dispatching a daughter to be brought up at Constantinople where she was given the name Helen.[35] The text survives of a marriage treaty, dated August 1074, in which the betrothed couple were accorded the title *basileis*, while Robert Guiscard himself was given the Byzantine rank of *nobilissimus* and many other gifts; he bound himself and his successors to friendship with Byzantium. Dölger has pointed out that the genuineness of the chrysobull is questionable on diplomatic grounds. But, with due caution, its date and purport are a guide to the probable course of events in the late summer of 1074.[36]

In the light of these events it would be surprising if the Byzantine emperor in 1074 renewed contact with the pope, and in the absence of evidence it may be presumed that he did not. Gregory, however, continued to hope for the obedient collaboration of Henry IV of Germany in the affairs of both Empires. On 7 December 1074 he sent the king two letters of admonition about them.[37] The second, which is one of five items in Gregory's Register inscribed *Dictatus pape*,[38] again canvassed an expedition to the East. Gregory said that he was prompted by pleas of Eastern Christians *(christiani ex partibus ultramarinis)*, most of whose number were daily suffering destruction and slaughter at the hands of the heathen. They had therefore asked him to send whatever help he could, lest the Christian religion perish in their time. Gregory's words suggest

---

35 Scylitzes, in George Cedrenus, 2:720, 724; Anne Comnène, *Alexiade,* 1.10.3, 12.2, ed. Bernard Leib, 1, rev. ed. (Paris, 1967) [hereafter cited as Anna Comnena], 37, 43, 171; John Zonaras, *Epitomae historiarum,* 18.17.7, ed. Theodore Büttner-Wobst, CSHB, 3 (Bonn, 1897), 714; Amatus, 7.26, pp. 318-320; Guillaume de Pouille, *La Geste de Robert Guiscard,* 3.501-502, ed. Marguerite Mathieu, Istituto siciliano di studi bizantini e neoellenici, Testi 4 (Palermo, 1961), pp. 190, 306.

36 The Greek text of the treaty is printed by P. Bezobrazov, "Chrisovul imperatora Michaila VII Duki," *Vizantiiskii Vremennik* 6 (1899), 140-143, with corrections by Eduard Kurtz in *Byzantinische Zeitschrift* 9 (1900), 280. For summaries and comment, Dölger, *Regesten,* 2:19, no. 1003, and Bernard Leib, *Rome, Kiev et Byzance à la fin du XIᵉ siècle* (Paris, 1924), pp. 172-174. Anna Comnena's statement that when Nicephorus III Botaniates was deposed in late March 1081 Constantine "had not yet reached his seventh year" is consistent with the date August 1074. Some Italian chronicles assigned Helen's dispatch to Constantinople to 1076: Lupus Protospatarius, *Chronicon a.* 1076, MGH SS 5:60; Romuald of Salerno, *Chronicon,* ed. Carlo A. Garufi, RIS² (Città di Castello, 1909-1935), p. 189.

37 *Reg.* 2.30-31, pp. 163-168; see Christian Schneider, *Prophetisches Sacerdotium und heilsgeschichtliches Regnum im Dialog, 1073-1077,* Münstersche Mittelalter-Schriften 9 (Munich, 1972), esp. pp. 85-91.

38 The five are *Reg.* 1.47, to Countess Matilda of Tuscany, 16 February 1074, pp. 71-73; *Reg.* 2.31 and 2.37 which concern Gregory's "crusading" plans, p. 165 and pp. 172-173; *Reg.* 2.43, to Bishop Hugh of Die, 5 January 1075, pp. 179-180; *Reg.* 2.55a, Gregory's twenty-seven theses on papal power entered between letters of 3 and 4 March 1075, pp. 201-208.

that he was responding, not to any official approach from the Byzantine emperor or court, but to "grass-roots" appeals of humbler, provincial Christians. He went on to say that he would himself endeavour, and would encourage other Christians, to bring help, to the point of laying down their lives for the brethren. He claimed that many both in Italy and beyond the Alps, to the number of more than 50,000, were already willing to follow him as general and pontiff *(dux et pontifex)* upon a campaign *(expeditio)* which should proceed in arms against the enemies of God and, under the pope's guidance, should reach the Lord's sepulchre at Jerusalem. Besides the military predicament of Eastern Christians, Gregory said that a second consideration moved him greatly *(per-maxime)* to contemplate such a task. The church of Constantinople, which differed from the apostolic see as regards the procession of the Holy Spirit, was looking for agreement with it; the Armenians—dissident since the council of Chalcedon (451)—were almost all estranged from the Catholic faith; and almost all Eastern Christians were awaiting what the faith of the apostle Peter might determine about their different beliefs.[39] Therefore it was time for Gregory to fulfil Christ's charge to St. Peter: *tu aliquando conversus confirma fratres tuos.*[40] Like his predecessors who had travelled eastwards to establish the Catholic faith—although, in fact, none had so travelled since Pope Constantine I (709-711)—Gregory must follow any way that Christ might open up to the twofold goal of confirming the faith and of defending Christian peoples *(pro eadem fide et christianorum defensione).* Gregory finally stated the role that he proposed for Henry, should an expedition take place. He sought Henry's counsel and, so far as the king was willing, his aid *(a te quero consilium et, ut tibi placet, auxilium)*; and he would leave Henry as protector of the Roman church during his absence. In face of all human doubts and conflicts Gregory trusted in the Holy Spirit to make clear to Henry what his plans and objectives were.

By 16 December Gregory was ready to issue a general summons—also inscribed in his Register as *Dictatus pape* — to all the *fideles sancti Petri,* especially those beyond the Alps.[41] Gregory presumed his hearers' familiarity with his purpose of bringing military aid to Christians beyond the sea in the Byzantine Empire, whom the devil was by his own devices striving to turn from the Catholic faith, and by his members the heathen was daily slaughtering like

---

39   For the Byzantine Church, see Runciman, pp. 1-78; the history of the Armenians is summarized by Arnold J. Toynbee, *Constantine Porphyrogenitus and his World* (Oxford, 1973), pp. 384-406.
40   Luke 22.32.
41   *Reg.* 2.37, pp. 172-173.

cattle. His plan had now matured beyond the hypothetical terms of his letter to Henry IV, for he called on some of his hearers to come to him as instructed by the bearer of his letter. He and they together would prepare the way for all who would journey beyond the sea. Gregory named no assembly date, but his dispatch on the same day of letters assuming his presence in Rome at the Lent council of 22-28 February 1075 shows that he did not plan to go before the spring.[42] On or soon after 16 December he revealed more of his plan to Countess Matilda of Tuscany in a letter bearing the marks of his own dictation.[43] He confessed that there were some whom he blushed to tell, lest he seem to be led by a mere fancy, how he was determined to cross the sea in aid of Christians who were being slaughtered like cattle. He made no mention of Henry IV, but he set out the part to be played by the group of pious women whose close spiritual association he had cultivated earlier in the year.[44] Henry's mother, the Empress Agnes, wished to accompany the expedition with Gregory and to bring Matilda with her; Gregory anticipated much strength from their prayers. Countess Beatrice was to stay in Italy and safeguard the interests there of the pope and of Countess Matilda.

Unlike Gregory's earlier plan, his winter preparations left no direct trace in sources other than his letters. From them it appears that he concentrated upon what were now more clearly defined than before as his twin objectives in the East: his military objective of freeing Eastern Christians from Muslim attacks, and his pastoral objective of bringing all Eastern Christians to unity in the faith of St. Peter. He made no express mention of the Normans; and his purpose as expressed in his general summons, that he and his retinue would prepare the way for a journey beyond the sea, will hardly bear Erdmann's interpretation that it was directed against Robert Guiscard.[45] The natural interpretation of his letter is not that a fully assembled host would first overawe the Normans and then proceed to the East according to his earlier plan; it is that an advance party to the East would be the forerunner of a larger company soon to follow. Gregory perhaps wished in December to exclude any such division of aims between South Italy and the East as had marked his first plan, and also any such feuds as had developed between the Pisans and the Salernitans.

42   *Reg.* 2.35-36, pp. 171-172.
43   *Briefsammlungen der Zeit Heinrichs IV.*, ed. Carl Erdmann and Norbert Fickermann, MGH Briefe 5 (1950), 86-87, Die Hannoversche Briefsammlung (1. Hildesheimer Briefe), no. 43; *The Epistolae vagantes of Pope Gregory VII*, ed. Herbert E.J. Cowdrey (Oxford, 1972), pp. 10-13, no. 5.
44   *Reg.* 1.85, pp. 121-123.
45   Erdmann, *Origin*, p. 167, n. 74.

There is, however, no evidence that this time forces ever assembled; indeed, Gregory's letter of 22 January 1075 to Abbot Hugh of Cluny already expressed his anguish of mind that his endeavours on the Church's behalf had been without avail. The Eastern Church had fallen away from the Catholic faith, and Satan was everywhere killing Christians by means of his members. In the West, there were no earthly princes who preferred God's honour and right-eousness to temporal gain; while his Italian neighbours, whether Romans, Lombards, or Normans, were worse than Jews and pagans.[46] Gregory clearly regarded his plans of 1074 as in total ruins. It was, indeed, the case that the plans and counter-plans of that year achieved nothing, whether for better or for worse. They did not improve matters in South Italy, for at his Lent council of 1075 Gregory again excommunicated Robert Guiscard, together with his nephew Robert of Loritello, as *invasores bonorum sancti Petri*.[47] The West brought no help to the East, nor were relations between the Churches improved. But they did not make matters worse. Despite the Emperor Michael VII's dealings with Gregory's adversary Robert Guiscard, about which Gregory may or may not have known, Gregory in 1078 excommunicated his supplanter, Nicephorus III Botaniates (1078-81); and in 1080, after Gregory renewed at Ceprano his alliance with Robert Guiscard, he praised Michael VII as *gloriosissimus imperator*.[48]

In the political world Gregory's plans came to nothing, but they may have had repercussions and interactions in the world of ideas. The first evidence for this is two odes written by Archbishop Alfanus I of Salerno to Prince Gisulf and his brother Guy.[49] Alfanus incited them to achievements whose scope matched Gregory's intentions. He urged the prince to continue his warfare against the Normans and to extend it against both Greeks and Turks.[50] Before Guy he opened up a yet more glorious prospect. He praised him for his past victories over the Normans — the *gens Gallorum* who had settled in Lombard Italy *velut una lues pecorum*. These victories were but an earnest of those to come, not only against the Normans but to win the Byzantine throne: *Evigilet studium Graeca trophaea tuum*.[51] The odes date from before Gisulf's quarrel

46   *Reg.* 2.49, pp. 188-190.
47   *Reg.* 2.52*a,* pp. 196-197.
48   *Reg.* 6.5*b,* p. 400; 8.6, 25 July 1080, pp. 523-524. For the latter letter and its circumstances, see Chalandon, *Domination normande,* 1:265-266, and Holtzmann, pp. 57-58.
49   *I carmi di Alfano I arcivescovo di Salerno,* ed. Anselmo Lentini and Faustino Avagliano, Miscellanea cassinese 38 (Montecassino, 1974), pp. 143-144, 150-152, carmi 17, 20; also PL 147:1256-1258, nos. 34-35.
50   Carme 17; see Anselmo Lentini, "Le odi di Alfano ai principi Gisulfo e Guido di Salerno," *Aevum* 31 (1957) [hereafter cited as Lentini, "Le odi"], 230-240, at p. 233.
51   Carme 20, line 100; see Lentini, "Le odi," pp. 234-236.

with Guy at an unknown date in 1075, before the end of which year Guy was in any case killed by the Normans.[52] No date before 1074 suggests itself, although Gregory's plans of that year provide a probable model. Despite attempts by Schipa and Lentini to date the odes precisely—in early 1074 and summer/autumn 1075 respectively[53]—it is not likely that they relate to any particular historical juncture in those years. They read like a talented court prelate's encomia of his political patrons. They play on such local Salernitan themes as hatred of the Normans whom Alfanus represents as flooding the land after the murder of Prince Guaimar V in 1052, and on a tradition of hostility to Byzantium. Indeed, Alfanus' call to Guy to seek the Byzantine throne fits uneasily with Gregory's continuing good will towards the Emperor Michael VII. Nevertheless, given the general similarity of purport, the odes probably took their inspiration from Gregory's call for an expedition having military aims in both South Italy and Byzantium, and illustrate its power to kindle the imagination of those towards whom it was directed.

Secondly, Gregory's plans call for comparison with Sibylline prophecies of the last emperor and comparable literature which were current in the eleventh century. Before 1074, Latin texts of the Tiburtine Sibyl had already coloured, in ways foreshadowing Gregory's plans, the ultra-imperialist Bishop Benzo of Alba's representation of Henry IV at the time of the Cadalan schism of 1061-3. Benzo then concocted a letter purporting to be from the Byzantine Emperor Constantine X Dukas (1059-67) to the antipope Honorius II. Constantine proposed that he and the antipope should form a league with the boy-king Henry, in which Constantine would pay soldiers who, under papal leadership *(te praevio)* would go *usque ad sepulchrum Domini,* destroying the Normans and restoring Christian *libertas* for all time.[54] These objectives were manifestly

52   Amatus, 8.12, pp. 352-353. For the date of Guy's death, see Michelangelo Schipa,"Storia del principato longobardo di Salerno," 10-12, *Archivio storico per le province napolitane* 12 (1887), 513-588 [hereafter cited as Schipa, "Storia"], at p. 572; Lentini, "Le odi," p. 238.

53   Michelangelo Schipa, *Alfano I, arcivescovo di Salerno. Studio storico-literario* (Salerno, 1880), pp. 17, 37-42; "Storia," p. 569; Lentini, "Le odi," pp. 232, 233, 238. Lentini's argument for 1075 fails because of his unsupported presumption that Michael VII's treaty with Robert Guiscard was made in 1075, and that Gregory knew of and reacted to it.

54   Benzo of Alba, *Ad Henricum IV imperatorem libri VII,* 2.12, ed. Karl Pertz, MGH SS 11:617. For the Tiburtine Sibyl, see Ernst Sackur, *Sibyllinische Texte und Forschungen* (Halle-an-der-Saale, 1898), pp. 177-187, at pp. 185-186). See also the texts and comment in Adso Dervensis, *De ortu et tempore Antechristi, necnon et tractatus qui ab eo dependunt,* ed. D. Verhelst, CC cont. med. 45 (Turnhout, 1976), pp. 26, 46-47, 53, 72, 101-102, 106-110, 123, 135, 140, 149 The indispensable discussion of the older material is Carl Erdmann, "Endkaiserglaube und Kreuzzugsgedanke i, 11. Jahrhundert," *Zeitschrift für Kirchengeschichte* 11 (1932), 384-414, also Prawer, *Histoire,* 1:172-173. The date and content of Constantine's supposed letter are discussed by Hugo M. Lehmgrübner, *Benzo von Alba, ein Verfechter der kaiserlichen Staatsidee unter Heinrich IV.* (Berlin, 1887), pp. 93-94, 99-111.

similar to Gregory's in 1074. If such ideas formed something of the background of his plans, they in their turn foreshadowed the programme which Benzo was to set before the grown-up Henry in 1085/6. Benzo recalled Charlemagne's legendary connection with Jerusalem and identified Henry as the future *signifer christianae religionis*. The whole world looked to him as a redeemer. Alluding to the mid-eleventh-century prophecy of the Cuman Sibyl, for which Erdmann suggested an origin in the circle of Gregory's ally Countess Matilda of Tuscany, Benzo set out how Henry would restore Apulia and Calabria to their pristine state before the Norman incursion, how he would wear his crown in Byzantium, and finally how he would proceed to Jerusalem where, having reverenced the Holy Sepulchre, he would also be crowned.[55] The similarities between Benzo's writings and Gregory's plans of 1074 are remarkable, and Erdmann raised the question whether Gregory knew at least the Tiburtine Sibyl's prophecy and sought to claim for himself something of the last emperor's role. In other words, by leading an army to the Holy Sepulchre, did Gregory seek to claim for the papacy a world role which the Sibylline literature associated with the emperor, while he relegated Henry, as emperor-to-be, to an ancillary role as protector of the Roman church? And was Gregory's bid to vindicate the faith of St. Peter among Eastern Christians a pre-empting of such an idea as Benzo's, that the whole world would look to Henry as a redeemer? Erdmann's own cautious answer should be decisive: the hypothesis of an influence upon Gregory is attractive — so attractive that historians would be wise to refrain from adopting it in default of positive evidence in the sources.[56]

Together with Gregory's plans of 1074, such flights of fancy as those in Alfanus' odes and in the Sibylline prophecies with their echoes in Benzo of Alba are mainly of interest as showing how, even before the First Crusade, men were beginning to envisage political and military actions on an international scale having the Holy Sepulchre in some way among their objects. As regards the direct bearing of Gregory's plans upon the crusade, at least one writer, with hindsight, declared that they inspired Pope Urban II's preaching of it. Urban's *Vita* in the *Liber pontificalis* records that Urban had heard how Gregory had called upon the *ultramontani* to go to Jerusalem for the defence of the Christian faith and to free the Lord's sepulchre from its enemies' hands; he successfully preached an expedition which Henry IV's hostility had frustrated.[57] But in 1074

---

55 Benzo of Alba, *Ad Heinricum,* 1.14-15, 17, cf. 19, pp. 604-607, for the date, see Lehmgrübner, *Benzo von Alba,* pp. 28-29. Erdmann edited the text of the Cuman Sibyl: "Endkaiserglaube," pp. 396-398, with comment on pp. 400, 406-408.

56 Erdmann, "Endkaiserglaube," p. 408.

57 *Le Liber pontificalis,* ed. Louis Duchesne, 2 (Paris, 1892), 293.

Urban was still a monk at Cluny, and the *Vita* seems to depend upon a reading of Gregory's letters, not upon a living tradition at Rome about what really happened. While it is likely that Urban became acquainted with Gregory's plans at least after becoming cardinal-bishop of Ostia in 1080, it is impossible not to agree with Professor Riley-Smith that they fell short of the armed pilgrimage that Urban's preaching called forth, and therefore of a crusade as a modern historian may reasonably define it: "Gregory's letters contain no clear link between the planned expedition and pilgrimages, no Indulgence and, again, no sign of the vow and resulting protection for crusaders."[58] Yet many ingredients of crusading preaching and motives were already discernible. Gregory repeatedly emphasized the martyrdom for the sake of Christian brethren and in the name of Christ, which was a main inspiration of crusading zeal. If he did not promise an indulgence even to the extent that Alexander II had foreshadowed it in 1063 to French knights before the Barbastro campaign,[59] he laid stress on the eternal reward which his warfare would convey: *per momentaneum laborem aeternam potestis acquirere mercedem.*[60] Above all, in 1074 Gregory twice issued general summonses, appealing to the military classes on both sides of the Alps to wage religiously motivated warfare for the liberation of Eastern Christians and for the promotion of Christian unity. Such plans for a papally directed campaign which enlisted the international military classes of Western Europe, which promised the crown of martyrdom and other spiritual rewards, and which encompassed worship at the Holy Sepulchre within its objectives, marked a significant stage in the development of the idea of crusade. It is more likely than not that Gregory's plans were powerfully present in Urban's mind when he preached his sermon at Clermont in 1095.[61]

---

58 Jonathan Riley-Smith, *What Were the Crusades?* (London, 1978), p. 75; cf. Paul Rousset, *Les Origines et les charactères de la première croisade* (1945; repr., New York, 1978), pp. 50-53.
59 *Epistolae pontificum Romanorum ineditae,* ed. Samuel Loewenfeld (1885; repr., Graz, 1959), p. 43, no. 82.
60 *Reg.* 2.37, p. 173.
61 Cf. Hans E. Mayer, *The Crusades,* trans. John Gillingham (Oxford, 1972), p. 22.

THE FIRST CRUSADE AND ST. PETER

JONATHAN RILEY-SMITH
Royal Holloway College, University of London

Certain saints were associated with the success of the First Crusade. Instances of devotion to them were reported; they were believed to be interceding with God for victory; some of them even appeared in visions to crusaders. St. Peter was one of them, but he was not nearly as prominent as one would have expected him to be: indeed it could be said that he was overshadowed by SS. Andrew and George. One gets the impression, moreover, of a saint associated with Antioch, his first bishopric, rather than with Rome, his second. This is very surprising and in the first part of this paper I will show why one might have supposed St. Peter, and the Roman St. Peter at that, to have been regarded preeminently as the patron of the expedition. Then, after drawing attention to the fact that he was not, I will try to explain why he appeared chiefly as Bishop of Antioch, rather than as Bishop of Rome, and why anyway he played a comparatively minor part in the ideology of the First Crusade. I will be using evidence provided by all the authors of contemporary or near-contemporary accounts of the crusade, whether eyewitnesses or not. Many of the most interesting ideas were in fact expressed by those senior and educated clergymen who stayed at home and wrote their narratives at second hand, and in a subject like this their views are as relevant as those of the men who took part in the expedition.[1]

---

1   I have used all the written evidence up to c. 1140, including Orderic Vitalis's account of the crusade. I have not referred, except in particular instances, to Caffaro's *De liberatione*, because, even though Caffaro was almost an adult at the time of the crusade, he did not write it until after 1140 and may have come under later influences. I accept many of the arguments

The crusade was launched by Pope Urban II, St. Peter's vicar. He claimed to have instigated it[2] and most contemporaries gave him the credit for it.[3] Nearly all the authors of accounts of the crusade reported his proclamation of war at Clermont[4] and several referred to the recruiting drive that followed.[5] His

of Suzanne Duparc-Quioc, *La Chanson d'Antioche*, 2 vols. Documents relatifs à l'histoire des croisades 11 (Paris, 1977-78), including the suggestion (2: 148-170) that the earliest version of the *Chanson d'Antioche* predated the narrative of Albert of Aachen, but the *Chanson* that has come down to us is the result of a reworking in c. 1180 and I have not thought it advisable to use it here, although it confirms what I have to say. And I have not used the Provençal fragment of the *Chanson*, ed. Paul Meyer, *AOL* 2 (1884), 467-509, because its text is corrupt.

2   Wilhelm Wiederhold, "Papsturkunden in Florenz," *Nachrichten von der Gesellschaft der Wissenschaften zu Göttingen*, Phil.-hist. Kl. (Göttingen, 1901), p. 313. See also Pope Paschal II's letter of 1100. Heinrich Hagenmeyer, *Die Kreuzzugsbriefe aus den Jahren 1088-1100* (Innsbruck, 1901), p. 179 [hereafter cited as Hagenmeyer].

3   Hagenmeyer, p. 164; Fulcher of Chartres, *Historia Hierosolymitana*, 1.1.1-5, ed. Heinrich Hagenmeyer (Heidelberg, 1913), pp. 120-123 [hereafter cited as Fulcher of Chartres]; Ralph of Caen, *Gesta Tancredi*, RHC HOcc. 3:606 [hereafter cited as Ralph of Caen]; Ekkehard of Aura, *Hierosolymita*, RHC HOcc. 5:15-17 [hereafter cited as Ekkehard of Aura]; Guibert of Nogent, *Historia quae dicitur Gesta Dei per Francos*, RHC HOcc. 4:136 [hereafter cited as Guibert of Nogent]; Bernold, *Chronicon*, MGH SS 5:464 [hereafter cited as Bernold]; *Narratio Floriacensis de captis Antiochia et Hierosolyma*, RHC HOcc. 5:356 [hereafter cited as *Narratio Floriacensis*]; Orderic Vitalis, *Historia aecclesiastica*, ed. and trans. Marjorie Chibnall, 6 vols. (Oxford, 1969-79), 5:4-6, 30, 228 [hereafter cited as Orderic Vitalis]. See also the references in notes 4-6 below. One should discount the stories of heavenly messages transmitted to the pope by others found in Albert of Aachen, *Historia Hierosolymitana*, RHC HOcc. 4:273 [hereafter cited as Albert of Aachen], who probably followed the early version of the *Chanson d'Antioche*, pp. 30-34; *Historia peregrinorum euntium Jerusolymam*, RHC HOcc. 3:169 [hereafter cited as *Historia peregrinorum*]; Caffaro, *De liberatione civitatum orientis*, in *Annali Genovesi*, ed. Luigi T. Belgrano, 5 vols. (Genoa and Rome, 1890-1929), 1:100-101; and also an original initiative by Bohemond of Taranto in William of Malmesbury, *De gestis regum Anglorum*, ed. William Stubbs, RS 90 (London, 1887-89), 2:390, 453 [hereafter cited as William of Malmesbury].

4   Baldric of Bourgueil, *Historia Jerosolimitana*, RHC Hocc. 4:12-16 [hereafter cited as Baldric of Bourgueil]; Fulcher of Chartres, pp. 132-143; Guibert of Nogent, pp. 137-140; Robert of Rheims, *Historia Iherosolimitana*, RHC HOcc. 3:727-730 [hereafter cited as Robert of Rheims]; *Gesta Francorum et aliorum Hierosolimitanorum*, ed. Rosalind Hill (London, 1962), pp. 1-2 [hereafter cited as *Gesta Francorum*]; Peter Tudebode, *Historia de Hierosolymitana itinere*, ed. John H. and Laurita L. Hill, Documents relatifs à l'histoire des croisades 12 (Paris, 1977), pp. 31-32 [hereafter cited as Peter Tudebode]; Bartolf of Nangis, *Gesta Francorum Iherusalem expugnantium*, RHC HOcc. 3:491-492 [hereafter cited as Bartolf of Nangis]; Ekkehard of Aura, p. 15; Gaufridus, *Dictamen de primordiis ecclesiae Castaliensis*, RHC HOcc. 5:348 [hereafter cited as Gaufridus]; Hugh of St. Maria, *Itineris Hierosolymitani compendium*, RHC HOcc. 5:363 [hereafter cited as Hugh of St. Maria]; *Narratio Floriacensis*, p. 356; Bernold, p. 464; William of Malmesbury, 2:393-398; Albert of Aachen, pp. 273-274; *Historia peregrinorum*, pp. 169-170; Orderic Vitalis, 5:14-18, 206-208.

5   *Narratio Floriacensis*, p. 356: Gaufridus, p. 348; *Gesta Andegavensium peregrinorum*, RHC HOcc. 5:345. See Baldric of Bourgueil, p. 15; *De reliquis sanctissimae crucis et dominici sepulchri Scaphusam allatis*, RHC HOcc. 5:336; *Notitiae duae Lemovicenses de praedicatione crucis in Aquitania*, RHC HOcc. 5:350, 352. And see also Frederic Duncalf, "The Councils of

authority over the crusade was recognised in a letter written to him on 11 September 1098 by the leaders of the army in Syria.

> Now we your sons ask you, our spiritual father, who initiated this journey and made us all leave all our lands and possessions by your sermons and ordered us to follow Christ, carrying our crosses, and exhorted us to exalt the Christian name, to complete what you encouraged and come, bringing whomsoever you can with you... Come, you who are father and head of the Christian religion... and finish this war *which is your own*... And so complete with us the journey of Jesus Christ begun by us and preached by you and open the gates of both Jerusalems to us and liberate the Holy Sepulchre and exalt the Christian name over all names... If you come and with us bring to an end the journey begun through you all the world will be obedient to you.[6]

Urban appointed churchmen to represent him in the armies[7] and he made it clear that Bishop Adhémar of Le Puy, the chief legate, was his personal representative, instituted in office by papal authority to exercise the powers granted by Christ to St. Peter.

> We have put (Adhémar) in our place as leader of this journey and labour and consequently (the crusaders)... should comply with his orders as if they were ours and should submit to his sentences of loosing and binding.[8]

The terms of Adhémar's appointment were well understood. It was known that he personally represented Urban and in September 1098 the leaders of the crusade reported to the pope the death of the legate, "whom you gave us as your vicar."[9] His powers of excommunication and absolution were men-

Piacenza and Clermont," *A History of the Crusades,* ed. Kenneth M. Setton, 2nd ed., 4 vols. so far (Madison, Wis., 1969-   ), 1:251.

6   Hagenmeyer, pp. 164-165.

7   See Jean Richard, "Quelques textes sur les premiers temps de l'église latine de Jérusalem," *Mélanges Clovis Brunel* 2 (Paris, 1955), 420-423.

8   Hagenmeyer, pp. 136-7. See also below p. 51. For Adhémar, see John H. and Laurita L. Hill, "Contemporary Accounts and the Later Reputation of Adhémar, Bishop of Puy," *Medievalia et Humanistica* 9 (1955), 30-38; James A. Brundage, "Adhémar of Puy. The Bishop and his Critics," *Speculum* 34 (1959), 201-212; Hans E. Mayer, "Zur Beurteilung Adhémars von Le Puy," *Deutsches Archiv* 16 (1960), 547-552; Jean Richard, "La papauté et la direction de la première croisade," *Journal des savants* (1960), 49-58.

9   Hagenmeyer, p. 164. See also Fulcher of Chartres, pp. 138-139; Guibert of Nogent, p. 140; *Historia peregrinorum,* p. 171; Orderic Vitalis 5:18. Fulcher of Chartres, p. 252, also referred to him as "vir apostolicus."

tioned,[10] as was the papal command to all to obey him.[11] He had been given the office of government[12] and the phrases used of it were revealing: he was "patronus noster,"[13] "rector et pastor"[14] and "like a father and lord."[15] His death meant the loss of one whose leadership had united the army: "there was no king in Israel."[16] One writer, describing his surrender on his deathbed of his powers to Arnulf of Chocques, made him speak of his "ministry of teaching," delivered to him by the pope, and of Arnulf's future "ministry for Christ" and power to absolve sins.[17] He was "necessary" and "useful" to the crusade and he comforted and strengthened the crusaders in the Lord.[18] He was

> counsel of the rich, consoler of those who mourn, sustainer of the weak, treasure of the indigent, reconciler of the discordant.[19]

Three authors, Robert of Rheims,[20] Baldric of Bourgueil and Ralph of Caen, compared him to Moses. To Baldric his sharing of the leadership with Raymond of St. Gilles was an example of the true relationship that should exist between Church and State.

> See the *sacerdotium* and *regnum*; the clerical order and the lay are in agreement on the leadership of the army of God. Bishop and Count are before us in the guises of Moses and Aaron.[21]

To Ralph he was, like Moses, the leader of the people on Christ's behalf, a voice mediating God's commands to them, zealous in instruction and in the giving of justice.[22] It will be noticed how closely all of this corresponded to the eleventh-century reformers' ideal of a good bishop, obedient to Rome.[23]

---

10   Ekkehard of Aura, p. 16: Guibert of Nogent, p. 210.
11   Baldric of Bourgueil, p. 15; Orderic Vitalis 5:18.
12   Guibert of Nogent, pp. 140, 210; Fulcher of Chartres, pp. 138-139; Robert of Rheims, p. 731. See also William of Malmesbury 2:398, 421.
13   Fulcher of Chartres, p. 196. See Baldric of Bourgueil, p. 15.
14   *Gesta Francorum,* p. 74.
15   Baldric of Bourgueil, p. 82; also Orderic Vitalis 5:132. But see Raymond of Aguilers, *Liber,* ed. John H. and Laurita L. Hill, Documents relatifs à l'histoire des croisades 9 (Paris, 1969), pp. 69, 73 [hereafter cited as Raymond of Aguilers].
16   Guibert of Nogent, p. 217. See Robert of Rheims, p. 839; Raymond of Aguilers, p. 84.
17   Ralph of Caen, p. 673.
18   Raymond of Aguilers, pp. 39, 84; Peter Tudebode, p. 44; Fulcher of Chartres, p. 252.
19   Robert of Rheims, p. 839. See Baldric of Bourgueil, p. 82; Orderic Vitalis 5:134.
20   Robert of Rheims, p. 731.
21   Baldric of Bourgueil, p. 16. See Orderic Vitalis 5:18.
22   Ralph of Caen, pp. 673-674.
23   For reforming bishops, see Ian S. Robinson, *Authority and Resistance in the Investiture Contest* (Manchester, 1978), pp. 163-169.

A feature of writings connected with the First Crusade was a predestinarian concept of the elect. The crusade's success was believed to have been divinely predestined[24] and the crusaders, "a blessed people chosen by God,"[25] were pre-elected especially for this task:[26] Guibert of Nogent remarked that Christ was now magnified by them in the same way as under the old dispensation God had been magnified by the Jews.[27] Their martyrs were the elect predestined for heaven;[28] even booty was predestined for their enjoyment.[29] The language used in the context of election was severely predestinarian, although in an extraordinary mixture of theologies Raymond of Aguilers wrote that God had chosen the crusaders from all mankind *because* they stood out in merit and grace.[30] The same writer referred to individuals among the elect divinely chosen for particular rôles: the visionary Peter Bartholomew, to whom was revealed the whereabouts of the Holy Lance, the most extraordinary of the relics discovered during the crusade, and Raymond of St. Gilles, for whom the Lance had been especially reserved.[31]

A group of writers equated the elect particularly with the Franks. Of course they wrote of the whole world, or at least all the West, being on the move at the summons of the pope and they stressed the many different nationalities taking part in the crusade.[32] Anselm of Ribemont, Guibert of Nogent and Robert of Rheims commented on the way the West now went to the aid of the East,[33] and Raymond of Aguilers expressed pride in being a Latin, fighting for the honour of the Roman Church as well as for that of the Franks.[34] The German Ekkehard of Aura, moreover, reacting against what he must have considered to have been French arrogance, stressed material rather than devotional reasons

---

24 Bartolf of Nangis, p. 515.

25 Raymond of Aguilers, pp. 79-80, 103, 154. See Robert of Rheims, p. 723.

26 Hagenmeyer, p. 149; Fulcher of Chartres, p. 306; Bartolf of Nangis, p. 516; Guibert of Nogent, p. 193; Robert of Rheims, p. 868; Henry of Huntingdon, *De captione Antiochiae a christianis,* RHC HOcc. 5:374 [hereafter cited as Henry of Huntingdon]; Orderic Vitalis, 5:30, 268.

27 Guibert of Nogent, p. 123.

28 Fulcher of Chartres, pp. 226-227; Hagenmeyer, p. 148. So were mortally wounded Turks baptised by Christian priests before their deaths. Fulcher of Chartres, p. 227.

29 *Gesta Francorum,* p. 95; Orderic Vitalis 5:88.

30 Raymond of Aguilers, p. 70.

31 Raymond of Aguilers, pp. 68, 69, 75.

32 Fulcher of Chartres, pp. 118, 202-203; Guibert of Nogent, pp. 124-125; Robert of Rheims, p. 730: *Narratio Floriacensis,* p. 356; William of Malmesbury 2:390, 399, 402; Orderic Vitalis 5:4-6, 30. See also Ekkehard of Aura, pp. 16-17; Sigebert of Gembloux, *Chronographia,* MGH SS 6:367; *Historia peregrinorum,* p. 172; Gaufridus, p. 348; *Narratio quomodo relliquiae martyris Georgii ad nos Aquicinenses pervenerunt,* RHC HOcc. 5:248.

33 Hagenmeyer, pp. 145-146; Guibert of Nogent, p. 221; Robert of Rheims, p. 740.

34 Raymond of Aguilers, pp. 79, 154.

for the success of crusade preaching in Francia.[35] But the sources reveal over and over again a pride in being Frankish, and Robert of Rheims made the Norman prince Bohemond declare, on learning in southern Italy of the crusade:

> Are we not of Frankish stock? Did not our ancestors come from Francia and liberate this land with arms? What disgrace! Will our blood-relatives and brothers go to martyrdom and indeed to paradise without us?[36]

Some French writers even seem to have believed that the Franks were now God's chosen people. They were the elect, that "blessed people whose Lord is its God."[37] Gaul, from whence they came, was that region of the world to be extolled above all others: like Israel, "how beautiful were its tabernacles" when its tents were pitched in Asia Minor.[38] God was especially the Franks' God; he loved them and had reserved them for this particular deed: their history, their special faith in God and their traditional devotion to the Holy See revealed this.

> If they were injured by neighbouring peoples it was customary for popes always to seek aid from the Franks. Popes Stephen and Zacharias fled to Kings Pippin and Charles, the first of whom... having campaigned as far as the Ticino, restored the Church's patrimony... I acknowledge, and it is worthy of everyone's belief, that God has reserved that people for such a great matter as this (crusade); especially since we know for certain that from the time they received the sign of faith at the hands of St. Remigius they have never caught the contagion of perfidy...[39]

It was claimed that the pope had preached the crusade in Francia because he knew that the Franks were the most warlike of western peoples.[40] The crusade

---

35 Ekkehard of Aura, p. 17.
36 Robert of Rheims, p. 741. See also Robert of Rheims, pp. 765, 767, 792, 855, 870; Guibert of Nogent, pp. 174-175, 192, 260; Baldric of Bourgueil, pp. 34, 47, 73; Raymond of Aguilers, pp. 79, 89: Bartolf of Nangis, p. 515; Ralph of Caen, p. 617; William of Malmesbury 2:396; Orderic Vitalis 5:66, 78, 86. Two contemporaries in the empire stressed that the chief recruitment from within the empire came from the Frankish parts of western Germany. Cosmas of Prague, *Chronicae Bohemorum libri III,* MGH SS 9:103; Ekkehard of Aura, *Chronicon universale,* MGH SS 6:208.
37 Robert of Rheims, pp. 723, 727. See Raymond of Aguilers, pp. 79-80.
38 Baldric of Bourgueil, pp. 28-29. See also Baldric of Bourgueil, p. 46; Albert of Aachen, p. 381.
39 Guibert of Nogent, pp. 135-136; also pp. 125, 192; Robert of Rheims, pp. 727, 812.
40 Robert of Rheims, p. 727: Hugh of St. Maria, p. 363; *Narratio Floriacensis,* p. 356. On their military virtues, see Robert of Rheims, p. 765; Guibert of Nogent, pp. 135-136. It was reported that in the East the word Frank became synonymous for westerner. Raymond of Aguilers, p. 52; Ekkehard of Aura, *Hierosolymita,* p. 24.

had been begun by them and was especially associated with them.[41] And the history of the expedition, of the deeds of "the pilgrim church of the Franks,"[42] was that of God acting through them: their power was not human but divine.[43] This was what distinguished them from the Turks, a people in many ways like them in military virtues, perhaps even, it was suggested, of the same stock, but alienated from God.[44]

Pride in being Frankish was reinforced by pride in ancestry. Robert of Rheims made Pope Urban II incite his audience at Clermont to crusade with the words:

> O most brave knights and children of unconquered parents, do not show yourselves to be degenerate, but be mindful of the power of your ancestors.[45]

Ralph of Caen made a Greek hermit living on the Mount of Olives speak of the fame of Tancred's grandfather, Robert Guiscard;[46] in fact the Norman contingent appears to have fought under what was called the *vexillum Wiscardigenae*, a flag depicting a cross on a background of costly material, which was perhaps an early example of a family standard, but may have been the *vexillum s. Petri* given by Pope Gregory VII to Robert Guiscard and somehow preserved by Bohemond, Robert's eldest but disinherited son.[47] This was a time of growing awareness among the West European nobility of family and patrimony. Most of the leaders of the First Crusade could trace their ancestry back to Charlemagne;[48] and three of them, Robert of Flanders, Godfrey of Bouillon and his brother Baldwin, seem to have been particularly conscious of this:

41 *Historia de translatione sanctorum magni Nicolai... ejusdem avunculi alterius Nicolai, Theodorique de civitate Mirea in monasterium s. Nicolai de Littore Venetiarum,* RHC HOcc. 5:273 [hereafter cited as *Historia de translatione*]. Note the titles of the *Gesta Francorum* and of the works by Bartolf of Nangis and Guibert of Nogent.

42 Raymond of Aguilers, p. 83.

43 Robert of Rheims, pp. 765, 824, 882; Fulcher of Chartres, pp. 116-117; Guibert of Nogent, pp. 117 (title), 224.

44 *Gesta Francorum,* p. 21; Baldric of Bourgueil, pp. 35-36; Guibert of Nogent, p. 162; Orderic Vitalis 5:62.

45 Robert of Rheims, p. 728.

46 Ralph of Caen, p. 685. See also *Historia peregrinorum,* p. 217.

47 Ralph of Caen, p. 666. For the *vexilla s. Petri,* see Carl Erdmann, *The Origin of the Idea of Crusade,* tr. Marshall W. Baldwin and Walter Goffart (Princeton, 1977), pp. 182-200 [hereafter cited as Erdmann]. The author of the *Chanson d'Antioche en provençal* (p. 485) described Bohemond of Taranto's standard as depicting a snake.

48 See Karl F. Werner, "Die Nachkommen Karls des Grossen bis um Jahr 1000," *Karl der Grosse,* ed. Wolfgang Braunfels and Percy E. Schramm, 5 vols. (Düsseldorf, 1965-8), 4:403-479.

Ralph of Caen stressed the fact that a descendant of Charlemagne came to sit, as King of Jerusalem, on the throne of David.[49]

The crusade was, in fact, suffused with the glow of Carolingian romance. Two images of Charlemagne seem to have inspired the crusaders. First, there was the conquering Christian emperor, waging warfare against the pagans in Spain and Saxony, familiar to contemporaries from the tales out of which had emerged or were emerging the Song of Roland and the William of Orange cycle: Ralph of Caen, writing of the Battle of Dorylaeum, exclaimed that one could say that Roland and Oliver were reborn.[50] Robert of Rheims made Pope Urban say at Clermont:

> Let the stories (*gesta*) about your ancestors move you and incite your souls to strength: the uprightness and greatness of King Charlemagne and of Louis his son and of your other kings, who destroyed the kingdoms of the pagans and extended into them the boundaries of Holy Church.[51]

Campaigns against the Muslims in Spain, bringing to mind scenes from the Song of Roland, encouraged this romancing. That Spain was in the minds of the crusaders is shown by an incident that occurred during the siege of Antioch, when Peter the Hermit and William the Carpenter, Viscount of Melun, fled from the Christian camp. Headed off and brought back, William was apparently reminded by Bohemond that once before, in Spain, he had betrayed his Christian comrades.[52] Secondly, Charlemagne was portrayed as protector of, and pilgrim and perhaps crusader to, the Holy Places in Jerusalem. The legend of his crusade to the Holy Land may not have developed by 1095 — although it may have inspired the report that the crusaders followed a road in Hungary built by him[53] — but of more significance to us than the exact date of its emergence is the atmosphere of Carolingian romance, drawing strength from the eschatological myth of the last emperor in occupation of

49   *Genealogia comitum Flandriae,* MGH SS 9:308; *Genealogia comitum Buloniensium,* MGH SS 9:300-301; Ralph of Caen, p. 633; William of Malmesbury 2:400, 431; Orderic Vitalis 5:118, 174.

50   Ralph of Caen, p. 627. See Robert Folz, *Le souvenir et la légende de Charlemagne dans l'empire germanique médiéval* (Paris, 1950), pp. 137-138.

51   Robert of Rheims, p. 728. See Etienne Delaruelle, "Essai sur la formation de l'idée de croisade," *Bulletin de littérature ecclésiastique* 55 (1954), 59.

52   *Gesta Francorum,* pp. 33-34; Guibert of Nogent, p. 175; *Historia peregrinorum,* p. 188.

53   *Gesta Francorum,* p. 2; Peter Tudebode, p. 33; Robert of Rheims, p. 732 (who wrote that the road had been built by Charlemagne's army); *Historia peregrinorum,* p. 174. For the legend of the crusade, see Folz, *Le Souvenir,* pp. 134-142; Paul Riant, "Inventaire critique des lettres historiques des croisades," *AOL* 1 (1881), 9-21.

Jerusalem and reflected in the rumour going round Germany soon after the crusade had been preached that Charlemagne had risen from the dead.[54]

The acceptance of papal authority, the pride in Frankish history and ancestry and the romance of Charlemagne should all have led to an exaltation of the Roman St. Peter. The pope's authority stemmed from St. Peter's principate. The First Crusade, moreover, was the culminating act of a period in which the popes and the reforming churchmen who supported them, engaged in a campaign to enlist western knighthood to the papal cause, had called for military support in terms of service to St. Peter, patron of war on the Church's behalf precisely because he had been first Bishop of Rome: the phrases *servitium s. Petri, vexillum s. Petri, militia s. Petri, milites s. Petri* and *fideles s. Petri* constantly recur in the propaganda of the decades before 1095.[55] It is clear with hindsight that with the crusade the idea of service to St. Peter had given way to something greater—I will return to this point later—but a sense of continuity with the immediate past must have been felt strongly by crusading leaders like Robert of Normandy, whose father had received a *vexillum s. Petri* from Pope Alexander II,[56] Robert of Flanders, whose father had been closely allied to Pope Gregory VII,[57] Bohemond of Taranto, whose father had been a *miles s. Petri,*[58] and Raymond of St. Gilles, who may have been a *fidelis s. Petri* himself.[59] And, turning to the authors of accounts of the crusade, the lives of Robert of Rheims and Guibert of Nogent suggest that they were in the reforming camp, and Baldric of Bourgueil, a cultivated man although hardly an enthusiastic reformer, wrote a biography of the saintly Robert of Arbrissel. Robert and Guibert became abbots, Baldric an archbishop: these senior churchmen must have been conscious of the part Petrine theory had been playing in papal propaganda.[60] Anyone with a knowledge of the history of Francia, moreover, would have known that the Frankish, and particularly the Carolingian, alliance with the Holy See had been marked by a strong devotion to St. Peter.[61] So had been the Reconquest of Spain and there is evidence that

54 Ekkehard of Aura, p. 19; Folz, *Le souvenir,* pp. 139-142.
55 Erdmann, pp. 182-228; Ian S. Robinson, "Gregory VII and the Soldiers of Christ," *History* 58 (1973), 173-183; Robinson, *Authority,* pp. 19-20, 102-103.
56 Erdmann, pp. 188-189. See also Herbert E.J. Cowdrey, "Pope Gregory VII and the Anglo-Norman Church," *Studi gregoriani* 9 (1972), 79-114.
57 Charles Verlinden, *Robert Ier Le Frison* (Paris, 1935), pp. 113-124.
58 Erdmann, pp. 205, 210.
59 Erdmann, p. 216. But *cf.* John H. and Laurita L. Hill, *Raymond IV de St.-Gilles* (Toulouse, 1959), pp. 10-21.
60 RHC HOcc. 3:xli-xliii, 4:iii-vi, xv-xvi. For Baldric, see also Orderic Vitalis 5:188-190.
61 See, for instance, Walter Ullmann, *The Growth of Papal Government in the Middle Ages,* 2nd ed. (London, 1962), pp. 51-228 passim.

the association of the *Reconquista* with St. Peter had established itself in the minds of ordinary people: in the Song of Roland Charlemagne's *oriflamme* was described as if it were a *vexillum s. Petri*.[62]

It would be natural to expect the patronage of St. Peter to be expressed in crusade ideology and a recent historian has in fact assumed that the crusade was a continuation of the *servitium s. Petri* propounded by Pope Gregory VII.[63] But what we find instead is a St. Peter who played a restrained part, except as Bishop of Antioch. Only in that rôle did he figure prominently. It was pointed out that it was at his first see that he had cultivated the Christian religion;[64] Antioch was, therefore, a fount of Christianity, but one now defiled by the infidels.[65] Peter was "claviger aethereus, Antiochenorum specialis episcopus."[66] In a vision experienced by a priest called Stephen of Valence on the night of 10 June 1098, when the crusaders were bottled up in Antioch by a strong Muslim army, he interceded with Christ for them precisely because Antioch had been his see.[67] Antioch was referred to as his heritage, presumably in the same way as Palestine was spoken of as Christ's inheritance.[68] It was his by right[69] and his conversion of it to Christianity had established the right of Christians to it.[70] He and his brother St. Andrew were supposed to have buried the Holy Lance under the floor of his cathedral in Antioch, and instructions on where in southern France it was to be kept in future were transmitted on his behalf to Raymond of St. Gilles.[71] The leaders of the crusade tried to resolve a dispute between Bohemond of Taranto and Raymond of St. Gilles at a conference held before his *cathedra*.[72] The most striking expression of the image of Peter as Bishop of Antioch came on 11 September 1098 in the letter from the

---

62   Erdmann, pp. 156, 166, 176, 195.
63   Robinson, "Gregory VII," pp. 191-192.
64   *Gesta Francorum*, pp. 27, 76; Baldric of Bourgueil, pp. 13, 40; Guibert of Nogent, p. 204; Robert of Rheims, p. 777; Gilo, *Historia de via Hierosolymitana*, RHC HOcc. 5:738 [hereafter cited as Gilo]; William of Malmesbury 2:416; Orderic Vitalis 5:68, 108.
65   Guibert of Nogent, p. 169; Baldric of Bourgueil, pp. 13, 40.
66   Guibert of Nogent, p. 195.
67   *Gesta Francorum*, p. 58: Guibert of Nogent, pp. 195-196. See also Baldric of Bourgueil, p. 66; Orderic Vitalis 5:100.
68   Hagenmeyer, p. 160; Bartolf of Nangis, p. 503. See Caffaro, *De liberatione*, p. 107.
69   Raymond of Aguilers, p. 78.
70   *Gesta Francorum*, p. 66; Peter Tudebode, p. 108; Baldric of Bourgueil, p. 74; Guibert of Nogent, p. 204. This supposedly was said by Peter the Hermit when on an embassy to the Muslim emir Kerbogha. In the same context St. Peter was called the *dux* of the Christian army in the account of Ralph of Caen, p. 664. This seems to have been a result of his episcopate of Antioch, but see also Ralph of Caen, pp. 653, 674.
71   Raymond of Aguilers, p. 88; Peter Tudebode, p. 101. See *Annales Augustani*, MGH SS 3:135.
72   *Gesta Francorum*, p. 76.

leaders of the crusade to the pope of all people, asking him to come out to "the original and first city of the Christian name," where, after St. Peter had been enthroned, those who had been called Galileans were first known as Christians.

> Afterwards St. Peter will be enthroned in his *cathedra*... We ask that you, who are father and head, should come to the place of your fatherhood, and that you, who are St. Peter's vicar, should sit on his *cathedra*.[73]

In connection with Antioch there were no references to the traditional Roman Petrine themes, except for the statement that the pope was St. Peter's vicar in the crusading leaders' letter and the title given to Peter of Prince of the Apostles.[74] And there is little else to be found in the sources for the rest of the crusade. St. Peter was reported appearing twice more, on both occasions to Peter Bartholomew: on c. 1 December 1098 he came with St. Andrew to reprove the crusaders for their sins and to report that God was willing to give them the fortress of Ma'arrat which they were besieging; and on 5 April 1099 he appeared as Christ's silent companion.[75] Pope Urban II apparently presented a *vexillum s. Petri* to Hugh of Vermandois, the brother of the King of France;[76] Adhémar of Le Puy may also have had one[77] and the South Italian Normans may have brought Robert Guiscard's with them.[78] It was stated that Adhémar was given by the pope the authority to bind and loose inherited from St. Peter, that the indulgence was granted to crusaders on the basis of St. Peter's power of the keys and that when Adhémar died "he deserved to have (St. Peter) open the heavenly gates."[79] It was noticed that he had died on the feast of St. Peter's Chains.[80] Apart from a statement in the *Liber pontificalis,* to which reference will be made later, that is the sum of the references to St. Peter and to Petrine theory that I have found.

It is on the face of it extraordinary that Petrine theory should have played so comparatively small a part in the crusade and that St. Peter should have been

---

73 Hagenmeyer, p. 164.
74 *Gesta Francorum,* p. 27; Baldric of Bourgueil, p. 40; Robert of Rheims, p. 777; Orderic Vitalis 5:68. See also Guibert of Nogent, p. 195; Robert of Rheims, p. 839.
75 Raymond of Aguilers, pp. 95-97, 113. Peter Tudebode, p. 123, seems to confirm the first of these visions, although only with reference to St. Andrew.
76 Anna Comnena, *Alexiade,* ed. Bernard Leib, 4 vols. (Paris, 1937-76), 2:213-214; Erdmann, p. 186.
77 Fulcher of Chartres, p. 254; Bartolf of Nangis, p. 504. Cf. William of Malmesbury 2:420. I do not find the counter-arguments of Erdmann (pp. 185-186 and note, based on Heinrich von Sybel, *Geschichte des ersten Kreuzzugs,* 2nd ed. [Leipzig, 1881], p. 371 note 4) convincing.
78 See above p. 47.
79 Ekkehard of Aura, p. 16; Guibert of Nogent, pp. 140, 210.
80 Robert of Rheims, p. 839; Guibert of Nogent, p. 210; Gilo, p. 780. See *Gesta Francorum,* p. 74; Peter Tudebode, p. 116.

associated with his first see and hardly at all with his second. Over forty years ago, with the percipience so characteristic of him, Carl Erdmann sensed that the crusade was not 'Petrine,' but he does not seem to have realised, or perhaps was reluctant to consider, the extent to which the Petrine language of the reformed papacy was absent. He suggested that Pope Urban II deliberately played down the idea of the *militia s. Petri* in favour of the concept of the *militia Christi* on pilgrimage to the Holy Sepulchre, but he did not believe that Petrine ideas were abandoned. He saw a "combination of continuity and revolution" and he maintained that the pope was in control of events.[81] It is certainly true that it was Urban himself who laid stress on the service of God or Christ in the crusade,[82] but there is some evidence that Rome was worried by what was happening to St. Peter: it was, after all, uncharacteristic of papal history before or since. The account of the crusade in the *Liber pontificalis,* written within the papal curia, emphasised the links with the ideas of Pope Gregory VII, and therefore presumably with the *militia s. Petri,* and stated that it had been fought under St. Peter's leadership.[83] And in 1100, writing to the Latins left in Asia, Pope Paschal II reminded them that

> since you began this pilgrimage through the vicar of St. Peter... you should abound always in the consolation of St. Peter and to the end hold him, whom you accepted as the foundation of such a great work, as your head in faith and obedience... You ought to submit to (the papal legate)..and through him to us, in fact to St. Peter.[84]

This is, of course, the typical language of papal primacy, but the emphasis on St. Peter may betray a concern lest he be completely overshadowed by the image of Christ as lord, an image that, at least in its feudal aspect, churchmen did not like.[85]

The first question to be answered is why Peter was prominent as Bishop of Antioch rather than as Bishop of Rome. It is understandable that in a moment of crisis, with the Christian army besieged in his first episcopal city, he should have been turned to, given the close association of saints with places where they had lived or where the inhabitants claimed to possess their relics: one has only to think of St. Mark and Venice, St. Nicholas and Bari and St. James and

---

81 Erdmann, pp. 334-343, 350-354.
82 See the references to pp. 59-63 below.
83 *Liber pontificalis,* ed. Louis Duchesne, 3 vols. (Paris, 1886-1957), 2:293. *Cf.* Erdmann, p. 353.
84 Hagenmeyer, p. 179. Paschal later presented a *vexillum s. Petri* to Bohemond for the crusade of 1107-08. Bartolf of Nangis, p. 538.
85 See Jonathan S.C. Riley-Smith, "An Approach to Crusading Ethics," *Reading Medieval Studies,* 6 (1980), 9-10.

Compostela. Another striking example, which also involved St. Peter and the Latins in the East, was reported by Caffaro. In 1101 the Latin army in Palestine laid siege to Caesarea, where Peter had baptised the first gentile converts (Acts 10-11). The Muslim garrison sent out two men to parley. They were met by the Latin patriarch Daimbert and the papal legate Maurice of Porto. Daimbert stated that Caesarea

> was St. Peter's and ought to belong to him, whom your ancestors (the Muslim invaders) drove from this city by force. And if we, who are St. Peter's vicars, wish to recover his land we are not stealing what is yours... And so we ask you to return to us the land of St. Peter.[86]

The emotions engendered throughout Christendom by the localization of saints were intense and their protective interest was strongly felt. They are confirmed if one looks at those saints who appeared in visions or were the objects of devotion during the crusade. Eighteen saints were reported making appearances to visionaries. Four were not named and the evidence for three others, SS. Maurice, Theodore and Ambrose, can perhaps be dismissed.[87] We are left with appearances by the archangel Gabriel,[88] the Blessed Virgin Mary,[89] and SS. Agatha,[90] Andrew,[91] Demetrius, George, Giles, Mark, Mercury, Nicholas[92] and Peter.[93]

---

86 Caffaro, *Annales Januenses*, in *Annali Genovesi*, ed. Belgrano, 1:10. Daimbert would have read the letter of Pope Paschal II referred to above, p. 52.

87 For the unnamed saints, see Raymond of Aguilers, pp. 90, 113, 127, 131-132. The names of SS. Maurice and Theodore were variants in or additions to the lists of Greek soldier saints. Robert of Rheims, pp. 796, 832; Peter Tudebode, pp. 100, 112; *Historia peregrinorum*, pp. 173, 183, 205. See also *Annales Augustani*, p. 135. The report of St. Ambrose's appearance while the crusade was being preached may be somehow linked to the fact that his relics were carried on the crusade of 1101. Albert of Aachen, pp. 415-416; Guibert of Nogent, p. 244.

88 Ekkehard of Aura, p. 40. See Riant, "Inventaire," pp. 110, 714; also Caffaro, *De liberatione*, pp. 100-101.

89 Raymond of Aguilers, pp. 73-74, 123-124, 127-128; *Gesta Francorum*, p. 57; Guibert of Nogent, p. 195; Baldric of Bourgueil, p. 66. See Fulcher of Chartres, p. 246.

90 Raymond of Aguilers, p. 127.

91 Hagenmeyer, pp. 163, 166; Raymond of Aguilers, pp. 68-72, 75-76, 77-78, 84-88, 89-91, 95-97, 98, 113, 119, 121, 123, 124, 131, 153; *Gesta Francorum*, pp. 59-60, 65; Peter Tudebode, pp. 100-101, 122; Guibert of Nogent, pp. 196-197, 203; Baldric of Bourgueil, pp. 67-68; Robert of Rheims, pp. 822-823; Bartolf of Nangis, p. 502; Gilo, p. 771; Henry of Huntingdon, p. 378; *Narratio Floriacensis*, p. 357. See Albert of Aachen, pp. 419-420. Fulcher of Chartres (pp. 235-241) was sceptical about these visions and Ralph of Caen (pp. 676-678, 682-683) was highly critical.

92 Raymond of Aguilers, pp. 116-117; and see also *Historia de translatione*, pp. 262, 286.

93 See above pp. 50-51. The Battle of Antioch took place on the vigil of the feast of SS. Peter and Paul and victory was believed to have been gained through the saints' intercession. Raymond of Aguilers, p. 83. For references to SS. Demetrius, George, Giles, Mark and Mercury, see below pp. 55-56.

Although these saints were all known and venerated in the West the proportion with important cults in the East was high. As far as we know this did not reflect the personal predilections of the crusaders. Anselm of Ribemont had a devotion to St. Quentin.[94] On coming home Robert of Normandy went to Mt. St. Michel to give thanks for his safe return.[95] Raymond of St. Gilles had a devotion to St. Robert, whose chalice he took with him on crusade.[96] He may also have regarded St. Giles, of whose abbey he was advocate, as a patron: it was reported that when early in August 1097 he was extremely ill St. Giles appeared to a Saxon count in the army to bring the assurance that he would not die.[97] Between 1100 and 1103, while a prisoner of the Muslims, Bohemond of Taranto made a vow to St. Leonard, the patron saint of captives, and on his return to Europe he visited the saint's shrine at St.-Léonard-de-Noblat to give thanks for his release, presenting it with silver fetters.[98] An interesting example of the concern for the cults at home is to be found in Peter Bartholomew's final message to Raymond of St. Gilles. Peter passed on the injunction that once the crusade was over the Holy Lance was to be kept in a church to be built five leagues from the cathedral of St. Trophimus at Arles, because St. Peter had promised to send it to Trophimus. The latter, an Ephesian disciple of St. Paul, was supposed to have been first bishop of Arles.[99] But the personal devotions of leading crusaders did not have much influence on the experiences of visionaries in the army. No less than four of these seem to have been followers of Raymond of St. Gilles and two others, the priest Stephen of Valence and one of Adhémar of Le Puy's chaplains, came from the same South French ambience. Raymond's entourage, moreover, contained two of the three most prolific visionaries, the priest Peter Desiderius and the poor servant Peter Bartholomew, and most of the evidence for the apparitions comes from an account of the crusade written by Raymond's chaplain, Raymond of Aguilers. There has been a tendency lately to treat this work as untrustworthy on the grounds that

---

94 *Sigeberti Continuatio Auctarium Ursicampinum,* MGH SS 6:471.

95 Orderic Vitalis 5:300.

96 Hill, *Raymond IV,* pp. 1, 19. Some crusaders may have regarded the patrons of houses endowed by them before their departure as special protectors. For an example of Godfrey of Bouillon's endowments before leaving, see *Chronicon S. Huberti Andaginensis,* MGH SS 8:615; Laurence de Leodio, *Gesta episcoporum Virdunensium,* MGH SS 10:497-498.

97 Raymond of Aguilers, p. 46; *Historia peregrinorum,* p. 184.

98 Ralph of Caen, p. 713; *Historia peregrinorum,* p. 228; William of Malmesbury 2:454; Orderic Vitalis 5:376, 378; *Acta Sanctorum,* Novembris 3:160-168 (according to which St. Leonard appeared to Bohemond in a vision).

99 Raymond of Aguilers, p. 88. For Arles, see *Lexikon des Mittelalters* (Munich, 1977-   ) 1:956.

the language and imagery used in it were biblical and liturgical.[100] But so were those of most contemporary accounts, and Raymond of Aguilers's evidence is sometimes corroborated in other sources, particularly with regard to the visions of Stephen of Valence and Peter Bartholomew. He included, moreover, much circumstantial detail, which suggests that he was writing up what he and others in his circle believed. And he was not the only participant to report that Raymond of St. Gilles took an intense interest in the supernatural experiences of his followers and implicitly believed the instructions transmitted by them.[101] But it is noteworthy that Robert and Giles, Raymond's own particular patron saints, never appeared to his followers. The saints who were seen by crusaders, therefore, did not necessarily have any relationship to the cults of western Europe.

A report of another appearance may be further evidence for the acceptance by westerners of the idea of the patronage of a familiar saint over an eastern locality. It was said that in the summer of 1098 a Syrian Christian had a vision of St. Mark, who had visited the church of St. Mary in Tripoli on his way from Alexandria to Antioch, whither Christ had summoned all his disciples to help the crusaders.[102] This, of course, was reported as the experience of an eastern Christian, but it is interesting to find in a western account St. Mark associated with Alexandria rather than with Venice.

The evidence for a growing devotion to Greek soldier saints is more significant. The first of their interventions in the crusade was supposed to have occurred on 1 July 1097 at the Battle of Dorylaeum, when it was said by Turkish deserters that the crusaders had been led by two horsemen with marvellous faces and glittering armour; later, perhaps in the light of subsequent events, some identified these as SS. George and Demetrius.[103] In January 1098 the Greek and Latin bishops with the army wrote of it being under the protection of SS. George, Theodore, Demetrius and Blaise, "soldiers of Christ accompanying us."[104] It was claimed that a turning point in the Battle of Antioch on 28 June 1098 came when an army of angels, saints and dead crusaders, carrying white banners and riding white horses, and led by SS.

100 John H. and Laurita L. Hill, introduction to Raymond of Aguilers, pp. 12-20.
101 Raymond of Aguilers, pp. 75, 153; Fulcher of Chartres, pp. 237-238, 241; Ralph of Caen, pp. 677-678, 682-683.
102 Raymond of Aguilers, pp. 117-118.
103 Raymond of Aguilers, pp. 45-46 (who did not name them); Bartolf of Nangis, p. 496; *Historia peregrinorum*, pp. 173, 183. According to the *Chanson d'Antioche* (pp. 79, 123, 211, 262-263), the archangel Michael and St. Denis also helped the crusade.
104 Hagenmeyer, p. 147. No one has been able to explain the reference to St. Blaise.

George, Demetrius and Mercury, appeared to lend the crusaders assistance.[105] St. George's reported interventions did not end there. Early in January 1099 Peter Desiderius received heavenly instructions to pick up some relics from a church in Antioch. Several reliquaries were found, but one of them was not identifiable, although some of the searchers thought that it might contain relics of St. Mercury. Shortly afterwards St. George appeared to inform Peter Desiderius that the reliquary contained his relics. He told him to collect it and reappeared when this was not done immediately.[106] By this time it seems that there was a growing devotion to him in the army and he was regarded as its standard-bearer.[107] When the crusaders reached Ramla, near Lydda where he was supposed to be buried, they chose a Latin bishop and held a service of intercession to him.[108] A leading devotee was Count Robert of Flanders, who became known as "the son of St. George"[109] and brought home with him an arm of the saint, which he gave to the monastery of Anchin.[110]

These saints were known in the West, where they were already occasionally venerated as military patrons.[111] But they were far more the objects of cults in the East and at this time there were other saints, apart perhaps from St. Theodore, who would surely have sprung to mind more readily as the patrons

---

105 The earliest reference to the heavenly host, although with no mention of the saints, comes in a letter in Hagenmeyer, p. 167. See also *Gesta Francorum,* p. 69; Peter Tudebode, pp. 100, 112; Baldric of Bourgueil, pp. 77, 96; Guibert of Nogent, pp. 206-207; Robert of Rheims, pp. 796-797, 830, 832, 835; *Historia peregrinorum,* pp. 173, 205; Henry of Huntingdon, p. 378; Hugh of St. Maria, p. 365; *Annales Augustani,* p. 135; Orderic Vitalis 5: 112-114 (who stated that not everyone saw them). William of Malmesbury (2:420) seems to have had doubts himself.

106 Raymond of Aguilers, pp. 131-134.

107 Raymond of Aguilers, p. 133; Robert of Rheims, p. 859; Orderic Vitalis 5: 154-156. Erdmann, p. 279 note 43 suggested that this title might echo the common Byzantine designation of George as *tropaiophoros.*

108 *Gesta Francorum,* p. 87; Raymond of Aguilers, p. 136; Guibert of Nogent, pp. 222-223; Baldric of Bourgueil, pp. 95-96; Robert of Rheims, p. 859; Bartolf of Nangis, pp. 508-509; William of Malmesbury 2:421; *Historia peregrinorum,* p. 212; Orderic Vitalis 5: 154-156. See Hagenmeyer, p. 177.

109 Walterus, *Vita Karoli comitis Flandriae,* MGH SS 12:540; *Genealogiae breves regum Francorum,* MGH SS 13:250; *Chanson d'Antioche,* p. 804.

110 *Narratio quomodo relliquiae,* p. 248; *Sigeberti Continuatio Auctarium Aquicinense,* MGH SS 6:395; *Historia monasterii Aquicinctini,* MGH SS 14:586; *Genealogia comitum Flandriae,* p. 323. For other relics sent home by the Count of Flanders earlier in his crusade, see Hagenmeyer, pp. 142-143.

111 Hippolyte Delehaye, *Les légendes grecques des saints militaires* (Paris, 1909), pp. 50, 92; Erdmann, pp. 273-281; Ernst H. Kantorowicz, *Laudes Regiae* (Berkeley, 1946), pp. 29 note 48, 45, 105, 107 note 137, 243; Louis Réau, *Iconographie de l'art chrétien,* 3 vols. (Paris, 1955-58), 3: passim; Georg Schreiber, "Christlicher Orient und mittelalterliches Abendland," *Oriens christianus* 38 (1954), 100-101.

of a largely Frankish enterprise. The saints invoked on behalf of Frankish armies in various *Laudes* from the eighth to the eleventh centuries included Hilary, Martin, Maurice and Denis. St. Maurice was particularly popular and his lance was one of the most important relics in the possession of the western emperors.[112] But, perhaps under the influence of the Greek bishops with the crusade, it was the Greek military saints who came to be adopted as patrons, and this confirms the bias towards eastern saints that has already been discerned.

This bias, it must be stressed, was in no sense a consequence of feelings of inferiority experienced by westerners overcome by the splendours of eastern Christianity. The sources reveal no such feelings at all. Of course Constantinople, the greatest city in Europe, was acknowledged to be rich, a royal city containing splendid buildings and the seat of an apostolic see; it was, in fact, Rome's equal except that Rome was the seat of the papacy and therefore the capital of Christendom. What really marked Constantinople out was not so much its size or splendour, as the fact that it contained the greatest collection of relics in the Christian world and was an important place of pilgrimage.[113] The Latins did not look on the Greeks as their superiors and, even though they may have disliked them, the emphasis in western writings connected with the crusade was on the brotherhood of equals. Only once were they described as being heretical,[114] and the shared inheritance of all Christians was very commonly stressed.[115] The easterners were brothers, and indeed to Baldric of Bourgueil, the most outspoken of the writers on this subject, they were full uterine brothers:

> Your brothers, members of Christ's body... your blood-brothers, your comrades, born of the same womb as you, for you are sons of the same Christ and the same Church.[116]

---

112 Erdmann, pp. 273-277; Robert Folz, *The Concept of Empire in Western Europe,* trans. Sheila A. Ogilvie (London, 1969), p. 73. Kantorowicz, *Laudes,* passim, did not really consider this question and at times (see p. 29 note 48) was too dismissive.

113 Fulcher of Chartres, pp. 176-177; Guibert of Nogent, pp. 132, 137; Robert of Rheims, pp. 747, 750-751; Hugh of St. Maria, p. 363; William of Malmesbury 2:411-413.

114 Hagenmeyer, p. 164.

115 Ekkehard of Aura, p. 15; Robert of Rheims, p. 746.

116 Baldric of Bourgueil, pp. 12-13; and see p. 74. For *fratres:* Raymond of Aguilers, p. 38; Bartolf of Nangis, p. 491; Hugh of St. Maria, p. 363; William of Malmesbury 2:396; Orderic Vitalis 5:68, 170; for *confratres:* Fulcher of Chartres, pp. 132-133; Albert of Aachen, pp. 462, 467, 469.

These relatives had suffered greatly from the pagans and needed help, which was an act of fraternal love.[117] It is not surprising that the crusaders were portrayed as being reluctant to fight or to take plunder from them.[118] The bias towards eastern saints was a consequence not of a feeling of inferiority but of a sense of geography. As the crusaders moved out of the confines of Latin Christendom they passed into an area in which familiar saints had different rôles — for instance Guibert of Nogent associated St. Paul with Iconium[119] — and in which saints who had played comparatively minor parts in western Europe were now prominent. It was the most natural thing in the world for the Antiochene Peter to be in the forefront of their minds at Antioch and for Greek soldier saints to be bringing aid to a Christian army fighting in their territory.

There remains the question why St. Peter played the comparatively minor rôle he did, a rôle that allowed his Antiochene personality to become prominent. The answer to that lies in something I have already touched on, the nature of the crusade itself and the difference between it and the *servitium s. Petri* demanded by popes in the previous few decades. Writing with reference to the crusade, Carl Erdmann pointed out that

> From the standpoint of the history of concepts, it is noteworthy that the episode of the papal *militia s. Petri* was over.[120]

He was right, but St. Peter's replacement by Christ as the lord to whom military service was owed was more complete and went even deeper than he realised. In the sources for the crusade the notion of fighting for, or under the leadership of, St. Peter only appeared, as we have seen, in connection with Antioch. It was swept aside by the idea of fighting for God or Christ, which had first been used by papal propagandists in rather a confused way alongside the concept of the *servitium s. Petri* in the 1070s[121] and, after a remarkably rapid development, now took over.

---

117 Fulcher of Chartres, pp. 132-133; Ekkehard of Aura, p. 15; Bartolf of Nangis, p. 491; Hugh of St. Maria, p. 363; *Narratio Floriacensis,* p. 356. For fraternal love, see Jonathan S.C. Riley-Smith, "Crusading as an Act of Love," *History* 65 (1980), 182-184.
118 *Gesta Francorum,* pp. 13, 25; Peter Tudebode, p. 47; Baldric of Bourgueil, p. 25; Guibert of Nogent, p. 164; Robert of Rheims, p. 746; *Historia peregrinorum,* p. 179, William of Malmesbury 2:431; Orderic Vitalis 5:44, 48, 168.
119 Guibert of Nogent, pp. 163-164.
120 Erdmann, pp. 341-342.
121 Robinson, "Gregory VII," pp. 177-179; Erdmann, pp. 201-203.

The crusade expressed the will of God: its battle-cry was *Deus vult.* [122] It was instituted by God, who alone was its instigator, not any prince or lord.[123] The crusaders, divinely inspired,[124] were called to battle by God or Christ, who spoke through the pope: Fulcher of Chartres made Urban state at Clermont

> It is not I who encourages you, it is the Lord... To those present I say, to those absent I enjoin, but Christ commands.[125]

It is not surprising that the crusade should have been described as *causa Dei,* [126] *opus Dei* or *Domini,* [127] *expeditio Dei,* [128] *expeditio dominica* [129] or *Dei et Domini Jhesu Christi expeditio;* [130] *bella fidei* [131] or *bella Christi;* [132] *negotium Christi* [133]—this phrase was to have a long history—or that it should have been treated as something sacred: *praelium sanctum,* [134] *negotium pium* or *labor pius,* [135] *expeditio beata* or *sanctissima.* [136] The same language was used of the army: *exercitus Dei,* [137] *exercitus Domini* or *dominicus,* [138] *exercitus Christi,* [139]

122 Albert of Aachen, p. 416; Guibert of Nogent, p. 221. For *Deus vult*: Fulcher of Chartres, p. 233; *Gesta Francorum,* pp. 7, 47; Peter Tudebode, pp. 40, 86; Ralph of Caen, p. 625; Bartolf of Nangis, pp. 496, 500, 515; Guibert of Nogent, pp. 151, 187; Robert of Rheims, pp. 729, 761; William of Malmesbury 2:414, 419; *Historia peregrinorum,* pp. 170, 174, 196.

123 Guibert of Nogent, pp. 123-124; Robert of Rheims, p. 730; Baldric of Bourgueil, p. 12; Ekkehard of Aura, p. 11.

124 Hagenmeyer, p. 142; Raymond of Aguilers, p. 47; Peter Tudebode, p. 40; Ralph of Caen, p. 611; Baldric of Bourgueil, pp. 9, 16; Guibert of Nogent, pp. 123-124; Robert of Rheims, pp. 729, 730, 739, 741, 747, 882; Gaufridus, p. 348; Hugh of St. Maria, p. 364; *Historia de translatione,* p. 255; *De reliquis,* p. 336; Orderic Vitalis 5:4, 16, 156.

125 Fulcher of Chartres, pp. 134, 135; Bartolf of Nangis, p. 491. But cf. the significant abbreviation in William of Malmesbury 2:396. See also Fulcher of Chartres, p. 116. For Christ initiating the crusade through an appearance to Peter the Hermit, see *Chanson d'Antioche,* pp. 32-33; Albert of Aachen, p. 273; *Historia peregrinorum,* p. 169.

126 Baldric of Bourgueil, p. 89; Orderic Vitalis 5:142.

127 Orderic Vitalis 5:28, 46.

128 Baldric of Bourgueil, p. 17; Orderic Vitalis 5:18.

129 Guibert of Nogent, pp. 223, 229, 235.

130 Albert of Aachen, p. 501. See Orderic Vitalis 5:6.

131 Guibert of Nogent, p. 177.

132 *Narratio Floriacensis,* p. 356; Gilo, p. 728. See Baldric of Bourgueil, p. 95.

133 Guibert of Nogent, p. 174.

134 Guibert of Nogent, p. 124.

135 Guibert of Nogent, pp. 182, 210.

136 Fulcher of Chartres, p. 117; Raymond of Aguilers, p. 134.

137 Hagenmeyer, pp. 138, 150, 168; Fulcher of Chartres, pp. 138-139, 215, 251-252; Raymond of Aguilers, pp. 35, 37, 54, 59, 84, 100; Baldric of Bourgueil, pp. 16, 17, 73; Robert of Rheims, pp. 779, 801, 830; Albert of Aachen, pp. 300, 302, 323, 328, 343, 386; *Historia peregrinorum,* p. 190.

138 Hagenmeyer, pp. 144, 157, 160, 166; Fulcher of Chartres, p. 308; Bartolf of Nangis, p. 503; Guibert of Nogent, pp. 226, 233, 253.

139 Hagenmeyer, p. 176; Peter Tudebode, pp. 69, 79, 129, 131; Ralph of Caen, pp. 618, 620; Baldric of Bourgueil, p. 22; Albert of Aachen, p. 418; *Historia peregrinorum,* pp. 190, 211.

phalanges Dei,[140] *agmen* or *numerus Christi,*[141] *militia Dei,*[142] *militia Domini* or *dominica,*[143] *coelestis regis militia,*[144] *summi Messiae militia*[145] and, above all, *militia Christi.*[146] Its camps were *castra Dei;*[147] its soldiers were called collectively *grex Domini,*[148] *populus Dei,*[149] *populus Domini*[150] or *populus Jhesu Christi;*[151] *plebs or gens Dei,*[152] *gens Deo dicata*[153] and *gens Christi.*[154] And it assumed the same sacred character as did the crusade: *christianissimus exercitus,*[155] *sacra Christi cohors,*[156] *sacra* or *sancta* or *beata* or *divina militia,*[157] *sanctum collegium,*[158] *sacra societas,*[159] *populus beatus,*[160] *populus sanctus Dei.*[161]

The crusaders, true followers of Christ,[162] fought under divine leadership.[163] They had no king but the Lord alone, no lord but Christ.[164] God was described

---

140 Orderic Vitalis 5:18.

141 Gilo, p. 739; Ralph of Caen, p. 624.

142 Guibert of Nogent, pp. 211, 234; Robert of Rheims, pp. 741, 776, 839; Raymond of Aguilers, p. 103; William of Malmesbury 2:398.

143 Hagenmeyer, pp. 146, 148; Ekkehard of Aura, p. 21; Guibert of Nogent, pp. 197, 219, 228. See *Historia peregrinorum,* p. 215.

144 Ekkehard of Aura, p. 17.

145 Orderic Vitalis 5:30.

146 *Gesta Francorum,* pp. 11, 14, 16, 82, 86; Peter Tudebode, pp. 117, 126, 131, 132; Ralph of Caen, p. 603; Baldric of Bourgueil, pp. 28, 82, 90, 93; Guibert of Nogent, pp. 164, 225, 229; Robert of Rheims, p. 740; *Historia peregrinorum,* pp. 181, 198, 207, 210; Orderic Vitalis 5:52, 54, 132, 144, 150, 188, 324. See Baldric of Bourgueil, pp. 14, 15.

147 Baldric of Bourgueil, p. 44; Robert of Rheims, pp. 746, 748.

148 Ekkehard of Aura, p. 21.

149 Hagenmeyer, p. 144; *Gesta Francorum,* p. 60; Peter Tudebode, p. 44; Ekkehard of Aura, p. 21; Baldric of Bourgueil, pp. 45, 72, 73, 80, 89, 97, 107, 108; Bartolf of Nangis, pp. 500, 501, 505, 516; Robert of Rheims, p. 873; Hugh of St. Maria, p. 365; Albert of Aachen, pp. 318, 320, 323, 325, 347, 348, 359, 373, 375, 378, 379, 380, 391, 403, 406, 412, 434, 435, 450, 455, 457, 472, 492; Orderic Vitalis 5:106, 108, 128.

150 Bartolf of Nangis, p. 515; Gilo, p. 758.

151 Albert of Aachen, pp. 348, 361, 367, 371, 423.

152 Ralph of Caen, p. 610; Peter Tudebode, p. 73; Baldric of Bourgueil, p. 73; Robert of Rheims, p. 746. See Gilo, p. 789.

153 Albert of Aachen, p. 320.

154 *Gesta Francorum,* p. 9; Guibert of Nogent, p. 153; Gilo, p. 736; *Historia peregrinorum,* p. 176.

155 Albert of Aachen, p. 463.   156 Orderic Vitalis 5:178.

157 Guibert of Nogent, pp. 225, 230; *Historia de translatione,* p. 255; Baldric of Bourgueil, p. 10; Robert of Rheims, p. 741.

158 Baldric of Bourgueil, p. 67. A feature of Baldric's work is his treatment of the crusade as a type of the early church.   159 Robert of Rheims, p. 781.

160 Ralph of Caen, p. 607.   161 Albert of Aachen, p. 380.

162 See Riley-Smith, "Crusading," pp. 178-179.

163 Hagenmeyer, pp. 150, 169; Raymond of Aguilers, pp. 127, 145; Ekkehard of Aura, p. 21; Ralph of Caen, pp. 651, 668; Baldric of Bourgueil, p. 104; Bartolf of Nangis, p. 515; Guibert of Nogent, pp. 154, 195; Robert of Rheims, pp. 747, 772, 882.

164 Guibert of Nogent, p. 243; *Historia peregrinorum,* p. 179; Peter Tudebode, p. 46; Raymond of Aguilers, p. 41. See Baldric of Bourgueil, p. 25.

as *dux solus,*[165] *dux et praeambulus,*[166] *dux et protector,*[167] *dux et conductor,*[168] *conductor et dominus.*[169] Christ was *signifer et praecursor,*[170] *imperator,*[171] *rex,*[172] *dux.*[173]

> Tu tuorum dux et rector, et in artis es protector
> Tu tuorum es adiutor et uictorum retributor.[174]

The campaign was marked for them and their contemporaries by signs of God's interventions on his soldiers' behalf. All Christians were, of course, the sons of Christ, but this was particularly true of the crusaders.

> These Christians are called the sons of Christ; and, by the mouth of the prophets, they are sons of adoption and promise, and, according to the apostle, they are the heirs of Christ, to whom Christ has already given the promised inheritance, saying by the prophets, "From the rising of the sun to its going down will be your bounds and no man shall stand against you."[175]

They were the friends of God or Christ[176] and were loved[177] and blessed[178] by the Deity. Besides *peregrini*[179] and *cruce signati* or *signati*[180]—early uses of what was to become the standard term for their successors in the thirteenth century—the ways they were described were expressive. They were *satellites Domini,* at war against the attendants of the Devil or the Antichrist;[181] *servi Dei* or *Christi,*[182] *vernulae Christi,*[183] *Dei* or *Christi proceres,*[184] *optiones*

165 Robert of Rheims, p. 858.
166 Baldric of Bourgueil, p. 92.
167 Robert of Rheims, p. 763. He was also described as "conviator et cooperator." Hagenmeyer, p. 170.
168 Raymond of Aguilers, p. 148.   169 Raymond of Aguilers, p. 124.
170 Guibert of Nogent, p. 140; and see p. 177.
171 Baldric of Bourgueil, p. 15.
172 Ekkehard of Aura, p. 16.
173 Raymond of Aguilers, pp. 94, 126; Baldric of Bourgueil, pp. 15, 66, 79, 110.
174 Orderic Vitalis 5:6.
175 *Gesta Francorum,* p. 54. Also Guibert of Nogent, p. 228; Albert of Aachen, p. 501. See Henry of Huntingdon, p. 377.
176 Fulcher of Chartres, p. 137; Albert of Aachen, p. 501. See Robert of Rheims, p. 839.
177 *Gesta Francorum,* p. 56; Fulcher of Chartres, p. 306; Hugh of St. Maria, p. 366.
178 Raymond of Aguilers, p. 151.
179 See Alphonse Dupront, "La spiritualité des croisés et des pèlerins d'après les sources de la première croisade," *Convegni del centro di studi sulla spiritualità medievale* 4 (1963), 453-483.
180 Albert of Aachen, p. 292; Ekkehard of Aura, p. 20. See Hagenmeyer, p. 165.
181 Robert of Rheims, p. 874; and for attendants of the Devil or the Antichrist, see for example Robert of Rheims, pp. 828, 876.
182 Raymond of Aguilers, pp. 51, 137, 148; *Gesta Francorum,* p. 66; Peter Tudebode, p. 104; Robert of Rheims, pp. 734, 836. See *Historia peregrinorum,* p. 215.
183 Orderic Vitalis 5:18.   184 Gilo, p. 746; Albert of Aachen, p. 328.

Christi,[185] *Dei coadjutores.*[186] Epithets referred to their rôle as warriors: *milites catholici,*[187] *pro populo Dei pugnatores,*[188] *belligeratores regis aeterni,*[189] *pugiles* or *pugnatores* or *bellatores Dei,*[190] *milites Dei,*[191] *athleta Dei* or *Christi,*[192] *Christi agonithetae,*[193] *Christi bellatores,*[194] *pedites Christi*[195] and especially *milites Christi.*[196] In a remarkable passage, echoing the values of the pre-Gregorian age, Raymond of Aguilers compared Godfrey of Bouillon's knights to the twelve apostles, and wrote that they treated their lord "as though he were vicar of God."[197]

It also seems that the authors of some of the accounts of the crusade consciously redirected military service, previously demanded by the popes for St. Peter, to God or Christ. One comes across the phrases *servitium Dei,*[198] *servitium viae Dei*[199] and *servitium Christi.*

> If, as one reads (wrote Guibert of Nogent of the participation of the heavenly army in the Battle of Antioch) there appeared once upon a time visible heavenly aid to the Maccabees, fighting for circumcision and abstinence from pork, how much more ought it to be the experience of those who, in order to cleanse devotedly the churches and propagate the faith, pour out their blood to give service to Christ.[200]

185 Orderic Vitalis 5:268.
186 Baldric of Bourgueil, p. 101.
187 Albert of Aachen, p. 287.
188 Baldric of Bourgueil, p. 15.
189 Robert of Rheims, p. 822.
190 Gilo, p. 773; Fulcher of Chartres, p. 141; Robert of Rheims, p. 747; Orderic Vitalis 5:108.
191 *Gesta Francorum,* pp. 23-24, 40; Raymond of Aguilers, pp. 37, 141; Baldric of Bourgueil, pp. 25, 89; Robert of Rheims, pp. 741, 787, 813, 816, 833; *Historia peregrinorum,* p. 184; Orderic Vitalis 5:142.
192 *Gesta Francorum,* pp. 29, 37; Peter Tudebode, pp. 33, 125; Ralph of Caen, pp. 651, 668; *Historia de translatione,* p. 273; *Historia peregrinorum,* pp. 187, 191, 195; Albert of Aachen, p. 288; Orderic Vitalis 5:104, 146.
193 Orderic Vitalis 5:6.
194 *Historia peregrinorum,* p. 223; *De reliquis,* p. 337.
195 Gilo, p. 740.
196 Hagenmeyer, p. 150; *Gesta Francorum,* pp. 11, 18, 19, 23, 24, 33, 70, 73, 89, 96; Fulcher of Chartres, p. 136; Peter Tudebode, pp. 39, 44, 58, 69, 81, 112, 115, 123, 129, 134, 135, 140, 145, 146; Raymond of Aguilers, p. 60; Ralph of Caen, pp. 617, 668; Baldric of Bourgueil, pp. 14, 22, 34, 42, 47; Bartolf of Nangis, pp. 496, 503; Robert of Rheims, pp. 762, 828, 843, 867, 876; *Historia de translatione,* pp. 273, 276; Hugh of St. Maria, pp. 366, 367; Gilo, pp. 735, 756; *Historia peregrinorum,* pp. 176, 184, 189, 194, 205, 208, 218, 220; Albert of Aachen, pp. 328, 393, 400, 402, 415, 416; Orderic Vitalis 5:174.
197 Raymond of Aguilers, p. 93. See Robert of Rheims, p. 866.
198 Hagenmeyer, p. 144; *Historia de translatione,* pp. 257, 272. See Ekkehard of Aura, p. 12.
199 *Historia de translatione,* p. 255.
200 Guibert of Nogent, p. 207. Also Robert of Rheims, p. 845. *Cf.* William of Malmesbury 2:420.

The crusaders made up the *familia Christi*[201] and one leader, Tancred, was called Christ's *vexillifer.*[202] Above all there were references to *fideles Dei* or *Christi,*[203] reminiscent of the *fideles s. Petri.*

What we have here is a transference, far more complete than Erdmann seems to have realised, of military service from Peter to Christ. The evidence for it comes from all types of source-material for the First Crusade, from letters written on the march to narrative histories composed by churchmen who never left France. The comparatively small part played by St. Peter in these writings can be explained by the fact that it was almost universally believed that this was not his war; it was Christ's. The pope was still St. Peter's vicar, but he had proclaimed the crusade not on Peter's behalf, but on Christ's. I have suggested earlier that St. Peter's diminished rôle may not have been entirely to the popes' liking. And I believe that we have here an example of one of the features of papal history: the way the ideas of the faithful ran ahead of official theory, forcing it up roads along which the popes, nearly always cautious, were reluctant to move too fast. The First Crusade was, in fact, a practical expression of the Vicariate of Christ before that concept had fully developed.[204] The idea of a war fought by Christ's army, called out by the pope on Christ's behalf, was, of course, a papal one, but it was taken up so enthusiastically by the faithful that afterwards there could be no turning back. The First Crusade was an important precedent for the most significant papal idea of the later Middle Ages.

---

201 Baldric of Bourgueil, p. 101.
202 Ralph of Caen, p. 604.
203 Guibert of Nogent, p. 211; Robert of Rheims, p. 781; Albert of Aachen, pp. 320, 330, 332, 339, 373, 375, 405, 407, 409, 417, 493. See Bartolf of Nangis, p. 496; Albert of Aachen, pp. 400, 402. For the word *fidelis* in feudal terminology, see Erdmann, pp. 207-208. For references to wages, calling to mind both paid military service and the parable of the labourers in the vineyard, see Fulcher of Chartres, p. 136; Baldric of Bourgueil, p. 15; *Historia peregrinorum,* p. 215. In the *Chanson d'Antioche* (p. 395) there was a reference to the crusaders as "Damedeu soldoiers".
204 For the history of the title, see Michele Maccarone, *Vicarius Christi: storia del titolo papale* (Rome, 1952), pp. 11-154.

THE FINANCING OF THE CRUSADES IN THE TWELFTH CENTURY*

GILES CONSTABLE

Dumbarton Oaks (Harvard University)

The two principal methods of financing the crusades in the twelfth century are illustrated in a document from Fleury recording three decisions made by the monks early in 1147.[1] They agreed, first, to take forty marks' worth of silver from the crucifix in order to feed the poor who were flocking to the abbey on account of the famine prevailing in France at that time, which had forced many nobles to sell their property and go to distant lands. Second, they ceded to Abbot Macharius two silver candelabra "of wonderful workmanship," weighing thirty marks, and a censer of eight marks of gold and three ounces[2] in

---

* This article is based on material gathered over the past thirty years, beginning with the research for a paper presented in the late Professor R.L. Wolff's seminar on the crusades at Harvard in the fall of 1951 and published as "The Second Crusade as Seen by Contemporaries," *Traditio* 9 (1953), 213-279. I was impressed at that time with the number of references to the crusades (especially their financing) in twelfth-century charters and was pleased to find, when asked to contribute to this Festschrift, that enough material had accumulated to be put together into an article. The collections of charters will be cited here, after the first reference, simply by the name of the institution.

1 *Recueil des chartes de l'abbaye de Saint-Benoît-sur-Loire,* ed. Maurice Prou and Alexandre Vidier, 1, Documents publiés par la Société historique et archéologique du Gatinais 5 (Paris, 1905-07), 340-343, no. 150. The document is dated by the editors 1146-1147, but since the passage describing the mortgage of the censer (see n. 2 below) refers to the third Easter "ab illo qui iam imminebat," the decisions were probably made before Easter (20 April) 1147. The document itself, however, was clearly drawn up later, since it refers to subsequent events.

2 The mortgage of this censer is the subject of *St.-Benoît-sur-Loire,* 1: 339-340, no. 149, which is dated 1146 in the tenth year of Louis's reign (that is, between 1 August 1146 and 29 March 1147). The censer was to be mortgaged on condition that it would be restored or replaced by one of equal value within three years, and eight *majores, servientes,* and *milites* guaranteed this agreement. The abbot was later authorized, however, according to the document cited in n. 1 above, to use the value of the censer to build a new dormitory.

order to meet the demand of King Louis "who was about to go as a pilgrim to Jerusalem in order with the help of God to protect and set free the Christians who lived there and were oppressed by many attacks from the Sarracens." The king extorted money "from the treasures of the churches of his realm in order to carry out this work" and asked at first for a thousand marks from Abbot Macharius, who replied that this was too much in view of his abbey's recent difficulties, the failure of the vineyards for seven years, and the exactions of the king and his servants. Louis then reduced his demand to five hundred marks, which Macharius said was still too much, and finally to the equivalent of about four hundred marks,[3] which the abbot, "recognizing that it was not right to oppose the king longer," agreed to try to raise.[4]

"At the same time," the document continued, going on to the third piece of business, "Joscerand the mayor of this town, wishing to journey as a pilgrim with the king, and Godfrey the butler of the lord abbot and Guido Belini and Adelard *de Porta,* being ready to go to Jerusalem, came into our chapter wishing to mortgage to us those things they held of us for a period of five years."[5] This the abbot and monks agreed to do on condition

> that the revenues deriving from these gages, both for their support and for the service owing to us, will for five years be considered ours for whatever we wish to do in this house and that if they have not returned after five years, or if they die, all the revenues... will be ours so long as they or their successors are unable to redeem them, as is contained in the charters written about this.

These particular charters have not survived, but the cartularies of the twelfth century, and to a lesser extent the chronicles and *Lives* of saints, contain many

---

3   The sum was defined as 300 marks of silver and 500 gold bezants, which were the equivalent of about 92 silver marks, according to information kindly given me by Professor Philip Grierson. F. Le Blanc, *Traité historique des monnoyes de France* (Paris, 1690), pp. 170-171, cited this passage, giving the value of the bezant as 9 s., and later (p. 403) gave the value of the silver mark at this time as 40 s. At Molesme, according to the charter of 1101/7, cited n. 109 below, 7 marks were equated with 300 s.

4   The accounts in these documents of the negotiations between the king and the abbot and between the abbot and the monks are of great interest, as are the descriptions of monastic finance and administration. It is tempting to think that some of the many noblemen who were ashamed to beg in their own country and "exteras ac procul remotas peterent regiones" may have joined the Crusade.

5   Joscerand mortgaged the dues owed him as mayor and for measuring for *septem viginti* (probably 27 but possibly 140) pounds; Godfrey, his fief for 30 pounds; Guido and Adelard, their fiefs for 10 pounds each. Joscerand and Godfrey were among the guarantors of the agreement concerning the censer (n. 2 above), where they were called *milites* as well, apparently, as *majores.*

references to transactions of this type, including sales and loans as well as mortgages, made by crusaders and pilgrims to the Holy Land who needed ready money to finance their trips. These records of the private financing of crusades, however, have on the whole attracted less attention from scholars than the type of levy demanded from Fleury by Louis VII and later institution-alized methods of financing the crusades.[6] In this paper I shall look briefly at both.

I

The precise nature of Louis's exaction to support his crusade in 1146-47 has long puzzled scholars, of whom some have said that it was basically a feudal aid, others that it was an exceptional general levy, and yet others that it was a series of arbitrary demands for money from particular churches. Many nineteenth-century French historians, who wanted to show the early origins of centralized royal power in France, argued that these levies were the first known general royal aids and even that the apparent lack of general opposition showed that they were based on earlier precedents.[7] Luchaire denied that they were feudal in character but was in doubt whether they were special levies on royal bishoprics and abbeys or, as he tended to think, a general imposition, the only known example between the reigns of Hugh Capet and Philip Augustus.[8] Flach agreed that it was a general aid in defense of the kingdom, as did Joranson, who called the 926 Danegeld the last collection of "anything resem-

---

6   Although charter evidence has not been widely used for the history of pilgrimage and the crusades, special mention should be made of the pioneering work of Reinhold Röhricht on German pilgrims and crusaders from 700 to 1300 in the second volume of his *Beiträge zur Geschichte der Kreuzzüge* (Berlin, 1878) and *Die Deutschen im Heiligen Lande* (Innsbruck, 1894). There are sections on crusading charters in the introductions to some cartularies, notably the *Cartulaire de l'abbaye de Saint-Père de Chartres,* ed. B.E.C. Guérard, Collection de documents inédits sur l'histoire de France (Paris, 1840), 1:cciv-ccv, and *Cartulaires de l'abbaye de Molesme,* ed. Jacques Laurent, Collection de documents publiés avec le concours de la Commission des Antiquités de la Côte-d'Or 1 (Paris, 1907-11), 1:138-141, and in some local and family histories, such as G. Tenant de la Tour, *L'homme et la terre de Charlemagne à St.-Louis* (Paris [1943]), pp. 362-363; Georges Duby, *La société aux XIᵉ et XIIᵉ siècles dans la région mâconnaise* (Paris, 1953), pp. 360-361; Robert Fossier, *La terre et les hommes en Picardie jusqu'à la fin du XIIIᵉ siècle,* Publications de la Faculté des Lettres et Sciences humaines de Paris-Sorbonne: Recherches 49 (Paris, 1968), pp. 610-612; and W.M. Newman, *Les seigneurs de Nesle en Picardie,* Bibliothèque de la Société d'histoire du droit des pays flamands, picards et wallons 27 (Paris, 1971), 1:26.

7   Alphonse Callery, *Histoire du pouvoir royal d'imposer depuis la féodalité jusqu'au règne de Charles V* (Brussels [1879]), pp. 25-32.

8   Achille Luchaire, *Histoire des institutions monarchiques de la France sous les premiers Capé-tiens (987-1180),* 2nd ed. (Paris, 1891), pp. 126-128, and *Manuel des institutions françaises* (Paris, 1892), pp. 578-579.

bling a general tax" before "the first royal aid" levied by Louis VII in 1146.[9] Many historians refer to it simply as a general levy on all subjects of the king.[10]

The evidence for this view comes from the chronicles of Robert of Torigny and Ralph of Diceto, both of whom were writing some time after the event. According to Robert, the Second Crusade "was for the most part undertaken out of plunder from the poor and despoiling of churches,"[11] and Ralph wrote under the year 1146 that, "A general census was made through all France; neither sex nor order nor dignity excused anyone from giving aid to the king, whose expedition was accompanied by many curses."[12] The close resemblance of this description to that of the levy to support Louis VII's siege of Verneuil in 1173 in Ralph's *Ymagines historiarum,*[13] however, was noticed by Lunt, who commented that, "There seems to be no adequate foundation for the assertion that the series of income-taxes began with the second crusade" and that "The meagre documentary evidence deals only with arbitrary sums demanded from the prelates by Louis VII."[14] Various recent scholars have followed this cautious view.[15]

9   Jacques Flach, *Les origines de l'ancienne France* (Paris, 1886-1917), 3:349-350, and Einar Joranson, *The Danegeld in France,* Augustana Library Publications 10 (Rock Island, Ill., 1924), p. 204.

10   Richard Hirsch, *Studien zur Geschichte König Ludwigs VII. von Frankreich (1119-1160)* (Leipzig, 1892), p. 45; Otto Cartellieri, *Abt Suger von Saint-Denis 1081-1151,* Historische Studien, ed. Ebering 11 (Berlin, 1898), p. 54; Alexander Cartellieri, *Philipp II. August, König von Frankreich,* 2: *Der Kreuzzug (1187-1191)* (Leipzig, 1906), p. 5; Charles Petit-Dutaillis, *La monarchie féodale en France et en Angleterre,* L'évolution de l'humanité 41 (Paris, 1933), p. 209; Marcel Aubert, *Suger,* Figures monastiques (Paris, 1950), p. 101; Sydney Knox Mitchell, *Taxation in Medieval England* (New Haven, 1951), p. 114; and Amy Kelly, *Eleanor of Aquitaine and the Four Kings* (London, 1952), p. 36.

11   *The Chronicle of Robert of Torigni,* ed. Richard Howlett, RS 82 (London, 1889), p. 154. See Charles Gross, *A Bibliography of English History to 1485,* ed. Edgar B. Graves (Oxford, 1975), p. 447, saying that the chronicle, which was written from time to time between 1150 and 1186, is of independent value after 1150.

12   *The Historical Works of Master Ralph of Diceto,* ed. William Stubbs, RS 68 (London, 1876), 1:256-257. See Gross, *Bibliography,* p. 418.

13   Ralph of Diceto, 1:372.

14   W.E. Lunt, *The Valuation of Norwich* (Oxford, 1926), pp. 1-2.

15   Emile Bridrey, *La condition juridique des croisés et le privilège de croix* (Paris, 1900), pp. 66-69, already expressed some doubts, saying that, "Il subsiste pourtant quelque doute sur la nature véritable de cette imposition." See also Carl Stephenson, "The Aids of the French Towns in the Twelfth and Thirteenth Centuries" (1922), revised tr. in *Medieval Institutions* (Ithaca, N.Y., 1954), p. 3, n. 5; Constable, "Second Crusade," p. 243, n. 161; James A. Brundage, *Medieval Canon Law and the Crusader* (Madison, Wis., 1969), p. 185, who omitted referring to the 1146 levy and wrote that, "The earliest of these schemes [to raise money for the crusades] dates from 1166"; Virginia Berry, "The Second Crusade," in *A History of the Crusades,* 1: *The First Hundred Years,* ed. Marshall W. Baldwin, 2nd ed. (Madison, Wis., 1969), p. 471; and John W. Baldwin, *Masters, Princes, and Merchants: The Social Views of Peter the Chanter and his Circle* (Princeton, 1970), 1:219.

An extraordinary event like a royal crusade could obviously not be financed simply out of normal royal revenues,[16] and the letters written by both Louis VII and Conrad III while they were on route show that they were chronically short of cash.[17] Louis's regent, Abbot Suger of St. Denis, was hard pressed to raise the necessary money and, according to his biographer, "either sent to the king on pilgrimage or set aside all the money paid from the royal fiscs."[18] The document from Fleury refers specifically to the king's efforts to raise money from "the churches of his realm," but the only other unambiguous reference is in a charter of 1145/7 confirming the privileges of the church of Le Puy, where Louis asked the bishop to help with the expenses of his pilgrimage to Jerusalem "out of the money of the city" and promised that "neither we nor any of our successors will exact this further on the basis of custom nor molest the church in this fashion."[19] The other documents cited by scholars as evidence of a royal levy at this time cannot with certainty be associated with the crusade,[20] and their number and precise nature remain unclear.[21]

Peter the Venerable of Cluny urged the king in a well-known letter to force the Jews to contribute to the expenses of the crusade,[22] but there is no evidence that he did so. Rabbi Ephraim of Bonn, writing probably in the 1170s, said that

16 J. Declareuil, *Histoire générale du droit français des origines à 1789* (Paris, 1925), p. 703.
17 See the letters of Louis VII to Suger in Achille Luchaire, *Etudes sur les actes de Louis VII* (Paris, 1885), pp. 171-176, nos. 224-225, 229-231, 236, and 240, and the letter of Conrad III to Wibald of Corvey in *Die Urkunden Konrads III. und seines Sohnes Heinrich,* ed. Friedrich Hausmann, MGH, Diplomata regum et imperatorum 9 (Vienna, 1969), pp. 354-355, no. 195.
18 William of St. Denis, *Vita Sugerii,* ed. A. Lecoy de la Marche, in *Oeuvres complètes de Suger,* Société de l'histoire de France (Paris, 1867), p. 395.
19 *Gallia christiana* (Paris, 1715-1865), 2 preuves 231; cf. Luchaire, *Institutions,* 1:127, n. 2 (who has two significant textual variants in his reprint of the text) and *Actes de Louis VII,* pp. 158-159, no. 185, dated 1 Aug. 1146/2 Feb. 1147.
20 See the lists of documents cited by Callery, *Histoire,* p. 26, and Luchaire, *Institutions,* 1:126, n. 2. These include several from the *Epistolae Sugerii abbatis S. Dionysii* published by François Duchesne in *Historiae Francorum scriptores coaetani* (Paris, 1636-49), 4:491-546, such as no. 24, p. 500, from the bishop of Amiens, which relates to the crusade but not necessarily to the king's financial demand, and no. 123, p. 532, from the abbot of Ferrières, which refers to a royal tax but not necessarily in connection with the crusade. The privilege for the church of Paris in *Monuments historiques,* ed. Jules Tardif (Paris, 1866), pp. 264-265, no. 494 (see Luchaire, *Actes de Louis VII,* p. 163, no. 200), relates to the tallage owed when the bishopric fell into the king's hand.
21 Abbé Gagnol, *Les décimes et les dons gratuits* (Paris, 1911), p. 16, stressed that these payments were not called tithes.
22 *The Letters of Peter the Venerable,* ed. Giles Constable, Harvard Historical Studies 78 (Cambridge, Mass., 1967), 1:327-330, no. 130; see Virginia Berry, "Peter the Venerable and the Crusades," in *Petrus Venerabilis 1156-1956: Studies and Texts Commemorating the Eighth Centenary of his Death,* ed. Giles Constable and James Kritzeck, Studia Anselmiana 40 (Rome, 1956), pp. 148-150.

many Jews in France lost their property owing to Louis's remission of debts owed by crusaders,[23] but in fact only the interest on loans was cancelled, and that by the pope, not by the king. Ephraim further wrote that, "We also gave our wealth as ransom for our lives.... Whatever they asked of us, either silver or gold, we did not withhold from them,"[24] but he is referring here not to the crusaders themselves or their leaders but to the persecutors of the Jews in the Rhineland, who used the pretext of the crusade to plunder the Jews.

The first known provision for a general tax in aid of the Holy Land was Louis VII's decree in 1166 that a penny for each pound of property and revenues should be sent to Jerusalem "for the defense of Christianity" annually for five years by himself and all his subjects, both clerical and lay.[25] Henry II of England, not to be outdone, issued a similar decree, doubling the amount to two pennies per pound for the first year.[26] The proceeds of this levy did not pay for a crusade, however, but were sent to Jerusalem, where they were used presumably for mercenaries and perhaps for fortifications. There were further levies in 1183 and 1185,[27] but the first specific crusading levy was the Saladin Tithe of 1188, which all non-crusaders, with a very few exceptions, were required to pay from all their moveable property and revenues.[28] Those who joined the crusade, according to the decree of Philip Augustus, were not only freed from payment but also entitled, if they were lords, to receive the tithes paid by their non-crusading vassals and, if they were knights, to receive the

23 Adolf Neubauer and Moritz Stern, *Hebräische Berichte über die Judenverfolgungen während der Kreuzzüge* (Berlin, 1892), pp. 64 and 195; *The Jews and the Crusaders: The Hebrew Chronicles of the First and Second Crusades,* tr. Shlomo Eidelberg (Madison, Wis., 1977), pp. 131 and 177, n. 59. Ephraim went on to say that the king of England protected the persons and property of the Jews.

24 Ibid., p. 122.

25 Robert of Torigni, pp. 227 and 230.

26 Gervase of Canterbury, *Historical Works,* ed. William Stubbs, RS 73 (London, 1879-80), 1:198-199. On these levies in England and France, see R.W. Eyton, *Court, Household, and Itinerary of King Henry II* (London, 1878), p. 93; Cartellieri, *Philipp II.,* 2:6-7; Benjamin Z. Kedar, "The General Tax of 1183 in the Crusading Kingdom of Jerusalem: Innovation or Adaptation?" *English Historical Review* 89 (1974), 342-343; and W.L. Warren, *Henry II* (Berkeley, Calif., 1977), pp. 105 and 377-378. They amounted to five-year capital levies of 2.08 percent in France and 2.5 percent in England.

27 See Cartellieri, *Philipp II.,* 2:14-17; Fred A. Cazel, Jr., "The Tax of 1185 in Aid of the Holy Land," *Speculum* 30 (1955), 385-392; and Kedar, "General Tax," 339-345.

28 *Oeuvres de Rigord et de Guillaume le Breton,* ed. H.F. Delaborde, Société de l'histoire de France (Paris, 1882), 1:88-90. That this was the first effort to impose a crusading tithe on the clergy was recognized in the eighteenth century by Louis Thomassin in his *Ancienne et nouvelle discipline de l'église,* ed. M. André (Bar-le-Duc, 1864-67), 6:254 and 270. See also Cartellieri, *Philipp II.,* 2:58-72, and Warren, *Henry II,* pp. 377-378, and the literature cited in Hans E. Mayer, *Bibliographie zur Geschichte der Kreuzzüge* (Hanover, 1960), p. 209.

tithes of their parents. The decree of Henry II of England likewise established, in somewhat different terms, that crusaders both paid no tithe themselves and might receive the tithes of their men.[29] The development of a system of public financing of the crusades reached its final stage in the elaborate provisions of the decree *Ad liberandam* of the Fourth Lateran Council in 1215.[30]

By this time it was also customary for vassals to contribute to the expenses of a lord's journey to Jerusalem. The monks of La Trinité at Vendôme, for instance, were obliged according to a charter of 1185 to give the count of Vendôme 3000 s. "the first time he goes to Jerusalem."[31] Such payments naturally roused opposition. Peter of Blois protested in his letter *On hastening the pilgrimage to Jerusalem* that, "The beginning of this pilgrimage should not come from injuries or seizures,"[32] and Stephen of Tournai complained in a letter to the bishop of Soissons, probably with reference to crusading levies, at "the new and unowed exactions... under which the Church groans today" and at "the tributes and tithes" paid by the clergy.[33] These payments, however, in spite of their unpopularity, helped to establish a reasonably clear financial basis for the crusades.

II

Most crusades and pilgrimages to the Holy Land in the twelfth century were financed privately. "All the pilgrims, once they were enrolled," wrote Vacandard of the Second Crusade, "including the king, feudal barons, simple knights,

---

29   "Benedict of Peterborough," *The Chronicle of the Reigns of Henry II. and Richard I.*, ed. William Stubbs, RS 49 (London, 1867), 2:30-31, which is excerpted in William Stubbs, *Select Charters and Other Illustrations of English Constitutional History*, 8th ed. (Oxford, 1905), p. 160. The phrase "sed de proprio suo et dominico" after the reference to the non-payment of tithes by crusaders was translated "except for [*or* from] their own property and demesnes" in Carl Stephenson and F.G. Marcham, *Sources of English Constitutional History* (New York, 1937), p. 96, and David Douglas and George Greenaway, *English Historical Documents 1042-1189* (London, 1953), p. 420. This makes nonsense of the exemption, and the phrase probably means that crusaders were expected to serve from their own property and demesne, as in the translation in *A Translation of Such Charters as are Untranslated in Dr. Stubbs' Select Charters* (Oxford, n.d.), p. 59. William of Newburgh, *Historia rerum anglicarum*, ed. Richard Howlett, RS 82 (London, 1884), 1:273, clearly stated that, "Quicunque autem clericus aut laicus crucem acceperit, nihil dabit."

30   *Conciliorum oecumenicorum decreta*, ed. J. Alberigo a.o., 3rd ed. (Bologna, 1973), pp. 267-271. See the references ibid., p. 271, and in Michel Villey, *La croisade. Essai sur la formation d'une théorie juridique*, L'église et l'état au Moyen Age 6 (Paris, 1942), pp. 179-185, and Mayer, *Bibliographie*, p. 209.

31   *Cartulaire de l'abbaye cardinale de la Trinité de Vendôme*, ed. C. Métais (Paris, 1893-1904), 2:445, no. 578.

32   Peter of Blois, *De Hierosolymitana peregrinatione acceleranda*, in PL 207:1068A.

33   Stephen of Tournai, Ep. 154 to Bishop Nivelo of Soissons, in PL 211:440B.

peasants, bishops, abbots, monks, were preoccupied with the costs of the crusade. Their first resource was to sell or mortgage their property, both moveable and immoveable."[34] A few crusaders may have hoped for pay from the Greek emperor[35] or from the Latin rulers of the Holy Land, and others may have had sufficient liquid resources to cover their costs, like the pilgrimage nest-egg stolen from a priest mentioned in the *De miraculis* of Peter the Venerable,[36] but the majority had to raise the necessary funds by sales or loans. "Jews and priests, who had the most money," wrote Röhricht, "received castles, woods, estates, and other property as security for loans, as gifts, and through sale."[37] Religious institutions even more than individuals acted as sources of credit. These transactions had incalculable social and economic effects.[38] They contributed not only to the enrichment of many institutions at the expense of crusading families, some of which beggared themselves to pay the costs of their journeys,[39] but also to the transfer into liquid form, or de-hoarding, as at Fleury, of treasure and other assets and consequently to the increased flow of money into the markets of both western and eastern Europe.

Guibert of Nogent, writing in the early twelfth century, said that the enthusiasm for the crusade of all classes of men was so great that they sold their houses, vineyards, and fields almost without regard for their value. Prices fell owing to everyone's efforts to sell their best property, he said, "at a lower price

---

34   E. Vacandard, *Vie de saint Bernard* (Paris, 1895), 2:274. The same point was made, with references to Vacandard and other works, by Eberhard Pfeiffer, "Die Cistercienser und der zweite Kreuzzug, 3. Hilfeleistungen der Cistercienserklöster an Kreuzfahrer," *Cistercienser-Chronik* 47 (1935), 78: "Die Finanzierung des II. Kreuzzuges blieb demnach der Privatinitiative einzelner Personen oder Personengruppen überlassen, wie denn überhaupt von einer eigentlichen päpstlichen Kreuzzugssteuer im ganzen 12. Jahrhundert keine Rede sein kann." Edmond-René Labande, "Recherches sur les pèlerins dans l'Europe des XIe et XIIe siècles," *Cahiers de civilisation médiévale* 1 (1958), 167-168, stressed that pilgrimages were well-known to be expensive.

35   As was proposed by Carl Erdmann, *The Origin of the Idea of Crusade,* tr. Marshall Baldwin and Walter Goffart (Princeton, 1977), p. 270 (and the long addition to n. 7 by the translators, who called the problem "obscure") and p. 326.

36   Peter the Venerable, *De miraculis* 1.23, in *Bibliotheca Cluniacensis,* ed. Martin Marrier and André Duchesne (Paris, 1614), p. 1283D.

37   Röhricht, *Beiträge,* 2:66 and 97, n. 29. See also Jonathan Sumption, *Pilgrimage: An Image of Mediaeval Religion* (London, 1975), p. 206.

38   A.L. Poole, *Obligations of Society in the XII and XIII Centuries,* Ford Lectures 1944 (Oxford, 1946), p. 32: "The crusade, involving the absence of many lords from their lands, doubtless worked a social upheaval."

39   J. Marc, "Contribution à l'étude du régime féodal sur le domaine de l'abbaye de Saint-Seine," *Revue bourguignonne de l'enseignement supérieur* 6 (1896), 71-73, who attributed the disappearance of knights by the fourteenth century in this part of France at least in part to the cost° of the crusades. On the family of Brancion, see A. Déléage, "Les forteresses de la Bourgogne franque," *Annales de Bourgogne,* 3 (1931), 167.

than if he were held captive in a harsh prison and needed to be speedily ransomed," and expensive things became cheap as a result of the movement which "drove innumerable men into voluntary exile."[40] Godfrey and Baldwin of Boulogne were said in the chronicle of Afflighem to have given "large benefices from their patrimonies to many poor monasteries" when they joined the crusade and "gathered an army from far and wide within the boundaries of this province";[41] and the crusaders were described in a chronicle from Tournai as "selling many of their lands and possessions and taking the proceeds with them."[42] In a document of 1152 the archbishop of Salzburg, presumably referring to the Second Crusade, said that at the time "when the expedition to Jerusalem inspired almost the entire West with a marvellous and hitherto unheard-of fervor, people began to sell their property as if they were never going to return, which the churches, looking out for their own interests, bought according to their means."[43]

According to the first known crusading bull, *Quantum predecessores,* issued by Pope Eugene III on 1 December 1145, crusaders were permitted "to pledge freely and without opposition their lands and other possessions to churches or clerics and also to other of the faithful, provided their relations and lords, to whose fief they belong, have been informed and are either unwilling or unable to lend the money." They were also freed from paying interest on existing debts, even if they had promised to do so.[44] Alexander III in 1162 interceded with Louis VII on behalf of a knight whose wife refused to allow him to sell or pledge his paternal inheritance in order to go to Jerusalem. The pope asked the king to allow the knight "to sell or pledge his possessions to whomever he wished" and to protect from harm or disturbance "those to whom he sold or

---

40 Guibert of Nogent, *Gesta Dei per Francos* 2.6, RHC HOcc. 4:140-141.

41 *Chronicon Affligemense* 17, MGH SS 9:415.

42 *Chronica Tornacensis,* in *Recueil des chroniques de Flandre,* ed. J.-J. de Smet, Collection de chroniques belges inédites (Brussels, 1837-65), 2:563, and MGH SS 14:326, n.**, where the quoted words appear as an addition to Herman, *Liber de restauratione S. Martini.* See also *Die Reinhardsbrunner Briefsammlung,* ed. Friedel Peeck, MGH Epp. sel. 5 (Weimar, 1952), 45-46, no. 49, for a letter written by an abbot of R. in 1103/44 containing a reference to a sale of land made "at the time when innumerable people from the regions of various peoples sold their lands and went to Jerusalem and captured it by siege."

43 *Monumenta canoniae ad S. Zenonem* 9, in *Monumenta Boica,* 3 (Munich, 1764), 540.

44 *Quantum predecessores,* in Otto of Freising, *Gesta Friderici I.* 1.36, 3rd ed. G. Waitz and B. von Simson, MGH Scriptores in usum scholarum (Hanover, 1912), 57; Jaffé-Löwenfeld, no. 8796. See also the text of the version of 1 March 1145 edited by P. Rassow as an appendix to E. Caspar, "Die Kreuzzugsbullen Eugens III.," *Neues Archiv* 45 (1924), 285-305. On the freedom from the obligation to pay interest, see Bridrey, *Condition,* pp. 199-233, and esp. Brundage, *Canon Law,* pp. 179-183 and (on the right to pledge) 176.

pledged."[45] Philip Augustus in his decree on the Saladin Tithe granted crusaders a respite of two years to repay debts contracted before taking the cross, allowed debtors who were unable to repay the loans to secure bondsmen and pledges, and defined the terms upon which both crusaders and non-crusaders could pledge lands and revenues.[46] By the end of the twelfth century, therefore, the right of crusaders to sell or pledge their property and to pay no interest on debts was established in both canon and civil law.[47]

The pledges made by crusaders technically carried no interest and could usually be redeemed for the amount borrowed, but since the lender received the revenues from the property until the principal was repaid (which was sometimes, as at Fleury, set for a specific period), these loans were often highly profitable for the lenders.[48] In most cases it is impossible to estimate how profitable, but Peter the Venerable, who was a shrewd financial administrator, gives an indication in his *Dispositio rei familiaris,* drawn up in 1147/8, where he refers to a pledge given by a crusader in return for a loan of 4000 s. and yielding 300 s. a year.[49] This represents a comparatively modest annual return of 7.5 percent, and it is probable that the effective rate of interest was often in fact considerably higher.

45 PL 200:187AB; Jaffé-Löwenfeld, no. 10796. The inheritance apparently belonged to the husband, not (as would seem more reasonable under the circumstance) the wife. Alexander justified his request on the grounds that the wife had withheld herself from her husband and committed adultery.

46 Rigord 58, ed. Delaborde, 1:85-87. See Brundage, *Canon Law,* p. 181. Philip said that the debts were to be paid in three annual installments.

47 Brundage, *Canon Law,* pp. 175-187.

48 Robert Génestal, *Rôle des monastères comme établissements de crédit étudié en Normandie du XIᵉ à la fin du XIIIᵉ siècle* (Paris, 1901), pp. 2-10, who contrasts these mortgages or dead pledges with the much rarer live pledges, where the principal was repaid out of the revenues of the property. Live pledges also carried effective interest when the revenues were estimated at less than their true value. The distinction between the two types of pledges is not always easy, but redemption by a lump payment is a sure sign of a mortgage.

49 *Recueil des chartes de l'abbaye de Cluny,* ed. A. Bernard and A. Bruel, Collection de documents inédits sur l'histoire de France (Paris, 1876-1903), 5:482, no. 4132. The arrangement was a complex one, by which the dean of Lourdon held the pledge (which was apparently a piece of land), presumably sold the produce, and gave the income to the chamberlain of Cluny, who used it to provide shoes and leggings for the monks, which could no longer be provided out of the revenues from England owing to the wars there. Peter stipulated that if the pledge was redeemed, the shoes and leggings should be provided out of the revenues of the manor of Letcombe-Regis, which was given to Cluny in 1136 by King Stephen in place of the annual cash gift given by Henry I: see *Letters of Peter the Venerable,* 2:138-139.

While some crusaders obtained loans from their relations and lords, as Eugene III provided, and some from bishops,[50] clerics, Jews, and even servile dependents, whose tenures were occasionally freed for the period of the crusade and who could win their freedom by joining the crusade themselves,[51] the vast majority turned to religious houses, which were the principal institutions of credit in the eleventh and twelfth centuries.[52] It was not unusual for monasteries to dispose of their treasures to raise the necessary funds, as did Fleury. The abbot of Capelle-Brouch plundered a reliquary of the Virgin and took gold and silver from some crosses in order to acquire some property from Baldwin of Ardre when he took the cross.[53] Bishop Godfrey of Langres used the liturgical vessels of his church and the gold and precious stones from the reliquary of St. Mamas in order to raise money for his crusade in 1147.[54] The abbot of Rolduc, who lacked the means to buy the allod of a crusader, arranged for it to be bought by some money-lenders "in such a way that the ownership thereof

---

50 *Cluny,* 5:108, no. 3755 (mortgage to brother-in-law ca. 1100); *Calendar of Documents Preserved in France, Illustrative of the History of Great Britain and Ireland,* 1:*918-1206,* ed. J. Horace Round (London, 1899), 93, no. 277 (mortgage to nephew 1188?); and, for examples of sales and mortgages to bishops, Bernard Bligny, *L'église et les ordres religieux dans le royaume de Bourgogne aux XIe et XIIe siècles,* Collection des Cahiers d'histoire publiée par les Universités de Clermont, Lyon, Grenoble 4 (Paris, 1960), p. 86, and Luchaire, *Actes de Louis VII,* p. 168, no. 215, where Louis VII in 1147 confirmed the mortgage of a crusader's fief to the bishop of Beauvais.

51 Poole, *Obligations,* pp. 31-32.

52 On monasteries as institutions of credit, see, in addition to the basic work of Génestal, Giuseppe Salvioli, "Il monachismo occidentale e la sua storia economica," *Rivista italiana di sociologia,* 15 (1911), 18: "Sappiamo come alle prime crociate abbiano largamente provvisto le risorce monetarie dei monasteri di tutto Occidente"; G.G. Coulton, *Five Centuries of Religion,* 3: *Getting and Spending* (Cambridge, 1936), 275 and 561-562; Georg Schreiber, "Cluny und die Eigenkirche" (1942) in *Gemeinschaften des Mittelalters* (Münster, 1948), p. 119; Paolo Grossi, *Le abbazie benedettine nell'Alto Medioevo italiano,* Pubblicazioni della Università degli studi di Firenze: Facoltà di Giurisprudenza NS 1 (Florence, 1957), pp. 121-124; Bligny, *Eglise,* p. 189: "Avant l'institution des dîmes spéciales par la papauté, c'est sur le monachisme, plus encore que sur l'épiscopat, qu'a reposé le succès de la croisade"; José Martoso, *Le monachisme ibérique et Cluny. Les monastères du diocèse de Porto de l'an mille à 1200,* Université de Louvain: Recueil de travaux d'histoire et de philologie 4.39 (Louvain, 1968), pp. 371-372.

53 Lambert of Ardre, *Historia comitum Ghisnensium* 139, MGH SS 24:632.

54 *Translatio S. Mamantis* 2.12, in *Acta sanctorum,* 17 August, 3:443D. See Pfeiffer, "Cistercienser," p. 78. In *Cartulaire de l'abbaye de Noyers,* ed. C. Chevalier, Mémoires de la Société archéologique de Touraine 22 (Tours, 1872), p. 583, no. 555, a crusader was given *in caritate* two silver cups, which he presumably used to finance his crusade.

passed to the church and the buyers were entitled to sustenance for their lifetimes, after which free ownership passed to the church."[55]

The crusades thus presented a favorable opportunity for institutions with liquid resources to acquire property and make profitable loans.[56] The dramatic increase at the turn of the twelfth century in the number of grants to the Cluniac house of Domène, in the kingdom of Burgundy, may be attributable to the needs of crusaders, who turned to this monastery rather than to the poorer houses of St. Barnard at Romans or St. Andrew at Vienne.[57] The six pan-chartes issued by Godfrey of Langres for Clairvaux in 1147, which incorporate 149 separate transactions, may reflect the rash of financial operations associated with the Second Crusade,[58] even though the Cistercians (perhaps owing both to poverty and to a desire to avoid secular affairs) seem to have been less involved than other orders in financing the crusades.[59] Sometimes churches took the initiative in acquiring the property of crusaders. A charter of the count of Soissons in 1146 recorded that the abbot and provost of St. Crispin,

---

55 *Annales Rodenses,* ed. P.C. Boeren and G.W.A. Panhuysen (Assen, 1968), p. 96 (fol. 19v s.a. 1146), see also p. 106 (fol. 22r s.a. 1153) for another example of the abbot's using money-changers to finance a purchase. The sale by the canons of Berchtesgaden to those of Reichen-hall in 1147 (cited n. 43 above) was presumably to raise money to lend to or buy from crusaders.

56 L. Bruhat, *Le monachisme en Saintonge et en Aunis (XIᵉ et XIIᵉ siècle)* (La Rochelle, 1907), pp. 17 and 173 (Saintes and St. Jean d'Angély); F.M. Stenton, *Transcripts of Charters Relating to the Gilbertine Houses of Sixle, Ormsby, Catley, Bullington and Alvingham,* Publications of the Lincoln Record Society 18 (Horncastle, 1922), pp. xii and 6-7, no. 15; Paul Schmid, "Die Entstehung des Marseiller Kirchenstaats," *Archiv für Urkundenforschung* 10 (1926-28), 206-207; Georges Duby, "Economie domaniale et économie monétaire. Le budget de l'abbaye de Cluny entre 1080 et 1155," *Annales* 7 (1952), 161: "En ce temps, les chevaliers du voisinage souhaitaient se procurer des espèces pour participer aux expéditions lointaines, en particulier à la croisade. Les moines en profitèrent et arrondirent à bon comte leur domaine en achetant ou en prêtant sur mort-gage." Indeed, some scholars have suggested that the principal interest of monks in the crusades was the opportunity they presented for profitable deals: J.R. West, *St. Benet of Holme 1020-1210,* [1]: *The Eleventh and Twelfth Century Sections of Cott. MS. Galba E. ii. The Register of the Abbey of St. Benet of Holme,* Norfolk Record Society 2 (n.p., 1932) and 2: *Introductory Essay,* Norfolk Record Society 3 (n.p., 1932), 2:205 ("Apparently the business side of the deal was more in the abbot's mind than the encouragement of the Crusaders.") and Coulton, *Five Centuries,* 3:283 and 670.

57 Bligny, *Eglise,* pp. 188-189. The number of "donations" was 18 ca. 1085, 33 ca. 1090, 24 ca. 1095, 55 ca. 1100, 22 ca. 1105/7, and 19 ca. 1110.

58 *Recueil des chartes de l'abbaye de Clairvaux,* ed. Jean Waquet, 1 (Troyes, 1950), pp. 20-45, nos. 13-18. See R. Fossier, "La fondation de Clairvaux et la famille de saint Bernard," *Mélanges saint Bernard. XXIVᵉ Congrès de l'Association bourguignonne des sociétés savantes Dijon 1953* (Dijon, 1954), p. 27, who associated these confirmations with the crusade.

59 Pfeiffer, "Cistercienser," p. 79: "In den für diese Arbeit zur Verfügung stehenden Urkunden- und Literaturbüchern finden sich denn auch nur zwei Beweise für diese materielle Unterstütz-ung von Kreuzfahrern durch Cistercienserklöster."

"hearing that I was going to Jerusalem," asked for the tithes and other property of the church at Estrées;[60] and when Archbishop Theobald of Canterbury heard that William of Oby had "taken the cross and intended to visit the Holy Sepulchre," he required him to return to St. Benet at Holme some property he held at farm, so that the monks would suffer no loss "on the occasion of his pilgrimage."[61] While these charters include no reference to a *quid pro quo,* one was probably given.

All types of property were involved in these transactions,[62] including lands, buildings (houses, mills, ovens), churches, cemeteries, fairs, ecclesiastical and secular revenues, both in cash and kind, tolls, rights of justice, and occasionally people. A tithe-collector was given to La Chapelle-Aude in 1095/6, a swineherd to Vigeois in 1106/8, and seven serfs to Moutier-Haute-Pierre in 1148 as the result of a vow made by an ill crusader.[63] Conditional grants or mortgages were sometimes changed into outright grants by crusaders, and obnoxious dues abolished. The grant of some tolls and taxes to Moutier-la-Celle by the count of Champagne in 1114 was confirmed by his nephew when he went on a crusade forty years later, and the monks of Vaux-de-Cernay in 1202 were given the right to buy and sell "foreign merchandise" for their own use without paying the customary dues.[64]

---

60 Newman, *Seigneurs de Nesle,* 2:45-49, no. 16.

61 *St. Benet of Holme,* 1:18-19, no. 27; Avrom Saltman, *Theobald, Archbishop of Canterbury,* University of London Historical Studies 2 (London, 1956), p. 354, no. 132 (dated probably 1153/61).

62 I have found no general evidence to support the view (based on evidence from the Auvergne) of Gabriel Fournier, "La création de la grange de Gergovie par les Prémontrés de Saint-André et sa transformation en seigneurie (XIIᵉ-XVIᵉ siècle)," *Moyen Age* 56 (1950), 314, that, "Ces opérations financières, plus ou moins camouflées sous des prétextes religieux, portent rarement sur des terres, mais plus souvent sur des droits, percières, cens et dîmes."

63 *Fragments du cartulaire de la Chapelle-Aude,* ed. M. Chazaud (Moulins, 1860), pp. 82-83 and 88-90, nos. 43 and 49; "Chartularium monasterii sancti Petri Vosiensis," ed. Henri de Montégut, *Bulletin de la Société archéologique et historique du Limousin* 39 (1890), 62, no. 104 (presuming that *suarius* means swineherd); Auguste Castan, *Un épisode de la deuxième croisade* (Besançon, 1862), pp. 10-11. For other examples see Ernest Petit, *Histoire des ducs de Bourgogne de la race capétienne* (Dijon, 1885-1905), 1:417, no. 100 (1100); *Molesme,* 2:26-28, 143, and 321-322, nos. 1.19 (1104), 1.146 (1100), and 2.173(A) (1104).

64 *Cartulaire de Montier-la-Celle,* ed. Charles Lalore, Collection des principaux cartulaires du diocèse de Troyes 6 (Paris, 1882), pp. 15 and 284-287, nos. 13 and 233; *Cartulaire de l'abbaye de Notre-Dame des Vaux de Cernay de l'ordre de Cîteaux,* ed. L. Merlet and Aug. Moutié (Paris, 1857-58), 1:122 and 136, nos. 103 and 118 (1202). See "Monumenta Baumburgensia II," in *Monumenta Boica,* 3 (Munich, 1764), 84, no. 226, concerning the grant in 1147 by a crusader of a small *taxatio* he held from his father, and "Cartulaire du prieuré conventuel de Saint-Pierre de La Réole en Bazadais du IXᵉ au XIIᵉ siècle," ed. C. Grellet-Balguerié, *Archives historiques du département de la Gironde,* 5 (1863), 140, no. 93 (1187).

The frequent use of the terms *dono* and *donatio* in the documents describing these transactions does not indicate that they were gifts in the modern sense of the term, nor, as is sometimes said, that they were disguised sales,[65] since *dono* and *donatio* were used in many regions to describe a variety of economic operations, including sales and loans.[66] Even in transactions referred to as gifts there was often a reference to a *quid pro quo,* which was recorded in order to avoid any possible future claims on the part of the donor. In a crusading charter from Vendôme, a payment of 12 d. to the youngest of four sons, who was said to still be in his cradle, was mentioned presumably as evidence that his interests had been considered, and when the count of Vendôme was going to Jerusalem he and his son granted part of a forest in return for a hundred pounds of pennies *de caritate monasterii,* "in order that this matter between us and the aforesaid monks may be better and more firmly established."[67] The "charity" of the purchaser in cases like this paralleled the "gift" of the seller.[68]

The terms for the redemption of loans and mortgages were usually spelled out in the charters, which often specified that the pledge would be forfeit if the crusader died or did not return and would belong to the monastery after his death even if he returned and redeemed it.[69] A pilgrim in the first half of the eleventh century pledged a manor to Vigeois in return for 5 s. on condition that "if he returned from Jerusalem... he would return the 5 s. he had received and would hold the manor for his lifetime and after his death it would belong to St. Peter without contradiction."[70] In 1140 Brogne allowed a crusader to redeem a pledge for half the amount given but would keep the property not only if he was killed on the crusade or died without heirs but also if his heirs ever had no

65   E. Perroy, reviewing Léon and Albert Mirot, *La seigneurie de Saint-Vérain-des-Bois,* in *Revue historique* 197 (1947), 140, n. 1; Fournier, "Gergovie," 314 (cited n. 62 above).

66   See the important article by G. Chevrier, "Evolution de la notion de donation dans les chartes de Cluny du IXe à la fin du XIIe siècle," *A Cluny. Congrès scientifique. Fêtes et cérémonies liturgiques en l'honneur des saints abbés Odon et Odilon 9-11 juillet 1949* (Dijon, 1950), pp. 203-209: "Du don à la vente, la transition est aisée et semble être sans conséquences" (p. 207).

67   *La Trinité de Vendôme,* 2:104-105 and 301-304, nos. 360 (ca. 1098) and 486 (1139).

68   *Noyers,* pp. 581, 583, and 584, nos. 553 (ca. 1146), 555 (see n. 54 above), and 556 (ca. 1146), where a crusader was given a total of 7 s. 4 d. *in caritate* in return for the census of four *censuales* and some other property. See *Cartulaire du prieuré de la Charité-sur-Loire,* ed. R. de Lespinasse (Nevers, 1887), pp. 126-127, no. 50 (ca. 1146), where the monks gave 300 s. for an oven *charitatis intuitu.*

69   According to Marc, "Contribution," p. 72, and Bligny, *Eglise,* p. 86, pledges were rarely redeemed. The number of agreements preserved in monastic cartularies (which were presumably kept as titles to property) also suggests that many pledges were not redeemed.

70   *Vigeois,* p. 4, no. 5 (1031/60).

heirs;[71] and St. Jean d'Angély agreed to divide a pledge with a crusader after his return, until he was able to give back the full value of the loan.[72] Occasionally there seems to have been no expectation of repayment, as in the grant by Admont to Rupert of St. George in 1147 "with the agreement that if he did not come back [the pledge] would pass to the monastery and that if he came back he would hold it for his lifetime and after his death it would pass to the monastery."[73] This looks like a "live" as contrasted with a "dead" gage (mortgage), since the lenders were apparently compensated by the revenues of the pledge as well, perhaps, as by the expection of eventual possession of the property.

Restrictions were sometimes put on when the pledge could be redeemed and by whom. An undated pledge to Aniane could not be redeemed before three years; a pledge to La Trinité at Vendôme in 1123 could be redeemed after two years by the crusader and after a further two years by his brothers and relations, but only for the entire sum paid "together at the same time" in the chapter of monks; and in a document from Chézery in 1147 two brothers who had pledged some land for ten pounds could each redeem it for five pounds for up to seven years, after which it belonged to the monastery.[74] Two brothers who went to Jerusalem in 1137 "gave and sold" their property to Savigny on separate terms: one sold his three-quarters of the property outright while the other gave his quarter but kept the serfs on condition that if he returned he would neither molest nor make demands of them before reaching an agreement with the abbot.[75] In a charter concerning the marsh at Fullerton made about 1147, the abbot of St. Benet at Holme "gave Philip [Basset] fifteen marks as a

---

71   A. Le Mire (Miraeus), *Opera diplomatica et historica,* 2nd ed. J.F. Foppens (Louvain, 1723-48), 1:689-90.

72   *Cartulaire de Saint-Jean-d'Angély,* ed. G. Musset, Archives historiques de la Saintonge et de l'Aunis 30 and 33 (Paris, 1901-3), 1:384, no. 319 (ca. 1101). It was specified in this charter that the monks would, as usual, keep the property if the crusader did not return and that he would give it to them at his death and, further, that they would receive him as a monk if he wished.

73   *Urkundenbuch des Herzogthums Steiermark,* ed. J. Zahn, 1 (Graz, 1875), 279, no. 266.

74   *Cartulaire d'Aniane,* ed. Abbé Cassan and E. Meynial (Montpellier, 1900), p. 200, no. 60; *La Trinité de Vendôme,* 2:225, no. 444; "Chézery. Chartes du XIIᵉ siècle," ed. Jules Vuy, *Mémoires de l'Institut national genèvois,* 12 (1867-68), 16 (separate pagination), where the redemption was for the lifetime of the redeemer only. See also "Cartulaire de Sauxillanges," ed. Henry Doniol, *Mémoires de l'Académie des sciences, belles-lettres et arts de Clermont-Ferrand,* 34 (NS 3; 1861), 721, no. 327, where the pledge could be redeemed only by the crusader himself and with his own money, and *Cartulare monasterii beatorum Petri et Pauli de Domina* (Lyons, 1859), pp. 218-219, no. 233.24, where the pledge could be redeemed by *aliquis suorum* but apparently not by a stranger, cf. Ulysse Chevalier, *Régeste dauphinois* (Valences-Vienne, 1912-26), 1:634-635, no. 3784, dating this document ca. 1147.

75   *Cartulaire de l'abbaye de Savigny,* ed. A. Bernard, Collection de documents inédits sur l'histoire de France (Paris, 1853), 1:503-504, no. 937.

premium and at the same time freed the marsh from rent for fifteen years from the coming feast of St. Michael following the departure for Jerusalem of the king of France and other barons and Philip himself."[76] Special arrangements like this were doubtless worked out to suit the needs of both parties, but the restrictions, particularly with regard to the timing of the redemption, usually benefitted the lender, who was thus assured a certain return.

Clerical pilgrims and crusaders also needed funds to pay for their trips. Bishop Godfrey of Langres, as has been seen, plundered the treasury of his own church. When Regenbert of Passau went to Jerusalem "in the service of this catholic and Christian army," he made a gift to his canons "to supplement their prebend" and "in order that Our Lord and God may direct our journey in the way of peace and salvation and bring us at the same time to the heavenly Jerusalem"—as indeed occurred, since he lost his life on the crusade.[77] It is uncertain what, if anything, he received in return, but he may have been permitted to keep the revenues of his position. A charter from St.-Martin-des-Champs in 1127/31 granting a priest a church in return for an annual rent of one mark specified that he might be absent for three years on a pilgrimage, and the Cardinal-Legate Otto of St. Nicola in Carcere in 1160/1 allowed a canon of Noyon to keep the revenues of his benefice for three years while he made a pilgrimage to Jerusalem.[78] These arrangements adumbrate the decree of the Fourth Lateran Council allowing crusading clerics to keep their benefices, and if necessary to mortgage them, for three years.[79] Such absences occasionally

---

76 *St. Benet of Holme,* 1:87, no. 155. The marsh, with 300 sheep, was granted for an annual rent of five marks, which was apparently remitted in return for the payment to Philip (for whose crusade this charter is the only evidence). Souvigny made a colossal loan of 500 silver marks to Archembald VI of Bourbon in 1147, when he was "about to go to Jerusalem with King Louis of the Franks and many other nobles," and who promised to repay it in five annual installments of 100 marks, thus apparently paying no interest, since the loan was unsecured; but the authenticity of this charter has been questioned: M.-A. Chazaud, *Etude sur la chronologie des sires de Bourbon (Xe-XIIIe siècles),* ed. Max Fazy (Moulins, 1935), pp. 253-254 (cf. pp. 362 and 366 on the date and authenticity of this charter); see also Max Fazy, *Les origines du Bourbonnais* (Moulins, 1924), 1:273-274, no. 316, and Léon Côte, *Contributions à l'histoire de prieuré clunisien de Souvigny* (Moulins, 1942), p. 45, no. 47, both accepting its authenticity.

77 "Codex traditionum ecclesiae Pataviensis... tertius," in *Monumenta Boica,* 28 (Munich, 1829), 2:227, no. 15. See Willibald Plöchl, *Das kirchliche Zehentwesen in Niederösterreich,* Forschungen zur Landeskunde von Niederösterreich 5 (Vienna, 1935), pp. 90-91, and (on Regenbert's death) *Acta sanctorum,* 8 August, 2:376F.

78 *Recueil de chartes et documents de Saint-Martin-des-Champs,* ed. J. Depoin, 2, Archives de la France monastique 16 (Paris, 1913), 3-4, no. 193, and *Papsturkunden in Frankreich,* NF 7: *Nördliche Ile-de-France und Vermandois,* ed. Dietrich Lohrmann, Abhandlungen der Akademie der Wissenschaften in Göttingen, Phil.-Hist. Kl. 3.95 (Göttingen, 1976), p. 362, no. 94.

79 *Conciliorum oec. decreta,* p. 267. See Brundage, *Canon Law,* p. 178, who said that, "This privilege is another which was not mentioned in the records of the early crusades and which first found a place in ecclesiastical law with the constitution *Ad liberandam.*"

created problems, and the bishop of Angoulême permitted a monk of St.-Amand-de-Boixe to serve a local church when its priest went to Jerusalem with the count of Poitiers.[80]

Crusaders needed not only money but also supplies and equipment, and protection for their property and dependents. Horses and mules were often included in these transactions,[81] and a grant to Aureil made before 1100 specified that, "If he [the donor] wishes to go to Jerusalem, the prior and canons will provide him with his equipment."[82] The canons of St. Vincent at Mâcon were given some property in 1060/1108 in return for looking after the donor's mother while he made a pilgrimage to Spain,[83] and a departing crusader in about 1146 arranged for the church of Saintes to protect his wife during her lifetime and to pray for both her and himself after they died.[84] Departing crusaders sometimes arranged for members of their families or themselves, after their return, to be received as monks or nuns. In an undated charter for Bèze a crusader specified that after his return he or a member of his family would have the right to become a monk.[85]

For many crusaders spiritual protection was no less important than material support. Viscount Gisbert of Dijon made a grant to the abbey of St. Stephen when he went to Jerusalem in 1145. "For my protection," he said, "I made the glorious protomartyr Stephen a partner in my worldly estate."[86] Many grants

---

80   This charter may have been printed elsewhere but came to my attention in the notes by E. Baluze to his edition of Pierre de Marca, *De concordia sacerdotii et imperii* (Frankfort, 1708), pp. 961-962.

81   See *La Trinité de Vendôme*, 1:385, no. 243 (1074); *Molesme*, 2:64 and 84, nos. 1.54 (1101/9) and 1.78 (1095/1100); *Cluny*, 5:52, 77, and 90, nos. 3703 (1096), 3727 (1097), and 3737 (1100); *St.-Jean-d'Angély*, 1:384, no. 319 (ca. 1101); *Steiermark*, 1:324, no. 338 (ca. 1150); *Sauxillanges*, pp. 882 and 967, nos. 566 (n.d.) and 697 (n.d.); *St.-Père de Chartres*, p. 511, no. 2.4.2 (n.d.).

82   *Cartulaires des prieurés d'Aureil et de l'Artige en Limousin*, ed. G. de Senneville, Bulletin de la Société archéologique et historique du Limousin 48 (Limoges, 1900), p. 29, no. 47. See also *Cartulaire de Saint-Vincent de Mâcon*, ed. M.-C. Ragut (Mâcon, 1864), pp. 321-322, no. 547 (1106), and *Molesme*, 2:113-114, no. 1.111 (1103/11), for examples of prospective crusades.

83   *Mâcon*, pp. 20-21, no. 24 (1060/1108).

84   *Cartulaire de l'abbaye royale de Notre-Dame de Saintes*, ed. T. Grasilier, Cartulaires inédits de la Saintonge 2 (Niort, 1871), pp. 99-100, no. 124. See also *Cartulaire des abbayes de Saint-Pierre de la Couture et de Saint-Pierre de Solesmes* (Le Mans, 1871), pp. 55-56, no. 52 (1140), for an example of an agreement by a monastery to defend a pilgrim's lands.

85   *Chronique de Saint-Pierre de Bèze*, ed. E. Bougaud and J. Garnier, Analecta Divionensia 9 (Dijon, 1875), pp. 472-473. See also *St.-Jean-d'Angély*, p. 384, no. 319 (ca. 1101); *Salzburger Urkundenbuch*, 1: *Traditionscodices*, ed. Willibald Hauthaler (Salzburg, 1910), pp. 411 and 413, nos. 292 (1147) and 296 (1147); *Aureil*, pp. 181-182, no. 245 (ca. 1147); *St.-Père de Chartres*, p. 646, no. 3.3.31 (n.d.).

86   Claude Fyot, *Histoire de l'église abbatiale et collegiale de Saint Estienne de Dijon* (Dijon, 1696), preuves p. 99, no. 157. On the desire of pilgrims for divine protection, see G. Mollat,

were made for the sake of the salvation or remedy of the souls of the donor and his relations and in return for liturgical services, such as prayers and masses during a pilgrimage and burial and commemoration if the donor died.[87] The abbot and monks of St. Andrew of Clermont were obliged, according to a charter of William of Auvergne in 1149, to seek and bring back his body "if I should die in the war against the Saracens or otherwise outside the kingdom of France and this duchy."[88] When Godescalc of Morialmé was "inspired by the heavenly desire of journeying to Jerusalem in the company of the faithful in order to free the promised land from the hands of the impious" in 1188, he gave a church to Floreffe "in order that his pilgrimage might be more pleasing and the effects of his pilgrimage more meritorious," asking that the revenues of the church be divided between two houses of nuns who were to pray for him, and the following year James of Avesnes "on the occasion of my departure to succor the land of Jerusalem" gave an annual rent of 100 s. to Brogne in order to maintain two lighted candles night and day before the cross.[89]

"La restitution des églises privées au patrimoine ecclésiastique en France du IXe au XIe siècle," *RHDFE* 4.27 (1949), 416, citing several examples of gifts and sales to churches by departing crusaders.

87 *Le cartulaire du prieuré de Notre-Dame de Longpont* (Lyon, 1879), pp. 173-174, no. 182 (ca. 1120); *Cartulaire d'Afflighem,* ed. E. de Marneffe, Analectes pour servir à l'histoire ecclésiastique de la Belgique 2.1 (Louvain, 1894), p. 121, no. 78 (ca. 1147); J.P. von Ludewig, *Reliquiae manuscriptorum,* 4 (Frankfort, 1722), 196-198 (charter of Duke Ottokar of Styria for Garsten in 1150). The request of the count of Brienne when going to Jerusalem in 1131 to replace canons with monks in the church at Brienne may have been motivated by his belief in the greater efficacy of monks' prayers: *Cartulaire de l'abbaye de la Chapelle-aux-Planches,* ed. C. Lalore, Collection des principaux cartulaires du diocèse de Troyes 4 (Paris, 1878), pp. 199-201, no. 75 (Bishop Hato of Troyes for Montiérender). Examples of provision for burial and/or commemoration made by relations after a crusader's death are found in *St.-Père de Chartres,* pp. 411-412, no. 2.2.14 (1102/22); Round, *Calendar,* p. 169, no. 476 (1105 for Troarn); *Gallia christiana,* 10 instr. 424E-425A (1118 for St. Arnulf at Crépy), *Urkunden- und Quellenbuch zur Geschichte der altluxemburgischen Territorien bis zur burgundischen Zeit,* 1 (Luxemburg, 1935), 512, no. 358 (1123 for the abbey of Our Lady at Luxemburg). Pfeiffer, "Cistercienser," pp. 79-80, gives some examples of prayers by Cistercians and of gifts given by crusaders to Cistercian abbeys probably in return for spiritual benefits. Sometimes, as in *Noyers,* p. 581, no. 553 (ca. 1146), spiritual benefits were combined with a cash grant *in caritate.*

88 C.-L. Hugo, *Sacri et canonici ordinis Praemonstratensis annales,* 1.1 (Nancy, 1734), cxliv.

89 "Documents concernant Sautour et Aublain, extraits du cartulaire de l'abbaye de Floreffe," *Analectes pour servir à l'histoire ecclésiastique de la Belgique,* 8 (1871), 365-366, no. 1, and "Obituaire de l'abbaye de Brogne ou de Saint-Gérard, de l'ordre de Saint-Benoît," ed. J. Barbier, *ibid.,* 18 (1882), 367-368, no. 7. See L. Genicot, "L'évolution des dons aux abbayes dans le comté de Namur du Xe au XIVe siècle," *XXXe Congrès de la Fédération archéologique et historique de la Belgique: Annales* (Brussels, 1936), p. 146, and *L'économie rurale Namuroise au Bas Moyen Age (1199-1429)*: 1: *La seigneurie foncière,* Université de Louvain: Recueil de travaux de l'histoire et de philologie 3.17 (Louvain, 1943), 146.

Many grants were the result of vows made at times of danger and sickness in the course of a crusade and of the testamentary dispositions of crusaders who died or were killed en route.[90] When Adjutor of Vernon (who later became a monk and saint) was ambushed near Antioch, he made a vow as a result of which, after his escape, he gave some property to Tiron;[91] and the archbishop of Besançon forced Bartholomew of Cicon to fulfill a vow, made when he fell ill at Jerusalem in 1148, to restore a mill and seven serfs to Mouthier-Haute-Pierre.[92] Shipwreck was another frequent occasion for vows. Count William of Nevers made some substantial concessions to Vézelay as a result of a vow made when he was shipwrecked on the Second Crusade,[93] and Count Waleran of Meulan founded La Valasse, probably in 1150, after being saved from shipwreck on his return from the crusade.[94]

Other new houses, such as Lironville in the diocese of Toul,[95] were founded by departing crusaders for the good of their souls or as substitutes for crusades. Among the most remarkable of these was St. Orens in the diocese of Toulouse, which was founded in 1098 by the would-be female crusader Emerias of *Alteias,* "who raised the cross on her right shoulder in order to go to Jerusalem" but was persuaded by the bishop to build a house of God instead.[96] The Cistercian abbey of Meaux was established by William of Albemarle "in

---

90 *Cartularium abbathiae de Whiteby,* ed. J.C. Atkinson, Surtees Society 69 (Durham, 1879), pp. 2-3; *Vigeois,* p. 68, no. 113 (1102/3); *Aureil,* p. 105, no. 153 (ca. 1115).

91 Hugh of Amiens, *Vita sancti Adjutoris monachi Tironensis,* in PL 192: 1347A. On Adjutor, who died in 1130/2, see A.M. Zimmermann, *Kalendarium benedictinum. Die Heiligen und Seligen des Benediktinerordens und seiner Zweige,* 2 (Metten, 1934), 79 and 81.

92 Castan, *Episode,* pp. 10-11. The archbishop heard the testimony of four witnesses (including a Knight Templar) who had been with Bartholomew when he made the vow and who later returned to France.

93 Hugh of Poitiers, *Historia Vizeliacensis* 2, in PL 194:1598D-1599A, and, better, *Monumenta Vizeliacensia,* ed. R.B.C. Huygens, CC cont. med. 42 (Turnhout, 1976), pp. 423-424.

94 Geoffrey H. White, "The Career of Waleran, count of Meulan and earl of Worcester (1104-66)," *Transactions of the Royal Historical Society* 4.17 (1934), 40-41. For another example of a church founded as a result of a vow during a shipwreck, see Fyot, *St Estienne de Dijon,* preuves pp. 154-155, no. 246 (1172), also in Petit, *Ducs de Bourgogne,* 2.352, no. 532.

95 *Gallia christiana,* 13 instr. 479-480. See Jacques Choux, *Recherches sur le diocèse de Toul au temps de la Réforme grégorienne. L'épiscopat de Pibon (1069-1107)* (Nancy, 1952), pp. 68 and 232.

96 C. De Vic and J. Vaissete, *Histoire générale de Languedoc,* 2 (Paris, 1733), 349, no. 323, and 2nd ed., 5 (Toulouse, 1875), 756-758, no. 401. See Elisabeth Magnou-Nortier, *La société laïque et l'église dans la province ecclésiastique de Narbonne de la fin du VIIIᵉ à la fin du XIᵉ siècle,* Publications de l'Université de Toulouse-Le Mirail A 20 (Toulouse [1974]), pp. 562-563.

redemption of his vow" to go on a crusade, which he was unable to fulfill "on account of his age and weight."[97]

The willingness of so many crusaders to make material grants in return for spiritual benefits is a reminder of the religious and penitential character of these expeditions and of the hopes of the participants for otherworldly rewards. When Robert II of Flanders went to Jerusalem in 1096, "at the instigation of the divine admonition, promulgated by the authority of the apostolic see, to free the church of God that has long been oppressed by barbaric peoples," he gave some land to St. Peter at Lille "in order that God Almighty may give effect to my effort, by which both the sanctified honor of His name may be spread and the gracious gift of the coin that never fails [i.e. salvation] may be given to me."[98] At about the same time in the Auvergne a father and son, who may have heard Urban II preach at Clermont, made a grant to Sauxillanges "in remission of their sins" and in return for a mule worth 200 s. and for burial and intercession for the father after his death, saying in their charter that, "When the persecution of the barbarians rose up to destroy the liberty of the eastern church, the entire strength and faith of the western peoples hastened to assist the destroyed religion at the exhortation of the pope."[99]

Individual crusades to Jerusalem were made throughout the twelfth century by pilgrims who made grants to monasteries in return for funds to pay their expenses and prayers to insure their eternal reward. When Geoffrey of Bero wanted to go to Jerusalem in about 1115, he confirmed a grant made by his father to St. Père at Chartres "fearing lest the sanctity of this undertaking be spoiled by the taint of some fraud."[100] A crusader sold some property to La Platière in 1139 "lest his labor be worthless and empty."[101] And William of

---

97 William Dugdale, *Monasticon anglicanum,* ed. John Caley, Henry Ellis, and Bulkeley Bandinel (London, 1846), 5:390. See David Knowles and R.N. Hadcock, *Medieval Religious Houses: England and Wales,* 2nd ed. (London, 1971), p. 122. William was advised to found a monastery by Abbot Adam of Fountains "when he found the earl nervous on account of the fulfillment of his vow." The archbishop of Rouen allowed Walter of Valmondois, who was unable to go to Jerusalem owing to physical impediments, to redeem his vow by giving a benefice to Pontoise: *Cartulaire de l'abbaye de Saint-Martin de Pontoise,* ed. J. Depoin, Publications de la Société historique du Vexin (Pontoise, 1895-1904), pp. 120-121, no. 155 (1165/9). See also the charters from Molesme cited nn. 108-109 below.

98 Fernand Vercauteren, *Actes des comtes de Flandre, 1071-1128,* Commission royale d'histoire: Recueil des actes des princes belges (Brussels, 1938), p. 63, no. 20.

99 *Sauxillanges,* pp. 966-967, no. 697. It is uncertain whether they joined the crusade, but the terms of the charter, especially the grant of a mule, suggests that they did.

100 *St.-Père de Chartres,* pp. 603-604, no. 2.4.114.

101 *Cartulaire lyonnais,* ed. M.-C. Guigue, 1 (Lyons, 1885), 35-36, no. 24.

Fossard gave some land to Watton in 1154/60 "above all for the journey that I am going to make to Jerusalem and for the remission of my sins and those of my relations both living and dead." [102] These charters show the element of personal spiritual motivation underlying the entire crusading movement, which included not only the great expeditions like that in 1148, when (according to a charter recording the purchase of an estate by Werden) "the *universitas christianorum* made the expedition to Jerusalem marvellous by its greater beginning than by its conclusion," [103] but also innumerable pilgrimages by individuals whose material sacrifices may collectively have been even greater than those made by members of the numbered crusades.

III

Although the arrangements made by crusaders to finance their expeditions had many common features, which have already been discussed, and were described in the sources in similar terms, each in fact dealt with a specific situation and reflected different needs and circumstances. It may therefore be of interest, by way of conclusion, to look at some individual examples, most of which are more elaborate than many such transactions but which illustrate their general characteristics.

Two, from the cartulary of Cluny, are dated 12 April 1096 and 15 June 1100 respectively. The first records a loan of 2000 s. of Lyons and four mules to Achard of Montmerle, who wished to join "in the multitudinous and mighty arousal and expedition of Christians going to Jerusalem in order to wage war for God against the pagans and Sarracens." The loan was secured by a pledge that could be redeemed only by Achard himself and would belong to Cluny either if he died on the crusade or if he did not return or if he returned and died without heirs. [104] The charter of 1100 first recorded a grant made by the crusader Stephen of Neublens, after settling his dispute with the dean of Lourdon, and by his brother and nephew and the compensation given to each and then described a further gift by Stephen, made for the sake of the monks and abbot

---

102 *Early Yorkshire Charters,* ed. William Farrer, 2 (Edinburgh, 1915), 396, no. 1095. See also Robert Wyard, *Histoire de l'abbaye Saint-Vincent de Laon* (St.-Quentin, 1858), pp. 196-197, where Anselm of Ribemont asked pardon of the monks of St. Vincent before he left with Godfrey of Bouillon in 1095.

103 *Urkundenbuch für die Geschichte des Niederrheins,* ed. T.J. Lacomblet, 1 (Düsseldorf, 1840), 249, no. 364. On the reaction to the failure of the Second Crusade, to which this charter refers, see Constable, "Second Crusade," pp. 266-276.

104 *Cluny,* 5:51-53, no. 3703. The specific reference to Achard's desire to join the expedition *armatus* suggests that he might have gone unarmed, simply as a pilgrim.

who, he said, "when I opened my heart to him concerning this journey and made this gift into his hand," had himself put "the sign of salvation, that is, the cross," on Stephen's shoulder and a ring on his finger, granted him confraternity, and promised him liturgical commemoration if he died on the crusade. "Although I did this especially for my soul," Stephen said, he also received 50 s. and "two excellent mules" from the dean of Lourdon.[105]

These two charters, in addition to showing the personal interest taken by Abbot Hugh of Cluny in the crusade, show an interesting contrast in motivation, since the second one, unlike the first, includes no reference to fighting aside from Stephen's half-apologetic references to himself as *quamvis miles* and as "involved in the temporal army in the secular habit." The long arenga of this charter is filled with biblical citations and moral commonplaces and with expressions of a sense of guilt that must be expiated by sacrifice and charity. "In view of the multitude of my sins," Stephen said, "and of the piety, gentleness, and mercy of Our Lord Jesus Christ, Who though rich became poor for our sake, I decided to give back to Him something for all those things that He gave to unworthy me. I therefore resolved to go to Jerusalem, where God the man was seen and kept company with men and to adore in the place where His feet stood."[106]

No such lofty sentiments are found in two groups of charters, one from La Trinité at Vendôme and the other from Molesme, showing some of the difficulties encountered by crusaders in raising funds and, incidentally, by monasteries in acquiring property. A grant made to La Trinité by Robert of Moncoutour when he became a monk in 1081 was opposed by his son Bertrand, who had not given his consent, until 1098, when he decided to go to Jerusalem and realized "that this journey to God would be worthless to him unless he dismissed his claim to the gift of his father." The details of the settlement are recorded in another charter, showing that in return for renouncing his claim he received 1800 s., his wife 100 s., his son Peter four pounds, his other three sons (one of whom was still a baby) 12 d. each, and the lord "of whose fief this obedience was" 20 s.[107]

---

105 *Cluny,* 5:87-91, no. 3737.

106 *Ibid.,* p. 88. The final words "ac in loco ubi steterunt pedes ejus adorare" are from Psalm 131.7 and resemble those used by Peter the Venerable in a letter to the patriarch of Jerusalem, saying that as a monk "nec adorare in loco ubi steterunt pedes domini possumus": *Letters of Peter the Venerable,* 1:220, no. 83. The sentiment, though a crusading commonplace, brings out the personal identification of the pilgrim with Christ.

107 *La Trinité de Vendôme,* 2:104-107, nos. 360-361, where it says that, "Tandem ipse Bertrannus, divina inspiratione compunctus, cum Jerosolimam ire disposuisset, et illam viam Dei sibi nihil posse prodesse certissime crederet si calumpniam, quam de elemosina patris sui faciebat, non dimitteret." Although the money may not have been used for Bertrand's trip to Jerusalem, his intention to go is clear.

An even more complicated arrangement is described in a series of charters for Molesme describing the gifts made by three crusading brothers of the family of Toucy: Iterius, who died on the First Crusade, Hugh, who died going to Jerusalem about 1100, and Norgaud, who died, also on the way to Jerusalem, about 1110.[108] The three brothers participated, between 1095 and 1100, in founding the priory of Crisenon, to which a final grant was renewed in about 1100 by Hugh and Norgaud, "when they both aimed at Jerusalem," in return respectively for a mule "of great price" and 30 s. They returned without reaching Jerusalem, however, and Hugh, worried at his failure to fulfill his vow, set out once more, after again renewing his gift, on an expedition from which he apparently never returned. Norgaud also decided to make another attempt, in 1101/7, when he mortgaged some property to Molesme for twenty silver marks and a mule worth 300 s. or seven marks. Meanwhile a lawsuit arose over an allod which the three brothers had given jointly to Molesme and of which Iterius had given his share, "when he was dying on his Jerusalem journey" and either forgetting or disregarding his previous grant, to Vézelay and La Charité. At least two papal legates were involved in the case, and Molesme had to grant compensation to both the other monasteries before finally establishing its claim to the entire allod in 1107/10.[109]

A different problem arose for the monks of Göttweig as a result of a loan to a noble named Wolfker, who "decided to go to Jerusalem, wishing to fulfill the evangelical precept 'If any man will come after Me' but since he was not well supplied with money" borrowed twenty marks from the monks in return for a pledge of some land which he could redeem for the same sum in the fifth year, if he returned, but which would belong to the abbey after five years or "if he remained on the journey, alive or dead." Wolfker apparently broke the agreement, however, and sold the land to another noble, whom the monks allowed to hold the property until his death "and then, by God's mercy, ... may it be restored to us."[110]

---

108 *Molesme,* 1:138-139 and 2:63, n.

109 *Ibid.,* 2:64, 84, and 105, nos. 54, 78, and 101. See *Gallia christiana,* 12 instr. 107-108, no. 12 (1110) and *Papsturkunden in Frankreich,* NF 6: *Orléanais,* ed. Johannes Ramackers, Abhandlungen der Akademie der Wissenschaften in Göttingen, Phil.-Hist. Kl. 3.41 (Göttingen, 1958), p. 115, no. 56 (1145), for a crusading grant to Fleury by another member of the family of Toucy.

110 *Die Traditionsbücher des Benediktinerstiftes Göttweig,* ed. Adalbert Fuchs, Fontes rerum Austriacarum 2.69 (Vienna, 1931), pp. 194-195, no. 55. The two parallel versions of this charter are substantially similar for the passages cited here. I am uncertain whether the words *quinto anno* mean "in the fifth year" or, more generally, "within five years."

Monasteries had to be perpetually on guard against acts of bad faith.[111] Gardrad of La Faie, for instance, according to a charter of 1111/7, gave his part of the mills at Alville to the abbey of Baigne but "a long time afterwards, when he wished to visit Jerusalem," he pledged this and some other property to the prior of Vitaterne, a dependency of St. Martial at Limoges. All turned out well this time, however, for Gardrad, when he was dying on his pilgrimage, remembered and confirmed his original grant, and Baigne was able to establish its claim in the court of the count of Angoulême.[112]

A deathbed gift to Sauxillanges was made by a crusader named Stephen, according to a charter of his cousin Bernard of *Rippa* in 1123. Stephen, "travelling to Jerusalem," left his entire property to Bernard, with a mansus for Sauxillanges in order to establish a general repast for the monks on the feast of St. Andrew. To this Bernard added on his own accord a pittance after Stephen's death. The monks in return offered prayers for Stephen's soul and received Bernard into association and confraternity, granting him a prebend at the priory of Taluyers "and in all houses belonging to Sauxillanges." Bernard further gave himself to God and the monks, according to the charter, in such a way that he could become a monk there and might neither enter another monastery nor journey to Jerusalem without their permission.[113] In return for the mansus and pittance, therefore, the abbey took on not only some liturgical obligations but also an anomalous member of the community.

Maurice of Glons seems to have made a similar arrangement in 1146, when he was "armed with the sign of the cross and ready to go to Jerusalem" and resigned the fief he held from the abbey of St. James at Liège on condition that half the revenues would belong to his mother during her lifetime and that it could be redeemed for 40 s. either while she was living or after her death. "He asked that the money we were going to give him *pro karitate* for the expenses of his pilgrimage should be given to his mother and children if he died in the meantime. It should also be known that if he returns from Jerusalem... he will settle in a dependency (*in obedientiam*) ready to serve either in the habit of a

---

111 Or what appear to be acts of bad faith in the surviving records, almost all of which derive from monastic sources.

112 *Cartulaire de l'abbaye de Saint-Etienne de Baigne,* ed. Abbé Cholet (Niort, 1868), pp. 23-24, no. 26.

113 *Sauxillanges,* pp. 1072-1073, no. 905. The precise nature of this arrangement is unclear, but Bernard appears to have become a quasi-monk. His right to a prebend in any priory and the restrictions on his liberty are unusual.

servant (*famulus*) or in the habit of a monk." [114] Here as with Bernard of *Rippa* the exact monastic status of the donor is uncertain, but the arrangement probably should be seen both as an act of piety and as a means of support for someone who had given his property to a monastery.

A final example of the difficulties of financing a crusade is found in a complicated (and in places obscure) charter from Auch describing a series of events between 1150 and 1180, beginning with a pledge of some property by Raymond-Aimeric of Montesquiou to the canons of Auch in return for 70 s. with which to pay a ransom. Raymond-Aimeric later brought a claim against the canons for some damage done to a church in the course of a dispute between his uncle the archbishop of Auch and the count of Armagnac. The canons agreed to restore the church, "but when Raymond-Aimeric decided to go to Jerusalem and asked his uncle the archbishop for the necessary expenses to do this," they demanded that he renounce his claims against them on behalf both of himself and of his heirs. He finally did so, but apparently only at the last minute, "when he had already started on his way to Jerusalem," and he presumably then received the necessary funds. [115]

These examples show that the financing of the crusaders affected almost every aspect of life in the twelfth century. They illustrate the broad appeal of the crusading movement and the sacrifices made by men and women of all classes in order to visit Jerusalem and to assist the Christians in the East. Above all, they show the importance of monasteries as institutions of credit and the importance of the crusades in contributing to the break-up of the old social and economic order by promoting the exchange of property, the transfer of treasure into liquid assets, the increase of circulation, and, through royal levies and feudal aids, the development of centralized financial administration. In the long run, indeed, how the crusaders got to the East may have had a more profound influence on the West than what they brought back with them when they returned.

---

114 Jacques Stiennon, *Etude sur le chartrier et le domaine de l'abbaye de Saint-Jacques de Liège (1015-1209),* Bibliothèque de la Faculté de philosophie et lettres de l'Université de Liège 124 (Paris, 1951), pp. 442-443, no. 6; see pp. 386-387. *In obedientiam* may mean simply "in obedience," that is, under the rule of the abbey. It is uncertain from the text whether the redemption was during or after Maurice's or his mother's lifetime.

115 *Gallia christiana,* 1 instr. 162-163, and *Cartulaires du chapitre de l'église métropolitaine Sainte-Marie d'Auch,* ed. C. Lacave La Plagne Barris, Archives historiques de la Gascogne 2.3 (Paris, 1899), pp. 128-132, no. 113.

HOSPITALS AND HOSPITAL CONGREGATIONS IN THE LATIN KINGDOM DURING THE FIRST PERIOD OF THE FRANKISH CONQUEST

JEAN RICHARD
University of Dijon

The Order of the Hospitallers of St. John of Jerusalem, with its exceptionally brilliant destiny and originality of development, has particularly attracted the attention of historians. Perhaps for this reason the Hospitallers have pushed into the background other establishments which, in the states founded by the crusaders, also undertook to carry out the same functions that had been in the beginning the only end and objective of the Hospital of St. John: the sheltering and upkeep of pilgrims, the care of the sick.

It may be useful to recall what constituted the originality of the Hospital of Jerusalem: about half a century before the crusader conquest of the Holy City, it was founded through the good offices of the same Amalfitan merchants who also established other hospitals, though of briefer duration, in other towns of the Orient. The patronage of the establishment seems to have been devolved by them to the only Latin congregation existing in Jerusalem before the crusades, St. Maria Latina, and not to the Holy Sepulchre, at which clergy of the Greek rite were then officiating. Following the First Crusade, the Hospital appears to have been separated from St. Maria Latina, but not placed under the jurisdiction of the Holy Sepulchre. This autonomy, which is not without equivalent in the history of hospitals in the West, was transformed into complete independence when the Master of the Hospital obtained from the papacy exemption from obedience to the patriarch. William of Tyre describes the effect of this independence, provocatively asserted, on the canons and the episcopal hierarchy of the Kingdom of Jerusalem, arousing their ire and bitterness.[1]

---

1   On all this cf. J. Riley-Smith, *The Knights of St. John in Jerusalem and in Cyprus, c. 1050-1310*

The foundation of the Hospital, like that of the others established by the Amalfitans in the eleventh century, forms part of the great movement that made the eleventh and twelfth centuries in Western Europe the epoch of the origin and proliferation of hospitals and infirmaries dedicated to the sheltering of the poor and of travellers, and the care of the sick.[2] A tradition going back to the early Middle Ages enjoined bishops to watch over the exercise of charity in their dioceses, and numerous hospitals had been founded by these prelates for the poor, travellers, lepers; the Aix-la-Chapelle rule had extended to the canonical chapters the obligation of providing shelter for the poor and for pilgrims in an annex to their cathedrals. At the same time, more and more frequently, laymen and ecclesiastics founded infirmaries along the routes taken by pilgrims, who represented simultaneously the categories of the poor and of travellers, who had the strongest claims to be the privileged beneficiaries of charitable endeavours.

The Westerners following the crusade to the East carried with them to their new habitations the pious customs of their regions of origin, and we witness the foundation of veritable hospitals, independent of any monastery or chapter, in the northern crusader states. Thus, in the county of Tripoli, where Raymond of Saint-Gilles and the first bishops of Tripoli constituted a fine endowment for the "poor of Jerusalem" represented by the Hospital,[3] we also encounter a *hospitale pauperum quod est in Monte Peregrino,* founded by the same Raymond of Saint-Gilles and more richly established by his successor Bertrand. Further to the north, in the proximity of another episcopal see, that of Rafaniyah, the same counts set up an endowment *ad hospitale pauperum construendum, sicut in carta scriptum est et legitur,* whose rector was a certain *Gualterius.* These are clearly two establishments, founded and endowed by the counts in the diocesan centres of their domains, for the benefit of the local poor and passing pilgrims. The bishop of the diocese probably had the privilege of presiding at the investiture of the rector presented to him by the count, patron of the hospital. At all events, it was Count Pons who, on 28 December 1126, put an end to the

---

(London, 1967), p. 32 ff., and also R. Hiestand, "Die Anfänge der Johanniter," *Ritterorden,* pp. 31-80. The latter draws attention to the fact that the Amalfitan hospital was not the only foundation of its kind in the 11th century.

2   See especially J. Imbert, *Les hôpitaux en droit canonique,* L'église et l'état au Moyen-Age 8 (Paris, 1947).

3   The church of St. John the Baptist near Mont-Pèlerin, the estates, revenues, tithes and parochial rights of the entire property of Nefin: Delaville, *Cartulaire,* no. 48, p. 40 and no. 72, pp. 69-70. Some material on hospitals in the Holy Land other than that of St. John has been assembled by M.L. Favreau, *Studien zur Frühgeschichte des Deutschen Ordens,* Kieler Historische Studien 21 (Stuttgart, 1974), p. 25 f.

independence of these two hospitals by transferring them to the proprietorship of the Knights Hospitallers of St. John of Jerusalem.[4]

An institution of the same kind existed in the county of Edessa; we know of a hospital at Turbessel which was annexed to a church called Saint-Romain, apparently endowed by Joscelin I of Courtenay and by King Baldwin II (when Baldwin was acting as regent of the county or when he was himself its titular incumbent, before 1118?). Joscelin II ceded it to the Hospitallers in 1134 with the agreement of the diocesan bishop, who was the archbishop of Doliché (*Tulupensis*).[5]

A different hospital system existed in the Kingdom of Jerusalem, not unlike that found in the West until the Carolingian period, and which co-existed with the newly created hospitals and infirmaries. The predominant form seems to have been the association of the hospital with the monastery or chapter officiating at the places frequented by pilgrims.

This situation is usually encountered in the institutions of the eastern churches prior to the crusades. Let us take as an example the monastery of St. Catherine at Mount Sinai, belonging to Greek monks. It was visited by great numbers of Latin pilgrims and benefited from Latin donations; it possessed in Jerusalem, according to a papal bull, a *hospitale et obedientiam Sancti Moysi, domos et furnum.*[6] The same consistent association of priory and hospital is encountered in the bull granted by Honorius III to the great monastery of St. Theodosius (Deir Dōsī, founded by the "cenobiarch of Berrie," that is, of the Judaean desert, in the Valley of Kidron, between Jerusalem and the Dead Sea).[7] At Jerusalem, this abbey possessed *ecclesiam Sancti Theodosii cum hospitali et apothecis et furno et vineis*; at Jaffa, apart from the church of St. Jonah (it was from Jaffa that the prophet embarked), *apothecas et hospitale*; at Ascalon, *terras et vineam cum hospitali*; at Gibelet (*Zevel*), an *obedientia cum apothecis et hospitale*; at Nicosia in Cyprus *ecclesiam Sancti Nicolaï cum hospitali*; at Constantinople, *ecclesiam Sancti Juliani cum hospitali*. We may suppose that other important communities, especially those of St. Sabas[8] and the Holy Cross, also had their satellite system of priories and hospitals.

---

4   Delaville, *Cartulaire*, no. 79, pp. 74-75.

5   Ibid., no. 104, pp. 89-90.

6   G. Hofmann, "Sinai und Rom," *Orientalia Christiana* 9 (1927), 262 (no. 19).

7   A.L. Tautu, ed., *Acta Honorii III et Gregorii IX*, Pontificia commissio ad redigendum codicem juris canonici orientalis, Fontes 3.3 (Città del Vaticano, 1950), p. 2. The editor has attempted to identify *Berria* as the name of the town of Verria, in Thrace; the name is in fact a Latin transcription of the French "la Berrie," which signifies the desert.

8   Cf. A. Ehrhard, "Das griechische Kloster Mar-Saba in Palästina," *Römische Quartalschrift* 7 (1893), 32-79 and Mayer, *Bistümer*, pp. 406-409. The possessions of this monastery during the period of Frankish rule are only partly known.

The Latin clerics' occupation of the Holy Sepulchre and the creation of a college of canons, later transformed into a regular chapter, put an end to the state of things that had existed at Jerusalem before the crusade;[9] and we have seen that, for Latin pilgrims, a hospital had been founded in the vicinity of the Sepulchre, which obtained its own statute after 1099. Besides, the exceptional importance of the pilgrimage to Jerusalem justified the separation of the various bodies entrusted with assuring different services. When a king of Aragon who was particularly devoted to the sanctuary of the Resurrection decided in 1131 to bequeath it his kingdom, he made an undivided donation, inviting the institutions concerned to share the revenues equally among themselves. These were the canons of the Holy Sepulchre, who performed the liturgical rites, the Hospitallers of St. John, who sheltered and tended the pilgrims and the poor, and the Knights Templars, who were responsible for the safety of the pilgrimage routes.[10]

From this it would seem that the canons of the Holy Sepulchre were entirely relieved of the obligation to provide hospitals in the Kingdom of Jerusalem. However, a recent study[11] has shown that they were still responsible for a certain number of hospitals which did not in any way cease to carry out their charitable functions, whether in Catalonia, Leon, Italy, Bohemia or Poland, and that the appellation of the Holy Sepulchre was more than once adopted for hospital establishments. We know too that laymen were associated by ties of confraternity with the canons of Jerusalem, and that among these "brothers" and "sisters" there were some who organized themselves in communities living according to a rule, although one cannot affirm that they specifically undertook to perform charitable works.[12]

The situation regarding the two other sanctuaries that attracted the veneration of the faithful visiting the Holy Land almost to the same degree as Christ's

9   Mayer, *Bistümer,* pp. 1-9.

10   We have shown that King Alfonso I's testament was not an isolated instance, and that other Spanish lords made donations that similarly associated the three establishments: J. Richard, "Quelques textes sur les premiers temps de l'église latine de Jérusalem," *Recueil de travaux offerts à M. Clovis Brunel,* 2 (Paris, 1955), 429-430 (reprinted in my *Orient et Occident au Moyen Age. Contacts et relations* [London, 1976], VII). Cf. E. Lourie, "The Will of Alfonso I El Ballador, King of Aragon and Navarre: a Reassessment," *Speculum* 50 (1975), 635-651.

11   G. Bresc-Bautier, "Dévotion au Saint-Sépulcre et histoire hospitalière (Xᵉ-XIVᵉ siècles)," *Actes du 97ᵉ congrès national des sociétés savantes. Philologie et histoire* (Nantes, 1972), pp. 256-272.

12   K. Elm, "Fratres et sorores Sanctissimi Sepulcri. Beiträge zu fraternitas, familia und weiblichem Religiosentum in Umkreis des Kapitels v. Heiligen Grabe," *Frühmittelalterliche Studien* 9 (1975), 287-333; id., "Kanoniker und Ritter vom Heiligen Grab. Ein Beitrag zur Entstehung und Frühgeschichte der palästinensischen Ritterorden," *Ritterorden,* pp. 141-169.

tomb—the basilica of the Nativity at Bethlehem and that of the Annunciation at Nazareth—was rather different. We have already referred to the fact that one of the Spanish testaments of the first half of the twelfth century linked the Church of the Nativity at Bethlehem with the Sepulchre, the Templars and the Hospitallers.[13]

We know the circumstances under which the church of Bethlehem had been elevated to the status of a cathedral by the Latins.[14] Very soon, however, the crusader princes caused Our Lady of Bethlehem to benefit from generous endowments.[15] The Westerners did not remain far behind; although the greater part of the church archives has disappeared, we can still form a notion, thanks to papal bulls, of the importance of the domain beyond the sea, which was to enable the bishop and his chapter to prolong the existence of their establishment for centuries after the fall of the Frankish colonies; on the one hand at Clamecy, where Count Guillaume IV of Nevers, who died in 1168 in the Holy Land and was buried at Bethlehem, had given them the elements of an establishment, and also at Varazze in Liguria, where the church of St. Ambrose was ceded to them in 1139.[16]

In this domain hospitals occupied a particularly important position. We may remark that when the bishop of Bethlehem appointed his delegate to visit the dependencies of his church in the West, he designated them by the words *ecclesias, hospitalia et pia loca.*[17] At Clamecy, the count of Nevers, in association with the knights and burgesses of the place, had founded an infirmary in 1147; it was this infirmary, with the chapel and "bourg" that accompanied it, which constituted the donation made in 1168 by Count Guillaume. The institution was complemented by another infirmary, that of Cercy-la-Tour; these houses were administered by hospitallers whom an act of 1124 calls *provisores et fratres dictorum locorum,* while the bishop of Autun, in 1211, addressed

13 Article cited in note 10 above.

14 Mayer, *Bistümer,* pp. 44-80. According to this author the bishopric was created in 1107-08; concomitantly, the rights over Bethlehem which the canons of the Holy Sepulchre had claimed until that date were cancelled.

15 For example, the counts of Tripoli: J. Richard, "Le chartrier de Sainte-Marie-Latine et l'établissement de Raymond de Saint Gilles à Mont Pèlerin," *Mélanges d'histoire du Moyen Age dédiés à la mémoire de Louis Halphen* (Paris, 1961), p. 609 (reprinted in *Orient et Occident,* VI).

16 Cf. P. Riant, *Etudes sur l'église de Bethléem,* 2 vols. (The first volume appeared in Genoa in 1889; the second was published by Ch. Kohler in *ROL* 1 [1893] and 2 [1894].) The count's burial is confirmed in *Recueil des chartes de l'abbaye de Cluny,* ed. A. Bernard and A. Bruel, 6 vols. (Paris, 1876-1903), 5, no. 4239.

17 Riant, *Etudes* 1:158-159.

himself to the *fratres de Bethleem* who live *in burgo de Bethleem apud Clameciacum.*[18]

These "Bethlehem brothers" are also mentioned in English texts of the mid-thirteenth century. When in 1247 Simon FitzMary, sheriff of London, founded the house of Bedlam, he made the provision that a prior and canons should live at this priory, as well as *fratres ac etiam sorores* who were to observe *regulam et ordinem dicte ecclesie Bethleem.*[19] Matthew Paris relates the foundation of the house of the *fratres Bethleemiti* at Cambridge, describing their garb as "resembling that of the Preachers, but their cope is marked over the breast with a red star with five points, in the centre of which is a circle of sky-blue, because of the star which appeared at Bethlehem at the birth of the Lord."[20]

The bulls issued by Gregory IX in 1227 and Clement IV in 1266, confirming the possessions of the church of Bethlehem, enumerate the numerous hospitals which belonged to it in France as well as in Italy.[21] These hospitals were not simply a source of revenue for the sanctuary of the Nativity, through the obligation undoubtedly imposed on them to pay a quit-rent for the maintenance of the church at Bethlehem and its clergy; they also constituted a veritable chain of establishments executing charitable works. The "Brothers of the Star" formed a congregation which, beside the canons who recited the canonical offices, also gathered brothers and sisters to tend the sick. The mention of a rule observed by them suggests that the congregation of Bethlehem was one of the important hospitaller orders which in the Middle Ages created a number of hospitals, and, especially, brought together many older infirmaries formerly administered by groups of brothers or sisters who experienced the need to follow a way of life based on the model offered them by these congregations.[22]

It seems that the manner in which the hospitaller vocation was expressed by the Brothers of the Star in their original house in the Holy Land attracted some

18   L. Chevalier-Lagenissière, *Histoire de l'évêché de Bethléem* (Paris, 1880), especially pp. 67, 74, 76.

19   Ibid., pp. 86-89; Riant, *Etudes* 1:95-100.

20   *Chronica Majora,* ed. H.R. Luard, RS 57 (London, 1880), 5:631.

21   Riant, *Etudes* 1:142, 143, 149. On the Scottish house of St. Germanus, in the diocese of St. Andrew, cf. E.R. Lindsay and A.I. Cameron, *Calendar of Scottish Supplications, 1418-1422,* Publications of the Scottish History Society 3.23 (Edinburgh, 1934), 1:83-85. As far as the famous convent of the Hieronymites at Belem, near Lisbon, is concerned, it is known that in 1496 it succeeded an "ermitage" called Our Lady of Bethlehem, but we have not found any proof that this establishment was connected with the Bethlehem congregation.

22   This need explains to some extent the expansion of the Order of St. John: cf. J. Richard, "Les Templiers et les Hospitaliers en Bourgogne et en Champagne méridionale, XII⁰ et XIII⁰ siècles," *Ritterorden,* pp. 231-242. On this phenomenon cf. P. Brune, *Histoire de l'ordre hospitalier du Saint-Esprit* (Lons-le-Saunier, 1892).

attention. As at Jerusalem, crowds of pilgrims came to Bethlehem, and it was necessary to come to their aid when they found themselves stranded, and to tend them when they were sick. The chapter of the Church of the Nativity did not dissociate itself from the duty of rendering assistance; it took into association, by giving them a rule, men and women hospitallers who served the poor and sick, and who were probably offered the privileges of a *fraternitas* so that they might enjoy the spiritual advantages of the liturgical service. We have no early texts concerning this exercise of hospitaller activity at Bethlehem; it is only in a letter of 3 February 1245 recommending those collecting for this church to the generosity of the faithful that Pope Innocent IV alludes to the heavy expenses it incurs in receiving *pauperes advenae et peregrini*.[23] But the concession of the infirmaries at Bethlehem during the thirteenth century suggests the organization of a hospital by the canons and the bishop of the place at an earlier period.

Establishments depending on Bethlehem proliferated in the Kingdom of Jerusalem as well. We do not know if the priories that the church of the Nativity possessed in the county of Tripoli, at Gibelet and at Mont-Pèlerin, were accompanied by a hospital, like those of Saint Theodosius "de la Berrie"; it is possible that the magnitude of the hospital network depending on St. John of Jerusalem seemed to make the creation of other hospitals in these localities unnecessary. But the bulls of 1227 and 1266 mention Bethlehem's possession of a hospital at Caesarea (one of the bulls designates it by the words *in archiepiscopatu Cesariensi hospitale cum oratoris*; the other, by the phrase *in urbe Cesareae Palestinae domum*).

It seems to us that it is possible to assume the existence of yet another congregation, which always remained more modest, and of which we know considerably less. It apparently arose in similar circumstances, near another sanctuary particularly dear to pilgrims: that of Nazareth. The Church of the Annunciation had also been elevated to the rank of cathedral by the Latins, who made it an archiepiscopal see.[24] The possessions of the archbishop and his chapter are very inadequately known. Well endowed in Galilee, where the archbishop governed an episcopal seigniory which was obliged to send a contingent of knights to the royal army,[25] they also possessed dependencies in the

23 E. Berger, *Les registres d'Innocent IV,* no. 980. In 1300, Boniface VIII authorized the solicitation undertaken by the brothers of the Order of Bethlehem; cf. a bull of 1455 repeating the earlier privileges: *Calendars of Entries in the Papal Registers relating to Great Britain and Ireland,* ed. W.H. Bliss, C. Johnson and J.A. Twemlow, 11 (London, 1921), pp. 7-8.
24 Mayer, *Bistümer,* pp. 89-97.
25 Richard, *Royaume,* p. 101 (English translation by J. Shirley [Amsterdam, 1979], p. 109).

West, including the priory of S. Maria of Barletta, which, according to an act of 1264, was served by canons obeying the rule of St. Augustine.[26] This allows us to class the chapter of Nazareth among those who adopted the communal life; like the Holy Sepulchre, Nazareth was therefore served by regular canons. This domain must have expanded in the course of time: as a result of a campaign waged by the Muslims in Galilee, during which a "grand casal" belonging to the church was sacked, Pope Alexander III addressed an appeal to the Christians of the West inviting them to succour the church of Nazareth (1170).[27]

The documents permitting us to assume the existence of hospitaller activity among the brothers of Nazareth are few in number, and our thanks are due to M. Alain Saint-Denis, assistant at the University of Dijon, for drawing our attention to them. It is in Champagne that references are found to the houses belonging to Nazareth.

The first of these is that of Chambry, "au bas de la colline de Laon," which a tradition recorded by an eighteenth-century savant attributed to certain Flemish monks who, returning there from the Holy Land, founded a hermitage in order to "live there as they had seen certain hermits do in Palestine," adopting the Virgin of Nazareth as their patroness.[28] This tradition seems primarily to prove that at that time only the memory of "la maison des religieux de Nazareth" had been preserved, without further details. In fact, the *fratres Nazarene ecclesie apud Chaumeriacum,* who received an annual income of three hogsheads of grain from the count of Troyes in 1174, and who negotiated in 1213 with the canons and bishop of Laon, depended on the archbishopric of Nazareth. This house had its dependencies in the shape of infirmaries; between 1160 and 1180 the "house of the sick" of Evergnicourt, which had been entrusted to them, was transferred to the larger hospital of Laon; a little later, the infirmary (*domum hospitalem*) of Pierrepont-en-Laonnois was placed under their control (*dominio et potestati fratrum Nazarene ecclesie*) by the local seigneur, *salva pauperum procuratione,* that is, on the condition that this house would continue to ensure the reception and the care of the poor. The rector of this establish-

---

26 J. Guiraud, *Les registres d'Urbain IV,* no. 2477. Another hospital is mentioned in a charter of the vicar of the bishop of Nazareth in the kingdom of Naples (*sic*), but the authenticity of this text (RRH no. 376, 1152/1162) is doubtful. We thank B.Z. Kedar, who drew our attention to this point.

27 RHGF 15:893 (no. 281). Appeals of this kind, evoking a quick flow of donations, are known to have been made on behalf of the Holy Sepulchre at the beginning of the 12th century; see my article cited in note 10 above.

28 Copy of Dom Varoqueaux (Bibl. Nat., collection de Picardie 186, p. 814). Text communicated by M. Saint-Denis.

ment had placed it in the hands of the bishop of Laon, who united it with the hospital of his episcopal seat in 1209. An agreement had to be negotiated, and in 1213 the monks of Nazareth relinquished their rights in return for an annual payment.[29] In the first case, it was a certain *R.,* appointed by the archbishop of Nazareth to rule the house of Chappes, who acted as mediator in the negotiations; in the second, it was a priest called Hugues, *privilegiatus a venerabili Nazareno archiepiscopo, a quo sub testimonio litterarum ipsius plenariam acceperat potestatem ordinandi et disponendi de rebus domorum de Chaumeri et de Capis.*

Yet another text is known, that of a letter written to Archbishop Henri of Reims, by Letard, archbishop of Nazareth (1154-1190) with the object of recommending to him a priest called Guillaume, charged with the responsibility of managing the affairs of the church of Nazareth, and in particular of recovering the house that the latter had owned at Chappes,[30] a house that can be identified with the Nazareth hospital known from a later text to have existed in this locality.[31]

Thus a group of two, then of four, infirmaries administered by the brothers of Nazareth, under the authority of the governor of the house of Chappes, with which that of Chambry was soon united, can be identified in this corner of Champagne. This is not enough in itself to justify the assumption of a congregation of a size and importance equalling that of the brothers of Bethlehem; however, it is sufficient to confirm that here too we have "brothers" with hospitaller duties, dependent on the archbishop of Nazareth while remaining distinct from the canons of his chapter. We think also that these brothers were originally entrusted with the administration of the hospital which must have existed beside the basilica of the Annunciation to shelter pilgrims and succour the poor. Neither Bethlehem nor Nazareth, therefore, handed this burden over to the Hospitallers of Jerusalem; the two churches were each endowed with a hospitaller congregation that radiated even beyond the borders of the Latin Kingdom.

---

29 Archives municipales de Laon, AA2, fol. 29v, 40v-41r. Pierrepont: Aisne, canton Marle; Evergnicourt: Aisne, canton Neufchâtel.

30 RHGF 16:192-193 (no. 156). This undated act should probably be assigned to a year ca. 1160. The priest in question was particularly commissioned to recover a revenue of 10 *livres provinois* deriving from the Coucy toll "et pro quadam domo recuperanda quam in Trecensi episcopatu in villa domini Clarembaldi de Cappes habere debemus." It is difficult to determine which of the seigneurs of Chappes, who transmitted this name to each other, is meant here.

31 A. Roserot, *Dictionnaire historique de la Champagne méridionale (Aube),* 1 (Angers, 1942), 334: a 16th-century inventory records, in the local church, a "Chapelle saint Thomas, aultrement dite l'Hostel-Dieu de Nazaret fondée en l'église du dit Chappes."

Another hospital can be found in the county of Champagne and related with a church serving a shrine in the Holy Land. Count Henry of Troyes, during his pilgrimage in 1179, visited the tomb of the Patriarchs Abraham, Isaac and Jacob in Hebron; he gave the bishop and canons a house in his own city of Troyes. This gift can be connected with the presence of a *domus Dei,* called the St. Abraham hospital (known from 1234 onwards), where a master lived together with some brothers and sisters. Probably their rule was that same *ordo* of the Augustinian canons of Hebron which Count Henry mentions in the charter of 1179, and which was observed by a hospital annexed to the church of Hebron itself, where the tomb of Abraham, "revealed" in 1129, was visited by many pilgrims.[32]

It should not be forgotten that it was again in the Holy Land that another hospitaller order arose, that which received lepers, enabling them to continue participating in the defence of the Latin Kingdom. This was the Order of St. Lazarus, which also migrated to France, where Louis VII gave it the house of Boigny, and to Sicily, where it was established by Frederick II.[33] At all events, this order, in spite of the originality conferred on it by the military vocation which allowed it to admit leper knights, did not achieve considerable expansion; there does not seem to have been an attempt to reorganize the numerous leper houses that existed in Western Europe in the twelfth and thirteenth centuries along the lines of the hospitals and infirmaries which were entrusted to the hospitaller orders.[34]

The Latin East, then, experienced a movement promoting aid to the poor, to pilgrims and to the sick, which compares very well with that known in the West; but the several hospitals founded on the pattern of the Western infir-

---

32   Count Henry's charter appears to call for the foundation of a priory (*canonicis ejusdem ecclesiae in terra mea manentibus domus honesta*), but the count authorizes the *clerici* et *laici* in his land, *tam sani quam infirmi,* to adopt the *ordo* of the Hebron church (H. d'Arbois de Jubainville, "Etudes sur les documents antérieurs à... 1285 conservés dans les archives de quatre petits hôpitaux de... Troyes," *Mémoires de la société académique de l'Aube* 21 [1857], p. j. xix and following). A. Roserot (*Dictionnaire* [note 31 above], 3 [Angers, 1948], 1566-1567) points out that the hospital would be transferred by 1200 to another Augustinian community, St Martin ès Aires, probably because of the disappearance of the Hebron chapter in 1187.

33   See especially P. Bertrand, *L'ordre de Saint-Lazare de Jérusalem en Orient* (Paris, 1924) and R. Petiot, *Contribution à l'histoire de l'ordre de Saint-Lazare en France* (Paris, 1914).

34   It is known that in the 17th century Louis XIV undertook to regroup all the small hospitals, infirmaries and leper houses still existing within the Order of St. Lazarus; this order, which in the 16th century bore the title of Saint-Lazare de Jérusalem, Bethléem et Nazareth, had been united with the new order of Notre-Dame du Mont-Carmel in 1608 by Henri IV. Cf. E. Vignat, *Les lépreux et les chevaliers de Saint-Lazare de Jérusalem et de Notre-Dame du Mont-Carmel* (Orléans, 1882), especially pp. 167, 183, 185, 207.

mary at the very beginning of the Frankish occupation were swiftly absorbed by the great Hospitaller congregation of St. John of Jerusalem. The multitudes of pilgrims to the Holy Land conferred particular importance on the hospitaller establishments annexed to the principal sacred sites. In Jerusalem, the Hospital of St. John avoided subordination to the patriarch and the chapter of the Holy Sepulchre; at Bethlehem and at Nazareth the hospitallers remained subject to the authority of the local bishop and bound to his chapter. This did not prevent either of these hospitals from developing a congregation to which were entrusted other foundations fulfilling the same charitable purposes in the West. This was done so as to allow the groups of brothers and sisters administering these establishments to benefit from the rules instituted for the communities of Bethlehem and Nazareth, and to express devotion to those two sanctuaries.

Of these orders, only that of Bethlehem may have survived the loss of the Latin states;[35] that of Nazareth seems to have disappeared very quickly.[36]

As we know, a new stage began in the middle of the twelfth century, with the establishment of hospitaller foundations intended to receive pilgrims from a specific region, for instance, the hospital founded at Jerusalem for the benefit of German pilgrims (1143);[37] or the hospital of the Holy Spirit, founded at Acre in the Pisan quarter and placed under the direction of one of the great hospitaller congregations of the West, the Crociferi of Bologna;[38] or again, but

---

35   This order should not be confused with that of Our Lady of Bethlehem founded in 1459 by Pius II, who granted it the properties of the Orders of the Holy Sepulchre and of St. Lazarus, to fight against the Turks.

36   In 1267 the pope placed the hospital of the Bretons at Acre under the jurisdiction of the archbishop of Nazareth. The hospital's archives were subsequently found in the charter-room of the Order of St. John: Favreau, *Studien* (see note 3 above), p. 54.

37   The history of this hospital, its integration into the Order of St. John, and that of the beginnings of the Teutonic Order, which seems to have originated in the hospital founded outside the walls of Acre during the siege of that city, have been definitively treated in the work cited in note 36.

38   Müller, *Documenti*, no. 63: by an act of June 1227, the rector of this hospital, founded before the taking of Acre by Saladin and re-established afterwards, recognized Pisa as its patron "salvo omni alio jure et potestate et reverentia ordinis cruciferorum et magistri predicti ordinis commorantium in diocesim Bononiensium." The Order of the Crociferi, called "of St. Clet," received its rule during the papacy of Alexander III; bulls issued by Gregory IX and Clement IV recognized its possession of the hospital of the Holy Spirit at Acre (whose brothers were lauded for going out to look for poor people who needed help instead of waiting for them to come) and of that of St. Julian of Nicosia, as well as others at Negroponte, in the Cyclades, on Crete and at Constantinople: B. Leoni, *L'origine et fondatione dell'ordine de' Crociferi* (Venice, 1598), fol. 13 and 16v. Reinhold Röhricht (RRH no. 982) erroneously associates the Holy Spirit of Acre with the Holy Spirit *in Saxia* at Rome, which belonged to the Order of the Holy Spirit founded by Guy de Montpellier.

rather later, the hospital of Saint-Martin of the Bretons founded in 1254 at Acre by Gilles de Saumur, archbishop of Tyre. All this did not encroach on the rights of the foundations of simultaneously hospitaller and military character: the Spanish order of Montjoye, the Teutonic Order,[39] the English order of St. Thomas the Martyr. This further stage implied a new wave of foundations, differing in many ways from those which we have tried to reconstitute.

39   This order had been purely hospitaller before assuming a military character, following the example of the Order of St. John.

CARVING UP CRUSADERS:
THE EARLY IBELINS AND RAMLAS

HANS EBERHARD MAYER
University of Kiel

In 1965 Count W.H. Rüdt de Collenberg[1] published a genealogy of the early generations of the house of Ibelin, later the most important feudal clan in the Latin Kingdom of Jerusalem. As the early Ibelins were already of great importance in the kingdom, their genealogy commands the interest of the crusading historian. Rüdt de Collenberg revised the family's genealogy as established by Ducange-Rey.[2] I accepted his findings at first, but later expressed reservations,[3] on which I now should like to elaborate. Two of his main points are in need of correction, and this will lead us back to Ducange-Rey: (1) that the founder of the family, Barisan-le-Vieux, Constable of Jaffa, must be split into two different Barisans succeeding one another in direct sequence; (2) that a whole additional generation must be inserted into the genealogy of the Lords of Ramla after Baldwin I of Ramla. This argument still seemed to be convincing to me in 1972. In order to understand its linkage with the Ibelin genealogy, one must remember that a Barisan of Ibelin (the second one according to Rüdt de Collenberg) married Helvis, daughter of, and heir to, Baldwin I of Ramla, indeed a match of considerable importance for the rising Ibelin family.

The first contention (p. 452 f.) is easy to refute. Rüdt de Collenberg deduced from RRH no. 135 that Barisan-le-Vieux was dead by the end of September

---

1   Weyprecht H. Rüdt de Collenberg, "Les premiers Ibelins," *Moyen Age* 71 (1965), 433-474.
2   *Les familles d'Outremer de Du Cange,* ed. Emmanuel G. Rey (Paris, 1869), pp. 360-379, with genealogical tree p. 375.
3   Cf. my review in *Deutsches Archiv* 22 (1966), 316 and my "Studies in the History of Queen Melisende," *Dumbarton Oaks Papers* 26 (1972), 119, n. 49f. Even then I regarded one of his conclusions which I now wish to disprove as "undoubtedly correct."

1145. In this charter Patriarch William I of Jerusalem, who died on 27 September 1145,[4] confirmed the statutes of the hospital of the Saviour founded by abbot Hugh of St. Mary of the Valley of Josaphat with the help of a confraternity.

> Nomina vero illorum, qui se primitus in hac confraternitate miserunt, sunt hec: domnus Balduinus rex primus et domnus Bernardus episcopus de Nazareth, Guillelmus de Buris, Guido de Miliaco, Goscelinus domnus de Tiberiade, domnus Balianus et ceteri plures, qui mortui sunt.

Combining the full printed version with Röhricht's abstract, Rüdt de Collenberg (p. 453) quoted this text in a fashion which never existed except in his own imagination:

> Balduini I (Rex), Guillelmi de Buris, Guidonis de Miliaco, Joscelini de Tiberiadis, Baliani et aliorum benefactorum mortuorum et ceteri plures qui mortui sunt.

By *his* insertion of the phrase *et aliorum benefactorum mortuorum* he was led to believe that all benefactors named in the confirmation by Patriarch William were dead, when William issued his charter some time during his term of office (after 27 September 1130—27 September 1145). In fact, because he assumed all benefactors to have been dead at the time of issue, he dated RRH no. 135 in the early 1140s, because William of Buris was still alive in early 1141 (RRH no. 201). If all benefactors listed were dead by 1145, this applied also to the *domnus Balianus* who is no doubt Barisan-le-Vieux. But it is this assumption by Rüdt de Collenberg which is wrong, and to which he was led by doubling the word *mortuus*. The only time it occurs is in the phrase *et ceteri plures, qui mortui sunt*. The relative clause clearly does not apply to all benefactors, but only to the *ceteri plures* whose names were no longer known because they had joined the confraternity in its early days but were long since deceased. This difficulty removed, we regain the old familiar Barisan-le-Vieux who was in the Holy Land before 1115 and was constable of Jaffa by this year (RRH no. 80), represented Jaffa at the Council of Nablus in 1120,[5] staked a claim together with Hugh of Jaffa in 1123 and 1126 for adding Ascalon to the county,[6] held fiefs from Hugh of Jaffa outside the county in 1127 which later reverted to the crown,[7] returned his fiefs in the county to the count when he led the Jaffa

---

4   WT, 16.17, p. 733. Rudolf Hiestand, "Chronologisches zur Geschichte des Königreichs Jerusalem um 1130," *Deutsches Archiv* 26 (1970), 229.
5   RRH nos. 89.90. Mayer, *Bistümer*, p. 145.
6   RRH nos. 102a.112.113. Mayer, *Bistümer*, pp. 137-156, 169f.
7   RRH no. 120. Mayer, *Bistümer*, pp. 143-145.

vassals into the king's camp during Hugh's revolt in 1134,[8] was enfeoffed in 1141 with the name-giving castle of Ibelin, took part in the great war council at Acre in 1148[9] and is mentioned alive for the last time in RRH no. 262 of early 1150.[10] Most likely still in the same year, his widow Helvis of Ramla married the kingdom's constable Manasses of Hierges.[11] By that time, but certainly not by 1145, as supposed by Rüdt de Collenberg, the formidable Barisan-le-Vieux, founder of the house of Ibelin, constable of Jaffa and first lord of Ibelin, was dead. By 1145 he was still very much alive. Only the *ceteri plures* who, together with Barisan, had founded the confraternity at Josaphat were dead by 1145.

Rüdt de Collenberg (p. 452 f.) adduced another argument in favour of his splitting poor Barisan in the middle. His first and his second Barisan were both married to a woman called Helvis. Rüdt de Collenberg clearly saw the improbability of having two Barisans, father and son, being both married to a Helvis. Yet he found this conclusion inescapable on account of RRH no. 100 of 1122, which shows a Barisan, Constable of Jaffa (Rüdt de Collenberg's Barisan I), to have been married to a woman named Helvis and having two sons named Hugh and Baldwin. That they were his sons is not expressly said in RRH no. 100, where they appear as giving their consent to Barisan's charter, but is proven by the confirmation RRH no. 423 and by RRH no. 252 of 1148, one of the cornerstones for the genealogy of the early Ibelins, as Rüdt de Collenberg clearly recognized. As they could give their consent, they both were apparently at least 8 years old.[12] Their brother Barisan the Younger could not give his

---

8   Ibid., p. 145. I argued for this date rather than 1132 in Mayer, "Queen Melisende," p. 104 f. Jean Richard, *The Latin Kingdom of Jerusalem* (Amsterdam, 1979), p. 96, remains unconvinced, but cf. p. 155, n. 22,24.

9   WT, 17.1, p. 759.

10   For the date of this charter see Mayer, "Queen Melisende," p. 138.

11   Ibid., p. 155.

12   The *venia aetatis* for males was reached with 15; cf. Mayer, "Queen Melisende," pp. 112-114. But Rudolf Hiestand, "Zwei unbekannte Diplome der lateinischen Könige von Jerusalem aus Lucca," *Quellen und Forschungen aus italienischen Archiven und Bibliotheken* 50 (1971), p. 28 n. 93, observed with his usual scholarly acumen that, perhaps, a limited legal competence, allowing a male to give consents, may have been attained at the age of eight, because it is at this age that the consent of the later King Baldwin III begins to appear. I expressed some reservations in "Queen Melisende," p. 112, n. 35, because Amalric I did not begin to give his consent until he was 10 or 11 years old. But his consents were definitely also a political matter. But already in 1972 I felt that Hiestand's line of thought should be pursued. I must now fully come over to his side, as otherwise the problem of Helvis's sons would be unsolvable. When using the age of eight in the following pages, this is, of course, an approximative figure, arrived at only by observation but without any definite statement in the sources to this effect. In reading Rüdt de Collenberg's article, one must bear in mind that he felt that full majority had to be attained by males before they could give their consent. This is certainly contradicted by both Baldwin III and Amalric I.

consent in 1155, because he was *infra annos,* but had reached the age of eight in 1158, when he did give his consent (RRH nos. 299.332). Disregarding the problem of when legal competence for consents started, if two sons Hugh and Baldwin were alive by 1122, they should have been born, at the latest, in 1121 and 1122. If their mother Helvis is supposed to have been 17 years old, when she gave birth to Hugh not later than 1121, she herself would have been born not later than 1104. This would have made her 47 years old when she married the Constable Manasses in 1150. But from him Helvis still had two daughters, the older one of whom cannot have been born later than late 1150 or early 1151,[13] because in the spring of 1152 Manasses was exiled for ever from the kingdom. The younger one would have been born in 1152, when Helvis was at least 49 — *if* her sons Hugh and Baldwin had been born just preceding RRH no. 100. If this was *not* the case, then Helvis would have been well over 50 when she had her last two daughters. There is a clear biological improbability, nay impossibility, here which Rüdt de Collenberg clearly saw. He resolved it by also splitting Helvis of Ramla into two women, an older one of uncertain extraction (wife of Rüdt de Collenberg's Barisan I, Constable of Jaffa) and a second one, daughter of the Lord of Ramla (wife of Rüdt de Collenberg's Barisan II) (p. 454). Disregarding Rüdt de Collenberg's argument as to the age of Helvis, because he assumes that consents could only be given after having come of age at 15, or rather adapting his argument to a limited degree of legal competence reached at 8, we get the following picture: Hugh and Baldwin, both sons of Barisan of Ibelin and Helvis of Ramla, gave their consent in 1148 (RRH no. 252). Both were therefore at least 8 years old. Consequently they were not born later than 1139 (Hugh) and 1140 (Baldwin). Then Hugh would possibly have been only 14 years old when participating in the siege of Ascalon in 1153,[14] but it was by no means uncommon that adolescents of this age were already engaged in warfare. King Baldwin III was still a minor, i.e. under 15, when he crushed a revolt in Oultrejourdain in 1144.[15] If Helvis of Ramla was about 17 when she gave birth to Hugh, she cannot have been born later than 1122. She could still have had daughters in 1151 and 1152, respectively, being then 30 or slightly above.

It seems sound if Rüdt de Collenberg (p. 455) reverses the order of the two marriages of the mother of this (second) Helvis (of Ramla). Twice the 14th century *Lignages d'Outremer*[16] assert that her mother was a Flemish woman

---

13   Ibid., p. 155.
14   WT, 17.21, p. 796.
15   Mayer, "Queen Melisende," p. 117.
16   *Lignages d'Outremer* 14, 26, RHC Lois 2:452, 462.

called Stephanie who *first* married Guy of Milly, founder of another famous *lignage* of the Latin East, and *then* took Baldwin of Ramla for a second husband after Guy's death. But Rüdt de Collenberg pointed out that before 1115 Guy had made a donation to Josaphat for his soul and that of his wife Elisabeth (RRH no. 80).[17] His silent inference is that Elisabeth had died between 1115 and 1120. Guy of Milly lived on to ca. 1126, when he is last mentioned in January (RRH nos. 112.113). Baldwin of Ramla, on the other hand, so far disappeared from sight in 1120, when he was a participant in the Council of Nablus of 23 January 1120 and a witness to a royal charter of 31 January 1120 (RRH nos. 89.90). This would make it impossible that Stephanie should have married first Guy, living up to ca. 1126, and then Baldwin, who seemingly died ca. 1120. Rüdt de Collenberg's reversal seems to make sense: Guy's first wife Elisabeth died not too long after 1115. He then married Stephanie. If she was also married to Baldwin of Ramla, she must have been married to him before 1120, as she could not have married him, as the *Lignages* have us believe, after 1126, when he was long dead. But, reversely, if Baldwin of Ramla really died very soon after the end of January 1120, Guy of Milly, then a widower, could have married the widow of this powerful vassal.

But Rüdt de Collenberg's reversal has a serious shortcoming. Stephanie and Guy of Milly had three well-known sons: Philip, Henry and Guy of Milly, of whom the first rose to be Lord of Oultrejourdain and Master of the Knights Templar. His brother Guy, however, is consistently called *Guido Francigena* in the charters. He had still been born in France, before his father came to the Holy Land, where he makes his first appearance in 1108 (RRH no. 52). This observation reverses Rüdt de Collenberg's reversal. As undoubtedly Philip, Henry and Guy *Francigena* were sons of Stephanie and Guy of Milly, since they are repeatedly called uncles of Hugh of Ibelin-Ramla (RRH nos. 299.332), and as Guy *Francigena* was born before 1108, the marriage of their parents must necessarily have preceded the one between their mother and Baldwin of Ramla. In this case we must extend the life of Baldwin of Ramla, which is easy enough to do. His supposed year of death, 1120,[18] rests only on the fact that in 1122 in RRH no. 100 his successor (and son, according to Rüdt de Collenberg) Hugh makes his first appearance, already as Lord of Ramla. We shall show RRH no.

---

17 Rüdt de Collenberg is, however, quite wrong in asserting that this Elisabeth was no longer mentioned in RRH no. 90, confirming RRH no. 80.

18 It was still accepted by Marie Luise Bulst-Thiele, *Sacrae domus militiae Templi Hierosolymitani magistri*, Abhandlungen der Akademie der Wissenschaften in Göttingen. Phil.-Hist. Klasse 3. Folge 86 (Göttingen, 1974), p. 77, n. 12, in her fine biography of Philip of Nablus, and by Hans E. Mayer, *Das Siegelwesen in den Kreuzfahrerstaaten*, Abhandlungen der Bayerischen Akademie der Wissenschaften. Phil.-Hist. Klasse, Neue Folge 83 (Munich, 1978), p. 47.

100 to be a forgery. With Hugh removed, a Baldwin of Ramla appears in 1136 and 1138 (RRH nos. 164.174.181) in the king's entourage among the barons or lords. William of Tyre[19] closes the case: In 1137 Baldwin of Ramla was *de regni proceribus* who retreated with the king into the castle of Montferrand and advised him in council.

The older Guy of Milly, then, was the first husband of Stephanie of Flanders. Their son Guy *Francigena* was born before 1108, ca. 1106. And now the difficulties begin. First of all, if he was the youngest son, as the *Lignages*[20] seem to say, then Philip of Nablus and Henry the Buffalo, his brother, were born even earlier, Philip ca. 1100. If his mother was then 17, she would have been born in 1083 and would have been already 43 years old, when her first husband died in 1126 and when she could have married Baldwin of Ramla, from whom she still had two children. This is not altogether impossible. But it is not certain that Philip was the oldest son.[21] As so much emphasis was placed on Guy

---

19 WT, 14.26, p. 645.
20 *Lignages d'Outremer* 14, RHC Lois 2:452. At least, he is called the third son, although Philip and Henry are not called the first and the second, but rather "one" and "another one" of three. Philip may have been listed first because he rose to the greatest prominence, while Guy, who died without offspring, was of little interest to the author of a genealogical source.
21 Philip succeeded in his father's fief in Samaria, and his brothers held rear-fiefs from him (RRH no. 366). This does not necessarily mean that he was the oldest son, because RRH no. 366 concerns almost only the family's holdings in Samaria, but not their very considerable feudal tenure in Galilee: (a) the fief which Philip had received from Rohard, former châtelain and viscount of Jerusalem, who went to Nablus with Queen Melisende after her downfall in 1152 and later called himself Rohard of Nablus. He was probably the father-in-law of Philip of Milly, better known as Philip of Nablus; cf. Bulst-Thiele, *Templi magistri*, p. 78; (b) the fief which Philip had received from his father Guy of Milly, who held money fiefs and land fiefs in Samaria (RRH no. 422a); (c) the fief which Guy *Francigena* had received from Rohard and later on held from Philip, obviously in Samaria and obviously a small fief, as a *Gui de Naples* (Guy *Francigena* much rather than his wealthy father Guy of Milly) owed one knight's service (*Livre de Jean d'Ibelin* 271, RHC Lois 1:424); (d) the fief which Henry the Buffalo, also one of the Milly brothers, held from Philip, obviously also in Samaria, because Henry retained his very large holdings in Galilee up to his death in or about 1165, i.e. beyond RRH no. 366 of 1161. On his Galilean possessions see Hans E. Mayer, "Die Seigneurie de Joscelin und der Deutsche Orden," *Ritterorden*, pp. 182-187; (e) the fief of Geoffroy Le Tort as he had held it from Philip. This and (f) Maron were both in Galilee. On the fief of Geoffroy Le Tort see last Marie-Luise Favreau, "Die Kreuzfahrerherrschaft Scandalion (Iskanderūne)," *ZDPV* 93 (1977), 22f. It is quite clear that at the time of RRH no. 366 Henry the Buffalo was already a crown vassal for his Galilean holdings (now or later mainly centred around St. George de Lebaene and Bouquiau, not far from Acre), because RRH no. 366 made no provision for a transfer of his service (for his Samaritan fief) from Philip to the king, whereas Guy *Francigena* and Geoffroy Le Tort only now became crown vassals, since such a transfer was expressly provided for. From the obvious exclusion of Lebaene and Bouquiau from RRH no. 366 we must conclude that old Guy of Milly's possessions had been divided after his death in the way provided for in case of several fiefs going to several sons: The sons chose individual fiefs from

Francigena having been born in France, his two brothers apparently were born in Palestine. Philip may have been the youngest and may have been the head of the family because he was the ablest. It should be remembered that both his brothers predeceased him. Sight is lost of Guy *Francigena* and Henry the Buffalo in 1165 (RRH nos. 412.422a), whereas Philip lived on to 1171.[22] If Guy was the oldest son, his mother's birthdate could be changed to ca. 1089, in which case she would have been only 37 when her first husband died in 1126.

But the real trouble comes with the two children she had from Baldwin of Ramla, Renier and Helvis. Renier was at least 8 years old when he witnessed a charter in 1141 (RRH no. 201). He was, therefore, not born later than 1133, when his mother was ca. 44. This is also still possible. Although genealogical trees are normally so arranged as to show Renier as the older of the two children, this is by no means certain. Helvis may have been the first-born. *If* her mother remarried immediately after Guy of Milly's death in 1126 (he is last mentioned in January), then with much luck Helvis could still have been born in the same year, but it is not very probable. But we have established (supra, p. 104) that she cannot have been born later than 1122, because she had Hugh of Ibelin-Ramla not later than 1139. Had she been born in 1126, for which there is no great probability, then she would have been only 13 when she had Hugh (and younger, if born later). While I have made a case for a woman of 13 giving birth,[23] one should preferably not multiply these cases. Yet one must either assume that her mother Stephanie not only remarried immediately upon the death of her first husband and also got immediately pregnant by him and that, furthermore, Helvis had her first child at the age of 13, or else assume that

their father's inheritance successively, according to their age. The oldest one had the first choice. Not before all heirs had chosen individual fiefs was there to be a partition of further fiefs remaining of the inheritance (*Livre au Roi* 28, RHC Lois 1:634; *Livre de Jean d'Ibelin* 148, RHC Lois 1:224). It may well have been that Henry the Buffalo chose Lebaene, in a fertile Galilean valley, before Philip had a choice. It could also have been that Guy *Francigena* chose Lebaene, if he predeceased his brother Henry. In this case he would also have been a crown vassal already before 1161. We do not know at what time Henry the Buffalo acquired Lebaene. We only know that he held it when he died ca. 1165 and when his inheritance gave rise to much legal dispute. Attention should be paid with regard to this problem to the fact that the *Lignages d'Outremer* (16, RHC Lois 2:454) have a chapter heading: *Ci devise et parole des hoirs de Guy le François,* but then the chapter opens with the statement that Guy le François = Guy *Francigena* died without heirs. In fact the complete chapter treats exclusively the succession not of Guy, but of his brother Henry the Buffalo. This might indicate that Lebaene came first to Guy and then to Henry. Philip would not have entered a claim, because by 1165 he had the much larger lordship of Oultrejourdain.

22 WT, 20.22, p. 981.

23 Hans E. Mayer, "Ibelin *versus* Ibelin: The Struggle for the Regency of Jerusalem 1253-1258," *Proceedings of the American Philosophical Society* 122 (1978), 47.

Stephanie's second marriage took place earlier than 1126, in other words that she remarried while her first husband was alive. This would necessitate the assumption that her first marriage was annulled. I find both options uncomfortable, but prefer the second over the first. Guy of Milly's "first" wife Elisabeth in RRH nos. 80.90 of 1115-20 must in any case be regarded as a misnomer for Stephanie. If Stephanie married Baldwin of Ramla in ca. 1121/22, Helvis could have been born in 1122 and could have had Hugh of Ibelin-Ramla in ca. 1139, so that he could have given consent in 1148 together with his brother Baldwin (born ca. 1140). The attraction of such a theory, which is based on an annulment of her first marriage to Guy of Milly, lies in the fact that Helvis of Ramla would have married Barisan-le-Vieux ca. 1137/38, when her father's life was coming to a close (supra, p. 106)[24] and when she was becoming a very desirable match, being about 15 years old and heiress to Ramla. It would also explain why her third son Barisan the Younger was not mentioned at all in RRH no. 252 of 1148. He was still *infra annos,* i.e. under the age required for consents in 1155, but could give his consent in 1158 (RRH nos. 299.332). If he was 8 in 1158, he was 5 in 1155 and had not yet been born in 1148.

Under this theory, Stephanie of Flanders could not have had any children from Guy of Milly after 1121/22. If Philip of Milly-Nablus was born about 1120, he would have been 18 when he made his first appearance in 1138 (RRH no. 174), 24 when he led a military expedition to Edessa in late 1144, 41 when he became Lord of Oultrejourdain in 1161 (RRH no. 366), 49 when he became Master of the Knights Templar in 1169, and 51 when he died ca. 1171. This is all possible, but he may well have been somewhat older. Dissolving Stephanie's first marriage ca. 1121/22 is, perhaps, not very good methodology, but it is surely better than reversing, with Rüdt de Collenberg, her mother's two marriages and letting her first marry Baldwin of Ramla and then Guy of Milly, as this is absolutely impossible, since Guy died in 1126 and Baldwin was still living in 1138 — unless the marriage with Baldwin was dissolved before he died, and then we would be in the same position as we are when we retain the traditional sequence of the two marriages.

If it is already *prima vista* improbable that there were two Barisans married to two Helvises in direct succession, there are two more objections which Rüdt de Collenberg chose not to see. First of all, his first Barisan, after all the famous Constable of Jaffa and formidable founder of the house of Ibelin, would have married a Helvis who was an *inconnue.* This is very unlikely in a

---

24   If it is true that Helvis was married off not by her father but by her half-brother Philip of
      Nablus (*Lignages d'Outremer* 14, RHC Lois 2:453), then the marriage should still be placed in
      1138 or very early in 1139 and Helvis would have had to become pregnant very quickly.

family which, at all times, placed great importance on concluding marriages which would accelerate the family's rise to the top. Also, Rüdt de Collenberg, precisely because he splits Barisan into two persons, must necessarily make Hugh of Ibelin-Ramla, Baldwin of Ibelin-Mirabel and Barisan the Younger sons of his Barisan II (p. 458), as this is established by RRH nos. 252.299. He also gives Baldwin of Ramla two sons, Hugh and Baldwin, because he must somewhere place Hugh, Lord of Ramla, and his brother Baldwin, Lord of Mirabel, mentioned in RRH no. 100 of 1122. His chief foundation for this assumption is that Hugh is styled Lord of Ramla.[25] But RRH no. 100 was not issued by Baldwin I of Ramla, who has so far been presumed to have been dead for two years, but who was really still very much alive (supra, p. 106). It was issued by the Constable Barisan of Jaffa, Rüdt de Collenberg's Barisan I. As, according to Rüdt de Collenberg, this Barisan never married into the Ramla family at all, whereas his Barisan II, supposed son of Barisan I, did so only ca. 1130 (p. 454, but cf. supra p. 107), one fails to see why a Lord of Ramla and his brother should have consented to a charter of Barisan I in 1122 — unless they were *his* sons. Even within the wrong genealogical system of Rüdt de Collenberg one cannot escape the conclusion that Barisan I had not only a son Barisan II, but also two sons Hugh (of Ramla) and Baldwin (of Mirabel). But so did Barisan II! If we start from Rüdt de Collenberg's position, we arrive at two Barisans being married to two Helvises and both having three sons named Hugh, Baldwin and Barisan.

25   There is a Hugh of Ramla who appears in 1126 and 1129 (RRH nos. 112.113.130). He is listed in the last of these charters after the viscount of Jerusalem, which indicates a not very high rank, but in the first two charters he is, after all, listed before the older Guy of Milly. Yet he cannot have been a son of Baldwin I of Ramla, who had only two children, Helvis and Renier. Nor can he have been a son of Barisan-le-Vieux, because his son Hugh of Ibelin-Ramla was not born until ca. 1139 (supra, p. 104). Nor can he have been a Lord of Ramla, because Baldwin I was alive until 1138. We could simply ignore him in this paper, but we should like to call the reader's attention to the fact that he gave two villages in the territory of Lydda to the Hospital of St. John in Jerusalem with the consent of his lord Count Hugh of Jaffa (RRH nos. 130.293). Now in RRH no. 105 of 1125, there occurs an enigmatic Lord of Lydda, where in the early days the bishop of Ramla-Lydda had held the position of a *seigneur*. This Lord of Lydda presented considerable difficulties already to the scribes who transmitted RRH no. 105. The original is lost. Two individual copies of the 12th and 13th centuries do not give a name at all, but simply let a Lord of Lydda witness the document. The two copies in the *Libri Pactorum* of Venice (late 13th and 14th centuries) call him Guy, whereas an otherwise not very good copy of the 13th century in the oldest manuscript of the Venetian statutes (Bibl. Marciana no. 3198) as well as a 17th century copy in the Bibl. Ambrosiana in Milan (A 141 inf.) call him Hugh. There may have been a short-lived attempt to create a lordship of Lydda as distinct from the lordship of Ramla which, technically speaking, was not yet a lordship, although Baldwin I carried on like a lord and had his own seal (Mayer, *Siegelwesen*, p. 47). This Hugh/Guy, Lord of Lydda, may have come from the town (not the family) of Ramla and may have taken his name with him into RRH nos. 112.113.130.

This is impossible. And indeed RRH no. 100 is the great stumbling-block in establishing the genealogy of the early Ibelins. Another experienced genealogist became confused by this charter. In a footnote, to which Rüdt de Collenberg once makes a fleeting reference, calling for considerable detective work in locating it, La Monte[26] confuses the matter beyond recognition, because he did not come to grips with RRH no. 100. He is still on seemingly safe ground when he states that Baldwin, brother of Hugh of Ramla, was the first known Lord of Mirabel and held it in 1122 (RRH no. 100). But then he goes on to say that, after Hugh's death, his brother Baldwin received Ramla as well and ruled there until 1138 (still correct) and that *he* married Stephanie, widow of Guy de Milly, and had by her Renier and Helvis. He confuses the Baldwin of Mirabel mentioned in RRH no. 100 with his grandfather Baldwin I of Ramla. Consequently, he arrives in his text at a startling conclusion: that Helvis of Ramla, wife of Barisan-le-Vieux, had an uncle called Hugh of Ramla and a father called Baldwin of Mirabel. In reality they were both her sons.

As the reader will by now be thoroughly confused, I reproduce on the adjacent page three genealogical tables, no. 1 being the traditional genealogy, no. 2 being La Monte's version, no. 3 being Rüdt de Collenberg's "revision." I must at the same time ask the reader to bear in mind that the traditional tree will be proven to be the correct one.

It will be noted that in the genealogical tree of Table 2 Hugh of Ramla and Baldwin of Mirabel are duplicated and that Barisan the Younger is not mentioned, because La Monte no longer knew whether to make him a son of Baldwin I of Ramla or of Barisan-le-Vieux!

Without RRH no. 100, the traditional tree (Table 1) would emerge very simply. As here is obviously the difficulty, we shall now look closer at this charter to show that the duplication of Hugh of Ramla and Baldwin of Mirabel in the trees of Tables 2 and 3 must be eliminated. The charter's authenticity has never been disputed, although it contains a number of irregularities. Admittedly it is not bad in style, but the oddities begin with the transmission. Today, there is no original, but only a mid-thirteenth century *inspeximus* drawn up by Adam, archdeacon of Acre (well attested in the 1250s), and by a prior of the Holy Sepulchre who occurs only here and styles himself strangely *J. abbas* (instead of *prior*) *sancti Sepulchri*. The title of *consul* given to "count" Hugh of Jaffa is certainly unique in the Holy Land, but it could reflect aspirations on

---

26   John L. La Monte, "The Lords of Le Puiset on the Crusades," *Speculum* 17 (1942), 116 n. 8.
Rüdt de Collenberg, "Premiers Ibelins," p. 438, n. 33, referred to La Monte, "op. cit." n. 5
(*sic,* and without a page number), but had listed five works by La Monte p. 433!

Table 1 (traditional)

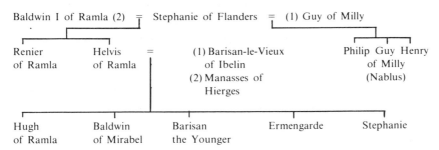

Table 2 (La Monte)

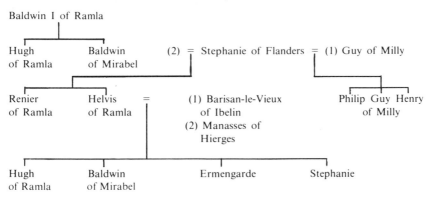

Table 3 (Rüdt de Collenberg)

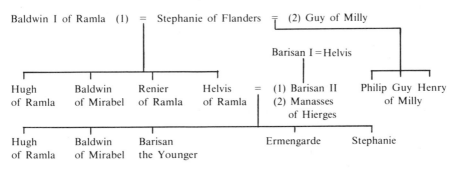

part of the count to gain a semi-independent position[27] and it did have an illustrious precedent in France, the *consul Andegavorum* in the charters of the counts of Anjou. The date is not correct. The indiction 8 ought to be corrected to 15, the *epacta* 11 is correct, the *concurrentes* 5 should have been 6 for 1122. Hiestand[28] correctly rejected the idea of Delaville Le Roulx that the charter ought to be dated 1160, in which case all other elements of its date would be in perfect harmony. But in 1160 Barisan-le-Vieux, who issued it, was long dead. RRH no. 100 is a donation to the royal hospital of St. John in Nablus, the history of which was elucidated by Hiestand.[29] But the hospital is called a *cutocothroffium*. The scribe must have thought of something evidently Greek, but what this was, remains unclear. That it was meant to be a corruption of *ptochotrofeion,* a poor-house, was an ingenious thought of Delaville Le Roulx, which Hiestand[30] passed on to his readers with cautious reserve. While it does fit the institution, one does not see how, palaeographically or otherwise, one could become the other. There is definitely something strange about it.

But the real proof of a forgery is the consent of a *Balianus,* a synonym for Barisan. The charter was issued by Barisan-le-Vieux, Constable of Jaffa, with the consent of his lord Hugh, "consul" of Jaffa, and the king and founder of the hospital, Baldwin II. This is perfectly in order. It was made for the salvation of the soul of Barisan-le-Vieux, of his ancestors (we wish we knew who they were) and of his wife Helvis. Consents are given by Hugh, Lord of Ramla, and his brother Baldwin, Lord of Mirabel. This is only possible, if one splits Barisan-le-Vieux into two different persons, as Rüdt de Collenberg did. If we paste this divided gentleman together again, it is impossible, because his wife Helvis of Ramla was not born until ca. 1122 (supra, p. 104) and his sons Hugh and Baldwin from this marriage perforce even later. Helvis of Ramla and Hugh and Baldwin of Ibelin cannot make an appearance in a document of 1122. But, quite apart from that, Barisan-le-Vieux and Helvis had a third son, Barisan the Younger. Nobody else but he can be the *Balianus* consenting to RRH no. 100. He is not expressly called the brother of Hugh and Baldwin, but that he was is apparent from the confirmation of RRH no. 100 issued by Baldwin of Mirabel in 1166 (RRH no. 423) and made with the consent of his brother Hugh of Ibelin (-Ramla) and his brother Balian (the Younger). Barisan the Younger, however, was 8 years old or older in 1158, was under 8 in 1155 and had not been born yet

---

27 So Mayer, "Queen Melisende," p. 108 where RRH no. 100 was, however, still accepted as genuine. Even without it, I believe that the rest of the evidence still supports my conclusions with regard to the aspirations of the Count of Jaffa.
28 "Zwei Diplome aus Lucca," p. 18, n. 47.
29 Ibid., pp. 17-25.
30 Ibid., pp. 23 f.

in 1148 (RRH nos. 332.299.252). Like his brothers Hugh and Baldwin of Ibelin, he could not possibly consent to a charter of 1122. Even if *infra annos* in RRH no. 299 were to mean "younger than 15," Barisan the Younger would not have been alive in 1122. Even Rüdt de Collenberg did not know what to do with him. While he made his two brothers in RRH no. 100 sons of Baldwin I of Ramla, he did not dare do this to Barisan the Younger. He mentions him once (p. 438) as having "signed" a document together with the Constable Barisan in 1122, but he does not refer the reader to RRH no. 100, although the reference is obviously to it, but cites La Monte in a way which is very hard to locate and the location of which reveals that La Monte there carefully avoided all reference to Barisan the Younger.[31] Rüdt de Collenberg seems to link him with the very old knight Bīran, born in 1106, who lived in Bethlehem in 1173 and entered the cave at Hebron with his father in 1119, after the discovery of the tombs of Abraham, Isaac and Jacob. This report by al-Harawī[32] is obviously wrong, if Bīran is to be equalled with Barisan the Younger, who had not yet been born in 1148.

If RRH no. 100 is a forgery, *cui bono*? It is of an unusual content, giving to the hospital at Nablus the *redecimatio* of all grain and vegetables in Mirabel and four other villages. What this means becomes clear in the confirmation of 1166 (RRH no. 423): *quoniam episcopus Sancti Georgii recipit primam decimam et hospitale secundam.* In other words, Mirabel was taxed twice for the ecclesiastical tithe. Baldwin of Mirabel first had to give one tenth of his income from Mirabel to the bishop of Lydda, then another tenth to the Knights of St. John, since 1166 the owners of the hospital of Nablus.[33] The normal arrangement

---

31 Supra, n. 26 and p. 110.
32 *Guide des lieux de pèlerinage,* trans. by Janine Sourdel-Thomine (Damascus, 1957), pp. 73 f.
33 Bernard Hamilton, *The Latin Church in the Crusader States. The Secular Church* (London, 1980), pp. 146, n. 1, and 148 has argued that this is to be understood to mean that the bishop received the tithe of the big summer harvest (of winter crops), while the hospital received the tithe on the poor winter harvest (of summer crops, sown in March and harvested in the fall), if I interpret him correctly. Surely the much bigger harvest was that of winter crops (including all grain), sown in November and harvested in April or May. On the rotation of winter and summer crops and on the difference in yield see Joshua Prawer, "Étude de quelques problèmes d'une seigneurie croisée au XIIIᵉ siècle," *Byzantion* 22 (1952), 47 = (with more conviction) idem, *Crusader Institutions,* p. 171 f. Hamilton's solution for the difficult problem of the *redecimatio* is ingenious but I am not convinced. Hamilton is certainly correct in his assumption that generally both harvests were tithed, because this is self-evident. But it should not be proven from RRH nos. 100. 423, which record an unusual arrangement. Since RRH no. 100 is a forgery, the Hospitallers would have been much wiser to forge themselves a charter entitling them to the *medietatem decime,* that is one half of the total tithe collected, as this was the usual arrangement when a bishop had to split a tithe with another religious corporation. For a *redecimatio* there is only one parallel known to me in the Holy Land (RRH no. 279), when

would have been a splitting of the ecclesiastical tithe between the two. But the bishop of Lydda may have been reluctant to do so, because the canons of the Holy Sepulchre in the church of St. Peter in Jaffa had the right to the ecclesiastical tithe in the whole county of Jaffa, of which Ramla, Mirabel and Ibelin were rear-fiefs.[34] Only two years after the confirmation of 1166, there was a conflict between the canons in Jaffa and the Knights of St. John, who were prohibited from adding a second church to the one they already had there.[35] We have no doubt that the *redecimatio* of Mirabel was not granted until 1166. In the already complicated tithing situation in the county of Jaffa, this boded ill. The Knights of St. John were probably well advised to forge for themselves a charter which threw their right to a *redecimatio* forward to 1122 and ascribed it to the formidable Barisan-le-Vieux. Baldwin of Mirabel could easily afford such generosity, because where he did grant the *redecimatio,* i.e. between Mirabel and Nablus, he had increased in the late 1150s corporal punishment for the Muslims in order to levy four times the head-tax customary in the country.[36]

RRH no. 100 of 1122 is forged. With its removal, the genealogy of the early Ibelins becomes simple. Baldwin I of Ramla (d. ca. 1138) had a son Renier and a daughter Helvis, who married Barisan-le-Vieux, Constable of Jaffa. Her half-brother Philip of Milly (Nablus) may have had a hand in this. The *Lignages d'Outremer*[37] assert that at this time Helvis was Lady of Ramla. This seems to be at first another of many wrong statements contained in this fourteenth-century source, because RRH no. 252 shows Helvis's husband Barisan-le-Vieux to have succeeded her brother Renier in the lordship of Ramla. But this charter also stresses in an unusual way Barisan's right to Ramla: *Ego itaque Barisanus et Hugo ac Balduinus filii mei ex honore prefato successores eius* (scil. of Renier). This was not customary. Normally the new lord issued charters, and if anybody disputed his rights, then this was a case for the courts. The phrase hints at difficulties having occurred in the succession of

---

the lord of Oultrejourdain granted to the Hospitallers *post decimationem beate Marie* the tithe of all his booty or other income taken from the Saracens. Here the booty is without a doubt taxed at 20% rather than at 10%, and the remainder of the lord's income subject to double taxation cannot refer to his share in the Saracen crops, not only because it was hardly possible to account separately his income deriving from their crops (to be taxed at 20%) and that deriving from the crops of Franks or Syro-Christians (to be taxed at 10%), but also because the Saracens living in this area were nomadic Bedouins not given to agriculture.

34   Mayer, *Bistümer,* pp. 122 f.

35   Ibid., p. 203.

36   Emmanuel Sivan, "Réfugiés syro-palestiniens au temps des croisades," *Revue des Etudes islamiques* 35 (1967), 137-139.

37   c. 14, RHC Lois 2:453.

Baldwin I of Ramla. A glance at the charters reveals that, in fact, Baldwin was first succeeded by his daughter Helvis, then by his son Renier. In February 1138 Baldwin himself had last attested a charter (RRH no. 174). By 4 December he was dead, because RRH no. 179 issued by King Fulk was attested, after the clerics but before the male lay witnesses, by the countess Hodierna of Tripolis (a daughter of King Baldwin II) and one *Halvisa*.[38] In 1142 a *domina Haloidis* was witness to a grant by King Fulk (RRH no. 210). Hiestand,[39] with regard to King Baldwin's daughter Melisende witnessing RRH nos. 121.137a of ca. 1129, insisted already that it was most unusual that women appeared among the witnesses of royal charters. In Melisende's case he explained this correctly as being due to her position as heiress to the throne. Fulk exercised in Jerusalem a *Samtherrschaft,* in which he and Queen Melisende ruled jointly, and both had a claim to the kingdom.[40] If Melisende, therefore, could inherit the kingdom jointly with her husband Fulk, it is clear that Helvis not only could not be prevented from inheriting Ramla from her father during the reign of King Fulk but had to be admitted as a witness in her capacity as Lady of Ramla. This is not to say that Helvis and Barisan-le-Vieux also had a *Samtherrschaft* in Ramla. He carefully avoided at all times the title of a Lord of Ramla, although he must have run the Ramla affairs at least with regard to the military service owed to the crown. But unlike Fulk who had, or at least claimed, the position of an heir to the Kingdom of Jerusalem together with his wife and was therefore much more than Prince-Consort, Barisan seems to have had the position of a consort in Ramla. Possibly Barisan's reluctance to emerge openly as Lord of Ramla had to do with the original law, which prohibited a vassal from accumulating more than one fief in his hands. This had been changed by ca. 1150, but we do not know exactly when the change occurred.[41]

Helvis's rule in Ramla did not remain uncontested. Her brother Renier entered a successful claim when he came of age. This was a different degree of legal competence than that of possibly eight years allowing to give consents. For males this majority, when they could claim their inheritance, was fixed at

---

38   A variant reading is *Alois.*

39   "Zwei Diplome aus Lucca," p. 27.

40   Hans E. Mayer, "Das Pontifikale von Tyrus und die Krönung der lateinischen Könige von Jerusalem," *Dumbarton Oaks Papers* 21 (1967), 165-167; Hiestand, "Zwei Diplome aus Lucca," pp. 26-31; Mayer, "Queen Melisende," pp. 98-114.

41   Joshua Prawer, "La noblesse et le régime féodal du royaume latin de Jérusalem," *Moyen Age* 65 (1959), 56 = idem, *Crusader Institutions,* pp. 25 f. Jonathan Riley-Smith, *The Feudal Nobility and the Kingdom of Jerusalem 1174-1277* (London, 1973), pp. 11 f.

15, for women at 12.[42] In 1141 a *Ramatensis Rainerius* witnesses a charter of
Patriarch William of Jerusalem (RRH no. 201). That he was identical with
Renier of Ramla is shown by RRH no. 244 of February 1146, concerning the
same business and having an almost identical list of witnesses, among them *de
baronibus... Rainerius Rametensis.* He also witnessed prominently, after
Barisan-le-Vieux, RRH no. 226 of 1144. As Helvis was still Lady of Ramla in
1142 (RRH no. 210), Renier must have reached his majority in 1143 or 1144,
which means that he was born in 1128 or 1129. He then entered a claim for the
Lordship of Ramla, which was successful, as we learn from RRH no. 252 of
1148, when he had already died but was recognized by Barisan-le-Vieux as
having been his predecessor in Ramla. I do not believe that the change from
Helvis to Renier had anything to do with King Fulk's death in November 1143,
because his widow Melisende continued to rule without much interference
from her son at first. Rather, Renier's claim was based on the principle that a
son, provided that he could perform military service, took precedence over all
daughters in inheriting a fief.[43] A man like Barisan-le-Vieux could see this
coming and act in time. Not that he could prevent it. But he could claim
compensation for the loss which would be sustained by his wife, if Ramla went
to her brother. Although we do not know the exact year in which King Fulk
built the castle of Ibelin in the south-west, William of Tyre[44] places it shortly
before his death; 1141 is a conventional and approximate date, probably not
far from the truth. Barisan was an old and trusted follower of the king, who
had decided in the king's favour the rebellion of the count of Jaffa. But the
king was not at absolute liberty to assign Ibelin to whomsoever he wished. He
was advised on this in council, and if Barisan argued that his wife had been
deprived, or would soon be deprived, of Ramla, here was an obvious compensation, especially as the importance of Ramla had rested in the fact that it had
to break the tides of Muslim attacks from Ascalon against Jaffa, Jerusalem and
the road between. This rôle was now taken on by the newly built castles of
Ibelin, Blanchegarde and Bethgibelin further south.

Later, fortune smiled on the Ibelins. While they had and held Ibelin, they
also got Ramla back, after Renier had died between 1146 and 1148, apparently
childless.[45] In 1148 Barisan-le-Vieux was running the affairs of Ramla, carrying

---

42 Supra, n. 12 and *Livre de Jean d'Ibelin* 171, RHC Lois 1:263 f. and *Abrégé des Assises des bourgeois* 23, RHC Lois 2:254.
43 Riley-Smith, *Feudal Nobility,* pp. 15, 128 f.
44 WT, 15.24, p. 696 f.
45 Rüdt de Collenberg (p. 457) gives him a son Baldwin alive in 1153, about whom he has already forgotten on p. 461 in the genealogical tree there. The reference is obviously to a Baldwin of Ramla in RRH no. 283 who, however, was nothing more than a vassal of the Prince of Galilee, witnessing one of his charters.

out last dispositions of Renier, who had died before he had been able to issue a charter about them (RRH no. 252). By that time Barisan had three children from Helvis: Ermengarde, Hugh and Baldwin. Later on they had Barisan the Younger (supra, p. 112 f.) and Stephanie who was still *infra annos* in 1158 but had come of age in 1160 (RRH nos. 332.360). Ermengarde rose to be Lady of Tiberias (RRH no. 299), probably by virtue of a marriage with Elinard of Tiberias. Hugh was the first of the family to call himself after the castle of Ibelin (RRH no. 291 of 1152). He was also the first of the Ibelins to call himself Lord of Ramla (RRH nos. 358.360 of 1160), but he did not do so until after his mother's death who is last mentioned alive in 1158 (RRH no. 335). In 1163 he married Agnes of Courtenay, the divorced wife of King Amalric I and the *femme fatale* of the Latin Orient.[46] He is last heard of in 1169, when he was about to make a pilgrimage to Santiago de Compostela (RRH no. 472), a typically grandiose Ibelin gesture. His brother Baldwin of Ibelin was Lord of Mirabel since ca. 1156[47] and is first styled so in 1162 (RRH no. 370b). As such he was under the close supervision of his elder brother in Ramla.[48] He himself appears as Lord of Ramla in 1171 (RRH no. 492) after his brother's death. There was a rumour that in 1177, having left his wife, he aspired to the hand of Princess Sybil, sister of King Baldwin IV, widow of the marquis William of Montferrat and possible heiress of the throne of Jerusalem.[49] The foundation for this may rest in the fact that when Sybil brought the crown of Jerusalem in 1186 to her second husband Guy of Lusignan, Baldwin refused to do homage to him, entrusted his fief to his brother Barisan the Younger and went to Antioch, where we find him in 1186 (RRH no. 649, although this probably precedes the *coup d'état* of October 1186 in Jerusalem). Barisan the Younger in 1177 married Maria Comnena, widow of King Amalric I, and thereby gained control of her dowry Nablus which, in fact although not in theory, he elevated to the position of a lordship.[50] In 1187 he became the defender of Jerusalem and disappears from sight in 1193 (RRH no. 716).

With RRH no. 100 having been eliminated as an authentic charter, there must be three alterations to the genealogies and history of Outremer: (1) The lifetime of Baldwin I of Ramla, father of Helvis and father-in-law of Barisan-le-Vieux, must be extended to 1138; (2) the succession of the Lords of Ramla must be: (a) Baldwin I, ca. 1110-1138; (b) his daughter Helvis of Ramla,

---

46   For the date see Mayer, *Siegelwesen*, p. 51.
47   Sivan, "Réfugiés," p. 138 n. 3.
48   Mayer, *Siegelwesen*, pp. 50 ff.
49   Ernoul, p. 33.
50   Mayer, *Siegelwesen*, p. 53.

1138-1143/44; (c) his son Renier of Ramla, 1143/44-1146/48; (d) Helvis of Ramla again, now being definitely represented by her husband Barisan-le-Vieux and later by her and Barisan's son Hugh of Ibelin, 1146/48-1158/60; (e) this same Hugh of Ibelin-Ramla, 1160-1169/71, but running Ramla's affairs since the death of Barisan-le-Vieux ca. 1150; (f) his brother Baldwin of Ibelin-Mirabel, 1169/71-1186; (g) their brother Barisan the Younger, 1186-1187; (3) the traditional genealogy of the early Ibelins and Ramlas must remain valid. Neither is there room for two Helvises or for two Barisans, nor may Hugh and Baldwin of Ibelin be split into Hugh and Baldwin of Ramla and Hugh and Baldwin of Ibelin, respectively. All these beautiful damsels and gallant knights of great renown must be pieced together again into one Helvis of Ramla, one Barisan-le-Vieux, one Hugh of Ibelin-Ramla and one Baldwin of Ibelin-Mirabel (later of Ramla).

Requiescant in pace nunc et in saecula saeculorum!

AN UNPUBLISHED CHARTER OF GEOFFREY, ABBOT OF THE TEMPLE IN JERUSALEM

AMNON LINDER

The Hebrew University of Jerusalem

Geoffrey, abbot of the Austin abbey of the Temple in Jerusalem between c. 1138 and c. 1160, was a leading ecclesiastic of his time in the kingdom of Jerusalem, and probably one of the more important members of the "Queen's party" in the conflict between Queen Melisende and King Baldwin III.[1] His position within the ecclesiastical hierarchy is indicated by the place he occupies among witnesses to charters. His name usually appears immediately after those of the archbishops and bishops and before those of all the other abbots and priors.[2] He is known to us as the author of the Continuation to Accard's *Carmen de Templo Domini*[3] and as the grantor of a charter recording the abbey's consent to a sale of property situated within the Temple's area.[4] We are now in a position to add to these a third document, preserved in a seventeenth-century copy, MS. Ash. 833 folio 351, now in the Bodleian Library, Oxford.

Folio 351 is the first page of a sheet of paper produced in France and imported to England at about the turn of the sixteenth century.[5] The other

1   H.E. Mayer, "Studies in the History of Queen Melisende of Jerusalem," *Dumbarton Oaks Papers* 26 (1972), 152, 175.

2   RRH nos. 174, 201, 205, 213, 226, 234, 244, 245, 262, 299, 307, 313, 323, 332, 354.

3   P. Lehmann, "Die mittellateinischen Dichtungen der Prioren des Tempels von Jerusalem Acardus und Gaufridus," *Corona Quernea; Festgabe K. Strecker,* Schriften der MGH 6 (Leipzig, 1941), pp. 306-307.

4   RRH no. 173b.

5   The watermark on folios 353-354, a Fleur-de-Lis on a crowned shield, is of the type classified in E. Heawood, *Watermarks* (London, 1950), under nos. 1672-1675, 1679, 1718, 1719. These variations were in use during the 17th century. The earliest recorded use is no. 1674, in the end papers of R. Knolles, *The Generall Historie of the Turkes* (London, 1603).

pages of this sheet (folios 352-354) were left blank. This sheet is inserted in the middle of three sheets of a larger size, the first pages of which contain a collection of copies of several English ecclesiastical seals (folios 345-350), while the last pages (folios 355-360) are blank. All four sheets belong to a rich miscellany of genealogical, heraldic and sphragistic material, most of which is in Elias Ashmole's handwriting. The latest piece in this collection refers to 1676,[6] and the entire collection is numbered consecutively in Ashmole's handwriting. We can conclude, therefore, that the copy on folio 351 was executed in the seventeenth century, and that its place in the arrangement of vol. 833 has not been changed since that order was fixed by Elias Ashmole some time between 1676 and his death in 1692. This volume, together with all the other manuscripts Ashmole bequeathed to Oxford University, was transferred to the Ashmolean Museum by 22 August 1692,[7] and, finally, to the Bodleian Library in 1860.[8]

The copy on folio 351 is a partial facsimile of the original document. Unlike the facsimiles executed for Sir Christopher Hatton,[9] which were designed to reproduce the originals faithfully, in all their details, our copy renders the general layout of the original charter, its seal and seal-cord, as well as the text, but it reproduces neither the script nor the exact physical appearance of the original document. The copyist was chiefly interested in the seal and in its cord, which he rendered in their minutest details. Yet his copy is detailed enough to give us some idea about the form of the original charter. The first four words of the charter, for example, were written in tinted ink, possibly red, as was the termination mark. The copy seems to be deficient in one important respect; the copyist omitted the main part of the confirmation clause that was appended to the original charter by its guarantor, because he was interested in Geoffrey's seal — hence also in the charter to which it was attached — rather than in the entire document. From this point of view, the guarantor's clause was of no importance and was consequently not copied.

The fact that the facsimile represents the sealed charter indicates that the copyist still had the original document in his hands, yet we are entirely ignorant about the provenance of the charter and about its subsequent history. We have to assume that it was kept in the archive of Woodbridge Priory until its

6   Fol. 361. See W.H. Black, *A Descriptive, Analytical and Critical Catalogue of the Manuscripts bequeathed into the University of Oxford by Elias Ashmole* (Oxford, 1845), col. 509-515 for a full description of this manuscript.

7   C.H. Josten, *Elias Ashmole,* 1 (Oxford, 1966), 301.

8   F. Madan (et al.), *A Summary Catalogue of Western Manuscripts in the Bodleian Library at Oxford,* 2.2 (Oxford, 1937), 1115.

9   L.C. Loyd and D.M. Stenton, *Sir Christopher Hatton's Book of Seals* (Oxford, 1950).

dissolution in 1537. Some manuscripts survived the dispersal of this archive. The priory's Register, for example, was consulted by Weever in the early seventeenth century,[10] and one charter — possibly two — in the British Library are probably remnants of the same archive.[11] In the present state of our knowledge, however, we have to assume that the original charter disappeared some time after it was copied, and that MS. Ash. 833 fol. 351 is the only facsimile known.

The text is as follows.[12]

> Galfridus dei gratia abbas Sancti Templi Domini Jerusalem et eiusdem loci fratres, universis sanctae matris Ecclesiae filiis ad quos praesens scriptum pervenerit salutem in domino.
>
> Sciatis nos communi assensu capituli nostri concessisse Ernaldo Rufo secundo, qui ad peticionem nostram caritatis intuitu et pro salute animae suae et antecessorum suorum, concessit et confirmavit nobis de Ecclesia Sanctae Mariae de Wudebregḡ, tunc temporis parrochiali, quam scilicet Robertus et Aluredus avunculi praedicti Ernaldi Ecclesiae nostrae dederunt, quod canonici ibidem ponerentur, qui Deo et Sanctae Mariae servirent, et Ordinem nostrum tenerent, et signum nostrum portarent; quod in dicta Ecclesia prior non erit electus nec factus, neque canonicus receptus aut remotus, nisi de assensu praedicti Ernaldi et haeredum suorum una cum assensu Norwicensis episcopi et canonicorum praedictae domus. Et ut nostra concessio robur optineat inperpetuum, illam sigilli nostri apposicione confirmavimus, et ad peticionem nostram et praedicti Ernaldi Willelmus Turbe, tunc Norwicensis episcopus, se testem concessit et contra omnes illos sententiam tulit qui huic confirmationi contrairent. Et isti sunt testes: Walkelinus archidiaconus, Michel de Meltuna clericus noster, Alanus decanus, Hugo clericus nepos noster, Baldewinus decanus, et multi alii.

10 J. Weever, *Ancient Funerall Monuments within the United Monarchies of Great Britaine and Ireland and the Ilands adjacent...* (London, 1631), pp. 752-753, 808.

11 BL Add. Ch. 7494 and BL Ch. Harl. 45A.50. The first charter is a record of a lease of tithes to Woodbridge Priory by Butley Priory. It was issued by the abbot of Butley at his priory, and was originally kept in Woodbridge Priory. BL Ch. Harl. 45A.50 is an indenture issued by Woodbridge Priory, recording an agreement between the priory and the tenants of Robert Ufford, who resided in the parish of Woodbridge. The text specifies that both parties should append their seals to the two halves of the indenture, while the bishop of Norwich should add his seal to that of the priory. As the surviving half bears traces of only two seals, it seems that this was the one sealed by the prior and by R. Ufford and left in possession of the priory, while the other half was kept by R. Ufford.

12 We have extended all contractions, divided the text into paragraphs, and introduced a uniform system of capital letters and division of phrases.

The seal was impressed on a cord attached to the charter through a fold at the bottom of the document. Obverse: +GAVFRIDUS DEI GRACIA ABBAS. The abbot, seated, blessing with his right hand and holding the crosier with his left. Reverse: +SIGILLVM TEMPLI DOMINI. The Temple (i.e., the Dome of the Rock) represented by a façade divided into five sections, with six intermediate columns and a gate in the middle section, and with a high dome based on a circular drum surmounted by a cross. This is identical with the only other known copy of Geoffrey's seal, a copy of a lead seal executed by A. Amico, now in Palermo.[13]

Like the Palermo copy, our charter lacks a dating clause, but it can be assigned, on grounds of prosopographical evidence, to the period between 1146 and 1166.

The abbacy of Geoffrey is documented from 1138, when he signed a document issued by William, Patriarch of Jerusalem, to 26 July 1160, when he attested a charter of Baldwin III.[14] His successor, abbot Hugo, was already in office by 6-11 April 1166, for on that date Amalric confirmed to him all the Temple's possessions in the Kingdom of Jerusalem.[15]

Ernald Ruffus the Second occurs for the first time in the Pipe Roll for the year 1158/9.[16] He was dead by 1186/7, when Ernald the Third, his son and heir, paid relief for his fee.

13   G. Schlumberger, F. Chalandon and A. Blanchet, *Sigillographie de l'Orient latin* (Paris, 1943), pp. xiii n. 2, 138; H.E. Mayer, *Das Siegelwesen in den Kreuzfahrerstaaten,* Abhandlungen der Bayerischen Akademie der Wissenschaften. Phil.-Hist. Klasse, Neue Folge 83 (Munich, 1978), p. 32 and Plate 1.5. For the content of this document see RRH no. 173b. The Palermo copy differs in one detail only — it reads GRATIA instead of GRACIA — but this difference is probably due to the carelessness of one of the two copyists. We wish to thank Dr. A. Manfrè, Director of the Palermo Municipal Library, for the photocopies of this manuscript which he kindly put at our disposal.   14   RRH nos. 172, 354.
15   RRH no. 422a. In the same year he witnessed a charter issued by William, bishop of Acre: RRH no. 372.
16   Ernald the Second was a son of Ernald the First and father of Ernald the Third — see John's confirmation on 17 May 1200 of the grant of Stradebroke: "Sciatis nos concessisse... Ernaldo Ruffo filio Ernaldi Ruffi... Ernaldus Ruffus, avus predicti Ernaldi" (*Calendar of the Charter Rolls preserved in the Public Record Office,* 1 [London, 1903], 46-47). He attested a charter of Walter fitz Robert, that gave to Robert, son of Ulf of Dunwich, land in Ubbeston, adjacent to the boundary of Laxfield (Loyd and Stenton, *Hatton's Book of Seals* [note 9 above], no. 305, p. 211). Owing to the geographical proximity of Ubbeston to Whittingham, the most plausible identification of the "Hern' Ruffo" mentioned in that document is with Ernald Ruffus the Second, rather than with Ernisius Ruffus from Essex (ibid.). This charter dates from the early years of Henry II. Ernaldus was probably the "Ernaldus filius Ernaldi" who gave Eye Priory seven acres in "Longeland pro remedio anime mee et filii mei et parentum et antecessorum meorum" (BL MS. Add. 19.089, fol. 214r = BL MS. Add. 8177, fol. 160v). In 1158/9 he paid for his fee (PR 5 Henry II, pp. 9,11); by 1186/7 he was dead, for in that year his son Ernaldus paid the Treasury part of a relief of £ 15 for his fee (PR 33 Henry II, p. 58).

William Turbe occupied the See of Norwich between his consecration in 1146 or early 1147 and his death on 16 January 1174.[17] Among the witnesses to the charter, "Walkelinus Archidiaconus" is probably identical with Walkelin, Archdeacon of Suffolk, who occurs in documents between c. 1137 and 13 January 1185/6,[18] while "Alanus decanus" might be identified with "Alanus de Bellafago," who occurs in Norwich documents between 1146 and 1170.[19]

William Turbe's consecration in 1146/7 and the end of Geoffrey's abbacy between 1160 and 1166 thus enable us to date the charter to the period between 1146/7 and 1166.

The charter is a public notification — by Geoffrey and the Chapter of the Temple — of an agreement concluded between them and Ernald Ruffus the Second concerning the church of St. Mary in Woodbridge. Ostensibly it is an exchange of confirmations and concessions. In response to Geoffrey's request and motivated by feelings of charity and concern for the salvation of his soul and those of his ancestors, Ernald concedes and confirms to the abbey the parochial church of Woodbridge, formerly bestowed on the abbey by Ernald's maternal uncles, Robert and Alured.[20] He also permits the conversion of the church to an Austin priory, linked to the Templum Domini through its use of that abbey's *ordo* and *signum*. Geoffrey and his Chapter, for their part, respond to Ernald's request and grant him the hereditary privilege of ratifying the election (or the "making") of the prior as well as the election and deposition of the canons, a privilege he was to share with the bishop of Norwich and the priory's Chapter. This privilege amounted, in fact, to a hereditary right of patronage over the new priory. At the request of both Geoffrey and Ernald, William Turbe witnessed the charter and decreed ecclesiastical censures against all future transgressors. Five other witnesses are mentioned by name and function, beside "many others" who were left unnamed. Among the witnesses we encounter "Hugo, our nephew." Both the paragraph that announces William's

---

17   J. Le Neve and D.E. Greenway, *Fasti Ecclesiae Anglicanae 1066-1300* (London, 1971), p. 56.

18   Ibid., p. 67. See also L. Landon, "The Early Archdeacons of Norwich Diocese," *Proceedings of the Suffolk Institute of Archaeology and Natural History* 20 (1930), 13-14.

19   B. Bodwell, ed., *The Charters of Norwich Cathedral Priory,* 1 (London, 1974), nos. 127, 129, pp. 72, 73.

20   In some medieval sources the word "avunculus" has the general meaning of "uncle," or even "relative," but we tend to assume that Geoffrey, who had obviously received a literary Latin education, employed this word in its correct sense. We do not know how the two brothers established contact with the Templum Domini, but it is worth noting that a strong contingent from Norfolk and Suffolk, under the command of Hervey de Glanvill, took part in the siege of Lisbon, that some of these crusaders arrived in Jerusalem in April or May 1148, while the others came after the siege of Tortosa in December 1148. See *De expugnatione Lyxbonensi*, ed. W. Stubbs, Rolls Series 38 (London, 1864), 1 : cxliv; G. Constable, "A Note on the Route of the Anglo-Flemish Crusaders of 1147," *Speculum* 28 (1953), 525-526.

confirmation and the paragraph that names the witnesses are phrased in first person ("Et ut nostra concessio... confirmavimus... ad peticionem nostram ...—clericus noster... nepos noster"), giving the impression that the witnesses are Geoffrey's. Yet we are inclined to believe that these are William's witnesses. The use of the first person in the charter's final paragraph does not, therefore, refer to the subject of the penultimate paragraph, which is undoubtedly abbot Geoffrey. Instead, it refers to a confirmation clause by William which, in the original charter, was found after the paragraph "Et ut nostra—confirmationi contrairent" and before "Et isti sunt—multi alii."

These witnesses were most probably members of the Suffolk and Norfolk clergy. Among them we encounter one "Michel de Meltuñ," whose surname points to Melton (Suffolk), a small locality near Woodbridge.[21] Another witness is "Walkelinus archidiaconus." As noted, a Walkelin served William Turbe as archdeacon of Suffolk during the period under consideration. One cannot dismiss *a priori* the possibility that another "Walkelinus archidiaconus," quite distinct from his namesake in Suffolk, and a different English canon who was a native of Melton just happened to be among Geoffrey's brethren in Jerusalem when he issued this charter; however, such a coincidence would be highly improbable. We assume, therefore, that they were William's witnesses. They attested the confirmation of the charter by William, not its issue by Geoffrey. Our seventeenth-century copyist omitted William's confirmation clause, but retained the names of his witnesses, apparently mistaking them for Geoffrey's witnesses.[22]

The parish church of Woodbridge is already mentioned in Domesday Book,[23] but its history before the thirteenth century is very poorly documented. Even the date of its conversion into an Austin priory is not known. John Leland was the first to identify a "Ruffus" as the founder of the priory,[24] and John Weever went one step further by attributing the foundation to "Sir Hugh

---

21   All three localities named "Meltuna" were in England. See J.G.T. Graesse, H. and S.-C. Plechl, *Orbis latinus,* 2 (Braunschweig, 1972), 544.

22   That confirmation must have been similar, if not identical, to the confirmation William Turbe granted to Eye Priory: "Si quis vero, quod absit, supradictum monasterium perturbare aut possessiones predictas auferre, diripere, aut ablata retinere, minuere seu quibuslibet vexacionibus fatigare temptaverit, nisi temeritatem suam digna satisfactione correxerit, reum se divino judicio de perpetrato facinore fore cognoscat, et a sacratissimo corpore et sanguine Domini nostri Iesu Christi alienus existat, atque in extremo examine districte ultioni subjaceat. Fiat, fiat, fiat, Amen. Salva sit auctoritate in omnibus Apostolice Sedis auctoritas, et nostre Norwicensis sedis justicia" (BL MS. Add. 19.089, fol. 198r-v; BL MS. Add. 8177, fol. 138v).

23   *Domesday Book, seu liber censualis Willelmi I regis Anglie...* 2 (London, 1783), 327.

24   J. Leland, *De rebus britannicis collectanea,* ed. T. Hearn (Oxford, 1715), p. 62.

Rous, or Rufus," based on the funerary monuments he inspected in St. Mary's church.[25] Yet some thirty years later Dugdale rejected this identification and proposed R. Ufford as the founder.[26] Later historians, however, adopted Leland's and Weever's identification, but were uncertain which member of the Ruffus family was the founder. Tanner,[27] Taylor[28] and Caley-Ellis-Bandinel[29] identified Hugo's three immediate ancestors—all of them bearing the name Ernald—as co-founders, but, curiously enough, still retained Weever's dating of the latter part of the twelfth century. A more precise date was suggested by Arnott. He hesitated between Ernald the Third and his son Hugh, but finally dated the foundation to c. 1193.[30] This date, based by Redstone on BL MS. Add. Ch. 7494,[31] has become accepted, and can be found in the works of Cox,[32] Copinger,[33] Dickinson,[34] Knowles-Hadcock[35] and Knowles-Brooke-London.[36] The most recent historian to pronounce on the subject, R. Mortimer, dates the foundation to "before 1200."[37]

Redstone, however, erred in his dating of BL Add. Ch. 7494 and in the way he tried to deduce from this date the foundation date of Woodbridge Priory. He dated the charter to c. 1193 because he believed that Geoffrey archdeacon

25 See note 10. Hearn's edition of this item in MS. Oxf. Bodl. Gen. Top.c.1 p. 60 is correct; Dugdale's different identification (see below) does not represent, therefore, a different reading of Leland's manuscript.

26 *Monasticon Anglicanum* 2 (London, 1661), 362: "Rufforde Fundator." This is certainly a mistaken reading for "R. Ufforde." The Uffords held extensive properties in Woodbridge, and a certain Robert Ufford is documented in one of the priory's charters; see note 11. This mistake in the *Monasticon* was repeated by the anonymous author of *Architectural Notes on the Churches and other Medieval Buildings of Suffolk* (London, 1855), who identifies a "Rufford" as founder of "a Benedictine priory" (*sic*) in Woodbridge (no. 46).

27 J. Tanner, *Notitia monastica* (Cambridge, 1787), *s.v.* Suffolk, no. L.

28 R. Taylor, *Index monasticus* (London, 1821), pp. 98-99.

29 *Monasticum Anglicanum: A History of the Abbies... A New Edition...* by J. Caley, H. Ellis and B. Bandinel, 6.1 (London, 1830), 600-601.

30 J. Arnott, "The Church and Priory of S. Mary, Woodbridge," *Proceedings of the Suffolk Institute of Archaeology and Natural History* 9 (1895), 338.

31 V.B. Redstone, "Woodbridge, its History and Antiquity," *ibid.,* pp. 346-347. The reference there (p. 347) to the charter "BM Add. Ch. 4947" must be corrected, of course, to BM Add. Ch. 7494.

32 J.C. Cox in *The Victoria History of the County of Suffolk* 2 (London, 1907), 111.

33 W.A. Copinger, *The Manors of Suffolk* 4 (Manchester, 1909), 324.

34 J.C. Dickinson, *The Origin of the Austin Canons and their Introduction into England* (London, 1950), p. 298.

35 D. Knowles and R.N. Hadcock, *Medieval Religious Houses, England and Wales* (London, 1971), p. 180.

36 D. Knowles, C.N.L. Brooke and V. London, *The Heads of Religious Houses, England and Wales, 940-1216* (Cambridge, 1972), p. 190.

37 R. Mortimer, *Leiston Abbey Cartulary and Butley Priory Charters* (Ipswich, 1979), p. 3.

of Suffolk and one of the witnesses named in it died in 1195. But recent research has established that Geoffrey was mentioned in documents as late as 1210.[38] Redstone was also mistaken when he deduced from the supposed date of that charter the foundation date of the priory, because BL Add. Ch. 7494 provides us with only the *terminus ante quem*, i.e., that by the end of the twelfth century (or the first decade of the thirteenth century) Woodbridge Priory was already served by a prior and by canons. It had thus been established earlier, but the charter supplied no information whatsoever as to how much earlier.

Geoffrey's charter throws new light on the whole question. It proves that Woodbridge church was bestowed on the Templum Domini by Robert and Alured, maternal uncles of Ernald the Second, and therefore suggests that this church did not belong to the Ruffus family before Ernald the Second. In 1086, in fact, it was held by Gislebert de Wissand (or Wistand).[39] The connection of the Ruffuses with Woodbridge probably began with the marriage of Ernald the First[40] to the sister of Robert and Alured (possibly relatives of Gislebert de Wissand) and with the transfer of inheritance rights from her to her son Ernald the Second. Our charter hints, however, that Ernald the Second did not recognize the grant made by his uncles. Hence the awkward but careful phrasing of the concession, in which Ernald the Second reiterates his uncles' grant and also makes it his own.

The full significance of the grant made by Ernald the Second can be appreciated only in the context of the entire agreement, which included two other important elements. These were the conversion of the parish church into an Austin priory and the bestowal of the patronage rights on Ernald. By giving to

---

38 Landon, "Early Archdeacons" (note 18 above), p. 14; Le Neve and Greenway, *Fasti* (note 17 above), p. 67.

39 *Domesday Book* (note 23 above), p. 327.

40 Ernald Ruffus, son of Roger, gave two parts of his tithes from Whittingham and Hasketon to Eye Priory upon its foundation, about 1080, and Robert Malet confirmed this donation among other "donaciones quas Barones et milites mei me annuente eis fecerunt" (BL MS. Add. 19.089, fol. 194r=BL MS. Add. 8177, fol. 131r). At the same time, Ernald attested a donation of William de Roville to Eye Priory (BL MS. Add. 19.089, fol. 213r=BL MS. Add. 8177, fol. 159v). After his son died he gave the priory eight acres of land in Whittingham (confirmation of the priory's properties by William Turbe, BL MS. Add. 19.089, fol. 198r=BL MS. Add. 8177, fol. 138v). In 1106 he was granted Stradbroke manor by Count Stephen of Mortain, and this grant was later claimed to have been confirmed by Henry I (*Calendar of the Charter Rolls preserved in the Public Record Office* 1 [London 1903], pp. 46-47; C. Johnson, H.A. Cronne and H.W. Davis, *Regesta regum anglo-normannorum 1066-1154* 2 [Oxford, 1956], 59-60). In 1130/1 he paid 60s. for his fee (PR 31 Henry I, p. 90). From Weever's account of the burial monuments of the Ruffus family in Woodbridge Priory (*Monuments* [note 10 above], p. 488), we can conclude that the name of the wife of either Ernald the First or Ernald the Second was Elisabeth.

the new priory the *ordo* and the *signum* of the Templum Domini, Geoffrey attempted to ensure that the new house would keep the liturgical observances, the customals and the "sign" (probably a cross sewn on the canons' habits, analogous to the distinctive sign allowed the Templars about that time)[41] of the mother house. Geoffrey obviously saw the future Austin priory of Woodbridge as belonging to a congregation headed by the Templum Domini, similar to the Austin congregation of the Holy Sepulchre which had gained a foothold in England a generation earlier.[42] In contrast to the strict dependence on the mother house as in the Holy Sepulchre congregation, our charter indicates a much looser type of dependence. The abbot of the Temple was not to enjoy rights of visitation, control or nomination over the new priory. Effective control over Woodbridge Priory was given, instead, to Ernald (and his heirs), when the abbot granted him authority over the admission and deposition of both the priors and the canons. Although Ernald was supposed to share these powers with the bishop of Norwich, it is obvious that he was granted what amounted to hereditary patronage over Woodbridge Priory. While this agreement satisfied the Templum Domini on the question of its proprietary rights, and perhaps offered it a way to preserve some hold over St. Mary's in the framework of a larger congregation, it also recognized the patronage of the Ruffus family over the new priory, probably legitimizing the *de facto* situation. The Ruffuses were henceforth known as "patrons of Woodbridge," and the church became the favourite burial place of the family for several generations.[43] This establishment of the Templum Domini *ordo* in Woodbridge was contemporaneous with its implantation in North Ferriby in the East Riding of Yorkshire, while the combination of a strong patronal authority with an Austin

---

41 "Postmodum vero, tempore domini Eugenii papae, ut dicitur, cruces de panno rubeo, ut inter caeteros essent notabiliores, mantelis suis coeperunt assuere...," WT 12.7, p. 521. See also H. Prutz, *Entwicklung und Untergang des Tempelherrenordens* (Berlin, 1888), pp. 259-261, for the relevant papal documents.

42 Dickinson, *Origin* (note 34 above), pp. 83-84, 133.

43 Ernald the Third, for example, was called "Ernaldus Ruffus quondam patronus de Wudebregg" in a verdict given by Apostolic judges-delegate in 1257 (BL MS. Add. 19.089, fol. 208r-208v=BL MS Add. 8177, fol. 152r). The direct line of the Ruffuses became extinct when William Ruffus died, before June 1253, leaving his daughter Alice as sole heiress (*Calendar of the Inquisitiones post mortem* 1 [London, 1904], nos. 282, 462, pp. 73, 128). Woodbridge Priory Register, still available to Weever, recorded the burial, in the church, of Ernald I, Ernald II, Ernald III, Hugo and William, with their wives, as well as "Sir Giles Rous," who is probably identical with the "Egidius Ruffus" who witnessed an indenture signed by the prior of Woodbridge and the burgesses of Ipswich in 1233 (BL MS Add. 19.147, fol. 311r).

foundation in Woodbridge heralded the similar activity of the Glanvills and their circle in Suffolk some decades later.[44]

If our interpretation of the charter is correct, it throws new light on a hitherto unknown chapter in the history of both the Templum Domini and Woodbridge Priory. At the same time it raises some questions about relations between the Latin Kingdom of Jerusalem and the Latin West.

Most, if not all, of the ecclesiastical establishments in the Holy Land held properties of varying types and importance in the West. The examples of St. Mary's in Josaphat Valley and of the Holy Sepulchre — more fortunate than the others in that their archives survived the disasters of 1187 and 1291, enabling historians to reconstruct their overseas properties — are highly revealing in this regard. The vast extent of the Templum Domini's properties in the Kingdom of Jerusalem, emphasized by William of Tyre[45] and recorded in detail in 1166,[46] suggests that the abbey held properties abroad too, and that they were at least as important as the properties held by the better documented establishments in Jerusalem. Finally one must bear in mind that some elements of proprietary relations were combined with other forms of control exercised from Jerusalem, for example in the framework of a congregation, an *ordo*. Here again the example of the Holy Sepulchre is better documented, but by no means unique.

These establishments obviously expected to derive profits from their properties, but we do not know how successful they were in this respect.[47] Neither do

---

44 The house at North Ferriby was probably founded by Eustace fitz-John (d. 1157). It administered, *inter alia*, a gift of land in Hessle, made to the Templum Domini in 1191. See E. Beck, "The Order of the Temple at North Ferriby," *EHR* 26 (1911), 498-501; D.M. Stenton, "Roger of Howden and Benedict," ibid. 68 (1959), 574-582. See also R. Mortimer, "Religious and Secular Motives for some English Monastic Foundations," *Studies in Church History* 15 (1978), 77-85.

45 WT 9.9, p. 376. The donations referred to in this passage were made by Godfrey of Bouillon.

46 See F. Chalandon, "Un diplôme inédit d'Amaury I, roi de Jérusalem, en faveur de l'abbaye du Temple-Notre-Seigneur (1166)," *ROL* 8 (1900/01), 311-317; C. Clermont-Ganneau, "Les possessions de l'abbaye de Templum Domini," *Recueil d'archéologie orientale* 5 (1902), 70-78; Mayer, *Bistümer*, pp. 222-229.

47 J. Riley-Smith's recent suggestion, that twelfth-century endowments in the West may have enabled — to some extent — the titular prelates of the Crusader States to maintain themselves until they were systematically employed by the Papacy from the middle of the thirteenth century, is very plausible, but the extent to which these endowments were actually exploited during the twelfth century is still largely a matter of speculation. See J. Riley-Smith, "Latin Titular Bishops in Palestine and Syria, 1137-1291," *Catholic Historical Review* 64 (1978), 1-15. [And see also the data on the European dependencies of the churches of Bethlehem and Nazareth, presented by Jean Richard, pp. 89-100 above. — Ed.]

we know what effect—if any—these proprietary links had on the proprietors and mother churches in Jerusalem as well as on their dependents in Europe. Judged from this point of view, our charter must be seen as a record of failure. The Templum Domini was obviously unable to exploit the parish church of Woodbridge, nor did it claim any revenue from the new priory. It is reasonable to assume that this failure was caused by the local gentry, and it was indeed in its settlement with Ernald the Second that the abbey renounced any profitable exploitation of its property. A similar renunciation might lie behind the list of properties the Templum Domini submitted to Innocent III in 1209 for confirmation: only properties situated in the Latin Empire of Constantinople were named, perhaps because by that time these were the only properties abroad which the abbey still hoped to administer and exploit.[48]

Unlike North Ferriby, whose adherence to the order of the Templum Domini is specific in records as late as 1442, it is doubtful whether the inhabitants of Woodbridge were much affected by the ties which Robert and Alured established with the abbey, and no trace of such effects can be detected from the period which opened with the settlement between the abbey and Ernald the Second. In violation of the agreement, Woodbridge Priory did not maintain any link with the Templum Domini. One looks in vain in the priory's later history for any evidence of even a memory of its past link with Jerusalem. The "sign" of the Templum Domini is not mentioned in any record bearing on Woodbridge Priory. The priors' seals, for example, depict St. Mary without any specific Jerusalem connotation.[49] If the history of Woodbridge church was typical of other properties of this abbey in Europe and of properties of other ecclesiastical establishments in Jerusalem in the twelfth century, it must be seen as an indication of an inherent weakness in one of the main ties that linked the Crusader States with the Latin West.

---

48 Potthast no. 3620; E. Baluze, *Epistolarum Innocentii III romani pontificis libri XX*, 2 (Paris, 1682), 263-264. The properties named were located in Constantinople, Athens, Thebes, Negropont and the diocese of Thermopylae.

49 For the first seal, see Cox in *Victoria History* (note 32 above), p. 111. The second seal, introduced in the fifteenth century, is reproduced in *Proceedings of the Suffolk Institute of Archaeology and Natural History* 4 (1864), 224. See also the accompanying note by C. Golding (pp. 223-224).

BOVARIA — BABRIYYA:
A FRANKISH RESIDUE ON THE MAP OF PALESTINE

MERON BENVENISTI
Jerusalem

The primary and secondary sources concerning the crusader period in Palestine contain more than 1200 place-names and topographical terms referring to places situated within the boundaries of the Latin Kingdom of Jerusalem. Nine hundred of these have been identified and mapped.[1] The comparison of Frankish nomenclature with biblical Hebrew or modern Arabic nomenclature reveals various types of influence and sources for the Frankish place-names on the map of Palestine.

The first and most common type of name is a direct transliteration from the Arabic. The transliteration is usually accurate, almost perfect, as in *Tarphin* = Khirbet Tarafein, or *Queffra* = Kafra; however one cannot identify any consistent rules of transliteration. Some Arabic names are corrupted beyond recognition: Deir Ibn ʻUbeid becomes *Dormibedi* and Meithalun — *Medeclala.* Sometimes the Franks transliterated names giving them a French turn: al-Kābri became *Le Quiebre.* There were some attempts to add French meaning to the French sound — thus Kawkab became *Coquet.*

The second type of Frankish names involves the literal translation of Arabic names into French or Latin. Such translations were done without apparent distinction between important and unimportant places. One cannot tell today why the Franks chose to honour specific places with French names and others

---

1 Joshua Prawer and Meron Benvenisti, "Crusader Palestine: Map and Index," in *Atlas of Israel*, 2nd ed. (Jerusalem and Amsterdam, 1970), Sheet 9.10. [For important additions see Dan Barag, "A New Source Concerning the Ultimate Borders of the Latin Kingdom of Jerusalem," *Israel Exploration Journal* 29 (1979), 197-217. Ed.]

not, but one can assume that when the Arabic meaning was known, the names were translated.

In most cases the translation is accurate. Thus, al-Fūla ('the broad bean') becomes *La Fève*; Tel aṣ-Ṣāfi ('the bright hill') is *Blanchegarde* and Khirbet al-Asad ('the ruin of the lion') was named *Gastina Leonis*.

Renewed biblical place-names are a special phenomenon in Frankish nomenclature. This is not the place to describe the *geographia sacra* of the Frankish period. It should just be noted that, of the dozens of renewed biblical names, some were based on erroneous, others on correct, identifications. It is interesting to note that in three cases the Franks transliterated ancient Hebrew place-names rather than the Arabic ones which are current at the present. For example, *Rahep* in the seigniory of Bethsan is a transliteration of biblical Reḥov, not of the present-day Arabic Tel as-Sarim. Biblical 'Efron ('Ofrah) was called by the Franks *Effraon*, and biblical Ḥafarayim—*Forbelet*; today, both places are called in Arabic aṭ-Ṭaiyiba ('the good'), as the Arabs replaced all names consisting of the root *'Afr* because of its negative connotation ('Afr—'Afrit means 'devil' in Arabic). The appearance of these three biblical names in Frankish garb suggests that at the arrival of the crusaders more biblical names—possibly in an Aramaicized form—were still in use than at the present.[2]

The third type of name in Frankish nomenclature is French and Latin place-names that came to replace Arab names. Some of these were given to places built or rebuilt by the Franks (like 'Atlit—*Chastiau Pelerin*), others were existing settlements whose names were changed for unknown reasons.

These original Frankish names were forgotten and are retained only in written records. Palestinian nomenclature did not absorb most of them. However, there are some notable exceptions. On the modern map of Palestine one can find four or five place-names of French or Latin origin. The village Sinjil retained the name of the St. Gilles family who owned it; Latrūn or an-Natrūn retained its name from *Le Toron des Chevaliers*; Kh. Dustri retains the name *Districtum* or *Casel Destreiz*. It is possible that Kh. Bablūn originated from the Latin *Casel Bubalorum* or *Casale Bufles*.

The fact that out of scores of Frankish names only a very few have survived indicates that the Arabic-speaking population never used them and when the Franks left the country they reverted to the old Arabic-Hebrew nomenclature. A comparable phenomenon happened at the end of the Byzantine period, when

---

2   The fact that neither Abū Shāma (n. 20 below) nor Yākūt (n. 33 below) speak of aṭ-Ṭaiyiba but of 'Afrabalā (referring to *Forbelet*) and 'Afrā (referring to *Effraon*), strengthens this hypothesis.

the Latin and Greek speaking authorities left Palestine, and all Roman-Hellenistic place-names, except for a very few, were replaced by the old Semitic names.

The same general picture appears in Frankish generic topographical names. The Franks translated generic names such as khirba into *gastina*, nahr into *flum*, 'ayn into *fountaine*, jabal into *mont*, kafr into *casale*. They also used Arabic names unaltered: *oedi* = wadi, *mezera* = mazra'a, *berquilia* = birka.

It is a strange phenomenon that one, and only one, French generic name, mentioned only two or three times in Frankish sources, has been preserved in the modern nomenclature of Palestine, with wide distribution and frequency. This name is *bovaria*.

bovaria or *boveria* in Latin, *boverie* in Old French, means farm or ox-shed.[3] The second meaning is still preserved in the French *bouverie* and in the English *byre*. A related word, *bouvium* or *bovarium*, means 'ox or cattle market.' In Frankish Acre such names appear in two different locations. In the north-eastern part of Montmusard, Marino Sanudo and Paolino of Pozzuoli mark on their maps a *bouaria* (or *boueria*) *Templi*; both locate also a *bouerel* within the Old City, to the west of the Hospitaller quarter.[4] A charter issued in 1198 mentions a gate named *porta boverie Templi* in the northern wall of the Old City, facing Montmusard.[5] It is customary to understand Frankish *bouerel* as cattle market, i.e., similar to the Latin term *bovarium*. In this context one should note that the cattle market in Jerusalem was called *buflaria*.[6] As for *bovaria* or *bouerie*, these terms are interpreted as ox-shed or also cattle-market.[7] An interpretation of *bovaria* as farm is offered only by Röhricht.[8]

It is difficult to determine the exact meaning of Frankish *bovaria*. The fact that it is mentioned only in an urban context makes it more difficult to accept Röhricht's assertion that it means a farm. An additional difficulty is that Frankish documents frequently use the term *curtile* to describe a farm.[9] Such

---

3   Charles du Fresne Du Cange, *Glossarium mediae et infimae latinitatis* (Niort, 1883-87), s.v. *bovaria, boveria*; Adolf Tobler and Erhard Lommatzsch, *Altfranzösisches Wörterbuch* (Wiesbaden, 1955-), s.v. *boverie*.

4   For a description of these maps see Joshua Prawer, "Historical Maps of Acre," *Eretz-Israel* 2 (1953), 175-184 (in Hebrew). [The maps are reproduced on p. 207 of the present volume. Ed.]

5   RRH no. 746. [For details on the location of this gate, and the problem of the second *boueria Templi* of Montmusard on Paolino's map, see David Jacoby, "Montmusard, Suburb of Crusader Acre: The First Stage of its Development," p. 209, n. 20 below. Ed.]

6   RRH no. 483.

7   For example, by Prawer, "Historical Maps," pp. 179, 181.

8   RRH, Glossarium, p. 513.

9   RRH nos. 169, 255, 283, 426, 483.

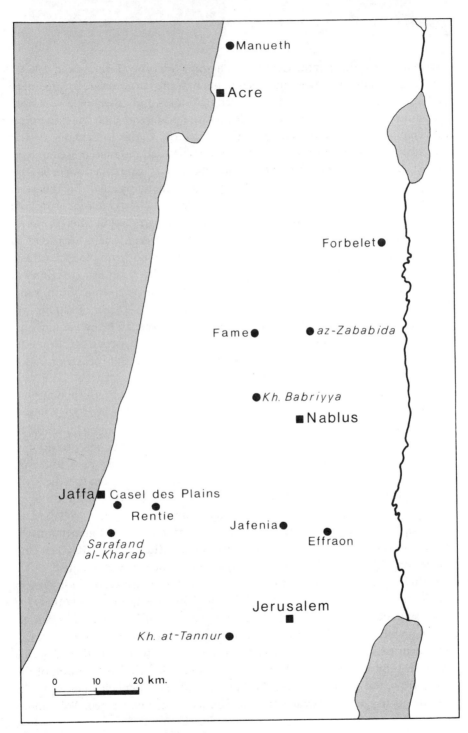

Fig. 1. *al-babriyya* ruins in Palestine

curtilia are mentioned in the vicinity of Caesarea, Hebron, Tiberias and Jerusalem. One can conclude from the documents that the *curtilia* were located near the built-up area of towns, and that dwelling houses and other structures were built around them. One should not dismiss the possibility that the *bouaria* of the Templars in Acre was, at least originally, a farm. In this context one should remember that Montmusard developed into a crowded residential area only in the last decade of the twelfth century and that the city-gate called *porta boverie Templi* had existed decades earlier. It is possible, therefore, that the Templars maintained a farm outside the city walls of Acre, which was later incorporated into the built-up area of Montmusard and its rural function altered.

Equipped with such scanty knowledge on the *bovaria*, one is surprised to discover that the same term is extensively used in the modern nomenclature of Palestine. The generic name *babriyya* or *babariyya* appears at least ten times in modern maps of Palestine or in name-lists.[10] The name is given to entire ruins (khirba) and also to buildings within villages and towns. These buildings are not similar in size, plan or function. They are, however, all Frankish remains. One served as a farmstead, two as watch-towers, one was part of a manor-house, one an administrative centre and five—unidentified structures situated in the midst of villages.

The fact that the name *babriyya* is linked in every case to Frankish buildings points to the relationship between it and the Frankish *bovaria*. That link is strengthened when one considers the fact that there is no meaning in Arabic to *babriyya* and that the Arab inhabitants themselves relate it to western origins, specifically to the middle ages. In the southern Ṭaiyiba we were told that *babriyya* is a corruption of *borboniyya*. The building, people say, was the work of "the prominent Frankish family al-Barbōn [=the Bourbons] hundreds of years ago." "Ignorant peasants," they say, corrupted it from *borboniyya* to *babriyya*. In the vicinity of Jerusalem villagers offer a different interpretation. The buildings, they say, were erected by Sultan Rukn ad-dīn Baybars and named after him *al-Baybarsiyya*; later the consonant s was eliminated.

In this context one should also note that the consonant v does not exist in Arabic and is usually replaced by b, f or w. Thus we can conclude that, for reasons unknown to us, a Frankish generic name, *bovaria*, took root in Palestinian nomenclature. The term, which originally meant a cow-shed or farm, became in its Arabic form *babriyya*, a generic term widely used to describe Frankish rural structures, and specifically vaults. The wide distribution of the name, from the plains of Acre to Judaea and the Shephela, points to its widespread usage and excludes the possibility of a coincidence. We cannot

10   See Fig. 1.

answer why the modest *bovaria* was privileged to be immortalized in the topography of the Holy Land, an honour that other, more illustrious, buildings did
not achieve. Perhaps the absorption of the term into local Arabic parlance
suggests that the crusader stable, in which beasts enjoyed a building especially
adapted to their needs, was an innovation in the country. In any case, this
curious occurrence sheds light on a neglected aspect of crusader history,
namely Frankish rural life in the Latin Kingdom.

1. *MANUETH* — KH. BABRIYYA, KH. AL-MANAWAT (PRESENT-DAY H. MANOT)[11]
GRID REFERENCE 164/271

This important ruin is situated on the southern slope of Wadi al-Qurayn
(Naḥal Keziv) where the gorge opens into the coastal plain. It commands a
fertile, well-watered valley in which the Franks grew sugar-cane.[12]

On the site there are three buildings: an elongated hall, with very thick walls,
and an entrance on the eastern side; a flour mill and a small, square tower
higher up the slope. The construction of the hall resembles that of the store-
house in Qula (*Chola*)[13] and seems to have served the same function. It was
known to the Arabs as al-Babariyya.

Manueth belonged in 1169 to Geoffroy le Tort the Younger and was apparently independent of the main, extensive le Tort fief.[14] In 1212 the Hospitallers
acquired it from King John of Jerusalem and Cyprus,[15] and during the first half
of the thirteenth century extended their estate. Riley-Smith[16] concludes that
the Hospitallers created a commandery of Manueth which was responsible for
the order's property in the northern plain of Acre. It seems that the existing
ruins, and especially the large hall, were built by the Hospitallers as part of
their elaborate system for collecting crops and distributing supplies.[17] In this,
its function is identical with that of the buildings found in Qula and aṭ-Ṭaiyiba
(*Forbelet*), both held by the order.

Manueth remained in Frankish hands until at least 1278.[18]

11   For a short description of "Kh. Bobrîyeh or Kh. el Menawât" see Horatio H. Kitchener and
      Claude R. Conder, *The Survey of Western Palestine. Memoirs*, 3 vols. (London, 1881-83),
      1:173 [hereafter cited as Kitchener and Conder, *Survey*].
12   RRH no. 468.
13   Meron Benvenisti, *The Crusaders in the Holy Land* (Jerusalem, 1970), pp. 227-229.
14   Gustav Beyer, "Die Kreuzfahrergebiete Akko und Galilaea," *ZDPV* 67 (1944/45), 197.
15   RRH no. 858a.
16   Jonathan S.C. Riley-Smith, *The Knights of St. John in Jerusalem and Cyprus, 1050-1310*
      (London, 1967), p. 430.
17   Ibid., p. 427.
18   RRH nos. 1374c, 1425a; cf. Benvenisti, *Crusaders*, p. 230.

Fig. 2. Manueth

Fig. 3. aṭ-Ṭaiyiba (North)

2. FORBELET—AṬ-ṬAIYIBA (NORTH), HEB. ḤAFARAYIM
GRID REFERENCE 192/223

The village of Ṭaiyiba is situated on the plateau of Issachar in Lower Galilee, 7 km W of Belvoir. Frankish Forbelet was part of an enormous Hospitaller estate centered on Belvoir.[19] In 1182 and 1183 two important skirmishes between Saladin's army and the Franks took place near it. The place is referred to as a "castle" by Abū Shāma[20] and as a "castle," "village" or "place" by William of Tyre.[21] Although it was certainly of military significance, the existing Frankish ruin al-Babariyya seems to have served as a depot, similar to other Hospitaller depots (see Manueth).

The Frankish building was raised on the foundations of a Roman fort. They consist of a strong, square outer wall, built of large, drafted-margin basalt ashlar. A Roman archway and traces of a vault can be seen on the N side of the ruin. The medieval remains are of a large hall (20×9 m), built E-W, with an entrance on the east. It is roofed by two cross vaults, with loopholes in each bay. A loophole on the west side was enlarged and widened into an entrance. The interior is built of smooth ashlar of good quality. No defensive devices are seen on the exterior walls. In later periods the hall was divided into a series of chambers in two floors.

3. FAME—FAHMA
GRID REFERENCE 167/198

Two Frankish buildings dominate the hilltop on which this Muslim village is situated. One of them, the large al-Babriyya (25×12.5 m), stands on the summit. Its eastern half is intact, with a barrel vault 6 m high (interior 11.30×7.50 m) and very thick walls of good masonry. It is used as a stable. The western half is destroyed and built over. Fifty metres south of al-Babriyya stands the village mosque, which is a converted twelfth-century Frankish church. The original entrance on the south side was blocked and transformed into a miḥrāb.

Fame, with the neighbouring village Age ('Ajja), belonged "with their appurtenances and half their tithes"[22] to the monastery of Mount Zion in Jerusalem. Fahma was a station on the route of the Mamluk royal mail (barīd) from Gaza to Safed, and a fire-signalling station of the Mamluk system.[23]

19   RRH no. 448; cf. Riley-Smith, Knights, p. 486.
20   Abu Shāma, K. ar-Rawḍatayn, RHC HOr. 4:221.
21   WT 22.16, pp. 1092-1094; 22.26, p. 1120.
22   RRH no. 576.
23   Maurice Gaudefroy-Demombynes, La Syrie à l'époque des Mamelouks d'après les auteurs arabes (Paris, 1923), pp. 243, 260.

Fig. 4. Fahma—*al-Babriyya*

Fig. 5. Fahma — *al-Babriyya*

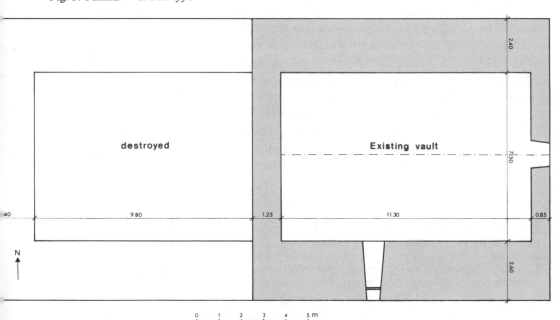

Fig. 6. Fahma — frankish church

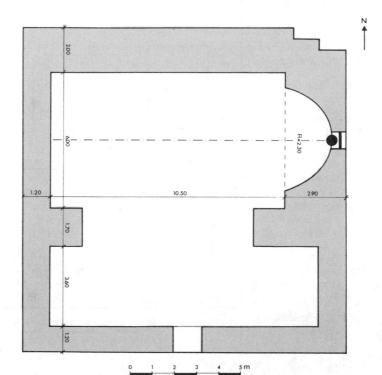

Fig. 7. Fahma —
Frankish church

Fig. 8. az-Zababida — *al-Babariyya*

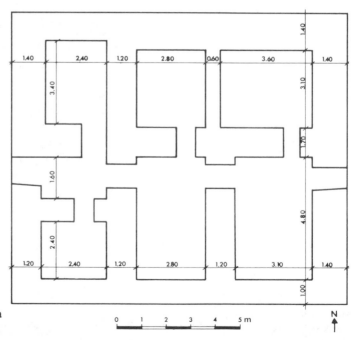

Fig. 9. az-Zababida
—*al-Babariyya*

0 1 2 3 4 5 m

N

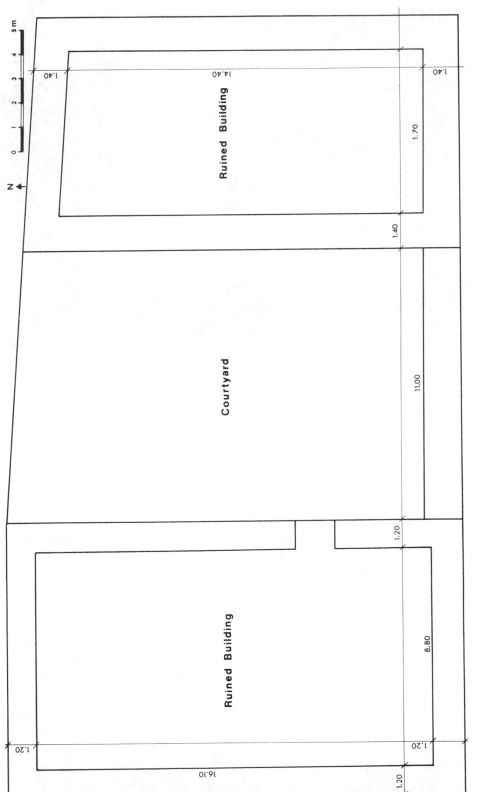

Fig. 10. Khirbet Babriyya, near Sabastiyy?

Fig. 11. Khirbet Babriyya, near Sabastiyya

4. AZ-ZABABIDA. FRANKISH NAME UNKNOWN
GRID REFERENCE 180/199

Zababida (or Zababdeh) is a village situated 8 km NW of Tubas in northeastern Samaria. The inhabitants are Christians who emigrated there in the sixteenth century from the vicinity of Karak in Moab. The area extending south
and west of the village, around the Valley of Sanur, was held in the first half of
the twelfth century by the viscounts of Nablus, and the tithes of its seven
villages were granted to the abbey of Templum Domini in Jerusalem.[24] The
structure known to the villagers as al-Babariyya is situated in the older part of
the village. It is 13.5 m long, 11.5 m wide, divided into six rooms with a long
corridor, and two entrances. It is built of large ashlar of exceptionally good
quality and from its appearance seems to date back to the Roman period. The
lack of windows suggests that its function was that of a depot of some sort.

24   RRH no. 422a.

Fig. 12. Yazur — *al-Babriyya*

Fig. 13. Yazur — vaults

5. KH. BABRIYYA. FRANKISH NAME UNKNOWN[25]
GRID REFERENCE 166/186

A large ruin, situated on a low ridge between the Nablus-Jenin and Nablus-Tulkarm highways, 2 km W of Sabastiyya in central Samaria. The medieval remains stand in the middle of an olive grove. They consist of two structures built east and west of a courtyard, of total length 32 m and width 18 m. The southern wall stands in parts to a height of 3.5 m. The corners are built of large size ashlar with drafted margins. The threshold of the entrance to the west building is of good masonry. Pottery collected there includes medieval samples.

6. *CASEL DES PLAINS* — YAZUR, HEB. AZOR
GRID REFERENCE 131/159

The history of this road-fort is well known, and especially the role it played during the Third Crusade.[26] Remains of the Templar fort are situated on a hilltop overlooking the plain of Jaffa. It is a square tower of the "Norman keep" type, completely preserved. North of it, on the northern slope, are remains of a girdle wall with ruined chambers. West of the tower stands the former village mosque, now closed. Its eastern part is probably of Frankish origin. The tower was known as al-Babriyya.[27]

7. *RENTIE* — RANTIYYA (PRESENT-DAY NOFEKH)
GRID REFERENCE 142/161

Frankish vaults, known as al-Babriyya according to the 1944 List of Antiquities,[28] situated 8 km NW of Ben-Gurion international airport (Lydda). The structure is 20 m long from north to south and 10 m wide from east to west, roofed by a barrel vault 4 m high. There are two entrances on the east side and four loopholes, two on the east and two on the west side. The walls are 2.30 m thick, built of medium-size drafted stones. On the west side there are remains of an outer wall.

Rentie is mentioned in a document of May 1122.[29]

---

25 *Archaeological Survey 1967-68* (Jerusalem, 1972), p. 222 (16-18/66/1).
26 Behâ ed-Dîn, *The Life of Saladin*, trans. Charles W. Wilson, PPTS 13 (London, 1897), pp. 314, 361, 371, 373.
27 Government of Palestine, *Official Gazette* 1375, Schedule No. 2 (24 November 1944).
28 loc. cit.
29 Delaville, *Cartulaire*, no. 59, p. 49.

Fig. 14. Rantiyya — *al-Babriyya* (southern side)

Fig. 15. Rantiyya — loophole in eastern wall

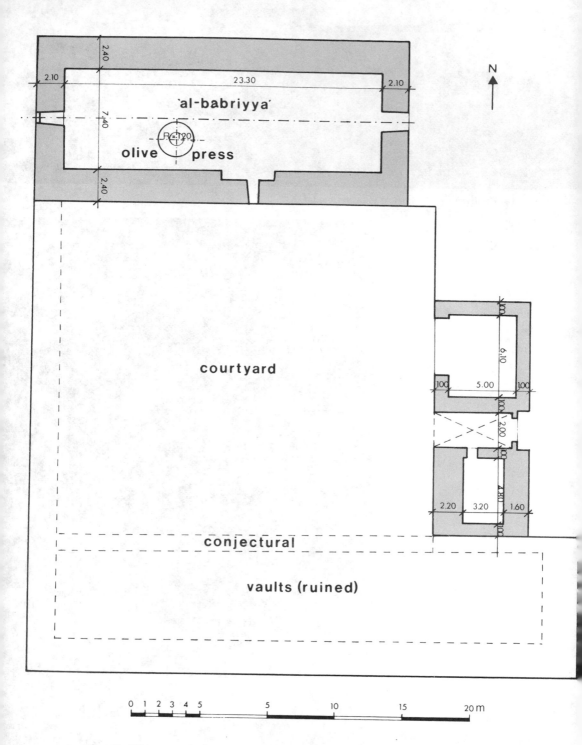

N

'al-babriyya'

olive press

R=1.20

2.40

2.10

23.30

2.10

7.40

2.40

courtyard

1.00

6.10

1.00

5.00

1.00

1.00

2.00

1.00

2.20

3.20

1.60

4.80

1.00

conjectural

vaults (ruined)

0 1 2 3 4 5   5   10   15   20 m

Fig. 16. Jifna — manor-house

8. JAFENIA—JIFNA, HEB. GOFNA
GRID REFERENCE 170/152

A large manor-house is situated in the middle of this Christian village.[30] Its general plan is that of a rectangle 30 m long (N-S) by 25.5 m (E-W) wide, enclosing an inner courtyard. The monumental entrance-gate is on the east, with portcullis. The lintel is made of Roman stone in secondary use. Two rooms are built on either side of the passageway. A long and narrow vault (6 m wide) occupied the southern side of the court, but most of it is ruined and built over. The northern side is occupied by a large and imposing barrel-vaulted hall (Interior 23.30×7.40 m). Its original entrance was from the courtyard but it is now almost completely blocked. The present entrance from the east is an enlarged loophole. The quality of the masonry is good. The vault is 6 m high, the walls are 2.40 m thick. In the middle of the hall stands an old olive press. This hall is still called by the villagers "al-Babariyya". In the outer walls of the manor-house there are no defensive devices, and its function is undoubtedly civilian. 50 m N of the manor-house stands a large crusader church, 10 m long, 5.60 m wide, with a single nave with a projecting round apse. The apse remains to a height of 2.5 m. Two columns stand *in situ*, one with a twelfth century capital. Other capitals and column bases are scattered. The modern church of St. Joseph is built on the western part of the crusader church.

Jifna is not mentioned in Frankish documents although *Raimundus de Jafenia* is mentioned as witness in a document dated 6 February 1182.[31]

9. EFFRAON—AṬ-ṬAIYIBA (SOUTH), HEB. 'EFRON, 'OFRA
GRID REFERENCE 178/151

The village is situated on a high hill and commands a panoramic view of the southern Jordan Valley, the mountains of Moab and Gilead. Its inhabitants are (like those of Zababida) Christians who emigrated there from Transjordan in the sixteenth century. The top of the hill is occupied by a large ruin, known to the inhabitants as al-Babariyya.

The ruin consists of an outer wall on the western side and an inner structure with vaults and a square tower. The line of the outer wall is irregular, with a bend opposite the centre of the inner structure. It is built of rudely drafted

---

30 Kitchener and Conder, *Survey* 3:437-438; *Archaeological Survey 1967-68*, p. 174 (17-15/02/1); Benvenisti, *Crusaders*, pp. 238-240.
31 RRH no. 613.

Fig. 17. Jifna—main gate

Fig. 18. Jifna—eastern inner wall

Fig. 19. aṭ-Ṭaiyiba (South) — outer wall and tower of *al-Babariyya*

masonry, except the NW angle which is built of smooth drafted ashlar of large size which forms a glacis. The *Survey of Western Palestine* mentions "An outer enceinte, surrounded with vaulted chambers opening inwards."[32] These chambers are now completely covered by topsoil which is under cultivation. The southeast and northeast sides of the wall have disappeared without trace and the area is covered with houses. Although the remains of the wall extend to a length of about 80 m, no defensive devices are visible, except the glacis, and it seems to be a retaining wall rather than a girdle wall of a castle. The inner structure consists of a large hall, approximately 20 m long by 6 m wide, barrel-vaulted, with two entrances from a square courtyard. On the opposite side of the hall a smaller vault is built. The side facing the courtyard is an enormous archway, now blocked. The archway is built of smooth ashlar of exceptionally good quality; its span is over 6 m and its height over 4 m. The courtyard was paved and underneath it is a large barrel-vaulted cistern. A third hall is situated on the western side of the courtyard. On the northwestern corner of the inner structure stands a rectangular tower to a height of 4 m above the roof of the inner vaults. It is built of medium-size, rudely dressed masonry with no loopholes.

32   Kitchener and Conder, *Survey* 2:370-372.

Fig. 20. aṭ-Ṭaiyiba (South)—courtyard and tower of *al-Babariyya*

Yākūt emphasizes the military significance of the site,[33] although its precise function is difficult to determine from an examination of the remains.

In the valley, east of al-Babariyya, is a crusader church, al-Khadr.

33   Guy Le Strange, *Palestine under the Moslems* (London, 1890), p. 385 (*'Afra.*)

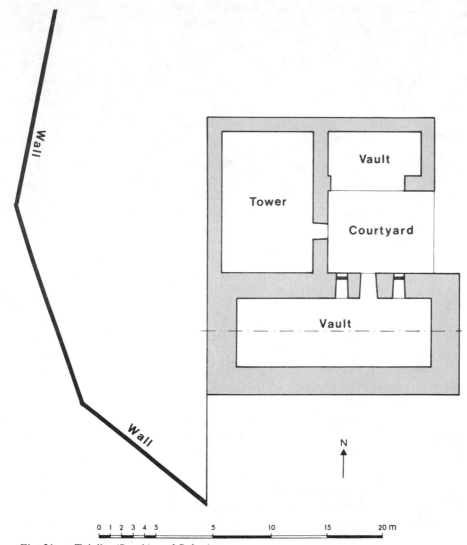

Fig. 21. aṭ-Ṭaiyiba (South)—*al-Babariyya*

10. SARAFAND AL-KHARAB (PRESENT-DAY YAD ELIʻEZER). FRANKISH NAME UNKNOWN GRID REFERENCE 131/149

Vaults known as al-Babariyya are cited in the 1944 List of Antiquities.[34] No trace is visible today.

34 See note 27 above.

Fig. 22. Khirbet at-Tannur—main structure (chapel?)

11. KH. AT-TANNUR ('ALLAR AS-SIFLAH).[35]
FRANKISH NAME UNKNOWN
GRID REFERENCE 154/124

An extensive Frankish ruin 14 km W of Bethlehem, not far from the ancient road to the Valley of Elah. It is built in a small, fertile valley near a spring ('Ayn al-Ḥasna). The ruin consists of two parts: (A) a hall, probably a chapel; (B) a farmstead with dwelling section and a farmyard.

The hall is 15 m long (E-W) and 10 m wide (N-S), roofed by a ribbed vault. Remains of the ribs survive in the north wall, which still stands to a considerable height and includes two windows. A third window is situated in the eastern wall, apparently above the altar. The entrance is on the south side. The walls are 3.50 m thick, built of small, rudely dressed stones. The interior is very beautifully constructed and plastered. Notable is the corniche that runs around the walls and the elegant corbels which supported the vault.

The west wall of the chapel adjoins the wall of the farmstead. It is a structure 40 m long and 35 m wide of farm buildings surrounding an inner courtyard. The east side is occupied by three or four barrel vaults, one of which is completely preserved. At the southwestern corner stands a long groin vault, and on the north side there is an elongated structure without internal subdivisions.

Kh. at-Tannur is not mentioned in Frankish documents. The entire area around it belonged until 1161 to John Gotmann.[36] In the nineteenth century the ruin was also known as al-Babriyya.[37]

---

35 Kitchener and Conder, *Survey* 3:62-63.
36 *Cartulaire de l'église du St.-Sépulcre de Jérusalem*, ed. E. de Rozière (Paris, 1849), no. 100, p. 197.
37 Charles Clermont-Ganneau, *Archaeological Researches in Palestine during the Years 1873-1874*, 2 (London, 1899), pp. 455-459.

THE VISIT OF KING AMALRIC I TO CONSTANTINOPLE IN 1171

SIR STEVEN RUNCIMAN
British Academy

There is no passage in all the great History of William of Tyre read with more relish than his account of the visit of his monarch, King Amalric, to Constantinople, in which he himself took part. William did not share the jealous suspicion of the Byzantines shown by most Crusader writers, though he at times disapproved of their policy. He had a genuine admiration and liking for the Emperor, Manuel Comnenus, about whom he was really more indulgent than was the great contemporary Byzantine historian, Nicetas Choniates. To William the visit was clearly one of the most interesting and enjoyable experiences of his life; and he tells of it in great detail. All students of Byzantine history must be very grateful to him, as his account of the Imperial Palace and its ceremonies, as seen by an intelligent and appreciative outsider, is unique.

His account is all the more valuable because of the curious silence of the Byzantine historians about the visit. Of the two contemporary Byzantine historians Cinnamus devotes three lines to it, merely saying that the King of Palestine came to Constantinople and admitted the suzerainty of the Emperor.[1] Nicetas Choniates does not mention it at all. It is probable that Nicetas was not yet in government employment, and he may have been away from Constantinople when the visit occurred; and no records of it may have survived when he wrote. But he gave a very full account of the visit of the Sultan Kilij Arslān to Constantinople, which took place nine years previously; and Cinnamus, too, devotes three pages instead of three lines to that visit. Amalric's sojourn in Constantinople clearly made no great impression on the Byzantine public.

---

1   Ioannes Cinnamus, *Epitome* 6.10, ed. B.G. Niebuhr, CSHB (Bonn, 1836), p. 280.

After all, earlier in Manuel's reign the rulers of Germany and of France had passed through the capital and been sumptuously entertained; and Amalric must have seemed small fry compared to such monarchs. Western knights were a not infrequent if not very welcome sight. On the other hand, a Muslim prince and his entourage presented a far more exotic sight; and in any case Manuel seems to have provided more splendid entertainment for Kilij Arslān than he did for any of his Christian guests, such as the naval tournament staged in the specially flooded Hippodrome: while the Turks provided additional amusement by producing a man who claimed to have discovered the secret of flight. He clothed himself in a vast garment pumped full with air and bound tight at the wrists and ankles, then flung himself from a high platform into the Hippodrome. But this human balloon proved ineffective. He crashed to the ground, to the cruel delight of the spectators. Amalric's party did not contain any such entertainer.[2]

The visit certainly established good will between the Imperial Court and the Court of Jerusalem. But was it the meeting of two sovereigns or of a vassal with his overlord? The Byzantines, as Cinnamus shows, held the latter view. William of Tyre, while never denying it, is anxious to emphasize the special honours that were paid to his king. Owing to contrary winds Amalric did not attempt to sail up the Sea of Marmora but landed at Gallipoli. But he embarked again at Heraclea so as to be able to arrive at the Palace at the small Imperial harbour of the Boukoleon, an honour reserved to royalty. When he reached the throne-room of the Chrysotriklinion Amalric advanced alone into the eastern apse where the Imperial throne was placed, and a great brocade curtain was lowered from its silver rod to hide his meeting with the Emperor. When the curtain was drawn back again, Manuel was seen seated on the throne and Amalric on a lesser throne a little below him. This was according to protocol. The Emperor's reception of a visitor was always veiled. But William suggests that the veil was specially lowered so that the Byzantine Court would not be shocked by the sight of the Emperor rising to greet his guest. Presumably this was what Amalric told him. On the other hand it could be suggested that the veil was tactfully lowered so that the visitors should not have to see their monarch received as a vassal.[3]

There is, I think, little doubt that Amalric was received as a very distinguished vassal, and that he was content to be so received. The whole question

---

2   Cinnamus, *Epitome* 5.3, pp. 204-208. Nicetas Choniates, *Historia, De Manuele Comneno* 3.5-6, ed. I. Bekker, CSHB (Bonn, 1835), pp. 154-159. Nicetas tells the story of the Turkish aeronaut.

3   WT, 20.22-24, pp. 981-987.

of whether the Byzantine Emperor was suzerain of the Crusader states has often been discussed; but it is impossible to give a clear-cut answer.[4] For all their respect for the Law, the Byzantines were not legally minded. They disliked exact definitions, preferring to state their case through symbols, of which the Imperial protocol was a supreme example. In theory the Byzantine Emperor was the Christian Emperor, the viceroy of God upon earth. But the emperors were at the same time pragmatical in their outlook. Long before the time of the Crusades they knew that they could not assert any suzerainty over the states of Western Europe. The Eastern Mediterranean was a different matter. Alexius I had hoped to establish suzerain rights over any Christian state that might be founded there by making the leaders of the First Crusade take an oath of allegiance to him, and to promise to restore to the Empire any lands that it had held before the Seljuq invasions. The oath was ignored by the Crusaders; and Alexius, who was essentially realistic, seems not to have worried himself about the Kingdom of Jerusalem. But he did worry about Antioch, that great fortress-city which had been Imperial until 1085 and which contained a mainly Greek population. The Treaty of Devol which he signed with Bohemond I in 1108 gave him unquestioned suzerain rights over Antioch but showed him content to have a Frankish vassal-prince there.[5] He was never able to implement his rights; but his son, John II, forced Raymond of Antioch to pay him homage in 1137 and was preparing to assert his rights again in 1143. He seems then even to have contemplated deposing Raymond and installing his own son Manuel as Prince in his stead.[6] Manuel, when he succeeded to the Empire, continued his father's policy and in 1159 was received in Antioch with great pomp as its sovereign.[7]

Whatever public opinion amongst the Crusaders might feel, the authorities in Jerusalem recognized Byzantium's special position over Antioch. When Prince Raymond appealed to King Fulk for help against the Emperor John, Fulk replied that the Emperor's claims were correct according to "the treaties

---

4   Notably by J.L. La Monte, "To what extent was the Byzantine Emperor the suzerain of the Crusading States?," *Byzantion* 7 (1932), 253-264.

5   Anna Comnena, *Alexiade* 13.12, ed. B. Leib, 3 (Paris, 1945), 125-129, gives the full text of the Treaty of Devol. For a commentary see F. Chalandon, *Essai sur le règne d'Alexis Ier Comnène* (Paris, 1900), pp. 246-249.

6   Cinnamus, *Epitome* 1.10, p. 23. See F. Chalandon, *Jean II Comnène et Manuel I Comnène* (Paris, 1912), pp. 184-185, who points out that it seems unlikely that John contemplated setting up a hereditary appanage, as Cinnamus suggests.

7   Manuel's triumphant sojourn at Antioch is not only recorded at length by Cinnamus, *Epitome* 4.18-20, pp. 181-186, and Nicetas, *Historia* 3.4, pp. 141-145, and by William of Tyre, *Historia* 18.23-25, pp. 859-864, but also by Armenian and Arab chroniclers.

made by our ancestors."[8] Amalric I on his accession wanted to be accepted as overlord of Antioch and sent to Constantinople to ask to be recognized as such, though presumably under the ultimate suzerainty of the Emperor. He received a prompt snub.[9] But in practice the Emperor's rights were only regarded when there was an Imperial army in the vicinity. When it was necessary to intervene in Antioch to protect the rights of the young heiress Constance against her mother, the Dowager Princess Alice, it was Alice's father, Baldwin II of Jerusalem, who came to settle the question. It could be said that he was acting as the head of the family; but he was certainly playing the part of an overlord.[10] The marriage of an heiress was always the concern of a feudal superior; and it was King Fulk that the Antiochenes asked to choose a husband for Constance; and when Constance herself chose her second husband she sought permission from King Baldwin III before she married him.[11] The Emperor clearly did not in practice enjoy the feudal rights over Antioch to which he was entitled.

If the position over Antioch was thus equivocal, the position over Jerusalem was far more complicated. Who, if anyone, was the overlord of the Kingdom? Some might say that it was the Papacy, which had organized the First Crusade. But in fact Papal intervention was only admitted over ecclesiastical affairs, over the episcopate and the Military Knights. Some might say that it was the King of France, who had been the suzerain of nearly all the princes that founded the Crusader states. It was the King of France whom Baldwin II asked to find a bride for his heiress Melisende.[12] But the King of France was far away; and when King Louis VII did appear on the Second Crusade he was given no special sovereign powers. The Byzantine claims of suzerainty over Jerusalem were clearly ignored by the earlier kings, whatever their lawyers might think about Antioch. It was only recognized when under Manuel the Byzantine army seemed to be a necessary aid for keeping in check the growing power of Nūr ad-Dīn. Both Baldwin III and Amalric I sought Byzantine brides; and their requests would certainly not have been granted had they not been made in suitably deferential terms.[13] When Baldwin III came to meet

---

8   Orderic Vitalis, *Ecclesiastical History* 13.39, ed. M. Chibnall, 6 (Oxford, 1978), 506-508.

9   Cinnamus, *Epitome* 5.13, p. 237.

10   WT, 13.27, pp. 599-601.

11   WT, 14.20, pp. 635-636, and 17.26, p. 802.

12   WT, 13.24, p. 593. The approval of the Pope was also sought and given: *Cartulaire de l'église du Saint-Sépulcre de Jérusalem*, ed. E. de Rozière (Paris, 1849), pp. 17-18.

13   WT, 18.16, 22, pp. 846, 857-858, and 20.1, pp. 942-943. In both cases two years elapsed between the king's request arriving in Constantinople and the bride's arrival in Palestine. This delay was due partly to the Emperor's insistence on certain political advantages before he would grant the request and partly to the time needed for negotiations over the dowry.

Manuel before Antioch in 1159 he was treated with great honour but according to the protocol for the reception of a vassal prince, though there is no evidence that he actually swore allegiance to the Emperor.[14]

The visit of Amalric to Constantinople was of a similar nature. Anyone versed in Byzantine etiquette would have known that the King was being treated as a vassal, but in so tactful a way that neither he nor his staff experienced any sense of humiliation. Indeed, it was a great success, much enjoyed by the participants. It lasted for about two months. Amalric left Acre on 10 March, and, though his journey was leisurely, he must have arrived in Constantinople fairly early in April; and it was not until 15 June that he set sail again for Palestine. His entertainment included a display of dancing in the Hippodrome and a trip up the Bosphorus to the Black Sea. During the latter part of the visit he left the Great Palace to stay in the more intimate atmosphere of the Palace at Blachernae, where Manuel ordinarily resided.[15]

William of Tyre's account leaves out much that we would like to know. In what language did the host and guests converse? It is unlikely that Manuel knew more than a smattering of Old French or that the King knew Greek.[16] The conversations must have been conducted through interpreters, of whom the most distinguished would have been the Empress, a princess of Antioch. Was the Orthodox Patriarch of Jerusalem, Nicephorus II, who resided in Constantinople, invited to any of the ceremonial functions? Presumably Amalric was spared the embarrassment of having to meet him. But religious affairs must have been discussed. Manuel certainly maintained the tradition that saw the Emperor as the suzerain of the Orthodox, wherever they might live; but he condoned the existence in Palestine of Orthodox prelates who recognized the authority of the Latin Patriarch of Jerusalem, such as Archbishop Meletus, who was a *confrater* of the Hospitallers and whose monastery at Bethgibelin he restored.[17] But most of the monasteries for whose repairs he paid were strictly Orthodox, such as that of St. John the Baptist in the Jordan valley and of St. Elias near Bethlehem.[18] When in 1169 he sent Greek artists to decorate with mosaics the Churches of the Holy Sepulchre at Jerusalem and the Nativity at

---

14   WT, 18.24, pp. 861-863.
15   WT, 20.22-24, pp. 981-987.
16   Manuel certainly did not know Latin. When the official interpreter mistranslated a speech of his to a Western embassy it was the Empress, who was German by birth, who had to correct him. Nicetas, *Historia* 4.6, p. 191.
17   See B. Hamilton, *The Latin Church in the Crusader States. The Secular Church* (London, 1980), pp. 182-183. He points out that the Orthodox bishops who accepted the authority of the Latin hierarchy seem all to have been Syrians, not Greeks.
18   Hamilton, *Latin Church,* pp. 166-167.

Bethlehem, both of them used by the Latins, this was probably a gesture to show his suzerainty. The Greek inscription on the Bethlehem mosaic is dated by the regnal year of "Manuel the great Emperor" and only mentions King Amalric in the second place.[19] Manuel's ecclesiastical good works in Palestine are perhaps a better indication of his suzerainty than his meetings with King Baldwin III and King Amalric.

Before he went home Amalric signed with the Emperor a treaty; but all that we know of it was that it committed both monarchs to joint action against Egypt.[20] It was to be more effective than the mismanaged joint expedition of 1169. But nothing came of it. During the next few years both monarchs had other distractions; and when the opportunity came in 1174, with the death of Nūr ad-Dīn, it was too late. Before any preparations could be made Amalric died, seven weeks after the great Muslim leader; and his kingdom was torn by internal feuds. Manuel for his part was having trouble now with his former guest, the Seljuq Sultan Kilij Arslān II, which was to culminate in the annihilation of the Byzantine army at Myriokephalon in 1176. Byzantium was no longer a great military power; and after Manuel's death in 1180 it fell into disarray. His successors, Alexius II who was a child, Andronicus I who was half-mad, and the Angelus brothers who were wholly incompetent, could none of them do anything to help the Kingdom of Jerusalem, even had they wished to do so.

Amalric's visit to Constantinople throws some light on Byzantine diplomacy and ceremony and on the personal and political relationship of the two monarchs. But it did nothing to alter the course of history.

19 C.J.M. de Vogüé, *Les églises de la Terre Sainte* (Paris, 1860), pp. 99-103, giving the Bethlehem inscriptions, which included the Nicene Creed with the *filioque* clause omitted. The Latin bishop of Bethlehem hung a portrait of Manuel in the sanctuary of the church: *The Pilgrimage of Joannes Phocas in the Holy Land*, PPTS 5 (London, 1896), 31.
20 WT, 20.23-24, pp. 984-987.

THE PREDICAMENTS OF GUY OF LUSIGNAN, 1183-87

R.C. SMAIL

Sidney Sussex College, Cambridge

Warfare is among the many aspects of life in Outremer illuminated by the work of Joshua Prawer. It is therefore fitting that a volume of essays written in his honour should include a contribution concerned with military affairs.[1]

In the early 1180s many Franks in the kingdom of Jerusalem were becoming aware of the growing imbalance of power between the crusader states and their Muslim neighbours.[2] In 1182 Saladin had subjected the military resources of the Latin kingdom to unprecedented strain by launching attacks in four different areas: east of Jordan, in Galilee, on Beirut and across the border between Egypt and the coastal plain of southern Palestine. In 1183, after nine years of effort, he at last acquired Aleppo, thus completing the conquest of Muslim Syria. With these lands, and the wealth and manpower of Egypt at his disposal,

---

1   Prawer, *Crusader Institutions*, in which pp. 469-500 are headed: Military History.
2   WT, 21.7, pp. 1014-1016.
    Almost every sentence in this paper could be supported by references to primary and secondary authorities. It deals, however, with well-known events in the reign of Baldwin IV and in the two following years which have been fully reconstructed and discussed by a succession of distinguished historians. In order that this short paper shall not be overloaded with notes, the reader is referred to easily accessible published works on that period of the kingdom of Jerusalem's history which is here discussed, and to the indications of source and secondary material which they provide. The best short accounts are by Hans Eberhard Mayer, *The Crusades*, trans. John Gillingham (Oxford, 1972), pp. 125-131; Marshall W. Baldwin in Kenneth M. Setton, ed., *A History of the Crusades*, 1, *The First Hundred Years*, ed. M.W. Baldwin (Philadelphia, 1955), 590-611. Outstanding among more detailed accounts are Prawer, *Histoire*, 1:539-649; Runciman, *Crusades*, 2:403-456. References will be given in this paper to identify quotations or to support points which are important to the argument.

he was better equipped than ever before to exert pressure on the Latin states. In the kingdom of Jerusalem, on the other hand, there were fresh signs of weakness. The need to raise additional military forces was so acute that a novel, though not wholly unprecedented, form of taxation was levied on the personal property and incomes of the whole population.[3] The project of sending a top-level mission to western Europe to persuade its rulers to raise reinforcements was probably already under discussion, since it was despatched in the following year. Most serious of all, the leprosy which afflicted King Baldwin IV reached so advanced a stage that he could no longer direct the royal government. He therefore handed over this responsibility to his brother-in-law, Guy of Lusignan. This transfer of power probably took place in September 1183. Before the end of the year, and probably in the following month, Guy was deprived of his office.

Guy's appointment weakened the kingdom because it sharpened the divisions already apparent among the leading men and women concerned in its government. Many historians have carefully described and analyzed two rival groups.[4] One of them was based on the royal court and household. It included the king's mother, Agnes of Courtenay, and Joscelin her brother, titular count of Edessa, who held the greatest of offices in the royal household, that of seneschal. The next most considerable of such offices, that of constable, was held by Aimery of Lusignan, a newcomer to the kingdom and a protégé, some said the lover, of Agnes. Other members of the group included Eraclius, the Latin patriarch of Jerusalem, who also owed his position to Agnes; Gerard of Ridefort, who at one time was marshal in the royal household but who subsequently became Master of the Temple, and Rainald, formerly prince of Antioch, but who by marriage had become lord of the major fief beyond Jordan. The second group was dominated by leading barons of the kingdom who had been born in the East. First among them was Raymond, count of Tripoli and also, in the right of his wife, prince of Galilee in the Latin kingdom. He enjoyed the consistent support of two members of the house of Ibelin, Baldwin of Ramla and Balian (Barisan) his brother, and also of Rainald of Sidon. On what issues were these two groups divided?

King Baldwin IV, through no fault of his own, created many problems. He came to the throne in 1174 as a child, so that it was necessary to appoint a regent. This office was a subject for dispute in the first weeks of the reign, and it

---

3   Benjamin Z. Kedar, "The General Tax of 1183 in the Crusading Kingdom of Jerusalem: Innovation or Adaptation?," *English Historical Review* 89 (1974), 339-345.

4   None better than Marshall W. Baldwin, *Raymond III of Tripolis and the Fall of Jerusalem (1140-1187)* (Princeton, 1936), pp. 35-45.

was only after one of the candidates had been removed by murder that Raymond of Tripoli was appointed. There was also a problem about the succession. Because of his leprosy the king was incapable of begetting heirs; who therefore was to be the next ruler? Until the last year of Baldwin's reign it was everywhere accepted that he would be followed by Sybil, his elder sister. A queen regnant, however, would not be able to discharge all the responsibilities of a head of government, particularly the military, and this made her marriage of particular importance. Her husband would become king in right of his wife. As early as 1176 she was married to a western magnate, William of Montferrat, but he died only a few months after the wedding. A search was made in Europe for an aristocrat of major importance who would replace him, and high hopes were placed in the duke of Burgundy. Those hopes were disappointed, and in 1180 Sybil was married to Guy of Lusignan, brother of that Aimery who was already constable in the kingdom. Guy was made count of Jaffa and Ascalon, a fief held by others in the recent past who were regarded as destined to become the next king of Jerusalem.[5] And when in 1183 the severity of the king's illness again made the appointment of a regent unavoidable, the choice fell on Guy.

The regency, the succession, the marriage of the Princess Sybil—these were the main issues on which the aristocratic factions were divided. From the beginning of Baldwin IV's reign, Raymond of Tripoli had aspired to the regency. More than this, the king believed, or was persuaded to believe, that the objects of Raymond's ambition included the crown itself, and there were other contemporaries who came to the same conclusion.[6] Some of the count's closest supporters showed themselves keen to become members of the royal family. Hugh of Ibelin had followed King Amalric as husband of Agnes of Courtenay; after Amalric's death, Balian of Ibelin had married that king's second wife, Queen Maria Comnena; and no one could have tried harder than his brother, Baldwin of Ramla, to marry the Princess Sybil.

Guy of Lusignan had thwarted these leading baronial figures in each area of their ambition. He married the heiress; he established the strongest claim to become the next king of Jerusalem; in 1183 he became regent. Small wonder that he became the object of venomous opposition. His enemies set themselves to deprive him of the regency, to exclude him from the succession, to nullify his marriage and to blacken his reputation. In this last process they were assisted by two writers of very different qualities and qualifications, both of whom were not only observers of political events in the Latin kingdom during the 1180s,

---

5   The fief had been held by Amalric, brother and heir of Baldwin III, and by William of Montferrat, Sybil's first husband. RRH nos. 353-355; WT, 21.13, p. 1025.

6   WT, 22.1, p. 1062; *Eracles*, p. 4; *The Travels of Ibn Jubayr*, trans. Ronald J.C. Broadhurst (London, 1952), p. 324.

but who took part in some of them. They also took sides in the political conflicts of the day, and it was the same side. William of Tyre, chancellor of the kingdom, its senior archbishop and one of the greatest historians of his age,[7] was often discreet on matters concerning the royal family and household; but in his *Historia* he could not conceal that he detested the Courtenays and their supporters.[8] For the ability of Raymond of Tripoli in politics and government he expressed, more than once, the highest admiration.[9] He thought that Guy, on the other hand, was unequal to the responsibilities thrust upon him.[10]

William's contemporary, Ernoul, who wrote in French, was an author of a different kind. Like William of Tyre, he was no run-of-the-mill chronicler, but neither did he have the archbishop's solemn sense of his responsibilities as an historian.[11] It was not his purpose to present an objective, straightforward account of events, but to give unity to his work by developing a single theme and to hold the attention of his readers by dramatizing that theme and by embroidering it with conscious literary art. The theme was to explain how the Christians lost the Holy Land and Cross to the Muslims in 1187 and 1188.[12] It is announced in what may well have been the very first sentence of his work and, by the art of the author, it is constantly recalled to the reader.[13] The theme

---

7 On William's life and work, see now Rainer C. Schwinges, *Kreuzzugsideologie und Toleranz* (Stuttgart, 1977), pp. 19-45.

8 WT, 22.9, pp. 1077-1078. Agnes is described as "mulier odibilis Deo" and associated with her, besides her brother, are "...viri impii... filii Belial et impietatis alumni."

9 WT, 21.5, p. 1012. "...mente compositus, providus multum, et in actibus suis strenuus..." The same author expresses similar sentiments at 22.9, p. 1078; 22.16, p. 1134.

10 WT, 22.25, p. 1117. "Impar enim et viribus et prudentia pondus importabile humeris imposuit."; also 22.29, p. 1127, quoted on p. 170 below.

11 Ernoul's work has not survived in the form in which he wrote it. The problems of assessing its scope and character have been the subject of a penetrating investigation by Margaret Ruth Morgan, *The Chronicle of Ernoul and the Continuations of William of Tyre* (Oxford, 1973). She has shown that Ernoul's chronicle dealt in a thin and unsystematic way with the history of the Latin kingdom from its beginning, became more detailed in its discussion of the 1180s, was most detailed of all on the year 1187, and extended to 1197. It was used by later compilers, the work of one of whom was edited by Louis, comte de Mas Latrie, under the misleading title of *Chronique d'Ernoul et de Bernard le Trésorier* (Paris, 1871). The work of other such compilers was used to continue the French translation of William of Tyre's *Historia*, so that they made use of Ernoul's chronicle for the years 1184-1197. Dr. Morgan's outstanding contribution to the elucidation of these problems has been to demonstrate that the closest contact with Ernoul's work can be made in a unique manuscript, Lyon, Bibliothèque Municipale 828, of which she has published an edition. M.R. Morgan, *La continuation de Guillaume de Tyr (1184-1197)*, Documents relatifs à l'histoire des croisades publiés par l'Académie des Inscriptions et Belles-Lettres 14 (Paris, 1982).

12 Ernoul, p. 4. "Oiés et entendés comment la tiere de Jherusalem et la Sainte Crois fu conquise de Sarrasins sour Crestiiens."

13 Ernoul, pp. 83, 114, 135, 178; *Eracles*, pp. 30, 34, 41, 46, 51, 57, 63.

is dramatized by its asssociation with particular individuals, who by their actions, conduct or incapacity contributed directly, in the author's view, to the loss of the kingdom: Gerard of Ridefort, Rainald of Châtillon, the patriarch Eraclius, Guy of Lusignan. In writing of such men, the author deploys skills which might be the envy of a modern journalist, especially those of ridicule and caricature. He also heightens the element of drama in his work by skilfully placed punch-lines, as pithy as they are memorable, relished by subsequent writers as material for the most telling of quotations. "Ceste corone vaut bien le mariage dou Botron." [14] "La prise de ceste carevane fu l'achaison de la perdicion dou roiaume de Jerusalem." [15]

For the period down to 1197 these traits are common to the texts edited by Mas Latrie and to the continuations of William of Tyre's *Historia*. They are works of literature as well as of history. The *Estoire d'Eracles* is also the *Roman d'Eracles*. And since, as Dr. Morgan has shown us, the lost chronicle of Ernoul is embedded in all of them, it was presumably marked by these same characteristics, "not so much history as *histoire romancée*, history being made to serve the end of good narrative." [16] It was studded with "cleverly turned phrases" and "purely literary devices used, successfully, to make the story live apart from the information it contains." [17] It was also a strongly partisan work. Ernoul was in the service of the Ibelins and wrote of the brothers Baldwin and Balian in terms of panegyric. [18] Their enemies were his enemies, and these included the newcomers from Poitou, who came off badly in his pages. Guy was "ne preus ne sages" and Baldwin of Ramla is made to refer to him in terms of biting scorn. [19] Ernoul presented his subject as a drama, with its heroes, villains and buffoons. He produced a skilfully contrived work of art, in which it was part of his purpose to ensure that the Poitevins did not get the best of it.

William of Tyre and Ernoul have provided posterity with the best narrative source material on the politics of the Latin kingdom in the 1180s. These writers, both supporters of one (the same one) of two bitterly opposed factions, naturally made partisan statements about the other; yet both have been used as if they were sources of objective evidence. Guy's opponents have therefore been seen as "the best element in the kingdom," whose "policy was that best calculated to promote its welfare." "The best interests of the kingdom pretty

---

14 *Eracles*, p. 29.
15 *Eracles*, p. 34.
16 Morgan, *Chronicle of Ernoul*, p. 156.
17 Morgan, op. cit., pp. 161, 165-166.
18 Ernoul, p. 44, where the author, describing the prowess of the brothers at the battle of Montgisard in 1177, compares them to Roland and Oliver at Roncesvaux.
19 Ernoul, pp. 60, 135.

clearly coincided with their own personal wishes."[20] Raymond of Tripoli has been regarded as "un politique prudent, sage, avisé, exercé, habile, excellent, le plus judicieux capitaine de l'armée, le seul espoir du royaume."[21] To M.W. Baldwin he was "a gentleman and good christian knight... the finest, the most attractive knight in the Latin East at the time of the kingdom's fall."[22] And what of Guy? Scholars of our own day have not minced their words. He was "a weak and foolish boy," "a man who was good-looking but worthless... chosen because of a woman's caprice and the weariness of a dying king."[23]

Was Guy genuinely incompetent, a figure of irredeemable "inability and weakness," or was his reputation exaggerated, or even manufactured, by his implacable political enemies? The question needs to be asked because of the evidence which exists to the contrary: his courage and decisiveness, shown only a few years later, in setting up the siege of Acre in the face of heavy odds; his resolution in upholding his rights as king after Ḥaṭṭīn and after the death of his wife; his success in establishing his government in Cyprus, after the failure to do so not only of an English administrator whose ability would one day make him seneschal of Anjou,[24] but also of those seasoned experts in Levantine affairs, the Order of Knights Templar.[25]

The first recorded episode in which Guy's enemies exerted themselves to destroy his career in the East was during and after his regency in 1183. It has already been stressed that the difficulties which faced the king's government were then particularly severe. Any head of that government, however able and experienced he might be, would stand in need of the counsel and support of the leading men of the realm in any test which might face him. The test which faced Guy immediately after his appointment as regent was an invasion of the kingdom by Saladin.

The military operations which ensued are easily described because they followed what had by then become conventional lines.[26] Since the Franks knew

20 Baldwin, *Raymond III*, pp. 55, 65.
21 The various elements of this vocabulary can be found in René Grousset, *Histoire des Croisades et du royaume franc de Jérusalem*, 2 (Paris, 1935), 616, 633, 699, 707, 708, 731, 732, 764.
22 Baldwin, *Raymond III*, pp. 95, 143.
23 Runciman, *Crusades*, 2:424; Grousset, *Croisades*, 2:690, 698; Adolf Waas, *Geschichte der Kreuzzüge*, 2 vols. (Freiburg, 1956), 2:131: "...der unfähige Guido, der nur König geworden war, weil er ein schöner Mann war."
24 "Benedict of Peterborough," *The Chronicle of the Reigns of Henry II and Richard I*, ed. William Stubbs, RS 49 (London, 1867), 2:167; Lionel Landon, *The Itinerary of King Richard I*, Publications of the Pipe Roll Society 51 (London, 1935), 50, 100.
25 Sir George Hill, *A History of Cyprus*, 4 vols. (Cambridge, Eng., 1948-1952), 2:34-44.
26 For the campaign in Galilee, September-October, 1183, see Prawer, *Histoire*, 1:620-623; Runciman, *Crusades*, 2:437-439; Grousset, *Croisades*, 2:723-730.

that Saladin would attack from the direction of Damascus, the army of Jerusalem was assembled at Saforie, a little town which had many advantages for any campaign in Galilee. It was well supplied with water; provisions could be concentrated there; it was well placed as a starting point to meet any enemy crossing of the Jordan either north or south of Lake Tiberias. On Michaelmas Day, 1183, Saladin's force crossed the river opposite Bethsan and entered the valley of Jezreel. Guy correctly led his army into the area by way of La Fève. His objectives were sensible and traditional: to place his troops in the immediate neighbourhood of the enemy; to occupy the sources of water supply; to remain tactically on the defensive so that his army would not be exposed to the risks of battle.

All this is firmly established by first-class evidence from the Muslim side. An official despatch to the Caliph, composed by al-Fāḍil, head of Saladin's chancery, is quoted verbatim in Abū Shāma's *Book of the Two Gardens*,[27] and the same compiler summarized the evidence of 'Imād ad-Dīn, Saladin's secretary,[28] who "accompanied Saladin almost without intermission from the summer of 1175 until his death."[29] Bahā' ad-Dīn, judge of the army, did not enter Saladin's service until 1188, but thereafter he was constantly in the company of men well able to give him first-hand testimony on the events of Saladin's earlier career.[30] All three, the chancellor, the secretary and the judge are in agreement that Saladin did his best to bring the Franks to battle, and that he tried to prise them from their defensive position by the provocation of archery and the lure of apparent retreat. The Franks were to be neither provoked nor tempted.[31] Even Muslim raids on surrounding towns and villages and interference with supply trains bringing much needed provisions to their camp did not lead them to abandon their passive watchfulness. After a few days Saladin withdrew his forces eastwards and returned to Damascus with nothing of lasting importance accomplished.

This account carries conviction not only because of the high quality of the Muslim evidence on which it is based, but also because it is entirely in keeping

---

27   Abu Shama, *Le Livre des Deux Jardins*, RHC, HOr., 4:245-248.

28   Abu Shama, *Deux Jardins*, pp. 244-245.

29   Sir Hamilton A.R. Gibb, "The Arabic Sources for the Life of Saladin," *Speculum* 25 (1950), 60.

30   Beha ad-Din, *Anecdotes et beaux traits de la vie du Sultan Youssof*, RHC, HOr., 3:74-76; English translation in *The Life of Saladin*, by Behâ ed-Dîn, PPTS 13 (London, 1897), 88-91.

31   Imad ad-Din in Abu Shama, *Deux Jardins*, p. 245: "…les Musulmans avaient harcelé (l'ennemi) de tous les côtés et accablé sous une nuée de flèches espérant qu'il prendrait l'offensive comme c'était sa coutume, mais il n'en fut rien." al-Fadil, op. cit., p. 247: "Nos flèches… venaient lui apporter le salut du défi, mais il n'y répondait pas. C'est en vain que nous cherchions à l'attirer dehors."

with what is known of Frankish military methods in the Latin East during the middle and later years of the twelfth century.[32] Christian control of the Holy Land depended on their possession of fortified places, that is, of the castles and walled towns which, as Joshua Prawer has shown, most of the European settlers inhabited.[33] When Muslim armies invaded Christian territory to achieve permanent reconquest rather than to raid, their primary objective was to win, by successful siege warfare, as many as possible of the Frankish strong places. In meeting such invasions the prime concern of the Syrian Franks was to prevent the formation of such sieges. They could succeed in this by taking their field army into the near neighbourhood of the invading forces. In this way they could hamper the Muslims' efforts to form siege lines or to set up siege apparatus, and could add to their difficulties of organizing adequate supplies. If in such ways the Franks could protect their fortified places during the summer campaigning season, then they won an important military success, because at the end of that season the invaders usually withdrew for reasons other than military pressure from the Franks. Any Muslim army strong enough to attempt reconquest was not made up wholly of troops maintained on a permanent footing. There were such men in the retinues of individual magnates, but a large invading force could be built up only by the addition of part-time soldiers recruited for a single campaign. At the end of the summer such men were anxious to return to their homes and families, especially if there were little prospect of abundant spoils of war. Even successful Muslim commanders of the highest prestige found it difficult to resist such pressure.

In the years when Saladin's growing military power put the Franks on the defensive, they could achieve the main military objective which has just been described without exposing their field army to the risks of battle. They knew what those risks were. They were aware of their own lack of human and material resources at a time when those of Saladin were being steadily augmented; hence the extraordinary taxation of 1183 and the mission to the West in 1184-85 to urge the preaching of a new crusade.[34] The field army, to which they assigned a key role in their defensive strategy, could be mustered only by drawing on the garrisons of those fortified places on which their control of the country ultimately depended. If that army were to be destroyed, or even

---

32 This paragraph and the next are based on Raymond C. Smail, *Crusading Warfare* (Cambridge, 1956). See especially pp. 74-75, 104-106, 135-136, 138-139.

33 Prawer, *Histoire*, 1:568-569; id., *Latin Kingdom*, pp. 66-67; id., *Crusader Institutions*, pp. 51-52, 182.

34 Alexander Cartellieri, *Philipp II August, König von Frankreich*, 2 (Leipzig and Paris, 1906), 18-25.

seriously weakened, by defeat in battle, then the all-important strong places were at risk, and might even be left virtually defenceless. This is what was to happen in 1187. In time of invasion, therefore, it was very much in the interests of the Franks of Jerusalem to secure their main military objectives, namely, to prevent the formation of sieges, to which the presence of their field army was essential, and to secure the withdrawal of the enemy without incurring the risks of battle. This degree of success was in fact achieved by the Franks in 1183.

The Muslim accounts of the short campaign of that year therefore acquire authority from the quality of the observers and the conformity of their information with well-attested Frankish military practice. On the Christian side there was a contemporary observer whose qualifications to report the episode were even higher than those of Saladin's officials. William of Tyre, even if he did not accompany the Christian army on the campaign, had a close knowledge of the kingdom's affairs and personal acquaintance with its greatest men and women, which put him in the strongest possible position for recording contemporary events.

It is to be expected, therefore, that his account of the campaign of 1183 will have much in common with those given on the Muslim side.[35] He tells us, as they do, of the various measures taken by Saladin to draw the Franks from their tight defensive formation: the apparent retreat towards Bethsan, the despatch of detachments to inflict damage on neighbouring Christian territory, the posting of troops all round the Christian position. William reports, too, that all attempts to provoke the Franks into offering battle were in vain, and that Saladin was obliged to withdraw his army from the kingdom with nothing of permanent importance accomplished.

There are, however, differences between the Christian and Muslim accounts of these events which are even more significant than the points of resemblance. As Saladin and his aides looked across at the defended Christian camp, from which no body of knights could be induced to come out and fight, they must have supposed that they were dealing with an enemy united in an inflexible resolve to present no more than a passive defence. William demonstrates the gulf between appearance and reality. The Christian ranks were riven by conflicting opinions.

Underlying the details of disagreement there was one root cause of division. To meet an invasion by patiently avoiding battle was likely to give rise to controversy. The Latin armies always included men, both among the leaders and the rank and file, who believed that military problems were best solved by

35   For that account, see WT, 22.26, 27, pp. 1118-1124.

carrying the attack to the enemy. To challenge him by all-out assault was the best way of preventing him from inflicting material damage through the agency of raiding parties and of driving him back into his own territory. The vigorous expression of such views by Gerard of Ridefort, Master of the Temple, both on May Day, 1187 and in the debates before Hattin two months later are among the best-known episodes in the history of the Latin kingdom.[36] To such men as Gerard, caution and restraint in the face of the enemy were simple cowardice. Such views were not exceptional. The whole history of warfare in the crusader states shows that leaders of recognized authority and established military reputation could encounter difficulty in restraining men under their command from premature and uncoordinated attacks against the enemy.[37]

In 1183 Guy of Lusignan, the newly-appointed regent, was at least nominally in command of the army. He was certainly not a leader of recognized authority and established military reputation. Because one so inexperienced in the affairs of the East had been given, without doing anything to deserve them, so many of its glittering prizes—a royal heiress, a major fief, the highest of offices, the prospect of a crown—there were many in the kingdom who wished him ill. Before 1183, however, he does not appear to have given his political enemies any opportunity to attack him openly; but in the campaign of that year he bore the full brunt of that criticism which was directed against the way in which the military operations had been conducted on the Frankish side. Inasmuch as the magnates allowed the hatred and resentment which they felt towards Guy to deprive him of that co-operation which, by reason of the oaths they had taken to him as regent, was his due, he was treated with monstrous unfairness;[38] but this was as nothing compared with the gross injustice meted out to him afterwards, both in his day and ours. His predicament in the campaign of 1183 may well do much to explain his fateful decision in that of 1187.

The Franks found difficulty in deciding how best to conduct the campaign of 1183. There were alternative courses of possible action, both of which could be supported and opposed by reasonable arguments. It was not always possible for the Franks to assemble a large army. In September 1183 the availability of pilgrims awaiting a return passage to the West and of the crews manning the

---

36   Prawer, *Histoire*, 1:645, 647-649; Runciman, *Crusades*, 2:453, 455-456.
37   Smail, *Crusading Warfare*, pp. 128-130.
38   WT, 22.27, pp. 1122-1123: "*Effusa est contentio super principes*... Nam qui negotia praesentia videbantur maxime promovere potuisse, ii, ut dicitur..., comitis Joppensis odio, cui regni curam nudiustertius rex commiserat, indigne ferentes, quod homini incognito, indiscreto et penitus inutili tantorum negotiorum summam in tantis periculis et tantae necessitatis articulo commisisset."

ships which were to carry them substantially reinforced the kingdom's normal forces. In this way the morale as well as the numbers of the army were raised, because the pilgrims included magnates of distinguished military reputation.[39] There were many to whom it made good sense to take advantage of these unusually favourable circumstances, which might not be quickly repeated, by launching a vigorous attack on the Muslims. This would presumably have obliged Saladin to call in the detachments which were inflicting such grave damage in the surrounding countryside. Victory in the field would have raised Frankish spirits; it might have eased some of their domestic problems; it might have deterred Saladin, at any rate for a time, from further invasions of the kingdom. On the other hand, the Franks well knew that the outcome of battle could never be certain. For them, military defeat could carry the gravest consequences, as events in 1187 were to show. Saladin, by contrast, had such resources and reserves at his disposal that he could quickly recover from a reverse in the field. He had shown this after he had been defeated in 1177, and was to do so again in 1191.[40]

There were always good arguments, therefore, why the Franks should avoid battle, especially if, by taking minimum risks, they could prevent the enemy from making permanent conquests and could secure his withdrawal to his own territory at the end of the campaigning season. All this was achieved in 1183. The objectives which mattered had been secured without the risks of battle, and from this point of view, however much men of spirit might chafe at the inaction, the campaign could be accounted a success.

Among writers in the fairly recent past this is the view taken, for example, by René Grousset and Sir Steven Runciman. In Grousset's view, Saladin in 1183 tried to provoke a Frankish attack, as he was to succeed in doing in 1187. On the earlier occasion, however, he failed; Grousset could describe the campaign of 1183 as "un Hattin qui a échoué."[41] Saladin was thwarted. To whom should the credit go on the Frankish side? Guy was regent and commanded the army; but Grousset regards the successful tactics adopted by the Franks as the work of the baronial magnates.[42] Runciman is even more explicit. "Guy hesitated and dithered; but Raymond and the Ibelins firmly insisted that to provoke a fight against such superior numbers would be fatal."[43]

39 WT, 22:27, p. 1122.
40 Smail, *Crusading Warfare*, pp. 136 n. 1, 165, 186.
41 Grousset, *Croisades*, 2:728.
42 Grousset, *Croisades*, 2:730: "...en se maintenant... dans une tactique purement défensive, Raymond III de Tripoli, les Ibelin et les autres barons avaient, avec un minimum de risques, délivré le royaume de la plus redoutable invasion qu'il ait jusque-là subie."
43 Runciman, *Crusades*, 2:439.

Agreement between historians of such eminence must carry great weight, yet their use of evidence seems open to question. Grousset cites a medieval source, but it records only that the barons took the lead in organizing the collection of provisions in the neighbourhood in order to relieve shortages which were causing hardship in the Christian camp.[44] Furthermore, the words which he quotes are taken from the French translation, made in the thirteenth century, of William of Tyre's *Historia*.[45] There is nothing about a baronial initiative in the original Latin text written by William himself. He refers to local officials responding to royal orders; and since the king was not present on the campaign, any order which can be termed "royal" can have come only from his deputy, who was his regent, Guy.[46] The only reference made by William to the magnates is to report the common belief that there was no attack on the enemy because of the hatred felt by those magnates towards Guy, and their wish to deny him any credit he might acquire by leading a successful action. In other words, the archbishop certainly tells us that the magnates disgracefully withheld from Guy the counsel and co-operation which they owed him by reason of the oaths they had sworn when he became regent. Whether his words also mean that the magnates formulated and executed a considered course of military action, as Grousset and Runciman would have us believe, seems much more doubtful. As to Guy's alleged dithering and hesitation, William says nothing about it, and the three other medieval sources cited by Sir Steven in support of his statement do not mention Guy at all.

Guy nominally commanded the Frankish army. Those historians just discussed allow that in 1183 the Franks achieved military success but deny credit to Guy. There were contemporaries, however, who believed that the Franks had failed, since they had not brought the Muslims to battle. For this failure they laid the blame squarely on Guy. King Baldwin was persuaded to take this view. "Rex... videns quod in supra dicto negotio apud fontem Tubaniacum comes Joppensis... minus strenue minusque prudenter se gesserat..."[47] So if the first injustice to Guy was the vassals' withholding of the counsel which they should have given him during the campaign, here is the second: by some he is denied the credit for success, as if he were not really the leader of the army at

---

44 Grousset, *Croisades*, 2:727. The words quoted by the author begin "Quant nostre baron virent..."
45 WT, 22.27, p. 1121.
46 WT, loc. cit.: "Mittuntur ergo legati ad urbes finitimas, qui earum praefectos pro mittendis cibariis sub omni celeritate sollicitent. Qui, debita diligentia, regiae parentes iussioni, certatim et sine dilatione, quanta possunt illuc dirigunt victualia."
47 WT, 22.29, p. 1127.

all; by others he was blamed for failure, as if he were solely responsible for the decisions taken.

Yet even if the available evidence is taken to mean that the baronial magnates were responsible for the decision to avoid battle with Saladin, the result was still injustice to Guy, because they allowed him to be blamed by those with whom that decision was unpopular. What is more, they took the lead in exacting penalties from Guy for his alleged incompetence. The king dismissed him from the office of regent and excluded him from the succession by arranging that Sybil's eight-year-old son Baldwin should forthwith be crowned to bear the royal title jointly with himself.[48] William of Tyre tells us that the elder Baldwin made these decisions by "taking sounder advice."[49] Whose advice? In a subsequent sentence the archbishop tells us that the coronation of the younger king was advised by a group which included Raymond, count of Tripoli, Rainald of Sidon, Baldwin of Ramla and Balian his brother. There could be no more striking illustration of the nature of politics in the Latin kingdom in the 1180s. They are sometimes represented as a conflict between, on the one hand, "the best element in the kingdom," led by "the gentleman and christian knight," and, on the other, "a group of upstart foreigners and court intriguers."[50] It seems easier to believe that two groups were in conflict which were equally uncompromising and equally hungry for power. Certainly in the months which followed the campaign of 1183 "the best element in the kingdom" were ruthless and unscrupulous enough to allow the career of one of whom they disapproved to be broken on account of decisions for which, as leading historians of our own day would have us believe, the magnates themselves were responsible. They used the opportunity to overthrow Guy and to replace him and his friends as the king's closest counsellors.

The penalties exacted from Guy were absurdly disproportionate to any fault which he might be held to have committed and were the third form of injustice to which he was subjected. Whoever commanded the army had needed to choose between alternative courses of possible action, each of which could be supported by sensible arguments. The course adopted had achieved the Franks' objectives; no one could be certain that the course rejected would have achieved them more effectively. The severest critics of the army's commander, and in the eyes of those critics that commander was Guy, could fairly accuse

---

48 On the measures taken against Guy, Prawer, *Histoire*, 1:624, 628-630; Runciman, *Crusades*, 2:439, 443.

49 WT, 22.29, p. 1127. "saniore usus consilio."

50 Baldwin, *Raymond III*, pp. 35, 57.

him of no more than an error of judgement. Yet he was treated as a guilty man whose failure was so extreme as to merit the most severe punishment. Not only was he dismissed from office and excluded from the succession, but an attempt was begun to dissolve his marriage to Sybil. At the time of the younger Baldwin's coronation, Guy was virtually expelled from the community of his feudal peers; when the vassals paid homage to the boy king, Guy was pointedly not required to join in doing so. Nor was this all. Baldwin IV authorized in his "will" that if both he and his nephew died, and the claims of Sybil to succeed were thus revived, those claims should be weighed against those of her half-sister Isabel by an *ad hoc* committee consisting of the pope, the western emperor and the kings of France and England.[51] The claims of Isabel to succeed had not been canvassed before; Sybil had always been regarded as the sole and undoubted heiress and it was for her that husbands had been sought in the West. It seems that the younger princess was brought into the reckoning as part of the attempt to exclude Sybil and Guy.

It is scarcely surprising that such frenzied and far-fetched attempts to ruin Guy should fail. When the two kings, the leper and the child, died in 1185 and 1186 respectively, the supporters of Sybil and Guy, first among whom was Joscelin of Edessa, had little difficulty in restoring the normal rules of succession and in securing their coronation. There was no popular movement in support of Baldwin IV's will and the western committee was never convened. A baronial plan to support Isabel's candidature by force collapsed literally overnight and, with two exceptions, the would-be rebels made their peace with the new king and queen. The exceptions were Baldwin of Ramla, who went into voluntary exile in the principality of Antioch, and Raymond of Tripoli, who withdrew to Tiberias, the capital of his principality of Galilee, and called on Saladin to send him Muslim reinforcements.

To recapitulate: Guy of Lusignan, as regent and the king's *alter ego*, had led the army of the kingdom from Saforie to make contact with Saladin's invading force west of Bethsan. Some contemporaries and some modern writers have concluded, for good reasons, that the Franks achieved military success by securing the withdrawal of the Muslims without serious loss, but some have given the credit for this success to the baronial magnates. Other contemporaries, less reasonably, rated the campaign as a failure, for which they blamed Guy and, as a consequence, they spared no effort in the months which followed to ruin Guy's career in the East and to exclude him from succession to the throne. The man who derived most benefit from Guy's fall was Count Raymond of

51 *Eracles*, p. 7.

Tripoli, who replaced him as regent and who, when Guy was crowned, went into a state of passive rebellion with Muslim support.

It seems scarcely possible that Guy's predicament when Saladin invaded the kingdom in 1187 should have been unaffected by his traumatic experiences of four years earlier. Once again he was in command of an army at Saforie which, as in 1183, some regarded as one of the largest forces assembled in the kingdom in recent years. Once again Saladin crossed the Jordan into Galilee, though on this occasion he attacked not Bethsan but Tiberias. How were the Franks to plan their campaign?[52] Guy was advised not only to attempt no attack on Saladin's army, but even to make no contact with it, and to stay in his base at Saforie sixteen miles away, and to allow the *caput honoris* of one of the great fiefs of the kingdom to be lost. As in 1183 there were excellent reasons for giving such advice. Any attempt to relieve the beleaguered citadel of Tiberias required a long march across waterless country, in midsummer heat, and in the teeth of Muslim resistance. To remain in Saforie, however, and to avoid contact with the Muslims, was a course of action similar to that for which Guy had been so savagely condemned in 1183, and the advice to pursue it was being given by the very man who had ousted Guy from office on that occasion and had since proved to be his inveterate enemy. Grousset believed that Guy, in rejecting Raymond's counsel, had taken leave of his senses; *quos vult perdere...*;[53] but Grousset, like Ernoul, his principal source, wrote with the benefit of hindsight. Is it so very surprising that Guy, without such benefit, finally decided not to be guided by Raymond, but listened instead to Gerard of Ridefort? The advice attributed to the Templar is sometimes represented as the product of his virulent hatred for Raymond; but, if the events of 1183-86 are called to mind, that advice was very much to the point:

> Sir, do you believe that traitor who has given you this advice? It is to shame you that he has given it. For it will be greatly to your shame and your disgrace if you, who have so recently been made king, and have as great an army as ever any king had in this land... if you allow a city only six leagues away to be lost. This is the first task which has fallen to you since you were crowned.[54]

---

52 Guy's predicament on that occasion is briefly discussed in Smail, *Crusading Warfare*, pp. 194-195.

53 Grousset, *Croisades*, 2:792.

54 *Eracles*, pp. 52-53. The translation, very slightly modified, is that of Baldwin, *Raymond III*, p. 113.

Like any other political figure, Guy of Lusignan had his enemies and detractors and, as much recent historical writing has shown, it will always be possible to make severely critical judgements on his career in the East. What is surprising is that there should only be hostile verdicts. General agreement on politics and politicians is not a common state of affairs. There are countless examples of men in public life who were subjects of controversy in their own day and have remained so in the debates of historians: Charles I and Cromwell, Napoleon, for and against, Gladstone and Disraeli, Roosevelt and Churchill.[55] Prawer has emphasized how Saladin had both his admirers and critics. In the propaganda disseminated on his behalf he was represented as the selfless champion of Islam, devoted to the destruction of the Franks; but to other contemporaries he was the ruthless politician who betrayed Nūr ad-Dīn, his patron and benefactor, and who built his fortune at the expense of that patron's family.[56] And among modern scholars Professor Ehrenkreutz has shown how it is still possible to interpret Saladin's character and achievement in terms very different from those used by Lane-Poole and Sir Hamilton Gibb.[57]

The same considerations could be applied to Raymond of Tripoli, about whom laudatory opinions, expressed in both the twelfth century and the twentieth, have already been quoted. As Professor Riley-Smith has remarked, Raymond "in recent years has had a good press."[58] There was much about his career to justify this, but equally there were flaws in that career which invited criticism in the twelfth century[59] and do so still. Although he may not have been involved personally, it has at least to be noticed that Raymond's first known political opponent, Miles of Plancy, was removed by murder.[60] In 1175

55   Pieter G.C. Geyl, *Napoleon, For and Against*, trans. O. Renier (London, 1949). The Hon. George Lyttleton, who had boyhood memories of Gladstone as a guest in his family home, remarks, in *The Lyttleton Hart-Davis Letters*, ed. Sir Rupert Hart-Davis, 1 (London, 1978), 201, on "the extraordinarily diverse views" on Gladstone, which were taken of him "throughout his long life, and (are) still rife half-a-century after his death." To some, "Mr. Gladstone was a hypocrite, a pompous, incoherent, hysterical gas-bag, a self-deceiver, a little Englander, a bore, a demagogue, an egoist." To others, he "was a far-sighted idealist, an unrivalled orator and debater, a man of burning sincerity and deep humility, magnanimous, courageous, a genius of finance, an indefatigable worker in great causes, living every moment of his life 'as ever in his Great Taskmaster's eye.'"

56   Prawer, *Histoire*, 1:540.

57   Andrew S. Ehrenkreutz, *Saladin* (New York, 1972).

58   Jonathan S.C. Riley-Smith, *The Feudal Nobility and the Kingdom of Jerusalem, 1174-1277* (London, 1973), p. 104.

59   Mayer, *Das Itinerarium peregrinorum*, Schriften der MGH 18 (Stuttgart, 1962), pp. 57, 256-257; Baldwin, *Raymond III*, p. 84, n. 35, 156-160.

60   Baldwin, *Raymond III*, p. 26.

he did not put pressure on Saladin when that leader's position was precarious.[61] Two years later he did not help the rulers of the kingdom to make the best use of the count of Flanders' presence in the Holy Land, but helped to draw that leader and his important following into a useless and ill-conducted expedition in northern Syria.[62] In 1180 he caused alarm and despondency in Jerusalem by appearing there with an armed force in the company of the prince of Antioch.[63] In 1183 he was the beneficiary of the unscrupulous means used to discredit Guy of Lusignan, and in the following year helped to engineer an exclusion crisis by changing the normal rules of succession.[64] In 1186 he showed unbelievable political ineptitude by allowing himself, immediately after the death of Baldwin V, to be outmanoeuvred by count Joscelin and to be kept away from Jerusalem.[65] When he heard that Sybil had been crowned, he was prepared to risk a civil war to secure the coronation of Isabel, but had so misjudged the mood of his political associates that the plan collapsed. He therefore found himself in a tiny minority which did not accept Guy and Sybil as king and queen, and did not hesitate to call on Saladin for help and to admit Muslim troops into Tiberias.[66]

Disagreement is still possible about the motives and abilities of Raymond of Tripoli, but there are few signs of differences of opinion about the career of Guy of Lusignan; judgements on his incompetence are commonplaces of historical writing. Yet in his own day he had supporters as well as opponents. There were those who approved of his appointment as regent in 1183, even though William of Tyre imputes to them unworthy motives.[67] The patriarch and the Masters of the Knights Templar and Hospitaller who interceded for him at the Council of Acre were not negligible friends,[68] and there was enough opinion in his favour in 1186 to secure his general acceptance as king of Jerusalem. He had virtues as well as defects, achievements as well as failures, as he showed before the walls of Acre and in the island of Cyprus. Modern scholarship should reflect that there is room now, as there was then, for more than one defensible view of Guy of Lusignan, just as Joshua Prawer has shown

---

61   Prawer, *Histoire*, 1:544.
62   Baldwin, *Raymond III*, pp. 32-33.
63   Ibid., p. 35.
64   Ibid., pp. 53-54, 57-59.
65   Ibid., p. 72.
66   Ibid., pp. 79-80, 82-83.
67   WT, 22.25, p. 1117.
68   Baldwin, *Raymond III*, p. 56.

that there is room for more than one such view about the activities beyond Jordan of Rainald of Châtillon.[69]

Certainly any verdict about Guy must take into account, first, the animosity against him displayed by those principal contemporary observers in the Latin kingdom whose historical writing has survived and who both sided with Guy's enemies; second, the unjust judgements and penalties to which he was subjected in 1183 and 1184; third, the extent to which those undoubted injustices may have affected his decision to march from Saforie to challenge Saladin in 1187.

---

69   Prawer, *Crusader Institutions,* pp. 480-481.

THE PATRIARCH ERACLIUS *

BENJAMIN Z. KEDAR

The Hebrew University of Jerusalem

Posterity has not been kind to Eraclius, the last Latin patriarch to reside in crusader Jerusalem. Thomas Fuller, in his *Historie of the Holy Warre* of 1639, called him "desperately vitious." In the *Dictionnaire historique et critique,* Pierre Bayle first presented him as "l'artisan de sa fortune," then adduced with obvious relish evidence for the "vie fort scandaleuse" he had led. François-Louis-Claude Marin, an adherent of the *philosophes* who in 1758 published a widely read *Histoire de Saladin*, denounced him as "l'infame Héraclius" and "le Prélat sacrilège." The climax came on April 14, 1783, with the patriarch ascending the Berlin stage as the compleat bigot in Lessing's *Nathan der Weise*; and as if this were not enough, it came to light with the publication of Lessing's private papers that the playwright once recorded his regret for having depicted the patriarch as far less of a villain than he had really been.[1]

Judgements passed by most modern historians on the patriarch have been hardly more reserved. Reinhold Röhricht regarded his election as patriarch an

* The present study, first discussed with Joshua Prawer and R.C. Smail in Jerusalem in 1971, assumed its final shape during a stay at the Institute for Advanced Study, Princeton, in 1981.

1   T. Fuller, *The Historie of the Holy Warre*, 4th ed. (Cambridge, 1651), p. 106; P. Bayle, *Dictionnaire historique et critique*, 3rd ed., 2 (Rotterdam, 1720), 1449, s.v. *Heraclius*; F.-L.-C. Marin, *Histoire de Saladin, sulthan d'Egypte et de Syrie*, 2 vols. (The Hague, 1758), 1:309, 2:4; *Nathan der Weise*, IV, 2. Lessing's expression of regret, appearing in *Gotthold Ephraim Lessings sämtliche Schriften*, ed. K. Lachmann and F. Muncker, 22.1 (Berlin and Leipzig, 1915), 114-115, is reproduced in Peter Demetz' fine volume on *Nathan der Weise* (Frankfurt/M, 1966), p. 178. Demetz documents also Lessing's utilization of the German translation of Marin's work.

"unheilvolle Wahl." For Gustave Schlumberger he was "de triste mémoire" and for René Grousset "un prélat indigne, sans coeur et sans énergie." Steven Runciman presented him as "a barely literate priest" and Jean Richard—in the original version of his masterful volume on the Kingdom of Jerusalem—as a cleric who was to dishonour the patriarchal throne by misconduct, cowardice and unfortunate participation in internal political struggles. Marshall W. Baldwin summarily dismissed him as "utterly worthless" and, as recently as 1967, Jonathan Riley-Smith referred to him as "the rascally Patriarch Heraclius of Jerusalem."[2] Wilhelm Hotzelt provided a dissenting if inaccurate sketch; but because his book was published in Cologne in 1940, and was therefore difficult to consult, that sketch for many years attracted little attention. It is only recently that the patriarch has become the subject of more balanced references and appraisals.[3]

The patriarch's age-old notoriety is almost exclusively based on his depiction in the chronicle of Ernoul, the one author who wrote about him at considerable length and was, one should hasten to add, a spokesman for a rival political faction. Ernoul's original work is not extant, but two adaptations, a longer and a shorter, survive.[4] The adaptations—both of which give the patriarch's name

2   R. Röhricht, *Geschichte des Königreichs Jerusalem, 1100-1291* (Innsbruck, 1898), p. 392; G. Schlumberger, *Renaud de Châtillon, prince d'Antioche, seigneur de la Terre d'Outrejourdain*, 3rd ed. (Paris, 1923), pp. 181, 265; R. Grousset, *Histoire des croisades et du royaume franc de Jerusalem*, 2 (Paris, 1935), 745 (also, 765, 787, 811); Runciman, *Crusades*, 2:425; Richard, *Royaume*, p. 95; M.W. Baldwin, "The Decline and Fall of Jerusalem, 1174-1189," in K.M. Setton, ed., *A History of the Crusades*, 1 (Philadelphia, 1955, 2nd ed. Madison, 1969), p. 597; J.S.C. Riley-Smith, *The Knights of St. John in Jerusalem and Cyprus, c. 1050-1310* (London, 1967), p. 81. The list may be easily prolonged.

3   W. Hotzelt, *Kirchengeschichte Palästinas im Zeitalter der Kreuzzüge, 1099-1291*, Kirchengeschichte Palästinas von der Urkirche bis zur Gegenwart, 3 (Cologne, 1940), pp. 131-139, 162-166; R.C. Schwinges, *Kreuzzugsideologie und Toleranz. Studien zu Wilhelm von Tyrus* (Stuttgart, 1977), p. 33; P.W. Edbury and J.G. Rowe, "William of Tyre and the Patriarchal Election of 1180," *English Historical Review* 93 (1978), 25; J. Richard, *The Latin Kingdom of Jerusalem*, trans. Janet Shirley (Amsterdam, 1979), p. 298, n. 2; and especially R. Hiestand, "Zum Leben und zur Laufbahn Wilhelms von Tyrus," *Deutsches Archiv* 34 (1978), 359-362 and B. Hamilton, *The Latin Church in the Crusader States: The Secular Church* (London, 1980), pp. 79-84. The judicious though inexact remark by J.L. La Monte, *Feudal Monarchy in the Latin Kingdom of Jerusalem, 1100-1291* (Cambridge, Mass., 1932), p. 34, n. 1, is also worth mentioning.

4   For the account of the patriarch's election and misconduct in the longer and shorter adaptations see *Eracles* 23.38-39, pp. 57-61 and Ernoul, pp. 82-87, respectively; the despatch of the True Cross is described in *Eracles* 23.29, p. 46 and Ernoul, pp. 155-156. For an attempt at delineating the relationship between the adaptations and the lost original see M.R. Morgan, *The Chronicle of Ernoul and the Continuations of William of Tyre* (Oxford, 1973), especially pp. 133-135.

as Eracle or Eracles—differ on several points. The longer first brings an account of Eracle's election as patriarch, an election which the God-fearing Archbishop William of Tyre attempted to prevent by reminding the canons of the Sepulchre of his misconduct and by adducing the minatory prophecy that an Eracles had brought the True Cross from Persia to Jerusalem and an Eracles was to carry it out of the city to its loss. Then it presents Eracle as a handsome, dissolute man of little learning, who became the favourite of the queen-mother and owed her his successive appointments as archdeacon of Jerusalem, archbishop of Caesarea and, finally, patriarch of Jerusalem. The shorter adaptation, in which the sequence of events is more coherent, starts by presenting Eracle as a native of the Auvergne who came to the East as a poor clerk; nothing is said about his little learning, the queen-mother's infatuation with him is described in somewhat less explicit terms and William of Tyre is portrayed as opposing his election solely on the basis of the prophecy about the two Eraclii.[5] The longer adaptation goes on to dwell on Pasque de Riveri, the mercer's wife from Nablus who became the patriarch's mistress; to repeat that William of Tyre, knowing about Eracle's misconduct, attempted to prevent his election; and to relate that the patriarch excommunicated William on Mount Zion on a Maundy Thursday. William appealed to Rome asking that Eracle be summoned before Pope Alexander at the council then to be convened, set out for Rome, but was poisoned on Eracle's orders. Eracle himself sailed in the meantime to Marseilles, continued to his native Gévaudan and returned to Jerusalem only upon learning about William's death. In the shorter adaptation, William refuses to pledge allegiance to Patriarch Eracle and appeals to Rome in an attempt to procure his deposition: the excommunication, the

---

The shorter adaptation is quite lapidary in its description of the Forbelet campaign of 1182 (Ernoul, p. 61) despite the fact, recorded by William, that Baldwin of Ramla and Balian of Ibelin excelled on it: WT 22.16, p. 1094. The Jezreel campaign of October 1183, on the other hand, is described with many a vivid detail and an accent on the deeds of Baldwin and Balian: Ernoul, pp. 98-102. It is therefore plausible to assume that Ernoul entered Balian's service at some point between the two campaigns.

For a discussion of Ernoul's partisanship see the article of R.C. Smail in this volume, pp. 162 ff. above.

5   In their detailed comparison of the accounts of the patriarchal election, Edbury and Rowe ("William of Tyre," p. 8) maintain that in the longer adaptation William assumes that the canons will postulate only one name for royal assent, while in the shorter adaptation his assumption is that they will postulate two. It should be noted, however, that in the longer adaptation William warns of the damage to ensue from the "nomeement de mei ou de l'arcevesque de Cesaire Eracle" (*Eracles* 23.38, pp. 57-58, MS D)—which seems to be short-hand for "a nomination (by the canons) out of which either I or Eraclius are to emerge victorious," as it is hardly conceivable that William cautioned against his own nomination.

pope's name, the impending council, all go unmentioned, but William is depicted as having been received in Rome with great honour and as having almost secured the deposition. Eracle goes to Rome — not Gévaudan — only after William had died there by poison and only upon his return does he become Pasque de Riveri's lover. While the longer adaptation relates that as the patriarch, the king and the magnates of the realm were once discussing matters of state in the patriarchal palace, a servant burst in and, to the patriarch's embarrassment, announced that Dame Pasque had given birth to a daughter, the shorter adaptation transposes the scene to the more spectacular setting of a council of war, with the uncalled-for messenger explicitly referring to Pasque as to the patriarch's wife. Again, while the longer adaptation states disapprovingly that in 1187 the patriarch excused himself from bringing the True Cross to the army assembled at Saforie, the shorter version, once more using a cruder brush, adds that he was unwilling to part with Dame Pasque. Finally, the shorter adaptation formulates more sharply, and at greater length, the assertion that Eracle's misconduct, and the sins of the clergy who were following his example, brought on the downfall of Jerusalem. (This formulation reached a considerable audience, as Jacques Bongars reproduced it in the preface to the pioneering collection of crusader chronicles he published in Hanau in 1611.)[6]

It is noteworthy that, in utilizing these repeatedly and not uni-directionally diverging adaptations of Ernoul's work, historians have exhibited a tendency to opt at every juncture for the alternative least complimentary to the patriarch's reputation, as if in response to some variety of Gresham's Law. (The prophecy linking the patriarch to Emperor Heraclius of Byzantium, which appears in both adaptations, seems to have influenced, along with humanist norms, the modern spelling of the patriarch's name: at any rate, the overwhelming majority of contemporary historians render it as *Heraclius* despite the fact that the patriarch's seals and letters invariably have *Eraclius*.) Yet the patriarch's portrayal in the Ernoul adaptations should be treated with considerable reserve. The assertion of the longer version that Eraclius — as we now should call him — *po savoit de letres*, is invalidated by a letter of Étienne of Tournai, the decretist and theologian, which indicates that Étienne and Erac-

---

6   J. Bongars, *Gesta Dei per Francos* (Hanau, 1611), praefatio, p. C (2); quoted by Bayle, *Dictionnaire*, p. 1450.

7   J. Desilve, ed., *Lettres d'Étienne de Tournai* (Valenciennes and Paris, 1893), no. 78, pp. 92-93 (more readily accessible in PL 211:355, no. 63); RRH no. 455. Étienne's letter, long known to historians of the University of Bologna, was noted but not commented on by R. Röhricht, "Syria sacra," *ZDPV* 10 (1887), 12, n. 14. The letter was utilized by Edbury, Rowe and Hiestand (all in n. 3 above) and, indirectly, by Hotzelt, *Kirchengeschichte*, p. 132.

lius had studied together at the nascent University of Bologna, and by a document of 1168 from Jerusalem in which Eraclius appears as a *magister*.[7] In the twelfth as in any later century, attendance at a university did not vouchsafe intellectual eminence, but a Bologna-trained master of the 1160's could not have been, comparatively speaking, a man of little learning, much less a barely literate one. Thus the one statement about Eraclius in the Ernoul adaptations which can be independently checked, points to a defamatory intent.

What about the other assertions? More than two decades ago, Hans Eberhard Mayer argued persuasively that the story about William's excommunication and death by poisoning must have been invented by Ernoul.[8] Indeed, even without Mayer's demonstration that William exercised his archiepiscopal office not long before October 17, 1186 and Rudolf Hiestand's recent discovery that he must have died on September 29 of that year,[9] excommunication and poisoning should have appeared suspicious in face of the absolute silence of well-informed contemporary European writers who dwell, however, on less spectacular events in the history of the Crusading Kingdom. Further, once the relevant evidence is examined in its entirety, there remains little sinister about the fact that Eraclius did not take the True Cross to the Battle of Ḥaṭṭīn, although another supporter of the rival faction, the anonymous author of the *Libellus de expugnatione Terre Sancte*, also criticized him severely on this account.[10] Fulcher of Chartres and William of Tyre mention between them eighteen instances from the years 1101-1179 in which the Cross was carried into a battle or siege: only in eight of these do the chroniclers specify that it was accompanied by a patriarch, in six it was attended by another prelate, while in four the identity of the escorting cleric is not stated.[11] Eraclius, who in 1182 was

8 H.E. Mayer, "Zum Tode Wilhelms von Tyrus," *Archiv für Diplomatik* 5/6 (1959/60), 182-201.

9 Hiestand, "Zum Leben," pp. 351-353. Hamilton errs in writing (*Latin Church*, p. 81) that Hiestand has shown that William died in Rome; also, Hamilton accepts Hiestand's dating apparently without realizing that it hinges on Mayer's argument based on the evidence of the *Inventaire Raybaud*, evidence that Hamilton, however, rejects.

10 *De expugnatione Terrae Sanctae libellus*, ed. J. Stevenson, RS 66 (London, 1875) [hereafter cited as *Libellus*], p. 219; on the author's support for Raymond of Tripoli see Prawer, *Histoire* 1:63-64. Hotzelt errs in writing that the *Libellus* claims that Eraclius did not carry the Cross "weil er des Augenlichtes beraubt gewesen sei" (*Kirchengeschichte*, p. 137): it states that he omitted doing so "quoniam lumen oculorum *cordis* jamdudum amiserat."

11 Fulcher of Chartres, *Historia Hierosolymitana*, ed. H. Hagenmeyer (Heidelberg, 1913), pp. 411, 453, 495, 625, 639-641, 648, 665, 736, 746; WT 11.3, 12.12, 12.14, 12.21, 14.26, 16.8, 16.11, 17.2, 17.21, 18.21, 20.19, 20.26, 20.27, 21.22, 21.28, pp. 455, 528, 533, 544, 647, 716, 723, 760, 795, 856, 974, 992, 993, 1042, 1054. In 1177 Patriarch Amalric of Nesle may have been too old to accompany the Cross to the crucial battle of Montgisard; but also at the Battle of Puthaha which Baldwin III waged shortly after Amalric's accession in 1158, the Cross was attended by Archbishop Peter of Tyre rather than by the patriarch. Normally,

with the Cross in the army assembled at the Fountains of Saforie on the eve of the Battle of Forbelet, who somewhat later went with the Cross on a deep raid into southern Syria and in 1183 accompanied it to La Fève in the Valley of Jezreel, and gave the sacrament to the large army which held Saladin in check there, thus followed numerous precedents when in 1187 he had the Cross carried into battle by Bishop Bernard of Lydda — whom he had appointed his vicar in Jerusalem when he left for Europe in 1184 — and Bishop Rufinus of Acre.[12] (It may be noted in passing that William of Tyre, unlike Fulcher of Chartres or Peter, an earlier archbishop of Tyre, is not known to have ever been in battle.)[13]

There remain the assertions that Eraclius led a dissolute life, owed his career to the queen-mother's favour and kept a mercer's wife for mistress, assertions which, however, did not receive much publicity in his own lifetime. An earlier patriarch of Jerusalem, Arnulf, in 1116 had to defend himself at the papal court against the charge that he had maintained relations with the wife of one Girardus as well as with a Saracen, who was said to have borne him a son;[14] Eraclius, on the other hand, is described as a *vir sanctus et prudens* by Peter of Blois, a *vir sanctus* by Gerald of Wales, as *vitae sanctitate non inferior* by Herbert of Bosham, with Rigord relating that in 1185 he was received in Paris "as if he were an angel of the Lord." Even Ralph Niger, a critic of "concubinarian" clerics in general, who was scandalized by Eraclius' ostentatious display of riches during his mission to Europe, knows nothing about his alleged

however, it was the patriarch who was expected to carry the Cross *in expeditionem*: *Cartulaire de l'Église du Saint-Sépulcre de Jérusalem*, ed. E. de Rozière (Paris, 1849), no. 167, p. 302 (a. 1169); no. 166, p. 297 (a. 1170); *Codice diplomatico Barlettano*, ed. S. Santeramo, 1 (Barletta, 1924), no. 6, p. 21 (a. 1182) [=RRH nos. 469, 474, 616]. Ernoul's remark that in 1187 Guy called on Eraclius to bring the Cross to the army and that Eraclius excused himself (see n. 4 above), points to the same conclusion.

12   WT 22.15, p. 1092 (Fountains of Saforie), 22.20, p. 1103 (raid), Ernoul, pp. 98-99 (La Fève in 1183; see also p. 101, where the chronicler points out that the news of the birth of Pasque's daughter was brought to Eraclius during a council held on that campaign). William of Tyre mentions the presence of the Cross but not of the patriarch on the 1183 campaign: WT 22.26, p. 1119. In face of the insistence of the shorter adaptation on Eraclius' presence there, and of William's mention of his presence on earlier occasions, the omission is probably meaningless. It allows the hypothesis, however, that Eraclius might have been present also on one or both of the subsequent occasions in which William mentions the presence of the Cross but not the name of the accompanying cleric: WT 22.22, 30, pp. 1108, 1130. On Bernard of Lydda as Eraclius' vicar see RRH no. 637a.

Contrary to Bernard Hamilton's assertion (*Latin Church*, p. 129), Amalric of Nesle was present on at least two campaigns: WT 20.19, 27, pp. 974, 993.

13   Fulcher, *Historia* (see n. 11 above), pp. 357-359, 416; WT 18.21, p. 856; cf. Hamilton, *Latin Church*, p. 131.

14   PL 163:410.

transgressions in the sexual sphere.[15] But even if Eraclius were indeed a "ver-liebter Pfaffe"—the expression is Hans Prutz's[16]—his conduct would not have been wholly exceptional for his time. The Second Lateran Council of 1139 and the Synod of Rheims of 1148 dealt with *bishops* and priests who had entered upon illicit matrimonial unions. Ralph of Domfront, patriarch of Antioch in the years 1135-1140, was accused of incontinence and the conduct of his succes-sor, Aimery of Limoges (1140-1193) may have also left something to be desired, since William of Tyre describes him as *conversationis non satis hones-tae*. The Third Lateran Council, in which both William and Eraclius took part, dealt with clerics in holy orders who kept "their little women" (*mulierculas suas*) in their houses—it is noteworthy in this context that the shorter adapta-tion of Ernoul emphasizes that Eraclius kept Dame Pasque in view of all, "fors tant qu'ele ne manoit mie aveuc li"—and priestly homosexuality, concubinage and marriage were matters of constant concern for the papacy throughout the century.[17] Moreover, the very requirement of clerical continence is reported to have been questioned by leading theologians of Eraclius' day. Gerald of Wales relates that he had heard Peter Comestor (d. c. 1180) publicly teach that the Devil had never deceived the Church so sorely as in the introduction of the vow of continence, and Robert de Courson reports that Peter the Chanter (d. 1197) used to call for the convocation of a general council at which that vow was to be revoked. (Robert does not spell out, though, which ranks within holy orders were to be affected by the proposed ruling.) The Chanter's followers expressed similar views until the issue was resolved by the stringent legislation of the Fourth Lateran Council.[18]

15   Peter of Blois, *Passio Reginaldi principis olim Antiocheni*, PL 207:966; Giraldus Cambrensis, *Expugnatio Hibernica* 2.27, ed. and trans. A.B. Scott and F.X. Martin (Dublin, 1978) [hereaf-ter cited as Giraldus, *Expugnatio*], p. 204; Herbert of Bosham, *Vita S. Thomae*, ed. J.C. Robertson in *Materials for the History of Thomas Becket*, RS 67.3 (London, 1877), 514; Rigord, *Gesta Philippi Augusti*, RHGF 17:14; Radulfus Niger, *De re militari vel triplici via peregrinationis Ierosolimitane* 3.65, 83, ed. L. Schmugge, Beiträge zur Geschichte und Quel-lenkunde des Mittelalters 6 (Berlin and New York, 1977), pp. 186-187, 193-194.

16   *Kulturgeschichte der Kreuzzüge* (Berlin, 1883), p. 127.

17   Concilium Lateranense II, c. 7 in Mansi, *Concilia* 21:527-528; Concilium Remense (a. 1148), c. 7, ibid., col. 715; WT 15.16,18, pp. 684, 688; Concilium Lateranense III, c. 11 in Mansi, *Concilia* 22:224. For general surveys see H.C. Lea, *An Historical Sketch of Sacerdotal Celi-bacy in the Christian Church*, 2nd ed. (Boston, 1884), pp. 313-326; G. Denzler, *Das Papstum und der Amtszölibat*, 1: *Die Zeit bis zur Reformation* (Stuttgart, 1973), pp. 87-95.

18   Cf. Lea, *Sketch*, pp. 325-326; J.W. Baldwin, "A Campaign to Reduce Clerical Celibacy at the Turn of the Twelfth and Thirteenth Centuries," in *Études d'histoire de droit canonique dédiées à Gabriel Le Bras*, 2 (Paris, 1965), pp. 1041-1053; Id., *Masters, Princes and Merchants. The Social Views of Peter the Chanter and his Circle*, 2 vols. (Princeton, 1970), 1:337-341. Gerald of Wales's statements appear in the *Gemma Ecclesiastica*, ed. J.S. Brewer in *Giraldi Cambren-sis Opera*, RS 21 (1861-1891), 2:187-188; Robert of Courson's *questio* has been edited by Baldwin, "A Campaign," p. 1052; Id., *Masters*, 2:231-232.

Despite Ernoul's unmistakable animosity toward Eraclius, he may be depended upon as far as details neutral to his intent are concerned. One such detail is Eraclius' place of birth. The shorter adaptation relates that he was born in the Auvergne; the longer is more specific and presents Gévaudan, in the southern part of that region, as his native land. His name, probably going back to the saintly bishop of Sens who might have been present at Clovis' baptism, was uncommon but not entirely unknown: one Eraclius was bishop of Tarbes between 1056 and 1065, another was archbishop of Lyons between 1153 and 1163 and the name recurred also in the family of the viscounts of Polignac, just north of Le Puy.[19] As unusual naming is more frequently encountered along the upper rungs of society, Eraclius' name may imply an origin of some standing. His easy student-day cameraderie with Étienne of Tournai suggests that they were of roughly the same age; and Étienne was born on February 18, 1128.[20]

Étienne's writings offer a few glimpses of the student life he shared at Bologna with Eraclius, the future cardinal Gratian, the future archdeacon of Lisieux and Ely, Richard Barre, and probably also with Uberto Crivelli, the future Pope Urban III.[21] It may have been at a farewell party like the one given to Richard Barre that Étienne read the rather puerile poem, occasionally verging on the burlesque, about the offerings the divinities of ancient mythology brought to a newborn son of Jupiter and Juno and about the branches of learning to which the infant was introduced. Law does not figure among them because, as Étienne puts it, distinctions between thieves who act openly and those who act in secret are not needed in Heaven, nor is usury known there.[22] It is an amusing example of in-group jesting about the subjects which the would-be poet and his companions were then studying. The same atmosphere is conjured up in the letter Étienne was to send Eraclius in the late 1170's. Here he mentions with ostensible regret those jocose conversations of old, when they referred to pleadings in the lawcourts as items of merchandise, to litigants' contentions as a battle of the blind, to the lecture-rooms of the Bolognese masters as artificers' workshops. (One is inclined to believe that the lively Étienne, who even as a septuagenarian Bishop of Tournai composed a quatrain

---

19 PL 159:958; RHGF 12:347A, 14:466D, 467C, 468D, 16:690C. The name is consistently spelled *Eraclius*.

20 For the date see J. Warichez, *Étienne de Tournai et son temps, 1128-1203* (Tournai and Paris, 1937), p. 2.

21 Desilve, ed., *Lettres*, nos. 44 (Gratian), 136 (Urban III), 275 (Richard Barre), pp. 57, 159-160, 346-347.

22 L. Auvray, ed., "Un poème rythmique et une lettre d'Étienne de Tournai," in *Mélanges Paul Fabre. Études d'histoire du moyen âge* (Paris, 1902), p. 290, lines 177-180.

which a scandalized biographer in the twentieth century thought sufficiently risqué to be relegated to a footnote,[23] coined most of these irreverencies, but Eraclius may have had a share.) Then, Étienne continues, they followed different inclinations, with him taking to the wagonmaker's workshop of Bulgarus—the noted Bolognese teacher of civil law—which he had formerly ridiculed, and Eraclius directing his steps to the Calvary of the Crucified.[24]

On the basis of this passage, Johann Friedrich von Schulte wrote that Étienne appears to have engaged in advocacy at Bologna.[25] If his reasoning were cogent, it would have applied to Eraclius as well; however, it is possible to poke fun at advocates without being one in person. Selmar Scheler and Rudolf Hiestand, on the other hand, deduced from the same passage that Eraclius was a student of theology.[26] *Studium calvarie Crucifixi* may indeed be so interpreted, but the subsequent sentence—"Blessed be your pilgrimage, which both atones for sins and uplifts you to heights"—suggests rather that Étienne had in mind Eraclius' departure for the Holy Land. However, if Eraclius really went on to study theology, he would have probably done so outside Bologna: Rolando Bandinelli, the future Pope Alexander III, taught theology at Bologna in the early 1140's, but the subject does not seem to have been pursued there later in the century.[27]

---

23   Warichez, *Étienne de Tournai*, p. 139, note.

24   "Iocosas olim confabulationes nostras fructuosis oro sepius orationibus expiari. Togatorum advocationes mercimonia, litigantium conflictus cecorum pugnam, Bononiensium auditoria fabriles diximus officinas. Inter hec, diversa sequti studia sumus; ego, quod irriseram, carpentariam Bulgari, vos calvariam Crucifixi. Beata peregrinatio vestra, que et culpas expiat et ad sublimia vos extollit. Interim, pater, obsecro, mementote Stephani vestri, qui sic memoriam vestram retinet, ut quasi iugi spectaculo vestram presentiam amplectatur." Desilve, ed., *Lettres*, no. 78, pp. 92-93. The letter must have been written after Étienne's election as abbot of Sainte-Geneviève in 1176 and before he received news of Eraclius' election as patriarch in 1180.

    As R.B.C. Huygens has already noticed, William of Tyre, too, refers to the *auditoria* of the Bolognese masters: "Guillaume de Tyr étudiant: Un chapitre (XIX, 12) de son *Histoire* retrouvé," *Latomus* 21 (1962), 823 with apparatus. The masters may have consciously revived the name given to the Higher School of Constantinople after its reorganization in 425, a name they must have encountered in C. 11.19.1.

25   J.F. von Schulte, *Die Summa des Stephanus Tornacensis über das Decretum Gratiani* (Giessen, 1891), p. xxiii: also, *Histoire littéraire de la France* 15 (Paris, 1820), p. 526.

26   S. Scheler, *Sitten und Bildung der französischen Geistlichkeit nach den Briefen Stephans von Tournai* (✝1203) (Berlin, 1915), p. 8; Hiestand, "Zum Leben," p. 360. Sarti and Fattorini mention Eraclius among the canonists: M. Sarti and M. Fattorini, *De claris archigymnasii Bononiensis professoribus a saeculo XI usque ad saeculum XIV*, ed. C. Albicinius and C. Malagola, 1 (Bologna, 1888-1896), 365-366.

27   F. Ehrle, *I più antichi statuti della Facoltà teologica dell' Università di Bologna. Contributo alla storia della scolastica medievale* (Bologna, 1932), pp. lxviii-lxix.

The years which Étienne spent in Bologna remain unknown. Joseph Warichez assumed that he studied there between 1145 and 1150, but the assumption, though repeated in the literature, is not supported by facts. Von Schulte reasoned from the biographies of Étienne's better-known fellow students that he must have been there in the 1150's, perhaps in the early 1160's.[28] The period during which Eraclius studied at Bologna, mentioned only in Étienne's letter, can be circumscribed only by the same vague limits.

The year is 1168 and the place Jerusalem when Eraclius makes his next appearance in the sources. From now on his doings are documented in considerable detail. In 1168 he witnessed two patriarchal deeds as *magister* Eraclius (it is noteworthy that another *magister*, Stephanus, was a further witness). In 1169 he was archdeacon of Jerusalem: in this capacity he succeeded in 1171 in mediating an agreement between Bishop Bernard of Lydda and Peter, prior of the Holy Sepulchre, but, more important, failed in 1172 in persuading Alexander III to comply with the wishes of Patriarch Amalric and King Amalric of Jerusalem and to reinstate Gilbert d'Assailly as Master of the Hospital. The pope pointed out in his decision, however, that Eraclius had pressed his case *sollicite et prudenter*.[29] In 1175 he was archbishop of Caesarea, one of the four metropolitan sees of the realm.[30]

The pace of Eraclius' preferment, though rapid by Palestinian standards — Abbot Bernard of Mt. Tabor, who became bishop of Lydda in 1168, died in that office in 1190 — appears less extraordinary when compared with the careers of some of his near-contemporaries at Bologna. Étienne of Tournai was elected in 1167 abbot of Saint-Euverte at Orléans, in 1176 of Sainte-Geneviève-de-Paris. Richard Barre went to the papal curia on delicate missions on behalf of Henry II both before and after the murder of Thomas Becket and by 1173 served as seal-bearer and chancellor to young king Henry.[31] Gratian, in 1168

---

28 Warichez, *Étienne de Tournai*, p. 17 (and, less definitely, p. 20); Ph. Delhaye, "Morale et droit canonique dans la 'Summa' d'Étienne de Tournai," *Studia Gratiana* 1 (1953), 438; J.A. Corbett, "Stephen of Tournai," in *The New Catholic Encyclopedia* 13 (New York, 1967), 701. — Schulte, *Die Summa*, p. xxiii.

29 RRH nos. 455, 456, 469, 492, 528; Delaville, *Cartulaire*, no. 434 (faultily summarized in RRH no. 492a). Eraclius is probably also the archdeacon of Jerusalem who, according to a fragmentarily preserved Hospitaller account, at an earlier stage backed Gilbert's request that the patriarch allow him to resign: Delaville, *Cartulaire*, no. 403, p. 277.

30 WT 21.10, p. 1021. RRH nos. 458b and 539 are the only extant acts in which Eraclius appears as archbishop of Caesarea.

31 *Gesta regis Henrici secundi*, ed. W. Stubbs, RS 49 (London, 1867) [hereafter cited as *Gesta*], 1:19-21, 43; Roger Howden, *Chronica*, ed. W. Stubbs, RS 51 (London, 1868-1871) [hereafter cited as Howden], 2:25-26, 46; Matthew Paris, *Chronica Majora*, ed. H.R. Luard, RS 57 (London, 1872-1883), 2:249.

subdeacon and notary of the Roman church—it was in that capacity that he drew up in 1172 Alexander III's negative though complimentary answer to Eraclius' pleading on behalf of Gilbert d'Assailly[32]—became in 1178 a cardinal-deacon. In the Kingdom of Jerusalem, Eraclius' preferment was closely parallelled by that of William of Tyre—archdeacon of Tyre in 1167, chancellor of the realm in 1174, archbishop of Tyre in 1175—whose studies in Europe are however far better documented.

In October 1178 Archbishop Eraclius set out for the Third Lateran Council, along with William of Tyre and six other prelates from Outremer.[33] Their performance at the council was far from impressive. The times boded ill for the Crusading Kingdom, hedged in as it now was between Saladin's possessions to the east and the west; but the eight prelates did not induce the council to issue a call for a new crusade, or at least to constrain to go east those who had already taken the cross. One suspects that they devoted their energy to ensure the adoption of canon 9 of that council, which defended episcopal authority against Templar and Hospitaller encroachments, and possibly also of canon 24, which prohibited naval assistance and the export of contraband to the Saracens.[34] More than a century ago, Hermann Reuter advanced the hypothesis that the ultramarine prelates did not press the cause of the crusade as they were elated by Baldwin IV's great victory over Saladin at Montgisard in 1177,[35] and it is indeed possible that contemporaries perceived that battle as reflecting the true military balance between the two sides rather than as a skillful exploitation of singularly propitious circumstances. Whatever the explanation, the prelates evidently exhibited shortsightedness. Eraclius shared their failure: even more so William of Tyre, who, on his own evidence, played an important role at the council and, in his *Historia*, presented the victory at Montgisard as miraculous and humanly undeserved.[36]

In October 1180 Eraclius became patriarch of Jerusalem. William of Tyre, who habitually dwells on the virtues and shortcomings of earlier incumbents, reports the elevation of Eraclius without wasting a word about his qualities—the only hint that William might have had reservations about the new patriarch. The adaptations of Ernoul relate, however, at considerable length that William strongly opposed Eraclius' candidacy, attempted to dissuade the

---

32 Delaville, *Cartulaire*, no. 434, p. 301.
33 WT 21.26, p. 1049.
34 Mansi, *Concilia* 22: 222, 230.
35 H. Reuter, *Geschichte Alexanders des Dritten und der Kirche seiner Zeit*, 3 (Leipzig, 1864), 424, 589.
36 WT 21.24, 26, pp. 1046-1047, 1051.

canons of the Holy Sepulchre from naming him in the election, proposed that they search for a candidate abroad, and was finally nominated himself alongside Eraclius, with King Baldwin IV bowing to the requests of the queen-mother and choosing Eraclius.[37] Peter Edbury and John Rowe have recently shown that the custom of dual postulation, recorded at this occasion for the first time, was roundly condemned by Pope Celestine III in the bull *Cum terra, que* of 1191, which made its way into the Decretals. The two authors suppose that the custom, which testifies to an increased royal control of the Church, arose during the 1180's out of the precedent of Eraclius' election.[38] The custom rejected by Celestine III applied however not only to patriarchal elections but to *alicuius prelati electio*, with the electoral bodies secretly postulating two persons *auribus patriarche vel principis*; in other words, it was a custom prevailing throughout the crusader East, reflecting not only temporal power over the church but, in the first place, a patriarchal curtailment of the *libertas* of local ecclesiastical bodies. It is hardly conceivable that so far-reaching an innovation could have become normative during the few, convulsive years separating Eraclius' election in October 1180 from the promulgation of Celestine's bull of 1191. Indeed, Celestine himself refers to the custom as having arisen *olim*, an expression hardly appropriate if it had emerged as recently as the 1180's.[39] It is plausible, therefore, to assume that the custom was introduced well before 1180 — probably, as Edbury and Rowe suggest, in imitation of Byzantine practice[40] — and that Eraclius was elected according to conventional though uncanonical practice. It is possible that William appealed to the papal court. The shorter adaptation of Ernoul says that he did so, though William himself, in his *Historia*, is silent on the matter. There was good precedent for such action. The archbishop of Caesarea and the bishop of Bethlehem had appealed to Rome in 1158, when it was said that the predecessor of Eraclius, Amalric of Nesle, had been elected through the intervention of the queen-mother of that time, Meli-

---

37   WT 22.4, p. 1068; *Eracles* 23.38, pp. 57-59; Ernoul, pp. 82-84.

38   X 1.6.14, to be read with the address, *arenga* and date discovered by W. Holtzmann, "La 'Collectio Seguntina' et les décrétales de Clément III et de Célestine III," *Revue d'histoire ecclésiastique* 50 (1955), 430; Edbury and Rowe, "William of Tyre," pp. 12-13, 19, 23. It should be noted that Paul Riant, though of course unaware of the *Collectio Seguntina*, understood that *Cum terra, que* dealt with crusader custom: *Haymari Monachi De Expugnata Accone liber tetrastichus*, ed. P. Riant (Lyons, 1866), pp. xxxviii-xl. Riant assumed, however, that the account of the 1180 election in the adaptations of Ernoul referred in reality to the later election of Monachus: *ibid.*, p. xxxix, n. 1.

39   Also, Hugh I of Cyprus and Innocent III refer in 1213 to the custom as to an *antiqua consuetudo*: PL 216: 733, 735. See also the argument of Hiestand, "Zum Leben," p. 350, n. 24.

40   Edbury and Rowe, "William of Tyre," pp. 19-20.

sende — whose *capellanus familiaris* he had been — and the support of Countesses Odierna of Tripoli and Sybil of Flanders, Melisende's sister and stepdaughter, respectively.[41] The appeal of 1158 was rejected and so was that, if it was ever made, of 1180.

As patriarch, Eraclius exhibited considerable skill and flexibility. In 1181 he headed a delegation to Antioch which worked out a compromise between Prince Bohemond III and Patriarch Aimery, deliberately leaving unresolved the most delicate issue, that of Bohemond's irregular marriage.[42] Eraclius displayed similar pragmatism in the case of the fragment of the True Cross which Patriarch Fulcher (d. 1157) had sent to Europe to serve as a proxy sanctuary for Christians unable to make the pilgrimage to the Sepulchre itself. The relic was forcibly seized while under way, with the connivance, so it would seem, of Duke Conrad II of Dachau, and the canons of the Sepulchre had been unable to recover it. During a pilgrimage to Jerusalem, Conrad III of Dachau begged Eraclius to allow him to possess the relic and the patriarch acquiesced, imposing on the duke, however, the responsibility of recovering other appropriated possessions of the Sepulchre.[43] He also successfully defended the archbishopric of Tyre against the claims of the patriarch of Antioch, repeatedly fending off attempts by Pope Lucius III to settle the issue, and thus preserved the status quo favourable to himself as well as to William of Tyre.[44] The relatively well preserved acts of St. Mary in the Valley of Josaphat disclose that Eraclius succeeded in settling two disputes concerning that abbey, in 1183 acting at the behest of Lucius III, in 1186 acting on his own.[45] In his dealings with the Jacobites Eraclius attempted to take advantage of an internal struggle in order to bring about their submission to Rome. Michael the Syrian, Jacobite patriarch of Antioch, denounces his rival, Theodore bar Wahbūn, for offering "the patriarch of the Franks of Jerusalem" to make the Jacobites obedient to Rome

41 WT 18.20, p. 854, gives a faulty reading. The full text, as transmitted by Vat. lat. 2002 (s. XIII), is brought by R.B.C. Huygens, "La tradition manuscrite de Guillaume de Tyr," *Studi medievali* 3.5 (1964), 302.

42 WT 22.7, pp. 1073-1074; cf. Hamilton, *Latin Church*, pp. 46-47.

43 Eraclius' letter to Conrad III, complete with its seal, is preserved in Munich, Allgemeines Staatsarchiv, KU Scheyern no. 10; facsimile in *Monumenta Boica* 10 (Munich, 1768), Plate 13 *in fine*; printed in *Chronicon Schirense*, ed. G.C. Joannes (Strasbourg, 1716), pp. 93-94. On the seal see H.E. Mayer, *Das Siegelwesen in den Kreuzfahrerstaaten*, Abhandlungen der Bayerischen Akademie der Wissenschaften. Philosophisch-Historische Klasse, NF 83 (Munich, 1978), p. 34, n. 112 and Plate 1.1,2. For the story of the relic, now at Scheyern, see M. Knitl, *Scheyern als Burg und Kloster. Ein Beitrag zur Geschichte des Hauses Scheyern-Wittelsbach sowie zur Geschichte des Benediktiner-Ordens* (Freising, 1880), pp. 64-69.

44 PL 214:466; cf. Hiestand, "Zum Leben," pp. 377-379.

45 RRH nos. 631, 657b. Eraclius probably had also a hand in the accord attained in 1185 between the bishop of Winchester and the Hospitallers: RRH no. 641a.

if he were helped in his bid to become the head of the Jacobite church, and adds that the patriarch gave him his support. Michael reports also that Theodore offered the patriarch 1,000 dinars for the Jacobite convent of Mary Magdalene in Jerusalem.[46] However, as Michael goes on to say that Theodore's proposal necessitated the despatch of messengers to Jerusalem, it transpires that Eraclius continued to maintain contacts with the patriarch in power. The convent seems to have remained under the control of Michael's men; at any rate, when the gates of Jerusalem were shut by Eraclius' faction during the controversial coronation of 1186, it was the abbot of *la Madeleine des Jacopins de Jerusalem* who opened a postern to let in a spy for the rival faction.[47] Eraclius' attempt at bringing about Jacobite submission to Rome, probably influenced by the success of Patriarch Aimery of Antioch in securing about 1182 the communion with the Maronites, thus appears to have remained within the bounds of tentative scheming.

Eraclius seems also to have displayed some of the skill in fiscal matters which he was to put to use after the capitulation of Jerusalem. In any case, in 1183 he and William of Tyre were appointed custodians of the prospective proceeds of the general tax then imposed on the kingdom, with the first supervising the collection in Jerusalem and the second in Acre: the appointments, in contrast with the account in the adaptations of Ernoul, presuppose a working relationship between the two. The structure of the tax decree of 1183 closely resembles the English and French orders of 1166, which established a levy for the relief of the Crusading Kingdom, and it is possible that Eraclius, who in 1166 might have still been in Europe, was one of the men to make the council in Jerusalem familiar with the English or French taxation schemes.[48] It is even more probable that the sudden appearance of the base unit of one hundred in the French and English tax ordinances of 1185 resulted from Eraclius' presence at the meeting between Louis VII and Henry II at which they were decided upon, as

---

46 *Chronique de Michel le Syrien, patriarche jacobite d'Antioche (1166-1199)*, ed. and trans. J.-B. Chabot, 3 (Paris, 1905), 386-387. Cf. P. Kawerau, *Die jakobitische Kirche im Zeitalter der syrischen Renaissance. Idee und Wirklichkeit* (Berlin, 1955), p. 59; Hamilton, *Latin Church*, p. 198. As Theodore's dealings with Eraclius took place in the days of Athanasius, Jacobite archbishop of Jerusalem from 1185 onward, it follows that the affair occurred after Eraclius' return from the West.

47 *Eracles*, pp. 27-28, MS D. On the Jacobite complex dedicated to Mary Magdalene see Prawer, *Latin Kingdom*, p. 228.

48 WT 22.23, pp. 1110-1112; cf. B.Z. Kedar, "The General Tax of 1183 in the Crusading Kingdom of Jerusalem: Innovation or Adaptation?" *English Historical Review* 89 (1974), 339-345. The argument that, in this tax decree, *civitas* means "town" rather than "diocese," is enhanced by the phrase *de universis civitatibus et castellis quae rex in praesentiarum possidebat*, which appears somewhat later in the chronicle: WT 22.25, p. 1116.

that unit, hitherto rare in the West, recurs several times in the Jerusalemite decree of 1183.[49]

In the internal struggles which convulsed the Crusading Kingdom from the closing years of Baldwin IV onwards, Eraclius initially appears as a decided supporter of Guy of Lusignan. He is mentioned, together with the queen-mother and unspecified nobles, as present at — and, one may assume, influential in bringing about — Guy's appointment as *bailli* early in 1183; in October 1183 he was with Guy on the inconclusive campaign in the Jezreel Valley; when, at the end of that year, Baldwin fell out with Guy and ordered Eraclius to initiate proceedings for Guy's divorce from his sister Sybil, the patriarch, or so William's account seems to indicate, did not concur and possibly even alerted Guy to remove Sybil from Jerusalem. At the general council subsequently convened at Acre to discuss the despatch of emissaries to the West, Eraclius, backed by the masters of the two military orders, interrupted the proceedings and besought Baldwin on bended knee to receive Guy back into his favour; when the three went unheeded, they left council and town in ire. (William of Tyre, who criticizes Eraclius for having left Acre "with untempered emotion" after failing in being "immediately" listened to, implies that a more patient approach might have borne fruit.)[50]

During the next year and a half Eraclius followed, however, a distinctly different course. At an unspecified moment in early 1184, probably some time after the appointment of Raymond of Tripoli as *bailli* with which William of Tyre's chronicle abruptly ends, it was decided to send Eraclius and the masters of the military orders on the mission to the West which had been on the agenda of the Acre council. Had the three attained their aims, the political fabric of the kingdom would have been radically altered and the ambitions of Guy and other local aspirants to the throne effectively undercut.

The three envoys sailed for Italy in the spring or early summer of 1184. For Eraclius it was the third crossing in twelve years, a crossing which, unlike those of 1172 and 1178, placed him for several months at the centre of European attention. As head and spokesman of the delegation he pleaded the cause of the endangered kingdom before Lucius III and Frederick I at Verona in November 1184, before Philip II Augustus in Paris in January 1185 and before Henry II in England from February to April 1185, and the sight of a patriarch of Jerusalem traversing the continent from Brindisi to Reading, imploring help, offering the

---

49 The point has been made by F.A. Cazel Jr., "The Tax of 1185 in Aid of the Holy Land," *Speculum* 30 (1955), 387, 391-392.

50 WT 22.25, p. 1116 (Guy's appointment); Ernoul, pp. 98-99, 101 (Jezreel Valley campaign). WT 23.1, p. 1133 (separation attempt and intervention at Acre.)

keys of the Sepulchre and preaching the cross had a considerable impact. Very little is heard of Eraclius' fellow envoys, especially after the death of the Templar master in Verona: it is the patriarch whom one chronicler after another mentions, rendering his mission one of the best recorded events of crusader history.[51] (The adaptations of Ernoul, on the other hand, ignore the mission altogether—a further measure of Ernoul's partiality.)

Eraclius' main purpose was to persuade a European ruler to accept the lordship over the Crusading Kingdom. Who empowered him to pursue this goal? Though he was in contact with Baldwin IV, reporting to him upon having landed in Brindisi and receiving in return an account of Saladin's summer campaign of 1184, and though the king seems to have made or acquiesced in a similar attempt two years earlier,[52] available evidence indicates that he did not make the proposals in the king's name. In the letter to Henry II which Eraclius conveyed to England and which may be taken to sum up the deliberations held at Verona, Lucius III writes that the Holy Land is lacking the protection of a king and its *proceres* had set their only hope on Henry's patronage. Gerald of Wales, who wrote on the mission within four years of the events, relates that Eraclius made his offer on behalf of the *primi* of Palestine, the Templars and the Hospitallers, and in accordance with the unanimous wish and approval of all clergy and people. And the anonymous chronicler of Laon reports that the patriarch offered the diadem of Jerusalem to many rulers, carrying with him letters patent in which Palestine's *principes* ratified in advance whatever settlement he was to arrive at.[53] In light of these sources, and

---

51   For a detailed description of the mission, based on most of the sources, see A. Cartellieri, *Philip II August, König von Frankreich*, 2 (Leipzig and Paris, 1906), 18-25; for Eraclius' itinerary in England see R.W. Eyton, *Court, Household and Itinerary of King Henry II* (London, 1878), pp. 261-264, to which should be added that, according to an inscription destroyed in 1695, Eraclius consecrated the Temple Church of London on February 10, 1185, and granted an indulgence of 60 days to those visiting the church yearly: *Royal Commission on Historical Monuments (England.) An Inventory of the Historical Monuments in London*, 4: *The City* (London, 1929), p. 137. For a survey of earlier missions see R.C. Smail, "Latin Syria and the West, 1149-1187," *Transactions of the Royal Historical Society* 5.19 (1969), 1-20.

52   Baldwin's letter—probably a mere fragment—appears in Ralph of Diceto, *Ymagines historiarum*, ed. W. Stubbs, RS 68.2 (London, 1876), pp. 27-28. The attempt of 1182 is mentioned in *Sigeberti continuatio Aquicinctina*, ed. L.C. Bethmann (1844), MGH SS 6:420; *Annales de Theokesberia*, ed. R.H. Luard in *Annales Monastici*, RS 36 (London, 1864-69), 1:52. Cf. Cartellieri, *Philip II August* 2:13; H.E. Mayer, "Kaiserrecht und Heiliges Land," in H. Fuhrmann, H.E. Mayer and K. Wriedt, eds., *Aus Reichsgeschichte und Nordischer Geschichte. Karl Jordan zum 65. Geburtstag* (Stuttgart, 1972), p. 202.

53   For Lucius' letter see, for instance, Howden 2:300-301; Giraldus, *Expugnatio*, 2.26, p. 200; *Chronicon universale anonymi Laudunensis*, ed. A. Cartellieri and W. Stechele (Leipzig and Paris, 1909), pp. 35-36 (more readily available in the partial edition of G. Waitz [1882], MGH SS 26:450).

especially of the papal letter, one may discard Roger of Howden's assertion that Baldwin and the *principes*, or Baldwin and the military orders, sent Eraclius on his mission, and assume instead that the envoys were empowered by an otherwise unknown council of early 1184, which despaired of Baldwin IV and V, Guy and Raymond alike.[54] The Templars and the Hospitallers, who had been involved in similar initiatives in 1181 and 1182,[55] were probably conspicuous among the supporters of the new departure, but it was Eraclius—evidently neither a diehard supporter of Guy nor a subservient tool of the "court party" —who became its main protagonist.

Of the many references to Eraclius' mission, a few shed some light on his personality. His sense for the dramatic, already exhibited while pleading on bended knee before Baldwin IV at Acre, finds further manifestation when he prostrates himself at Henry II's feet and entreats him in tears to come in person to the rescue of the Holy Land. The retort he made to Henry's offer of money—"we seek a man who stands in need of money, not money that needs a man"—attests to some rhetorical capacity. He seems to have had no compunction about placing himself at centre stage: Herbert of Bosham relates that when, during his stay in England, conversation turned to Thomas Becket, Eraclius asseverated that he knew in Jerusalem about Becket's martyrdom within fifteen days of the event and that he spread the news throughout the realm, having learned about it through a cenobite's vision. The strain of irascibility, revealed in his rash departure from the Acre council, reappears when he reacts to Henry's definite refusal by harshly rebuking him "while many stood by and listened." Gerald of Wales, who describes this scene in a work completed before Henry's death, adds in a later treatise that in a subsequently held private audience Eraclius went so far as to accuse Henry to his face of having murdered Becket: when the enraged king gave him his customary stare, Erac-

---

Hans Eberhard Mayer has ingeniously suggested that William of Tyre, in a last-second addition to the *Historia*, intended to warn Eraclius against basing his offer on the conception that the Kingdom of Jerusalem was a fief depending on its patriarch: Mayer, *Bistümer*, pp. 25-28. In fact, Eraclius is not known to have used this argument; in England, he stressed the blood ties with the Angevins.

54 *Gesta* 1:331; Howden 2:299. Mayer, "Kaiserrecht," p. 203, suggests that the mission may have been decided upon at the council which appointed Raymond as regent. However, in his account of that council William of Tyre does not mention the mission and presents Raymond's appointment as the "unica et singularis salutis via." Also, as William mentions that the king was present at the council, it would follow that the envoys acted on his behalf, too—a conclusion which may be rejected on the basis of Lucius' letter.

55 For the letter of Alexander III which *Templarii et Hospitalares Jerusalem* conveyed to the kings of England and France see *Gesta* 1:272-274, Howden 2:255-258. For the initiative of 1182 see note 52 above.

lius bent his neck and dared him to cut off his head. The gesture is in character, though the ensuing dialogue is probably either embellished or imaginary.[56] (Little affection seems to have been lost between the two, with the king sarcastically commenting, in response to Gerald's plea on the patriarch's behalf, on clerics who can afford to call him boldly forth to battles, knowing well that they are not going to sustain a blow in them.)[57] A further trait emerges from Ralph Niger's bitter lines about the jingling of the patriarch's gold and silver furnishings, the fragrance spreading from his garments and the extravagance of his moveable chapel.[58]

After a final meeting with the kings of England and France at Vaudreuil on May 1, 1185, where he received more promises of money and men, Eraclius hastened home, "greatly dismayed," writes Roger of Howden, "at having achieved so little."[59] As in 1172, when his mission was to Alexander III, he gained respect for his pleading, but dismally failed in attaining his objective. Skirting the Curia on his return voyage so as to avoid the showdown planned by Lucius III on the conflicting claims of the patriarchates of Jerusalem and Antioch, Eraclius arrived in Jerusalem before August 1, 1185.[60] His political influence reached its nadir: with Baldwin IV having finally succumbed to his illness some time before May 16, 1185,[61] the country was ruled by Raymond of Tripoli, regent for Baldwin V and opponent of Guy of Lusignan. Even the minor successes Eraclius had been able to achieve in Europe turned out to be hollow: when the English and French who took the cross under the impact of his preaching arrived in Jerusalem after Easter 1186 and learned that a long-term truce with Saladin was in effect, most of them promptly returned to

56 *Gesta* 1:335, Howden 2:299, Giraldus, *Expugnatio* 2.26, p. 200 (prostration); Giraldus, *Expugnatio* 2.27, pp. 202-204 (retort and rebuke); Herbert of Bosham, *Vita S. Thomae* (see n. 15 above), pp. 514-516; Giraldus, *De principis instructione* 2.28, ed. G.F. Warner, RS 67.8 (London, 1891), p. 211 (accusation of murder).

57 *De principis instructione* 2.26, p. 207.

58 See n. 15 above. Ralph Niger's description may be compared with that of Dame Pasque's garments in the adaptations of Ernoul.

59 *Gesta* 1:338, Howden 2:304.

60 The date of arrival in Jerusalem is given in *Gesta* 1:341, Howden 2:307. As Eraclius neither sent a written statement on the Jerusalem-Antioch issue nor returned to the Curia on his way back from France, Lucius III, some time before his death on November 25, 1185, set a new date for the proceedings, but Eraclius chose to ignore it: PL 214:466.

61 The traditionally adduced date of his death, March 16, is unfounded: Röhricht, *Geschichte*, p. 415, n. 2. Baldwin V's earliest charter extant dates from May 16: RRH no. 643. Rudolf Hiestand has promised to prove that Baldwin IV died on April 15, 1185: "Zum Leben," p. 374.

Europe.[62] Eraclius' own activities during Raymond's regency remain unknown, but they seem to have been in a minor key. His support for Theodore bar Wahbūn probably began in this period and he may also have wrestled with the issue of Genoese privileges, for in two letters of March 13, 1186, Pope Urban III — still another fellow student of Étienne of Tournai — ordered him, first, to urge Baldwin V and Raymond of Tripoli to give back the Genoese their possessions and, second, to make the canons of the Sepulchre set up again in their church the inscription which recorded, in letters of gold, the rights enjoyed by the Genoese in the kingdom.[63]

After Baldwin V's death in the summer of 1186,[64] Eraclius returned once more to the centre of the stage. His role in the proceedings leading to Guy of Lusignan's coronation was probably more complex than might appear from the adaptations of Ernoul, hitherto considered the main source for this event. The chronology of the relevant part of the adaptations is questionable. While William of Tyre, recording the events shortly after their occurrence, gives November 20, 1183 as the date of Baldwin V's coronation and places Raymond's appointment as *bailli* at some later point, and while Baldwin IV's letter to Eraclius leaves no doubt that he was still alive in mid-September 1184, the adaptations claim that the coronation took place *after* Raymond had accepted, on his own terms, the regency, and that Baldwin IV died a short time after the coronation.[65] The adaptations describe at considerable length the succession arrangements which were to come into force after the death of Baldwin IV, but in that description the possibility is not mentioned that, should the mission of Eraclius to the West prove successful, a European ruler might become king of Jerusalem. This omission casts doubt on the accuracy and comprehensiveness

---

62   *Die lateinische Fortsetzung Wilhelms von Tyrus*, 1.9, ed. Marianne Salloch (Leipzig, 1934) [hereafter cited as *Fortsetzung*], pp. 63-64; *Gesta* 1:359, Howden 2:316. Howden's assertion that Guy was king when the crusaders arrived may be discarded.

63   *Codice diplomatico della Repubblica di Genova dal MCLXIII al MCLXXXX*, ed. C. Imperiale di Sant'Angelo 2 (Rome, 1938), nos. 157, 160, pp. 301, 303-304. For a recent discussion of the background see H.E. Mayer and Marie-Luise Favreau, "Das Diplom Balduins I für Genua und Genuas Goldene Inschrift in der Grabeskirche," *Quellen und Forschungen aus italienischen Archiven und Bibliotheken* 55/56 (1976), 22-95 (but the original of Alexander III's letter to Amalric [p. 27, n. 15] can be consulted in Genoa's Biblioteca Universitaria, Manoscritti, scatola D.VIII.1, no. 5).

64   The exact date is unknown. Remnants of his funerary monument have been recently discovered and described by Zehava Jacoby, "The Tomb of Baldwin V, King of Jerusalem (1185-1186) and the Workshop of the Temple Area," *Gesta* 18 (1979), 3-14.

65   WT 22.29, 23.1, pp. 1128, 1134; Baldwin's letter: n. 52 above; *Eracles* 23.4-5, pp. 6-9, Ernoul, pp. 115-119. Runciman, *Crusades* 2:443, n. 2, notes the discrepancy but, believing that William wrote his last pages in Rome, prefers the account of the adaptations.

of the narrative to be found in the adaptations.[66] The subsequent account that the patriarch crowned Sybil, let her place another crown on Guy's head and then anointed him, arouses similar doubts, as it makes Eraclius break with coronation custom without any compelling motive. It has been suggested that owing to Guy's unpopularity Eraclius was unwilling himself to place the crown on his head;[67] but to have Sybil do so and to anoint Guy with his own hands immediately afterwards could not—and indeed did not—effectively obscure Eraclius' responsibility for the coronation, yet added still another irregularity to an already highly unorthodox ceremony. Furthermore, Eraclius' open-ended call on Sybil, "Dame, vouz estes fame, il covient que vouz aies avec vos qui vostre roiaume vos aide a governer, qui masle soit; prenez ceste corone, si la dones a tel home, qui vostre roiaume puisse governer,"[68] would have been, under the circumstances spelled out by the adaptations, an empty charade, as Sybil could have crowned only her husband, the spectacle of a queen crowning a regent yet remaining married to another man being inconceivable.

The clue to the understanding of the rather puzzling moves described in the adaptations may be found in two independent accounts of the coronation written by chroniclers who arrived in the Crusading Kingdom less than five years after the event: Guy de Bazoches who landed near Acre in July 1190 and Roger of Howden who came east with King Richard about ten months later.[69] Their accounts, like that of the adaptations, are marred by factual mistakes; however, the two were in a position to get the inside story of the 1186 ceremony from Guy of Lusignan's followers, with whom they shared camp during the siege of Acre, whereas the adaptations present the essentially outsider view of the barons who at the time of the coronation were assembled at Nablus. Now,

---

66   As Baldwin IV died before May 16, 1185, he must have made the succession arrangements at a time at which Eraclius' fiasco in the West could by no means have been known in Jerusalem. Indeed, Arnold of Lübeck, whose account conflicts with that of the adaptations on numerous points—and who presents Eraclius as recommending Baldwin V's coronation and as agreeing to Raymond's regency—has Raymond assert that he accepts the guardianship of Baldwin V "nisi forte rex Anglie vel per se, vel per filium suum huic regno subvenire voluisset." Arnold of Lübeck, *Chronica Slavorum*, ed. I.M. Lappenberg (1869), MGH SS 21:166.

67   H.E. Mayer, "Das Pontifikale von Tyrus und die Krönung der lateinischen Könige von Jerusalem," *Dumbarton Oaks Papers* 21 (1967), 158. For the Sicilian parallels of 1130 and 1151, in which a layman imposed the crown and a cleric performed the anointment, see C. Brühl, "Kronen- und Krönungsbrauch im frühen und hohen Mittelalter," *Historische Zeitschrift* 234 (1982), 5.

68   *Eracles* 23.17, p. 29, MS D; cf. Ernoul, p. 134.

69   On Guy's arrival see *Liber epistularum Guidonis de Basochiis*, ep. 35, ed. H. Adolfsson, Acta Universitatis Stockholmiensis. Studia Latina Stockholmiensia 18 (Stockholm, 1969), pp. 152-154 and Röhricht, *Geschichte*, p. 522, n. 8; on Roger see Doris M. Stenton, "Roger of Howden and *Benedict*," *English Historical Review* 68 (1953), 574-582.

both Bazoches and Howden relate that before her coronation Sybil was urged upon to divorce Guy and marry an abler or nobler man.[70] The verisimilitude of this account is considerable. A generation earlier, Eraclius' predecessor Amalric — whom William of Tyre writes off as "practically useless" — crowned Sybil's father, Amalric, only after having made him consent to the annulment of his marriage to Sybil's mother;[71] it is conceivable that, in the far more unsettled circumstances of 1186, assent to Sybil's coronation was made dependent on her divorce from Guy. (A similar situation was to recur after Sybil's death in 1190.) Perhaps it was believed in Jerusalem that a divorce, or its mere discussion, might break the ranks of the barons assembled at Nablus; again, some of the supporters of Sybil's claims who convened in Jerusalem might have considered Guy unacceptable. The "court party," which most modern historians credit — or rather debit — with the coronation of 1186, must not have been of a single cloth.

Bazoches goes on to assert that Sybil, though granted permission to part with Guy and recommended to marry a more capable man, retorted that she could confer the crown only on her husband, "and thus, by the wish and decision of his most faithful spouse, Count Guy of Jaffa was crowned with her as king." The anonymous crusader who wrote his versified chronicle in the camp before Acre between October 1189 and July 1190, echoes this assertion:

Namque videbatur absurdum spernere sponsum,
Quem sibi legitime junxerat ipsa fides.[72]

70 *Ex Guidonis de Bazochiis Crono graphie libro septimo. Letzter Teil bis zum Schluss (1199) für akademische Übungen*, ed. A. Cartellieri and W. Fricke (Jena, 1910), p. 2. As this edition is difficult to consult, I bring here the relevant passage, transcribed from the unique manuscript, BN lat. 4998, fol. 63vb: "Quarto quippe Balduino Iherosolimorum rege defuncto, soror eius comitissa Iopensis, ad quam moderamina regni redierant, cum ei persuasum esset atque concessum, ut Guidonem de Lizinnon, militem strenuum satis et nobilem, quia regio culmine minor et nomine videretur, proprium dimitteret et novum aliquem potentie maioris admitteret, virum quem Deus ei coniunxerat separare (MS: sperare) se nolle respondit, quia non liceret ei, quam debebat ferre, conferre coronam alteri, quam cui promiserat fidem, et corporis commiserat proprii potestatem. Igitur pro voluntate iudicioque fidelissime coniugis sue cum eadem in regem coronato comite Iopensi Guidone..." The passage appears, with several changes, in the *Chronica Albrici monachi Trium Fontium*, ed. P. Scheffer-Boichorst (1874), MGH SS 23:859.
   Roger of Howden's account, originally appearing in *Gesta* 1:358-359, is repeated with several changes in Howden 2:315-316; *Fortsetzung* 1.10, pp. 64-65; Roger of Wendower, *Flores Historiarum*, ed. H.G. Hewlett, RS 84.1 (London, 1886), 138-139. For a similar but apparently independent account see Robert de Clari, *La Conquête de Constantinople*, 33, ed. Ph. Lauer (Paris, 1924), p. 35.
71 WT 19.4, pp. 888-889; for Patriarch Amalric's characterization see WT 18.20, 22.4, pp. 854, 1068.
72 H. Prutz, ed., "Ein zeitgenössisches Gedicht auf die Belagerung Accons," *Forschungen zur deutschen Geschichte* 21 (1881), 458, lines 41-42.

Howden goes one step further and relates that Sybil actually assented to the divorce on the condition that she might freely choose her next husband and, once crowned, chose Guy *in regem et maritum.* At first sight, the scene appears far-fetched — until one realizes how well it explains the above-quoted, hitherto unintelligible call which, according to the adaptations, Eraclius made on Sybil during the coronation ceremony. It would seem that Ernoul, through genuine misunderstanding or inattention, once more omitted an element vital to his account.

Eraclius' reasoning can only be guessed at. Having recently conferred in person with Frederick I, Philip II and Henry II, he must have had ample grounds for believing that if these three and Pope Urban III were allowed to decide between the claims of Sybil and her sister Isabel, in accordance with the succession arrangements made while he was out of the country, then the kingdom would be left for an indefinite period in the hands of Raymond of Tripoli, a situation which Eraclius was evidently unwilling to contemplate. His earlier endeavour to import a European ruler and make Jerusalem directly dependent on a European power having failed, he may have decided to support Guy as the best of the local candidates and used the divorce scheme merely as a device to outmanoeuvre Guy's opponents who, as the adaptations reveal, expected at the crucial moment solely the coronation of Sybil; on the other hand, Eraclius may have seriously considered, at some early stage, Sybil's remarriage. In any case, when he made his call on Sybil in the Church of the Holy Sepulchre, many in the audience could not have known upon whom her choice was to fall — and this effective deception, as well as the subsequent coronation of Guy by Sybil which was noted even by a Muslim chronicler,[73] probably appealed also to his sense of drama.

On October 21, 1186, Eraclius was with King Guy in Acre and witnessed there three royal charters, in telling contrast to his absence from similar functions during Raymond's regency.[74] In April 1187, aiming at a reconciliation with Raymond, Guy and Eraclius sent envoys to Tiberias. A Genoese, writing in the thirteenth century, believed that the patriarch led this delegation, as he had that sent to Antioch in 1181. In fact Eraclius did not accompany this ultimately successful mission,[75] neither did he, some two months later, go with

---

73 Ibn al-Athīr in RHC HOr. 4:674. Other contemporary sources, too, do not warrant the presentation of Sybil as a tool of the "court party."

74 RRH nos. 653-655.

75 *Libellus,* p. 211; *Regni Iherosolimitani brevis historia,* in *Annali Genovesi di Caffaro e de' suoi continuatori,* 1, ed. L.T. Belgrano (Genoa, 1890), p. 138. See also Abū'l Fidā' in RHC HOr. 1:56. For the envoys' names see *Eracles* 23.25, pp. 36-37; Ernoul, p. 143; also, *Libellus,* p. 217.

the True Cross to Saforie but had it carried, as already mentioned, by the bishops of Lydda and Acre. So it came about that after the catastrophe at Ḥaṭṭīn he found himself in charge of Jerusalem.

Eraclius decided to resist Saladin to the best of his ability. When Balian (Barisan) of Ibelin, a supporter of Raymond, arrived under Saladin's safe-conduct to fetch his family to Tripoli, Eraclius, eager to place the defense of Jerusalem in the hands of an experienced warrior, absolved him from the oath that he had sworn to Saladin to stay in the city for just one night. Moreover, although Queen Sybil was still in town, he acceded to Balian's demand to be recognized as lord of Jerusalem and receive homage and fealty. In order to save the city, Eraclius was evidently willing to accept a political solution still more radical than the one he had propagated during his European mission three years earlier. He gave his full support to Balian, to the point that he had the silver coverings of the edicule of the Sepulchre dismantled and their metal used to strike the coins with which the city's defenders were daily paid.[76] (As Joshua Prawer has surmised, these are probably the crusader coins which, devoid of a king's name, bear silent testimony to Balian's ambition.)[77] When on September 4, 1187, Saladin offered generous terms to a delegation from Jerusalem, the envoys, doubtless on instructions from Eraclius and Balian, refused to surrender the city.[78] And in a recently discovered letter written a few days before Saladin invested Jerusalem on September 20, Eraclius implored Pope Urban III to send immediate help, for otherwise Jerusalem and Tyre would fall within less than six months. The letter brims with hyperbole — the "pitiable patriarch" addresses "the supreme pontiff and universal pope" and, characteristically, falls at his feet in tears — but it forcefully conveys the urgency of the situation, with the inhabitants of Jerusalem no longer able to move freely outside the walls and with the arrival of Saladin daily expected. Significantly, Eraclius presents the capture of the True Cross and the defeat of the army as due to unaccounted-for divine wrath, not as a punishment for Christian sins.[79]

---

76 Ernoul, pp. 174-176; *Eracles*, p. 68, MS G; pp. 70-71, MSS C and D. The MSS on which the bold-lettered version is based (23.46, pp. 68-71) dispense with mentioning Balian's oath and its revocation by Eraclius: *Eracles* 23.46, pp. 68-71. (In 1758 Marin will rebuke Eraclius for this act: *Histoire de Saladin* 2:51. Marin is also indignant at the "paroles insensées" with which Eraclius dared to address Henry II — and believes that the bishops of Lydda and Acre who carried the True Cross to Ḥaṭṭīn were offspring of Eraclius' incestuous liaison with Pasque de Riveri: ibid., 1:340-341, 2:4.)

77 Prawer, *Histoire* 1:673, n. 60.

78 *Eracles*, 23.52-53, pp. 79-81; Ernoul, pp. 185-186.

79 A fragment of this letter appears in *Chronica Fuldensis. Die Darmstädter Fragmente der Fuldaer Chronik*, ed. W. Heinemeyer (Cologne and Vienna, 1976), pp. 87-91. For the full text, edited from Clm 28195 (s. XII-XIII), fol. 48va-49ra, see B.Z. Kedar, "Ein Hilferuf aus Jerusalem vom September 1187," *Deutsches Archiv* 38 (1982), 112-122.

During the thirteen days of the ensuing siege, Eraclius went on buttressing the resistance. An anonymous defender attests that after the enemy had breached the wall, he heard with his own ears a herald announce that the patriarch and other magnates promised to pay 5,000 besants, and distribute arms, to 50 sergeants willing to guard the breach for one night, yet even this lavish offer failed to procure fifty defenders.[80] With Saladin's final assault imminent, the remaining burghers, knights and sergeants decided on a suicidal night sortie, preferring — in the language of the adaptations — honourable death in battle to disgraceful slaughter within the walls. At this critical juncture, Eraclius mobilized his considerable expertise in pleading to dissuade the Jerusalemites from taking this desperate step. Wisely starting by praising the plan on principle, he is said to have advised against its adoption in the prevailing circumstances, stressing the Christian duty of his listeners towards their kinsfolk and astutely avoiding all reference to their self-preservation. If the men were to fall in battle, he argued, their women and children would be forced by the victorious Saracens to apostatize from Christianity and thus, by attaining for themselves salvation on the battlefield, the men would allow the women and children to lose their souls. Therefore he advised them to negotiate for an evacuation. The patriarch's opinion carried the day and Balian was despatched to make terms with Saladin.[81] René Grousset — ironically enough, in 1935 — sternly rebuked Eraclius for this display of "defeatism" and went on to evoke with sorrow the memory of anterior patriarchs, "défenseurs de la cité et animateurs de la Vertu franque";[82] a less *gloire*-thirsty observer may conclude that but for Eraclius the number of sanguinary pages in the annals of the crusades might have been still larger than it already is.

The adaptations of Ernoul insist that when the ransom dues were agreed upon after considerable haggling, Eraclius and Balian threw all their weight into ensuring the safe departure of as many as possible of those citizens of Jerusalem who could not afford to pay. First they persuaded the Hospitallers to place at their disposal the treasure sent by Henry II and earmarked its 30,000

---

80   *Libellus*, p. 245. According to the longer adaptation, a sergeant guarding the breach was paid one besant per day and one besant per night: *Eracles* 23.56, p. 85. The problematic letter of an otherwise unknown Bishop William has the following story: "Die vero septima ceperunt turrim novam, quam construxerant fratres Hospitalis, et intraverunt eam cum tribus signis. Quod cernens patriarcha accepta cruce domini promisit multa munera, quicumque eam liberaret, nec est inventus, qui se tali opponeret periculo, nisi Swevus quidam miles, qui superne remuneratione gratia diu serviverat infirmis. Hic constanter ascendens turrim tribus occisis liberavit eam." *Epistola episcopi Wilhelmi de excidio terre Jehrosolimitane*, ed. R. Röhricht, in his *Beiträge zur Geschichte der Kreuzzüge* 1 (Berlin, 1874), 191.

81   *Eracles* 23.56, p. 86; Ernoul, pp. 214-215.

82   Grousset, *Histoire* 2:811.

besants for the ransom of 7,000 of the poor. Then they appointed two men in each street to have every resident declare his wealth on oath, to determine the number of those in need of aid and to take from those to be ransomed with the help of King Henry's gold all money in excess of the sum necessary to reach Christian-held territory. Through this ingenious scheme, the surplus taken from the 7,000 who were to be redeemed by English money could serve to buy freedom for others who could not have afforded the payment due. Subsequently Eraclius and Balian appealed to the Templars, Hospitallers and burghers to help to ransom the remaining poor, but the response was lukewarm. Then Eraclius went up to Saladin and begged to let him have some of those still unransomed; the sultan gave him five hundred. Balian fared likewise. Still more were allowed to depart at the behest of Saladin and his brother, and thus there remained only 11,000 in the city, but when Eraclius and Balian offered to become hostages in their stead, Saladin refused. Finally, when the ransomed Franks began to depart in three large convoys, Eraclius and Balian chose to lead the last of the three so that they might gain still more opportunities of persuading Saladin to release the remaining Christians, but their efforts were to no avail.[83]

This detailed account in the adaptations should be taken with more than a grain of salt, for it is quite obvious that Ernoul, Balian's squire in 1187, aimed at defending his erstwhile master against accusations that he had abandoned thousands of Jerusalemites to Saracen servitude. (His repeated references to *le patriarche et Balian*—always in that order in the variant closest to the original—imply that Balian was acting on the patriarch's moral authority.) The sympathetic depiction of Eraclius' activities in October 1187 appears therefore to have been secondary to the chronicler's main purpose; yet this description contrasts so starkly with the devastating portrayal of Eraclius' character and morals in the chapters dealing with the 1180 election, that one may seriously question whether the two sections were penned by the same man. In any case, the account's veracity is dubious. The anonymous author of the *Libellus de expugnatione Terre Sancte* writes that the ransom arrangements "pleased the lord patriarch and the others who had money," and says nothing at all about attempts at saving the poor.[84] Indeed these attempts seem to have been less exhaustive than they might have been. It is permitted by canon law to break up, melt down and sell sacred vessels, and redeem captives with the proceeds; Gregory I, in a passage incorporated by Gratian into his *Decreta*, explicitly denounces as sinful the preservation of a church's possessions, especially if that

83   *Eracles* 23.59-64, pp. 88-100, MS D; Ernoul, pp. 217-231.
84   *Libellus*, p. 247.

church is deserted, rather than using them to ransom its people.[85] However, 'Imād ad-Dīn, Saladin's secretary and an eyewitness of the conquest of Jerusalem, relates that the Franks cleared their churches of all precious objects and that the "grand patriarch" took from the Church of the Holy Sepulchre its gold and silver, its fabrics and its silk tapestries.[86] 'Imād ad-Dīn's assertions may not be entirely accurate — the silver of the edicule he claims that Eraclius took away with him, had been used, according to the adaptations, to strike the coins with which the city's defenders were paid and according to the *Libellus* the Sepulchre and Calvary were plundered upon the conquest[87]— but Eraclius undoubtedly left Jerusalem with some valuable objects, as the sight gave occasion to an exchange between 'Imād ad-Dīn and Saladin. Eraclius may not have been willing to part with precious furnishings of the kind which had aroused the ire of Ralph Niger; again, it is possible that his religiosity, quite in line with the crusader reverence for holy objects, was more matter-oriented than that of an Ambrose, a Gregory I or a Gratian. In any case, it is noteworthy that no Christian writer, not even the bitter author of the *Libellus*, criticizes Eraclius on this account.[88]

Having left Jerusalem, where his palace soon became a Ṣūfī convent, Eraclius made his way to the unconquered Frankish possessions along the Syrian littoral.[89] Nothing is known about his whereabouts and doings during the next year and a half. In the summer of 1188 he probably took part in the assembly in which the *clerus regni* decided to absolve the recently liberated Guy of Lusig-

85 C. 12 q. 2 cc. 13-15, 70; the passage from Gregory I appears in C. 12 q. 2 c. 16. See also E.L. Sadlowski, *Sacred Furnishings of Churches*, Catholic University of America. Canon Law Studies 315 (Washington, 1951), p. 7.

86 'Imād al-Dīn al-Iṣfahānī, *Conquête de la Syrie et de la Palestine par Ṣalāḥ al-Dīn*, ed. C. de Landberg (Leiden, 1888), p. 60; French trans. by H. Massé (Paris, 1972), p. 49; 'Imād al-Dīn, *Barq*, quoted in Abū Shāma, RHC HOr. 4:339. Ibn-al-Athīr's claim that the patriarch took with him the treasures of the Dome of the Rock and of al-Aqṣa as well (RHC.HOr. 1:704) is hardly convincing.

87 See the previous note and *Libellus*, p. 250.

88 In his letter to Béla of Hungary, written in Tyre in January 1188, Conrad of Montferrat merely mentions "qualiter [Saladinus] patriarcham et canonicos sepulchrum colentes, monachos omnes et heremitas, virgines deo dicatas servituti sue redegit et redimere fecit." The letter is edited in A. Chroust, *Tageno, Ansbert und die Historia Peregrinorum* (Graz, 1892), pp. 199-201.

89 Ṣūfī convent: 'Imād al-Dīn, *Conquête*, trans. Massé, pp. 58-59. According to the anonymous author of the *Itinerarium peregrinorum*, probably an English Templar who wrote his account in the Crusading Kingdom some five years later, Eraclius went to Antioch: *Das Itinerarium peregrinorum. Eine zeitgenössische englische Chronik zum dritten Kreuzzug in ursprünglicher Gestalt*, ed. H.E. Mayer, Schriften der MGH 18 (Stuttgart, 1962) [hereafter cited as *Itinerarium*, ed. Mayer], p. 266.

nan from the oath he had sworn to Saladin to go overseas for good;[90] Balian's absolution by Eraclius, less than a year earlier, may have served as a precedent. At any rate, Eraclius decided once more to back Guy and gave him the advice to lay siege to Acre and thus start the reconquest of the country.[91] It was sound advice, for the lackland king had no choice but take the military initiative and attract thereby to his banner the crusaders who were continuously arriving from the West.[92] The siege began on August 29, 1189 and a few weeks later Eraclius joined Guy at his camp at Toron, the ancient *tell* just outside the walls of Acre, exhibiting once more a willingness to expose himself to danger. (Arnold of Lübeck relates that his arrival heartened many of the besiegers.)[93] Later, when the crusader camp swelled with newcomers to the point that it became feasible to seal off the city all around, Guy moved to the northwest but Eraclius remained on Toron, accompanied by the bishops of Acre and Bethlehem and several nobles.[94] Eraclius used to bless the crusaders as they went into battle,[95] but his authority over the heterogeneous host must have been rather limited: when in July 1190 Guy and the other leaders forbade unauthorized attacks and Eraclius, in his last public act on record, threatened to excommunicate all transgressors, the *vulgus* nonetheless went on an ill-conceived raid which ended in disaster.[96] Like most of his major efforts, Eraclius' final move failed to have the effect he had hoped for.

As patriarch of Jerusalem in the agitated 1180's, Eraclius certainly faced unprecedented difficulties, but his repeated failures should not be ascribed solely to external constraints. An acute observer who in 1184 comprehended the stabilizing potential of a new dynasty and in 1189 perceived the necessity of risking aggressive warfare, an able manipulator who in 1186 helped to mislead and paralyze the opposing faction, a man of considerable courage who in 1187 assumed the hopeless defence of Jerusalem, a deft administrator of ecclesiastical affairs and an able pleader all along, Eraclius failed in his major initiatives also because of an inadequate assessment of the forces at work. To assume that

---

90   *Itinerarium*, ed. Mayer, p. 304.
91   *Gesta* 2:93; Howden 3:20. *Eracles*, p. 125, MS D, ascribes the advice to besiege *aucune cité* to Guy's brother Geoffrey. The otherwise unknown bishop William claims to have been sent to the pope *consilio legis (regis?) et patriarche nec non primatus totius terre: Epistola Wilhelmi*, ed. Röhricht (see n. 80 above), p. 193.
92   Cf. R.C. Smail, *Crusading Warfare (1097-1193)* (Cambridge, 1956), pp. 37-38. For a different appraisal see Runciman, *Crusades* 3:22.
93   *Gesta* 2:95, Howden 3:22, Arnold of Lübeck, *Chronica* (see n. 66 above), p. 177.
94   Ralph of Diceto, *Ymagines historiarum* (see n. 52 above), p. 80. The disposition postdates October 7, the day of Frederick of Swabia's arrival.
95   This can be safely deduced from *Itinerarium*, ed. Mayer, p. 349.
96   *Itinerarium*, ed. Mayer, pp. 330-331; *Libellus*, p. 254; *Gesta* 2:142; Howden 3:70.

Henry II or Philip II would accept direct rule over troubled Outremer was about as unrealistic as to believe that a coup d'etat executed in the teeth of a sizable opposition would inaugurate a stable reign. It was similarly unreasonable, though relatively harmless, to expect that support for a Jacobite pretender might lead to an effective submission of his church. Eraclius' remarkably active career nevertheless yielded some unquestionable benefits for the Crusading Kingdom, especially the part he played in preventing massacre and wholesale destruction in Jerusalem in 1187 and in focusing the Christian counter-attack on Acre in 1189. It may also be said that Eraclius' imagination ran ahead of his times, for the offer Henry II and Philip II spurned in 1185 would have been eagerly seized by a Frederick II or a Charles of Anjou.

In the fall of 1190 Eraclius fell ill and Archbishop Baldwin of Canterbury, whom he had met during his European voyage, had to bless the outgoing crusaders in his stead.[97] Roger of Howden writes that after the death of Sybil —which must have occurred in October 1190—Eraclius was among those who advised that the marriage of her sister Isabel to Humphrey of Toron should be annulled and that she should be married to Conrad of Montferrat. The more reliable sources on this event do not, however, mention Eraclius as playing a role in it and the well-informed author of the *Itinerarium peregrinorum* notes that Archbishop Baldwin, taking the place of the sick patriarch, vehemently censured the scheme.[98] It is a measure of the decline in Eraclius' importance that none of the chroniclers of the siege of Acre troubled to record the date of his death, but one may safely assume that he succumbed there to his illness in the closing months of 1190.[99] He must have then been about sixty years old. His erstwhile fellow students at Bologna, pursuing their careers far from the excitement of Outremer and the deprivations of camp life, survived him by several years: Cardinal Gratian died in 1197, Richard Barre in 1202, Étienne of Tournai in 1203.

---

97 *Itinerarium*, ed. Mayer, p. 349.
98 *Gesta* 2:141; Howden 3:70-71; Ralph of Diceto, *Ymagines*, p. 86; *Eracles* 25.11, p. 152; Ernoul, p. 267; *Itinerarium*, ed. Mayer, p. 353.
99 *Gesta* 2:147, Howden 3:87, list him among the dead during the siege; so does Ambroise, *L'Estoire de la Guerre Sainte*, ed. G. Paris (Paris, 1897), lines 5591-5592. The statement in *Eracles*, p. 203, MS D, may be discarded. It is noteworthy that Archbishop Monachus of Caesarea, who dedicates several lines of his poem to the death of the archbishops of Ravenna, Canterbury and Besançon and the bishop of Faenza, does not mention the death of Eraclius— or of Sybil—at all: *Haymari Monachi liber*, ed. Riant (n. 38 above), pp. 37-38.

MONTMUSARD, SUBURB OF CRUSADER ACRE: THE FIRST STAGE OF ITS DEVELOPMENT

DAVID JACOBY
The Hebrew University of Jerusalem

Crusader Acre maintained in the twelfth and thirteenth centuries many of the physical features it had inherited from the preceding Arab period,[1] yet a major change occurred in its urban area and configuration with the emergence and expansion of a new suburb. This suburb, known as Montmusard, appears on the mid-thirteenth century map of Acre by Matthew Paris, as well as on the map drafted by Pietro Vesconte for Marino Sanudo and the one prepared for Paolino Veneto shortly after 1320;[2] the growth of the suburb is also well documented by written sources. So far, however, it has not been the subject of any specific study. It is my purpose to make a contribution towards filling this gap as a tribute to Joshua Prawer, who was the first to draw attention to the existence of Montmusard prior to the conquest of Acre by Saladin in 1187.[3]

The first reference to the suburb appears in 1120, sixteen years after the conquest of Acre, when Baldwin II confirmed a grant of two *carruchae* of land in the *suburbio Tholomaidis* to the monastery of St. Mary in the Valley of Josaphat.[4] It has been convincingly argued that this suburb was situated to the north of what we may call, for the sake of convenience, the Old City of Acre, in

---

1 See David Jacoby, "Crusader Acre in the Thirteenth Century: Urban Layout and Topography," *Studi medievali* 3.20 (1979), 1-45, especially 39-45.
2 On the nature, dating and degree of accuracy of these maps, see ibid., 2-7, 14, 24.
3 Joshua Prawer, "L'établissement des coutumes du marché à Saint-Jean d'Acre et la date de composition du Livre des Assises des Bourgeois," *RHDFE* 4.29 (1951), 335-337.
4 Henri-François Delaborde, *Chartes de Terre Sainte provenant de l'abbaye de N.-D. de Josaphat* (Paris, 1880), p. 34, no. 8: the text mentions the grant by King Baldwin I of *terram arabilem quatuor carruchiis sufficientem in territorio Joppe (...) et in suburbio Tholomaidis, que alio nomine Achon appellatur, terram duarum carruchiarum.*

the area in which we later find Montmusard.[5] The language used in the charter of Baldwin II, especially the term *carrucha*, clearly implies that arable land was granted to St. Mary in the *suburbium* of Acre, as in the vicinity of Jaffa and Beirut.[6] This land extended over approximately 70 hectares,[7] an area considerably larger than that later covered by Montmusard when it was enclosed by walls.[8] It follows that in the charter of 1120 the term *suburbium* was loosely applied to a territory not clearly delineated beyond the city wall.[9] The suburb had a predominantly rural character and was no doubt thinly populated. Its existence at this date does not reflect, therefore, any rapid economic development of Acre in the early years of Latin rule.[10]

These conclusions are strengthened by what we may assume about the first stage of the suburb's existence. As revealed by later sources from the Third Crusade onward, the name of the suburb was Montmusard.[11] This seems to be a composite name combining the French word *Mont* with the French version of a previous Arabic name, an assumption all the more likely if we take into consideration the location to which it was originally applied.[12] A small area included in the suburb of Montmusard, as depicted by two medieval maps of Acre, retained the name of *contrata de Mumusart* (figs. 1 and 2).[13] *Mazār* was the Arabic term used for a holy place, a saint's tomb, a shrine or a place of pilgrimage, which were often flanked by a group of buildings that occasionally

---

5   See Mayer, *Bistümer,* pp. 360-361, and cf. pp. 321-323. The author is the first to have detected the interest of the charter for the history of Montmusard.

6   See text above, n. 4. *Carruca* applied to arable land is widely attested in sources referring to the Latin Levant: see Prawer, *Crusader Institutions,* Index, s.v. *carruca.*

7   Ibid., pp. 157-158, for the size of the *carruca.*

8   On which see below, p. 216.

9   Examples of such a use in the West in the first quarter of the twelfth century in J.F. Niermeyer, *Mediae latinitatis lexicon minus* (Leiden, 1954-76), s.v. *suburbium,* and also *suburbanum.*

10   As suggested by Mayer, *Bistümer,* p. 361.

11   In September 1189 Muslims from Acre and Christians clashed *de deça devers Mont Musart*: Ambroise, *L'Estoire de la guerre sainte*, ed. Gaston Paris (Paris, 1897), lines 2901-2904. Ralph of Diceto, *Ymagines historiarum*, ed. William Stubbs, RS 68 (London, 1876), 2:79, mentions that in 1190 *ante montem Musardi supra mare sunt Geneuenses*; his chaplain William, who was in Acre, supplied him with information about the siege: see ibid., p. 80. The only map to mention the name of the suburb is the one drafted by Matthew Paris in 1252 or somewhat later: see Jacoby, "Crusader Acre," fig. 3, and p. 7 for the date.

12   There is at present no trace of a hill or mound in this area, yet this may be due to changes in the nature of the terrain in the late eighteenth century: see below, p. 215.

13   The inscription appears only on the map of Pietro Vescote, close to the street running parallel to the northern wall of the Old City (fig. 1); the name has been omitted on the three extant copies of the map appearing in Paolino Veneto's universal chronicle (fig. 2).

accommodated pilgrims or travellers.[14] The location of a sacred tomb at a road junction is not uncommon in the Muslim world, and this was precisely the case with the small *contrata de Mumusart*. It was situated in an area, close to the Old City, in which the main urban thoroughfare leading from Acre's harbour northward joined the coastal road from the north and the Galilee road from the east (figs. 1 and 2); after the walls of Montmusard had been completed, these roads reached the outer wall of the suburb at the Gate of the Evil Step (*porta de malo passu*) and the Gate of St. Anthony (*porta sancti Antonii*), respectively.[15] We may conjecture, therefore, that some dwellings close to a sacred tomb already existed in the area of the *contrata de Mumusart* in the Arab period preceding the crusader conquest. It is doubtful whether, in view of the still unstable military situation, new structures were erected in the area in the early years of Latin rule, although this possibility is not to be totally excluded.[16] It is perhaps significant in this respect that the charter of Baldwin I issued in 1115, on which Baldwin II relied in 1120, does not mention the suburb; the different wording of the two documents may well indicate that building activity in this area started between 1115 and 1120.[17] The road junction and the tomb nearby provided a likely site for new construction, and we may safely assume that the *contrata de Mumusart* was the first quarter beyond the city wall in which a new urban settlement developed; this is also borne out by the fact that eventually this quarter gave its name to the whole suburb.

The expansion of Montmusard in the years following 1120 must have been rather slow: the suburb is not attested even once until 1187, while the evidence referring to the Old City in the same period is abundant. It seems most likely, therefore, that the suburb retained its rural character down to Saladin's conquest. Near-contemporary narrative sources of the Third Crusade do not provide any information about the urban development of the suburb. On the other hand, documentary evidence seems to imply that the suburb expanded from

---

14 For *mazār*, see Reinhart Dozy, *Supplément aux dictionnaires arabes*,[3] (Leyden, 1967), and Francis Joseph Steingass, *A Comprehensive Persian-English Dictionary*, (London, 1892).

15 The urban thoroughfare is more accurately depicted on Paolino Veneto's (fig. 2) than on Vesconte's map (fig. 1): see Jacoby, "Crusader Acre," p. 4; it also appears on my conjectural reconstruction of the Old City's topography: ibid., fig. 4. On the gates of the suburb, see below, p. 216.

16 Sidon and Beirut were captured by the Christians only in 1110, and Tyre as late as 1124. The incursion of Mawdūd into Galilee in 1113 must have deeply impressed the Latins: see Prawer, *Histoire*, 1:289-294.

17 Delaborde, *Chartes*, p. 29, no. 6: *et in Joppe terra quatuor carruciis et Achon duobus*; cf. the text of 1120 above, n. 4. Yet it may well be that the charter of 1115 is just more concise, as it does specify neither the territory of Jaffa, nor that of Acre in which the granted territory was situated.

the *contrata de Mumusart* westward, toward the shore, along the dry ditch protecting the northern wall of the Old City.[18] Unfortunately, the nature of the sources makes it virtually impossible to know whether the evidence reflects a development that occurred before the Muslim conquest of 1187, or after the Latin recovery of Acre in 1191.

Two almost identical charters issued after Saladin's conquest, one by Conrad of Montferrat in October 1187 and the other by Guy of Lusignan two years later, speak of the *burgus novus* and confirm the existence of the suburb of Montmusard without mentioning it by name.[19] The second charter mentions "the house of the Temple" (*domus Templi*) in an area which later became known as *burgus Templi*, close to the Gate of the Bath (*porta balnei*) of the Old City (figs. 1 and 2).[20] Various factors strongly suggest that these charters, or at least the topographical data they contain, are forgeries made by a notary active in Acre approximately between May 1192 and October 1200, at any rate after the Christian reconquest of the city.[21] It is impossible to ascertain, therefore, whether the "house of the Temple" existed in the suburb prior to 1187, the period to which the charter of 1189 refers, or whether it was built after the Christian reconquest of Acre. Ralph of Diceto mentions that in 1190 Genoese forces camped on the shore "opposite Montmusard,"[22] which would indicate that by then the suburb had already reached the sea. This location is too vague,

18 See above, n. 11, for sources relating to the Third Crusade, and below, n. 39, for the ditch.
19 Müller, *Documenti*, no. 25, p. 30, and no. 32, p. 38; see also above, n. 3.
20 For the location of the *domus Templi*, see Jacoby, "Crusader Acre," pp. 20-21 and especially n. 103. The name of the Templars' quarter in which it was situated is *burgus Templi* on Vesconte's map (fig. 1), but *boveria Templi* on that of Paolino (fig. 2), although both maps concur in applying the latter name to another quarter of the Templars situated along the eastern flank of Montmusard. The author of Paolino's map was obviously mistaken, as a charter of 1240 clearly indicates that the *boveria Templi* was close to the house of St. Lazarus, situated at the northern tip of Montmusard (figs. 1 and 2): Comte de Marsy, "Fragment d'un cartulaire de l'Ordre de Saint-Lazare en Terre Sainte," *AOL* 2 (1884), part B, pp. 155-157, no. 38. A charter issued in 1198 by Amalric II mentions a house bordering the *porta boverie Templi* to the west and the *furnus Malvicini* to the south; as this oven is mentioned in 1235 as being close to the *porta nova*, the reference is in fact to the *Boverel*, a quarter *within* the Old City (figs. 1 and 2): for the charters, see respectively Sebastiano Pauli, *Codice diplomatico del sacro militare ordine gerosolimitano oggi di Malta*, 2 vols. (Lucca, 1733-1737), 1:287, no. 8, and Delaville, *Cartulaire*, 1:173-174, no. 72. On the *porta nova*, see Jacoby, "Crusader Acre," p. 21, n. 103. The reference to the *boveria Templi* in the charter of 1198 is puzzling: it may be due to a slip of the scribe or an erroneous emendation made at a later date, when the *boveria Templi* already existed at the location indicated by the maps; it may also reflect the existence in what later became known as the *burgus Templi* of a *boveria* or stable, transferred to the other quarter of the Templars in Montmusard when the latter developed.
21 On forgeries or alterations in these documents, see Jacoby, "Crusader Acre," pp. 20-24.
22 See above, n. 11.

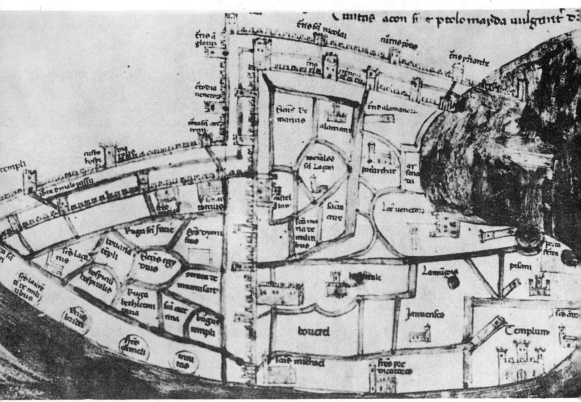

Fig. 1. Map of Acre by Pietro Vesconte (c. 1320). Oxford, Bodleiana, Ms. 10,016 (Tanner 190), fol. 207r.

Fig. 2. Map of Acre in the chronicle of Paolino Veneto (original in 1323?). Rome, Vaticana, Ms. Lat. 1960, fol. 268v.

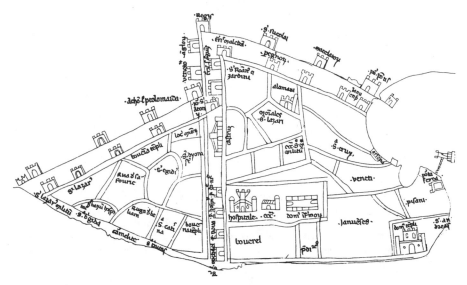

however, to warrant any definitive conclusion. It seems more likely that the Templars expanded beyond the city wall only after 1191.

It should be noted that the same charters also mention Pisans owning houses in Montmusard.[23] It would appear, therefore, that some of them settled in the suburb, either before Saladin's conquest of Acre or slightly after the Third Crusade. However, as the topographical data contained in these charters were forged in order to sustain Pisan territorial claims, it is most likely that these documents reflect aspirations rather than reality;[24] all the more so as it is doubtful that Pisans should have been interested in settling in Montmusard, in view of its minor economic importance in the twelfth century.[25]

Whether the *burgus Templi* existed prior to 1187 or not, there can be no doubt that the urban expansion of the suburb was considerably hastened after the Latins reconquered Acre, for the same reasons that prompted the development of the Old City. From 1191 onward, Acre replaced Jerusalem as the capital of the Latin Kingdom. It absorbed numerous Latins and Oriental Christians who had fled the cities captured by the Muslims in 1187, as well as ecclesiastical institutions that had to be relocated.[26] This migration continued afterwards, especially in the second half of the thirteenth century, parallel to the pace of the Muslim conquest. It was reinforced by an influx of newcomers from other cities of the Latin kingdom of Jerusalem, as well as by western immigrants attracted by the increasing prosperity of Acre.[27] The settlement and urban expansion of Montmusard were obviously connected with a substantial increase in Acre's population. Yet the speed at which it proceeded also depended upon the protection provided to the area in which it was located.

There is no evidence nor any reason to believe that Montmusard was protected by a wall prior to Saladin's conquest. The existence of one or several

23 See above, n. 19.
24 This also appears to be the case with a charter issued in 1200 by Theobald, bishop of Acre: it refers to Pisans living outside an area extending to the north as far as the *burgus novus* and implies that some of them settled in Montmusard: Müller, *Documenti*, pp. 82-83, no. 52. The topographical data contained in this charter, roughly similar to those of the two documents mentioned above, are equally suspicious: see Jacoby, "Crusader Acre," pp. 21-23, and especially n. 104.
25 Even at a later date only few Pisans seem to have inhabited the suburb, and there is no trace of a Pisan quarter within its area.
26 In December 1198 Innocent III mentions the refugees who *perpetuam elegerant mansionem* in Acre, where the bishops of their former cities persist in taxing them: PL 214:476, no. 516. See also Jacoby, "Crusader Acre," p. 44.
27 See, e.g., David Jacoby, "L'expansion occidentale dans le Levant: les Vénitiens à Acre dans la seconde moitié du treizième siècle," *Journal of Medieval History* 3 (1977), 244-248, reproduced in idem, *Recherches sur la Méditerranée orientale du XIIᵉ au XVᵉ siècle. Peuples, sociétés, économies* (London, 1979), VII.

clusters of buildings just north of the Old City wall would not have warranted the construction of a wall surrounding the large territory later enclosed by ramparts, nor were there any demographic or economic factors that would have prompted the Franks to do so before 1187.[28] It is generally assumed that Montmusard was enclosed by walls in the middle of the thirteenth century and that their construction was ordered by Louis IX of France, who stayed in the Holy Land from 1250 to 1254.[29] This dating of Montmusard's walls implies that the development of the suburb preceded the construction of its defences. A careful reading of contemporary documents, however, points to a different course of events.

Acre was surrounded by a single wall in 1103, at the time of the unsuccessful siege of the city by Baldwin I.[30] This was still the case in 1189, when the crusader army attacked the Accursed Tower (*turris maledicta*), the main stronghold along this wall.[31] The location of the tower on the Paolino map (fig. 2) is duly substantiated by sources describing the siege and conquest of Acre by the Muslims in 1291: the tower was situated at the northeastern angle of the wall surrounding Acre at the time of the Third Crusade; this same wall later became the inner wall of the Old City when a second rampart was added.[32] Extensive repairs of the battered wall were carried out from August 1191 onward.[33] The eastern flank of the Old City was still protected by a single wall in 1193, when Henry of Champagne granted to the Hospitallers a section of the

28   A wall built along another line would have appeared on the medieval maps of Acre, like the northern wall of the Old City which lost its primary military function after the construction of the double wall of Montmusard.

29   See below, n. 45.

30   [Rex] *urbem Accon (...) obsedit, sed quia muro et antemurali fortis erat valde, non potuit eam tum comprehendere*: Fulcher of Chartres, *Historia hierosolymitana (1095-1127)*, ed. Heinrich Hagenmeyer (Heidelberg, 1913), pp. 456-457.

31   *Est et turris, quam maledictam nominant et muro, qui urbem amplectitur, insidet*: Hans E. Mayer, *Das Itinerarium peregrinorum*, Schriften der Monumenta Germaniae Historica 18 (Stuttgart, 1962), p. 318, lines 6-7; Ambroise, *L'Estoire*, lines 4751-4766, 4909-4914, 4945-4947.

32   *Les Gestes des Chiprois*, ed. Gaston Raynaud (Genève, 1887), indicate that the Accursed Tower was *as segons murs* (§490) and *une tourete neuve as premiers murs devant la tour maudite* (§491, p. 244). In 1291, after penetrating between the two walls enclosing the city, the Muslims reached the Accursed Tower and entered through its gate into the quarter of St. Romans, located within the Old City (§§497, 499). The inscription *turris maledicta* appearing on the Vesconte map (fig. 1) next to the northeastern corner of the *outer* wall is thus erroneous.

33   Sources differ in their description of the fortifications: Ralph of Diceto, *Ymagines*, 2:95, who was well informed (see above, n. 11), speaks of one wall (*civitate (...) muro plenius communita*), while Ambroise, *L'Estoire*, line 5384, uses the plural (*Si fist les murs d'Acre refaire*). This also occurs in charters, yet the topographical evidence contained in the latter is decisive in pointing to the existence of a single wall: see below.

wall extending from the Gate of Geoffroy le Tort to the Gate of St. Nicholas.[34] As the former gate had been opened shortly before 1181 in the single wall existing then,[35] it is obvious that the latter was situated on the same line of defence; this is also confirmed by the existence of the Gate of St. Nicholas at the time of the Third Crusade.[36] The situation remained unchanged in 1198, when Amalric II granted to the Teutonic Order the tower above the Gate of St. Nicholas, through which "one enters and goes out of the city."[37] Yet by 1212 Acre was protected by two walls. Wilbrand of Oldenburg, who visited the city in this year, has left us the following description:

> This is a fine and strong city situated on the seashore in such a way that, while it is quadrangular in shape, two of its sides forming an angle are girdled and protected by the sea; the other two are encompassed by a fine, wide and deep ditch, stone-lined to the very bottom, and by a double wall fortified with towers according to a fine arrangement, in such a way that the first wall with its towers does not overtop the main [second] wall and is commanded and defended by the second and inner wall, the towers of which are tall and very strong.[38]

---

34 The grant is preserved in an eighteenth-century summary: Delaville, *Cartulaire*, 1:594, no. 938; see also two other grants of 1193 to the Teutonic Order referring to the same section of the wall: Ernestus Strehlke, *Tabulae Ordinis Theutonici* (Berlin, 1869), pp. 24-25, no. 28-29. On these grants, see Marie-Luise Favreau, *Studien zur Frühgeschichte des Deutschen Ordens*, Kieler Historische Studien, 21 (Stuttgart, 1974), pp. 57-59.

35 Delaville, *Cartulaire*, 2:909, no. 20: *ante domum Gaufridi Torti, ubi nunc porta civitatis facta est.*

36 *Eracles*, p. 130.

37 Strehlke, *Tabulae*, pp. 28-29, no. 35: *per quam intratur et exitur de villa.* It is only later that the name of St. Nicholas was transferred to a new gate built opposite the old one in the outer wall, as illustrated by the fourteenth-century maps (figs. 1 and 2).

38 *Hec est civitas bona et fortis, in littore maris sita, ita ut, dum ipsa in dispositione sit quadrangula, duo eius latera angulum constituentia a mari cingantur et muniantur; reliqua duo latera fossa bona et larga et profunda funditus murata et duplici muro turrito pulchro ordine coronantur, eo modo, ut prior murus suis cum turribus ipsam matrem non excedentibus a secundo et interiore muro, cuius turres alte sunt et validissime, prospiciatur et custodiatur: Peregrinatores medii aevi quatuor*, ed. Johann Christian Moritz Laurent (Leipzig, 1864), p. 163. My translation is an amended version of the one published in Meron Benvenisti, *The Crusaders in the Holy Land* (Jerusalem, 1970), p. 94. In his own German translation, the editor of the text provides what amounts to a different interpretation of the nature of the first wall's towers: according to him, *ipsam matrem non excedentibus* means *welche aus der Mauer selbst nicht hervorragen*. This interpretation, however, contradicts the depiction of the outer wall with its protruding towers as found on the maps of Acre; see figs. 1 and 2. Burchard of Mount Sion, who visited Acre in 1283, considers that the city has a triangular shape, ibid., p. 23: *Accon autem civitas munita est muris, antemuralibus, turribus et fossatis et barbicanis fortissimis, triangulam habens formam, ut clypeus, cuius due partes iunguntur magno mari, tercia pars campum respicit, qui ipsam circumdat.* Benvenisti, ibid., p. 94, argues that the quadrangular plan of Acre which Wilbrand

As no second wall ever covered the northern flank of the Old City, it follows from this description that the two walls of Montmusard which appear on the fourteenth-century maps of Acre (figs. 1 and 2) had been completed by 1212 and that their construction had taken place between 1198 and this date.[39]

The completion of the double wall of Acre and its suburb in this period, much earlier than generally assumed, is indirectly confirmed by later sources. A charter issued in 1217 by King John of Brienne for the first time explicitly mentions two walls when referring to a section of the eastern flank of the Old City, close to the Gate of Geoffroy le Tort.[40] The fourteenth-century maps of Acre (figs. 1 and 2) clearly illustrate that the defence system of Montmusard was closely linked with that of the Old City. It is obvious, therefore, that the strengthening of the latter entailed the construction of the former. Indeed, compelling strategic considerations rule out the building of an outer wall confined to the eastern side of the Old City. Such a wall could have been easily outflanked by the enemy at its northern extremity, as it ran parallel to the inner wall without ever joining it.[41] A double rampart was devoid of military value, unless it extended from coast to coast to the north and east of Acre and surrounded the entire territory of the city and its suburb. Once the construction of the outer wall had started, it was imperative to complete it within a short span of time in order to ensure the safety of Acre in the event of a new Muslim attack. Exactly in which year the walls of Montmusard were completed remains unknown; we can be certain only that the work had been done by 1212.

Additional evidence confirms that the suburb was protected by an elaborate defence system prior to the arrival of Louis IX in the Holy Land. Coming from Tyre in 1241 Riccardo Filangieri, bailiff of the kingdom of Jerusalem on behalf

mentions in 1212, as well as the triangular shape attributed to Acre by Burchard in 1283, reflect two different stages in the fortification of Acre, respectively prior to and after the surrounding of Montmusard by walls. This interpretation is not warranted in view of the documentary evidence assembled above, all the more so as a source almost contemporary with the Third Crusade, thus prior to the fortification of Montmusard, also refers to the triangular shape of Acre: Mayer, *Das Itinerarium*, p. 317, lines 23-25.

39   For 1198 as a *terminus a quo*, see above, p. 212. The period of construction was perhaps even shorter. The severe damage inflicted on the wall of the Old City by the earthquake of 1202 may have prompted the Franks to strengthen the defences of Acre. On this earthquake, see Hans E. Mayer, "Two Unpublished Letters on the Syrian Earthquake of 1202," in Sami A. Hanna, ed., *Medieval and Middle Eastern Studies in Honor of Aziz Suryal Atiya* (Leiden, 1972), pp. 295-310. The dry ditch running along the single northern wall of the Old City, between the latter and the suburb, was still in existence in 1291: *Gestes*, §503.

40   Strehlke, *Tabulae*, p. 41, no. 50: *totam (...) barbacanam infra duos muros civitatis*. On this gate, see above.

41   The line joining the two walls at the northeastern corner of the Old City on my reconstruction of Acre (Jacoby, "Crusader Acre," fig. 4) is mistaken and should be erased.

of Emperor Frederick II, entered Acre through a false postern. The garden of the Hospitallers in which he gained access to the postern was situated outside the suburb, close to the Gate of the Evil Step.[42] The gardens close to that gate are again mentioned in connection with another episode: in 1267 one of the Frankish leaders avoided a battle with a Saracen army larger than his by fleeing to the suburb "through the gardens in front of the Gate of the Evil Step."[43] It follows that this gate opened in the outer wall of Montmusard and the latter already existed in 1241, nine years before Louis IX arrived in Acre.[44] The French king fortified Montmusard while staying in the Holy Land, yet unfortunately we do not know the precise nature of the work performed.[45] It evidently differed from that executed in Jaffa, where Louis IX enclosed the suburb, till then undefended, with a wall extending from coast to coast and including twenty-four towers.[46]

The location of the two walls of Montmusard remains a mystery, and the same holds true of its various quarters.[47] It is rather surprising that the urban

42 The text of *Gestes*, §222, is somewhat misleading: *une fauce posterne quy est au borc en .j. jardin de l'Hospital (...) Encore est apelée cele posterne la Porte de Maupas.* It would seem that the garden was within the suburb, but the chronicle later refers to the same area as being outside the walls, which anyhow appears more plausible: see next note. Filangieri escaped from Acre through the same postern after being besieged for six months in the main structure of the Hospitallers, which was located in the Old City.

43 *Gestes*, §351.

44 The name of the gate is inscribed on a copy of Vesconte's map of Acre between the two walls of Montmusard (fig. 1), but several sources clearly indicate that the gate was in the outer wall: in 1281 the Hospitallers were granted the guard of the section of the outer wall extending from the gate of St. Anthony to that of Maupas, and Marino Sanudo mentions the construction of a barbican between these two gates in 1287: Delaville, *Cartulaire* 3:420, no. 3771, and Sanudo, *Secreta*, 229. The two gates are also mentioned together in a letter written in 1291 by John of Villiers, Master of the Hospitallers, which describes the fall of Acre: Delaville, *Cartulaire* 3:592-593, no. 4157.

45 The sources are vague. According to Joinville, Louis IX strengthened the city of Acre, but there is no mention of the suburb in this context. The papal legate decided to spend all his money *à fermer le fors-bourc d'Acre* after the king's departure: Jean, sire de Joinville, *Histoire de Saint Louis*, ed. Natalis de Wailly (Paris, 1874), §§616 and 612, respectively. The exact meaning of *fermer*, or *firmare*, *fortificare* and *reparare* in the Latin sources is not clear. The "Annales de Terre Sainte," ed. Reinhold Röhricht et Gaston Raynaud, *AOL* 2 (1884), part B, p. 444, version B, mentions without specifying that the king *frema une partie dou Bourc*, i.e., only part of Montmusard. A later well informed source claims that the king *fortificò di mura et fozze il borgo, comminciando dala porta de San Antonio verso la marina sino a San Lazaro*: Florio Bustrone, *Chronique de l'île de Chypre*, ed. René de Mas Latrie, Collection de documents inédits sur l'histoire de France, Mélanges historiques 5 (Paris, 1885), p. 109. This somewhat ambiguous statement seems to hint at the existence of the two gates prior to the work ordered by Louis IX.

46 Joinville, *Histoire*, §§516-517, 561-562, on Haifa, Caesarea and especially Jaffa.

47 Only few remnants of the Crusader period have been found. Systematic excavations remain a desideratum.

layout of the suburb should have been completely blurred, while that of the Old City has been relatively well preserved;[48] all the more so as the suburb's area was not resettled from the fall of Acre in 1291 till the beginning of this century, and even then only to a small extent.[49] The total disappearance of Montmusard may well go back to the late eighteenth century, when it was essential for defence purposes to flatten the ground and ensure thereby a free field of fire for artillery mounted on the walls of the Old City.[50] About a century ago Rey claimed that he had found the course of the suburb's walls starting from a point on the coast.[51] This would have implied that the northern tip of Montmusard was located some 900 metres to the north of the Old City and that, compared to the latter, the suburb was considerably larger than it appears to have been according to the fourteenth-century maps of Acre (figs. 1 and 2). Although not drawn to scale, the Vesconte map provides a fairly accurate representation of the shape and size of the various quarters of the Old City.[52] It may therefore be considered on the whole reliable in its depiction of Montmusard, from which it follows that the shore of the suburb was substantially shorter than assumed by Rey. Some fifty mangonel stones have been found about 750 metres to the north of the twelfth-century Old City, probably on the site from which they were to be hurled at the walls of Montmusard during the Muslim siege of 1291.[53] If so, the northern tip of the suburb must have been close to a small bay some 500 metres north of the Old City wall.

The almost flat terrain enabled the construction of a short and efficient defence line for the suburb (figs. 1 and 2). From the bay the walls followed a straight or almost straight course to the southeast, and the inner wall of the suburb joined the wall of the Old City somewhat to the east of the royal

---

48   See Jacoby, "Crusader Acre," p. 2.

49   As illustrated by aerial photographs taken during World War I: see Gustaf Hermann Dalman, *Hundert deutsche Fliegerbilder aus Palästina,* Schriften des Deutschen Palästina Instituts 2 (Gütersloh, 1925), photos 60-62.

50   As done in 1567 by the Venetians around Nicosia in Cyprus: see Rupert Gunnis, *Historic Cyprus. A Guide to its Towns and Villages, Monasteries and Castles* (London, 1936), p. 29. Aḥmad Jazzār Pasha, governor of Acre since 1774, fortified the city in the years preceding the siege by Bonaparte in 1799.

51   See Emmanuel G. Rey, *Les colonies franques de Syrie aux XIIme et XIIIme siècles* (Paris, 1883), pp. 452-454, 461-462, and the plan between pp. 462 and 463. Rey's plan is based on that drawn by Colonel Jacquotin during the siege of Acre by Bonaparte. It implies the existence of a wall along the maritime flank of the suburb, contrary to the information provided by the medieval maps.

52   See Jacoby, "Crusader Acre," pp. 2-7.

53   See ibid., p. 42, n. 214. Such an attack could not have taken place at a later date, as the suburb's walls were destroyed in 1291 and never rebuilt afterwards.

castellum. It is obvious that the course of Montmusard's walls was deliberately chosen so as to take advantage of this important structure. Hidden behind the two walls of the suburb, it had lost its primary military function as the main stronghold along the northern city wall, yet its location at the juncture of the inner wall of Montmusard and the Old City lent substantial support to one of the weakest points along the defence line of Acre. The names of the three gates opening in the outer wall of the suburb are known (fig. 1). Close to the Old City's northeastern angle we find the Gate of St. Anthony, which derived its name from the nearby church and hospital;[54] the road from Safed in upper Galilee and St. George de Lebeyne in central Galilee probably reached Acre at this gate.[55] The coastal road coming from Tyre and Montfort, the castle of the Teutonic Order, arrived at the Gate of the Evil Step.[56] The Gate of St. Lazarus was situated in the vicinity of the church and hospital bearing the same name, close to the northern tip of Montmusard.[57] The main streets leading to these gates and joining them are well marked on the Vesconte map (fig. 1).

The completion of the two walls was of considerable importance for Acre. First, these walls substantially enlarged the city's protected territory: as illustrated by the medieval maps of Acre, Montmusard was about half the size of the Old City and may have covered around 16 hectares.[58] Moreover, the walls ensured the safety of an area in which a much needed urban development could rapidly proceed. Unfortunately, there is hardly any evidence bearing on the suburb's history in the period immediately following the construction of its two walls, yet it is obvious that the future course of its expansion was largely determined in these years. Unlike the Old City, Montmusard lacked any substratum conditioning its development and grew, so to speak, on virgin soil. The curved streets depicted on the medieval maps prove that there was no master plan nor any supervision governing its development, and eventually its layout

---

54   Gestes, §492.

55   On this road, see Henri Michelant et Gaston Raynaud, *Itinéraires à Jérusalem et descriptions de la Terre Sainte rédigés en français aux XIe, XIIe et XIIIe siècles* (Paris, 1882), p. 102, no. 20, and Delaville, *Cartulaire* 2:775, no. 2721: *via magna qua itur ad Saphettum et Sanctum Georgium*. See also *Atlas of Israel* (Jerusalem and Amsterdam, 1970), Sheet 9.10. On the gate, see also above, n. 42.

56   See *Gestes,* §§222, 351, and above, p. 207.

57   The name of this gate is inscribed behind the inner wall on all the medieval maps of Acre (see figs. 1 and 2, as well as Jacoby, "Crusader Acre," fig. 3, for the map of Matthew Paris), yet it definitely opened in the outer wall: see *Gestes*, §491 (p. 245).

58   For the area of the Old City in the Crusader period, see Jacoby, "Crusader Acre," p. 41.

greatly resembled that of the Old City.[59] On the other hand, the two parts of Acre considerably differed in their landscape. The mingling of imported western styles, Romanesque and Gothic, with those of the Levant was characteristic of the Old City, a former Muslim urban centre inhabited by western immigrants and their descendants.[60] Such a mingling of styles was not to be found, or to a small extent only, in the new suburb that developed to the north of the city wall inherited from the Arab period preceding the crusades.

59 The maps reflect the urban layout in the last years before the Muslim conquest of 1291: see ibid., pp. 7, 19, 35-36.
60 See ibid., pp. 43-45.

STRUCTURE AND AIMS OF THE LIVRE AU ROI*

MYRIAM GREILSAMMER

The Hebrew University of Jerusalem

Modern historians of the Latin Kingdom of Jerusalem regard the *Livre au Roi* as a juridical source of primary importance. In addition to the later works of Philippe de Novare and Jean d'Ibelin, the *Livre au Roi* "fills the gap to some extent between the time of Baldwin II and the middle of the thirteenth century."[1]

The two existing editions of the *Livre*, those of E.H. Kausler[2] and A.A. Beugnot,[3] are based on two manuscripts: Fr 19026 and Codex Gallus 51.[4] One of the primary reasons for the necessity of a critical edition lies in the existence of a third manuscript, Codex Gallus 771, which was revealed by M. Grandclaude in 1926.[5] This manuscript remains unedited (although Joshua Prawer has cited parts of it in his studies),[6] and has never been the subject of detailed study. The readings of CG 771 seem to be of great value, since they throw light on certain problems posed by the *Livre au Roi*. In order to illustrate the interest

---

* This study is based on my M.A. thesis, *Le 'Livre au Roi' et les réalités féodales du royaume latin de Jérusalem au XIIᵉ siècle* (unpublished, The Hebrew University of Jerusalem, 1977), written under the direction of Professor Joshua Prawer.

1 J. Prawer, "Etude sur le droit des assises de Jérusalem: droit de confiscation et droit d'exhéredation," *RHDFE* 4.39 (1962), 30, reprinted in his *Crusader Institutions,* p. 457.

2 E.H. Kausler, ed., *Les Livres des Assises et des Usages dou reaume de Jérusalem* (Stuttgart, 1839), chs. 298-349, pp. 353-395.

3 RHC Lois 1:601-644.

4 For further details see M. Grandclaude, "Classement sommaire des manuscrits des principaux livres des assises de Jérusalem," *RHDFE* 4.5 (1926), 458-460.

5 Ibid., p. 419.

6 Prawer, "Etude," pp. 40-41.

of this manuscript, we shall cite its contribution to two such important matters as 1) the structure of the *Livre au Roi*; 2) the origin and inspiration of the *Livre au Roi*.

1) STRUCTURE OF THE *LIVRE AU ROI*

Beugnot believed that the *Livre au Roi* was a code of law established by a jurisconsult "sans s'astreindre à aucun ordre méthodique."[7] In 1923, M. Grandclaude suggested that it was a treatise of feudal law dealing primarily with the juridical obligations of the king and his vassals.[8] In 1926, he altered his opinion and stated that the *Livre au Roi* was "une série de bans et de records simplement mis bout à bout par un auteur anonyme."[9]

We believe that what we possess is in fact a "coutumier" of feudal law which contains legislative, judicial and feudal common law practices of the period.[10] The *Livre au Roi* reproduces assizes, judgments and certain customs of the Latin Kingdom, though it has no official character. This hypothesis permits a better understanding of the text without denying its incorporation of judgments and laws.

We also believe, contrary to the view held by Beugnot and Grandclaude, that the *Livre au Roi* possesses a fairly definite and deliberate structure. The editor of the text clearly explains his priorities in beginning his work in the rubric of the first chapter:[11]

> *Por ce que* la raison commande que se la cort as chevaliers con claime la haute cort ne doit nus hom coumencer a retraire les iugemens con ne doit coumencier tout premier au chief, ce est au roi ou a la rayne, de qui tos les biens et tous bons essamples si devent venir et toutes bones droitures, *et por ce coumande la raison con deit tout premier a luy coumencer*, por ce con doit saver et counoistre *quel poer a li rois* de bien faire a ces homes liges, *et quel poer il nen a* de mau faire, par dreit et par lassize.

Thus, his object is to begin by describing the prerogatives of the king.

Later in the text, we find several references to a methodical construction.

---

7   A.A. Beugnot, "Introduction," in RHC Lois 1:lxvi.
8   M. Grandclaude, *Etude critique sur les livres des Assises de Jérusalem* (Paris, 1923), p. 41.
9   M. Grandclaude, "Caractère du Livre au Roi," *RHDFE* 4.5 (1926), 309.
10   J. Prawer has already stated ("Etude," p. 522) that: "Le *Livre au Roi*, rappelons-le, est une collection privée composée après la chute de Jérusalem..."
11   I shall always refer (if not stated differently) to Kausler's edition of the *Livre*. Kausler himself seems not to have understood the reason for the parallelism between the two parts of the sentence since, contrary to common sense, he omits in his edition the "et" of the second "et por ce" [my italics in text].

These explain the division and the content of the book, serving as proof that it does not consist of texts placed one after the other by mere chance:

> *Puis que vous aves oy la raison et le poer dou roi,* si coumande le dreit que vos oies la raison et le dreit de quei est tenus le mareschau dou reaume de servir au roi, et ques est son office de la marechaussie, par dreit.[12]

And further on:

> *Puis que vous aves oy le dreit et la raison des homes liges,* si comande la lei et l asise que vos oies et entendes la raison des femes veves liges, quel poier elles ont de leur cors marier sans conge de son seignor ou de sa dame de sous cui elle sera, et quel poier a le seignor ou la dame de sa feme marier segont se qui li afiert.[13]

This evidence, contained within the text itself, prompted us to try and reconstitute the original plan of the work, or at least what remains of it. The *Livre au Roi* contains three major subdivisions: 1) The king; 2) the liege men; 3) the fief. These can be further broken down and their contents described as follows:

First part: The king
a) Rights and obligations of the king
    — The king's obligations toward the realm and his vassals (chs. 298-300)
    — Rights of succession (chs. 301-303)
    — Royal rights: *auxilium* to be given in the event of the king's ransom or debt (chs. 304-305)
b) Royal institutions
    — The office of the 'mareschau dou reaume' (chs. 306-310, 312)
    — The office of the 'counestable' (ch. 311)
    — The king's right of confiscation without 'esgard de cort' (ch. 313)
    — Royal jurisdiction in the High Court: cases of offences between burgesses and noblemen (chs. 314-317)

The rights and obligations of the king described here are those of a strong monarchy, in which power is not yet usurped by the high nobility. The obligations of the king are primarily presented as general principles designed to safeguard the abstract institution of royalty. These obligations are minimal and seem to do little to interfere with the king's freedom of action. The precautions safeguarding the inheritance of the kingdom do not adversely affect the king but in fact protect the property of the crown, without regard to the royal person. Upholding the acts of previous kings and guaranteeing royal acts with

---

12 *Livre au Roi* 306, pp. 358-359.
13 Ibid., 327, p. 375.

the signature of the vassals of the kingdom constitute current practice. Similarly, it would be contrary to the practice of the time for the king to dispose of the possessions of his vassals without their prior agreement (the right of the king to transfer part of his own property is well protected).

A distinction should be made between these general princlples and the chapters which follow. The latter correspond to the situation which in fact existed at the time: the right of succession to the throne, the obligation of coming to the aid of the king in case of ransom or debt. The following chapters then go on to describe certain royal institutions. Here we find a description of officials who enjoyed great power. In addition, as Prawer has already noted, the much-debated chapter on the right of confiscation without "esgart de cort" brings us back to a period preceding the reign of Amalric I: confiscation without judgment seems impossible at the time the *Livre* was written.[14]

Second part: The liege men
— Disposition against heretic or renegade liege men (chs. 318-320)
— Rights and obligations of the liege men (chs. 321-326)
— Rights and obligations of female vassals (chs. 327-329)
— Feudal succession rights (chs. 330-335)
— Judicial rights of the liege men: a) barons (ch. 336); b) knights (chs. 337-338)

In this part, too, the rights and obligations described are those of an earlier period when the authority of the king was unequalled. We again find contemporary concerns: the *Livre* devoted no less than three chapters to cases of heresy and treason committed against the state and Christianity. The fact that at the end of the twelfth century these cases should have been accorded such importance is noteworthy and suggests that this threat was real and disturbing.

If we compare the rights of the king and his vassals, we are struck by the severity and the force of the former and by the banality which characterizes the latter. While seeming to grant the liege men fairly extensive rights (the right to judgment by peers, the case of liege men recommending their fief for one year and one day, the case of the king's non-payment of allowances, the case of a fief reconquered by the Saracens, the case of required service outside the kingdom), the *Livre* merely sets down current practice in writing. Moreover, the punishment for deviating from the obligations of the vassal is always

---

14   Prawer, "Etude," p. 531. Amalric II's interest in this assize might have been related to his attempt to confiscate the feudal possessions of Raoul of Tiberias without prior judgment. See R.C. Smail, *The Crusaders in Syria and the Holy Land* (London, 1973), pp. 48-49, and J. Riley-Smith, *The Feudal Nobility and the Kingdom of Jerusalem, 1174-1277* (London, 1973), p. 156.

present and testifies to the authority of the suzerain, even if judgment of peers is demanded.

The rules concerning the wardship of a vassal's widow stipulate that the king may force her to marry one of his three nominees. This is an intermediate stage between that in which he had the right to impose a single nominee and that in which the widow could, under certain circumstances, refuse all three.[15]

Finally, having developed the law of feudal succession (the inheritance of fiefs and burgage tenures), the author devotes a chapter to the *Assise de cors* which permits a liege man to possess several fiefs. This assize allows the vassal already provided for to inherit a fief which has lapsed, by placing it in the service of a salaried knight. Again, this is a minor concession which does not really take into account developments begun several decades earlier. In view of its antiquity and its importance, it would have been impossible not to include the *Assise de cors* in the text. After this assize, which permits the concentration of feudal lands in the hands of a small number of great vassals, the author goes on to describe their rights and obligations. He reduces their prerogatives to the right to "tenir cort" and to "poer d'aver coings et de ceeler leur dons," specifying that the right to "tenir cort" must be applied "si com est establi en ce livre et non autrement." In describing the rights of the barons of the kingdom, the author bases himself on an obsolete text, describing a situation at least thirty years old, with the apparent aim of firmly establishing these rights in order to prevent any further evolution.[16]

Third part: The fief

— Leprous knight (ch. 339)
— Fief succession of a nun (ch. 340)
— The sale of a fief (chs. 341-342)
— The infringement of privileges (ch. 343)
— Aging or disabled liege men (chs. 344-345)
— Vassals' use of fiefs for borrowing or pledges (chs. 346-347)
— Liege men without surviving heirs (ch. 348)
— Obligation of *consilium* at royal summons (ch. 349)

The aim of the chapters in this part is first of all to maintain the vassal's service to his lord. This section envisages the case in which the service is

---

15 *Livre au Roi* 327, p. 375. For the early and final stages see J. Prawer, "La noblesse et le régime féodal du royaume latin de Jérusalem," *Moyen Age* 65 (1959), 51, 56 = idem, *Crusader Institutions*, pp. 26-27, 30-31. [For a detailed discussion of the final stage see now J.A. Brundage, "Marriage Law in the Latin Kingdom of Jerusalem," *infra* pp. 258-271. Ed.]

16 P. Meynial, "De quelques particularités des successions féodales dans les assises de Jérusalem," *RHDFE* 4.16 (1932), 419-420. See also Prawer, "La noblesse," p. 55 = idem, *Crusader Institutions*, pp. 29-30.

rendered impossible or in which an adjustment is necessary (a leprous liege man, a clerical heir, an aged or disabled vassal, an heirless liege man), then deals with the sale of fiefs in order to protect the obligations related to it. Similarly, other chapters deal with the usurpation of a privilege, and with pledges and loans—transactions related to the fief. Finally, the last chapter deals with a question of procedure related to the obligation of *consilium*: the punishment in the event of refusal is the confiscation of the fief, which is why it is included in this section. Thus, this third and last part of the *Livre au Roi* also seeks to protect and guarantee the rights of the king (here as suzerain).

CG 771 contributes to our effort to define the structure of the *Livre*, as it seems that the scribe of this manuscript attempted to preserve the original, tripartite structure of the work. Evidently he made an effort to conclude the last chapter of the second part on fol. 231r, clearly going beyond the space allotted to the text and encroaching on the margin. The verso of folio 231 was left blank, and the scribe drew on it a large spiral to which no text is attached. Then, on fol. 232r, begins the third part of the treatise. Since both the first and the second parts of the *Livre* begin on the recto of a folio and not on the verso,[17] it may be suggested that the scribe, wishing to preserve the original partition of the work, decided to begin each part on a recto side.

2) ORIGIN AND INSPIRATION OF THE *LIVRE AU ROI*

Beugnot was the first to try and situate the *Livre au Roi* in time, placing it between the years 1271-1291.[18] Paulin Paris criticized his conclusions without proposing an alternative.[19] The large majority of the historians of the crusades accept the dating of M. Grandclaude,[20] which places the composition of the *Livre au Roi* between 1197 and 1205; any other solution can be dismissed.

However, a close reading of the chapters dealing with succession to the throne seem to refute the hypothesis put forward by Grandclaude on the inspiration of the *Livre*: the idea that the author could have been a "devotee" of Queen Isabel[21] cannot be accepted. Indeed, if chapter 302 seems to guarantee the rights of Marie de Montferrat (as Grandclaude tells us), the following chapter considers other solutions which move in the opposite direction and

---

17 First part, fol. 188r; second part, fol. 206r.
18 Beugnot, "Introduction," in RHC Lois 1:lxvi.
19 P. Paris, "Comptes-rendus," *Journal des savants* (1841), 292-294.
20 Grandclaude, *Etude,* pp. 46-47.
21 Ibid., p. 50.

which seem to demonstrate that Amalric II was the inspiring force behind this treatise:

> Sy ores du seignour mari ces doussegont Roi et desses enfans et quel don vaut dou bailliage que li peres thient tant coume celuy cien fis au quy eschiet le Roiaute est merme daage pour quy le pere tient celuy bailliage du Roiaume.
>
> Encement ce il avient que la Roine non ait heu nul enfant du premier baron ou les oit mais ne vesquerent rien et elle ot puis autres enfans que vesquerent du seignour baron ceest du segont Roi. La raison iuge et coumande que apres la mort de la Roine leur mere de par quy meut celui Roiaume le Roiaute sy vient au plus prochain ainsne des enfans si coume est dessus dit.

Obviously, Amalric inserted this text in order to secure for himself the bail of the kingdom, should Isabel and her heiress die, and to ensure that the succession should then revert to his heirs. He alludes cynically to the possible death of the princess Marie, which would clear the way for his own children to inherit the throne. Amalric reveals himself as a far-sighted and meticulous man who left nothing to chance.

CG 771 here adds an additional element concerning the probable role of Amalric II in initiating the treatise, as it brings a prologue (fol. 32v) to the works of Jean d'Ibelin and the *Livre au Roi* which does not figure in the other two manuscripts. The prologue contains a text very close to the first rubric of chapter 1 of the *Livre*, though differing from the version given in CG 771, and concludes with the statement:

> Lesquelles assizes furent recordez et renouvellez et mist en escrit par le Roy heimeri de bonne memoire, et par messire Raoul de Tabar et messire philippe de novaire que Dieus lor doint la gloire de paradis.

Thus, while Philippe de Novare and Jean d'Ibelin [22] merely recount the abor-

---

22 *Livre de Philippe de Navarre* 38, 47 and 94, RHC Lois 1:515, 522-523, 569; *Livre de Jean d'Ibelin* 239, 273, RHC Lois 1:384, 428. It is not impossible that Amalric II himself gave precise instructions concerning the composition of the *Livre au Roi*; Philippe de Novare recounts that he: "sot meaus les us et les assises dou reaume que nul autre." He asked Raoul of Tiberias to assist him in this task, placing ten vavassours at his disposal (only two according to d'Ibelin). Raoul refused and, according to Philippe de Novare and Jean d'Ibelin, this refusal aborted the enterprise begun by Amalric. We can however ask whether Amalric would have been ready to abandon the project which he considered so important. The importance attributed by Philippe and Jean to Raoul of Tiberias seems frankly exaggerated. One can easily understand how they deliberately tried to erase any evidence concerning this new codification of the assizes, which was not approved by these two defenders of pure feudalism.

tive effort of King Amalric to codify the assizes, the additional prologue[23] of CG 771 asserts that Amalric's attempt at codification resulted in the assizes contained in the *Livre au Roi*.

Any serious study of the *Livre au Roi*, whether of its structure or its inspiration, must take into consideration the unique contribution of CG 771. It establishes with greater certainty the fragmentary nature of Fr 19026,[24] and allows us to understand the significance of the copyist's choices in this manuscript. In effect, Fr 19026 was drawn up under circumstances different from those which formed the basis of the writing of the *Livre au Roi*. The chapters which were advantageous to the high nobility of the kingdom were carefully copied (for example, the *Assise de cors*), and if others were omitted, this was because they were to its disadvantage (for example, the chapter on the rights of the barons). Royal authority no longer appears as in the original text; royal prerogatives are for the most part removed, contrary to the duties. In Fr 19026:

The first part, devoted to the king, is fairly complete, although it should be noted that the word "roi" is frequently replaced by the word "seignor." The chapter on booty was omitted as was the assize on confiscation without "esgart de cort."[25]

Of the second part, devoted to liege men, only certain chapters remain (a fief recaptured by the Saracens, the inheritance of a burgage tenure, the *Assise de cors*, rights and obligations of the vassals to the High Court).

Of the third part, the scribe left out the chapters dealing with the sale of fiefs, the service of aged or disabled vassals, and the obligation of *consilium* towards the king.

23   We know that this prologue dates at least from the first part of the fourteenth century, since it is part of a dated manuscript copied by one Pol Castressio on 4 August 1344 and retranscribed in CG 771. This dating is reinforced by the existence of another manuscript, the "Nancy" MS, no longer extant, of which Beugnot learned after having published the first volume of the assizes. He was struck by two passages contained in this manuscript, the first of which corresponds to the prologue. On this point we can rely on Beugnot's testimony, since he had never heard of CG 771. Grandclaude already cited this prologue but with numerous inaccuracies: "Caractère du Livre au Roi," p. 317.

24   Fr 19026 contains 31 chapters of the *Livre au Roi* (with their rubrics); CG 771 and 51 contain 52 chapters.

25   Contrary to what Grandclaude believed ("Classement sommaire," p. 420), it is possible to determine with accuracy the original placement of this assize. CG 51 and 771 place it in the 16th position (first part), and Fr 19026 in the 27th position (third part). I believe that CG 771 and 51 give us the correct position, because it fits in naturally in the section describing the royal prerogatives.

Fr 19026 corresponds to a period in which the great vassals had seized the royal prerogatives and royal authority had irrevocably declined.

A critical edition thus seems necessary.[26]

3) CONCLUSIONS

Philippe de Novare and Jean d'Ibelin present the interests of a kingdom based on the upper aristocracy, in which the institution of the monarchy has lost its meaning. The work of Jean d'Ibelin is most characteristic of this evolution.

The aim of the *Livre au Roi* is an opposite one. It tries to present the image of a strong monarchy, like that existing at the beginning of the twelfth century, and to reestablish its authority.[27] Its content constitutes a detailed program gaving two definite goals:

1) The *Livre* describes the royal prerogatives, but aims primarily at reestablishing certain of these, which were already archaic at the time.

2) In addition, while seeking to attribute quite extensive rights to the liege men and to protect them, the author seeks more to establish these rights in order to prevent any further evolution. He describes an obsolete situation which does not take into account the growing strength of the great vassals, which had occurred several decades earlier.

We can conclude that the *Livre au Roi*, despite appearances, does not represent an exact reflection of the monarchy's situation of its time. At first glance, the treatise seems simply to describe the respective rights and obligations of the king and his vassals, basing itself on old and new assizes, and incorporating contemporary customs. However, by a judicious choice of assizes, the author deliberately described an obsolete situation, that of a quasi-omnipotent monarch, whose vassals still had very limited rights. Given the fact that the work was most certainly prepared for King Amalric, this monarch's aim was to facilitate the restoration of a strong monarchy rather than to set down in writing the old assizes lost in 1187.

---

26   See the critical edition in my *Le "Livre au Roi" et les réalités féodales du royaume latin au XIIe siècle*, to be published shortly.

27   For a similar view see Richard, *Royaume*, p. 69; also, H.E. Mayer, *The Crusades*, trans. J. Gillingham (London, 1972), p. 158; J. Riley-Smith, *The Feudal Nobility and the Kingdom of Jerusalem, 1174-1277* (London, 1973), p. 36.

CROCUSES AND CRUSADERS: SAN GIMIGNANO, PISA AND THE KINGDOM OF JERUSALEM

DAVID ABULAFIA

Gonville and Caius College, Cambridge

Famous now for its medieval towers, the town of San Gimignano possessed a more special reputation in the thirteenth century, when tall towers adorned factious communities of Italians as far afield as Acre. San Gimignano was then the prime centre of production in Tuscany of saffron; from its crocuses was extracted this prized dye, condiment and medicine—the most valuable of the colouring agents made in and exported from western Europe in the Middle Ages.[1] At a time when northern Italy was dependent on Muslim lands for most of the finest dyes, exports of Tuscan saffron to the east helped to pay for these luxury imports. Thus the development of an active saffron trade with the eastern Mediterranean indicates a slight shift towards a more equal trading relationship between western Europe and the Levant. Certainly, western saffron fetched a very high price in eastern markets during the thirteenth century; it was more than worth its weight in Pisan silver, provided the saffron was not too severely adulterated. And in this respect the produce of San Gimignano achieved particular respectability.[2] Nor, indeed, was it only the crocuses of San Gimignano which were known in Acre or Aleppo. The town's inhabitants went east too, and they themselves sold their native dye to Saracen merchants.

The men of San Gimignano did not directly receive any known commercial privileges from the rulers of the Latin states in the east; they traded under a Pisan flag, and even then by tacit agreement rather than by treaty. The picture

---

1   Antonio Petino, *Lo Zafferano nell'economia del medioevo*, Studi di economia e statistica, ser. 1.1 (Catania, 1950-51).
2   Enrico Fiumi, *Storia economica e sociale di San Gimignano*, Biblioteca storica toscana 11 (Florence, 1961), pp. 33-40. Hereafter cited as Fiumi.

presented by Boccaccio in his *Decameron* of informal co-operation between Sangimignanesi and Pisans living in Messina seems to hold true for thirteenth-century Acre: in the story of the pot of basil a young Pisan, Lorenzo, lodges with and works for three brothers from San Gimignano, but when he seduces their sister he pays a terrible penalty.[3] Fortunately Boccaccio's characters have their counterparts in the historical record—in the jailbird Muczus, who absconded with the Prince of Antioch's funds; in the destitute Dandus, importuning Tuscan merchants in Acre. The source of information for these colourful figures lies in the extensive records of commercial litigation from the podestà's court in San Gimignano, which date back as far as 1221. Preserved in the State Archives at Florence there are lengthy fragments of the transcripts made by court notaries of evidence presented by plaintiffs and witnesses —carefully compiled, and checked through with those who gave evidence.[4] Several law-suits say much about Acre, and have been known to scholars in outline since 1900, when Robert Davidsohn published his register of documents from or about medieval San Gimignano.[5] But it is impossible to gain from Davidsohn's terse summaries in Latin and German a real sense of the conflict of evidence in the podestà's court; sometimes, indeed, Davidsohn presents as statements of apparent fact remarks which were bitterly contested by an opposing party. The *Carte di San Gimignano* pose in a very acute form the difficulty of choosing between the evidence of several witnesses, even eye-witnesses; moreover, what survive are only fragments of the record, so that cases are encountered when already well under way, or lost from sight before judgment has been delivered. Fortunately, less contentious merchant operations are briefly illuminated by a notarial cartulary dated 1257-62, once again preserved in Florence, but devoted to the affairs of San Gimignano.[6]

I

The first mention of Acre in the *Carte* is in documents of 1224; but they refer back in time to about 1221, when the armies of the Fifth Crusade were occupy-

3   Giovanni Boccaccio, *Decameron* 4.5; David Abulafia, "The reputation of a Norman king in Angevin Naples," *Journal of Medieval History* 5 (1979), 142-143.

4   Florence, Archivio di Stato, Carte di San Gimignano—hereafter cited as Carte. Most *buste* of the Carte examined here take the form of a notebook composed of about six to ten leaves of paper, folded and (in the best preserved examples, e.g. Carte 138) sewn together at the fold, and on occasion bound within a parchment cover (e.g. Carte 45); but pages are often inserted loose or higgledy-piggledy (Carte 45, perhaps Carte 1) and folios have certainly disappeared (Carte 44, between fols. 2 and 3). Usually each notebook contains material from several law-suits in the hand of more than one notary.

5   Robert Davidsohn, *Forschungen zur Geschichte von Florenz, 2: Aus den Stadtbüchern und Urkunden von San Gimignano* (Berlin, 1900); hereafter cited as Davidsohn.

6   Florence, Archivio di Stato, Notarile antecosimiano A 943: Arrigo di Janni, 1257-62.

ing Damietta.[7] Seracenus Grugnoli claimed in court in San Gimignano that a certain Gradalonis owed him one gold besant, on the grounds that Seracenus had lent Gradalonis' son, Dandus, money for clothes when Dandus and Seracenus were together in Acre. Dandus had sailed east, had apparently taken the cross, and had served at Damietta; after the defeat of the Fifth Crusade he had escaped to Acre, where he pestered his compatriots for loans and hung about "quasi nudus." He was fitted with a tunic at the shop of Rainerius the Florentine, after which Seracenus left for Aleppo on business and lost contact with Dandus; but he did not forget his loan and insisted that Dandus' father must bear responsibility for it. Gradalonis for his part denied that he had encouraged Dandus to go on crusade, but he agreed that Dandus "efectus est miles" while abroad — the confusion whether Dandus had taken the cross may indicate that he left home as a merchant and joined the crusade army as a *miles* once in the east; on his departure, indeed, Dandus was still quite well off. Crusader or not, the court decided, his debts must be repaid by his father to Seracenus.[8] Now, although the exact events are difficult to recover amid inelegant notarial Latin and vigorous counter-claims, these pages of the *Carte* are rich in information. Seracenus Grugnoli reappears in later court cases not as a plaintiff but as a busy Levant trader, spending part of the year "ultramare" with other prominent merchants of San Gimignano.[9] And the presence in Acre of a specialist Florentine merchant, here dealing in cloths, is echoed in later documents from this series.

Dandus escaped from Damietta, but there were men of San Gimignano who died there. Evidence was presented in 1224 that Bernardinus Villanus and Cigolinus Alberti fell ill at Damietta during the occupation of the city; they were cared for in separate houses by women from San Gimignano who had accompanied the armies of the crusade to the east. Cigolinus recovered and bore witness in San Gimignano to the death of his friend, who had been buried outside the city walls at the church of St. Bartholus (perhaps a converted mosque, to judge from the case of the cathedral of Frankish Damietta).[10] What the court in Tuscany needed to know was whether it was certain that Bernardinus had died, and whether it was certain that the person in San Gimignano who claimed to be his wife, and the inheritor of his estate, was in fact that; and while these points were being resolved information about Bernardinus' eco-

---

7   See e.g. J.P. Donovan, *Pelagius and the Fifth Crusade* (Philadelphia, 1950).

8   Carte 2, fols. 31r and 96r; this is a larger *busta* than the others examined. Davidsohn, no. 2303 summarises part of fol. 96r. See also Fiumi, pp. 56, 48.

9   Carte 42, fol. 15r; Carte 44, fol. 3v.

10   Carte 2, fols. 133v-134r; Davidsohn, no. 2304; Fiumi, p. 55. For events in Damietta see e.g. Runciman, *Crusades*, 3:162-169; Pràwer, *Histoire*, 2: 149-169, esp. 160-161.

nomic standing emerged. According to one witness his wife's dowry was worth £40, plus £18 in furnishings, so that Bernardinus must have had a fairly prosperous household.[11] But it is not clear whether he was himself a crusader, though there is no reference to a merchant's effects in the description of his death. Moreover, it was important to be very careful to have accurate proof of the death of a crusader overseas.[12] And it is well known that the army occupying Damietta included a group of ambitious Bolognese citizens.[13] Finally, even if the Sangimignanesi in Damietta were not all crusaders, they were there because of the crusade and because of the opportunities, spiritual or material, which it offered.

It is clear already that the merchants of San Gimignano used Acre as a base from which they traded to Aleppo. Seracenus Grugnoli had several rivals along this route: Aleppo appears no less often than Tripoli in the San Gimignano law-suits.[14] Contemporary documents from Marseilles indicate that Latin merchants favoured the alum on sale in Aleppo, though there is no specific reference to visits to the Muslim hinterland by Provençal traders.[15] The San Gimignano documents, by contrast, reveal that the markets of Aleppo absorbed western saffron as well as a variety of other products—a document of 1245 mentions "vj barilos blanche," six barrels of lac, which Ristorus entrusted to his agent Bonome, to be carried to Aleppo. Bonome's base seems to have been Acre, for it was there that Bonome claimed to have settled his debts upon his return; unfortunately, those who brought Bonome to court in

11   Carte 2, fol. 133v: testimony of Gascha uxor Ricoueri, who believed Bernardinus had married at least twenty years before.

12   James Brundage, *Medieval Canon Law and the Crusader* (Madison, Wis., 1969), pp. 126-127: "adequate proof of his [a crusader's] death was necessary, in the first place, lest the heirs to his estate be forced to redeem his vow. Second, proof of the husband's death was required before a widow could remarry", and so on. Brundage cites a thirteenth-century MS from my own college library: Tancredus, Apparatus to Compilatio Prima, 4.22.3, ad v. *vita*, in: Gonville and Caius College, Cambridge, MS 28/17, p. 107b: "Sed quid faciet si nunc per magistrum militum ut ibidem dicitur certificari [non] poterit de morte uiri, sicut sepe accidit in magnis preliis et precipue sarracenorum et christianorum ubi multi pereunt de quibus nichil nouerunt hii qui ducebant exercitum? Mittat ad uicinas ciuitates si posset; alias contrahat [*scil.* uxor]. La[urentius]."

13   Reinhold Röhricht, *Studien zur Geschichte des Fünften Kreuzzuges* (Innsbruck, 1891), pp. 58, 64, 70-74.

14   Aleppo: Carte 2, fol. 96r; Carte 32, fol. 12r; Carte 42, fol. 15r; Carte 44, fol. 4r; Carte 45, fols. 1av, 2ar, 2av, 2br (Carte 45 contains two folders of paper, one of 4 fols., here numbered fol. 1a, etc., and one of ten fols., here numbered fol. 1b, etc.). Tripoli: Carte 45, fols. 2ar-v, 2br; Carte 138 is, as will be clear, rich in reference to Tripoli.

15   L. Blancard, ed., *Documents inédits sur le commerce de Marseille au moyen âge*, 1 (Marseilles, 1884), no. 47 of the edition of Manduel charters; David Abulafia, "Marseilles, Acre and the Mediterranean, 1200-1291," in *Coinage in the Latin East*, ed. P.W. Edbury and D.M. Metcalf, British Archaeological Reports, supplementary series (Oxford, 1980).

San Gimignano did not believe he had been so diligent.[16] Elsewhere in the *Carte* is a statement that a merchant of San Gimignano had, among his stocks at Aleppo, textiles, raw cotton and felt, possibly purchased for export to Acre.[17] Yet the key to the presence of Sangimignanesi in the Syrian hinterland seems to lie in the evidence that, in the same decade, quantities of "boni et puri groci," of best saffron, were being shipped via Pisa and Acre to Aleppo; other favoured destinations were Alexandria and "Turchia," but merchants tended to base themselves in the Holy Land.[18] Acre was the servicing centre for a wider saffron trade that remained partly under the control of men of San Gimignano even in Muslim lands. The Sangimignanesi were, in fact, expert dealers in all grades of saffron; they did not only bring Tuscan saffron to the east, but interested themselves in saffron produced outside their homeland.[19]

These attempts to penetrate beyond the frontiers of the Latin states were not always free of impediment. Although they might be warmly welcomed in Muslim cities, the Latin merchants encountered the disapproval of the Frankish rulers in the east, who feared the loss of revenue from the royal markets at Acre, where the Italians often purchased the oriental goods they required, and often sold their imports to Saracen and native Christian merchants.[20] From the same decade as the *Carte* which refer so frequently to Latin trade in Acre comes the complaint of the Venetian *bailli* in Syria, Marsiglio Zorzi: "if anyone from Venice wishes to go to Damascus or to any Muslim country and buys merchandise and he wishes to bring it to Acre by land, he must pay nine and seven twenty-fourths per cent if he wants to sell it in Acre." The only way to protect what the Venetians saw as their special rights to tax exemption was to make a special deal with the king's officers in Acre — perhaps, Marsiglio means, to bribe them.[21] It is not clear to what limitations the Tuscans trading to Aleppo were subjected; the Sangimignanesi posed as Pisans, as will be seen, when trading between Acre and Aleppo, so that their position may have been similar to that of the Venetians who traded to Damascus. What is clear is that

16   Carte 32, fol. 12r-v; photograph of fol. 12r in Fiumi, fig. 6, facing p. 76, and Fiumi, p. 35, note 77, for a brief reference.
17   Carte 42, fol. 13v; Carte 44, fol. 4r; Davidsohn, no. 2307.
18   Carte 32, fol. 7r records a price of £11 for 4 1b. of saffron, and a visit to Acre; photograph in Fiumi, fig. 5, facing p. 60.
19   Fiumi, pp. 34-35. In the early 1270s Muczus Ardinghelli bought saffron in Acre and carried it to Alexandria: Carte 138, fol. 1r; Davidsohn, no. 2310.
20   Jonathan Riley-Smith, "Government in Latin Syria and the Commercial Privileges of Foreign Merchants," in *Relations between East and West in the Middle Ages*, ed. D. Baker (Edinburgh, 1973), pp. 109-132.
21   G.L.F. Tafel and G.M. Thomas, eds., *Urkunden zur älteren Handels- und Staatsgeschichte der Republik Venedig mit besonderer Beziehung auf Byzanz und die Levante*, 2 vols., Fontes rerum austriacarum, 2.13.2 (Vienna, 1856), pp. 397-398; translation here from Riley-Smith, "Commercial Privileges," p. 120.

the merchants of a second-rate Tuscan town saw Aleppo as a very desirable target for trade both in saffron and in more general wares.

Within the Mediterranean, the Sangimignanesi also used Acre as a base for operations over a wide area. They visited Alexandria, of course.[22] And there were little groups in Sicily and perhaps in north Africa who traded directly with the Holy Land. Paganellus son of Rusticus of San Gimignano agreed in 1260 to take £67 belonging to Bonacursus Tedaldini from Messina to Acre; in the early 1270s both businessmen were again active in Acre.[23] It was difficult to prevent merchants from visiting other Mediterranean ports for trade on their return to Tuscany from Acre: Ugolinus Burnetti was accused of ignoring instructions to return directly from Syria to Pisa and San Gimignano, for he had stopped in Messina and had even diverted to Tunis. Admittedly, his plans had been thrown awry, because a partner had died in Tripoli while returning from Aleppo to Acre.[24] The unhappy venture generated accusations of dishonesty and deceit, but others took more calmly the common emergency presented by the death of a merchant overseas. Ubaldus Iudex of San Gimignano fell ill at Acre in about 1261; he entrusted 140 besants and his coat to two other Tuscan merchants, one from his home town, the other a Florentine spice-dealer. Shortly thereafter his heirs in San Gimignano commissioned another merchant, who was about to leave for Acre, to make use of Ubaldus' property in the east. Moreover, Ubaldus had entrusted 33 besants to a merchant named Strenna, who was due to return from Acre to San Gimignano. But Strenna too died, this time in Palermo, so Ubaldus' heirs sought out another merchant to redeem his property. Their choice fell on Maffeus olim Petri, whose family had good experience of Syrian trade too.[25]

There is rich information in the *Carte* about the economic standing of the Acre merchants. Ildebrandus Coni fulfilled a number of judicial and political tasks for the commune of San Gimignano; he and his sons operated from an important textile warehouse in their native city, and they were active in the Levant trade.[26] Paganellus Rusticus thought in 1277 that he possessed about

22 Davidsohn, no. 2305, showing that the Pisans in Alexandria allowed other Tuscans to trade under their flag; Fiumi, p. 59.
23 Davidsohn, no. 2300 (=no. 2309), from the cartulary of Arrigo de Janni (A943) in Florence; no fol. reference is given. I did not see this document when I examined A943; Fiumi, p. 63, also bases himself on Davidsohn's report. The document was drawn up originally in Messina, in the house of Guilielmus, in the Jewish quarter—"contrata yudeorum." For the activities of these merchants in the 1270s: Carte 138, fols. 4v and 10r-v.
24 Carte 45, fols. 1av-2av, fol. 2br; Davidsohn, no. 2308.
25 Notarile antecosimiano A943, fols. 204v, 205r, 205v, 206v-207r, 207r—six documents, of which the third and the last are cancelled; Fiumi, p. 58. Maffeus' father appears among a list of witnesses with knowledge of Syrian trade; Carte 42, fols. 14v and 15r.
26 For instance, Carte 4 fol. 1r; Carte 25, fols. 1r, 2r-v, 3r, 5v, 9v, 12r, 14r; Fiumi, pp. 249-250.

£200 in worldly goods; he was then at least 36 years old.[27] The same year some Tuscan merchants with experience of Acre were asked to state their age and minimum wealth, at the end of their testimony in court. Only two of the San Gimignano merchants were worth more than £200; but Pisan merchants who knew Acre were generally worth £1,000. The Pisans were indeed senior partners in the affairs of Acre.[28]

DECLARED AGE AND WEALTH OF TUSCANS FORMERLY IN ACRE

Source: Carte di San Gimignano, 138 (anno 1277).

	minimum wealth	*approximate age*
1) *Merchants of San Gimignano*		
Jacobus	£100 (in common with his father and brothers)	36
Ranerius	£100	38
Gratianus Tancredi	—	26
Terius Gentilis	£200	40
Dinus Guccii	£200	28
Maffeotus Seraceni	£800	36
Corsus Danielli	£200	37
Dietiguardi	£900	35
Ghese de Diotavive	£100	30
2) *Merchants of Pisa*		
Dominus Loiterius Corbinus	£500	50
Pellarius filius domini Ranerii de domo Lanfrancorum	—	30
Oddo Gaytonis	£1000	30
Oddinus de Sala	£1000	25
Lorrentius Ruffelmini	£1000	40
3) *Pisan consuls in Acre*		
Dominus Andrioctus Seraceni	£1000	38
Dominus Guido de Caprona	£1000	
4) *Pisan notaries from Syria*		
Vitalis de Cola	£100	30
Benencasa olim Leonardi de Casana	£100	56
5) *A servant to a Pisan merchant*		
Henricus famulus Oddi Gaytani	£100	30

For some individuals, e.g. Guido son of Andrioctus Seraceni, neither age nor wealth is indicated. Note that these witnesses described events when they were at least six years younger.

27 Carte 138, fol. 4v.
28 These figures are appended to the testimony of witnesses in Carte 138. The Pisans included Andrioctus Seraceni (38 years, £1,000) and Guido de Caprona (no age given, £1,000), both of whom had been Pisan consul in Acre—Carte 138, fols. 7v, 9v. The figures for age need not be taken too seriously; some witnesses confessed uncertainty. The figures for wealth are the witnesses' own approximate minimum.

II

The close relationship between Pisa and San Gimignano—between country town and maritime outlet—is apparent at the Tuscan and Levantine end of the trade route to Acre. Davidsohn printed some lines from a series of documents of 1245, which show that merchants of Florence, Pistoia, Lucca, Siena and San Gimignano, "et omnes alii de Tuscia," presented themselves as Pisans in Acre; so too, it seems, on their visits to Aleppo and Alexandria.[29] This relationship poses several problems. Why did the Pisans allow the Sangimignanesi to take their name? And what did the "pseudo-Pisans" offer the true Pisans in exchange? It is also necessary to separate the interests and involvement of the commune of San Gimignano in Tuscany from the choice or custom prevailing among Sangimignanesi living in or visiting Acre. In other words, is this an official, regulated association, formulated perhaps on a legal basis between the government of Pisa and that of San Gimignano, or is it an *ad hoc* relationship formed out of the requirements of Tuscan traders in the Levant? It is necessary to remember that the practice of sailing under the flag of a more privileged trading city was well established in the thirteenth-century Mediterranean. For a time "merchant of Marseilles" subsumed merchant of Montpellier too, in Cyprus and Acre.[30] The Genoese were quite open in their desire to make Savonese merchants trade under their patronage; and a clause the Genoese inserted in their treaty with William I of Sicily in 1156 forbade French and Provençal merchants direct access to Sicily only, it seems, so that these merchants would have to travel there under Genoese licence.[31] Sometimes, too, the definition of a privileged community of merchants was left very loose: in 1197 Henry VI allowed the Luccans and "universi homines totius Tuscie" the same rights as the Pisans in his newly conquered Kingdom of Sicily; while the earliest genuine privilege welcoming the merchants of Marseilles to the Holy

---

29 Davidsohn, no. 2307: what Davidsohn printed were not statements of fact by witnesses (although these were offered later), but a series of questions emanating from the court about the real status of Tuscan merchants in Acre. His source was not, as may appear, the continuous text of the law-suit in Carte 42, but a separate sheet of paper in a clear hand inserted loose among the pages of the notebook. Davidsohn prints lines 7 to 19 out of a total of 23 lines. This sheet seems to be a list to be kept before the court of the issues the court wished to resolve. Aleppo: Carte 44, fol. 2v. Alexandria: Davidsohn, no. 2305. Cf. Tafel-Thomas, pp. 62-66, 256-260, for Aleppo.

30 Abulafia, "Marseilles," p. 29; H.E. Mayer, *Marseilles Levantehandel und ein akkonensisches Fälscheratelier des XIII. Jahrhunderts* (Tübingen, 1972), pp. 84-88, also p. 65 for a reference to San Gimignano. In the twelfth century Provençal merchants too took the cover of a Pisan flag, as Mayer shows.

31 David Abulafia, *The Two Italies: Economic Relations between the Norman Kingdom of Sicily and the Northern Communes* (Cambridge, Eng., 1977), pp. 95-96, 169-170.

Land names several other prominent Occitanian towns, and also Barcelona.[32]

Two legal cases, fought at San Gimignano in 1245 and 1277, concern in different ways the jurisdiction of Pisa over men of San Gimignano who traded in Acre and posed as Pisans. Both cases reveal that the commune of San Gimignano possessed little exact information about the status of its citizens in Acre—no treaties, with Pisa or anyone else; no copies of the *breve*, or instructions, given to the Pisan consuls in Acre; little knowledge of who the consuls were or what they did. But, precisely because the judges were so unclear about these matters, they extracted lengthy explanations from witnesses at each trial.

In 1245 Avitus, the legal guardian of Subilia, daughter of Cambius, brought an action against Guido Actaviani, who had been with Cambius in Aleppo "cause mercantie," and who had received merchandise from Cambius in commenda.[33] But Cambius died out east, and Guido failed to make full restitution to Subilia for the property of her father that had been entrusted to him. Giving evidence, Guido stated firmly that it had long been the custom that a third part of the goods of any merchant "qui pro Pisano cognoscitur," who died in Syria, should be surrendered to the consul of the Pisans at Acre.[34] Guido claimed he had brought Cambius' effects, which included a quantity of raw cotton, from Aleppo to Acre, where he was subjected to this ruling. Against this, Subilia's *tutor* maintained that the Pisan consul was not the highest authority in Acre, and it had therefore not been right to accept his judgment: "in civitate Acon est dominus qui preest consulibus omnibus comunitatum e[x]istentibus in civitate iam dicta." Quite recently, he said, the "dominus" had instructed the Pisan consul to hand over to him two towers in Acre, constructed at the expense of the commune of Pisa; and the consul had complied.[35] It is noticeable that Avitus dwells on the problem of Pisan jurisdiction and does not seek to deny that there are non-Pisans in Acre who submit themselves to Pisan authority; it is simply that the "dominus" gives judgment in cases where even true Pisans wish to appeal against the decisions of their own consul.

The court decided to test the validity of Guido's case by searching for precise information on the following points:

i. Who elected the Pisan consuls? Was it the Pisans in Acre or the commune of Pisa, and how was the election conducted?

---

32 Abulafia, *Two Italies*, pp. 260-261, for Lucca; Mayer, *Marseilles Levantehandel*, pp. 40 and 181-183, document no. 4, for the privilege to St Gilles, Nîmes, Montpellier, Marseilles, Barcelona—also Abulafia, "Marseilles," p. 20.

33 Carte 42, fols. 13v-15r; Carte 44, fols. 2r-4v; extracts in Davidsohn no. 2307.

34 Carte 42, fol. 14r. Guilelmus Gobbecti de Ripa Fracta was Pisan consul "ante Galitianum nunc consulem."

35 Carte 42, fol. 14r, mostly printed by Davidsohn, no. 2307, p. 296.

ii.   What authority did the Pisan consuls have to administer justice or punishment, and on the basis of what statutes or documents?

iii.   How is it known that the Pisan consuls possess rights over "omnibus de
Tuscia in Accon pro tempore existentibus"?

iv.   Even if it is true that all these Tuscans call themselves Pisans, do those
who know what they really are treat them still as Pisans while in Acre?

v.   If the consuls do deliver judgment in all matters brought to their attention by Tuscans of whatever sort, what happens if a Tuscan refuses to submit
to the penalty imposed—has anyone seen the consuls actually impose their will
on a pseudo-Pisan, perhaps by force?

vi.   Above all, what is done in the case of Tuscans who die somewhere in
Syria? Has any witness seen the Pisan consuls take a third of the property of
the deceased, and has any witness knowledge of some law or custom by which
this is done?[36]

Witnesses were to be called not just from San Gimignano but from Pisa and
from Syria too—Seracenus Grugnoli was to be interviewed on his return from
the east, as were several Florentines and a certain Simon of Jaffa, whose name
seems to reflect a very close tie to the Kingdom of Jerusalem.[37] The evidence of
these witnesses, as far as it survives, tended to support Guido's contention in
many respects, while also revealing further complications. Thus Galligaius
Bonacursi said that many Tuscans, including Sangimignanesi, did indeed submit to the Pisan consuls, but "illi qui nolunt non subsunt et non coguntur nisi
velint se conficeri Pisanos"; this statement raised the problem whether Cambius had indeed posed as a Pisan, but it seemed certain that he had.[38] Ildebrandus Coni, who has already been identified as a wealthy and important citizen,
pointed out that non-Pisans who assumed a Pisan identity gained the enormous advantage of passing as Pisans through the "catena de Acon"—the *cour
de la chaine*, where the king's officers checked most merchants.[39] The fact of
being "franchi ad catenam" and of enjoying Pisan tax privileges was stressed
by several witnesses, but few knew much about the election of the Pisan consul.
One witness thought the Pisans in Acre sent to their mother-city for a nominee
of their choice; but Dominus Acoppus Iudex thought the election took place in
Pisa, and that the consul was sent over to Acre to be installed in office there.

---

36   This is a paraphrase of a text inserted loose in Carte 42: see note 29 *supra*.
37   Carte 42, fols. 14v, 15r.
38   Carte 44, fol. 2v for the testimony; also Carte 42, fol. 15r for the question whether "dictus
     Guido et dictus Cambius erant et habebantur et censebantur pisani in acon et in partibus
     Syrie et alappi."
39   Carte 44, fol. 2v; cf. Riley-Smith, "Commercial Privileges," pp. 112-114.

Acoppus was present at the installation of Guillelmus Gobbecti as consul; the ceremony took place in the church of St. Peter—the main church in the Pisan quarter—and the statutes of the consulate in Acre were read aloud.[40] Those who knew about the matter were sure that the Pisan consuls in Acre did usually claim their share of the property of deceased merchants; Guillelmus Gobbecti had taken his share of the goods of Ristorus, who died "in turchia"; another consul, Ildebrandus Pallarosa, followed the same practice.[41] When Cambius' goods were divided, Ildebrandus Coni and others went to see the consul in Acre and asked that no part of his property should be seized, but the consul demurred; Cambius' goods were in the end put up for sale outside the church of St. Peter in Acre.[42]

The evidence of the witnesses does not directly answer all the questions that worried the court; Subilia's *tutor* had himself advanced several other suggestions about which the witnesses had nothing to say. Either the court was unimpressed by Avitus' argument that the consuls were subject to a higher authority in Acre, that of the "dominus," or the court records have survived very incompletely. The absence of questions to the witnesses about this "dominus" suggests that the court did not find Avitus' statements very relevant; they were a long shot, really, at an attempt to hold Guido rather than the Pisan consul responsible for the abstraction of part of Cambius' cargo. Recently, however, David Jacoby has suggested who this "dominus" might have been: if

40 Evidence of Ristorus quondam Tineosi: Carte 44, fol. 3v; cf. Acoppus: Carte 44, fol. 3r. A *breve* of 1286 survives, but does not necessarily reflect exact conditions over forty years earlier: Müller, *Documenti*, pp. 380-381. In the early fourteenth century the Venetian vice-consul at Trani was elected by the merchant community there from the Venetian aristocracy; but the Venetian consul in the Kingdom of Naples was expected to supervise the election: David Abulafia, "Venice and the Kingdom of Naples in the last years of King Robert the Wise, 1332-1343," *Papers of the British School at Rome* 48 (1980). Pisan overseas consulates had already developed in the twelfth century: David Abulafia, "Pisan Commercial Colonies and Consulates in Twelfth-century Sicily," *English Historical Review* 93 (1978), 68-81, printing a document where consuls are referred to in the plural (Messina, 1189); but in Acre there was only one consul at a time during the 1240s and 1270s, as Carte 42, 44, 138 indicate. Compare also Arthur Hibbert, "Catalan Consulates in the Thirteenth Century," *Cambridge Historical Journal* 9 (1949), 352-358.

41 Carte 44, fols. 3v-4r. Seracenus Grugnoli saw the goods of a certain Peruccius brought before Consul Ildebrandus Pallarosa. Fiumi, p. 270, mentions a Peruzzi family of San Gimignano with overseas trading interests; "Peruccius" probably does not signify "of Perugia."

42 Carte 44, fols. 2v and 4r; Ildebrandus Coni mentions the visit to the Pisan consul in his own evidence; it is interesting to see another witness single him out as leader of the group that called the consul—confirming, perhaps, the impression of Coni's special status among the Sangimignanesi of Acre. For St. Peter's church: David Jacoby, "Crusader Acre in the Thirteenth Century: Urban Layout and Topography," *Studi medievali* 3.20 (1979), 24-25.

the towers which Avitus insisted were handed to the "dominus" were transferred in about 1242 or 1243, the mystery figure could be Balian d'Ibelin, lord
of Beirut, then becoming very active inside Acre.[43] At that time the Pisans were
vigorously supporting Frederick II's party in the Kingdom of Jerusalem; perhaps, therefore, the towers were handed over as a guarantee of good conduct;
and perhaps too Balian's grip on Acre encouraged the Pisans to side with
Balian in June 1243 when, according to Philippe de Novare, they recognised
Alice of Cyprus as *bailli* of Jerusalem—a half-measure against their preferred
patron, Conrad of Hohenstaufen, the absentee king. Although Jacoby has
found in Balian an excellent candidate for the rôle of "dominus," it is not in
fact clear that the Pisans attended Balian's conference about Conrad and
Alice; only Philippe de Novare names them, though the other sources mention
just the Genoese and the Venetians.[44] Avitus' information about the towers in
Acre inspires a little confidence; but in other respects his knowledge is very
vague and arouses suspicion: he may have heard rumours of current events in
Acre, including events after 1243, since Cambius' death; but he could not
name his "dominus." Perhaps he was merely hazarding a guess at the special
constitutional position of the Italians in the Kingdom of Jerusalem; probably
he was trying to capitalise on the simple fact that the podestà's court in San
Gimignano was very ignorant of the laws and customs of the Italian colonies in
Syria; but in the event he failed.

The law-suit does not specify one advantage non-Pisans may have gained, at
least for a time, as a result of calling themselves Pisans. Not merely were Pisans
"franchi ad catenam," free of customs dues on the passage of most goods
through the port of Acre; a privilege of 1187 gave them a unique right to
supervise the movement of Pisan goods through the *catenae*, markets and gates
of Acre, Tyre and Jaffa. This generous privilege was soon countermanded, but
the Pisans seem to have struggled to maintain this freedom from royal oversight.[45] Certainly, non-Pisan factors of Pisan merchants and Tuscan pseudo-
Pisans could expect to benefit from such a right; it may in consequence have
been easier to pose as a Pisan than as a Genoese or Venetian, for in the latter

---

43   Jacoby, "Crusader Acre," p. 25, note 120.
44   *Les Gestes des Chiprois*, ed. G. Raynaud (Geneva, 1887), para. 226; cf. John La Monte,
      Feudal Monarchy in the Latin Kingdom of Jerusalem, 1100 to 1291 (Cambridge, Mass., 1932),
      pp. 71-72, note 2. It would be reasonable to expect Marsiglio Zorzi to mention the Pisans in
      his own account of the conference: Tafel-Thomas, *Urkunden*, 2: 345-347.
45   Müller, *Documenti*, nos. 24-5, 27-8, 31-2; for Henry of Champagne's less generous provisions,
      see Müller, no. 37 and now Marie-Luise Favreau-Lilie, "Graf Heinrich von Champagne und
      die Pisaner im Königreich Jerusalem," *Bollettino storico pisano* 47 (1978), 97-120; valuable
      remarks also in Riley-Smith, "Commercial Privileges," p. 114.

cases a merchant would always undergo a royal check. The principal limitation on the activity of the Sangimignanesi was apparently electoral. They witnessed the arrival of new Pisan consuls in Acre, but they did not participate, in Pisa or in Acre, in the slightly mysterious process of appointment.

It is not too difficult to suggest what advantages the Pisans found in the presence of other Tuscans sailing under their flag to Acre. The references in the San Gimignano text to "factitiis Pisanis," Pisan factors, who were accepted as real Pisans, confirms that Pisans and non-Pisans often worked together in financial ventures through Acre: analogies to better-documented Genoese and Venetian practice can be assumed.[46] Added to the possibilities such co-operation raised for the injection of outside capital into Pisan enterprises, there was the advantage gained from the expertise of specialist traders who worked alongside the Pisans in Acre: Florentine cloth merchants, rising to prominence during the thirteenth century; Florentine spice-dealers, financiers from Siena (visible in large numbers, though with limited Levantine interests, in the Marseilles documents); experts in the production of and handling of saffron from San Gimignano, Volterra and Siena; even the prestigious cloth-dealers of Lucca, who generally expressed a preference for the Genoese flag, seem on occasion to have hoisted a Pisan banner in Acre.[47] Much of the trade of the Tuscan hinterland with the Levant was, of course, channelled through Pisa, and Sangimignanese or Volterran capital no doubt stimulated the shipping industry. Not surprisingly, therefore, the Pisan commune began to assume legal rights over these surrogate Pisans, and even encouraged them in their wish to claim Pisan privileges in the ports of Syria—but all this was achieved, not through formal agreements with the Tuscan communes nor even with the rulers of Jerusalem; it was achieved by an accidental or deliberate process of slow absorption. In 1245 the podestà's court in San Gimignano was itself beginning to learn what advantages the town's merchants had acquired in Acre apart from a lively market for Tuscan saffron.

---

46 "Factitiis pisanis": Carte 42, fol. 15r; Carte 44, fol. 4r; etc. As examples of contracts between Italians from the leading maritime cities and Italians from commercial centres inland, see Abulafia, *Two Italies*, p. 144 (Verona and Venice, 1176), and pp. 256-260 (Lucca and Genoa, 1179-91).

47 Siena: in 1248, Dioteviva Alberto of Siena sent 171 lb of saffron, worth over £160 (perhaps, therefore, not best quality merchandise) from Marseilles to Acre; but his factor was in fact Provençal—Blancard, *Documents*, Cartulaire d'Almaric no. 230. Volterra: Fiumi, p. 34, also p. 55. Lucca: Carte 42, inserted sheet (note 29 *supra*); but elsewhere in the law-suit the Luccans disappear, though the Sienese and Florentines tend to remain among those listed as "pseudo-Pisans."

By 1277 the Pisan relationship with merchants of San Gimignano in Acre was no longer a serious matter for investigation in the court of San Gimignano. A case examined that year took it for granted that the Pisan consul should imprison a San Gimignano merchant against whom the agents of the prince of Antioch-Tripoli had a serious case. This law-suit, which has a quire all to itself in the *Carte di San Gimignano*, may originally have occupied several quires: the beginning has been lost, but a rough reconstruction of the charges is still possible.[48] Bonacursus Tedaldini, who has already been encountered, sued Lambertus olim Guidi Ardinghelli, a member of an important Sangimignanese clan, for the recovery of money invested with Lambertus and his brother Muczus, who had disappeared about six years before.[49] Muczus Ardinghelli was said to have mislaid or abandoned a cargo while in Syria; but this was in fact only one of a series of heady accusations. Muczus' career in crime seems to have begun in Tripoli. He absconded from there "cum bizantinis quinque milia de hominibus principis de Tripuli"—these words are from the testimony, secured in Pisa, of the sometime consul in Acre, Andrioctus Seraceni.[50] Before suspicion was aroused about his embezzlement, Muczus seems to have found backers for a business trip from Acre to Alexandria; at any rate, he carried a cargo worth £105 to Egypt, much of it saffron bought in Syria, some of it honey.[51] The ship which carried Muczus also carried "plures mercatores Florentini et Pisani" to Alexandria; and it was owned by a Venetian merchant (according to other testimony, a Pisan merchant)—the absence of Genoese surely reflects conditions in Acre after the War of St. Sabas, when they lost their quarter and went to Tyre.[52] Muczus, perhaps because he was in a sense on the run, had paid a rather high price for the goods he brought to Alexandria; now he sold them in Egypt to Saracen merchants at a loss, taking no account of seasonal changes in price ("propter mutationem temporis et rerum," as one witness expresses a simple economic law).[53] But he did return to Acre and he

---

48 Carte 138, containing testimonies but no statements of charges.
49 Carte 138, fol. 10v; excerpts in Davidsohn, no. 2310, pointing out (p. 302) that Lambertus was an Ardinghelli; also Fiumi, pp. 234-235. Fiumi, p. 78, notes that "nel 1274-75 risiedono in Lombardia i fratelli Lamberto e Muzzo Guidi degli Ardinghelli," so that northern Italy seems to have become Muczus' place of refuge.
50 Carte 138, fol. 7v.
51 Carte 138, fol. 1r.
52 Carte 138, fol. 1r (Venetian ship), fol. 3v (Pisan).
53 Evidence of Terius Gentilis, Carte 138, fol. 3r. Earlier (fol. 2v) the same witness indicated that some at least of Muczus' losses were through incompetent trading rather than through the abstraction or mishandling of his cargo: "ipse testis erat in Ciuitate acon et recepit leteras a dicto Muçcio qui erat in alesandria continentes quod ipse Muçcio disschapitauerat de endica suprascripta. Item quod ipse Muççonis post quam reddidit ad ciuitatem acon obstendit ipsi

did bring a cargo or possessions with him — some coats are mentioned, in particular.[54] At some stage he lost even this cargo, either *en route* to Acre or while in Acre.

For he stayed in Acre two years or so — in prison. On his return he was arrested by the *masnaderii*, the armed police, of Andrioctus Seracenus, the Pisan consul.[55] He was conducted to the "Pisan tower which is in the city of Acre at the top of the Pisan quarter [or street]" — "in turri pisana que est in Ciuitate Acon in capite Rughe pisane."[56] David Jacoby has argued persuasively that the term "rua," "ruga," "rugha" stands for the whole quarter occupied by a merchant community overseas, and not merely for the street of a particular commune in a foreign port; the tower at the top of the Pisan quarter would then most probably be the "new" tower built in about 1240, and standing on the edge of the old Genoese quarter of Acre — it may even be one of the towers which Avitus insisted had been surrendered to the "dominus" over the communes.[57] Several witnesses in the trial had seen Muczus languishing in the tower, though they did not stay constantly in Acre but travelled to and fro to the west.[58] Those who had heard why he had been arrested said it was because he had absconded with the Prince of Antioch's funds; unfortunately neither Andrioctus Seraceni nor his successor as consul, Guido de Caprona, has much to add to this observation.[59] The court, however, was less concerned with the claims of Prince Bohemond than with the need to gain satisfaction for merchants of San Gimignano. What, then, had happened to his cargo? Perhaps it had simply disappeared while he was in prison, through no direct fault of his own. Some witnesses implied so, but another described the fury of the mer-

---

testi per librum raciocinei qualiter ipse Muççius perdiderat de endica suprascripta negotiando silicet emendo et vendendo et obstendat ei in ipso libro ... quod non remanserant ipsi Muççio de dicta endica nisi LXX bisantii seracinati." Terius had even heard that Muczus had lost over 200 besants, but this may represent confusion between his losses in Alexandria and in Tripoli.

54   Carte 138, fol. 5r.
55   Carte 138, fol. 7v: "uidit ipsum capi per masnaderios domini Andriocti domini Saraceni qui tunc erat consul."
56   Carte 138, fol. 1v.
57   Jacoby, "Crusader Acre," pp. 14-15, also p. 25 and map 4, following p. 45. Confirmation of Jacoby's interpretation of "rugha" is provided by Carte 138, fol. 5r: "domini Andriotti Seraceni de Pisis tunc consulis rughe Pisane ciuitatis predicte [Acon]." But the origins of a quarter often lay in the grant of a street, or in concentrated settlement in one: the "rua Florentinorum" in Messina (1193) seems to be a street name — David Abulafia, "Pisan Commercial Colonies," p. 78.
58   Thus Ranerius "ibat et reddat mercando" to Acre: Carte 138, fol. 1v.
59   Carte 138, fols 7v, 9v; also fols. 7r-v (evidence of a notary then living in the Latin East).

chants in the "rugha Pisana" when they heard that Muczus had brought such losses upon them.[60] In any case, since six or more years had passed, most witnesses could not remember what had happened to Muczus' goods. What they did remember was a more dramatic episode: Muczus escaped "secretim" from prison — according to one witness, he escaped twice, but the first time was soon recaptured.[61] When he did succeed in escaping, the Pisan consul, Guido de Caprona, searched throughout Acre without luck.[62] And this, the witnesses insisted, was "publica fama" in Acre. It seems that in 1277 he had still not returned to San Gimignano, since Lambertus Ardinghelli had to face the court without his brother's perhaps dangerous assistance.

The career of Muczus sheds a little light on the Pisan quarter in Acre: on the powers of coercion of the consuls, on the Pisan prison in the new tower, on the existence of a squad of police, or *masnaderii*. The most important conclusion to be drawn from the law-suit of 1277 is, however, the existence of great mixing among the Tuscans in the Pisan quarter at Acre, who used the "rugha Pisana" as the focal point of local trading activities northwards and southwards along the Syrian coast, commissioning factors and expecting these factors to show better judgment and honesty than Muczus seems to have possessed.

There is no evidence that the inhabitants of San Gimignano grew wealthy specifically on their Levant trade; their interests were spread around the Mediterranean and extended into France.[63] For most of the town's merchants the horizon was bounded by the city of Pisa. Local commercial rivalry with, say, Volterra counted for more than competition on the high seas with the professional maritime merchants.[64] Thus the significance of the *Carte di San Gimignano* lies to a considerable extent in the information the court cases convey about the activities of merchants in Acre who had arrived from much larger and more influential towns — Pisa and Florence. Secondly, the importance of the *Carte* lies in the emphasis they place on the saffron trade. Thirdly, it is worth considering whether the cumulative significance of the merchants from

---

60 Carte 138, fol. 4v (evidence of Paganellus Rustici).
61 Carte 138, fol. 7v.
62 Carte 138, fol. 1r-v.
63 Even the royal court in Paris is mentioned in a jotting on fol. 2r of the parchment cover of Carte 45.
64 The ancient Etruscan foundation of Volaterrae had a much longer pedigree than San Gimignano, which is first mentioned in a document of 929, a privilege of Hugh of Provence; Fiumi,. p. 17.

"lesser" towns present in thirteenth-century Acre may not have been high.[65] The inland Tuscan towns, for their part, were not precocious participants in the commercial expansion of medieval Italy; the great age of Florentine business success really begins just as the Kingdom of Jerusalem nears extinction. But from the mid-thirteenth century the Tuscan towns were beginning to acquire profits from a regular and successful Levant trade; and unlike the Pisans, they did not apparently have to work hard to win privileges.[66] Nor did their governments become involved, like that of Pisa, in the vicious battles among merchants in the streets of Acre. The Tuscans simply followed where the Pisans led them. But they did not necessarily damage Pisan interests through competition, because they offered special services. Indeed, by the mid-thirteenth century Pisa had lost some of its pioneer vigour; Pisan merchants may have remained wealthy men, but it is not impossible that they maintained their status partly through the impetus of non-Pisan investments.[67]

65 In my article "Marseilles," note 39, I suggest that the Sienese may have valued their privilege of 1268 from Conradin (Müller, *Documenti*, no. 70) more for its advantages in Sicilian than in Levantine trade; Sicily was certainly more important to Sienese businessmen, but I surely underestimated the Tuscan interest in the Holy Land. For these and other "lesser" merchants, see W. Heyd, *Histoire du commerce du Levant au moyen âge*, transl. F. Raynaud, 1 (Leipzig, 1885), 318-319.

66 Even without written privileges, some towns claimed special trading rights in the Mediterranean during the thirteenth century: David Abulafia, "Dalmatian Ragusa and the Norman Kingdom of Sicily," *Slavonic and East European Review* 54 (1976), 412-428, showing that oral agreements between the inhabitants of Dubrovnik and those of other towns were respected. The government of San Gimignano did worry about ease of access for its saffron to Pisa and Genoa: Carte 25, fol. 34v (Pisa, 1238; see Davidsohn, no. 2314); Carte 31, fol. 6br (Genoa, 1241; see Davidsohn, no. 2315); but it looked no further.

67 Petino, *Zafferano*, shows how the Tuscan saffron trade was supplanted in the late Middle Ages by that from the Abruzzi in particular; San Gimignano remained famous as a source of sweet wines. By the late fifteenth century the term "zafferano" had become an insult — as it were, 'yellow-bellied': Bartolomeo Scala da San Gimignano to the Dieci di Balià in Florence, 16 October 1479, in Florence, Archivio di Stato, Dieci Responsive 25, fols. 332-3; I owe this reference to Alison Brown. I should also like to thank Anna Sapir Abulafia for her help and interest in Florence and during the composition of this article.

THE ROTHELIN CONTINUATION
OF WILLIAM OF TYRE

M.R. MORGAN
Girton College, Cambridge

The text known as the Rothelin continuation of William of Tyre is found in twelve extant manuscripts of the *Estoire d'Eracles*, and covers in them the years 1229 to 1261. It is printed in the *Recueil des Historiens des Croisades* in volume 2 of the series *Historiens Occidentaux* as a separate text, after the end of the alternative version for the period 1229 onwards. Let us clarify immediately where the Rothelin continuation fits in to the *Eracles* as a whole. All the manuscripts which give it begin with the translation of William's *Historia*, then go on to the continuation 1184-1229 in the *g* version, then immediately on to the Rothelin continuation 1229-1261. The reader of the *Recueil* can thus reconstitute this version of the *Eracles* for himself by reading the Old French translation of the *Historia* given below the text of the *Historia* in volume 1, followed by the continuation as given in volume 2 in the *g* variant version as far as the end of the long variant ending at book 33 chapter 12,[1] followed immediately by the Rothelin continuation.[2] Two points are worth noting at the outset. No manuscript that gives the Rothelin continuation for the period 1229-1261 gives anything other than the *g* version for the earlier period of the continuations, 1184-1229. And with the exception of two manuscripts in which a French translation of the *De Excidio Urbis Acconis* has been tacked on by the compiler, the narrative ends in all the manuscripts at exactly the same point.[3] What the

1   RHC HOcc. 2:379, *g* variant.
2   Ibid., pp. 489-639.
3   The *De Excidio* is found in MS 2825 fonds français of the Bibliothèque Nationale, Paris, and MS Reg. Lat. 737 of the Biblioteca Apostolica Vaticana, Rome. There are also three Rothelin MSS that stop short of 1261 merely by virtue of being mutilated at the end, namely MS Palais

significance of these two features is we shall see. The second, meanwhile, has had the happy if coincidental result of causing all the manuscripts we shall be considering to fall into the same section of the various classifications of the *Eracles* manuscripts made successively by Mas-Latrie,[4] by Riant,[5] and by Folda,[6] since the end-date is the criterion used by all of them.

We thus use as our point of departure in this study the fourth section of Folda's inventory. From that section however we except immediately three manuscripts: Folda 59, which is nothing more than an 18th century copy of Folda 60; Folda 56, the text of which is an adaptation rather than a true exemplar of the *Eracles*; and Folda 57, MS *a* of the *Recueil*, which gives only the 1248-1261 section of the Rothelin continuation, having followed the alternative version up to that point. We shall discuss this last compilation later as a case apart. The remaining twelve manuscripts of this section are those we shall be primarily considering, that is nos. 52-55 inclusive, 58, and 60-66 inclusive. They form a genuine family of manuscripts textually speaking, unlike those of Folda's section 5, a fact which we owe partly to the chance that most of them fulfil the condition of ending at 1261 and partly to the fact that Riant, and his successors after him, chose to overlook the exceptions to this rule, that is the two manuscripts that add the *De Excidio*,[7] and should thus strictly have been put in section 5, and the three that are mutilated at the end and so stop short of 1261.[8] They were of course quite right to do so. The manuscripts which give the *De Excidio* do not continue the narrative from 1261 to 1291, but simply tack the *De Excidio* on to the end of the Rothelin continuation as elsewhere extant, leaving a gap from 1261 to 1288. It thus forms an addition rather than a continuation proper, and that is how we shall treat it here. The three incomplete manuscripts on the other hand give no sign of being other than copies of the text we know, and we are in our rights to assume, in default of evidence to the contrary, that they ended in 1261 like all the manuscripts to which they are related.

We have thus twelve manuscripts of the Rothelin version of the *Eracles*. These we may divide immediately into two sub-families. The reader of the

---

des Arts 29 of the Bibliothèque de la Ville, Lyon, and MSS L.I.5 and L.II.17 of the Biblioteca Nazionale, Turin, both damaged in the fire of 1904.

4   L. de Mas-Latrie, "Essai de classification des continuateurs de l'Histoire des croisades de Guillaume de Tyr," *Bibliothèque de l'École des Chartes* 5.1 (1860), 38-72 and 140-178. Reprinted in his *Chronique d'Ernoul et de Bernard le Trésorier* (Paris, 1871), pp. 473-639.

5   P. Riant, "Inventaire sommaire des manuscrits de l'Éracles," *AOL* 1 (1881), 247-252, 716-717.

6   J. Folda, "Manuscripts of the History of Outremer by William of Tyre: a Handlist," *Scriptorium* 27 (1973), 90-95.

7   Folda 58 and 64.

8   Folda, 55, 65, 66.

Recueil will notice that MSS *E* and *F* of that edition (Folda 55 and 58) omit ch. 30 and part of ch. 31, which are given by MSS *H*, *I* and *K* (Folda 60, 61 and 63); and that on the other hand *E* and *F* give chs. 45-58, which are omitted by *H*, *I* and *K*. Between *E* and *F* there is one further major difference, namely the inversion of material noted by the *Recueil* editors from ch. 69 onwards,[9] and which we suggest must originally have been provoked by a homeoteleuton committed by a scribe copying from a model in which the words *que il ne feroit jamais trives aus Crestiens* appeared at either the head or the foot of two columns on adjacent folios. We may therefore regard the *F* version as merely an aberrant form of *E*, and take the *E* and *F* manuscripts together as one sub-group of the Rothelin family, the *H*, *I* and *K* manuscripts as the other. Between these two groups the manuscripts in question are distributed as follows: in the family of *HIK* we place Folda 52, 60 (*H*), 61 (*I*), 63 (*K*), and 65, while the family of *EF* contains Folda 53, 54, 55 (*E*), 58 (*F*), 62, 64 and 66. Among these latter, we may specify further that 53 and 64 belong with *F*, while 54 and 62 belong with *E*.[10] In the case of 66 it is impossible to be certain on this point, since this manuscript is mutilated at the end and the section in which the inversion occurs is not present. Let us note too that MS *E* itself is mutilated in several places, and that even in the sections that remain complete it offers some very bad readings. A much better copy of this text is to be found in Folda 54. However, to avoid confusion, we shall continue to refer to this text as the *E* text, as the *Recueil* editors do.

With five manuscripts of the *HIK* text and seven of the *EF* text surviving, even allowing for the possible loss of some exemplars of one or the other, we must suppose the two recensions of the Rothelin continuation to have been roughly equally popular among compilers. This is not without interest for us, since the differences between them bear witness to a fairly substantial difference in interests and tastes. The sections omitted by the *EF* manuscripts contain two songs, one against the military Orders composed by Philippe de Nanteuil, the other an anonymous piece said to be one of many composed by the Christians in the army of Thibaut de Navarre, criticising the leaders of the crusade. Of these the second at least was certainly in the original model of the *EF* family, since we read in all the *EF*, as well as in the *HIK* manuscripts:

> Aucunz des Crestienz meismes en firent plusseurz chanconz. Maiz nous n'en metronz que une en nostre livre.[11]

---

9   RHC HOcc. 2:622, n. 22, and 624 n. 13.
10   For what it is worth, Folda 56 appears to have been adapted from a MS of the *F* group.
11   RHC HOcc. 2:550.

This the *HIK* manuscripts then do, but the *EF* manuscripts do not. Evidently the *EF* compiler simply found the song or songs offered by his model without interest, while the compiler of *HIK* kept them in, fortunately for us.

The opposite is however the case for the other major variation between the two recensions, namely chs. 45-58. The reader cannot but notice how badly placed these chapters are, and how separate from the narrative into which they are, we can immediately state, inserted. Their content has nothing whatsoever to do with the chronicle as a whole, consisting as it does of a description of various perils to be met with at sea, followed by an account of the journey of Cato across Africa, and finally a story about Alexander the Great. Between these various elements we may discern some minimal connexions. The compiler apparently proceeds by a combination of word-play and association of ideas. Thus the initial idea for this digression comes to him while he is recounting the sea-voyage of St. Louis and comes to the phrase

> Nous fusmes sus mer .xxii. jourz et moult eumes de contrairez et de travaux en la mer.[12]

This mention of the sea is enough to set him off on a detailed description of a number of *perilz et tormenz qui sont en mer*, destined to enlighten the *genz des terrez qui sont loingtaingnes de la mer*,[13] and which fills the whole of ch. 45. From this topic to the journey of Cato may seem a large step, indeed he says he is now turning to something else, but he makes the connexion by the word *perilz*, which reminds him that Cato and his companions suffered many such.[14] From Cato to Alexander the Great the transition is equally simple: Cato arrives at the Nile, where Alexander began one of his adventures. At the end of this excursus, the compiler simply takes up the main narrative again at the point where he had left it without further attempt at reconciling the irreconcilable:

> Mes or retornons a conter de nostre estoire que nous avionz devant lessiee.[15]

We are thus entirely in agreement with the *Recueil* editors in considering these chapters a blatant interpolation in the original version of the Rothelin continuation.[16] But their identification of the sources of this interpolation, as Lucan

---

12   Ibid., 2:571.
13   Ibid., 2:571.
14   Last paragraph of ch. 45, ibid., 2:573.
15   Ibid., 2:589.
16   Ibid., 2:571 note a.

(books 9 and 10 of the Pharsalia) and pseudo-Callisthenes, must now be recti-
fied. The source of ch. 45 remains unidentified, but chs. 46-58 consist entirely,
not of adaptations of Lucan, but of verbatim extracts from *Li Fet des
Romains*.[17] This remarkable work, composed in the Ile-de-France about 1213
or 1214 and based on Lucan, Sallust and Suetonius, was essentially a work of
popular historiography, popular both in that it was a work of vulgarisation,
with a generous admixture of legend and literary anecdote, and in that it
enjoyed an enormous vogue. Some fifty manuscripts of it survive, together with
Italian and Portuguese translations and about twenty-five later compilations
for which it served as the model. The first printed edition of it appeared in 1490
and was rapidly followed by a second in 1500. The passages used by the *EF*
compiler come from two different sections of the third book: the story of Cato
is taken from parts of chs. 14 and 15, the story of Alexander from ch. 4.[18] The
way he chooses and puts together the extracts he makes is quite clever, and
contrasts markedly with the total lack of dexterity with which he sets this whole
excursus into the Rothelin continuation, right in the middle of the account of
St. Louis's voyage and indeed in the middle of the letter of Jean Sarrasin, one
of several letters used by the original Rothelin compiler.[19]

So between the *EF* text on the one hand and the *HIK* text on the other, this
large, irrelevant and ill-placed excursus creates a major difference. From a
literary point of view there can be no doubt that *HIK* has by far the more
satisfactory structure; from an historiographical point of view its superiority is
equally evident. Yet we cannot ignore the fact that not one but several copyists
copied the *EF* texts without thinking it necessary to remove these visibly super-
fluous chapters. Most copyists would of course just copy. But MS *a*, whose
compiler shows marked originality, nevertheless keeps in his version this otiose
section. We shall return to this curious point.

Leaving aside now the particularities of the two sub-groups, let us look at
what the Rothelin continuation as a whole has to offer its readers. The reader
who reads consecutively the text given at RHC HOcc. 2:379, *g* variant, and the
beginning of the Rothelin continuation at RHC HOcc. 2:489 finds in the latter
a first chapter so short as to be a mere paragraph, which is a reprise of the
chapter next but last preceding (RHC HOcc. 2:378 *g* variant), a very obvious

---

17   *Li Fet des Romains*, ed. L.-F. Flutre and K. Sneyders de Vogel, 2 vols. (Paris and Groningen,
     1938).
18   In the edition of Flutre and Sneyders de Vogel the passages in question are to be found in ch.
     14, paragraphs 18-19, 25-27, 32-33, 35-44, 47-50; ch. 15 paragraphs 20-24; and ch. 4 para-
     graphs 2 and 3.
19   Jean Sarrasin, *Lettre à Nicolas Arrode*, ed. A. Foulet (Paris, 1924). See especially pp. vii-viii.

way of attaching the Rothelin continuation firmly to the preceding, independently existing text. We already know of course that there is a clear break in the
Eracles at this point,[20] and we need be in no doubt at all that what the Rothelin
compiler was doing was adding his piece to a text which had had a well-
established independent existence for some time before he began to work on it.
That text is the one contained in the manuscripts of section 3 of Folda's
inventory, all of which give the *g* version of the continuations, stopping at
1231. This is why all the Rothelin manuscripts give the *g* text for the pre-1229
period. Having established the link, however, between this and his own work,
by recalling Frederick II's treaty and the attack on Jerusalem that followed his
departure from the Holy Land, the compiler proceeds to leave this subject
aside entirely for the next seventeen chapters, returning to Frederick and his
treaty only in ch. 19. The intervening chapters offer the sort of varied fare that
is familiar to readers of the short chronicles related to the continuations,[21]
indeed not only are these chapters similar in nature to the short chronicles but
the contents of the two are to a large extent identical. We have first (in chs. 2-9)
a very long description of Jerusalem, which is a version of that found in MS *c*
of the continuations (Folda 50), and of which versions are also found in all
manuscripts of the short chronicles (Folda 16-26). This is followed in chs. 10
and 11 by a description of the Holy Places and the pilgrimages, a description
which is apparently peculiar to the Rothelin text, but which fulfils much the
same purpose as the *Devise des Sains Lieus* in Folda 24, 25 and 26. Next comes
that popular piece, the *Profecie le Fil Agap*, which is also found in manuscripts
of unrelated texts, for example MS 307 of the Bürgerbibliothek, Berne. The
next section of the Rothelin continuation (chs. 15-18) also appears in Folda 24,
25 and 26 (that is to say all the medieval manuscripts of section 2C), and in
Berne 307, and in the work of Jacques de Vitry. A later chapter, 24, appears
along with chs. 15-18 in all these texts too. From ch. 19 onwards we return to a
relatively straightforward historical narrative, covering the crusades of Thibaut
de Navarre and Richard of Cornwall, the excommunication of Frederick II and
its consequences in the Empire, the invasions of the Tartars, the first crusade of
St. Louis, and miscellaneous events in the Holy Land during the seven years
following his return to France. The narrative stops quite abruptly, in a fashion
that suggests that its compiler expected someone to continue his work as he
had continued that of his predecessors. If so, his expectations were to remain

---

20   M.R. Morgan, *The Chronicle of Ernoul and the Continuations of William of Tyre* (Oxford,
        1973), ch. 1.
21   Folda's sections 2A, 2B and 2C.

unfulfilled. This is all the more ironic in view of the fortuitously prophetic note on which his work ends, for the last event he recounts is the murder of the sultan Sayf ad-Dīn Quṭuz, Quṭuz's murderer being that same Baybars whose depredations among the Franks' remaining possessions in the East over the next sixteen years were to be the beginning of the end of the Latin Kingdom. The last chapters of the Rothelin continuation offer thus a clear invitation to future compilers to add an account of the next thirty years. But none took it up.

As it stands, then, the Rothelin continuation resembles in its mixture of contents the short chronicles related to the continuations rather than the other versions of the continuations themselves. The historical narrative it contains, like that of the short chronicles and the other continuations, is interesting and, with the usual provisos, informative. But the impression given by the whole, in the *HIK* version and *a fortiori* in the *EF* version, is of a medley of more or less related material destined for the general reader rather than a specifically chronicular account of the crusades intended to inform, or to excite to action.

This, then, was one of the two alternatives that offered themselves to compilers of the *Estoire d'Eracles* for the period from 1229 onwards, and the one that was preferred by twelve known copyists. The other version, that printed by the editors of the *Recueil* as their main text, survives in ten known medieval manuscripts, though these manuscripts give redactions of varying length. We propose to call this version the Acre continuation, since the earliest manuscripts of each of its redactions all come from there. The shortest redaction, that of MS *d* (Folda 72), ends at 1248, after the first few sentences of book 34. We must here enter a caveat: the last two folios of this manuscript are in a different hand and appear to replace lost folios. If this is so, we cannot know how many lost folios there were, that is, whether the scribe who set out to replace them reached the end of his task or not. However, there are good internal reasons for supposing the compiler of the *d* text to have worked about the year 1250,[22] and on balance we must conclude that the manuscript as it stands does represent the complete extent of his work. Indeed given the striking change in method that is visible at this point in the Acre version of the continuations, it is easy to suppose that it first existed in a redaction ending here, to which the abysmally dull book 34 was then added bit by bit. The first extension took it down to the year 1264, thus producing the text contained in Folda 71 and 78. Ostensibly MS *b* of the *Recueil* also ends at 1264. However the reader of the *Recueil* will note that MS *b* (Folda 73) stops in the middle of a clause, while Folda 71 and 78 stop at the end

---

22 Morgan, *Chronicle*, p. 111.

of the clause before. In view of this, we must regard Folda 71 and 78 as genuine examples of the 1264 redaction, but 73 (MS *b*) as an incompleted copy of the next longer redaction, continued to the year 1275, of which Folda 69 contains a complete copy. The last and longest redaction of this version was composed in about 1290, and takes the narrative as far as the year 1277. But it exists in only one manuscript (Folda 70), and appears to have remained without imitators. It was the 1275 redaction that was evidently brought to Europe, since we find copies of it being made at Rome in 1295 (MS *g*, Folda 77), in Lombardy at about the same time (Folda 74), and in the 15th century in Flanders (Folda 67) and in Northern France (Folda 68). Of these four copies we should mention that 74 and 67 are today incomplete at the end, but that there is every textual reason to suppose that they are, or rather were, true copies of this same redaction of which the other two survive as complete versions.

To summarise, then: of the four redactions of the Acre version, ending respectively at 1248, 1264, 1275 and 1277, all were composed in the East, but only one, the 1275 redaction, was recopied in Europe. Thus of the ten extant manuscripts of this version, six (Folda 69, 70, 71, 72, 73 and 78) come from Acre, and only four (Folda 67, 68, 74, and 77) are of European provenance. The Rothelin version, by contrast, is a purely European production: it seems to have been written in or near Soissons,[23] and all its twelve manuscripts come without exception from the Ile-de-France or Northern France or Flanders. Continuing then to take numbers of extant manuscripts as a rough guide, we can see that though the apparently similar numbers of manuscripts of the two possible continuations for the post-1229 section of the *Estoire d'Eracles*, that is twelve of the Rothelin continuation, ten of the Acre continuation, might at first sight suggest that they were equally popular choices with compilers, when we consider the provenance of the manuscripts, a quite different picture emerges. Compilers working in the East did not have a choice: only the Acre continuation was available, in four redactions gradually extended over the years. Compilers working in Europe on the other hand, at least from 1295 onwards (the date of the earliest known European copy of the Acre text) had the choice of two versions for the post-1229 section of their work, and of the sixteen copies they have left us, twelve chose the Rothelin continuation and only four the Acre continuation. Evidently for them the Rothelin version had a much stronger appeal; nor is the reason for this preference very far to find when we examine the contents of the Acre version.

---

23 See Foulet, *Lettre à Nicolas Arrode*, p. vii. Cf. the end of ch. 75 of the Rothelin continuation, RHC HOcc. 2:630.

For the reader of the *Eracles* who has been following the *b* version up to 1229, the Acre continuation flows on smoothly at this point from what precedes.[24] In the *g* and *d* versions, by contrast, there is here an overlap of material betraying insufficient skill on the part of the compiler in reconciling two sources. But after that the narrative proceeds smoothly, clearly and very logically, unlike that of the Rothelin text which, as we have seen, throws something of everything into the melting pot. The Acre text continues to the end of book 33 with a mixture of historical topics, cutting from one to the other in much the same way as the first part of the continuations had done. We hear of the career of Frederick II, with especial attention devoted to the Imperialist-Cypriot war; of the defence of the remaining fragments of the Latin Kingdom against various threats; of succession problems and dynastic marriages; of the crusade of Richard of Cornwall; and of St. Louis's taking of the cross. In book 34, by contrast, we immediately note a marked change. Gone is the lucid discursive treatment, the attempt at a wide-ranging examination of the various aspects of a situation. We are left merely with a catalogue of events so perfunctory that the whole of St. Louis's first crusade, for example, is reduced to a series of notes scattered among others through the first chapter of the book. Most of the rest of book 34 continues in the same fashion, and though we find here and there fairly long discursive passages,[25] these neither redeem book 34 as a whole, nor make of it a work of historiography. It is rather an inventory, of some use as a work of reference, but no use at all as a book to read from cover to cover, or even to read sections of, as we do, and as our medieval predecessors doubtless did, in the case of the earlier parts of the continuations.

This being so, it is hardly surprising that European compilers, faced with the choice of the Rothelin continuation or the Acre continuation, chose the former in twelve cases and the latter in only four. They judged, rightly, that the Rothelin version simply offered a more readable narrative. One compiler, however, was more enterprising. His work, composed in the Ile-de-France at the beginning of the fourteenth century, survives in MS *a* of the *Recueil*, and what he did is quite simple. Up to 1229 he follows the *b* text (and let us note too that this is the only European manuscript of any version other than *g*). Then, having to hand both the Acre and the Rothelin versions, he realised that while the first was extremely weak after 1248, and particularly deficient for a French audience in that it provided no proper account of St. Louis's first crusade, the second omitted the very substantial historical narratives offered by the Acre continuation for the period 1229-1248. So he simply combined the two in the

---

24   Ibid., 2:379-380, main text.
25   For example, chs. 22-24, 25, 28-30, 35.

most advantageous way, following the Acre continuation as far as 1248 (the end of book 33) and the Rothelin continuation from that point on. By this elegantly simple device, he gave his readers the best of both worlds.

So it may surprise us that this intelligent historian, choosing what are to us undoubtedly the most worthwhile parts of each of his sources, did not trouble to eliminate the irrelevant vagaries of chs. 45-58 of his model (evidently a member of the *EF* family) of the Rothelin continuation. We cannot possibly suppose this inclusion to be the result of slavish copying, since he plainly looked at the whole content of both his sources at the outset in order to combine sections of each in his work. Rather this decision on the part of a compiler who plainly knew what he was at must suggest to us that while our taste coincides with that of his readership to the extent that we applaud the basic choice he made when combining the Rothelin and the Acre continuations, it departs from theirs when there is a question of what we see as irrelevance. In the light of this we must also judge his rejection of the first half of the Rothelin continuation not as a negative decision against these meandering chapters, but as a positive decision in favour of the rich 1229-1248 section of the Acre version.

In other words, given the intelligence that is evident in the work of the *a* compiler, we must suppose that he knew what would appeal to his audience. He knew they wanted to be informed about events in the East, especially as they concerned their compatriots, and so chose the most informative parts of his sources. But he also knew that they wished to be entertained, that for them history was not only a record but a diversion. *Li Fet des Romains* itself is a prime example of history as diversion, and given its wide dissemination, it is quite possible that the *a* compiler actually recognised these extracts from it, and decided that a link with so successful a book of this kind could not but enhance the appeal of his own work. Be that as it may, he plainly did believe that these chapters were entirely in accordance with prevailing taste, and the development of the whole corpus of works of which his is a part suggests strongly that he was right. William's *Historia*, its French translation, and its continuations of the first period, may all be described as history as record. The authors of these texts might have more than one purpose in writing. They might wish to amuse, to amaze, to instruct their readers, or to incite them to go on crusade, but always they wished to inform, simply to tell people what was happening or had happened, either in order to fulfil one of their other possible purposes, or just for the sake of the thing. William tells us of his intention to record facts for posterity,[26] and his last successors in the Acre development of

26   WT, 23. Praefatio, p. 1132.

the text, that is the successive compilers of book 34, though their work could not resemble the *Historia* less, were still struggling to record facts. But in Europe their work was overtaken by a change in fashion towards history as diversion. Three elements of the *Eracles* corpus bear witness to this fashion: the popularity of the Rothelin continuation, with its very diverse contents, the compilation of *a*, which did not attempt to eliminate that diversity, and the compilation during the thirteenth century of the short chronicles related to the *Eracles*, with much the same variety of elements as the Rothelin compiler selected. That is not to say that these compilations failed to inform, but that such was not their sole or even perhaps their primary purpose. To put it more bluntly, the nature of their work, compared with that of their predecessors, suggests that their readers were not taking the crusades as seriously as an earlier generation had done. What had formerly been an aspect of current events was now a literary topos, a central thread around which to weave multicoloured patterns. Of these the least remote are the topographical descriptions, the most farfetched the excesses of the *EF* Rothelin compiler, and the most shameless the innovations found in Folda 21, an exemplar of the *Estoires d'Oultremer et de la Naissance Salahadin* whose compiler, into his historical narrative, interpolates two well-known independent works of fiction without any warning or apology whatsoever.[27] It is significant too that this large manuscript contains, before the *Estoires d'Oultremer*, the *Saint Graal*[28] and *Merlin*.[29] The compiler clearly expected all three to appeal to the same tastes, if indeed he was not actually commissioned to copy all three together. His readers were demanding above all excitement and adventure; whether fact or fiction they did not know or care. So while in Acre diligent compilers were still striving to record the state of affairs obtaining in their homeland *tam prosper quam adversus*, in Europe stories of the crusades and the East were being drawn into the ever more attractive orbit of a thriving vernacular adventure literature.

By no stretch of the imagination could the Acre continuation be expected to gain popularity in such a market. But the Rothelin continuation could, and did. Its main contents, like those of the short chronicles, were just what was required: exciting stories centred on French heroes — Thibaut de Champagne, the count of Bar, Geoffroi de Sargines, and above all St. Louis himself — together with descriptions of unknown lands, strange peoples and other exotica and mirabilia able to compete with the most extravagant imaginings of the most successful writers of romance. For the same reason, the compiler of *a* allowed his work to retain the outrageous *digressio* of chs. 45-58, knowing that

27　Morgan, *Chronicle*, p. 14.
28　Fols. 1r-120v.
29　Fols. 121v-312v.

it was just the kind of thing his readers were accustomed to. As the material of crusade history proved itself so eminently suitable for a romance-reading audience, so too its style and techniques become more akin to those of romance.

In other words, during the thirteenth century in Europe, the *Estoire d'Eracles* passed from the realm of current events into that of literature, from the primary world of reality into the secondary world of art. This, I suggest, also offers us an explanation, or rather two explanations, of what is otherwise the most curious feature of the whole *Estoire d'Eracles*, namely the fact that having been added to repeatedly so that it formed a continuous history of the crusades from their beginning until the mid-thirteenth century, all continuation then stops abruptly and for good. The Rothelin continuation stops at 1261. The Acre continuation did receive several additions while it remained in Acre, but none in Europe, and even its longest redaction only reaches 1277. Yet reality continued to provide would-be continuators with highly dramatic material at least up to the end of the century. Why did they not use it?

The first reason, I suggest, is precisely that the *Estoire d'Eracles* had come to be seen as a story, or a collection of stories, and as such, had become disconnected from the actuality that had first given it birth. This tendency may indeed have been inherent in the corpus from its earliest beginnings. R.H.C. Davis has proposed the theory that the *Historia* itself failed of its purpose because, whereas William had written it "to explain how [the Holy Land] could be saved, and to persuade men to come and save it," his readers loved his work above all for its picturesque qualities, and treated it as a story collection.[30] However that may be for the *Historia* itself and its French translation, it is certain that the direction taken by later compilers in the West, those who produced the Rothelin continuation and the short chronicles, does suggest strongly that while they might be expecting their readers to absorb some serious points they were above all answering a demand for stories and descriptions and for what Davis calls "the literary equivalent of *chinoiserie*."[31] The *EF* compiler in particular seems to have had this demand very clearly in mind, and to have seen his book as something akin to *Li Fet des Romains*, which itself may be best described as *histoire romancée*, and which displays exactly the kind of tendencies Davis describes. Only in the Acre continuation, whose authors were perforce more closely in touch with the reality of the declining Latin Kingdom, is this tendency not apparent, a difference which further supports the view that while for Franks in the East, from William onwards, the purpose of the *Estoire*

30 R.H.C. Davis, "William of Tyre," in *Relations between East and West in the Middle Ages*, ed. D. Baker (Edinburgh 1973), pp. 64-76. The quotation is from p. 74.
31 Davis, "William of Tyre," p. 74.

d'Eracles was real and earnest, for Western readers, as the thirteenth century wore on, it became more and more a part of the flourishing empire of vernacular romance.

This brings us to the second reason why they did not trouble to prolong the Rothelin continuation after 1261, even though copies of it continued to be made through the fourteenth and fifteenth centuries: they were used to unfinished adventure stories. Of the five major romances of Chrétien de Troyes, to take but one famous example, one, the *Perceval*, was left unfinished by him and circulated in unfinished form in four manuscripts; another, the *Lancelot*, was given to Godefroi de Lagny to finish, after a fashion; and a third, *Yvain*, has an ending so abrupt and weak as to be hardly worth the candle. These books were not read for their dénouement. In fact just as Davis suggests that William's readers would have said, "Tell me another story from William of Tyre," [32] so Chrétien's readers could well have read one adventure of any one of his heroes in isolation. If they did, they would of course miss the overall psychological development he depicts so well, just as William's readers would miss his overall purpose. But they were accustomed too to the idea that literature, both romance and epic, was cyclic, so that even a work complete in itself might well be only a part of a greater whole. One way and another, they did not mind much about books having proper endings.

One compiler of the *Estoire d'Eracles*, however, did mind. Two manuscripts, Folda 58 and 64, give us his work. We cannot regard this compiler as a continuator in the same sense as his predecessors in the evolution of the *Eracles*. They had normally continued the history in the sense of carrying on chronologically from where the preceding text left off. There might be overlaps, as in *d* and *g* around the years 1229-1231, there might be small gaps, and there would often be shorter or longer stretches consisting merely of sketchy notes, like most of book 34 of the Acre continuation. This last compiler however, to a narrative ending in 1261, simply tacks on an account of the loss of Acre, with no attempt even to sketch in the intervening thirty years. His account is a translation, not always a very good one, of the Latin text published by Martène and Durand under the title *De Excidio Urbis Acconis Libri II*.[33] According to the editors, one manuscript of this text was available in the library of St. Victor by 1298. Both the manuscripts in which the French translation of it follows the Rothelin text were written in the Ile-de-France, Folda 58 about the year 1300, Folda 64 in the first quarter of the fourteenth century, which ties in exactly.

---

32   Davis, "William of Tyre," p. 75.
33   E. Martène and U. Durand, *Veterum Scriptorum et Monumentorum Amplissima Collectio*, 5 (Paris, 1729), 757-784.

The translation is free, a wise policy perhaps on the part of a man whose Latin is so weak that he renders

Prima igitur narratio est de his quae ante Aconis obsidionem evenerunt [34]

by

La premiere narracion est de ceus qui vindrent a Acre avant que elle feust assegiee.[35]

But however poorly he understood the detail of his source, he had chosen it well. It represented, at the time when he was working, an up-to-date account of what had recently been happening in the Holy Land, indeed more than that, the last tragic chapter in the history of the Latin Kingdom. It was thus a most satisfactory addition to the *Estoire d'Eracles* and we must applaud his judgement in making it. But even as we applaud, we must also admit that his tastes were apparently unfashionable. While he was telling his readers of the final ruin of the Latin Kingdom, all the other compilers were content to leave the Rothelin continuation as it stood, regaling their readers with stories of the exotic East as "places and circumstances where westerners could have adventures."[36] His is the voice of a solitary historian crying in the wilderness of a romance-reading public, pleading the cause of the Holy Land. For the last rhetorical chapter of the *De Excidio* laments the lost city, inveighing against those who desert the ways of wisdom and spend their days hunting, or who extort money from the poor under pretence of concern for the crusade, but in reality for their own profit. All these men, neglecting the crusade for their own affairs, are the unpromising material from among whom must come the rescuers of the Holy Land, and it is on the theme of the recovery of the Holy Land that the text ends:

Toutes foiz je pri que Nostre Sirez veille visiter son puesple et l'en doint bones volantés que il delaissent la gloire mondainne qui rienz ne vaut, et puissent seulement la gloire de Dieu avoir, et recouvrer la Sainte Terre.[37]

How ironic and how pathetic, but also how fitting, that while the short chronicles and the Rothelin version of the *Eracles* signal the final absorption of a serious historical and apologetic corpus into the fairytale realm of heroic literature, this last compiler should bring it to a close on the same note on which the crusades had begun: with a lament for the Holy Land, and a plea for men to come and save it.

34   Martène and Durand, *Amplissima Collectio* 5:758.
35   MS Vatican Reg. Lat. 737, fol. 384ra.
36   Davis, "William of Tyre," p. 73.
37   MS B.N.f.fr. 2825, fol. 361vb (The Vatican MS is incomplete at the end).

MARRIAGE LAW IN THE LATIN KINGDOM OF JERUSALEM

JAMES A. BRUNDAGE

University of Wisconsin-Milwaukee

Every European society has created legal norms to regulate the formation and dissolution of marriage, and the Latin Kingdom of Jerusalem was no exception to this rule. Like other medieval Western societies, Outremer treated matrimony as both sacred and secular. Marriage in Outremer, as elsewhere, was controlled in part by the legal norms and courts of the church and in part by the customary law of the earthly kingdom. This paper will address the problems raised by the intersection of the two jurisdictions and will examine the impact of this situation upon the marriage law and institutions of the Latin Kingdom.

This subject is especially appropriate as a contribution to a volume in honor of Joshua Prawer, for it is a subject on which he himself has done much of the basic research.[1] Indeed Prawer is the preeminent modern pioneer in the study of the legal records of the Latin States and their social implications. In part this essay will retrace some of Prawer's work on the marriage law of the Latin East; but my approach differs from his, since I shall be looking at the texts from the vantage point of a historian of canon law. My aim is to compare and contrast the marriage law of Outremer with the marriage law of the canonists and to

---

1   Especially his "Etude préliminaire sur les sources et la composition du 'Livre des assises des bourgeois,'" *RHDFE* 4.32 (1954), 198-227, 358-383, and his "Etudes sur le droit des *Assises de Jérusalem*: droit de confiscation et droit d'exhérédation," *RHDFE* 4.39 (1961), 520-551 and 4.40 (1962), 29-42. [For updated versions of these studies see now his *Crusader Institutions*, pp. 358-411, 430-468. Ed.]

suggest some areas in which each may have influenced the development of the other.

The marriage law of the Latin Kingdom has been transmitted to us in a group of treatises that are sometimes referred to collectively as the *Assises de Jérusalem*. All of the surviving legal texts of Outremer date from the thirteenth century, save for one twelfth-century record of the *acta* of the Parlement of Nablus (1120), which was published by Mansi.[2] The main corpus of the Latin Kingdom's legal records was edited nearly 150 years ago by Count Beugnot in the *Recueil des Historiens des Croisades*.[3] The principal legal treatises in this corpus are the *Assises de la cour des bourgeois* (ca. 1240), Jean d'Ibelin's *Assises de Jérusalem* (ca. 1260), and the book which bears the name of Philippe de Novare (also ca. 1260).[4] Aside from the isolated record of the Parlement of Nablus, it is impossible to speak with any certainty about the law of Outremer in the twelfth century, because all of the other early legal records of the kingdom vanished when Jerusalem fell to Saladin's army in 1187.[5]

Since we know the law of Outremer only as it appears in mid-thirteenth century records, this study will concentrate on the canon law of the same period, that is the canonical sources included in the *Decretum* of Gratian (ca. 1140) as modified by the later rules and decisions incorporated in the *Liber Extra* of Pope Gregory IX (1234), together with the standard glosses and commentaries on those collections.[6]

The marriage law of the Latin Kingdom, according to Philippe de Novare, took shape only gradually following the conquest of Jerusalem by the army of the First Crusade in 1099. Philippe tells us further that women in Outremer

---

2   Mansi 21:262-264.

3   RHC Lois 1-2 (Paris, 1841-1843).

4   Prawer, "Etude préliminaire," p. 199; Jean Richard, "Le statut de la femme dans l'Orient Latin," *Recueils de la Société Jean Bodin* 12 (1962), 378.

5   Jonathan Riley-Smith, *The Feudal Nobility and the Kingdom of Jerusalem, 1174-1277* (London, 1973), pp. 121-144; also his "The *Assise sur la ligèce* and the Commune of Acre," *Traditio* 27 (1971), 185.

6   The texts of the canon law will be cited throughout from the standard edition of the *Corpus iuris canonici* by E. Friedberg, 2 vols. (Leipzig, 1879; repr. Graz, 1959), while the *glossa ordinaria* will be cited from the 4 vol. edition published at Venice in 1600. Texts of the *Corpus iuris civilis* will be cited from the critical edition by Paul Krueger, Theodor Mommsen, Rudolf Schoell, and Wilhelm Kroll, 3 vols. (Berlin, 1872-1895; numerous reprintings). On the state of the canon law by the mid-thirteenth century see A. Van Hove, *Prolegomena ad Codicem Iuris Canonici*, 2d ed. (Malines, 1945), pp. 337-348, 357-363; J.A. Clarence Smith, *Medieval Law Teachers and Writers, Civilian and Canonist* (Ottawa, 1975), pp. 19-20, 38-39; Gabriel Le Bras, Charles Lefebvre, and Jacqueline Rambaud-Buhot, *L'age classique, 1140-1378: sources et théorie du droit*, vol. 7 of Histoire du droit et des institutions de l'église en Occident (Paris, 1965), pp. 17-50, 133-152.

were originally allowed to marry as they pleased. This caused such problems for the kings of Jerusalem, however, that they and their barons imposed limits upon freedom of marriage; the peculiar marriage law of the Latin Kingdom slowly began to take form.[7] This may or may not be what actually happened. It is clear, however, that by the mid-thirteenth century the matrimonial law of Outremer made a basic distinction between the marriage law that applied to noble persons, especially noble women, and the marriage law that applied to the bourgeoisie.[8] The legislative history of the Latin Kingdom is so poorly documented that the stages by which this distinction developed are, however, completely hidden from us.[9] But Prawer's studies have demonstrated that the marriage law of the bourgeoisie borrowed heavily from the Roman civil law tradition, expounded in the Provençal paraphrase of the *Codex Justiniani* which is known as *Lo Codi*.[10] This work, which may be dated to about 1149, was certainly one important vehicle for the transmission of Romano-canonical legal doctrine to the Latin East.[11] But the marriage law of the Western church also underwent major changes during the last half of the twelfth century and the first decades of the thirteenth century, and those changes, too, are reflected in part in the marriage law of the *Assises des bourgeois*, as well as in the marriage law sections of the treatises of Jean d'Ibelin, Jacques d'Ibelin, and Philippe de Novare.[12]

"A good marriage is very pleasing to God and highly profitable to man," declared the *Assises des bourgeois*.[13] Since both God and man had a stake in marriage, both the courts of the church and the secular courts of the Latin Kingdom undertook to regulate it. To be sure, the *Assises des bourgeois* went on to assert that the ecclesiastical courts enjoyed primary competence in matrimonial affairs.[14] Nonetheless, the attention devoted by the *Assises* to matri-

---

7 *Livre de Philippe de Navarre* 86, RHC Lois 1:558-559; Richard, "Statut de la femme," p. 379.
8 Richard, "Statut de la femme," pp. 380-381.
9 Prawer, "Etude sur le droit," p. 521.
10 Prawer, "Etude préliminaire," pp. 205-213.
11 The texts that I have used are *Lo Codi in der lateinischen Übersetzung des Ricardus Pisanus*, ed. Hermann Fitting (Halle, 1906; repr. Aalen, 1968) and *Lo Codi: eine Summa Codicis in provenzalischer Sprache aus dem XII. Jahrhundert*, ed. Felix Derrer (Zurich, 1974).
12 Charles Donahue, "The Policy of Alexander the Third's Consent Theory of Marriage," in *Proceedings of the Fourth International Congress of Medieval Canon Law*, ed. Stephan Kuttner, Monumenta iuris canonici, ser. C, vol. 5 (Vatican City, 1976), pp. 251-281; Georges Duby, *Medieval Marriage: Two Models from Twelfth-Century France* (Baltimore, 1978), pp. 15-22; Christopher N.L. Brooke, *Marriage in Christian History: An Inaugural Lecture* (Cambridge, 1978), pp. 17-34.
13 *Assises des bourgeois* 159, RHC Lois 2:108.
14 *Assises des bourgeois* 181, RHC Lois 2:121.

monial matters makes clear that secular courts were prepared to deal with marriage cases when the interests of secular society would be served.

The bourgeois *Assises*, following *Lo Codi*, explicitly accepted the basic Romano-canonical principle that consent is essential to marriage, and that marriage is contracted by the consent of the parties.[15] This principle was modified, as we shall see, when the marriage of female holders of military fiefs was at issue.

Another basic tenet of canon law figures in the treatise of Jean d'Ibelin, the principle that within the marriage relationship equity demands that men and women be treated as equals.[16] True, Jean d'Ibelin follows the canonists in limiting this equality to the sexual rights of the married parties.[17] Even so, the acknowledgement of this principle by a leading jurist of thirteenth-century Outremer underscores the dependence of Outremer's marriage law upon the canonistic sources.

As for the substantive law of marriage, the jurists of Outremer were concerned with the problem of canonical irregularities which might invalidate marriages.[18] One common irregularity occurred if the partners to a marriage had not yet attained the minimum age for marital consent. On this matter the jurists of Outremer took a curious position. They accepted the conventional Romano-canonical rule that the minimum age for marriage of females was twelve, but ruled that boys might be allowed to marry at age 13.[19] The canonists had established fourteen as the minimum age for marriage by males and *Lo*

---

15 *Assises des bourgeois* 158-159, RHC Lois 2:107-108, quoting the Roman law definition of marriage from *Inst.* 1.9.1; cf. *Lo Codi* 5.1.7, ed. Fitting, pp. 150-151; ed. Derrer, p. 110. See also John T. Noonan, Jr., "Power to Choose," *Viator* 4 (1973), 424.

16 *Livre de Jean d'Ibelin* 228, RHC Lois 1:364.

17 Noonan, "Power to Choose," p. 431; Elizabeth M. Makowski, "The Conjugal Debt and Medieval Canon Law," *Journal of Medieval History* 3 (1977), 99-114; Kari Elisabeth Børresen, *Subordination et équivalence: nature et rôle de la femme d'après Augustin et Thomas d'Aquin* (Oslo, 1968), pp. 204-205; Hans Zeimentz, *Ehe nach der Lehre der Frühscholastik: eine moralgeschichtliche Untersuchung zur Anthropologie und Theologie der Ehe in der Schule Anselms von Laon und Wilhelms von Champeaux, bei Hugo von St. Viktor, Walter von Mortagne, und Petrus Lombardus* (Düsseldorf, 1973), p. 220. The principle was well stated by the anonymous author of the mid-twelfth century *Fragmentum Cantabrigiense* to the *Decretum* of Gratian, C. 27 pr., in Cambridge University Library, MS Add. 3321, vol. 1, fol. 10v: "Matrimonium enim inter coniuges parilitatem iure exigit, altero enim debitum exigente, alteri continere non licet; et hoc de matrimonio non solum iniciato, sed etiam per sexuum commixtionem consummato. Si matrimonium enim solum iniciatum fuerit, alteri continere licebat altero etiam inuito."

18 *Assises des bourgeois* 158, RHC Lois 2:107.

19 *Livre de Jean d'Ibelin* 171, RHC Lois 1:263-264; *Assises des bourgeois* 159, RHC Lois 2:108.

Codi, an ultimately Roman source, agrees with this.[20] On this point, then, the marriage law of Outremer followed neither the canon law nor the Roman authorities known in the Latin East.

The marriage law of Outremer did incorporate in its own rules the canonical ban on marriage during the solemn fasting seasons of the ecclesiastical year.[21] Likewise the *Assises* incorporated canonistic rules concerning consanguinity, affinity, and incest.[22]

The provisions of the marriage law of Outremer treated thus far are, with a few minor variances, in accord with the matrimonial rules of contemporary canonists. There are some other points, however, where the law of Outremer diverges sharply from the general law of the Western church. One such discrepancy is a provision in the *Assises des bourgeois* that resurrected in modified form a long-obsolete Constantinean prohibition of intermarriage between free persons and those of unfree or freed status. The *Assises* limited the prohibition to marriage between the owner's son and the freedman's daughter.[23] The church had rejected this policy long before the mid-thirteenth century and it is startling to see it reappear in a legal text of this period.[24] This anachronistic peculiarity may perhaps reflect the special social hierarchy of the Holy Land under the Latins. Unfree and freed persons there were virtually always members of the conquered populations, rather than Latin settlers. Hence the prohibition of interclass marriage may have been intended to forbid intercultural unions between Latins and Muslims, Jews, or Eastern Christians. That such marriages had taken place fairly commonly during the early years of Latin rule in the Levant was noted by Fulcher of Chartres, writing about 1125. In a passage obviously intended to impress his readers back in Western Europe, Fulcher boasted of the speedy assimilation of Latin settlers in the Holy Land.

---

20 *Lo Codi* 5.1.2-4, ed. Fitting, pp. 149-150; ed. Derrer, p. 109. See also W. Onclin, "L'âge requis pour le mariage dans la doctrine canonique médiévale," in *Proceedings of the Second International Congress of Medieval Canon Law*, ed. Stephan Kuttner and J.J. Ryan, *Monumenta iuris canonici*, ser. C, vol. 1 (Vatican City, 1965), pp. 237-247.

21 *Assises des bourgeois* 158, 179, 180, RHC Lois 2:107, 120-121, relying on Gratian, C. 33 q. 4 c. 10.

22 *Assises des bourgeois* 158-159, 161, RHC Lois 2:107-111; Gratian, C. 33 q. 2 & 3, d.p.c. 21; cf. *Dig.* 38.10.4.

23 *Assises des bourgeois* 158, RHC Lois 2:107; cf. *Dig.* 23.2.23, 44.

24 Gratian, C. 29 q. 2 c. 1, 3; X 4.9.1. See also Miguel Falcão, *Las prohibiciones matrimoniales de caracter social en el Imperio Romano* (Pamplona, 1973), pp. 43-58; Jean Gaudemet, *Sociétés et mariage* (Strasbourg, 1980), pp. 67-73, reprinted from *Revue internationale des droits de l'antiquité* 2 (1946), 329-336; Peter Landau, "Hadrians IV. Dekretale 'Dignum est' (X 4.9.1) und die Entstehung Unfreier in der Diskussion von Kanonisten und Theologen des 12. und 13. Jahrhunderts," *Studia Gratiana* 12 (1967), 514-515.

Part of the assimilation process that Fulcher described consisted in the marriage of Latin men to Syrian, Armenian, or Saracen women who had been converted to Christianity.[25] The ban on interclass marriage that we find in the *Assises des bourgeois* may indicate, if my reading is correct, that this aspect of the social policy of the Latin states had changed by the mid-thirteenth century. This would account for the decision by the author of the *Assises* to appropriate a long-moribund provision on interclass marriage. Possibly he hoped to bolster a new policy with an ancient authority.

Both intermarriage and concubinage relationships between Latins and the Muslim inhabitants of Outremer were, as might have been expected, disapproved by the law of the Latin Kingdom.[26] What is noteworthy here is that the law of Outremer seems to have been slightly more lenient on this point than was the law of the church. The canon law on this matter underwent a long and complex development, but by the mid-thirteenth century the teaching was clear that *dispar cultus* was a diriment impediment to marriage and that therefore Christians might not validly marry pagans, Jews, Muslims, or heretics.[27] The *Assises des bourgeois* declare that marriage cannot *iuste* take place between Christians and heretics. This is not the same thing as saying that there can be no valid marriage between them. Validity and licitness are two different concepts: what the *Assises* seem to say is that such marriages are not licit. Whether this was intended to imply that, although illicit, such marriages might be valid (and hence the children of those marriages might be legitimate) is at the very least a possible reading of the text. As for concubinage, the prohibition and penalties enacted by the Council of Nablus are consistent with the usage of

25 Fulcher of Chartres, *Historia Hierosolymitana* 3.37.3-4, ed. Heinrich Hagenmeyer (Heidelberg, 1913), pp. 748-749; Richard, "Statut de la femme," p. 385.

26 *Assises des bourgeois* 158, RHC Lois 2:107; Mansi 21:264; Richard, "Statut de la femme," pp. 383-384.

27 While Gratian and later authorities considered marriage between two infidels valid, the doctrine that a Christian could not validly marry either an infidel or a heretic had been accepted by most authorities by the mid-twelfth century; see C. 28 q. 1 c. 15-17 and *glos. ord.* to c. 15 ad v. *omnem alienam*, as well as *glos. ord.* to c. 16 ad v. *hereticis.* When two Christians were married, the lapse of one party into heresy, paganism, Islam, or Judaism did not terminate the marriage; C. 28 q. 2 d. p. c. 2; Bernardus Papiensis, *Summa de matrimonio* 3.4, ed. E.A.T. Laspeyres (Regensburg, 1860; repr. Graz, 1956), pp. 291-292; Tancredus, *Summa de matrimonio* tit. 10 as transmitted by Raymond of Peñafort, *Summa de matrimonio*, ed. Xavier Ochoa and A. Diez (Rome, 1978), col. 951-955. (The *Summa de matrimonio* of Tancredus was edited by Raymond after the appearance of the *Liber extra* in order to bring the legal references up to date; the text of the *Summa*, however, was substantially unchanged.)

other Western Christian kingdoms; the matter was not explicitly treated by the canonists.[28]

Some marriage provisions in the *Assises des bourgeois* may be characterized as efforts to spell out in detail matters that were either implied or assumed in canon law. Such would be, for example, the provision that a declaration of freedom and capacity to marry must be made at the time of betrothal,[29] the provisions for formal termination of betrothal,[30] and the provisions for disposition of property rights arising from betrothal.[31] In this connection it is worth noting, too, that the *Assises des bourgeois* accepted without comment the principle that the property of married couples was held in common.[32] This view of marital property was adopted in French customary law during the thirteenth century, but at the time of the redaction of the *Assises des bourgeois* it must have been a comparative novelty.[33] As for acquest property, this was not only held jointly by husband and wife, according to the *Assises des bourgeois*, but it was also freely disposable by testament.[34] This view of marital property was also quite new in French law at this period.

The bourgeois *Assises* follow the Roman law, as reported in *Lo Codi*, in excluding inter-vivos gifts between husband and wife.[35] This did not, of course, bar antenuptial gifts, nor did it prohibit legacies to a wife in a will. A much more novel provision in the *Assises* not only allowed husbands to make a small monthly allowance to their wives for household expenses, but even gave such practices, or agreements concerning them, the status of quasi-contracts binding upon the husband and his agents.[36] Although this passage is drawn in part from *Lo Codi*, the text in the *Assises* goes far beyond the provisions of *Lo Codi*,

---

28 Susan M. Stuard, ed., *Women in Medieval Society* (Philadelphia, 1976), pp. 85-86; Frederic William Maitland, "The Deacon and the Jewess; or Apostasy at Common Law," *Law Quarterly Review* 2 (1886), 153-165; James A. Brundage, "Concubinage and Marriage in Medieval Canon Law," *Journal of Medieval History* 1 (1975), 1-17.

29 *Assises des bourgeois* 162, RHC Lois 2:111-112.

30 *Assises des bourgeois* 163, RHC Lois 2:112; *Lo Codi* 5.2.5, ed. Fitting, pp. 151-152; ed. Derrer, pp. 110-111.

31 *Assises des bourgeois* 164-165, RHC Lois 2:112-113; *Lo Codi* 5.2.6, ed. Fitting, p. 152; ed. Derrer, p. 111.

32 *Assises des bourgeois* 181, RHC Lois 2:121.

33 Charles Donahue, Jr., "What Causes Fundamental Legal Ideas? Marital Property in England and France in the Thirteenth Century," *Michigan Law Review* 78 (1979), 69-73. The Roman law rule in *sine manu* marriage was that the married woman retained ownership and, if she wished, control of her nondotal property, the *parapherna*; *Dig.* 23.3.9.3; *Cod.* 5.14.9.

34 *Assises des bourgeois* 183, RHC Lois 2:122-123; Prawer, "Etude préliminaire," p. 382, n. 83.

35 *Assises des bourgeois* 173, RHC Lois 2:117; *Lo Codi* 5.16.2, ed. Fitting, p. 169; ed. Derrer, p. 122. Both the *Digest* and Justinian's *Code* devoted whole titles to this problem: *Dig.* 24.1, *Cod.* 5.16.

36 *Assises des bourgeois* 174, RHC Lois 2:117.

which merely permit such gifts but stop far short of giving them binding force *quasi ex contractu.*[37] The position taken on this matter by the *Assises des bourgeois* seems to have no parallel in Roman law. As for the canonists, none of them have much to say on this subject beyond general statements to the effect that husbands have an obligation to provide for their wives and children.[38] The *Assises des bourgeois* also go far beyond the canonists in their provisions for the child-support obligations of husbands, both with respect to legitimate children following separation of the spouses and as regards the maintenance right of natural children.[39] Here the *Assises* are clearly dependent on *Lo Codi,* as Prawer has noted.[40] The *Assises* also contain remedies for safeguarding a married woman's dowry against an improvident husband and seek to protect her economically from the follies of her spouse.[41] Although there is some allusion here to Roman law provisions on this subject as reported in *Lo Codi,* the *Assises* go into greater detail than the Roman law in specifying the protection accorded to the wife.[42] As for the dower rights of a surviving widow in the estate of her deceased husband, both the *Livre de Jean d'Ibelin* and the treatise of Jacques d'Ibelin describe her as the usufructuary possessor of half of the estate.[43] This contrasts strikingly with the Romanist doctrine, which did not consider the wife a full-fledged member of her husband's family and hence accorded her only minimal claims upon his property at the time of his death.[44]

Although the *Assises des bourgeois* restated the principle that marriage was a lifelong relationship that ended only at the death of one of the parties,[45] this was modified by provisions for the nullification of marriages that failed to meet the minimum legal requirements for validity.[46] Such matters, the *Assises*

---

37   *Lo Codi* 5.16.13, ed. Fitting, p. 170; ed. Derrer, p. 123.

38   Raymond of Peñafort, *Summa de matrimonio* 25.5, ed. Ochoa-Diez, col. 995, citing *Dig.* 23.3.7, 10. See also Richard H. Helmholz, *Marriage Litigation in Medieval England* (Cambridge, 1974), pp. 67-68, 106; A. Esmein, *Le mariage en droit canonique,* 2 vols. (Paris, 1891: repr. New York, 1968), 2:95-96.

39   *Assises des bourgeois* 177-178, RHC Lois 2:119-120.

40   *Lo Codi* 5.18.1-2; 5.20.1-3, ed. Fitting, pp. 171-173; ed. Derrer, pp. 124-125; Prawer, "Etude préliminaire," pp. 378-379.

41   *Assises des bourgeois* 171-172, RHC Lois 2:116-117; cf. X 4.20.7; Raymond of Peñafort, *Summa de matrimonio* 25.7, ed. Ochoa-Diez, col. 997-998.

42   *Lo Codi* 5.11.2, 5.14.1-3, ed. Fitting, pp. 163-164, 167; ed. Derrer, pp. 119, 121.

43   *Livre de Jean d'Ibelin* 117, RHC Lois 1:279-280; *Livre de Jacques d'Ibelin* 68, RHC Lois 1:467.

44   *Nov.* 53.6, 112.5; W.W. Buckland and A.D. McNair, *Roman Law and Common Law,* 2d ed. (Cambridge, 1965), pp. 184-185.

45   *Assises des bourgeois* 158-159, RHC Lois 2:107-109.

46   *Assises des bourgeois* 160, RHC Lois 2:109.

declared, were within the exclusive competence of the courts christian. If a complaint about marriage matters was brought to the royal court, that court should refuse to hear the case and should remand it to the ecclesiastical judges.[47] This reflects the conventional practice of mid-thirteenth century European jurisdictions. Although ecclesiastical claims to exclusive competence in determining whether a marriage was valid had been contested in earlier periods, the church's jurisdictional claims were generally conceded by the thirteenth century.[48]

But it is also apparent that the authorities in the Kingdom of Jerusalem were prepared in some circumstances to express their views on questions of validity. This is demonstrated by an interesting and unusual chapter of the *Assises des bourgeois* that provides for the separation of spouses on the grounds that the wife had become quarrelsome and difficult to live with. Under such circumstances, according to the *Assises*, the husband could seek a judicial decree of **separation from bed and board** (*divortium a mensa et thoro*) from the ecclesiastical courts.[49] This is very interesting, for what is described here is separation **on the grounds of cruelty** (*sevitia*) or hatred (*odium*), for which neither the classical texts of the canon law nor the Romanist treatise followed by the author of the *Assises des bourgeois* made any provision at all.[50] These grounds for action were developed by academic canonists. Separation because of cruelty or hatred was not something that legislative authorities created, but rather it was brought into being by the interpretative legerdemain of the teachers in the law faculties of the medieval universities. Although the history of the development of this doctrine is obscure, the reference to separation on these grounds in the *Assises des bourgeois* is very early indeed.[51] Also interesting

---

47   *Assises des bourgeois* 181, RHC Lois 2:121.

48   Esmein, *Le mariage* 1:25-31; Duby, *Medieval Marriage*, pp. 17-22; Pierre Daudet, *L'établissement de la compétence de l'église en matière de divorce et consanguinité (France, Xème-XIIème siècles)* (Paris, 1941).

49   *Assises des bourgeois* 175, RHC Lois 2:118.

50   Esmein, *Le mariage* 2:93-95; Helmholz, *Marriage Litigation*, p. 100; *Lo Codi* 5.17, ed. Fitting, p. 171; ed. Derrer, pp. 123-124.

51   The date at which this cause for separation came to be accepted has never been determined. The text on which the commentators usually base their treatment of this topic is X 4.19.1, but the thirteenth-century commentators whom I have consulted say nothing of *odium* or *sevitia* as grounds for *divortium a mensa et thoro*. The earliest explicit reference to the matter that I have located occurs in the *Commentaria facundissima in quinque decretalium libros* by Petrus de Ancharano (ca. 1330-1416), 5 vols. (Bologna, 1580-1581), 4:135, commenting on X 4.19.1. It is possible, however, that an obscurely phrased passage in the *Summa super titulis decretalium* of Goffredus de Trano (d. 1245), to X 4.19 (Lyon, 1519; repr. Aalen, 1968), fol. 191rb, might refer to this idea. Goffredus' *Summa* was composed between 1241 and 1243, or, in other words, at almost exactly the time when the *Assises des bourgeois* was written.

in this same chapter of the *Assises* are the passages that deal with proof of allegations of *sevitia*, and the provision that women and men have the same right to seek separation on these grounds.[52] Separation *a thoro et mensa* obliged the husband to restore his wife's dowry to her or, if she was entering a religious house, to her convent.[53] Here the *Assises* seem to be following the canon law rules on the restitution of dowry.[54]

Up to this point we have looked at the marriage law of Outremer principally as it is set forth in the *Assises des bourgeois*. When we turn to deal with marital property rights in feudal estates, as those are treated in the books of feudal law, we find a complex set of regulations which for the most part have little to do with Romano-canonical treatments of marriage. There are a few areas in the law of feudal property, however, that impinge upon canonistic notions of marriage in interesting and suggestive ways. I shall deal briefly with three of these topics. They are, first, the mechanism devised by the jurists of Outremer to limit freedom of choice when female fief-holders married; second, the treatment of the remarriage of widows; and, third, the problem of the marriage or remarriage of the elderly.

One well-known peculiarity of the feudal law of the Latin Kingdom was the liberality with which the law accepted the rights of women to hold fiefs either in their own right (as, for example, by purchase), or by succession to a deceased father or husband. At the same time the military needs of the kingdom demanded that female fief-holders be married, so that the king would not be deprived of the personal military service attached to the fief, which a woman could not render.[55] Accordingly the feudal law of Outremer was much concerned with the conditions under which noble women might be required to marry and also with the profits that the lord might realize from these marriage arrangements.[56]

The ability of a feudal lord to control the marriage of an heiress who held a fief from him constituted a limitation on the woman's freedom of choice and on the very freedom of consent that was essential for the validity of her marriage contract in canon law. For this reason the legal writers of the Latin Kingdom took special pains to set limits to the lord's rights. The lord could only require a woman to marry when she held from him a fief for which

---

52   *Assises des bourgeois* 175, RHC Lois 2:118.
53   *Assises des bourgeois* 176, RHC Lois 2:118-119.
54   X 4.20.1-3.
55   Richard, "Le statut de la femme," pp. 378-379; *Livre de Jean d'Ibelin* 148-150, 177, 187, 277, RHC Lois 1:224-225, 279-282, 297, 359.
56   Richard, "Le statut de la femme," p. 380; *Livre de Jean d'Ibelin* 171, RHC Lois 1:264.

personal military service was owed.[57] Women who held other types of fiefs could not be required to marry, although if they did marry they were required to secure their lord's permission first. Further, the lord could not indefinitely refuse to grant this permission. If he delayed permission, the woman or her relatives had the right to demand that she be allowed to marry; if the lord then refused to give permission, he might lose his veto rights over candidates for her hand.[58] The procedures for exercising the lord's rights over the marriage of heiresses are spelled out in detail by Jean d'Ibelin and seem to have been framed in order to prevent, so far as possible, a successful attack upon the validity of the marriage in the courts christian.[59] One notable feature of the law on this matter is that the lord was required to offer a female heiress a choice of three men nominated by the lord as prospective husbands. The nominees must be suitable to her rank and station. Prawer has argued convincingly that this provision of the law is a response to the pressure to assure the widow's family some input into the marriage decision.[60] Should the widow fail to choose one of the three candidates, she might be summoned by her lord to explain her reasons. If she failed to appear, she might be deprived forthwith of her fief. If she appeared, but failed to satisfy her lord that she had adequate reasons for refusal to marry one of his nominees, he might take control of her fief for a year and a day. At the end of that time he could require her once again to choose a husband from among three different candidates. Failure to make a choice the second time presumably resulted in permanent loss of the fief.[61] These regulations seem to reflect an effort to compromise between the canonists' insistence that the free consent of the parties was essential to a valid marriage and the interest of the feudal lords of Outremer in securing the service of acceptable male warriors by marrying them to heiresses of desirable fiefs. That the woman was given a choice of three candidates for her hand suggests a need to argue that she had been able to exercise choice in selecting her husband; the lord's nominating power, of course, enabled him to ensure that she only considered marriage to men who were acceptable to the lord.[62]

---

57   *Livre de Jean d'Ibelin* 177, RHC Lois 1:279.
58   *Livre de Jean d'Ibelin* 171, RHC Lois 1:264-265.
59   *Livre de Jean d'Ibelin* 228, RHC Lois 1:362.
60   *Livre de Jean d'Ibelin* 171, 227, RHC Lois 1:265, 359; *Livre de Jacques d'Ibelin* 67, RHC Lois 1:467; Prawer, *Crusader Institutions*, pp. 30-31.
61   *Livre de Jean d'Ibelin* 227, RHC Lois 1:359-361; *Livre de Philippe de Navarre* 86, RHC Lois 1:559.
62   On the legal doctrine of marital choice see especially Noonan, "Power to Choose," pp. 419-434.

The treatment of the remarriage of widows in the legal treatises of Outremer also reflects the social and military conditions of Latin settlements there. Maintaining the military posture of the Latin states required that widows who held fiefs from which military service was due remarry.[63] Although there had been some controversy on the matter early in the history of the Christian church,[64] and although there was some feeling that second marriages were not desirable on moral grounds,[65] the law of the church by the twelfth century allowed remarriage following the death of a first spouse.[66] Nonetheless the church discouraged the practice by denying the nuptial blessing to couples who married for a second time and by forbidding such marriages to be celebrated with solemn ceremony.[67] Theologians and canonists criticised second marriages, but they were not the only ones.[68] There was widespread popular disapproval of the remarriage of widows and widowers, in France and probably elsewhere. Such marriages commonly aroused local protests, which took the form of charivaris. While demonstrations of this sort were most common in rural communities, they also occurred in cities and seem to indicate that popular sentiment was offended by the spectacle of remarriage.[69] In the face of disapproval of second and subsequent marriages both among the clergy and the general public, it is striking that the jurists of thirteenth-century Outremer expected widows to

---

63 *Livre au Roi* 30, RHC Lois 1:626-627.
64 Willy Rordorf, "Marriage in the New Testament and in the Early Church," *Journal of Ecclesiastical History* 20 (1969), 193-210; Esmein, *Le mariage* 2:120; Joseph Freisen, *Geschichte des kanonischen Eherechts bis zum Verfall der Glossenliteratur* (Paderborn, 1893; repr. Aalen, 1963), pp. 665-676. The sharpest arguments against second marriage were voiced by Tertullian (ca. 150-240), especially in his *De monogamia* 10.7, 12.1-5, ed. P. Dekkers, CC 2 (Turnhout, 1954), pp. 1243, 1247-1248. The opposite view, however, also dates from a very early period in Christian history, as shown in the *Pastor* of Hermes 4.4, ed. R. Joly in Sources chrétiennes (Paris, 1958), pp. 162-163.
65 Gratian, D. 26 c. 5; see also John T. Noonan, Jr., "Novel 22," in *The Bond of Marriage*, ed. William Bassett (Notre Dame, 1968), p. 84; André Rosambert, *La veuve en droit canonique jusqu'au XIVe siècle* (Paris, 1923), p. 92.
66 Gratian, C. 31 q. 1 c. 10-13; C. 32 q. 4 c. 1.
67 Gratian, C. 31 q. 1 c. 8; Bernardus de Montemirato (Abbas antiquus; ca. 1225-1296), *Commentaria ad libros decretalium* to X 4.21.1 (Venice, 1588), fol. 132ra-rb; Hostiensis, *Summa aurea,* lib. 4 tit. De secundis nuptiis (Lyon, 1537; repr. Aalen, 1962), fol. 224vb.
68 For example, St. Bonaventure, *Commentaria* to 4 Sent. 42.3.2, in his *Opera*, ed. A.C. Peltier, 15 vols. (Paris, 1864-1871) 6:443-444; Nicholas de Lyra, *Postilla* to Deut. 24.4 ad v. *ne peccare facias* (Strasbourg, 1492; unpaginated). The most savage critic of second marriages among the late twelfth-century canonists was Johannes Faventinus (d. ca. 1187), who held that second marriages should not be tolerated because they were a sign of sexual incontinence; see his *Summa* to C. 31 q. 1 c. 8 ad v. *secundis nuptiis* and to C. 31 q. 1 c. 9 ad v. *secundum ueritatis ratione*, in London, British Library, MS Royal 9.E.VII, fol. 140 vb.
69 Natalie Z. Davis, "The Reasons of Misrule: Youth Groups and Charivaris in Sixteenth Century France," *Past and Present* 50 (1971), 45, 53-54, 65-66.

remarry as a matter of course and provided that they could be forced to remarry, if need be on pain of forfeiture of their fiefs.[70] It is also surprising to find the law books of the Latin Kingdom resurrecting an ancient Roman rule that required a mandatory waiting period for widows before remarriage.[71] Although the early medieval church had accepted that rule, it had been obsolete in canon law since the ninth century and had been specifically condemned by Pope Alexander III (1159-1181).[72]

Finally, a word about the marriage, or remarriage, of the elderly. This was a topic on which neither canonists nor civilians had much to say. Although both recognized a minimum age for marriage, neither contemplated a maximum limit on age at marriage. Jean d'Ibelin, however, enunciated a novel principle in marriage law, that after a woman had attained the age of sixty, the lord from whom she held a fief might no longer require that she marry as a condition of retaining her feudal holding.[73] She retained the right to marry if she wished, but she could no longer be compelled to do so.

This remarkable doctrine is founded upon two arguments. First, Jean d'Ibelin reasoned that requiring women of advanced age to marry was contrary to God's will and to the dictates of reason. This was essentially a natural law argument, based on the premise that marriage of very elderly women is inappropriate because there is no possibility that the marriage will produce offspring.[74] Jean d'Ibelin also specified that a woman who declined to marry on the grounds of advanced age could not be allowed to do this in order to lead a life of licentious sensuality. Rather she must avow a "ferme propos de tenir chasteté de son cors et garder sei de peché."[75]

The second reason advanced in justification of Jean d'Ibelin's doctrine was based on an analogy with the military service obligations of male fief-holders. Men, Jean declared, are excused from military service when they reach the age of sixty and this is the "usage custom, or assise of the Kingdom of Jerusalem and of Cyprus."[76] The implications of this analogical argument are far-

---

70 *Livre au Roi* 30, RHC Lois 1:627.
71 *Livre au Roi* 30, RHC Lois 1:626-627; also *Assises des bourgeois* 166-167, RHC Lois 2:113-114. For the Roman *tempus luctus* see *Dig.* 3.2.10-11; Paul Frédéric Girard, *Manuel élémentaire de droit romain*, 8th ed. (Paris, 1929), pp. 178-179.
72 X 4.21.4; Esmein, *Le mariage* 1:401-402.
73 *Livre de Jean d'Ibelin* 228, RHC Lois 1:362-364.
74 *Livre de Jean d'Ibelin* 228, RHC Lois 1:363, John T. Noonan, Jr., *Contraception: A History of Its Treatment by the Catholic Theologians and Canonists* (Cambridge, Mass., 1965), pp. 289-292, discusses the problems raised by sterile marriage.
75 *Livre de Jean d'Ibelin* 228, RHC Lois 1:364.
76 *Livre de Jean d'Ibelin* 228, RHC Lois 1:362.

reaching, for it implies that just as male fief-holders render "servise de leur cors" through military service, female fief-holders render a comparable bodily service through marriage in the interest of their feudal lord. Thus the ladies of the Latin Kingdom, in the view of one of the kingdom's most eminent jurists, constituted a branch of the kingdom's army. Side by side with the chivalrous army of knights, who fought in the field, and the *militia celestis* of clerics, who fought on the kingdom's behalf through prayer and spiritual service, Jean d'Ibelin implies that the women of Outremer made up a third echelon of Jerusalem's army. We might facetiously label this the *militia cubiculi*, since its members served the interests of the kingdom's rulers in the nuptial chamber, rather than on the battlefield.

If we can, with Paul Rousset, speak of the "stratégie spirituelle" of the clergy during the First Crusade,[77] it is perhaps not too farfetched to regard the marriage law of the Latin Kingdom as the codified rules of a "stratégie matrimonielle," whose successful pursuit was also a vital element in the social and political fortunes of Outremer.

---

77   Paul Rousset, *Les origines et les caractères de la première croisade* (Neuchâtel, 1945), p. 88.

THE TEUTONIC KNIGHTS IN ACRE
AFTER THE FALL OF MONTFORT (1271):
SOME REFLECTIONS

MARIE-LUISE FAVREAU-LILIE
University of Kiel

Elsewhere in my writings, I have already shown that the Teutonic Knights had no intention of withdrawing from Palestine after they had lost Montfort, their main castle, and the greater part of their territories in the Kingdom of Jerusalem to the Mameluk Sultan Baybars in 1271. They were, on the contrary, looking for new opportunities to establish a fresh territorial basis and set up a new domain of the Order in the seigniory of Scandalion.[1] Interesting in this connection are three documents,[2] deposited among the records of the Teutonic Knights in the state archives of Venice, which have gone practically unnoticed by historians and are discussed below. They were drawn up in 1273 and 1274 at the Court of Burgesses under the chairmanship of the viscount of Acre and concern the sale of burgage tenures.[3]

---

1   Marie-Luise Favreau, "Die Kreuzfahrerherrschaft Scandalion (Iskanderūne)," *ZDPV* 93 (1977), 12-29, especially pp. 18-29.

2   Archivio di Stato, Venezia. S. Maria dei Teutonici (SS. Trinità) Busta 3, nos. 62, 64, 66. Riccardo Predelli, "Le reliquie dell'ordine Teutonico in Venezia," *Atti del Reale Istituto Veneto di Scienze, Lettere ed Arti* 64 (1904/05), 1444, 1445, nos. 62, 64, 66 = RRH no. 1400; Louis de Mas-Latrie, *Histoire de l'île de Chypre* 3 (Paris, 1855), 677, note 2, reproduces the text faultily.—The documents have been used by Hans E. Mayer, *Das Siegelwesen in den Kreuzfahrerstaaten*, Abhandlungen der Bayerischen Akademie der Wissenschaften. Phil.-Hist. Klasse, Neue Folge 83 (Munich, 1978), p. 82 and (RRH no. 1400 only) by Joshua Prawer, "The Origin of the Court of Burgesses," in his *Crusader Institutions*, p. 295.

3   On the term *borgesie* cf. *Abrégé des Assises de la Cour des Bourgeois* 1.21, RHC Lois 2:251 and the comment of Prawer, "The *Assise de Teneure* and the *Assise de Vente*: A Study of Landed Property in the Latin Kingdom," *Economic History Review* 4 (1951/52), 82f., reprinted under the title "The Evolution of Landed Property in the Latin Kingdom: The *Assise de Teneure* and the *Assise de Vente*," in his *Crusader Institutions*, p. 350f.; id., *Latin Kingdom*, pp. 74f.,

On 4 August 1273 (Predelli no. 62), viscount Pierre of Amineis and eleven jurors of the Court of Burgesses,[4] who are mentioned by name, documented in writing the sale of an heritage[5] situated in the district of Acre known as *rabat*.[6] This must be placed within the residential area of Acre's non-Latin population, which is also described as located *en amont*.[7] The heritage is described here as being on the street leading to the Church of *St. Jorge des Grifons* (St. George of the Greeks)[8] and adjacent to the houses of the Greek Convent of St. John. For the heritage, a rent of five and three Saracen besants respectively was to be paid

78f., 149f. Prawer's interesting comments on "burgage tenure" in his *Crusader Institutions*, pp. 250-262 could unfortunately not be given consideration as the manuscript of this article was already handed in when that book was published. See also Jonathan Riley-Smith, *The Feudal Nobility and the Kingdom of Jerusalem, 1174-1277* (London, 1973), p. 82. In the thirteenth century, entire villages could be owned service-free as *borgesies*, as emerges from *Eracles* 34.28, p. 474.

4   The jurors of the Court of Burgesses apparently remained in their posts much longer than the viscounts. Jofrei de Tabarie, Johan Jordan (both mentioned in *Abrégé* 1.14, RHC Lois 2:247; RRH no. 1364; Predelli, "Reliquie," nos. 62, 64, 66 = RRH no. 1400; Johan Jordan also in RRH no. 1291) and perhaps also Reimont Odde (RRH nos. 1209, 1364; Predelli, nos. 62, 64, 66 = RRH no. 1400) apparently held their positions for more than two decades. Andre le Berton (Breton), Giles de Conches, Marc dou Chastiau, Martin de Nefin, Pelerin Coqueriau and Pierre le Hongre filled this function for at least five years between 1269 and 1274 (all appear in RRH no. 1364; Predelli, nos. 62, 64, 66 = RRH no. 1400, Pierre le Hongre also in RRH no. 1368; Pelerin Coqueriau entered the Order of St. John about 1281: RRH no. 1443a). Guillaume des deux Chevaus and Hugue Blanchon appear, however, only in 1273 and 1274 (Predelli, nos. 62, 64, 66 = RRH no. 1400). On the required number of members of the Court of Burgesses see *Livre des Assises de la Cour des Bourgeois* 275, ed. Eduard H. von Kausler, *Les Livre des Assises et des Usages dou reaume de Jérusalem* 1 (Stuttgart, 1839), p. 333f.; *Abrégé* 1.2, RHC Lois 2:236f. However, by no means all jurors had to be present at every court function; *Livre des Assises de la Cour des Bourgeois* 12, ed. Kausler, p. 51f.; *Abrégé* 1.52, RHC Lois 2:279f. — On the Court of Burgesses see now the important comments of Prawer, *Crusader Institutions*, pp. 263-295, which unfortunately could not be considered in detail.

5   The term *heritage* or *hereditas* appears but rarely in the documents: RRH nos. 418, 424, 1198d, 1291, 1364; Predelli, "Reliquie," nos. 62, 64.

6   The *rabat* is mentioned also in RRH nos. 1098, 1234.

7   For this localisation see *Assises de la Cour des Bourgeois* 238, ed. Kausler, p. 282. For the localisation east and north of the royal market of Acre cf. Jean Richard, "Colonies marchandes privilégiées et marché seigneurial. La fonde d'Acre et ses 'droitures'," *Moyen Age* 59 (1953), 334f. The Muslim "ghetto" is disputed between Joshua Prawer and Claude Cahen, "A propos des coutumes du marché d'Acre," *RHDFE* 4.41 (1963), 287-290.

8   The addition *des Grifons* serves undoubtedly to differentiate it from a Latin church "Seint George" mentioned in the *Pelrinages et Pardouns de Acre* (about 1280), ed. Henri Michelant and Gaston Raynaud, *Itinéraires à Jérusalem et descriptions de la Terre Sainte rédigés en français au XIe, XIIe et XIIIe siècles* (Geneva, 1882), p. 236. Cf. the parallel case of the "ecclesia sancti Georgii Jacobitarum" in the *burgus* of Tripoli, mentioned in RRH no. 1270b. In the crusader chronicles (*Eracles, Gestes des Chiprois*) there are numerous examples for the use of the term *Grifon* in the sense of "Greek."

to the Churches of *St. Antoine* and *St. Sarguis*.[9] This could give rise to the conjecture that the heritage was situated on an estate (if it was a house) or was a tract of land of which the greater part belonged to the Church of St. Antoine and the lesser to the Church of St. Sarguis.

The owner of the heritage had hitherto been a woman named Set Lehoue, who had sold the property, with the consent of her husband Jorge le Haneisse and her son Faet, for 280 Saracen besants to a certain *dame* Ysabiau, the daughter of a man named Jorge. It cannot be ascertained whether Ysabiau, the buyer of the heritage, was a relative of the seller and her family; as a relative, she would at least have had the right of pre-emption, which precedes that of the neighbours.[10] All of them — sellers and buyers — were certainly not Latins, as their names show, but probably Syrian Christians whose church affiliation (Armenian-Jacobite or Greek Orthodox) must remain uncertain. It is not surprising that non-Latin residents of Acre appear as proprietors of the adjoining real estate, namely Lorens, son of Houdeir, the Greek priest Joseph, and Nassire, son of Halef, as well as a non-Latin religious institution. The document is important in showing that free non-Latins, not only Syrian Christians but even Muslims, could acquire a so-called *tenure en borgesie*.[11] The document of sale confirms the conjecture made by Jonathan Riley-Smith[12] that for the burgage tenures of non-Latin house and estate owners, the Court of Burgesses was likely to be the competent authority rather than their own court. In Acre in the mid-thirteenth century this was the Court of the Market in place of the Court of the Syrians.[13] Thus the Court of Burgesses of Acre was not only competent for cases of litigation concerning burgage tenures (*carelle de borgesie*[14]) between Syrian Christians but also for sales and, without question, for other types of property transactions among non-Latins as well.

---

9   Though a Church of St. Sergius is not known in Acre, the Church of "Seint Antoyne," mentioned in the *Pelrinages et Pardouns de Acre*, p. 236, was situated not far from the "Porta Antonii" in the suburb of Montmusard, namely north of the citadel and south of the Franciscan convent. See the plan of Acre in the reprint of Sanudo, *Secreta* (Jerusalem, 1972) [and the two plans of Acre attached to the article of David Jacoby in this volume. Ed.]. — Though Sergius was a particularly popular saint of the Eastern Church, it is quite possible that the church in question was Latin, even if Sergius appears but rarely as patron of Latin churches and monasteries in the crusader states; the only known instance is the Cistercian monastery of St. Sergius in Gibelet (RRH nos. 1028, 1044, 1082, 1103).
10   *Assises de la Cour des Bourgeois* 30, ed. Kausler, p. 65; *Abrégé* 1.33, RHC Lois 2:260-265.
11   RRH nos. 606a, 682, 697b, 848, 1098a.
12   Riley-Smith, *The Feudal Nobility*, p. 82.
13   Ibid., p. 90f.
14   *Livre de Jean d'Ibelin* 4, RHC Lois 1:26.

The references to the Church of *St. Jorge des Grifons*, the nuns of *saint Johan des Grifons* and the *prestre Josep le Grifon* permit the supposition that in the early 1270s there existed a Greek-Orthodox community in Acre, whose beginnings are shrouded in darkness.[15] By the mid-thirteenth century at the latest, there were Greeks in Acre, among them traders and merchants,[16] and at the latest since 1255 there existed a second Greek institution, the *domus S. Margarethae Graecorum*.[17] It should at least be considered whether one of the two Greek establishments which moved to Acre might not have been the successor community of that hitherto nameless Greek convent known to have existed in Jerusalem in 1167.[18]

In the other two documents deposited in the state archives of Venice, the Teutonic Order in Acre is touched on directly. The viscount and the Court of Burgesses, enlarged by one member,[19] authenticate on 1 September 1273 (Predelli no. 64) that Thomas of Bailleu, who is otherwise unknown to us, had sold his heritage in Acre, with the consent of King Hugh III of Jerusalem and Cyprus, to the Teutonic Knights. The heritage had once belonged to James of Amigdala, and the sale, amounting to 6620 Saracen besants, included 175 besants and 22 corroubles in rent (*censive*)[20] for a number of houses in town. The transaction was concluded by the Grand Commander Konrad of Nevel[21] representing the Master and the brothers of the order. The heritage was apparently situated in the north-east of the town, between *ruga St. Samuelis* in the south, the moat of the citadel in the north,[22] the heritage of the Syrian money

---

15 It would be somewhat hypothetical to assume that it reached as far back as the time of the Byzantine princess Theodora who received Acre from her husband Baldwin III as a marriage gift and, as supposed by Rudolf Hiestand, ''Zum Leben und zur Laufbahn Wilhelms von Tyrus,'' *Deutsches Archiv* 34 (1978), 364, assembled there a Greek court around her.

16 RRH no. 1273a.

17 RRH no. 1234.

18 RRH no. 431.

19 ˌGui de Laon appears otherwise only in Predelli, "Reliquie," no. 66 = RRH no. 1400.

20 For the transfer of a *censive (encensive)* to third parties cf. RRH nos. 590, 1271a and the stipulations in the *Assises de la Cour des Bourgeois* 92-94, 100-102, ed. Kausler, pp. 115-117, 122-124.

21 On him see Frank Milthaler, *Die Großgebietiger des Deutschen Ordens* (Königsberg, 1940), p. 35 and, after him, Marian Tumler, *Der Deutsche Orden im Werden, Wachsen und Wirken bis 1400 mit einem Abriß der Geschichte des Ordens von 1400 bis zur neuesten Zeit* (Montreal, 1955), p. 616.—It may be worth considering an incorrect rendering of the name and an identity, already imputed by Milthaler, with the Grand Commander Konrad von Anefeld, who in February 1272 signed a contract with the lady of Scandalion (RRH no. 1384); cf. Favreau, "Scandalion," p. 17.

22 By 1291, the citadel had a moat only on one side, toward Montmusard: *Gestes des Chiprois* 503, RHC DArm. 2:815.

changer Brehin (Ibrahim)[23] in the east, and the monastery of St. Samuel in the west.[24] The location of the latter is vaguely established here for the first time. The houses whose rent revenues were sold (they themselves appear to have remained the property of Thomas of Bailleu) were situated east of the citadel in the garden of Acre's castle.[25]

In view of the considerable purchase price, the property bought by the Teutonic Order must have been fairly large. The knights had to accept the condition that for one year from the date of the sale the king or his representative would be entitled to repurchase the property, provided the full purchase price for the heritage and rent was returned. The Grand Commander was also obliged to agree that the previous owner and seller would have the benefit of both heritage and rents for the duration of one year at the minimal interest of one *denier*. That is, at least, how I understand this passage of the text, which is both difficult to read and awkwardly formulated.

Just over a year later, on 14 October 1274 (Predelli no. 66), viscount William of Flori and his jury authenticated the transfer without time limit of all the rents from houses in Acre belonging to *dame* Marguerite to the treasurer of the Teutonic Order, Johan Sas.[26] *Dame* Marguerite, widow of the much respected Acre resident Nicole de la Monee—an erstwhile member of the Court of Burgesses[27]—made the transfer in lieu of payment of her debts to the Teutonic Knights. The order sometimes gave this kind of help to nobles who were embarrassed by debt.[28] For herself Marguerite retained merely an annual sum of 60 besants to cover her living expenses.[29]

The explicit mention of royal consent for the sale, documented in Predelli no. 64, made by Thomas of Bailleu to the Teutonic Knights, and the clause contained in the same document concerning the king's right to repurchase the

23   He was still alive in 1281 (RRH no. 1443a).
24   On its possession, founded in Acre in 1185, see Hans E. Mayer, "St. Samuel auf dem Freuden-berge und sein Besitz nach einem unbekannten Diplom König Balduins V.," *Quellen und Forschungen aus Italienischen Archiven und Bibliotheken* 44 (1964), 62f., 69f.
25   See the plans of Acre (note 9 above), where the church "Sanctus Romanus a zardini" is marked; it was probably also situated in the garden of the citadel.
26   He is undoubtedly identical with the treasurer Johannes de Saxonia who signed a contract with Agnes of Scandalion in August of the same year (RRH no. 1399); Favreau, "Scandalion," p. 19.
27   *Abrégé* 1.14, RHC Lois 2:246.
28   Favreau, "Scandalion," pp. 15-19, 24-27.
29   Perhaps she had still other property on which she could draw. In RRH no. 311, for instance, a noblewoman did indeed donate her total real estate to the Knights of St. John, but made it conditional on retaining one house and eighty besants a year for the duration of her life.

property sold, and its limited lease to the seller, are singular features demanding a closer examination. Neither in Predelli no. 62 nor in Predelli no. 66 is there any question of consent by the crown or repurchase on the part of the seller.

A glance at the treatment of the question of consent in connection with acquisition and sale of burgage tenures in the law books shows the following picture: though the relatively early *Livre au Roi* from the turn of the twelfth century offers the unadorned statement without further substantiation that churches and orders may not own any burgage tenures and that none may be bestowed on them,[30] the author of the *Abrégé du Livre des Assises de la Cour des Bourgeois* in the mid-fourteenth century holds a different opinion. He treats the problem of property and sales rights of burgage tenures and the question of the necessity of consent at some length.[31] *Chevaliers, dames, prestres, clers, gent de religion et de coumunes* were allowed, in his opinion, freely to sell *heritages* they owned. However, they could purchase them only with the *speciale grace* of the lord of the city. Especially, this was permitted to them if they were relatives of the proprietor or at least his neighbours.[32] Thus they normally obtained burgage tenures through inheritance, donation or marriage. These provisions show, after all, that the legal conceptions in this field had become considerably more generous since the twelfth century. If one follows the *Abrégé*, Thomas of Bailleu would not have needed the consent of the ruler of Acre, that is, the King of Jerusalem and Cyprus, if he wanted to sell his town property to the Teutonic Order. It was rather the Teutonic Order which had to obtain royal agreement for the purchase of these properties. In the document things are indeed turned around, and it appears as if the lost charter of Hugh III was addressing its consent[33] to Thomas of Bailleu; in truth it was surely addressed

---

30 *Livre au Roi* 43, RHC Lois 1:637f.; cf. also 42, p. 637. This prohibition was, however, not quite so rigorously applied in the twelfth century. RRH no. 418 shows, for instance, that the acquisition of *hereditates* (=*heritages*) through purchase or donation was possible for orders if the appropriate lord gave his consent.

31 See *Abrégé* 1. 21-28, 33-34, 40; ibid. 2.15, 16, 19, RHC Lois 2:251-258, 263, 265, 272, 310-315, 317f.

32 *Abrégé* 1.24, 33, RHC Lois 2:255, 263. — In the twelfth century, the free repurchase of burgage tenures was not permitted to the military orders as a matter of course; permission had to be given them in each case specifically, as can be deduced from RRH no. 424.

33 The deperditum seems to have been issued between 24 September 1269, the day Hugh was crowned as king of Jerusalem, and 1 September 1273, the day Predelli, "Reliquie," no. 64 was drawn up; it is probable that it was issued only a few days before the latter date.

to the Teutonic Order.[34] The maxim of Cypriote law written down in the *Abrégé* in the mid-fourteenth century, according to which also the *gent de religion*, among others, had to obtain the consent of the appropriate ruler for the purchase of burgage tenures, had already been declared binding by King Henry II of Cyprus in the summer of 1298. He had ordered at that time that in future burgage tenures could be owned only by those who could prove they had acquired them with royal consent, either by means of purchase or as a gift.[35] How far was this principle valid on the mainland prior to the collapse of the crusader states in 1291? A perusal of the quite fragmentarily preserved documentation on Jerusalem, Tripoli and Antioch seems to indicate that religious institutions, monastic or military orders had always needed the consent of the town ruler for the purchase of town property. Now and then, separate confirmative documents have survived;[36] otherwise, mention of consent can always be found in the documents whose full text is preserved.[37] The purchase in 1276 by the Templars of the village of La Fauconnerie near Acre, a burgage tenure acquired from a knight without asking prior consent of the crown, thus rightly incurred the anger of King Hugh III.[38]

The absence of a consent in Predelli no. 62 and no. 66 is easily explained by the fact that, prior to the aforementioned edict of 1298, all who did not belong to the nobility or to the different groups of clergy or communes did not need to obtain consent when they wished to buy or sell burgage tenures. In addition, the transfer of income to a military order in payment of debts did not require consent.

---

34 In similar fashion as in Predelli, "Reliquie," no. 64, the following documents also indicate that the consent of the lord to a sale had already been received: RRH nos. 217, 265, 1364. Whether the disposal of his property by the viscount of Caesarea to the Order of St. John mentioned in RRH no. 139, which came about with the consent of the lord of Caesarea, was a sale or a donation, can no longer be certified, owing to the vague formulation in the document. RRH no. 430 mentions the consent of the patriarch of Jerusalem to a previous sale in the Patriarch's Quarter in Jerusalem made to the Order of St. John; he gave his agreement in this instance in his capacity as ruler of that part of the town.

35 *Abrégé* 2.16, RHC Lois 2:315; *Bans et Ordonnances des rois de Chypre* nos. 9, 18, RHC Lois 2:361, 366.

36 Confirmations of sales are RRH nos. 217, 256, 299, 416, 424, 514, 590 (the deperditum mentioned herein). Though the term *hereditas* is used only in one of the documents quoted in connection with the confirmed property, the other properties are evidently also burgage tenures (for a definition of the terms *bourgesie* or *heritage* see *Abrégé* 1.21, RHC Lois 2:251f.). Some of them were parts of fiefs and thus could be sold only in the High Court. It is especially the absence of the Court of Burgesses and the presence of the barons, documented in the lists of witnesses, which permits us on some occasions to assume that this type of burgage tenure was dealt with (RRH nos. 217, 256, 416, 514, 812, 953, 954).

37 See the documents quoted in note 34 above.

38 *Eracles* 34.28, p. 474; Riley-Smith, *The Feudal Nobility*, p. 225f.

It remains to consider whether a court fee was due for the authentication of burgage tenures transferred as collateral to a creditor, as happened in Predelli no. 66, or for the authentication of donations.[39] Few documents of this kind have come down to us, and with the exception of Predelli no. 66 they are concerned only with donations.[40] In none of them, however, is there a fee fixed which donor or recipient, or alternatively debtor or creditor, had to pay. Added to this is the evidence of the law books. In the *Abrégé*, in particular, detailed mention is made of law fees in connection with the sale of heritages and also of cases of exchange or partition of inherited properties for which some fees were due.[41] However, nowhere is there any mention of fees to the town ruler which would be due on the occasion of heritage donations to third parties.[42] In view of the care with which the law books were compiled, it is hardly an oversight that donation fees are not mentioned. Hence the sources support our supposition that a fee was levied only for sales, exchanges and partition of heritages, and thus also, and rightly so, for the sales documented in Predelli nos. 62 and 64. When both documents stipulate that the fees have to be borne by the buyer this also corresponds exactly to the stipulations of the *Assises*.[43]

Jonathan Riley-Smith took the view that a vendor of a burgage tenure usually had to pay one mark of silver to the Court of Burgesses as a fee.[44] This was not the case in the sales discussed here. Actually, Riley-Smith is only partially correct; he overlooked a clause in the relevant regulation of the *Assises*,[45] according to which the vendor had to pay the mark of silver only if

---

39 RRH no. 1291.

40 RRH nos. 311, 1065, 1291, 1383a.

41 For the sales fees see *Assises de la Cour des Bourgeois* 31, 295, ed. Kausler, pp. 66, 350; *Abrégé* 1.22, 26, 27, 42, 50, RHC Lois 2:253, 256, 257, 273, 278; for the exchange fees see *Abrégé* 1.41, 42, RHC Lois 2:273, and for the fees due for partitions see *Abrégé* 1. 49, 50, RHC Lois 2:277, 278.

42 For the treatment of burgage tenure as debenture see *Assises de la Cour des Bourgeois* 32, 82, ed. Kausler, pp. 66f., 107f.; *Abrégé* 1.52, RHC Lois 2:279f. For disposal as donation to third parties, *Abrégé* 1.34-39, RHC Lois 2:265-271. In case of pious donations to the church, which according to *Abrégé* 1.38, RHC Lois 2:269 were only possible with royal consent, the viscount and the Court of Burgesses had to take part.

43 Over a period of roughly two hundred years, a slight rise in the purchase fee can be observed: from 1 besant and 1 *rabouin (Assises de la Cour des Bourgeois* 295, ed. Kausler, p. 350) to 2 besants and 2 soldi in the 1170's (RRH nos. 534, 590) and 3 besants as of 1269 at the latest (RRH no. 1364; Predelli, "Reliquie," nos. 62, 64; *Assises de la Cour des Bourgeois* 31, ed. Kausler, p. 66), the fee rose after 1273, but perhaps only in the fourteenth century, to 3 besants and 2 soldi (*Abrégé* 1.22, 26, 27, 42, 50, RHC Lois 2:253, 256, 257, 273, 278).

44 Riley-Smith, *The Feudal Nobility*, p. 86.

45 *Assises de la Cour des Bourgeois* 31, ed. Kausler, p. 66.

the heritage concerned was situated on crown lands and quit-rent was due to the king. The vendor had to pay nothing if the land or house was free of taxes (*franche*) and quit-rent was hence not due to the crown. The buyer was obliged in any case to pay the Court of Burgesses the fee already mentioned. If this regulation is in accordance with the law as practised around 1270, none of the vendors of burgage tenures in Acre known from that period[46] would have had to pay the mark of silver, since their heritages were rent-free.

Regarding the clause mentioned above about the king's right to repurchase the property, it was evidently laid down in Predelli no. 64 just because this arrangement deviated from the customary judicial norm. This appears to be confirmed by the absence of such a clause in other comparable documents. The author of the *Abrégé*[47] held the opinion that the heritage could once more become the property of the vendor or his heirs if he, the heirs or their proctor refunded to the buyer the purchase price and, in addition, the purchase fee within a given time limit, usually one year, though this could be fixed as desired. Should the time limit expire without the vendor having asked or received the heritage back, then it would become the legitimate property of the buyer. The time limit set for property repurchase in Predelli no. 64 therefore remained within normal bounds. It would also surely not have been included in the text of the document if it had not been stipulated at the same time that in place of the vendor Thomas of Bailleu it was the consent-giving king who ensured for himself the right of repurchase, and this in spite of the fact that the purchase price was not payable to him.

Concerning Thomas of Bailleu's motive for selling his Acre property and the reasons of Hugh III for claiming the repurchase right, only conjectures can be made. Debts could have induced Thomas of Bailleu to sell. Perhaps, after paying his debts, he no longer had the financial means to buy back the properties he had sold. Under such circumstances, the assignment of the right of repurchase to the king would have been easy enough for him. It is also possible that Thomas of Bailleu simply intended to return to Europe, the situation in the Holy Land after the fall of Antioch (1268) and Montfort (1271) no longer appearing to him sufficiently safe for Christians. Hence he looked for a buyer of his property in Acre and found one in the Teutonic Order. Unable to depart immediately, however, either because he had not yet obtained a passage by sea or still had other business to attend to, Thomas of Bailleu made the condition that for a symbolic rent he could continue to live for another year in the house, of which the Order was already proprietor. He was evidently firmly convinced

46   RRH no. 1364; Predelli, "Reliquie," nos. 62, 64.
47   *Abrégé* 1.28, RHC Lois 2:257f.

that he would return to Europe within that year and hence was no longer interested in the repurchase right which the king took over.

It is more than likely that it was to please Thomas of Bailleu that Hugh III gave his consent to the transaction requested by the Teutonic Order, stipulating only that the property was left to the vendor for another year for a minimal rent, which would serve to guard the ownership rights of the Order. However, an actual interest in the property and the repurchase rights on the part of the king cannot be excluded. Inasmuch as Hugh III was thinking of extending the citadel of Acre or perhaps filling in the southern part of the moat facing the inner city — we do not know whether this was so — he must have been interested in the heritage of Thomas of Bailleu, as it bordered directly on the said moat. The fact that in 1291 the citadel had a moat only in the direction of Montmusard[48] does not prove conclusively that Hugh III made use of his purchase rights and did fill in the southern moat. This alteration could have been accomplished at a later date.

The Grand Commander of the Teutonic Order would surely not have agreed to the transaction had it not so closely concerned the interests of the knights. Buying the rent from several houses, the Order simultaneously acquired the pre-emption right on these heritages[49] and thereby created the pre-conditions for an eventual further enlargement of the real estate which it possessed in the eastern part of town. More attractive to the Teutonic Order was, without question, the possibility of buying Thomas of Bailleu's property, because it had previously been the heritage of James of Amigdala who had died in Acre at some time between 5 November 1265 and 21 February 1271.[50] The Teutonic Order had quarrelled for years over property rights and brought law suits against James of Amigdala, grandson of Joscelin III of Edessa and heir of half the "Seigneurie de Joscelin."[51] The Order had financed the debt-ridden only son of James, William II of Amigdala, and his spouse Agnes of Scandalion. As security, the Order had already in 1263 ensured itself access to part of the income from James's fief, and in 1272 it had taken in mortgage the whole seigniory of Scandalion which was, after all, connected with the name of Amigdala in a certain manner.[52] The wish of the Order to purchase the heritage of James of Amigdala which, apart from everything else, was not far from the establishment of the Teutonic Knights in Acre, was only natural and was fully in keeping with its policy of acquisition.

48   Cf. note 22 above.
49   *Abrégé* 1.46, RHC Lois 2:275f.
50   For date of death see Favreau, "Scandalion," p. 17.
51   Ibid., p. 16f.; Hans E. Mayer, "Der Deutsche Orden und die Seigneurie de Joscelin," *Ritterorden*, pp. 171-216.
52   RRH no. 1384; Favreau, "Scandalion," pp. 17-19.

The three documents in the Venetian state archives illustrate the activity of the Court of Burgesses in Acre in the early 1270s and stimulate reflections on the judicial position regarding sales of burgage tenures at that period. Above all, the documents provide an insight into the activities the Teutonic Order was able to develop only a few short years after the fall of its fortress Montfort and barely two decades before the collapse of crusader rule in Syria and Palestine. It is correct to say that the document of 4 August 1273 can only be drawn upon conditionally as evidence of the Order's expansionist drive in Acre. Presumably, though, it finally reached the records of the Teutonic Order precisely because the very heritage dealt with in the document came into the possession of the Order by one means or another; and with it the Teutonic Knights received the document, which was quite normal procedure. The documents of September 1273 and 14 October 1274 throw a clearer light on the financial power of the Teutonic Order and on its ambitions to enlarge its property in Acre. Perhaps the knights hoped to consolidate their real estate into a separate quarter of their own at some later date. The setback of 1271 did not, at any rate, deter the Teutonic Order from continuing to see the centre of its activities in the Holy Land and to consolidate its position in Acre.

APPENDIX[1]

Archivio di Stato di Venezia. S. Maria dei Teutonici (SS. Trinità), Busta 3, no. 62; Summary: Riccardo Predelli, "Le reliquie dell'ordine Teutonico in Venezia," *Atti del Reale Istituto Veneto di Scienze, Lettere ed Arti* 64 (1904/05), 1444 no. 62. — Original.

Nos, Pierre d'Amineis, visconte d'Acre au jor, et nos, Johan Jordain, Reimont Odde, Jofrei de Tabarie, Pierre le Hongre, Marc dou Chastiau, Gile de Conches, Andre le Berton, Martin de Nefin, Pelerin Coqueriau, Guillaume des .II. Cheuaus, Hugue Blanchon, jures de la cort des borgeis d'Acre, faisons assaveir a toz ceaus qui sont et seront que Set Lehoue, par l'otrei et la volonte de son espous Jorge le Haneisse et de Faet son fiz, vint en nostre presence et vendi un heritage que il avoient au rabat en la rue si con l'on vait a l'iglise saint Jorge des Grifons, o totes ses apartenances et ses raisons et ses droitures et ses teneures o tot son vent, por .CC. et .LXXX. besanz sarrazinas a dame Ysabiau, fille de Jorge. Et ce dit heritage est en la censive de saint Antoine et de saint Sarguis et doit chascun an .VIII. besanz sarrazinas de cens, c'est assaveir a saint Antoine .V. besanz et a saint Sarguis .III. besanz. Et ce devant dit heritage

---

1   I would like to thank Professor Jean Richard, Dijon, for his kind advice during the establishment of the text.

siet en tel maniere: vers levant joint a un heritage de Lorens, fiz de Houdeir, et a une gastine de prestre Josep le Grifon, et vers couchant li est une rue comune, et joint a un heritage de Nassire, fiz de Halef, et vers boire li est la dite rue comune si con l'on vait a l'iglise saint Jorge des Grifons, et vers oistre joint as maisons des nonains de saint Johan des Grifons. Et se dessaisirent dou dit heritage la dite Set Lehoue et son dit espous Jorge et Faet son dit fiz, et en saisirent le vesconte; lequel en saisi maintenant la devant nomee dame Ysabiau qui paia par la main dou dit visconte les .CC.LXXX. besanz sarrazinas a la dessus nomee Set Lehoue et a Jorge son espous et a Faet son fiz, et a nos la dite cort .III. bezans por la raison dou dit achat. Et la dite Set Lehoue jura le sairement use de la cort. Et porce que nos volons que chascun sache que ceste devant dite vente, en la maniere come ele est dessus devisee, fu faite en la presence de nos la dite cort, avons nos fait faire ceste presente chartre seeler de nostre seel de cire pendant. Escrite par la main de Bienuenu nostre escrivain. Ce fu fait en l'an de l'incarnation nostre seignor Ihesu Crist .M.CC. et .LXXIII. a .IIII. iors dou meis d'aost.

Archivio di Stato di Venezia. S. Maria dei Teutonici (SS. Trinità). Busta 3, no. 64; Summary: Predelli, "Reliquie," p. 1444 no. 64. — Original.

Nos, Pierre d'Amineis, visconte d'Acre au jor, et nos, Johan Jordain, Reymont Odde, Jofrei de Tabarie, Pierre le Hongre, Marc dou Chastiau, Gile de Conches, Andre le Berton, Martin de Nefin, Pelerin Coqueriau, Guillaume des .II. Cheuaus, Hugue Blanchon, Gui de Laon, jures de la cort des borgeis d'Acre, faisons assaveir a toz ceaus qui sont et seront que mon seignor Hugue, noble roi de Jerusalem et de Chipre, dona pooir de vendre a mesire Thomas de Bailleu son heritage qui fu jadiz de mesire Jaque de la Mandelee et cent et setante cinc besanz et vinte deus carobles de censive que il a es maisons qui sont au jardin dou chastiau o totes les raisons et les droitures que il y a et avoir doit. Et le dit mesire Thomas de Bailleu vint en nostre presence et vendi l'eritage qui fu de mesire Jaque de la Mandelee qui est en la rue de saint Samoel et la censive des maisons qui sont dedenz le jardin dou chastiau qui sont .C. et .LXXV. besanz sarrazinas et .XXII. carobles o totes luer apartenances et luer raisons et luer droitures et luer teneures o tot luer vent, por ssis mile et set cens et vint besanz sarrazinas, a frere Conrat de Neuel, grant comandeor de la maison de l'Hospital de Nostre Dame des Alemans a Acre et en leu de maistre, et as freres de cele meimes maison. Et ce devant dit heritage siet en tel maniere: vers levant joint a l'heritage de Brehin le Changeor et vers couchant joint a la maison saint Samoel et vers boire joint au foce et vers oistre li est la dite rue comune de saint Samoel. Et la dite censive est dedenz le jardin qui fu dou chastiau. Et ce dessaisi le dit mesire Thomas de Bailleu dou dit heritage et de la dite censive et en saisi le vesconte; lequel en saisi maintenant le dessus nome frere Conrat por lui et por les freres de la dite maison des Alemans qui paia par la main dou dit visconte les .VI.M et .VII.C et .XX. besanz sarrazinas a mesire Thomas de Bailleu, et a nos la dite cort .III. besanz por la raison dou dit achat. Et le dessus nome frere Conrat, par l'assent et la comune volente des freres de la dite maison des Alemans, dist que totes les feis que le devant nome roi de Jerusalem et de Chipre [ou son][2] comandement vodront avoir le dessus nome heritage et la dite censive, par tot le meis d'aost prochein venant pro les [.VI.M][3] et .VII.C et .XX. besanz sarrazinas que il lor en feront vente. Et loerent le dit heritage et la dite censive a mesire Thomas de Bailleu por un denier jusques a un an. Et porce que nos volons que chascun sache que ceste devant dite vente en la maniere come ele est dessus devisee fu faite devant nos la dite cort, avons nos fait faire ceste presente chartre seeler de nostre seel de cire pendant. Escrite par la main de Bienuenu nostre escrivain. Ce fu fait en l'an de l'incarnation nostre seignor Ihesu Crist .M. et .CC. et .LXXIII. le premier jor del meis de setembre.

Archivio di Stato di Venezia. S. Maria dei Teutonici (SS. Trinità). Busta 3, no. 66; Summary: RRH no. 1400; Predelli, "Reliquie," p. 1445 no. 66; Printed: Louis de Mas-Latrie, *Histoire de l'île de Chypre* 3 (Paris, 1855), 677 note 2 (faulty). — Original.

Nos, Guillaume de Flori, visconte d'Acre au jor, et nos, Johan Jordain, Reimont Odde, Jofrei de Tabarie, Pierre le Hongre, Marc dou Chastiau, Gile de Conches, Andre le Berton, Martin de Nefin, Pelerin Coqueriau, Guillaume des .II. Cheuaus, Hugue Blanchon, Gui de Laon, jures de la cort des borgeis d'Acre, faisons assaveir a toz ceaus qui sont et seront que dame Marguerite espouse qui fu de sire Nicole de la Monee vint en nostre presence et dist que ele metoit totes les rentes des maisons que ele avoit a Accre en la garde et au poeir de frere Johan Sas, tresorier a Acre de la maison de l'Hospital de Nostre Dame des Alemans, por ses dettes paier, sauf ssissante besans de rente que ele en retenoit chascun an por son vivre. Et ensi se dessaisi la dite Marguerite des rentes de ses dites maisons et en saisi le dit tresorier de la maison des Alemans. Et porce que nos volons que chascun sache que la dite comande en la maniere come ele est dessus devisee fu faite en nostre presence, avons nos fait faire ceste presente chartre seeler de nostre seel de cire pendant. Escrite par la main de Bienuenu nostre escrivain. Ce fu fait en l'an de l'incarnation nostre seignor Ihesu Crist .M. et .CC. LXXIIII. a .XIIII. iors del meis de huitovre.

2   Free space for 4 to 5 letters, mildew. Legible under quartz-lamp: *ou son*. Kindly suggested by Professor Jean Richard.
3   Likewise free space at the end of the line, mildew. The text must be completed here to: VI.M

CHRISTIAN PILGRIMS IN THE THIRTEENTH CENTURY AND THE LATIN KINGDOM OF JERUSALEM: BURCHARD OF MOUNT SION

ARYEH GRABOIS
University of Haifa

There are still problems about Christian pilgrimage to the Holy Land in the Middle Ages which need to be studied. While the late Roman and Byzantine period, up to the end of the sixth century, has been the subject of distinguished research,[1] work published on the subsequent medieval centuries has often lacked the precision to be expected in modern investigation.[2] General conclusions on pilgrimage to Jerusalem have been based on the verdicts of scholars

---

1   Bernhard Kötting, *Peregrinatio Religiosa. Wallfahrten in der Antike und das Pilgerwesen in der alten Kirche* (Regensburg, 1950). This earlier period is also favoured by critical publications of sources, including new editions of texts already published, e.g., the *Itineraria et alia geographica,* Corpus Christianorum, Series Latina, 175-176 (Turnhout, 1965), with an excellent bibliography and important remarks. The result of previous works on the period before the First Crusade and their bibliography figures in the study of John Wilkinson, *Jerusalem Pilgrims before the Crusades* (Jerusalem, 1977). For the later period, see the excellent *Regestum* by Reinhold Röhricht, *Die Deutschen im Heiligen Lande (c. 650-1291)* (Innsbruck, 1894), completed by his *Deutsche Pilgerreisen nach dem Heiligen Lande*, 2nd ed. (Innsbruck, 1900). See also Paul Riant, *Expéditions et pèlerinages des Scandinaves en Terre Sainte au temps des croisades* (Paris, 1865). Similar works do not exist for other European countries.

2   Among them, cf. Raymond Roussel, *Les pèlerinages à travers les siècles* (Paris, 1954); Raimond Oursel, *Les pèlerins du Moyen Age* (Paris, 1963); Alan Kendall, *Medieval Pilgrims* (London, 1972); Pierre-André Sigal, *Les marcheurs de Dieu* (Paris, 1974). More relevant are the papers presented to the symposium of Todi (1961), *Pellegrinaggi e culto dei santi in Europa fino alla prima crociata* (Todi, 1963) as well as the remarks by Raymonde Foreville, "Pèlerinages, croisade et jubilé au moyen âge," *Amis de Saint-François* 7 (1966), 48-61 and, especially, Edmond-René Labande, "Recherches sur les pèlerins dans l'Europe des XIe-XIIe siècles," *Cahiers de civilisation médiévale* 1 (1958), 159-169 and 339-347; id., *"Ad limina;* le pèlerin médiéval au terme de sa démarche," *Mélanges René Crozet* (Poitiers, 1966), 1: 283-291 (both reprinted in his *Spiritualité et vie littéraire de l'Occident* [London, 1974]), and Giles Constable, "Monachisme et pèlerinage au Moyen Age," *Revue historique* 246 (1971), 3-27.

who have studied those made to Santiago of Compostela[3] or Mont-Saint-Michel.[4] With all due respect to the use of comparative methods in the study of history, this has led to unnecessary confusion.

Joshua Prawer has already emphasized that Christian pilgrims to the Holy Land during the period of the crusades were not generally travellers interested by the *realia* of the actual Latin Kingdom of Jerusalem. Their votive purposes brought them to shrines related to the Old and New Testament and, moreover, to any place in the Holy Land which faith or superstition might connect with the cult of a saint, with or without some historical basis.[5] The study of one of the best accounts by a twelfth-century pilgrim, that of John of Würzburg (*ca.* 1160), clearly leads to the conclusion that a pilgrim from western Europe then viewed the Holy Land in terms of its biblical past, and that he had little or no interest in the contemporary conditions of Palestine.[6] Such an approach was different from that of Muslim or Jewish travellers. Benjamin of Tudela and Petaḥyah of Ratisbon, John's contemporaries, were interested in the holy sites, but they were also aware of the realities of their time. The crusade has been considered as an armed pilgrimage, but the aims and views of crusaders were quite different from those of pilgrims proper.[7] It may even be asked whether pilgrims were not disappointed in the Latin kingdom, where they found lay structures and a society conducting itself in ways far removed from that idea of holiness which had impelled them to undertake the long and difficult journey to the land of Christ.[8]

3   Cf. Luis Vazquez de Parga, José-Maria Lacarra, Juan Uria y Riu, *Las Peregrinaciones a Santiago de Compostela,* 3 vols. (Madrid, 1948-1949) and the review by Yves Renouard, "Le pèlerinage à Saint-Jacques de Compostelle et son importance dans le monde médiéval d'après quelques travaux récents," *Revue historique* 206 (1951), 254-261.

4   Jean Laporte et Raymonde Foreville, eds., *Millénaire du Mont-Saint-Michel,* 4 vols. (Paris, 1968-1971).

5   Prawer, *Latin Kingdom,* ch. 11.

6   Aryeh Graboïs, "Le pèlerin occidental en Terre sainte à l'époque des croisades et ses réalités: la relation de pèlerinage de Jean de Wurzbourg," *Mélanges Edmond-René Labande* (Poitiers, 1974), pp. 367-376.

7   This question, the relations between pilgrimage and crusade, has been discussed by Paul Alphandéry and Alphonse Dupront, *La Chrétienté et l'idée de croisade,* 2 vols. (Paris 1954-1955). On the other hand, Labande ("Recherches sur les pèlerins," pp. 166-167) clearly emphasizes the difference between crusaders and pilgrims visiting the Holy sites, who did not show any interest for the profane Jerusalem of the terrestrial realm of the crusaders.

8   This would be the reason for the curious "ignorance" of the *realia* in the pilgrims' relations, as it has been represented by the Latin Kingdom and its institutions, as well as by the city of Acre, the most representative "mirror" of the Crusader lay society. Cf. Aryeh Grabois, "Acre as the Gateway of Pilgrimage to the Holy Land in the Crusaders' Period," *Studies in the History of the Jewish People and the Land of Israel* 2 (1972), 93-106 (in Hebrew). Breaking with that "ignorance," Burchard of Mount Sion openly criticized the crusader society, and his criticism will be discussed below.

Did such attitudes remain unchanged in the thirteenth century? In view of so many important new developments in European society,[9] it would be rash to assume that they did, without a close examination of the evidence. The spectacular growth of urban society, the influence of the Friars and of intellectuals trained in the universities, brought new attitudes to pilgrimage, though its primary aims, the expression of religious feeling by the visit to a holy place and the cult of relics, remained constant.[10] The study of these new trends in pilgrimage has to be closely connected with the new realities in the world of the crusaders. These begin with changes in the idea of the crusade [11] as well as with the political and social structures of what became the "kingdom of Acre." A good illustration of this new reality and its impacts is provided by Burchard of Mount Sion's *Descriptio Terrae Sanctae*; it is undoubtedly the best account by a thirteenth-century pilgrim and it became one of the most popular descriptions in the late Middle Ages. It served as a source for Marino Sanudo and other theorists of the crusade in the fourteenth century [12] and was largely quoted by fifteenth-century travellers and guides.[13]

Burchard, or Brocardus, was a Dominican friar of German origin, who came either from Strasbourg or Magdeburg. He was connected with the Dominican House at Magdeburg and sent them a manuscript of his description.[14] There are no sources at our disposal concerning his family, education or career, either before his pilgrimage or after his return to Europe. Even the year of his death is

---

9 The difference between the twelfth and thirteenth centuries, as a consequence of the structural changes of the Western European society, has been discussed by many historians, who have dealt with its impacts on various fields. Among the works, see Joseph R. Strayer, *Western Europe in the Middle Ages*, 2nd ed. (Santa Monica, 1974), especially pp. 141-147.

10 See Labande, *"Ad limina"*; Jean Leclercq, "Monachisme et pérégrination du IXe au XIIe siècle," *Studia Monastica* 3 (1961), 33-52; Adriaan Bredero, "Jérusalem dans l'Occident médiéval," *Mélanges René Crozet*, 1:259-271, and especially Prawer, *Latin Kingdom*.

11 See Palmer A. Throop, *Criticism of the Crusade. A Study of Public Opinion and Crusade Propaganda* (Amsterdam, 1940).

12 Sanudo, *Secreta*. See Aziz S. Atiya, *The Crusade in the Later Middle Ages* (London, 1938), passim.

13 *Un guide du pèlerin en Terre Sainte au XVe siècle*, ed. Régine Pernoud, Cahiers d'histoire, 1 (Paris, 1940). For other quotations see Röhricht, *Deutsche Pilgerreisen*, pp. 32, 164, 213.

14 This dedication figures in the Bratislava Ms., as mentioned and copied by J.C.M. Laurent in his preface to the edition of Burchard's relation: *Peregrinationes medii aevi quatuor: Burchardus de Monte Sion, Ricoldus de Monte Crucis, Odoricus de Foro Julii, Willebrandus de Oldenburg* (Leipzig, 1864) [hereafter cited as Burchard, ed. Laurent].

uncertain, though hypotheses have been formulated.[15] Our knowledge about him is limited to some autobiographical remarks which appear in different variants of his book, or to notices by copyists of the fourteenth and fifteenth centuries, written merely for purposes of identification.[16] According to events mentioned in his description, he visited the Holy Land after the Second Council of Lyons (1274) and before the death of Hugh III, king of Jerusalem and Cyprus (1284). The fact that he mentions the Mameluk Sultan Qalā'ūn (1279-1290) as the living Muslim sovereign allows us to suppose that at least the first draft of the description was written between 1280-1283. While in the Holy Land he was intensively active; he visited both those areas of the Latin Kingdom still under Christian rule and the major part of its former territories under Mameluk domination. Burchard had thoroughly prepared himself for his pilgrimage: his readings of the Old and New Testament were completed by those of the *Onomasticon* by Eusebius of Caesarea, the writings of Saint Jerome and the *Historia Orientalis* by James of Vitry. These were his principal authorities, but he also used previous descriptions and *itineraria* by pilgrims.[17] Unlike twelfth-century pilgrims, Burchard subjected his authorities to critical scrutiny and confronted their evidence with his own observations. This is illustrated by the account of his visit to Mount Gilboa, where, according to the biblical verse, i.e., the curse of King David, there was no rainfall; but the personal experience of our author led him to write: "it is not true"; during his visit on Saint-

---

15   Victor Le Clerc, *Histoire littéraire de France*, 21 (Paris, 1850), 180-215, considered him as a "Frenchman," i.e. Alsatian, originally of Strasbourg. Laurent was opposed to this hypothesis and suggested that his origins were either of the family of the counts of Barby, or of Magdeburg (Burchard, ed. Laurent, pp. 3-4). Röhricht, *Die Deutschen im Heiligen Lande*, p. 129 and in his *Bibliotheca geographica Palestinae* (Berlin, 1890), no. 143, suggested that he might have been either a count of Barby, sent in 1283 by Rudolf I to the Holy Land, or a relative of his, bearing the same name. See also Berthold Altaner, *Die Dominikanermissionen des 13. Jahrhunderts* (Habelschwerdt, 1924). The existing data cannot support any of the hypotheses formulated; all that might be said about Burchard is that he was a Dominican friar, born and educated in Germany, who had connections with the order's House of Magdeburg before he had undertaken his pilgrimage.

16   The 26 existing manuscripts of Burchard's description, including the variants, were described by Laurent in his edition, pp. 5-11.

17   Among these sources of the pilgrims, which are not mentioned by their authors' names, it is possible to identify the *Descriptio* of John of Würzburg and Theodorich's *Libellus de locis sanctis*, dating to 1160-1170, as well as the *Descriptio* of Thietmar, of *ca.* 1220. While the Bible, Eusebius, Jerome and James of Vitry were considered by Burchard as authorities, his attitude to the other sources was critical, denying the veracity of their statements when they did not correspond to his own observations or theories.

Martin's Day (November 11), it rained and he became "wet to the skin."[18] But this critical attitude in no way affected his piety. Christian devotion had led the pilgrim to undertake his difficult journey; his primary interest was the biblical past of the land. However, the past became combined with the present, and his description of the Holy Land includes *realia*, even though this reality was not always a pleasant one.

The geography of the Holy Land was for Burchard primarily that of the Old Testament. While he was aware of other administrative divisions, such as the *Decapolis*, which he found in James of Vitry,[19] the cis-Jordan country remained for him the "land of the ten tribes of Israel."[20] This land was also that of Christ and the Apostles and it was the aim and goal of his pilgrimage. While he states that he followed the authority of James of Vitry when describing the adjoining countries, even though he visited part of them and was able to add his personal remarks, the "land which fell to the lot of the ten tribes" he explored with special care. There the Bible was his main guide, while the other sources remained secondary.

This "holy geography" is however described in a particular way, and is made to include five main territorial divisions. One of them is Jerusalem and its surroundings, while the other four do not represent regions, but merely territories radiating from the city of Acre along the main roads which connected the capital of the crusader kingdom with various settlements in the north, northeast, east and south. Burchard was aware that such a description was unusual and needed the explanation which he provided in his preface: his wish to place the Scripture-sites in subdivisions corresponding to the four, and then, twelve winds of heaven, implied the choice of a central point, in order to "arrange the whole land around it in due order. For that I choose the city of Acre, as being known better than the others. Yet it is not in the midst (of the land), but stands

---

18 *Nec verum est, quod dicunt quidam, quod nec ros nec pluvia veniat super montes Gelboe, quia, cum in die beati Martini essem ibi, venit super me pluvia ita, quod usque ad carnem fui madefactus* (Burchard, ed. Laurent, p. 52). In this case the *quidam* was the Bible itself (2 Reg. 1.21: *Montes Gelboe, nec ros, nec pluvia veniant super vos*). Choosing this way of referring to an anonymous source, Burchard was able to oppose his own experience, without contradicting the sacred text of the Bible.

19 Burchard, ed. Laurent, p. 23.

20 Ibid., pp. 45-46. James of Vitry is always mentioned by Burchard with great deference, including the title *dominus* and his qualities: *patriarcha Hierosolymitanus et Romanae sedis legatus*, despite his death in 1240. Burchard is the sole source qualifying James as patriarch of Jerusalem, while he was bishop of Acre. It seems that this intitulation reflects the later union of the two offices. About James's career, see Robert B.C. Huygens, *Lettres de Jacques de Vitry* (Leiden, 1960), p. 1.

on its western boundary by the sea-side."[21] Yet it seems that this reason for choosing a method, later adopted by Marino Sanudo and other pilgrims of the later Middle Ages,[22] is only part of the truth. While Burchard states that he decided to describe the country *utiliter* for his readers, he chose a travel system profitable for himself. Apart from Jerusalem, which is not included in these territorial *divisiones* and which he visited while staying at the monastery of Mount Sion (where he probably wrote his *Descriptio* and hence the name by which he is known), Burchard used Acre as his headquarters while travelling and exploring the country along the main roads. Thus, the description is also his travel diary, reflecting the logic of a systematical exploration of the land.

The result of such an approach implies a lack of priorities in the description of the sites visited. Indeed, Burchard adopted a selective attitude, but this selection is the outcome of his personal impressions. In some cases, these impressions were the reason for his dealing at length with certain places, such as the dissertations about several mounts named *Seyr-Sanyr* and *Hermon*, and why there are two rivers named *Cisson*,[23] or for expressing his feelings about the glory and the decay of the ancient city of Sebaste.[24] On the other hand, he contented himself with relatively short remarks on several places, even though they were as important as Saforie. Even Nazareth, second only to Jerusalem in the holiness of its shrines, is but briefly described, though he stated "that he said many Masses there."[25] Such an approach is characteristic of earlier pilgrims; but while they did not neglect to add any information on hagiographical traditions and on shrines connected with the worship of saints, the hagiography of Burchard is limited to the Old and New Testament, so that when, for example, he described Bethsaida and Capernaum, he made no reference to Saint Peter's house.[26]

Another important feature that symbolizes the beginning of a new era is related to Burchard's critical remarks concerning palaeo-Christian hagiography. Nobody will attempt to doubt his piety and especially his firm belief

---

21 Burchard, ed. Laurent, p. 21. It is possible that he concluded his description at the monastery of Mount Sion, where many guides for pilgrims were compiled in the later Middle Ages (see Röhricht, *Deutsche Pilgerreisen*, p. 43).
22 Concerning Marino Sanudo and other Christian travellers, see Steward's introduction to his translation of Burchard's work for the PPTS 12,1 (London, 1896), p. VI. During the first quarter of the fourteenth century, the Jewish explorer Ashtori ha-Parhi adopted a similar method, but choosing as central point the town of Beth-Shan, his residence. See his *Kaftor va-Perah* in Abraham Yaari, ed., *Travels in Palestine* (Tel-Aviv, 1946, in Hebrew).
23 Burchard, ed. Laurent, pp. 33, 35, 41-43, 48-49, 51.
24 Ibid., pp. 52-54.
25 Ibid., pp. 46-47.
26 Ibid., p. 40.

that he has seen the genuine sites connected with the biblical period and the life of Christ;[27] his critical remarks are merely concentrated on the unusual places of such sites. Such is the case of a note added to the account of his visit to Cana in Galilee. Pilgrims from Western Europe found it perfectly natural to visit tombs in the crypts of churches. However, when Burchard was shown the sites of the Annunciation at Nazareth, the Nativity at Bethlehem or the underground site of the famous wedding at Cana, he was astonished to find a contrast between what he saw and what he had learned from the Scriptures. As his inquiries were not satisfactorily answered, he himself produced a logical explanation: "The only reason I can find for this is, that owing to the frequent destruction of churches built over these places, the ruins raised the soil above them, and then, after they had been somehow levelled, other buildings were erected upon them. But Christians who by piety visited these places and wished to reach the very place where the thing occurred, had to clear the places and construct steps in order to come down to them. And so, almost all these places seem to be in crypts."[28] This explanation of the creation of a *Tel*, with a number of *strata* and of the diggings, precedes scientific archaeology by hundreds of years.

This critical attitude, combined with the desire to find a reasonable explanation for things which he observed and which aroused his curiosity, is also manifested in Burchard's description of Jerusalem. The city of Jerusalem, its monuments, churches and shrines, were well known in the West, as a result of the oral and written accounts given by the pilgrims who visited the Holy City and described its topography and holy history. One of the original questions raised by Burchard was whether a change had occurred in the site of the city since the era of Christ. He was told that such a change had indeed taken place, the consequence of which would mean that the site of the Passion, which according to the Scriptures had been *extra muros*, was included within the walled city of his times.[29] Burchard was vehemently opposed to ideas of topographical changes: "they do not know what they say and want to (seem to)

---

27 For example, the stone near Tyre upon which Christ stood when he preached to the Tyrians and "is never covered by the sand" (ibid., p. 25); the house of Mary the Magdalen at Magdala (ibid., p. 40); the stone upon which Christ stood at the *Mensa Christi* (ibid., p. 35) and the whole description of the Jerusalem, Bethlehem and Hebron shrines (ibid., pp. 63-85).

28 Ibid., p. 44.

29 Ibid., p. 63. Here there is no need to discuss this theory, already dealt with by modern research. See Louis H. Vincent, *Jérusalem de l'Ancien Testament*, 3.2 (Paris, 1956), summarizing the works which had appeared since the publication of his *Jérusalem nouvelle*, in collaboration with Félix M. Abel (Jerusalem, 1926).

know what they have not seen." He argues that the site of the Temple "has always been the same." His own theory was that, since the times of Christ, the city had spread so that the Holy Sepulchre and the Calvary were included within its walls. But he also remarks: "such a great city has a small population," attributing the phenomenon to the terror which reigned there. While he did not make any allusion to the destruction of Jerusalem by the Khwarismians in 1244,[30] his affirmation is identical to that of Naḥmanides who, some twenty years before Burchard's pilgrimage, worked for the restoration of the Jewish settlement of Jerusalem.[31] Burchard's attempt to explain facts in terms of the dynamics of urban development, of which he had been aware in Europe, is an important innovation. Because of the holiness of Jerusalem in the eyes of previous pilgrims, such questions were never raised by them, as they felt no need for concordance between the text of the Scriptures and the sites of shrines which they were shown.

The main interest of medieval pilgrims was the biblical geography and history of the Holy Land, especially as exhibited in its shrines and relics. Burchard himself was no exception, though his interest was broader. It included observations both of the fauna and flora, with which he was able to describe the rural economy, and of the society ("the religions"), to which he dedicated special chapters of his book. This interest also led him to include, while describing localities, many remarks on the contemporary situation. He mentioned, for example, the state of the fortifications of cities held by the crusaders (e.g., Acre, Tyre, Sidon, 'Atlith[32]), and he referred to places recently lost by them. In certain instances, he made short allusions to the circumstances of their loss. He did so in the case of Saphet, with its "most powerful fortifications," where the use of expressions such as "shameful sort of fall"[33] is an open charge against

---

30 See Runciman, *Crusades*, 3:224-225.

31 For a critical edition of Naḥmanides' letter see Benjamin Z. Kedar, "The Jews of Jerusalem, 1187-1267, and the Role of Naḥmanides in the Re-Establishment of their Community," in *Jerusalem in the Middle Ages. Selected Papers*, ed. B.Z. Kedar (Jerusalem, 1979; in Hebrew), pp. 135-136. For the Jewish resettlement of Jerusalem see Prawer, *Latin Kingdom*, ch. 13 and Kedar, "Jews," pp. 122-133.

32 Burchard, ed. Laurent, pp. 23, 24-25, 83. Burchard also supplies correct information about the lords who held various cities and about their feudal dependence. Such information does not supply new data and proves that his knowledge was accurate.

33 *Inde ... est castrum et civitas Sephet, pulchrius et firmius meo iudicio omnibus castris, que vidi, situm in monte altissimo. Quod fuerat milicie templi, sed proditum et captum ignominiose nimis ad iacturam tocius christianitatis, quia Soldanus de illo tenet totam Galileam, ... et omnem terram usque Accon et Tyrum et Sidonem.* Burchard, ed. Laurent, p. 34. Should this allusion be part of the degradation of the Templars by public opinion, that finally led to the trial of their leaders by Philip IV of France and to the abolishment of the order?

the Templars, whom he accused of betrayal, thus enabling the Mameluks to dominate Galilee.

The allusions to the *actualia*, condensed in the form of short remarks, bring us to consider Burchard's attitude to the realm of the crusaders and its society. A first remark, emphasizing that Acre "has never been (part) of the Holy Land,"[34] may already indicate his attitude to the capital of the realm and explain why pilgrims, during the period of the crusades, preferred not to mention the most important city of the Latin Kingdom in their descriptions. The absence of biblical and palaeo-Christian traditions in Acre alienated the pilgrim from it, even though he had disembarked and lodged there. Such a statement as that just quoted expressed the criticism made by many pilgrims of crusader society, or in contemporary terms, "the Latins of the Holy Land." The pilgrim who did not consider Acre to be part of the Holy Land also considered the "Latins" to be the dregs of its society. Burchard did not spare harsh criticism of the crusader society and, as in other instances, he gave his reasons:

> When someone was a malefactor, such as a murderer, a robber, a thief, or an adulterer, he used to cross the sea, either as a penitent, or else because he feared for his skin and therefore did not dare to stay in his own country; and so, they come thither from all parts, such as Germany, Italy, France, England, Spain, Hungary and other parts of the world. And while they change the sky above them, they do not change their minds. Once being here (i.e., in the Holy Land), after they had spent what they had brought with them, they have to acquire new (funds) and, so, they return to their "vomit," doing the worse of the worst. They lodge pilgrims of their nation. These men, who do not know how to take care of themselves, trust their hosts, and lose their goods and honour. And so they breed sons who imitate the crimes of their fathers, and from bad parents descend worse sons, and from them the worst grandchildren, who tread upon the holy places with polluted feet. Hence it comes that, because of the sins of the inhabitants against God, this land, together with the place of sanctification, is brought into contempt.[35]

34 *Sciendum tamen, quod hec civitas nunquam fuit de terra sancta, nec a filiis Israel possessa, licet in distributione terre Asser tribui fuerit assignata, quia Asserite nunquam possederunt eam.* Ibid., p. 23. Though Burchard did not refer in this case to his favourite authority, James of Vitry, and reached the conclusion by his own reading of the Bible, there is an interesting analogy with James's feelings in 1216, when he wrote to his former colleagues, the Parisian masters, that he saw from the windows of his palace in Acre the Holy Land, but *Ego vero terram promissionis, terram desiderabilem et sanctam, nondum intravi* (*Lettres de Jacques de Vitry*, ed. Huygens, p. 89).

35 Burchard, ed. Laurent, pp. 86-88.

This criticism of the "Latins" corroborates many details of the picture of society in Acre given by James of Vitry in 1216, in his letter to the Parisian masters,[36] a letter that was probably not known to Burchard. Even if its contents had been communicated to him, Burchard's approach would have been a special one, because he did not content himself with describing the vices of this society, but attempted to identify their causes. Such an attempt led him to adopt a psycho-sociological approach to a colonial society which included criminals, or more specifically, people deserving the death penalty who had settled on Palestinian soil in order to escape that punishment in their countries of origin. Such people had absolutely no connection with the idea of the crusade or the Holy War. One wonders where the "good Latins" were, and it is difficult to understand why Burchard omitted them. Furthermore, Burchard's approach is genetic; the descendants of the founding fathers inherited negative traits and became even worse than their parents. There is a clear distinction between this Frankish society (*habitatores terrae*) who, by their presence in the land, "pollute the holy soil," and the pilgrims, described as innocent persons, whose aim was to seek holiness, and who found themselves so abused by these Franks that they lost not only their belongings, but also their honour. This statement became a terrible charge against the "Latins," compared with the hospitality which the pilgrims were offered by the Muslims.[37]

The statement made about the "Latins" was intended to be more than a description and social analysis of crusader society; it was even a revenge by the idealistic pilgrims against the profane Frank, whose behaviour had nothing to do with the expected rule of life in the Holy Land. It seems that Burchard decided to reveal the truth (*ut veritatem dicam*) in order to prepare the public in the West for the fall of the crusader states. Like the other moralists of the twelfth and thirteenth centuries, this Dominican friar believed in divine punishment for sins and could not find an explanation other than this for the failure of the crusades. While William of Tyre, in the years preceding the battle of Ḥaṭṭīn, warned of the consequences of vices which he criticized during the reign of Baldwin IV,[38] and James of Vitry still hoped that his preaching would have salutary effects, Burchard remained sceptical and did not see any hope for

---

36   *Lettres de Jacques de Vitry*, pp. 86-89.
37   Burchard, ed. Laurent, p. 89.
38   WT, 21.7, pp. 1014-1016. See especially: *Considerantibus ergo nobis et statum nostrorum diligenter discutientibus prima occurit causa in Deum auctorem omnium respiciens, quod pro patribus nostris, qui fuerunt viri religiosi, et timentes Deum, nati sunt filii perditissimi, filii scelerati, fidei Christianae praevaricatores, et sine delectu per omnia currentes illicita...* (p. 1015).

the realm, populated by a society he considered unworthy to be part of the *societas christiana*, as defined by the Augustinian concept. Perhaps a Christian-populated Palestine, under a tolerant Mameluk domination, would for him have been a better choice than a hated profane society such as that of the "Latins" whom he found in the country.

The description of the other "religions" may support such a hypothesis. Burchard adopted a liberal attitude to the various Eastern Christian sects, particularly praising the Greeks and Armenians for their piety and behaviour.[39] Even the Nestorians, though heretics, are presented in liberal terms, because of their influence in the East,[40] that is, in the Mongol Empire. The only exceptions to this charitable attitude were the Syrians, the major element of the Christian population of Palestine, for whom he had no liking, and who faithfully served the Muslim authorities.[41] Our author was persuaded that Christians were still the great majority of the Palestinian population,[42] while the Muslims, who had been the dominating element in the country, remained in a minority. Though he criticized the "followers of Mahomet," this criticism is less vehement than that of the "Latins."[43] Burchard's knowledge of Islam was, however, superficial, and cannot be compared with that of Ricoldo da Monte Croce, his contemporary, but his image of Muslims was influenced by the new trends he might have become aware of during his sojourn at the monastery of Mount Sion.[44]

This detailed description of the population and religions of the Holy Land is, however, incomplete. Burchard did not mention the Jewish element in the country, although it is unlikely that he did not meet any Jews at Acre or Jerusalem, as well as in other places. It is natural to seek the reason for such an omission, but no satisfactory answer can be provided.

Burchard's *Descriptio* is an interesting document, written by a man who was the product of Western scholasticism. By its pious approach to holy geography and history and to the *terra sancta* as a concept, even though it lacks the intensity of feeling evinced by those who were primarily concerned with the worship of saints, it belongs to the long series of *itineraria* written by genera-

---

39   Burchard, ed. Laurent, pp. 89 and 91-93. The last description is dedicated to the Armenians, whose realm he visited; their behaviour left a deep impression upon him, diametrically opposed to that of the "Latins."

40   Ibid., p. 91.

41   Ibid., p. 89. The sole recognized reason for this dislike is that the Syrians were misers.

42   *...audivi, quod ... pro uno Sarraceno triginta vel plus invenies Christianos.* Ibid., p. 90.

43   Ibid., pp. 89, 90.

44   See Norman Daniel, *Islam and the West: the Making of an Image* (Edinburgh, 1962).

tions of pilgrims. On the other hand, by its critical methods and the author's need to find reasonable answers to the questions he posed, it opens a new way leading to a systematic exploration of the Holy Land. This kind of exploration is based on the confrontation of the normative texts with the observations of the traveller who was an eye-witness, and who wished, not only for himself, but also for the benefit of his readers, to express the truth as he himself had experienced it.

THE PATRIARCHS OF JERUSALEM
IN THE LATE THIRTEENTH CENTURY—
SEIGNORS ESPIRITUELES
ET TEMPORELES?[*]

SYLVIA SCHEIN
University of Haifa

Writing around 1265, Jean d'Ibelin declared that "il y a ou reiaume de Jerusalem deus chiefs seignors, l'un esperituel et l'autre temporel: le patriarche de Jerusalem est le seignor espirituel et le roi dou reiaume de Jerusalem le seignor temporel doudit reiaume."[1] It is by now almost generally agreed that though Ibelin's statement reflected the situation in the kingdom during the first three decades of its existence, the political reality after 1130 was different and the ecclesiastical hierarchy did not play any decisive role.[2] Yet a closer examination of the position of the patriarchs of Jerusalem in the kingdom around 1265 suggests not only that Ibelin's statement was hardly out of place but that, in describing the patriarch as the spiritual lord of the kingdom, Ibelin was perhaps deliberately concealing the fact that the patriarch was increasingly taking upon himself the function of its temporal lord as well.

    This major change which occurred in the status of the patriarch in the kingdom can be ascribed to a number of factors, including the absence of a

---

[*]   This study is based on my M.A. thesis, *The Political Theories of Philippe de Novare and Jean d'Ibelin* (unpublished, The Hebrew University of Jerusalem, 1974), prepared under the supervision of Professor Joshua Prawer.

1   *Livre de Jean d'Ibelin* 260, RHC Lois 1:415.
2   J.L. La Monte, *Feudal Monarchy in the Latin Kingdom of Jerusalem, 1100-1291* (Cambridge, Mass., 1932), pp. 203-225; Prawer, *Latin Kingdom*, pp. 159-163; but see J. Richard, *The Latin Kingdom of Jerusalem*, trans. Janet Shirley (Amsterdam, 1979), pp. 382-383 and recently B. Hamilton, *The Latin Church in the Crusader States. The Secular Church* (London, 1980), pp. 243-281. For a different view see G. Dodu, *Histoire des institutions monarchiques dans le royaume latin de Jérusalem, 1099-1291* (Paris, 1894), pp. 207-360.

king as well as a deliberate papal policy. First of all, the king's rights in the election of the patriarch, which seem to be unquestioned during the twelfth century, disappeared in the thirteenth. At that time the king's influence, in ecclesiastical matters in general and particularly in the election of bishops and in making appointments to ecclesiastical benefices, considerably weakened. In the course of the century the papacy increasingly arrogated to itself the appointment of prelates. Thus the king's prerogative of choosing the patriarch from candidates presented to him by the concourse of bishops became a mere shadow. The election of the patriarch now became almost completely a papal affair; some of the patriarchs were even appointed, like James Pantaleon (the future Urban IV), in spite of the strenuous opposition of certain sections of the Latin hierarchy in the East.[3] Except for Thomas Agni of Lentino, who served as titular bishop of Bethlehem (1255-1267), and Patriarch Elias (1279-1287), who served before his election as patriarch as administrator of the Church of Acre, the patriarchs were nominated from Western clergy.[4] Thus already by the middle of the thirteenth century the patriarchs of Jerusalem were becoming direct agents of the pope.

It also became customary to appoint the patriarchs as *legati nati* in the Holy Land and in about 1220 the post of the papal legate began to be joined to that of patriarch of Jerusalem. From the time of the Fifth Crusade (1217-1221) onwards the patriarchs were given almost without a break "full power to exercise the legation both in the ecclesiastical province of Jerusalem and in the Christian army wherever it may be sent in that province to succour the Holy Land."[5] Moreover, from the 1250's no *legati a latere* were sent to the Holy Land and from 1272 only the patriarch of Jerusalem carried the title of *legatus natus* in that province.[6]

The office of the patriarch was united not only with that of papal legate but also with that of the bishop of the kingdom's capital, Acre. The fact that the patriarch resided in Acre became a most dangerous source of friction between

---

3   Richard, *Latin Kingdom*, pp. 261-262. J. Riley-Smith, *The Knights of St. John in Jerusalem and Cyprus c. 1050-1310* (London, 1967), p. 409. For the twelfth century see Dodu, *Histoire*, pp. 339-344.

4   R. Röhricht, "Syria sacra," *ZDPV* 10 (1887), 9-11; L. de Mas Latrie, "Les patriarches latins de Jérusalem," *ROL* 1 (1893), 24-27; J. Riley-Smith, "Latin Titular Bishops in Palestine and Syria, 1137-1291," *Catholic Historical Review* 64 (1978), 6-7.

5   Richard, *Latin Kingdom*, pp. 262-264 and n. 18.

6   Thomas Agni was the last who as bishop of Bethlehem carried the title of legate (1255-1267). He stayed in Acre during the years 1259-1263. See RRH nos. 1264, 1269, 1271, 1279, 1288, 1293, 1294, 1298, 1312, 1314, 1315, 1318, 1320, 1323, 1325. Mas Latrie, "Les patriarches," pp. 25-26. Hamilton, *Latin Church*, p. 269. The last *legatus a latere* was Eudes de Châteauroux, bishop of Tusculum (d. 1273). See RRH nos. 1174, 1191, 1206, 1216, 1219, 1437.

him and the city's bishop. The problem could be solved only by the union of the offices of patriarch and bishop. This was done in a series of moves from 1261 to 1263 by Pope Urban IV, who, as mentioned above, had himself been patriarch of Jerusalem (1255-1261) and had experienced the difficulties of living in Acre as a neighbour of its bishop. He therefore transferred Bishop Florence of Acre to the see of Arles, while the see of Acre was united, until the Holy City should be recovered, with that of Jerusalem.[7]

The patriarchs gained yet additional influence through their control over troops and funds sent to the aid of the kingdom by the papacy. Due to the absence of royal power those troops and funds were entrusted by the popes directly to their legates, who were the patriarchs of Jerusalem, and not to the secular rulers of the kingdom. In January 1264, for example, Pope Urban IV wrote to the archbishop of Tyre about a sum of money intended for repairs to the fortifications of Jaffa, explicitly instructing him to transfer the money not to the lord of Jaffa, Jean d'Ibelin, but to the patriarch of Jerusalem, then William II, "who devoted much effort to the well-being of the city of Jaffa "[8] In 1267 we find Patriarch William II (1262-1270) hiring for the papacy, for a period of six months, fifty knights who had arrived with Odo of Burgundy, count of Nevers and Erard of Valéry; this patriarch also hired, besides crossbowmen, forty-eight other knights for five months. On 16 June of the same year Pope Clement IV instructed the patriarch to dispatch military aid to Armenia and Antioch. Five years later, in 1272, Patriarch Thomas Agni (1272-1277) was given the responsibility of military command by Pope Gregory X, who ordered him to conduct a contingent of 500 mercenaries to Syria. He and his forces arrived in Acre on 8 October 1272.[9] One of Gregory X's successors on the papal throne, Hadrian V (1276), managed during his pontificate of

---

7   Röhricht, "Syria sacra," p. 21, contra G. Fedalto, *La chiesa latina in Oriente*, 2 (Verona, 1976), pp. 26-28, 133-135, who claims (ibid., p. 134 n. 1.) that the two sees were united by Gregory X on 10 May 1272. Actually in his *Crescit apud Deum* Gregory X only confirms the union, referring explicitly to Urban IV, who "curam et administrationem spiritualiter et temporaliter Acconensis ecclesie tunc vacantis, bone memorie patriarche Jerosolimitano... duxerit specialiter committendam..." *Les Registres de Grégoire X (1272-1276)*, ed. J. Guiraud and E. Cadier (Paris, 1892-1960), no. 8. For Urban IV see *Les Registres d'Urbain IV (1261-1264)*, ed. L. Dorez and J. Guiraud (Paris, 1899-1958), nos. 168, 189-191 bis, 235-236. See also *Eracles*, p. 447 and n. 9. Riley-Smith, "Latin Titular Bishops," p. 5.

8   Prawer, *Histoire*, 2:477.

9   *Annales Ecclesiastici*, ed. C. Baronius, O. Raynaldus et al. (Lucca, 1738-1750), ad a. 1267, no. 69. R. Röhricht, *Geschichte des Königreichs Jerusalem (1100-1291)* (Innsbruck, 1898), pp. 965-966. P.A. Throop, *Criticism of the Crusade: a Study of Public Opinion and Crusade Propaganda* (Amsterdam, 1940), p. 229. Richard, *Latin Kingdom*, pp. 379, 382. Thomas Agni was raised, on 21 April 1279, to the see of Jerusalem. See above n. 6.

forty-nine days to send to Patriarch Thomas Agni the sum of 12,000 *livres tournois* "pro galeis construendis, vel aliis magis bonorum virorum indicio opportunis." [10]

This deliberate papal policy of strengthening the position of the patriarch is reflected also in the papal attitude towards the military orders in the Kingdom of Acre and the issue of their relations with the patriarch of Jerusalem. Both the patriarchs and the orders were acting in the kingdom as executors of papal commands and were encouraged by the popes to take up much of the responsibility that would have been held by a resident king; both were often acting as advisors and as agents of papal policy. Moreover, Innocent III had instituted a system whereby regular reports on conditions in the Latin East were to be sent to Rome by the patriarch and the masters of the main orders of the Holy Land, namely the Hospital and the Temple. [11] However, probably because of the jealousy and rivalry among the orders in Acre, and probably also due to the growing criticism of their conduct, [12] the papacy, from the time of Alexander IV (1254-1261) onwards, began to rely more and more upon the patriarch and less upon the military orders in its handling of the affairs of the Latin Kingdom. In 1258 Alexander IV, recommending Patriarch James Pantaleon as apostolic legate, ordered the Hospitallers to observe his admonitions and commands "notwithstanding the existence of an indulgence by the Holy See to you or your servants, communally or individually, from interdiction, suspension, excommunication or calling its judgement outside certain places." [13] The pontificates of Alexander IV and of Urban IV reflect the preoccupations of both popes with the jealous guarding of the rights of the See of Jerusalem. [14] In 1272 Pope Gregory X gave his apostolic legate in the East, namely, the patriarch, extensive powers to take action against the military orders as well as against all religious if they refused to obey him. [15] This was repeated by Pope Nicholas IV on 27 August 1288. [16]

Not only had Rome's support of the military orders in the disputes with the patriarch, and indeed with the local clergy, diminished in the second half of the

---

10   *Eracles,* p. 477. Sanudo, *Secreta,* p. 927.
11   Riley-Smith, *Knights,* pp. 145-147.
12   For that criticism see ibid., pp. 385-389. Throop, *Criticism,* pp. 230-231. J. Prawer, "Military Orders and Crusader Politics in the Second Half of the XIIIth Century," *Ritterorden,* pp. 217-229.
13   Delaville, *Cartulaire,* no. 2797. Riley-Smith, *Knights,* p. 390.
14   Delaville, *Cartulaire,* nos. 2772, 2775, 2787, 2797, 2901, 2902, 2993, 2995. Riley-Smith, *Knights,* pp. 402-403.
15   Delaville, *Cartulaire,* no. 3442. Riley-Smith, *Knights,* p. 409.
16   Delaville, *Cartulaire,* no. 4015.

thirteenth century, but the papacy ceased to grant the orders the responsibility of deciding how papal subsidies to Latin East were to be spent.[17] From the pontificate of Alexander IV the patriarchs became normally entrusted with control over the subsidies.[18] Characteristic of this shift in papal policy is the fact that on the eve of the Second Council of Lyons Pope Gregory requested Patriarch Thomas Agni for advice regarding the crusade planned for 1276; of the three announcements of the council containing a request for such a memoir, one was addressed to the patriarch (1 April 1272).[19] This request had its precedent. In 1267 Patriarch William II of Jerusalem had outlined, in a letter to Amaury de la Roche, commander of the Temple in France, a detailed military plan for the defence of the crusader kingdom.[20]

By the middle of the century the patriarchs had already become regular participants in the sessions of the High Court and played there, it seems, a similar role to that of other non-feudal elements, for example, the representatives of the Italian and other communes, of the burgesses and of the military orders.[21] The power of the patriarch in the kingdom reached its peak by the end of the 1280's.[22] The career of Nicholas de Hanapes, who resided in Outremer in the last years of the kingdom's existence (1288-1291), demonstrates that the spiritual lord became the head of state and the real sovereign of what was left of the former Latin Kingdom. Addressed by the papacy with regard to temporal affairs of the kingdom, the patriarch assumed in those crucial and final years the burden of government. He was assisted by a council of war in which the *bailli* of the kingdom was a mere member.[23] This council included, except

17 Delaville, *Cartulaire*, no. 2789. Riley-Smith, *Knights*, p. 118.

18 Here above n. 8, 9, 10 and below n. 30, 31. See also M.L. Bulst-Thiele, *Sacrae domus militiae Templi Hierosolymitani magistri*, Abhandlungen der Akademie der Wissenschaften in Göttingen, Phil.-hist. Klasse, 3. 86 (Göttingen, 1974), p. 243.

19 Potthast, no. 20527; Mansi 24:39. Cf. Throop, *Criticism*, p. 19.

20 G. Servois, "Emprunts de Saint Louis en Palestine et en Afrique. Appendice," *Bibliothèque de l'École des Chartes* 19 (1858), 291-293.

21 J. Riley-Smith, *The Feudal Nobility and the Kingdom of Jerusalem, 1174-1277* (London, 1973), pp. 195-196. J. Prawer, "Estates, Communities and the Constitution of the Latin Kingdom," in his *Crusader Institutions*, pp. 80-81. Writing in 1273 to the king of Jerusalem and Cyprus, Pope Gregory X referred to the king, the patriarch and the magnates as the rulers of the kingdom: *Annales Ecclesiastici*, ad a. 1273, no. 36. See also *Eracles*, p. 474 (for 1276).

22 Writing on 1 October 1278 to the Dominican General Jean de Verceil *seu* Ayglier "Hierosolymitanus electus," who refused to assume his office, Pope Nicholas III declared "Terrae Sanctae statum a pastoris ejusdem... maxime... dependere." *Annales Ecclesiastici*, ad a. 1278, no. 80. Jean, who never assumed the office, resigned it in the following year, and Elias, then administrator of the Church of Acre, was elected in his place. Ibid., ad a. 1279, nos. 21-24, 47. RRH nos. 1441, 1467, 1471. Mas Latrie, "Les patriarches," pp. 26-27. For Elias see Hamilton, *Latin Church*, pp. 277-278.

23 Richard, *Latin Kingdom*, p. 380.

for the *bailli*, Bernard II the bishop of Tripoli, Otho de Grandison, Jean de Grailly, the Venetian *bailli* and the Pisan consul as well as Guillaume de Beaujeu, the grand master of the Temple, and Jean de Villiers, the grand master of the Hospital.[24]

A Dominican from the diocese of Rheims, Nicholas de Hanapes served as a penitentiary at the papal court until being elected by the cardinals, according to Bernard Gui entirely on account of his virtues, as patriarch of the Holy City of Jerusalem.[25] After being consecrated by Pope Nicholas IV himself (30 April 1288), he was granted the direction of the church of Acre "donec eadem Hierosolymitana ecclesia, bonis suis recuperatis, de adepta ipsorum possessione laetetur."[26] Later (27 August 1288) Nicholas was nominated papal legate for Syria, Jerusalem, Cyprus and Armenia.[27] During the three years when he resided in Acre as patriarch, papal legate and the city's bishop, Nicholas took upon himself the task of both the government of the realm and its defence. This partly resulted from papal policy.

Nicholas IV (1288-1292), the first Franciscan pope, was the first in the rapid succession of popes who followed Gregory X to revive the latter's crusader policy. Like Gregory, he made the Holy Land the *leitmotiv* of his pontificate and took a vivid interest in the inner affairs of the kingdom of Acre. Until the fall of Acre (18 May 1291) he aimed to follow Gregory X's plan of a general pacification of Europe, the union of the Catholic and the Greek Churches, and the recruitment of Europe for a massive and coordinated action in the East. As far as the kingdom of Acre was concerned he aimed to pacify the various competing and ever-fighting parties by placing the patriarch at its head.[28] Significantly, on 27 August 1288 Nicholas IV renewed in favour of Nicholas de Hanapes the bull *Antiqua sanctorum patrum* (19 March 1272) granted by Gregory X in favour of Thomas Agni.[29]

24   Ibid., p. 425.
25   *Les Registres de Nicholas IV*, ed. M.L. Langlois (Paris, 1886-1891), nos. 93-95. Delaville, *Cartulaire*, no. 3997. V. Le Clerc, "Nicholas de Hanapes, Patriarche de Jérusalem," *Histoire littéraire de la France* 20 (1842), 51-52.
26   *Registres de Nicholas IV*, nos. 85-92. Potthast, no. 22693. *Annales Ecclesiastici*, ad a. 1288, no. 41.
27   *Registres de Nicholas IV*, nos. 219-226. Potthast, no. 22784. *Annales Ecclesiastici*, ad a. 1288, no. 41.
28   For Gregory X see V. Laurent, "La croisade et la question d'Orient sous le pontificat de Grégoire X (1272-1276)," *Revue historique du Sud-Est Européen* 22 (1945), 104-137; L. Gatto, *Il pontificato di Gregorio X, 1272-1276* (Rome, 1956), pp. 63-106. For Nicholas IV see Richard, *Latin Kingdom*, pp. 430-431; S. Schein, *The West and the Crusade. Attitudes and Attempts, 1291-1312* (unpublished Ph.D. thesis, Cambridge 1980), pp. 28-49.
29   *Registres de Nicholas IV*, nos. 93-95. Delaville, *Cartulaire*, no. 4015. *Registres de Grégoire X*, no. 11. According to Hamilton, *Latin Church*, p. 278, Nicholas was granted more extensive privileges than any of his predecessors.

As he envisaged the patriarch as the head of the kingdom, on 9 September 1289 Pope Nicholas transferred to him a sum of 4,000 *livres tournois* as a loan to be spent on repairing the fortifications of Acre, building war machines and redeeming prisoners.[30] When in the following year a fleet of some thirteen galleys, carrying a force of about 1500 North Italian crusaders, was sent by Nicholas IV to Acre, it was the patriarch who was nominated by the pope "ad regimen galearum et gubernationem Christiani populi." The patriarch was authorized to appoint commanders of the fleet and the crusading army. He was also granted the administration of a sum of thirty thousand gold florins dispatched by the pope for their maintenance. Otho de Grandison, the Swiss knight who represented Edward I of England in the kingdom, Jean de Grailly, a knight from Gascony representing the king of France, the Venetian *bailli*, the Pisan consul, Amalric, lord of Tyre and *bailli* of the kingdom, the grand masters of the military orders, Henry II, king of Cyprus and Jerusalem, all were ordered by the pope (on 15 October 1290) to assist the patriarch by aid and counsel to enable him to govern the affairs of the kingdom.[31] When in August 1290 the sultan presented Acre with an ultimatum, it was the patriarch who headed the council of war that met to consider it.[32] During the meeting of this council, which included the Bishop of Tripoli, Amalric of Lusignan, Otho de Grandison, Jean de Grailly, the Venetian *bailli* and the Pisan consul, as well as the heads of the three chief military orders of the kingdom, the patriarch delivered a speech aimed to pacify the ever quarelling leaders of Acre and called the people of the city to unite as if they were "of one heart and soul" (Acts 4:32) against the enemy.[33]

Thus, though Jean d'Ibelin defined the patriarch's status in the kingdom in purely spiritual terms, that hierarch was already participating in the government of the realm, together with other non-feudal figures, before Jean had completed his *Livre des Assises de la Haute Cour*. As the result of the transfor-

---

30 *Registres de Nicholas IV*, no. 1357. RRH nos. 1495, 1500.

31 *Registres de Nicholas IV*, nos. 2269, 2270, 4385-4401. For the extensive financial powers of Nicholas see also Hamilton, *Latin Church*, p. 290.

32 *Le Templier de Tyr*, ed. G. Raynaud, *Les Gestes des Chiprois* (Paris, 1887), p. 249: "...tous les seignors d'Acre c'est asaver au patriarch et leguat, et au maistre de l'Ospitau, frere Johan de Villiers, et au coumandour des Alemans... au cons[e]le de Pize, et au baill de Veneize..." *Annales Mediolanenses anonymi scriptoris*, RIS 16:682: "Qui [Soldanus Babylonie] aggressus civitatem Acon quam custodiebat Frater Nicolaus Ordinis Praedicatorum Patriarcha Hierosolymitanus ipsam obsedit." Giovanni Villani, *Cronica*, ed. F. Gherardi Dragomanni, 1 (Florence, 1844), 472. Ptolemy of Lucca, *Historia Ecclesiastica*, RIS 11:1196.

33 *De excidio urbis Acconis libri II*, in E. Martène and U. Durand, *Veterum Scriptorum et Monumentorum Amplissima Collectio*, 5 (Paris, 1729), 764. Le Clerc, "Nicholas de Hanapes," p. 57.

mation of his status in the kingdom which occurred during the thirteenth century, in the very last years of the existence of the kingdom the patriarch became, *de facto*, the temporal as well as spiritual head of state.

The patriarch's activities as head of state reached a new climax during the siege of Acre. It was he who acted as the overlord of the leaders of the besieged stronghold; as such he took an active part in the war effort and according to Taddeo of Naples "totus flagrans et calens zelo fidei christiane... non parcens laboribus periculorum, dispendiis nec expensis, in civitatis custodia diffensioneque sollicita die noctuque vigil et sedulus persistebat."[34] In the last days of Acre the patriarch became also more than head of state; he was the spiritual leader of the city's population. As such the patriarch is depicted as a wholly saintly figure, whose self-sacrifice and devotion to the people of Acre was boundless and his activities relentless. It was, for example, the patriarch who, in a sermon delivered on 17 May, the eve of the city's fall, consoled its defenders and encouraged them to die fighting, as befitted those who had been personally chosen by God from among all the Christian people to defend his rights. Those who did so, the patriarch promised, would "exchange their temporal heritage for an eternal one."[35]

Following his sermon the patriarch celebrated mass in Acre for the last time, gave the last kisses of peace and received the last confessions.[36] When on the following day (18 May 1291) the enemy launched the final assault and it became evident that the city was lost, the last defenders decided to hold back the enemy at the harbour entrance to cover the evacuation of the city's Christian population. One of the evacuees was the patriarch. When he died it was in yet another act of Christian charity. According to the French version of the *De excidio urbis Acconis*, which bears witness to the opinions current among the lower classes of European society following the loss of the Holy Land, when the patriarch was brought to the boat it was against his will and by force. It is said that he protested in these words: "Baiu (*sic*) signour, il samble que vous me tenès pour fol et hors de mon sens, quant vous me traiiés encontre me volente, et me faites laissier en si grant peril les elles que Jhesus racatu (*sic*) de se precieus sanc, et les mes carga a garder."[37]

---

34 Taddeo of Naples wrote in December 1291, in Messina, a treatise about the fall of Acre. Thaddeus Neapolitanus, *Hystoria de desolacione et conculcacione civitatis Acconensis et tocius Terre Sancte in A.D. MCCXCI*, ed. P. Riant (Geneva, 1873), pp. 16-18.

35 *De excidio*, col. 774-775. Le Clerc, "Nicholas de Hanapes," pp. 59-61.

36 *De excidio*, col. 775. See also col. 778.

37 V. Le Clerq, "Relation anonyme de la prise d'Acre en 1291," *Histoire littéraire de la France*, 20 (1842), 88.

According to the *De excidio* and Taddeo of Naples, the patriarch, who had been slightly wounded, was put into a small skiff by his servants but out of charity allowed so many refugees to climb in with him that the boat sank with their weight and they were all drowned. Characteristically, however, there is more than one version of the patriarch's death.[38] The author of the English *Chronicle of Lanercost* claims that the patriarch was the first to flee from the city, followed by "other rich folk."[39] And the so-called *Templier de Tyr* relates that a sailor who was helping the patriarch on board let him slip and drown.[40] However it must have been the first of these versions which was best remembered, for this last patriarch of Jerusalem to exercise his office from Acre was later canonized, one of the very few saints of the Latin Kingdom.[41]

---

38   *De excidio*, col. 781. Thaddeus Neapolitanus, *Hystoria*, p. 77. For this version see also *Chronicon Parmense*, RIS² 9:62.
39   *Chronicon de Lanercost*, ed. J. Stevenson (Edinburgh, 1839), pp. 139-140.
40   *Le Templier de Tyr*, p. 254; also, *Annales Ecclesiastici*, ad a. 1291, no. 10.
41   Ricoldo da Monte Croce, *Epistolae V commentatoriae de perditione Acconis 1291*, ed. R. Röhricht in *AOL* 2 (1884), 269-270, 289-294, esp. 290.

GENIZA SOURCES FOR THE CRUSADER PERIOD: A SURVEY*

S.D. GOITEIN
The Institute for Advanced Study, Princeton

The so-called Cairo Geniza, a treasure trove of medieval manuscripts, mostly written in Hebrew script (originally found in Old Cairo and now dispersed in many libraries), contains, besides religious and other literary texts, thousands of complete and fragmentary papers of documentary character. The late eleventh through the early thirteenth centuries, the period of the main crusades, are well represented in the Geniza, for that was a time of vibrant communal life for Egyptian Jewry, which also participated vigorously in international, especially the India, trade. Our survey, naturally, is confined to sources of direct relevance to the history of the crusades. Following suggestions by Joshua Prawer, who himself has contributed so much to a meaningful interpretation of the Jewish sources for this period,[1] and others, I collected the sources published by me, adding to them still unedited texts. The material is discussed here in more or less chronological order. Most texts deserve full translation.[2]

---

*   I wish to reiterate my deepfelt thanks to the Librarians and staffs of the Bodleian Library, Oxford, the University Library and Westminster College, Cambridge, and the Library of the Jewish Theological Seminary of America, New York, for their unfailing support of my work on the manuscripts used here, studied by me in the course of the last thirty years. See also n. 9, below.

1   Prawer, *Latin Kingdom*, pp. 233-251, and in numerous Hebrew publications.

2   S.D. Goitein, *Palestinian Jewry in Early Islamic and Crusader Times in the Light of the Geniza Documents* [in Hebrew] (Jerusalem, 1980) [hereafter cited as *Palestinian Jewry*]. For the Geniza in general and the marks of the manuscripts noted below see S.D. Goitein, *A Mediterranean Society: The Jewish Communities of the Arab World, as Portrayed in the Documents of the Cairo Geniza*, 3 vols. so far (Berkeley and Los Angeles, 1967-78), 1:xix-xxvi and 1-28; some additional marks, 3:xix-xxi [hereafter cited as *A Mediterranean Society*].

Crusader times began for Palestine, and in particular for Jerusalem, before the crusades. The ceaseless wars between the Seljuqs, their auxiliary hordes, and Fatimid Egypt and the merciless devastation of the country by the successive invasions made life in Jerusalem unbearable. For reasons understandable in the light of the explanations provided in n. 30, below, the women, in particular, must have refused to remain in a place so insecure. The Yeshiva, or Jewish High Council, left the city in the course of the 1070s and moved to Tyre, Lebanon, where its presence is attested by Geniza sources.[3] The same was done by the Sheikh of the Shāfi'īs, a Muslim *madh-hab*, or "school" dominant in the region, who also had his seat in Jerusalem. It is likely that the action of the Muslim leader induced the Head of the Yeshiva to follow his example.[4] After that exodus the Rabbanite community, that is, the bulk of the Jewish population, was depleted to such an extent that during the last quarter of the eleventh century we do not hear of a single Rabbanite personality active in Jerusalem. The yearly contributions for the Holy City collected in Egypt (consisting partly in gifts and partly in revenue from houses donated for this purpose) were now delivered in Cairo itself to trustworthy persons, preferably Jerusalemites, to be forwarded by them to "the elders of the Rabbanites still remaining in Jerusalem."[5] We are able to form an idea of the size of the decimated Jewish population by a comparison with the effects of the Bedouin upheavals and atrocities of 1025/6 ("the like of which had never occurred in Islam"), when only "fifty men," perhaps meaning: heads of households, had remained in the city—and that at a time when the High Council was still there and very active.[6]

---

3   Jacob Mann, *The Jews in Egypt and in Palestine under the Fāṭimid Caliphs*, 2 vols. (London, 1920-22, repr. New York, 1970), 1:188-189. [hereafter cited as Mann, *Jews in Egypt*]. The Yeshiva of Jerusalem was not an educational institution, but a council of seven members, whose head, the Gaon, was recognized by the Fatimid government as the highest religious and communal authority for the Jews of the empire, cf. *A Mediterranean Society*, 2:5-17.

4   *Palestinian Jewry*, p. 24. "Region" stands for Arabic *Shām*, a term comprising Syria, Lebanon, and Palestine.

5   A document to this effect from 1085, TS 13 J 5, fol. 2 (not 1, as printed in Mann) was published by Mann, *Jews in Egypt*, 1:192. For corrections see *A Mediterranean Society*, 2:415, section 13. The corrected text and English trans. in M. Gil, *Documents on the Jewish Pious Foundations from the Cairo Geniza* (Leiden 1976), pp. 212-214.

    A fragment of a similar document is preserved in TS NS Box 320, fol. 24, ed. in *Palestinian Jewry*, p. 257. The writer, Joseph ha-Kohen b. Solomon was probably the son of Solomon b. Joseph, a descendant of a Gaon of Jerusalem, who, in January 1077, composed a long Hebrew poem in honor of the caliph al-Mustanṣir and his viceroy Badr al-Jamālī on the occasion of their victory over the Seljuqs menacing Cairo. J.H. Greenstone, ed. and trans., "The Turkoman Defeat at Cairo, by Solomon ben Joseph ha-Kohen," *American Journal of Semitic Languages and Literatures* 22 (1906), 144-175. This poem shows also that the devastation of Palestine by the Seljuq invaders was far more serious than commonly assumed.

6   Mann, *Jews in Egypt*, 2:181, line 13.

Thus, in Jerusalem, the crusaders liquidated a Jewish community already in a state of liquidation. In contemporary letters related to the capture of Jerusalem, not a single person who died in the massacre is mentioned by name. Compare this with the persecutions of 1096 in Germany, where scores of men and women who suffered martyrdom were remembered in reports written forty years later, and dirges were composed in their honor, which are still recited in synagogues. No dirge for the victims of Jerusalem in 1099 has become known thus far, while the fall of Acre in 1291, then a seat of Jewish learning, evoked a lament, praising with poetic exaggeration, inter alia,

> Noble girls, fed by the breast of the Holy Language
> Even before being nursed by their mothers.[7]

Moreover, a letter by a refugee woman from Jerusalem, writing from Tripoli, Lebanon, in the early 1070s, speaks at length of a crate of books which her husband had brought with him.[8] He was certainly not the only one who acted thus, and the Head of the Yeshiva, who presided also over a *midrash*, or house of study, no doubt carried his books with him while leaving Jerusalem for Tyre. This would explain why the Rabbanite letter translated below—in contrast to that of the Karaite community—speaks solely of Torah scrolls, not of books lost during the fall of Jerusalem.

This letter was identified by me in July 1975, when I examined the hitherto uncatalogued Geniza fragments of the Additional Series of the Taylor-Schechter Collection in the University Library Cambridge.[9] As its contents show, the letter was written immediately after the first reports of the fall of Jerusalem on 15 July 1099 had arrived in Cairo. Since Jews were found in the entourage of the Fatimid commander of the citadel, to whom free conduct had been granted by the crusaders,[10] and since Egypt could be easily reached by sea via Ascalon, the happenings related in the letter probably took place only two or three weeks after the conquest. This assumption is corroborated by the

---

7   A dirge by Joseph b. Tanḥum Yerushalmi, ed. by H. Schirmann, "Dirges on Persecutions in Palestine, Africa, Spain, Germany and France," *Kobez al Jad*, NS 3 (Jerusalem, 1939), 64, line 23 (in Hebrew).

8   Westminster College, Cambridge, England, Fragmenta Cairensia, fol. 35, ed. and trans. by S.D. Goitein, "Tyre-Tripoli-'Arqa: Geniza Documents from the Beginning of the Crusader Period," *Jewish Quarterly Review* 66 (1975), 79-83 [hereafter cited as "Tyre-Tripoli-'Arqa"]. Revised in *Palestinian Jewry*, pp. 278-282.

9   TS AS 146, fol. 3, ed. in *Palestinian Jewry*, pp. 254-256. I use this opportunity to express my special thanks to Dr. Stefan C. Reif, M.A., Director, Taylor-Schechter Genizah Research Unit, and his staff.

10   As reported in the Karaite letter, see n. 28, below.

detail reported that the Nagid (pronounce *nahgueed*), or Head of the Egyptian Jews, who was also a physician and counsellor to the viceroy al-Malik al-Afḍal, was found sitting on the floor with his clothes rent. This was a ritual to be observed during the first week after one had received tidings of the death of a close relative or a martyr. Some notables visiting the Nagid collected on the spot 123 dinars "for redeeming the Torah scrolls and ransoming the captives" (in this sequence), to be sent to Ascalon for action. This sum appears to be small, as compared with that of 500 dinars expended by the Karaites for the same purpose[11] and over a thousand dinars collected in Egypt for the ransoming of persons captured by pirates around 1150.[12] But this was only a first step, probably aimed at the immediate rescue of the Torah scrolls, while the redemption of the prisoners would be an affair requiring negotiations.[13]

Since our letter is probably the oldest document showing the reaction of the indigenous population to the fall of Jerusalem, it is translated here in full. It is a short missive, sent by the Jewish community of Cairo to that of Ascalon, concerned mainly with the difficulty of transmitting the money collected to the Palestinian seaport in view of the prevailing insecurity. What we have, of course, is the draft. The first four lines are mostly lost, but can be approximately restored by comparison with similar letters. Lines 5, 7, and 8 are longer than the others because of the many words written above them.

TRANSLATION

University Library Cambridge, TS AS 146, fol. 3[14]

(1) *Boundless* [*blessings...*] (2) *from the Lord of Peace, who makes peace,* [*and the angels of peace, and from the Torah,*] (3) [*the per*]*fect,*[15] *all the paths of which are peace,* [*may come upon*] (4) *the excellent* [*congrega*]*tions,*[16] *the communal*

---

11   Mentioned in the letter referred to in the preceding note.

12   *Palestinian Jewry*, p. 254.

13   One must remember, of course, that a dinar was made of gold, not of paper. Two dinars were regarded as a sufficient monthly income for a family in modest circumstances. Moreover, it was a time, when, owing to a great plague, even the well-to-do families had become impoverished. See notes 32 and 33, below. Also, only a handful of Jews lived at that time in Cairo, the residential city; the bulk of the Jewish population was to be found in Fustat, the ancient capital of Islam in Egypt. Even a hundred years later, Moses Maimonides, although a physician in attendance at the court in Cairo, had his domicile in Fustat.

14   Arabic original and Hebrew translation in *Palestinian Jewry*, pp. 255-256. Words in Hebrew are italicized.

15   The reading in *Palestinian Jewry*, p. 255: [*ḥḥkh*]*mh*, should be replaced by [*ḥtmy*]*mh*, see Psalm 19.8.

16   In the plural, because Jews from different places had settled there.

assembly of Ascalon [*with greetings from us,*] (5) *the community at Cairo, known as the residential city,*[17] *your loving brothers, who inquire about your welfare and wish you all the best. May it please our God to accept from us all prayers and supplications on your behalf.*

(6) We beg to inform you—may God grant you permanent welfare and bestow upon you his mercy and grace—(7) that we received tidings of the great disaster[18] and all-comprising visitation, which befell *our brothers, the Jews living in the Holy City,* (8) *may God restore it forever, the holy Torah scrolls, and the captives,* suffering multiple vexations inflicted upon them *by the enemies of God and haters of* (9) *his people. We assembled at his Excellency, our lord, his Hon(or), Great(ness), and Hol(iness), our master and teacher Mevōrākh, "Leader* (10) *of the Deliberations," "Sage of the Yeshiva," "the Great Council,"* etc.,[19] and found him, his garments (11) rent, sitting on the floor, and shedding tears about what had happened. He addressed us, admonishing (12) and urging us to donate sums for redeeming *the Torah scrolls* (13) *and the people of God held in captivity by the wicked kingdom, may God destroy and exterminate it.*

(14) We were moved by his warm and *heart-winning* words—*may God preserve his high rank*—(15) and, responding to him, collected one hundred twenty-three dinars (16) for retrieving the Torah scrolls and ransoming *the remnants of Israel who had escaped from the sword.*

This sum we handed over (17) to Mr. Manṣūr, son of Mr. ————, known as "the Son of the Schoolmistress,"[20] to bring it to Ascalon. (18) He will let you know what he is carrying and how he acted. We explained to him how he should proceed in (19) this matter.[21] We are sending you these lines in a great hurry because we (20) are afraid *lest our sins might cause failure and, God*

---

17 An allusion to the Arabic name of Cairo: *al-Qāhira al-Mu'izziyya*, "Cairo of (i.e., founded by) the caliph al-Mu'izz."

18 Ar. *al-raṣiyya* is not a misprint for *raziyya*, and certainly not a slip of the excellent clerk who wrote that draft (Hillel b. Eli, see *A Mediterranean Society*, 2:231), but was pronounced thus.

19 Honorific titles bestowed on Mevōrākh by the heads of the yeshivas of Jerusalem and Baghdad, and other Jewish dignitaries. Just as a Judge was called "Court," a member of the yeshiva was honored with the title "Great Council." In the final text of the letter all his titles would be written out. At the time of his death Mevōrākh possessed fourteen.

20 The father of this man had disappeared so long before the writing of this letter that even the court clerk, who knew everyone in the community, did not know his name. The Geniza has preserved a letter to him, addressed to "the Synagogue (that is, school) of the Schoolmistress, to the Sheikh Abū Manṣūr, Son of the Schoolmistress," in which he is asked to help a relative "in this hard year." On female teachers see *A Mediterranean Society*, 2:183-185, 3:344-346.

21 Manṣūr probably carried a *suftaja*, or letter of credit, but for the safety of the person who was to convert the *suftaja* into cash, everything was done in a veiled form.

forbid, our iniquities will be visited upon us.[22] *For indeed* (21) *we are unable to control and console ourselves. Our kidneys are in flames, because of the burning of the house of our God,* (22) *our glorious sanctuary, may God forgive*[23]—, *our sun*[24] *has darkened and our stature is bent..."*[25]

The burning of the synagogue, reported by Muslim historians, appears here for the first time in a Jewish source. The crusaders did not burn the spacious mosques, because they needed them for their own use. The "glorious" synagogue must have been a very modest structure. It is mentioned nowhere in the Geniza prior to its destruction. The yearly contributions sent from the Jewish diaspora to Jerusalem were destined for its scholars and the poor, never for building operations.[26] The solemn pilgrims' assembly on the Feast of Tabernacles was held on the Mount of Olives, not in the synagogue, nor do we ever hear about any other special ceremony taking place there. It was certainly too small for such purposes.[27] Its burning was an event of religious significance rather than a great material loss.

The comprehensive but incomplete letter of the Karaite elders of Ascalon describing the fall of Jerusalem and the subsequent rescue activities, published by me in 1952, was recently complemented by the identification of a Geniza fragment containing its end and most of its beginning.[28] The new addition established what was previously in doubt, namely, that the senders of the letter were Karaites, a Jewish sect which believed only in the Bible, but developed themselves a large theological and juridical literature, and emphasized the religious duty of living in the Holy Land. Consequently, they did not leave Jerusalem in the 1070s as completely as the Rabbanites did. As a result, their invaluable treasures of books and Bible codices fell into the hands of the crusaders. About 350 manuscripts were bought from the conquerors, but how

---

22   The rescue mission might fail.

23   Heb. *we-ḥās*, abbreviated from the phrase "God forbid." Excessive mourning is disapproved by the sages of the Talmud. One must accept God's judgment.

24   Heb. *qṣr* is a misprint for *qdr*. The manuscript is correct.

25   Here the clerk had arrived at the bottom of the page. The concluding phrases would be added by him in the final copy.

26   The situation was different after the Muslim reconquest of the city, as reported in the sources referred to in n. 55, below.

27   The reason for this probably was that in Jerusalem one prayed not in a synagogue but "at the gates of the Temple" and other holy sites, as we so often read in Geniza letters.

28   TS 20.113, ed. in *Palestinian Jewry*, pp. 241-248, English translation in my "Contemporary Letters on the Capture of Jerusalem by the Crusaders," *Journal of Jewish Studies* 3 (1952), 171-175 [hereafter cited as "Contemporary Letters"]; see Hans Eberhard Mayer, *The Crusades*, trans. John Gillingham (Oxford, 1972), pp. 60-61, The new fragment, TS 10 J 5, fol. 6, ed. in *Palestinian Jewry*, pp. 241 and 249.

many were lost? From the newly discovered beginning we learn that a letter of credit[29] had been sent from Egypt and its equivalent paid out in cash. The recipients laud the sender's generosity, the more praiseworthy because times in Egypt itself were so difficult, but the extremely polite letter does not conceal the fact that the funds available were still inadequate.

The letter of the Karaite elders from Ascalon is so rich in content that I must forego even trying to recapitulate its contents. I must, however, correct one important detail. In lines 24-25 we read:

> We have not heard—thank God, the Exalted—that the cursed ones known as *Ashkenaz* violated or raped women, as others [do].

Ashkenaz was a general term for non-Mediterranean western Europeans, later confined to Germans and Germany. In 1952 I understood "as others" to mean other *crusaders,* and tentatively took the term to refer to the Lorrainers; in 1980, following B.Z. Kedar's suggestion (made in another connection), I suggested Normans. But *Ashkenaz* must be taken here in the general sense as it was used in that time, and the meaning of the sentence is: Those crusaders did not do what Muslim invaders used to do, namely raping women and boys whenever they took a city.[30]

A second letter published by me in 1952 was written by a Jerusalem Pilgrim from the Maghreb, in the spring of 1100, after having been detained in Egypt for a full five years. A civil war raged in the country; Alexandria, where the traveler stayed, was twice besieged by the viceroy al-Malik al-Afḍal, who finally took the city; the roads to Jerusalem had become impassable because of unruly bedouins and other bandits; and, above all, the country was ravaged by a plague and other illnesses, which raged four years. This is what he writes:

---

29 In the article mentioned in the preceding note, p. 175, I translated *suftaja* as "bill of exchange," which then was customary, but meanwhile more has been learned about the nature of this term, see *A Mediterranean Society*, 1:242-245.

30 "Contemporary Letters," p. 167; *Palestinian Jewry*, p. 235, n. 17. I apologize to Raymond and his Frenchmen.
   The first of the two Ar. terms, *qaharū* and *istaṭawhā ghaṣban*, tentatively translated as "violated" and "raped," probably refers to the practice of *'azl* (coitus interruptus), applied when one expected to receive a higher ransom for the woman violated.
   Jacob Mann, *Texts and Studies in Jewish History and Literature* 2 (Philadelphia, 1935), 43, n. 83, notes sources in which *Ashkenaz* may refer to crusaders on their way to Palestine. But the discussion of the sources adduced there would lead too far afield. The Jews writing in Germany discerned, of course, between Germans and Frenchmen (*Ashkenaz-im* and *Ṣarfat-im*), see Adolf Neubauer and Moritz Stern, eds., *Hebräische Berichte über die Judenverfolgungen während der Kreuzzüge,* 2 (Berlin, 1892), 36.

You know, my lord, what has happened to us in the course of the last five years. The plague,[31] diseases, and illnesses have continued unabated for four successive years. As a result of this, the wealthy have become poor; the majority of the population died *of the plague*, so that entire families have been wiped out by the plague. I, too, was affected by a grave illness, and did not recover from it until last year; then I was taken ill again the following year so that I remained incapacitated by illness for four years.[32]

The letter of the elders of Ascalon, too, speaks of "that plague," in which some of the ransomed died upon arriving in Egypt, and repeatedly refers to the impoverishment of the once well-to-do families. One may wonder whether the feeble resistance of the Egyptians to the onslaught of the crusaders was not largely due to the exhaustion of the country by civil war, anarchy, and, in particular, the plague and its corollaries, impoverishment and dearth of funds.[33]

Also noteworthy in the Maghrebi's letter is his expectation that the viceroy would launch a new offensive "this year" (1100) and retake Jerusalem, whereupon he would visit and "see" the Holy City and return home. After Palestine had changed hands so often in the past, the crusader invasion was regarded as a transient phenomenon.

The letter of the Karaite elders from Ascalon emphasized that it was possible to ransom so many captives because the Crusaders demanded for them far less than the usual 100 dinars for three persons. It mentioned, however, that a boy of eight from a most prominent Karaite family had been offered by his captors the opportunity of being baptized and becoming a Christian priest,[34] whereupon the boy replied: How could I convert, after the Jews have already spent so much on my ransom? A similar case is reflected in TS AS 147, fol. 5, a draft of an appeal to the congregations of Egypt: the Rabbanite elders of Ascalon had already paid 80 dinars (with funds sent from Egypt) for a person for whom, it seems, a threefold ransom had been demanded; now "the small sum

---

31 The technical word for plague, *wabā*, is used here as well as in the letter of the elders of Ascalon, who add two other well known terms, *fanā'* (lit., annihilation), and *balā'* (spelled *bl'*, lit., affliction or decomposition): *Palestinian Jewry*, p. 241, TS 20.113, line 6. Once, the biblical term *dever* (Heb.) is introduced. The plague is clearly differentiated from other diseases, *'ilal*, and illnesses, *amrāḍ*.

32 Bodleian MS Heb. b 11 (Cat. 2874), fol. 7, lines 39-43, and margins, ed. in *Palestinian Jewry*, p. 253. English translation of the entire letter in my "Contemporary Letters," pp. 175-177.

33 The plague, which later affected also the crusaders, was known, but the historical significance it might have had for the outcome of the war was perhaps not sufficiently recognized.

34 In the midst of the Ar. text the Heb. word *kohen* is used!

still remaining" should be raised. This draft seems to be some years later than 1100.[35]

The ransomed captives became refugees, and, if they were not of a noble family, or learned, or otherwise prominent, had to beg their way through the communities of Egypt. The moving appeal of "a captive woman with a boy from the Land of Israel" to the community of Fustat is translated in *A Mediterranean Society* 2:169-170.[36]

The process of ransoming could take years: until the whereabouts of the captives were ascertained, the captors, on dangerous voyages, reached, the negotiations successfully completed, and the necessary funds raised. In a highly interesting letter (62 lines) from Palestine the sender reports that he succeeded in redeeming his brother, mother, and little sister, after his father had already died seven years before. He wished to renew business relations with his well-to-do relatives in blessed Egypt (who had kept silent all those years, but reports about whom had reached the writer constantly). He twice emphasizes that normal conditions had returned to the country, using Hebrew phrases:

> Praised be God who made me fertile in the land of my affliction. Take notice that God has ensured our survival in the country and saved the lives of a large remnant.[37]

A similar letter (69 lines), written by Zadok b. Josiah, a high religious dignitary, to another in Egypt, states that the sender had to linger against his wish "in this little town" (unfortunately he does not mention the name), because "some of the boys are still captive in Antiochia"; the little girl had been already freed; now he hoped that "our prince and lord, my son-in-law, The Prince of the House of Israel" (no name added) might soon be ransomed. Zadok intended to travel to Egypt, but it is evident that his main purpose was promotion for himself or some other communal affair. The ransoming of captives had become a routine of daily life. Our letter was written before 1111, since Zadok intended to renew his connection with the Nagid Mevōrākh, who died in that year.[38]

---

35   The draft, summarized in *Palestinian Jewry*, p. 257, was written by the clerk Halfon b. Manasse, and, as script and arrangement show, at an early stage of his career (dated documents 1100-1138).

36   The original is ed. in *Palestinian Jewry*, pp. 288-289.

37   TS 16.250, line 19, and margin, lines 9-10, ed. in *Palestinian Jewry*, pp. 289-294. The quotations are from Genesis 41.52 and 45.7.

38   TS 24.65, ed. in *Palestinian Jewry*, pp. 283-288. (On the date of Mevōrākh's death see now Mark R. Cohen, *Jewish Self-Government in Medieval Egypt* [Princeton, 1980], p. 147, n. 148.)

Captives were being taken continually. A legal document tells this sad story. A group of ransomed women and girls arrived in a place seeking sustenance. A woman in modest circumstances, a mother of three girls and two boys, "adopted" one of those unhappy girls. When the children grew up, one of the boys married her, but she immediately repudiated him and refused to share his company even if he would heap gold on her head. The boys turned her out of the house.[39]

A rather close relationship between a Frankish warrior and a local Jew seems to be reflected in another story with a romantic touch about a captive girl. In a letter from Ascalon (written after its capture by the crusaders in 1153) the sender recounts that he had visited Nablus, where the girl was being kept, together with her brother and obtained from her captor the permission to take her with him in order to raise 60 dinars still due for the ransom. (She must have been a very beautiful girl, since the ransom demanded was a multiple of the sum internationally accepted for this purpose, see above.) All the endeavors of the writer to raise the money in Ascalon, including his readiness to give his son as a collateral for a loan, failed. Therefore the brother traveled with his sister to Egypt, probably with the wishful intention that a rich boy would cast his eye on her and present her the ransom money as his marriage gift. At the time of writing nothing had been heard from the travelers, but the Frankish knight had come down from Nablus to Ascalon and demanded either the money or the return of the girl.[40]

Amalric, King of Jerusalem, took the Egyptian border city of Bilbays on 3 November 1168, and, after the carnage visited upon the city the following day, carried with him many prisoners on his way back. The ransoming of the Jewish captives caused major repercussions in the community. Moses Maimonides, who had arrived in the country not long before, had already attained the position of Great Rav, corresponding approximately to that of a Muslim Grand Mufti, that is, the highest juridical authority. Experienced in public disaster from his homeland, the Muslim West, he took the initiative in the rescue of the captives and sent the two most respected Jewish judges as ambassadors to Palestine, probably to Amalric himself. They had to negotiate with the captors and partly also the captives, some of whom had the means for

---

39   Jewish Theological Seminary of America, New York, ENA 2808, fol. 15a, ed. in *Palestinian Jewry*, pp. 309-311, trans. in "Tyre-Tripoli-'Arqa," pp. 87-88. Neither Jewish nor Islamic law knows formal adoption.

40   TS NS J 270, ed. in *Palestinian Jewry*, pp. 306-309. "I am sitting here in Ascalon in 6000 states of well-being"—not a bad testimony for how a Jew was feeling in a town ruled by crusaders. For problems concerning this document see Joshua Prawer, "Notes on the History of the Jews in the Latin Kingdom of Jerusalem," *Shalem* 2 (1976), 103-105 [in Hebrew].

ransoming themselves. In addition, he circulated appeals for a comprehensive drive, a number of which, mostly fragments, but some almost complete and most eloquent, have been preserved. The Geniza contains also a letter from a female prisoner from Bilbays dealing with her redemption, as well as a legal document showing Maimonides personally active and collecting the funds pledged.[41]

It is perhaps not far-fetched to assume that Maimonides' meteoric rise to the office of *Ra'īs al-Yahūd,* official head of Egyptian Jewry, in 1171, when he, the foreigner, was only 33 years old, was partly due to his energetic action for the unhappy victims of Bilbays.

Even around 1230, when the crusaders were confined to Acre and a few other fortified places, we read about female prisoners taken by them. A letter sent from Cairo to Alexandria at that time contains this passage:

> You enquire about the women captives — may God grant their release; no news has arrived about them; but boats from Acre are coming and going in your place.

These women were probably taken during some raid of northern Palestine.[42]

I have put these references to captives together to impress upon the reader that ransom money probably formed a considerable part of a crusader's income.[43]

In the following a number of stray Geniza texts of some historical significance are summarized.

This remark in a letter about the fall of Beirut to the Crusaders in 1110 emphasizes that the siege of the city had come to its people as a surprise:

> My heart stood still, when a person escaping from Beirut during the night — as he said — reported that there lived in it thirty-five Jewish families, besides the foreign merchants visiting there and were about to leave

---

41 *Palestinian Jewry,* pp. 312-320, see S.D. Goitein, "Moses Maimonides, Man of Action, a Revision of the Master's Biography in the Light of the Geniza Documents," *Hommages à Georges Vajda,* ed. G. Nahon and Ch. Touati (Louvain, 1980), pp. 155-167, where the more important texts are translated.

42 TS 20.138, lines 30-32, ed. in *Palestinian Jewry,* p. 230, n. 3. The letter was written by Solomon, son of the judge Elijah.

43 I believe I have read other such references but failed to note them. The fragment of a letter to a Nagid, it seems Mevōrākh, wishes him, *inter alia:* "May God let you dwell in safety and save us and you from captivity, famine, and exile" (*ṭilṭūl,* Heb.). Twice, "the Land of Edom," Christian Europe, is mentioned. TS 8 J 39, fol. 7, lines 1, 4-5.

when they were overtaken by the siege and forced to remain. Praised be The True Judge.[44]

Acre was taken by Baldwin and the Genoese in 1104, but the Jewish community there seems to have quickly recovered. A remarkable calligraphic letter by the cantor and ritual slaughterer of the Acre congregation (whose family hailed from Tiberias) castigates the Jewish purple shell-gatherers from Alexandria "who drank beer in the taverns"[45] and took a stand against him in the dissensions caused by the "Christian" ban on the Jewish way of killing cattle. This ban was by no means particular to the crusaders, and was a matter for the market police rather than a religious affair.[46] The Jewish population seems to have suffered by dearth of provisions. Cheese, the main protein food for the poor, probably sent by coreligionists in southern Italy, Sicily, or Crete, was distributed as a handout, in which the cantor's household, comprising five daughters and four other females, was passed over. The names mentioned indicate that the letter was written either before, or shortly after 1111.[47]

Tyre capitulated to the crusaders in July 1124, after prolonged fighting, and those of its inhabitants who wished to do so were permitted to leave the town with their belongings.[48] Among these was probably the Jewish judge Nathan ha-Kohen b. Solomon, who, as early as 1102 signed, as first, a court record in Tyre and again one in 1125 in Fustat, where he appears as signatory for

---

44 TS 13 J 15, fol. 10, lines 15-18, ed. in *Palestinian Jewry*, pp. 294-296. The benediction is said on the reception of the news that someone has died.

45 TS 18 J 3, fol. 5, lines 36-37, ed. in *Palestinian Jewry*, pp. 302-305. Professor Mark R. Cohen draws my attention to J. Braslavsky, *Studies in Our Country, its Past and Remains* (Tel Aviv, 1954; in Hebrew), pp. 85-87, 89-90, where the text is printed (without translation) and discussed. I regret this oversight. I am, of course, familiar with Braslavsky's work; this book is cited in *A Mediterranean Society* countless times. In this particular case, however, B.'s understanding of the text is so completely off the mark that I must have written it off many years ago, for TS 18 J 3, fol. 5, is used in each of the first three volumes of *A Mediterranean Society* but never with a reference to B. I apologize for this, too, here. Ar. *mākhūr* from Persian *mā*, wine, *khūr*, taking something. *Mizr*, beer, made according to Maqrīzī (*Khiṭaṭ*, 1 [Bulāq, 1270 H], 44, bottom), from wheat, is not religiously taboo for a Jew, but those taverns might also have served other purposes.
The crusaders probably admitted those Alexandrian purple shell-gatherers, who had a bad reputation in their hometown too (see *A Mediterranean Society*, 2:62-63), because the purple shells were needed for dyeing and probably also because the gatherers had to pay a sales tax.

46 See *A Mediterranean Society*, 2:282.

47 Zadok the Third (see Mann, *Jews in Egypt*, 2:232 [3]), is probably identical with Zadok b. Josiah, see n. 38, above. "The Great Nagid" might refer to Mevōrākh, who died in 1111, as distrinct from his elder brother and predecessor Judah, or Mevōrākh's son and successor Moses.

48 The fight for Tyre is described in great detail in *Encyclopaedia of Islam*, 3:603-604, s.v. *Ṣūr* (E. Honigmann).

another twenty-five years.[49] However, he longed to return to the Holy Land and applied to the flourishing Jewish community of Aden, South Arabia, to make this possible for him financially. Owing to dissensions in that community nothing came of this, as we learn from a letter dated September 1133. But Nathan's action shows that the situation of the Jews in the crusader realm must have been bearable at that time.[50]

Since Ascalon remained a Fatimid outpost in Palestine until 1153 it is not surprising that Jewish communal life continued there without interruption. We even possess a copy of a marriage contract from Ascalon, dated January 1100, in which an Egyptian Jewish notable, Shela, "The Prince of the House of Israel," remarries his divorcée. He is almost certainly identical with the prominent government agent Sahl b. Yūsha', who, a few months later, conducted a caravan of ransomed captives from Ascalon to Egypt.[51] Records dated 1135-1143 about the lease of apartments and stores belonging to the community also betray "business as usual." The fact that these records found their way into the Geniza seems to prove that the papers of the rabbinical court of Ascalon were brought to Cairo after 1153.[52]

In the years preceding the end of crusader rule over Tiberias (July 1187), the town was in the possession of Echive, the wife of Count Raymond III of Tripoli. A Jew who owed them money — probably a tax farmer who, as so often happened with tax farmers, was unable to pay what he had promised — fled to Egypt, whereupon the Countess put the fugitive's wife and son into prison. As his father-in-law complains in his letter to him, he was in no hurry to return, but enjoyed Egyptian food, drink, music,[53] and good company. The writer lauds the example of the Jewish communities of Damascus, Tyre, and Acre (the latter two being then under Christian domination), "who exerted themselves for the foreigners," and exhorts his son-in-law to return; ways would be found to come to an agreement with the Count and the Countess.[54]

The Geniza is particularly rich in information about Jerusalem after its reconquest by Saladin in 1187. At no time do we find such close and construc-

---

49 1102: TS 8 J 4, fol. 18 c, ed. and trans. in my "Tyre-Tripoli-'Arqa," pp. 74-78. Fustat: *A Mediterranean Society*, 2:518, section 17.

50 TS 20.173, ed. Mann, *Jews in Egypt*, 2:366-367. The writer, a Yemenite notable and savant, Jacob b. Salīm, is known also otherwise. The letter was sent to Nathan from al-Juwwa, a town in Yemen. The circumstances are discussed in my *Documents on the India Trade from the Cairo Geniza* (in progress), nos. 181 and 246.

51 Details in *Palestinian Jewry*, p. 236.

52 Ibid., p. 296.

53 TS 18 J 2, fol. 10, line 24. Ar. *li'b*. I translated literally "play." But in such a connection the word means "music."

54 *Palestinian Jewry*, pp. 259-260, 265-267.

tive relations between an Islamic government and its Jewish subjects as during the first half of Ayyubid rule.[55] Here, naturally, only texts which have direct relevance to crusader history will be cited.

Saladin, who, because of his ceaseless wars, was always short of money, tried to reinstate the ancient Muslim law according to which non-Muslims had to pay twice the customs due on a Muslim. He soon was forced to renounce this attempt. A letter from Alexandria addressed to Cairo has this to report:

> A proclamation by our lord Saladin — may God make his rule eternal — arrived and was read out in Alexandria in the presence of the head of the customs house, who confirmed its content; whereupon the amīr Fakhr ad-Dīn — may God let him live as long as Time exists — proclaimed it in the town, saying: neither Jew nor Christian, foreign nor local, must pay more than half the customs. Our coreligionists made a procession *with the holy Torah scroll* and prayed for the Sultan, may God make his rule eternal.[56]

The arrival in Egypt on their way to Palestine of "invaders" from France and England, this time, Jews, in the year 1211, was known from a late Hebrew literary source, which, with the usual exaggeration, speaks of 300 rabbis involved. A more realistic picture emerges from this passage in a letter written in Alexandria on 23 September 1212:

> In the very night I am writing you, my lord, there arrived here seven of the rabbis, the great scholars, accompanied by one hundred persons, men, women, and children, in need for eating bread, as if we had not enough beggars here! There are forty beggars in town and most people are in trouble because of the sluggish business. And now this great expenditure! We shall see how we manage.[57]

The way in which "the rabbis, the great scholars" are introduced (with the article) shows that these were not the first arrivals of immigrants from France; thus the date given in the source referred to above was probably correct; nor must we assume that those preceding them were as poor as these; otherwise the writer would have said something like "and these were penniless like the others."

---

55 Cf. ibid., pp. 260-263, 268-275, 298-300, 321-335.

56 Ibid., pp. 296-298. This double tax for non-Muslims has a long and complicated history. See ibid.

57 Ibid., pp. 338-343, esp. pp. 342-343. TS 12.299. The court clerk and cantor Judah Ibn al-'Ammānī of Alexandria writes to another Alexandrian, Meir b. Yakhīn, who held the same office in Fustat.

Robert Chazan has suggested that this emigration of French Jews to Palestine was motivated not only by religious enthusiasm, but "by the immediate problems stemming from the wide-ranging royal confiscation [of Jewish property] of 1210."[58] This reasonable assumption is confirmed by the date of another letter from Alexandria, which says that travelers arriving from Marseilles had reported that a large number of French Jews were on their way to Egypt, adding: "May God beware us from the trouble they will cause."[59] The letter is dated 25 May 1235, a year after continuous harrassments had culminated in a new royal decree making the existence of Jews in northern France next to impossible.[60]

As is known from literary sources as well as from Geniza documents, the presence of the learned French Jews was immediately felt in Jerusalem. They could not have enjoyed their stay there for a long time, since the city, with exception of the Muslim holy sites and the Holy Sepulchre, was laid waste by the Sultan al-Malik al-Mu'azzam in 1219, who was afraid that the crusaders, after taking the Egyptian seaport of Damietta, would proceed to the Holy City. As so often before, refugees from Jerusalem would appear in Geniza documents written in Fustat.[61]

When, in 1229, Jerusalem was ceded by the Egyptian Sultan al-Malik al-Kāmil (al-Mu'azzam's brother) to Emperor Frederick II, Muslims were not permitted access to the Holy City (except the Temple area), and it stands to reason that the same applied to Jews, although this seems not to be stated in literary sources. This assumption is confirmed by a letter from Tiberias, dated 30 November 1236, which among business and personal matters, contains this passage, the beginning of which, unfortunately, is torn away:

> Ghāndār[62] came saying: the ruler greets you [and grants] your requests.[63]
> They brought us fruit and other things.[64] I met with them and discussed

58 Robert Chazan, *Medieval Jewry in Northern France* (Baltimore and London, 1973), p. 87.
59 TS Arabic Box 54, fol. 66, and 53, fol. 67; discussed in S.D. Goitein, "Chief Justice Hananel b. Samuel, In-law of Moses Maimonides," *Tarbiz Jubilee Volume* (1981), n. 52 [in Hebrew; in press].
60 Robert Chazan, *Medieval Jewry*, pp. 109-116.
61 *Palestinian Jewry*, pp. 336-337. TS NS J 66, and TS 8.167: "When we, the undersigned, lived in Jerusalem, which is now destroyed, may God, in his great mercy, grant its building up anew..." The second of the two documents, one in Heb. and one in Ar., but almost identical in content, is dated April 1229.
62 Since the word is not preceded by the article, I took it as a Frankish name, cf. German Günther, but the late Uri Ben-Horin suggested Ar. ghāndār, "Keeper of arms" [cf. D. Ayalon, "Studies on the Structure of the Mamluk Army," *Bulletin of the School of Oriental and African Studies* 16 (1954), 63], which might be preferable.
63 Probably concerning commercial matters.
64 Such as sweetmeats, since Jews would not take cooked or baked things or wine.

with them their refusal to let Jews live in Jerusalem. After long deliberations they agreed to let Jews visit the holy places and that a Jewish dyer should stay with them. With this the meeting came to an end. A Jewish dyer lives now in Jerusalem, thank God, the beneficient, the benefactor.[65]

Frankish Acre was the main refuge of Jewish scholarship in Palestine in the thirteenth century. At its fall in 1291, Christians and Jews suffered the same cruel fate. Reference has been made above, n. 7, to a dirge bemoaning the dead. Some prisoners were taken. About one, "a girl who had lost her virginity because she was captured in Acre by Muslims together with other Jewish women a short time ago," we have the draft of her marriage contract, the most bizarre Geniza document, both in its content and outer appearance, I have ever seen. Her redeemer from Muslim captivity and future husband bore the title Ṣafī [al-Dawla] "Confidant of the Goverment" and his father and grandfather are lauded as scholarly and beneficent. But he must have been quite assimilated to his Muslim superiors, since he had stipulated in the marriage contract with his first wife that he was permitted to marry a total of four wives (as Muslims), a condition not seen in any other Jewish marriage contract. The draft emphasizes repeatedly that the captive was now a free woman and free to marry whomever she wished, but she preferred to become the wife of the man who had delivered her from captivity, and the first wife also agreed to this arrangement. How far these agreements were really free choices must be left to the imagination of the reader. The Mamluk period was a time of ruthless oppression in every respect.[66]

I have described this document in some detail to bring home the truth, unfortunately known to us only too well, that great historical catastrophes do not minimize the personal sufferings of those who happened to be involved in them. If this survey of Geniza sources has any value it is this, that it shows us an easily forgotten aspect of history: the population over whose bodies rapacious men fight their unsavory wars.

---

65 ENA 2559, fol. 178, ed. in *Palestinian Jewry*, pp. 300-302. The dyer was needed by the Christians for his work and by the Jewish visitors for lodging and meals. Since the letter was written in late November, certainly several months had passed since the writer's visit in Jerusalem, and meanwhile a dyer had settled there.

66 TS 8 K 13, fol. 11, edited and discussed by Mordechai A. Friedman, "Polygamy in the Documents of the Geniza," *Tarbiz* 40 (1971), 346-356 [in Hebrew; facsimile provided], with his usual exactness and ample attention to the legal and human aspects involved.

Added in proof

In my comments (above, p. 315) on Moses Maimonides' circular for the ransoming of the captives from Bilbays (1168), I assumed that he had sent the two judges to whom the circular was addressed (only their first names are mentioned) from Egypt to Syro-Palestine. However, in a private communication (20 May 1982), Professor Joshua Prawer rightly remarks that the wording of the text suggests, rather, that they were local judges and that R. Ephraim was none other than the eminent judge Ephraim al-Miṣrī ("the man of Fustat"), whom Benjamin of Tudela met in Tyre and who is extensively mentioned in the Responsa of Moses Maimonides. Thus it appears that the captives were sent to the Mediterranean ports to be sold to slave dealers from Europe, but that it was finally deemed more preferable for both sides if the prisoners were ransomed against a reasonable sum.

SOME NEW EDITIONS OF ORIENTAL SOURCES ABOUT SYRIA IN THE TIME OF THE CRUSADES

CLAUDE CAHEN
University of Paris I (Panthéon-Sorbonne)

In my thesis *La Syrie du Nord à l'époque des croisades et la principauté franque d'Antioche* (Paris, 1940) I had given a rather wide study of the oriental sources which were published at that date or could be read in manuscript. This study is still valuable. However, I made additions in the article "Crusades" in the new edition of the *Encyclopaedia of Islam* in 1960. I shall say here a few words about more recent publications.

ARABIC SOURCES

There is nothing for the first half of the twelfth century. For the period of Saladin, the main source, the *Barq al-Shāmī* of 'Imād ad-dīn al-Iṣfahānī, is known to us, with the exception of a few directly preserved passages,[1] only through the very extensive quotations by Abū Shāma in his *K. ar-Rawḍatayn*. However, we know that a slightly abridged version had been made by the same al-Bundārī who had done an analogous work for the *History of the Seljuqs* of 'Imād ad-dīn. A manuscript of the first part of al-Bundārī's version of the *Barq* has now been discovered and published down to 577 H. by Ramazan Shōshan.[2] The question must be asked whether Abū Shāma made use of the original *Barq* or of al-Bundārī's version, which appears to have been completed about 630 H.

---

1   H.A.R. Gibb, "al-Barq al-Shāmī. The History of Saladin by the Kātib 'Imād ad-Dīn al-Iṣfahānī," *Wiener Zeitschrift für die Kunde des Morgenlandes* 52 (1953), 93-115 (years 573 H.—beginning of 575 H., 578 H.—part of 579 H.)
2   Al-Bundārī, *Sanā al Barq al-Shāmī*, ed. Ramazan Shōshan (Beirut, 1974).

The same problem arises for other writers of the mid-thirteenth century such as Sibṭ ibn al-Jawzī and Ibn Wāṣil. The editor indicates a few additions by al-Bundārī. He thinks that the *Bustān*, which I published a long time ago,[3] is part of al-Bundārī's version because the copyist of the manuscript calls the author also ʿImād ad-dīn. It is obvious that Dr. Shōshan has not seen the text, as it bears no similarity at all to the *Barq*, not to speak of the reasons which I had given in 1937 and which exclude the possibility of the *Bustān* being from the pen of the illustrious *kātib*.

As is well known, ʿImād ad-dīn had written a special work about the conquest of Jerusalem by Saladin. In spite of the extremely flourished style, the historical value of the content made it desirable to have a tentative translation done in an occidental language. This has now been done by Henri Massé (posthumous; the edition was seen through the press by Charles Pellat).[4]

Muḥammad b. Taqī ad-dīn ʿUmar b. Shāhanshāh b. Ayyūb, prince of Hamā, d. 617/1220, *Miḍmār al-Ḥaqā'iq wa sirr al-Khalā'iq*.[5] This unique manuscript of a part of the historical work of the nephew of Saladin and ancestor of Abū'l-Fidā' bears on the years 575-581 H., that is, the period when Saladin conquered the main part of upper Mesopotamia and northern Syria. *Grosso modo*, the text tells the same events as the *Barq* in an abridged form. However, it differs from it firstly because every year begins with a rather long narration of Baghdad and Iraqi events for which the sources must still be found (as the *Muntazam* by Ibn al-Jawzī stops before; perhaps the source was his continuator al-Qādisī, who was used by Sibṭ ibn al-Jawzī in Damascus). Secondly, the author stresses the role of his father al-Malik al-Muẓaffar and himself. Thirdly, for the same reason he speaks at length of the expeditions of al-Muẓaffar's freedman Qarāqūsh in Eastern Maghreb, which are known to us through Abū Shāma's quotations of the Aleppine chronicler Ibn abī Ṭayyī; still for the same reason we are told of the conquest of Yemen. Relations between our author and Ibn abī Ṭayyī (who knew ʿImād ad-dīn) must be looked for. Lastly, a few letters from the Sultan are quoted, only written to Baghdad (perhaps to be found there?) and only one ascribed to a special redactor, al-Fāḍil, none to ʿImād ad-dīn.

---

3   Claude Cahen, "Une chronique syrienne du VIᵉ/XIIᵉ siècle: Le Bustān al-Jāmiʿ," *Bulletin d'études orientales* 7-8 (1937-1938, published 1938), 113-158.

4   ʿImâd ad-Dîn al-Iṣfahânî, *Conquête de la Syrie et de la Palestine par Saladin (al-Fatḥ al-qussî l-fatḥ al-qudsî),* trans. Henri Massé, Documents relatifs à l'histoire des croisades 10 (Paris, 1972).

5   Al-Malik al-Manṣūr Muḥammad ibn ʿUmar, *Miḍmār al-ḥaqā'iq wa-sirr al-khalā'iq,* ed. Ḥasan Ḥabashi (Cairo, 1968).

For the Ayyūbid period after Saladin, Kamāl ad-dīn's *Zubda* has at last been brought to its end by its editor Sami Dahan.[6] The first volume of the *Bughya* (geographical introduction) has been announced by the Academy of Damascus. It is badly needed that we should have at least a photostatic edition of the nine good and unique other volumes preserved. Sa'd ad-dīn's *Memoirs* are reproduced in translation in Cahen's *Les peuples musulmans* from his previous, almost unavailable translation.[7]

In 1960 I had not been able to mention the facsimile edition that Gryaznevitch in Moscow had given of the *Ta'rīkh Mansūrī* by Ibn Naṭīf (or Naẓīf). The author had previously written a large general chronicle which disappeared in the fire of the Escorial (1671) but of which he does not seem to have made use for his shorter chronicle, as, for the whole of the narrative down to the time of Saladin, he merely copies the *Bustān* published by myself in 1937 (a fact of which Gryaznevitch does not appear to have been aware). For the first third of the seventh/thirteenth century it has important information about Mesopotamia and Asia Minor, partly used by Gottschalk and myself;[8] some other information about the Franks and Frederick II had been made known by Amari in his *Biblioteca Arabo-Sicula*.[9] It is highly to be regretted that the complete translation once planned under Gottschalk did not actually appear.

The edition of Ibn Wāṣil has been brought to vol. 5 (645 H.) by Shayyāl's successor in this respect, H. Rabie,[10] and will be continued. It is hoped that a French translation by Bruno Halff will appear shortly.

The edition and translation of the *History of the Patriarchs* of the Coptic church of Alexandria has at last been brought to its completion (640 H.) for the

6 Kamāl ad-Dīn 'Umar ibn Aḥmad ibn al-'Adīm, *Zubdat al-Ḥalab min Tārikh Ḥalab*, ed. Sāmī ad-Dahhān, 3 vols. (Damascus, 1951-1968).

7 Claude Cahen, "Une source pour l'histoire Ayyūbide: Les Mémoires de Sa'd al-Dīn ibn Ḥamawiya Djuwaynī," *Bulletin de la Faculté des Lettres de Strasbourg* for 1950, pp. 320-337, reprinted in Claude Cahen, *Les peuples musulmans dans l'histoire médiévale* (Damascus, 1977), pp. 457-482.

8 Ibn Naẓīf = Muḥammad al-Ḥamawī, *at-Ta'rīkh al-Mansūrī* (Moscow, 1960), 228 folios plus introduction in Russian and Arabic index. Hans L. Gottschalk, "Der Bericht des Ibn Naẓīf al-Ḥamawī über die Schlacht von Jasyčimen," *Wiener Zeitschrift für die Kunde des Morgenlandes* 56 (1960), 55-67; Claude Cahen, "Questions d'histoire de la province de Kastamonu au XIIIᵉ siècle," *Selçuklu Araştirmalari Dergisi* 3 (1971), 145-158.

9 Michele Amari, *Biblioteca Arabo-Sicula. Versione italiana. Appendice* (Torino, 1889), pp. 42-65.

10 Ibn Wāṣil, *Mufarrij al-kurūb fī Akhbār Banī Ayyūb*, ed. Jamal ad-Dīn al-Shayyāl, vol. 5, ed. Hassanein Rabie (Cairo, 1977).

Coptic Archaeological Association by O.E.H. Burmester and A. Khater.[11] The narrative gives a rather large consideration to non-ecclesiastical events.

The life and reign of Baybars is known to us through two works which, though largely used by later authors, were not directly accessible. A complete manuscript of Ibn ʿAbd aẓ-Ẓāhir's *Life of Baybars* has been discovered and prepared for press by Khowayter as a thesis in London, and has been printed in Riyad in 1976, but is not commercially available. Qalāʾūn's life (*Tashrīf al-ayyām*) by the same author has appeared in 1961.[12] The *Life of Baybars* by Ibn Shaddād is not entirely preserved; the second part of it, prepared for the press by A. Hoteit (Beirut), will hopefully be published. The *Aʿlāq* (Historical geography of Syria and Mesopotamia) by the same author will at last be completely published from Anne-Marie Eddé's recent thesis.

From the continuation of Sibṭ Ibn al-Jawzī's *Mirʾāt* by Yūnīnī which preserves much of Ibn Shaddād's *Life of Baybars*, four volumes have been published (inaccurately) in Hyderabad;[13] it is hoped that the whole of the chronicle, which goes down to 1314 A.D., will be published by a young Lebanese scholar within a few years. The sources for this period have been studied by Haarmann and Little.[14] Dhahabī's middle-sized *History* has been translated by Arlette Nègre,[15] but the large *Taʾrīkh al-Islām* is still unedited (except for the first two centuries of Islam) and untranslated.

The third volume of Maqrīzī's *History of the Fāṭimids (Ittiʿāz)* which has something to teach about Syria, has now been published (not very well) by Muḥammad Ḥilmī Muḥammad Aḥmad.[16] From the large history of Ibn al-Furāt, extracts bearing on the Franks have been published (partly from Zurayk's previous edition) and translated by Lyons.[17] The volumes bearing on

---

11 Sāwīrus ibn al-Muqaffaʿ, *History of the Patriarchs of the Egyptian Church, known as the History of the Holy Church*, ed. and trans. A.S. Atiya, Yassā ʿAbd al-Masīḥ, O.H.E. Burmester and A. Khater, Publication de la Société d'archéologie copte, 4 vols. (Cairo, 1943-1974).

12 Muḥyī al-Dīn ibn ʿAbd al-Ẓāhir, *Tashrīf al-ayyām wal-ʿuṣūr fī sīrat al-Malik al-Manṣūr*, ed. Murād Kāmil (Cairo, 1961).

13 Kutb al-dīn Mūsā al-Yūnīnī, *Dhail Mirʾāt al-Zamān*, 4 vols. (Hyderabad, 1954-61).

14 U. Haarmann, *Quellenstudien zur frühen Mamlukenzeit*, Islamkundliche Untersuchungen 1 (Freiburg i. Br., 1970). D.P. Little, *An Introduction to Mamlūk Historiography*, Freiburger Islamstudien 2 (Wiesbaden, 1970).

15 al-Dhahabī, *Kitāb Duwal al-Islām, années 447/1055-6 à 656/1258*, trans. Arlette Nègre, Institut Français de Damas (Damascus, 1980).

16 Al-Maqrīzī, *Ittiʿāẓ al-Ḥunafā*, vol. 3, ed. Muḥammad Ḥilmī Muḥammad Aḥmad (Cairo, 1973).

17 *Ayyubids, Mamlukes and Crusaders. Selections from the Tārīkh al-Duwal waʾl-Mulūk of Ibn al-Furāt*, text and translation by U. and M.C. Lyons, historical comment and notes by J.S.C. Riley-Smith, 2 vols. (Cambridge, 1971).

Saladin's reign have been published (inaccurately) by al-Shammā'.[18] The volumes bearing on the first two thirds of the twelfth century (being the more important ones, as they preserve Ibn abī Ṭayyī's Syrian and Ibn Ṭuwayr's Egyptian chronicles), though promised for some time by a young scholar, still await publication.

I take the liberty of pointing out *Le Testament d'al-Malik al-Ṣāliḥ Ayyūb* which Ibrahim Chabbouh and myself took from the *Nihāya* of Nuwayrī and published in volume 1 of the *Mélanges H. Laoust* (Institut français de Damas, Damascus, 1978), pp. 97-114. This is a document of a human interest and a precision of contents which are rare in this kind of literature. It is contemporary with the disembarkation of King Louis IX of France at Damiette.

NON-ARABIC SOURCES

The *Anonymous Syriac Chronicle* published more than half a century ago by J.B. Chabot had remained of no use to the ordinary historian except for excerpts translated by Chabot himself and by Gibb and Tritton.[19] Now at last it has been translated by Father Abouna with an introduction by Father Fiey.[20] According to the latter scholar, there could be only one author for the whole chronicle, since he speaks of himself in the first person as being present at events of 1139, 1187, and down to the end of his work in 1235. But surely the man who lived in 1139 cannot be the same man who wrote in 1235. The question is whether the man who speaks of himself in 1139 is identical with the one of 1187, or whether the one of 1187 is the same as the author of 1235. It can only be one or the other. To me it seems more probable that there was a first author, writing before 1187, because he is well acquainted with the events of Edessa at the middle of the century and because, whereas he used the sources known to his illustrious contemporary Michael the Syrian for earlier times, he

18   Ibn al-Furāt, *Tārīkh Ibn al-Furāt (Commonly Known as Tārīkh al-Duwal wa'l-Mulūk)*, ed. Ḥasan Muḥammad al-Shammā' (Basra, n.d.).
19   *Anonymi auctoris chronicon ad annum Christi 1234 pertinens*, ed. J.B. Chabot, Corpus scriptorum christianorum Orientalium 81, 82, 109 (=Scriptores Syri 14. 1, 2 and 15) (Paris and Louvain, 1917-1937). The Latin translation in vol. 109 does not cover the period of the crusades. J.B. Chabot, "Un épisode de l'histoire des croisades," *Mélanges offerts à M. Gustave Schlumberger* 1 (Paris, 1924), 169-179. A.S. Tritton and H.A.R. Gibb, "The First and Second Crusade from an Anonymous Syriac Chronicle," *Journal of the Royal Asiatic Society* for 1933, 69-101, 273-305. More recently excerpts in J.B. Segal, *Edessa. The Blessed City* (Oxford, 1970).
20   *Anonymi auctoris chronicon ad A.C. 1234 pertinens*, trans. A. Abouna with an introduction and notes by J.M. Fiey, Corpus scriptorum christianorum Orientalium 354 (=Scriptores Syri 154) (Louvain, 1974).

knows nothing of the important chronicle completed by Michael in 1197. The first author was particularly aware of affairs in Edessa; I doubt whether the second one could have lived in the monastery of Mar Barsauma, where he could have known the last part of Michael's chronicle.

The *Chronicle ascribed to the Constable Smbat* (Sempad) which Gérard Dédéyan has recently translated,[21] is the most important Armenian chronicle from Cilicia. However, it had remained unknown even to the scholars who had prepared the Armenian volume for the *Recueil des Historiens des Croisades* when at the close of the nineteenth century Father Leonce Alishan made known some extracts which he cautiously ascribed to an anonymous Royal Historian. The value of the text for the history of the Latin Orient has been made clear in my *La Syrie du Nord* (p. 99), but necessarily I evaluated it only on the basis of the short translated extracts. In 1956 the complete Armenian text appeared in Venice and a few years later Miss S. Der Nersessian translated important parts of it into English.[22] Dédéyan now offers a French translation of the whole of the original part (the first part being a pure copy of Matthew of Edessa), with notes bearing mostly on comparisons with other sources, mainly Armenian. The question whether the chronicle is the work of the famous constable Sempad, the brother of King Hethoum, or of somebody close to him, must be left open. In any case it is an official history dealing with the Cilician kingdom, partly from archival material, but also giving valuable information about events in neighboring countries.

The *History of the Nestorian Patriarchs* was published about eighty years ago by Gismondi[23] but has very rarely been used by other than church historians. However, it has recently been photomechanically reproduced[24] and, although it has almost no bearing on Syrian history, this may be an opportunity to draw attention to a single sentence: During the patriarchate of Isho'yab (1159-1183), says the author, "the Frankish martyrs were martyred and they were buried in the church of the *sūq al-thālatha* in Baghdad..."[25] Now, as it was not the

21   *La chronique attribuée au Connétable Smbat*, trans. Gérard Dédéyan, Documents relatifs à l'histoire des croisades (Paris, 1980).

22   *Smbatay Sparapeti taregirk'*, ed. by S. Akelian, Matenagrow'iwnk' nakhneats 46 (Venice— San Lazzaro, 1956). S. Der Nersessian, "The Armenian Chronicle of the Constable Smpad or of the Royal Historian," *Dumbarton Oaks Papers* 13 (1959), 141-168. Russian translation by A.G. Galstian, *Smbat Sparapet Letopis'* (Erevan, 1974).

23   *Maris, Amri et Slibae De Patriarchis Nestorianorum commentaria*, ed. H. Gismondi, 4 vols. in 2 (Rome, 1899, 1896/97).

24   Published in two volumes and without the Latin translation in Baghdad, n.d.

25   The text adds (p. 107) *qadām al-bāṣlūt bayna* (correct thus a mistake in the edition) *al-Kuddayn*. Prof. Gérard Troupeau, using Graf and Fiey, kindly explains to me from the Syriac that the meaning is that the martyrs were buried in the oratory between the two choirs of the Nestorian church.

custom to kill prisoners of war, these Franks must have been something special. Of course we cannot tell anything certain, but there is a probability that they were men who had participated in the expedition launched by Rainald of Châtillon in the Red Sea and against the Holy Cities of Islam. It is known that a number of these Franks were killed on the spot, others were sent to Egypt where Saladin had them executed. Nothing is reported of others having been sent to the Caliph in Baghdad, but this is altogether likely, as is the fate they met.

APPENDIX. SUMMARY OF THE CHAPTERS OF THE *MIDMĀR* RELATING TO SALADIN

Year 575

p. 15:   What happened to the Sulṭān Ṣalāḥ ad-Dīn in Syria and Egypt.
p. 16:   Battle of Marj'uyūn.
p. 18:   Reasons why al-Muẓaffar Taqī ad-Dīn 'Umar, father of the author, was absent from the battle.
p. 24:   Attack of Bayt al-Aḥzan.
p. 31:   Raid of 'Izz ad-Dīn Farrukhshāh against Safad.
p. 32:   Extract from a letter of the Sulṭān to Baghdad.
p. 33:   Expedition of 'Abd al-Mu'min to Ifrīqiya.
p. 34:   Expedition of Sharaf ad-Dīn Qarāqūsh al-Muẓaffarī.

Year 576

p. 42:   The Sulṭān enters the country of the Armenians and takes Ḥiṣn al-'Anqar.
p. 43:   Death of Sayf ad-Dīn Ghāzī b. Mawdūd b. Zenki.
p. 52:   Ṣalāḥ ad-Dīn returns to Egypt.
p. 53:   Expedition of Qarāqūsh al-Muẓaffarī to the Maghreb.

Year 577

p. 59:   Death of Ismā'il b. Maḥmūd b. Zenkī, prince of Aleppo.
p. 60:   Letter of the Sulṭān to 'Abd ar-Raḥmān b. Unur to invite him to go and help Taqī ad-Dīn 'Umar.
p. 62:   Correspondence of the Sulṭān with the Ustādh ad-Dār to describe the treachery of the people of Mosul.

p. 66: Departure of Ẓahīr ad-Dīn Tuktekīn to Yemen.

p. 67: Capture of a Frankish fleet at Dimyāṭ.

p. 67: Wars of Sharaf ad-Dīn Qarāqūsh al-Muẓaffarī in the Maghreb. — Al Shahrazūrī comes to Baghdad as envoy from Ṣalāḥ ad-Dīn.

Year 578

p. 93: What happened to the Sulṭān Ṣalāḥ ad-Dīn in Syria and Egypt.

p. 94: Raid against Dabūriya.

p. 95: Raid against Ṭabariyya and Baysān.

p. 96: The Sulṭān marches towards Aleppo, crosses the Euphrates and takes possession of Mosul and Jazīra.

p. 104: Death of Farrukhshāh.

p. 105: Capture of Edessa. — Capture of Raqqa.

p. 106: The Sulṭān besieges Mosul.

p. 107: Arrival of envoys from the Caliphate.

p. 109: The Shaykh ash-Shuyūkh at Mosul.

p. 110: The Sulṭān goes to Sinjār and takes it.

p. 111: The Sulṭān goes to Naṣībīn and the Shaykh ash-Shuyūkh returns to Baghdad.

p. 114: Extract from a letter to the Dīwān al-'Azīz written by al-Fāḍil.

p. 115: The Sulṭān besieges Āmid.

Year 579 (?)

p. 136: Expedition and conquest (of Āmid) by Ṣalāḥ ad-Dīn in this year.

p. 138: Āmid is given to Nūr ad-Dīn b. Qarā Arslān.

p. 139: Letters sent by the Sulṭān about the capture of Āmid.

p. 141: The Sulṭān besieges Aleppo.

p. 142: 'Imād ad-Dīn Zenkī b. Mawdūd asks for peace.

p. 144: Death of Tāj al-Mulūk Būrī. — The Sulṭān enters Aleppo and stays in the Citadel.

p. 145: Capture of Ḥārim.

p. 146: Governors appointed to the fortresses.

p. 147: Abbreviated extracts from letters of the Sulṭān to announce the capture of Aleppo.

p. 150: The Sulṭān receives news from Egypt about the victory of al-Malik al-'Ādil over Frankish troops on land and at sea.[26]

---

26   Cf. Abū Shāma, *K. ar-Rawḍatayn* 2:27.

p. 151: Return of the Sulṭān from Aleppo to Damascus.

p. 152: Raid against Baysān.

p. 153: Raid against al-Karak.

p. 154: al-Malik al-Muẓaffar is appointed to the governorship of Egypt.

p. 158: al-Malik al-'Ādil is appointed to the governorship of Aleppo and its province.

p. 161: The Sulṭān comes back from al-Karak to Damascus.

p. 162: Mosul affairs.

p. 164: Wars of Qarāqūsh al-Muẓaffarī during this year.

Year 580

p. 196: Embassies between the Sulṭān and the Caliph.

p. 201: Reign of Ya'qūb b. Yūsuf b. 'Abd al-Mu'mīn.

p. 202: Wars of Sharaf ad-Dīn Qarāqūsh during this year.

Year 581

p. 212: What happened to the Sulṭān Ṣalāḥ ad-Dīn in Syria and Egypt.

p. 215: Extract from a letter of the Sulṭān to the Ustādh ad-Dār about affairs of Antioch and Mosul.

p. 217: The Sulṭān returns from Mosul towards Diyār Bakr with Nāṣir ad-Dīn Muḥammad b. Shīrkūh and Muẓaffar ad-Dīn ibn 'Alī Kütshük as his vanguard; march towards Khilāt and arrival of Pahlavan Ibn Ildeguz.

p. 219: Capture of Mayāfāriqīn.

p. 221: The Sulṭān goes from Mayāfāriqīn to the banks of Qaramān.

p. 222: Arrival of envoys from the Sulṭān of Egypt to announce the capture of Mayāfāriqīn. — The Sulṭān returns from the banks of Qaramān to Mosul.

p. 226: Letter from the Sulṭān to his brother Sayf al-Islām, King of Yemen, announcing the capture of Mayāfāriqīn, from the pen of al-'Imād al-Iṣfahānī. — Something about the virtues of Ṣalāḥ ad-Dīn.

p. 227: War of Qarāqūsh al-Muẓaffarī. — People who died in this year.

CRUSADE AND "PRESENCE OF JERUSALEM" IN MEDIEVAL FLORENCE

FRANCO CARDINI

University of Florence

In two fundamental passages of the *Divine Comedy*—it is not surprising that our Florentine enquiry begins here—Dante supplies us with the ideological coordinates of his thoughts on the crusade.

In the *Inferno*, Federico da Montefeltro, the formerly prestigious political and military Ghibelline leader who later joined the Franciscan Order, blames Pope Boniface VIII for his damnation; since Boniface with "deceit" and "bad faith" persuaded him to participate in the crusade against the Colonna. Montefeltro and Dante comment that this was a false crusade, as it contended "not with Saracen and not with Jew."[1] We have here the condemnation of the *crux cismarina*, the crusade *contra christianos*, a condemnation which was a stock theme dear to Ghibelline propaganda. From these verses a certain disagreement emerges with those canonistic theses of which Cardinal Hostiensis was a clear spokesman, and of which Dante was certainly aware.[2]

The crusade returns in the *Paradiso*; but this time it is the true crusade, in all the splendour of a holy war and Christian faith maintained to the point of martyrdom. Against the background of the sphere of Mars shines the *signum* characteristic of crusaders—but of the Florentine *Popolo* too[3]—the cross. It is

---

1   *Inferno*, 27.86, transl. L. Binyon (London, 1947); see also G. Miccoli, "Crociata," *Enciclopedia dantesca* 2: 275-277.

2   See M. Villey, "L'idée de la croisade chez les juristes du moyen âge," *10° Congresso Internazionale di Scienze Storiche. Relazioni*, 3 (Florence, 1955), 565-594.

3   In Florence, the red cross in a silver field was the arms of the *Popolo*. For the origins of such a symbol in the world of Duecento Italian cities and its reference to the crusade, see E. Dupré Theseider, "Sugli stemmi delle città comunali italiane," in his *Mondo cittadino e movimenti*

made up of a myriad lights: they are the spirits of the *milites Christi*, the martyrs fallen in battle for the Faith, soldiers of the Lord, free at last, unlike other spirits, of any part of their physical likeness.

Within the cross of the martyrs, from which rises a triumphal hymn to Christ, the victor over death and victorious king,[4] the principal *athletae Christi* shine for a moment with such intensity that they can be recognised as they are named by Cacciaguida, ancestor of Dante and himself a crusading martyr.[5]

But Cacciaguida's words are themselves polemical: the Holy Land, which justly belongs to the Christians (and here one is reminded of the famous argument of Hostiensis) is usurped by the Saracens "per colpa de' pastor,"[6] that is, because of the negligence and the injustice of the heads of the Church, the pope first and foremost. Cacciaguida's discourse finishes thus, converging with the invective of Federico da Montefeltro.

It is important at this point to underline the fact that the crusader ideal of Cacciaguida (that is, of Dante), always viewed within the context of polemics against contemporary degeneracy, is inserted as a main element of Cacciaguida's praise in memory of the Florence of the good times past, of "Fiorenza dentro della cerchia antica,"[7] the small, temperate, strict Florence of the mid-twelfth century, placed in dramatic contrast with the avidity, pride and discord of the rich, sinful city of Dante's time.

Thus we are presented with the outline of an "ideological code": the crusade of the knights-martyr, the just war fought in pureness of spirit against the infidel, cannot be carried out except as a product of a regulated, harmonious, just society. Where, on the other hand, society does not adhere to such a model, any opposition to the infidel becomes impossible: it is impossible mainly because the prime reason for lack of success is *in capite* besides *in membris* of Christianity, in its spiritual guide ("per colpa de' pastor"). However, the loss of the Holy Land is, at the same time, a sign of the corruption of Christians and a divine punishment for their sins.[8]

What were the authentic crusader records of Florence in Dante's time? In order to give a correct reply, which for reasons of space we must cut short, it

---

ereticali nel Medio Evo (Bologna, 1978), pp. 103-145, and L. Paolini, "Le origini della Societas Crucis," *Rivista di storia e letteratura religiosa* 15 (1979), 173-229.

4   *Paradiso*, 14.125.

5   *Paradiso*, 18.37-48; ibid., 15.148.

6   *Paradiso*, 15.144.

7   *Paradiso*, 15.97.

8   It is the basis of anti-crusading thought which already begins to emerge in the West with the failure of the Second Crusade and which increases in the following century. See P.A. Throop, *Criticism of the Crusade. A Study of Public Opinion and Crusade Propaganda* (Amsterdam, 1940), and Prawer, *Histoire*, 1:387-394, 2:14-15, 336-338, 379-395.

would be necessary to examine first and foremost those ties with the Holy Land and the Christian Orient which were alive in Tuscany and in Florence from the most ancient times. As in all Christendom, the first patrons of Florence — Reparata, Zanobi — were of oriental origin.[9] Famous relics which arrived in Florence were also oriental, from those of Saint Genesius, which passed through the city escorted by the *comes* Scrot between the end of the eighth and the beginning of the ninth centuries,[10] to the bodies of the "Innocents" brought to Tuscany by Romano, bishop of Fiesole in the first thirty years of the ninth century.[11] Pilgrims, both Tuscan and those who crossed the region coming from the North and following the Via Francigena — the original route of which, however, passed some distance from Florence [12] — must have been a not unusual sight. However, it is a fact that at the beginning of the crusading movement Florence was still a relatively unimportant city, and though she took a passionate part in matters concerning ecclesiastical reform,[13] there is no trace of intervention by her citizens, or even of their interest, in the events of 1096-1099.[14] Much later were born those legends, of a clearly heraldic-genealogical character, about the contribution of certain families or personages to the capture of Jerusalem.[15] However, the only certain fact is that Urban II, travelling from Rome to the North, stayed in the city for an undefined period at the beginning of 1095, or, as Davidsohn prefers, perhaps even from the end of the previous year. Certainly the only document which proves that Urban was in

---

9   For the connection between the Orient and the establishment of Christianity in Florence, see R. Davidsohn, *Storia di Firenze*, Ital. transl. by G.B. Klein, 1 (Florence, 1956), pp. 54-65; for Tuscan churches whose dedication recalls a Jerusalem-centred cult, see P. Aebischer, "Sancta Hierusalem," *Bollettino storico lucchese* 11 (1939), 81-92.

10   See *E miraculis sancti Genesii*, ed. G. Waitz, MGH.SS. 15:169-172; and Davidsohn, *Storia* 1:120.

11   Davidsohn, *Storia* 1:1056.

12   G. Plesner, *Una rivoluzione stradale al dugento* (Florence, 1979), passim.

13   Cf. Davidsohn, *Storia* 1:207-446; G. Miccoli, "Aspetti del monachesimo toscano del secolo XI," in his *Chiesa gregoriana* (Florence, 1966), pp. 47-73, an article in which there are, in addition, bibliographical indications of specific stages in the politico-religious struggle of Florence during the 11th century; F. Cardini, "L'inizio del movimento crociato in Toscana," in *Studi di storia medievale e moderna per Ernesto Sestan*, 1 (Florence, 1980), pp. 135-157, where the struggle for reform is briefly referred to within the perspective of the crusade which began shortly after.

14   The crusade is referred to in general terms in the more reliable Florentine sources, which seem to be more interested in the later expeditions. Both Giovanni Villani, *Cronica* 4. 24, ed. F. Gherardi Dragomanni, 1 (Florence, 1844), pp. 171-172, and Ricordano Malispini, *Storia fiorentina* 64, ed. V. Follini (Florence, 1816), pp. 60-61, refer in vague and unconvincing terms to a Florentine participation in the event, both using as a source for their facts, however, a "book of the pilgrimage" about which they say nothing more. Granting the Villani-Malispini polemic, we might note here that those two texts seem incontestably interdependent.

15   See *infra*, notes 34, 35, 58, 59, 60.

Florence is dated 1 February 1095,[16] at a time when the crusade, at least in its later form, was still unforeseeable.

It is known that some crusader contingents passed along the Via Francigena in the autumn of 1096, and we have documented evidence of the departure of Tuscan crusaders, for example from Lucca,[17] and especially the famous Pisan expedition led by Archbishop Daimbert.[18] Florence, it seems, was not involved; perhaps it was too far from the Via Francigena and the sea-ports. It has been assumed that members of the Guidi family took part in the First Crusade, but the supporting evidence is weak and may be the result of misunderstanding.[19]

Hence we cannot know how the news of the crusader conquest of Jerusalem was received in the city, since there are no contemporary chronicles. There is documentary evidence of pilgrimages some time after 1099, but nothing authorises us to think that the ancient custom of pilgrimage received a new impetus in Florence because of the capture of the Holy Land. Certainly this happened elsewhere, but with a lack of documentary evidence it is dangerous to draw analogies. One indirect proof of the fascination exercised upon the Florentines by the crusader epos would be in their contribution to the Pisan enterprise in the Balearics, but here too information regarding Florence is very late and legendary.[20]

Some Florentines may have arrived in the Holy Land after the end of the First Crusade. Here too we must be wary of insufficient evidence. Some would seek Florentines in the many references to Pisans and Tuscans, since we know that in the Holy Land Florentines used to pass themselves off as Pisans. It is possible that pilgrims and settlers from Florence were sometimes included in such references, but nothing more definite can be said. We are on firmer ground with *Rogerius de Florentia*, however, who must have been a man of importance. A document of 1118 shows that he had then already bestowed on the Knights Hospitaller a "casale... in terminio de Harenc."[21]

16   Jaffé — Löwenfeld, no. 5539.

17   Cardini, "L'inizio," pp. 152-154.   18   Ibid., pp. 156-157.

19   Ibid., pp. 146-157; R. Fantappiè, "Nascita d'una terra di nome Prato," *Storia di Prato*, 1 (Prato, 1980), 187.

20   Davidsohn, *Storia* 1:554-561, who emphasises certain information, the basis for which is the famous *Liber Maiolichinus*, but which in the memories and the mythopoetic of the people was soon transformed into legends on the one hand, and anti-Pisan arguments on the other. Cf. Villani, *Cronica* 4, 31, pp. 177-178, and Malispini, *Storia* 31, p. 64; on a pilgrim of the Florentine *contado* who, in 1127, in order to depart for the Holy Land, gave a field in pledge to the abbot of Coltibuono, see Archivio di Stato di Firenze, *Diplomatico. Coltibuono*, April 1127; Davidsohn, *Storia* 1:1057.

21   Delaville, *Cartulaire*, no. 45: a confirmation by Roger of Antioch of earlier grants to the Hospitallers.

Not even the Second Crusade, the "crusade of Cacciaguida," aroused much enthusiasm in the city: people were busy fighting to consolidate certain advantageous positions gained in the *contado*. However, we cannot underestimate the fact that one of the papal legates in the expedition, Cardinal Guido di San Crisogono, was a Florentine: but if this will allow us to put forward the hypothesis that the cardinal might have "transmitted" to his city, as it were, some of his experiences, or that he might have had with him some Florentine servant or collaborator, and that of these one might have remained in the Holy Land, it is the furthest we can speculate.[22]

Must we disbelieve Dante? There seems to be no reason. It is possible that Cacciaguida and others with him followed the "Emperor" Conrad to the Levant: however, we do not have any certain proof. On the contrary, the fact that the Florentines attacked and conquered the castle of Monte di Croce during the absence of its lord, Count Guido Guerra, and that this episode is strictly connected with the interdict imposed on the Florentines — a fact easily understood if the Count was a crusader, and hence under the tutelage of the Church — we may conclude that the Florentines preferred to take advantage of the confusion caused by the crusade and the losses in the local nobility in order to advance their political and military control of the *contado*.[23]

In the second half of the twelfth century the city started to grow, and with the Third Crusade there is better information about Florentine *cruce signati*. This may have been a consequence of the loss of the Holy City to Saladin, which so profoundly shocked the whole of Christendom; or it may have been the result of the emergence of Florence as a well-established political and

22 Davidsohn, *Storia* 1:652-653, demonstrates that the more reliable urban tradition, which maintains that Guido belonged to the Bellagio family, is not based on any reliable fact. For the part played by the cardinal in the crusade, see P. Alphandéry and A. Dupront, *La Cristianità e l'idea di crociata*, Ital. transl. by B. Foschi Martini (Bologna, 1974), p. 180, and Prawer, *Histoire* 1:385. A document in the Hospitaller *Cartulaire* (see previous note) 1, no. 210, shows that Guido was still legate in the Holy Land in 1152.

23 Substantially, this is the thesis of Davidsohn, *Storia* 1:643-651. In the article "Dante e i conti Guidi," in his *Italia medievale* (Naples, 1966), pp. 336-337, Ernesto Sestan has taken a clear position both on the historicity of Cacciaguida's participation in the crusade, and on the fact that he was accompanied by Count Guido Guerra III. The fact is not proved by any document; but the coincidence of the Dantean tradition with the question of the capture of Monte di Croce and of the interdict against the Florentines suggests that the vision of the great Italian historian should be accepted. Naturally, the case of Cacciaguida does not prove that there were too many Florentines with the count. At most some of his *homines* would have left with him: such must have been the one who in February, 1147, in Altomena near Pelago, a locality belonging to the Guidi, pledged some of his land to the Abbey of Vallombrosa for 25 *soldi*, with the clause that the abbey could appropriate it should he not return from the Holy Land within three years (see Archivio di Stato di Firenze, *Diplomatico. Vallombrosa*, February 1147).

economic centre which preachers of the crusade could no longer ignore. From this period we have the picturesque record of the ceremony in which the cross was given to the Florentines on 2 February 1188, the Feast of the Purification of the Virgin, in the Church of San Donato a Torri in Polverosa. The papal legate Gerardo, the Cistercian archbishop of Ravenna, gave the crosses and at the same time consecrated the new church which had recently been built there. The crusaders received as a gift the banner that was flying on the roof of the building.[24] However, we do not know for sure that this contingent actually departed. According to Ralph of Diceto, some Florentine crusaders took part in the siege of Acre: this chronicler mentions numerous contingents, among them Florentines and Pisans.[25] It is well known that the Pisan contingent, commanded by Archbishop Ubaldo, had a special importance, and it is probable, though solid proof is lacking, that some Florentines had sailed in company with Pisans. We have in any case to be somewhat sceptical with regard to Giovanni Villani's assertion that Florentines "fecero oste e squadre di loro medesimi oltremare."[26] Furthermore, this bold and rather irritated assertion

24 Davidsohn, *Storia* 1:866; Prawer, *Histoire* 2:9-16; see the document edited in J. Lami, *Sanctae Ecclesiae Florentinae monumenta*, 2 (Florence, 1758), 1208-1209, and in Müller, *Documenti*, no. 26, p. 32, a narrative which is followed by both Villani, *Cronica* 5. 13, p. 198, and Malispini, *Storia* 78, p. 68-69. A banner "bianco e rosso da Damiata" is recorded in the inventory of San Giovanni of 1314, and was flown during feast days (Davidsohn, *Storia* 2:86). The fact that the reference is to "da Damiata" demonstrates that in the city memory the true Florentine crusading glory was in Damietta, not in Acre (see here, *infra*, notes 32, 33). Of course, nothing clearly demonstrates that the banner of 2 February 1188 and the one from Damietta were the same banner, brought by Florentine contingents in the expedition of 1188 and in the expedition of 1219: but it is possible.

25 Cf. S. Painter, "The Third Crusade: Richard the Lionhearted and Philip Augustus," in *The Later Crusades 1189-1311*, ed. R.L. Wolff and H.W. Hazard (Madison, Wis., 1969), p. 66 (*A History of the Crusades*, ed. K.M. Setton, 2); Radulfus de Diceto, *Ymagines historiarum*, ed. by W. Stubbs, RS 68 (London, 1876), 2:79-80. In general for Tuscans and the Third Crusade, cf. also A. Mundò, "Lettera inedita di Clemente III ai crociati toscani (1188)," *Rivista di storia della Chiesa in Italia* 13 (1959), 289-292.

26 Villani, *Cronica* 5. 13, p. 198, to which correspond, as usual, Malispini, *Storia* 78, p. 69. See F. Wilken, *Geschichte der Kreuzzüge*, 4 (Leipzig, 1832), 303 ff., and Davidsohn, *Storia* 1:869. The Florentine contribution to the Third Crusade is briefly examined, but with useful accuracy, also by S. Borsari, "L'espansione economica fiorentina nell'Oriente cristiano sino alla metà del Trecento," *Rivista storica italiana* 70 (1958), 478. In the city chronicles also the restitution of the Florentine rights of jurisdiction on the *contado*, within ten miles of the walls, is connected with the Third Crusade (Villani, *Cronica* 5. 13, p. 198; Malispini, *Storia* 1, p. 69; see also P. Santini, *Quesiti e questioni di storiografia fiorentina* (Florence, 1903), p. 106. In fact, such rights were restored, and not so largely, by Emperor Henry VI in a document of 24 June 1187 (Davidsohn, *Storia* 1:874). It is with regard to the Third Crusade that we see the initiation of a *Societas peregrinantium* in Florence like in other Tuscan cities, e.g. in Pistoia (Davidsohn, *Storia* 7:150).

of Villani has all the air of an *excusatio non petita*: in times of resurgent urban patriotism and of irreconcilable enmity with Pisa (an enmity not yet existing in the twelfth century), it was unpleasant for the great Guelf and Florentine chronicler to recall those times when his fellow citizens had shared the glory of the Holy Land with their rivals.

If we accept that the Florentine participation in the Third Crusade was brought about, as the document of San Donato a·Torri seems to prove, by massive propaganda, we must not forget that on the eve of this crusade there stayed in the city Haymarus Monachus, a refugee from the Holy Land after the terrible events of 1187, and author of the celebrated *De expugnata Accone*.[27] Haymarus was a Florentine and, after becoming *magister* in the city, he emigrated to the Holy Land around 1160. It seems that in Outremer he became a friend of Emperor Manuel Comnenus. Having been nominated canon of Acre's church of the Holy Cross, in 1171 he was promoted chancellor of the Holy Sepulchre by the patriarch of Jerusalem. He held this office for about ten years, and then gave it up to succeed Eraclius as archbishop of Caesarea. When in 1187 his city fell to Saladin, Haymarus fled to Tyre and from there embarked for Italy: he returned to the Holy Land with the wave of Christian recovery and took part in the siege of Acre, which he describes in his masterpiece.

Once restored to his archiepiscopal city, which was recovered by the forces of the Third Crusade, he stayed there until he was proclaimed patriarch of Jerusalem. He could not, however, occupy his patriarchal see, which remained in Saracen hands. During his patriarchate he favoured his relatives; he brought his nephew Graziano from Florence and persuaded Henry of Champagne to give him a fief in money and land near Acre.[28]

The name of Haymarus is linked with the transfer to Florence of the arm of the Apostle Philip, a famous relic which constitutes one of the most prestigious tokens of the connection between Florence and the Holy Land. According to the tradition of the Florentine *Translatio*,[29] the relic of the apostle had been

---

27   *Haymari Monachi de expugnata Accone liber tetrastichus*, ed. P. Riant (Paris, 1865), pp. 69-118; in this work is published also the *Instrumentum translationis brachii sancti Philippi Florentiam*, edited from the original preserved in the Opera del Duomo, and which is published also as *Translatio brachii sancti Philippi Hyerosolymis Florentiam*, in AA.SS., Maii 2:15-17. The thesis of Riant, that Haymarus belonged to the Corbizi family, based on a reference in Malispini, Storia 79, p. 69 (but cf. Villani 5.14, pp. 199-200, where the reference is merely to "messer Monaco"), depends on a copy by a clerk of Corbizi household, who might have interpolated it in the text (see Follini in his notes to the Malispini text, p. 315).

28   See Davidsohn, *Storia* 1:866-867, who follows Riant; and G. Fedalto, *La Chiesa latina in oriente*, 2 (Verona, 1976), pp. 60, 134.

29   See note 27, *supra*.

given in dowry by Emperor Manuel to his great-grandniece Isabel, daughter of Amalric I of Jerusalem and Maria Comnena. Haymarus, who died in 1202, asked for the relic and obtained it as a gift; the bishop of Florence, Pietro, asked for it in turn so that it might honour their city. Haymarus, who was already ill, entrusted it to another Florentine of the Holy Land, Ranieri, dean of Jaffa, who had begun his career as chaplain of Polvereto in Val di Pesa and was later transferred to the Church of the Holy Sepulchre. The king and the Frankish clergy opposed the departure of the relic, which left, eventually, only through the intervention of another Florentine, Gualterottus, who had been a canon in Florence before he became bishop of Acre.[30]

Ranieri was able to leave for Italy only in 1205, when he was entrusted with the task of escorting to the Holy Land the bishop of Vercelli, newly elected patriarch of Jerusalem. It was then that the relic of the arm entered Florence, awaited at the southern gate by Bishop Giovanni da Velletri and by the *podestà* Rodolfo di Capraia.[31] It is interesting that this relic, with its miracles, created confusion among the heretics who, in Florence, were rather powerful. The entrance of the relic into the city was used as a pretext to renew the harsh persecution of the Cathars: it is a noteworthy sign of the already implicit relationship between the idea of the crusade and the struggle against heresy. The importance of the *Instrumentum translationis* is all the greater because it presents, from Haymarus to Ranieri and Gualterottus, a far from negligible Florentine ecclesiastical élite transplanted to the Holy Land.

By this time, a growing familiarity with the eastern shore of the Mediterranean, economic interest and the ideals of the crusade were well established on the banks of the Arno, and it was with the Crusade of Damietta that the city's tradition found its first bold and concrete expression. Once more, however, we know very little about the effective participation of Florentine crusaders in this episode. Urban sources tell us that they were present at the battle of 5 November 1219; they also tell us about that famous red and white banner which, according to Florentine tradition, had been brought from Damietta and was kept in San Giovanni to be solemnly exposed during feasts.[32] To this crusade and to this banner is related a small but significant florilegium of urban legends. Both Villani and Malispini, for example, have left an impressive list of families which might have taken part in the crusade.[33] It was said that the

---

30   Gualterottus should be identified with Gualterus, on whom Fedalto, *Chiesa*, 2:27.
31   For this person, see F. Cardini, "Capraia, Rodolfo da", *Dizionario biografico degli Italiani* 19:139-142.
32   See Davidsohn, *Storia* 2:86, and note 24, *supra*.
33   Villani, *Cronica* 5.40, pp. 220-221; Malispini, *Storia* 51, p. 82.

banner kept in San Giovanni (which both Villani and Malispini identified as, or probably confused with, that which had been given at San Donato a Torri to those who were setting out on the Third Crusade) had been the first to fly on the walls of Damietta. This story is an adaptation of the "first crusader" legend in other cities, which generally refers to the conquest of Jerusalem in 1099.[34] According to a tradition, perhaps not without political and polemical meaning, this Florentine hero at Damietta was a member of the Bonaguisi della Pressa family.[35]

However, we are not so much interested here in the actual presence of Florentine warriors under the walls of Damietta, which anyhow is difficult to verify. What is really of interest is the well authenticated fact that the preaching of that crusade in Tuscany was very successful. One of the preachers was Cardinal Ugolino d'Ostia, who, on this occasion, paved the way to those good relations with Florence which became customary after his election as Pope Gregory IX. We hear of great enthusiasm, of special monetary contributions to the enterprise and many crusading vows taken.[36] The importance of all this, however, must not be exaggerated. We know that there is no sure connection between the number of those who, dragged in the wake of the enthusiasm aroused by the crusade preaching, or for mere political calculation, took the cross (thus profiting from the protection of the Church in order to avoid payments of debts or to escape criminal jurisdiction) and the number of those who really did depart.[37] In fact, these continuous abuses constitute one of the main causes for the widespread antipathy that crusade propaganda aroused during the thirteenth century.[38] However, since the time of the Crusade of

---

34   The tradition of the "first crusader" is found, for example, in Genoa and by way of competition, though less credibly, in Pisa with her Cucco Ricucchi and Coscetto del Colle (the latter an illustrious name in the political life of Pisa in the early fourteenth century, which lends this legend a forceful political significance, and which perhaps constitutes a mode of dating, at least *post quem*). With regard to these Pisan traditions, corroborated also by certain amusing "false" ones, see, e.g., P. Tronci, *Memorie istoriche della città di Pisa* (Livorno, 1862), pp. 35-46; Idem, *Annali pisani*, 1 (Pisa, 1868), 182; R. Roncioni, *Delle famiglie pisane*, ed. F. Bonaini (Pisa, 1844). Unfortunately, these municipal traditions of the crusades—"false" as such, but useful for aspects of customs, mentality and social life at that time—have not yet been adequately considered by historians. A first example of their treatment, however, can be found in A. Vasina, *Le crociate nel mondo italiano* (Bologna and Padua, 1973), pp. 46-50.

35   For Bonaguisa de' Bonaguisi as the first conqueror of Damietta, see Malispini, *Storia* 51, p. 82. Bonaguisi, according to Malispini, went to the Holy Land with the Marquis of Ferrara, who dubbed him knight and conceded him the use of his arms.

36   Davidsohn, *Storia* 2:85-88.

37   A Volterran example of these abuses, which must have been frequent, is in Davidsohn, *Storia* 2:87.

38   See note 8, *supra*.

Damietta, Florentines seem to have kept the custom, later traditional in both this and other cities, of legacies *pro remedio animae*, or donations *pro recuperatione Terrae Sanctae*.[39]

It is not certain, however, that all those Florentines who joined the crusader ranks did so as pilgrim-fighters: on the contrary, we have the distinct impression that, at least in the thirteenth century, the crusade appealed to them mainly as a good opportunity for doing business. In the first crusade of Saint Louis, directed against Egypt, the presence of Florentines in the army is well documented, but they were all bankers and merchants.[40]

It is well known that many Florentine bankers made a fortune as collectors of and bidders for the tithes, especially after the levying of the great tithe by Gregory X in 1274.[41] The businessmen who lived in Syria, or who were at least resident in those areas for a good part of the year, could not have been few;[42] and for this reason too the fall of Acre in 1291 was felt in the city as a great tragedy, even though some bankers—those holding the deposits of operators fallen victim to the Saracens—ultimately took advantage even of this event.[43] The ten years following 1291 were, as is well known, a period of intense though inconclusive propaganda for the crusade. During this period, as indeed before and after, the donations in favour of the *passagium* were many, but the Florentines who perfectly well understood the difficulties of organizing a new venture, at the same time as they donated, vied one with another in imposing as many limiting clauses as possible, so as to prevent their money, officially destined for the Christian recovery of the Holy Land, from going elsewhere, even if canon law should legitimize such diversion.[44]

At the end of the thirteenth century Florentine interest in the Near East was still very much alive. We find Florentines in Little Armenia,[45] in Cyprus, in

---

39 Archivio di Stato di Firenze, *Diplomatico. Passignano*, 9 October 1220: legacy of *Bernardus filius quondam Scolai de Montebuoni* for the crusade.

40 Borsari, "L'espansione," pp. 479-483; Davidsohn, *Storia* 2:478; 6:750.

41 Davidsohn, *Storia* 3:97, 287, 306, 310, 447, 616; 6:572.

42 Borsari, "L'espansione," p. 497; Davidsohn, *Storia* 3:75; 6:751-752.

43 Such would seem to be the case of the Peruzzi (but see Borsari, "L'espansione," p. 480); Borsari, however, reports the information of the Peruzzi's increased wealth after the fall of Acre (p. 488), but without taking a definite position on the question. See also Davidsohn, *Storia* 6:753-754.

44 A few examples in Davidsohn, *Storia* 7:150; see also Archivio di Stato di Firenze, *Diplomatico. Cistercensi*, 21 February 1284; also ibid., *Notarile Antecosimiano. Protocollo di Matteo di Biliotto*, 291, 1, c. 103r.

45 Davidsohn, *Storia* 6:755; Borsari, "L'espansione," p. 489.

Rhodes, where the relations with the Knights Hospitaller were close,[46] in Crete[47] and on the Black Sea.[48] However, it was mainly in Romania that families such as the Acciaiuoli and the Buondelmonti found the basis for their feudal empires;[49] while at the beginning of the fifteenth century and with the acquisition of Pisa's harbour, Florence also made its modest but firm debut as a sea-power.[50]

At this point, the ideals of the crusade did not much appeal to the Florentines. Only during the pontificate of Pius II, in the fifteenth century, does it seem that the Republic showed a certain interest in the *passagium*: but after the battle of Varna and after the fall of Christian Constantinople, everything petered out in vague declarations of principle and dilatory diplomatic manoeuvres.[51] The only sure evidence of Florentine politics of the time is of the obvious attempt to avoid paying tithes for crusading enterprises.

Still, the crusade survived as an idea which could be the mainspring of vigorous action. It did this both as a basic conception which inspired attitudes and, on the popular level, as a set of what sociologists call *idées données*.[52] It existed also as a latent force, ready to explode when a particular combination

46 Davidsohn, *Storia* 6:756-761; Borsari, "L'espansione," pp. 489, 494-498 and passim; A. Luttrell, "Interessi fiorentini nell'economia e nella politica dei Cavalieri Ospedalieri di Rodi nel Trecento," *Annali della Scuola Normale Superiore di Pisa. Lettere, storia e filosofia* 2.28 (1959), 317-326; Idem, "The Hospitallers at Rhodes, 1306-1421," in *The Fourteenth and Fifteenth Centuries*, ed. H.W. Hazard (Madison, Wis., 1975), p. 291 (*A History of the Crusades*, ed. K.M. Setton, 3).

47 Davidsohn, *Storia* 6:763; Borsari, "L'espansione," passim.

48 Davidsohn, *Storia* 6:765; Borsari, "L'espansione," passim.

49 Borsari, "L'espansione," passim; C. Ugurgieri della Berardenga, *Gli Acciaioli di Firenze alla luce dei loro tempi* (Florence, 1962); Idem, *Avventurieri alla conquista di feudi e di corone* (Florence, 1963); A. Carile, *La rendita feudale nella Morea latina nel XIV secolo* (Bologna, 1974), pp. 46-52 and passim; K.M. Setton, *Catalan Domination of Athens, 1311-1388*, rev. ed. (London, 1975), pp. 65-78; Idem, "The Catalans and Florentines in Greece, 1380-1462," in *The Fourteenth and Fifteenth Centuries* (note 46, *supra*), pp. 225-277.

50 See M.E. Mallett, *The Florentine Galleys in the Fifteenth Century* (Oxford, 1967).

51 For the relations between Florence and Pius II with regard to the crusade, see R. Black, "La storia della prima crociata di Benedetto Accolti e la diplomazia fiorentina rispetto all' Oriente," *Archivio storico italiano* 131 (1973), 3-25, and F. Cardini, "La repubblica di Firenze e la crociata di Pio II," *Rivista di storia della Chiesa in Italia* 33. 2 (1979), 455-482.

52 As in the anti-Muslim attitude which can be seen, e.g., in the accounts of pilgrims—a good example of which is in the pilgrimage made by a group of Florentines in 1384, among whom were Lionardo Frescobaldi, Giorgio Gucci and Simone Sigoli, all of whom left a diary: see L. Frescobaldi and S. Sigoli, *Viaggi in Terrasanta*, ed. C. Angelini (Florence, 1944); G. Gucci, *Viaggio ai Luoghi Santi*, ed. C. Gargiolli (Florence, 1862). See now R. Delfiol, "Su alcuni problemi codicologico-testuali concernenti le relazioni di pellegrinaggio del 1384," in *Toscana e Terrasanta nel medioevo*, ed. F. Cardini (Firenze, 1982), pp. 139-177.

of circumstances was set in motion. A conspicuous crusading, or rather "chivalrous-crusading," theme runs through the romances and songs of the fourteenth and fifteenth centuries up to the *Morgante* of Luigi Pulci.[53] In fact, when the *Morgante* came fresh off the press, there had been, some little time before in Florence, the tragedy of the Pazzi family and their unfortunate plot against Lorenzo il Magnifico. This was that same family of Pazzi which, traditionally and up to the present, has been associated with the most popular account of the crusade and the "presence of Jerusalem" in Florence, the "Scoppio del Carro," which seems to record and reproduce the descent of the "Holy Fire" into the edicule of the Holy Sepulchre in Jerusalem on the day after Good Friday.

The whole question of the "Scoppio del Carro" is complicated, consisting of at least two elements: first, the ceremony of kindling the "Holy Fire," which the Florentine Church celebrated since the twelfth century, and which —though we cannot exclude its ties with the remains of pagan customs of Germanic origin, typical of agricultural spring festivals—has a notable similarity to the famous ceremony of Holy Saturday in the Holy Sepulchre Church;[54] second, the connection between the ceremony and the Pazzi, a great Guelph family which distinguished itself in Florentine affairs from the second half of the thirteenth century and received magnate status in 1293. A member of the Pazzi family had the customary privilege (acquired perhaps by payment, as was still done in Jerusalem in the eighteenth century, according to Mariti),[55] of being the first to light his torch at the "Holy Fire" offered in Florence by the canons of San Giovanni. This we know from a reference by Giovanni Villani[56] and a provision of 1478 (though, after the attempt on Lorenzo's life, the Medici sympathisers wanted to condemn the whole house of Pazzi to a sort of *damnatio memoriae*) which attests that the connection between the ceremony of the lighting of the "Holy Fire," patronised by the Pazzi, and the popular holiday was consolidated by this time.[57] To this can be added the story according to

---

53   For the *Morgante*, see R.M. Ruggieri, "La serietà del 'Morgante'," in his *L'umanesimo cavalleresco italiano* (Rome, 1962), and P. Orvieto, *Pulci medievale* (Rome, 1978).

54   See R. Davidsohn, "Le origini storiche dello Scoppio del Carro, lettera al sindaco," *Il Nuovo Giornale*, 3 June 1909. I thank my colleague and dear friend Sergio Raveggi who, for this and following information, allowed me to use an unpublished article of his regarding the Pazzi family legends and the "Scoppio del Carro" tradition See now S. Raveggi, "Storia di una leggenda: Pazzo dei Pazzi e le pietre del Santo Sepolcro," in *Toscana e Terrasanta* (note 52, *supra*), pp. 299-316.

55   Cf. G. Mariti, *Viaggi per l'isola di Cipro e per la Soria e Palestina fatti dall'anno MDCCLX al MDCCLXVIII*, 3 (Florence, 1770), 254.

56   Villani, *Cronica* 1. 60, pp. 82-83.

57   See Don Ristori, "Una nota sopra la lettera del dottor Roberto Davidsohn al sindaco," *La Nazione*, 8 July 1909; also, Davidsohn, *Storia* 1:1067-1068.

which one of the Pazzis was the "first crusader" to climb, as usual, the walls of Jerusalem, a story recorded for the first time in the 1480s, in a short poem about Florence by the humanist Ugolino di Vieri, called Verino, though it may not have originated with him.[58]

It is only in a book of memoirs written in 1535 by Ghinozzo di Uguccione de' Pazzi, copied, he says, from a more ancient source, that we find the story in its definitive form: a personage who has all the air of being an eponymous hero, Pazzo de' Pazzi, received from Pope Urban II the military command of the Tuscan crusaders; he was the first to climb the walls of Jerusalem to plant the crusader flag; back in Florence he gave three silicone stones from the Holy Sepulchre edicule to the church of San Biagio: with these stones, the "Holy Fire" of Florence was lit each year.[59] The story, repeated during the seventeenth century by genealogists and students of heraldry,[60] did not stand up to the doubts cast on its authenticity during the Enlightenment and was shattered by the critique of positivist historiography.[61] But to us its "falsity" is more interesting than any authentic account. The story arose apparently between the fourteenth and the fifteenth centuries: not before, since Villani, who mentions the "Holy Fire" and its connections with the Pazzi family, does not recall these events; but later, at a time when patrician Florentine families looked to the crusades to establish their surreptitious merits and their doubtfully "noble" origins. In fact, it is in the accounts of the Pazzi family that we find a "Christian" glory (from the Guelph point of view; and Florentine Guelphs loved to call the Ghibellines, if not "infidel," at least "heretics") and a crusader banner, at least in the sense of a standard with a cross. The story concerns Messer Iacopo del Nacca Pazzi, who carried the banner of the Florentine *Commune* (or perhaps the flag of the *Popolo* with its red cross) at the battle of Montaperti in 1260, and whose arms were hacked off by the Ghibelline Bocca degli Abati so that the flag would fall.[62] His son was Pazzino, whose name recalls the legendary crusader hero, and who was one of the outstanding political figures of the city at the time of Dante.[63]

---

58   *Ugolini Verini De illustratione urbis Florentiae*, 3 (Florence, 1636), p. 67.
59   The memoir of Ghinozzo di Uguccione is edited by G. Richa, *Notizie istoriche delle chiese fiorentine*, 3. 1 (Florence, 1755), 232-236.
60   See mainly G.F. Negri, *Prima crociata* (Bologna, 1658), CLXII-CLXIV.
61   See D.M. Manni, *Dei fuochi d'allegrezza artifiziati per la famiglia Pazzi di Firenze nel Sabato Santo* (Florence, 1867); Davidsohn, "Le origini."
62   See Malispini, *Storia* 171, pp. 137-138; Villani, *Cronica* 6. 79, p. 301; Marchionne di Coppo Stefani, *Cronaca fiorentina*, ed. N. Rodolico, in RIS² 30:123.
63   Cf. Dino Compagni, *Cronica*, ed. I. del Lungo, in RIS² 9.2, passim.

For the Pazzi of the fourteenth and fifteenth centuries to place the origins of their glory in the time of the crusades (as the crusades were no longer a reality of political and military life) was, without doubt, more prestigious and more fashionable than any reference to the turbid and unpleasant period of the civil war between Guelphs and Ghibellines, Blacks and Whites, magnates and *popolani*. In fact, the only certain connection between the Pazzi and the crusade was that they, like other Florentine bankers of the time, were collectors of crusade tithes in Germany.[64]

With the slow growth of the legendary fame of the Pazzi — a fame which perhaps took as models such Pisan stories as those of the "first crusaders" Cucco Ricucchi and Coscetto del Colle, with which there are numerous analogies and chronological coincidence[65] — the references to Jerusalem in Florence increased in number and importance. Domenico Maria Manni commented, with regard to the "Scoppio del Carro," that in Florence there were stones, besides those conserved in San Biagio, which were said to originate in the Holy Sepulchre; one of them, which in his day was in San Iacopo in Campo Corbolini, had been there since 1206.[66] No one could help but notice the almost perfect coincidence with the transfer to Florence of the arm of the Apostle Philip. There were in the city two reproductions of the edicule of the Holy Sepulchre which dated from the Trecento: the first is conserved in Fiesole, the second was on the bridge called "Ponte alle Grazie," now destroyed.[67]

Two masterpieces of the Florentine Quattrocento refer to Jerusalem and the Church of the Holy Sepulchre. They are, of course, Masaccio's famous fresco in Santa Maria Novella depicting the Crucifixion, which includes the Calvary Chapel in exact detail, and the no less famous edicule of the Holy Sepulchre, an outstanding work of Leon Battista Alberti, commissioned by Giovanni Rucellai in San Pancrazio.[68]

At the end of the fifteenth century the Holy Land thus constituted a real and tangible presence in Florence: relics, crusader legends, records of pilgrims,

---

64   R. Davidsohn, *Forschungen zur Geschichte von Florenz*, 3 (Berlin, 1901), Regesten, 160.
65   See note 34, *supra*. Also the legend of the relic of the "Santo Cingolo" (the Holy Girdle of the Virgin) of Prato has its origins in Holy Land, in the First Crusade and in a legend of a "first crusader," who is of course, in this case, a citizen of Prato (Fantappiè, "Nascita" [note 19, *supra*]), p. 187.
66   Manni, *Dei fuochi* (note 61, *supra*), pp. 16-18.
67   On the edicule of "Ponte alle Grazie," see F. Sacchetti, *Le lettere*, in his *Opere*, ed. A. Chiari, 2 (Bari, 1938), 103.
68   Cf. U. Schlegel, "Observations on Masaccio's Trinity Fresco in Santa Maria Novella," *Art Bulletin* 45 (1963), 19-33.

reproductions of Holy Places. The dream of a new crusade, forgotten with the death of Pius II and only ephemerally stirred up by the events of Otranto in 1480, and during the campaign of Charles VIII of France who regarded the conquest of Naples as a stage in the reconquest of Jerusalem, was now indeed nothing but a dream. The illusion might still exist in the mind of some pilgrim who contemplated the abject condition, according to his lights, of the Holy Places, now in the hands of the infidel; the dream of conquest might live on in popular songs of the marketplace, with the audience riding again with Roland against the Moors. The crusade became propaganda, a collective illusion, a rather harmless *idée donnée* (especially among merchants who went on to trade with the Sultan), a pretext for heraldic symbolism.